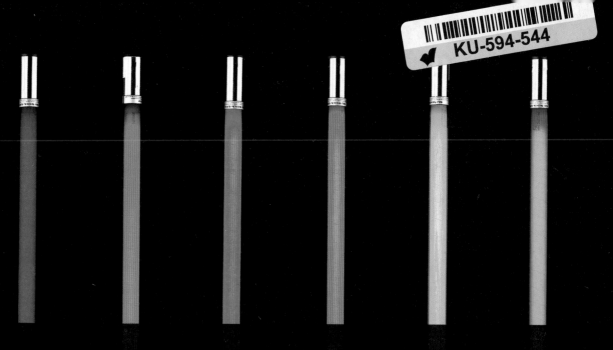

introduction to BUSINESS LAW

THIRD EDITION

Lucy Jones

OXFORD
UNIVERSITY PRESS

OXFORD
UNIVERSITY PRESS

Great Clarendon Street, Oxford, OX2 6DP,
United Kingdom

Oxford University Press is a department of the University of Oxford.
It furthers the University's objective of excellence in research, scholarship,
and education by publishing worldwide. Oxford is a registered trade mark of
Oxford University Press in the UK and in certain other countries

© Oxford University Press 2015

The moral rights of the author have been asserted

First edition 2011
Second edition 2013
Impression: 3

Public sector information reproduced under Open Government Licence v2.0
(http://www.nationalarchives.gov.uk/doc/open-government-licence/open-government-licence.htm)

Published in the United States of America by Oxford University Press
198 Madison Avenue, New York, NY 10016, United States of America

British Library Cataloguing in Publication Data
Data available

Library of Congress Control Number: 2014957586

ISBN 978–0–19–872733–0

Printed in Great Britain by Bell & Bain Ltd., Glasgow

To Allan, Sophie, Nick, and Rosie and to all the students who have inspired me over the years.

New to this Edition

- A chapter on Intellectual property law which includes coverage of Copyright, Patents, Design Rights and Trade marks and changes in the law made by the Intellectual Property Act 2014.

- Coverage of recent changes made to consumer law including changes to cancellation of consumer contracts and reforms proposed by the Consumer Rights bill.

- Discussion of the new 'employee shareholder' introduced by the Growth and Infrastructure Act 2013.

- Further case authority illustrating issues in Employment law.

- Updated case law including coverage of the recent Supreme Court's decision relating to piercing the corporate veil.

- Updated legislation and regulation coverage throughout.

Outline Contents

Detailed Contents

PART 6 STUDY SKILLS & REVISION

Guide to the Book

Introduction to Business Law is enhanced with a range of features designed to help support and reinforce your learning. This guided tour shows you how to fully utilise your textbook and get the most out of your study.

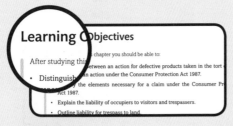

Learning Objectives

Each chapter begins with a bulleted outline of the main concepts and ideas you will encounter. These provide a helpful signpost to what you can expect to learn from the chapter.

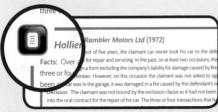

Cases

Expanding on the facts and decisions of key cases, these boxes illustrate important precedents set in case law.

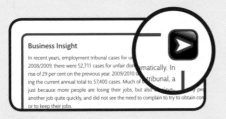

Business Insights

Situations from the recent past are highlighted and explained to show how the topics in the book relate to real world business scenarios.

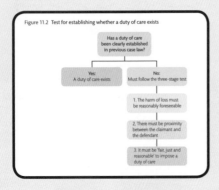

Tables and Figures

Full colour tables and figures help define complex issues and highlight key points to remember.

Viewpoint Boxes

Throughout the book are accounts from real business people who need to interact with the law as part of their job. Read their stories to see how the law might apply to your career.

Key Concepts

Important ideas from within the chapters are distilled into bullet points that can be used as summaries or aids to revision.

Basic Terminology

A useful reference for all the key words and phrases used within each chapter. A full glossary of terms is available online.

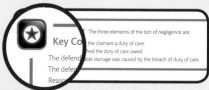

Summaries

The central points and concepts covered in each chapter are collated into end-of-chapter summaries. These reinforce your understanding and can be used for quick revision. All chapter summaries are available for reference and download online.

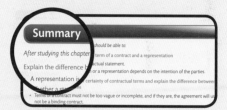

Questions

Self-test questions at the end of each chapter help you to develop analytical and problem solving skills. Presented in both essay and problem style, these questions will give you a chance to consolidate your knowledge and develop your own successful approach to assessments and examinations. Outline answers are available online.

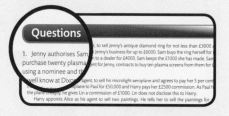

Multiple-Choice Questions

Each chapter is linked to an online multiple-choice question test. These can be accessed by following the web address.

Guide to the Online Resource Centre

The Online Resource Centre that accompanies this book provides students and lecturers with ready-to-use teaching and learning resources. They are free of charge and are designed to maximise the learning experience.

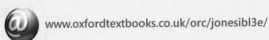

www.oxfordtextbooks.co.uk/orc/jonesibl3e/

For Students

Accessible to all, with no registration or password required, enabling you to get the most from this textbook.

- Updates on case law and legislation
- Interactive flashcard glossary of key terms from the book
- Chapter summaries
- Multiple-choice questions
- Outline answers to end-of-chapter questions
- Exam help

For Lecturers

Password protected to ensure that only lecturers can access these resources. Registering is easy: click on 'Lecturer Resources' on the Online Resource Centre, complete a simple registration form that allows you to choose your own username and password, and access will be granted within 48 hours (subject to verification).

Instructors' manual

Includes:

- PowerPoint slides for each chapter with accompanying teaching notes, and selected tables and figures from the text
- Assignment questions to accompany each Part of the text
- Research exercises to accompany each chapter
- Group exercises to accompany each chapter

Test bank of multiple-choice questions

- A fully customisable resource containing ready-made assessments.

Table of Cases

Court of Justice of the European Union

European Court of Human Rights

Australia

Canada

Table of Legislation

PART 1

THE ENGLISH LEGAL SYSTEM

The Nature of English Law

Introduction

All legitimate businesses need to operate within the framework of the law. It is essential for persons working within the business world to have an understanding of how law works and affects their businesses, for example a contract will only be of value to a business if it is legally enforceable. The law sets down rules for the setting up and administration of certain types of business and governs areas of employment of staff. Although specialist legal advice is usually obtained on specific legal issues, it is essential to understand the core principles of business law and to know when to seek legal advice.

The United Kingdom of Great Britain and Northern Ireland (UK) has three distinct legal systems and sets of laws, those relating to England and Wales, those relating to Scotland, and those relating to Northern Ireland. Although there are many similarities between them, this book is concerned with the laws of England and Wales. References in this book to Acts of Parliament refer to Acts made by Parliament sitting in Westminster, London, which is the supreme law-making authority in the UK and can pass laws relating to the whole of the UK. However, students should be aware that the Scottish Parliament sitting in Edinburgh may pass Acts of the Scottish Parliament which relate only to Scotland.

The UK has been a member of the European Union (EU) since 1 January 1973 and as such has agreed to be bound by EU law. Each of the 28 Member States of the EU has its own domestic laws in addition to being bound by EU law. The UK is also a signatory to the human rights treaty, the European Convention for the Protection of Human Rights and Fundamental Freedoms 1950 which was incorporated into English law by the Human Rights Act 1998.

Learning Objectives

After studying this chapter you should be able to:

- Explain what is meant by law.
- Outline the historical development and characteristics of English law.
- Understand the difference between Public and Private Law and the difference between Civil and Criminal Law.

What is Law?

All societies or groups require rules in order to regulate the behaviour of their members. Although people in society have a right to freedoms, those freedoms cannot be absolute because one person's use of freedom may adversely affect another person's freedom or rights. Usually one looks for justice and fairness in laws; however, justice and fairness is subjective; for example, in looking at the tax burden one might ask how far the employed hardworking person should support the poor unemployed.

Laws are rules and regulations which govern the activities of persons within a country. They provide necessary rules, and balance the various interests of different members of the community. Both natural persons (human beings) and legal persons (companies) are bound by laws of the country they reside in. From these laws they can ascertain what they are permitted to do and what they are not permitted to do. Some laws prohibit certain actions, such as theft and murder, while other laws state that persons must fulfil conditions before commencing certain activities or must comply with specified regulations. For example, a special licence must be obtained prior to legally running a riding school, and a company must have a registered office. Laws are not the same in every country around the world, although often countries will have similar laws. The law of each country is only binding within its territory.

Viewpoint Alexey Petrov, Accounts Manager, Google

The knowledge of law is very important in a modern business environment—it allows for a better planning ahead and predicting consequences of any decisions made. It also structures the approach to any sort of business project—and I can say this confidently having done an industrial placement in Intel in the UK and currently being an Account Manager at Google in Ireland straight after graduation. However, the legal knowledge can come in handy in the variety of personal situations. Having just completed my second year of a Degree at the University of Brighton, I was unfortunate enough to be involved in a motorcycle accident which wasn't my fault. I had to pursue the claim myself from the other party's insurer, which resulted in the County Court action, preparing the claim form and witness statements. I won the action, despite representing myself against a major legal company representing the insurer. Hearing 'the claimant won his case' from the District Judge was the best possible reward for the effort.

Nature of English Law

In England and Wales, laws are composed of three main elements: legislation which is created through Parliament, common law, and directly enforceable EU law. An **Act of Parliament**, sometimes referred to as a **statute**, is the highest form of UK law. Some of the characteristics of English law differ from the domestic law of other EU countries; however, English law does share some similarities with countries such as New Zealand, the United States of America, and Australia which have a historical connection with the UK.

The Characteristics of English Law

Continuity

English law has developed over many centuries and its origins can be traced back to the Norman era in the 11th century. There have been numerous important developments and changes in the law but these have been brought into effect in a piecemeal fashion through **case law** and legislation. English laws do not become inoperative due to old age and even statutes (laws made by Parliament) dating back to the 13th and 14th century may still be effective today. The Treason Act 1351 was cited in a case decided in 2003, *R (on the application of Rustbridger) v AG* (2003).

A criminal offence set out in a statute was used two hundred years later in *R v Duncan* (1944). In the 1940s Helen Duncan was convicted of fortune telling under the Witchcraft Act 1735 despite the fact that there had not been any prosecutions under the Act for over a hundred years. The Witchcraft Act 1735 had not been repealed and was still effective. (Note, the Witchcraft Act 1735 has now been repealed.)

It is not only statutes that remain good law until they are repealed; cases (decided by judges) may be referred to and followed in later cases even though they may date back centuries. The rule in *Pinnel's Case* (1602) was cited and followed in *Foakes v Beer* (1884), which in turn was cited and applied in *National Westminster Bank plc v Bonas* (2003). These cases all concerned promises made by creditors to debtors to accept a smaller sum of money than was actually owed in settlement of a debt. Following the law set out in the old cases, the debtors could not enforce the creditors' promises, and were bound to pay off the full amount of the debt.

Absence of a legal code

English law is uncodified. This means that unlike other European countries the laws have not been systemised into codes. In Spain there is a Code of Commerce, a Civil Code, and a Criminal Code. A Code is a systematic collection of laws designed to deal with main areas of law.

A codified system of laws should not be confused with codification of the law into a statute which does happen in English law. Codification into a statute is where English law has been developed by judges through the medium of case law and is then collected together and restated in a statute. The common law relating to the sale of goods was originally codified in the Sale of Goods Act 1893. The principal duties of company directors, previously found in case law, have been codified in the Companies Act 2006.

Law-making role of judges

Although the traditional view is that the role of English judges is to decide cases according to existing laws, it is accepted that judges do make and change the law. Judges make law when deciding both criminal and civil cases in two main ways:

(a) *Interpreting statutes*

On occasions the meaning of a statute will be unclear and a judge will be called upon in a case to interpret it. There are various rules and presumptions that judges use when interpreting statutes (see Chapter 2). Such interpretation is often, arguably, tantamount to law-making.

(b) *Developing the common law*

There are significant areas of Civil Law, for example early contract law, and the law of torts, where the courts have developed the law through decisions in cases. Criminal Law has also developed in part through decisions in cases. Murder is a common law crime and there is no definition of what constitutes murder in a statute. However, if Parliament chooses to legislate in an area which is already covered by case law, the provisions of the statute will take precedence over the case law.

Doctrine of binding precedent

The doctrine of binding **precedent** means that in deciding a case an English judge does not just look at earlier decisions of judges in similar cases for guidance, but is actually bound to apply the law decided by those earlier cases, if the earlier cases were heard in a court of superior status (and sometimes one of equal status) and have involved similar facts in that area of the law. In other European countries, judges are guided as opposed to being bound by previous cases. The doctrine of judicial precedent is also known as '*stare decisis*' meaning to stand by decisions. The earlier decisions of previous courts which are relied upon are known as precedents.

Adversarial system of trial

The usual type of procedure in English courts is described as adversarial. In both civil and criminal cases each side presents their case to the judge, who supervises the proceedings. The judge remains neutral and decides the case on the evidence presented to him by the parties or their lawyers. Where courts use an inquisitorial procedure a judge plays a more active role in the proceedings, which may involve cross-examining the defendant and questioning witnesses himself (see Figure 1.1).

Figure 1.1 Characteristics of the English Law

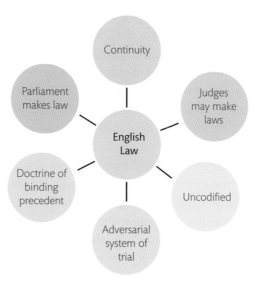

Key Concept The doctrine of binding precedent is part of English law which means that judges must apply the law as set out in relevant decisions of previous superior courts and sometimes courts of the same status. This is different from other European countries where judges are guided rather than bound by previous cases.

The Historical Development of Common Law and Equity

Prior to the Norman conquest of England in 1066 there was no national legal system, and the laws, administered through local courts, were based on what appears to have been the local custom of particular regions of the country. When William the Conqueror (1066–1087) came to the throne in England he began a process of centralisation, by imposing national government over the country. Later Norman monarchs recognised that in order to achieve strong national government there was a need to have a system of national law and order.

Henry II (1154–1189) began the process of applying the same law to the whole country. Royal Commissions, who later became known as circuit judges, travelled from London to all parts of the country hearing cases, checking on the procedure of the local courts, and applying the same laws to each region. This national law became known as common law as it was common to all parts of the country, as opposed to the local customs which applied to the different regions. Over a period of time the decisions of circuit judges were recorded and followed in subsequent cases.

Originally the King's courts were part of the King's Council, *Curia Regis*, but in time the courts developed into three distinct courts: the Courts of Exchequer, Common Pleas, and King's Bench. The rules of evidence and procedures of these courts became very rigid and formalistic. There were limited types of claims and if there was no appropriate claim for the type of action a citizen wanted to commence, then no action could be started. Even small mistakes made on a claim form would mean the action would fail, and if an action was successful the only remedy available was payment of damages (monetary compensation).

Citizens unable to gain access to the Common Law Courts or a suitable remedy in the courts sought to petition the King. The Lord Chancellor, as the King's most senior clergy-man, dealt with the petitions. Clergymen were trained in church law which was based on the ideals of conscience, morality, and justice. There were no complex rules of procedure and the Chancellor could dispense justice in accordance with what he considered to be fair in the circumstances. As the number of petitions increased the Lord Chancellor set up a specific court, the Court of Chancery, to deal directly with the petitions and administer justice on principles of equity (fairness). Decisions of the Court of Chancery became as important as the decisions of the Common Law Courts and a body of equitable laws developed. Equity did not provide a complete system of laws. It only covered certain areas, and it was intended to supplement the common law where the common law was inadequate. It gave new rights in areas where the common law had provided no right, and did not have the strict time limits that applied to common law claims. There were additional remedies provided under the law of equity, other than the common law remedy of damages (compensation) that could be awarded to a successful party. But these equitable remedies were not available to a party as a right even if they won their case. Judges in a Court of Equity had discretion to award a remedy, such as specific performance (forcing a party to carry out their part of a contract), if they considered the winning party had acted fairly and it was just in all the circumstances. However, there were areas of overlap and conflict between common law and equity. In the *Earl of Oxford's Case* it was decided that in a conflict between equity and common law then equity would prevail and be used in preference to common law.

The two court systems ran alongside each other for several hundred years, until eventually the two systems were merged in the Judicature Acts 1893–5 which created one court system but provided that all courts had the power to decide cases in accordance with both common law and equity. Today the two systems co-exist, and a court may, at the judge's discretion, use principles of equity where common law principles or remedies cause injustice. Both the rules from common law and equity are known as case law today although they are often referred to under the one term of 'common law'.

Meanings of the term 'common law'

The term **'common law'** has several different meanings. It is usually used to mean the law that is not the result of legislation but is the law created by the decisions of the judges. When common law is given this meaning it encompasses cases that have used both, or either, equity and common law.

An alternative meaning of the term common law is when it is used to distinguish common law from equity, and refers to case law that has been developed through the old Common Law Courts as opposed to the old Chancery Courts.

An archaic meaning of the term common law is law that is common to the whole of England as opposed to local law. However this is no longer the usual meaning of the term.

Finally, the term may mean the law that is not foreign law; in other words, the law of England, or of other countries (such as America) that have adopted English law as a starting point. In this sense it may be contrasted with Roman, Islamic, or French law, and here it includes the whole of English law; even local customs, legislation, and equity.

Classification of Different Types of Laws

Laws can be classified in different ways, for example they can be classified into Private and Public Law, or into Civil and Criminal Law. Civil Law may be either Public or Private Law. Criminal Law is part of Public Law. Sometimes it is important to know whether a civil matter is a Public Law issue as opposed to a Private Law issue, as there are different court procedures for civil Public Law issues.

Public and Private Law

Public Law involves the relationship between individuals and the state and is concerned with the decisions by, and control of, government bodies. Public Law is made up of Criminal Law, Constitutional Law, and Administrative Law (see Figure 1.2). Criminal Law makes certain types of behaviour against the law and gives the state power to prosecute persons who

Figure 1.2 Classification of law into Public and Private Law.

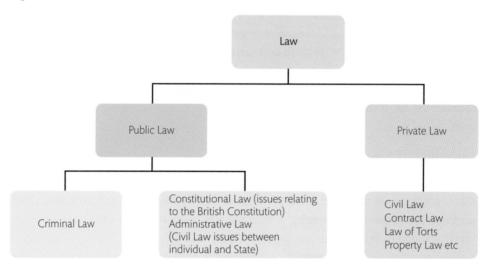

disobey the law. The term 'person' refers to both individuals (human beings) and legal persons such as companies. A legal person is an organisation that has a separate legal identity from the persons running or owning the organisation. Constitutional Laws are the laws relating to the British Constitution. An example of a Constitutional Law is the Fixed-term Parliaments Act 2011 which provides fixed days for parliamentary general elections.

Administrative Law is concerned with the powers and duties of government bodies and ensuring that the government acts within its legal powers. Disputes may arise between a citizen and a government body; for example, if a citizen's house has been compulsorily purchased by a government department in order to build a motorway, the citizen may take the government department to court alleging that the action taken by the government department was outside the powers given to it by Parliament.

Private Law is concerned with the rights and duties between individuals and covers areas of law such as contract, tort, property, company, and family law. The individuals may be private persons, companies, or even a state body such as a local authority if, for example, a citizen has a contract with that local authority.

Criminal Law and Civil Law

An alternative method of classifying English law is into Civil Law and Criminal Law. The distinction between Civil Law and Criminal Law is important in terms of which court a case is heard in and the burden of proof that is required. There is also different terminology for civil and criminal issues.

In Civil Law, an aggrieved person commences court action and is called the **claimant** (prior to April 1999 a claimant was known as a **plaintiff**). The other party is called the **defendant**. A claimant taking the action before a court is said to sue a defendant. A claimant must prove his case on the balance of probabilities which means the claimant must show the court that the evidence is more in his favour than in the defendant's favour. A civil action is commenced in either a County Court or the High Court. If a claimant successfully wins the case, judgment will be entered in favour of the claimant. The purpose of a civil action is to compensate the person who has incurred a loss or an injury, or to provide some other remedy, such as an order to ensure the other party carries out their contractual obligations or an order to prevent the other party from acting in a wrongful manner.

In Criminal Law, both natural persons and legal persons, such as companies, can be prosecuted. In England and Wales a child reaches the age of criminal responsibility at the age of 10 and therefore children cannot face prosecution for crimes committed when they were younger than 10. The person who is being prosecuted is called the defendant or is sometimes referred to as the accused. A crime is regarded by society as a crime against the state and prosecutions are usually commenced by the state prosecution body, the Crown Prosecution Service (CPS). The police will pass the file on to the CPS who will decide whether to start an action. There are other state bodies, for example, County Councils and District Councils (part of local government) which also have prosecuting powers in areas such as trading standards. In addition, ordinary persons may bring private prosecutions against defendants, if the CPS declines to mount a prosecution. Some crimes, such as manslaughter, assault, and burglary have specific victims whereas other crimes, such as carrying an offensive weapon and breach of the Official Secrets Act, have no specific victims.

In a criminal trial, the case is heard either in a Magistrates' Court by three non-legally qualified magistrates or by a legally qualified District Judge (Magistrates' Court), or the trial is heard in a Crown Court before a judge and jury. A prosecutor prosecutes a defendant and the prosecutor must prove the facts of the case beyond reasonable doubt. This is a very high standard of proof and, unless the prosecution meets this standard of proof, then the defendant must be acquitted. The defendant does not have to prove his innocence; in fact a defendant does not have to give evidence at his own trial. A defendant is convicted if he is found guilty and acquitted if found not guilty. The purpose of a criminal prosecution is to determine the guilt of the defendant. If a guilty verdict is pronounced, the defendant will be sentenced by the judge. The purpose of imposing the sentence may include punishment of the defendant.

In both criminal and civil cases, if the losing party has grounds for an appeal then in the appeal case the party who brings the appeal will be known as the **appellant** and the other party will be called the **respondent** (See Table 1.1).

Certain circumstances will give rise to both criminal and civil actions. For example, a car accident caused through careless driving may give rise to both a criminal prosecution of the careless driver and a civil claim in the tort of negligence against the careless driver by the other driver.

Business Insight Laws tightened to prevent businesses gaining advantages through corruption

Old anti-bribery laws have been replaced by a suite of offences under the Bribery Act 2010. This Act makes it easier to bring successful prosecutions against UK corporate bodies for corruption offences committed at home and abroad. The Act also makes it an offence for commercial organisations to fail to prevent bribery. An organisation can be prosecuted if a person working on their behalf bribes another (in the UK or overseas), to obtain a business advantage for that commercial organisation. The organisation will only have a defence if it can show it had adequate procedures in place designed to prevent such bribery occurring. The aim is to ensure that businesses take responsibility for establishing an anti-corruption culture. Persons can also be convicted of giving or receiving bribes. The first person to be prosecuted and convicted under the Bribery Act 2010 was a clerk in a Magistrates Court who accepted a bribe in exchange for omitting to record a traffic offence on a court database. He was given a three-year sentence under the Act. A student was recently sentenced to 12 months imprisonment for offering £5,000 to a lecturer to move his dissertation mark to a pass.

Table 1.1 Differences between Civil and Criminal Law

Civil Law	Criminal Law
Disputes between persons.	Offences committed by persons.
Action taken by the claimant (one of the parties).	Action taken by the state (the state body responsible for prosecutions is the Crown Prosecution Service).
The action is first heard either in the County Court or the High Court.	The trial of the defendant is heard in either the Magistrates' Court or the Crown Court.
Case is cited by the names of the parties: *Claimant's name v Defendant's name.*	Case is usually cited: *R v Defendant's name.*
A claimant sues a defendant.	A prosecutor prosecutes a defendant.
The claimant must prove his case on the balance of probabilities, i.e. he must show that he has a greater right than the defendant.	A prosecutor must prove the defendant is guilty beyond reasonable doubt. The defendant does not have to prove his innocence.
Judgment will be entered for the claimant where the defendant is found to be liable, or if the defendant is found to be not liable, judgment will be entered for the defendant.	A defendant must be convicted if he is found guilty and acquitted if found not guilty.
In an appeal, the person bringing the appeal (who lost the case in the first court) is called the appellant and the other party (who won the case in the first court) is called the respondent.	In an appeal, the person bringing the appeal (who lost the case in the first court) is called the appellant and the other party (who won the case in the first court) is called the respondent.

Table 1.1 (*continued*)

Civil Law	Criminal Law
The purpose of a civil action is to provide a remedy for a civil wrong and is not to punish the person who loses the action, and therefore remedies include court orders that the losing party pays damages to the other party or carries out the contract as previously agreed.	The purpose of a criminal case is to determine the guilt of the defendant. Sentences such as imprisonment or fines may be imposed on conviction.

Case Names

In a civil action, the parties' names are used with the claimant's name first followed by 'v' and the defendant's name, e.g. *Fisher v Bell*. The 'v' is pronounced 'and', therefore the case would be read as *Fisher and Bell*. In an appeal case, the original claimant's name is still shown first even though the appeal may have been commenced by the original defendant.

Criminal prosecutions taken by the state (sometimes called the Crown) will usually be brought in the name of the Queen against the defendant. A prosecution against John Brown will be known as *R v Brown*. 'R' stands for *Regina* which means queen in Latin. (If there is a king on the throne then the 'R' will stand for *Rex* which means king in Latin). Just as in civil cases, although written 'v' this should be spoken as 'and'.

In certain complex cases and some specific offences, the prosecution is brought in the name of the head of the Crown Prosecution Service, namely the Director of Public Prosecutions (DPP) or the Attorney General (AG); therefore, the case is cited *Director of Public Prosecutions (DPP) v Defendant's name*, or *Attorney General (AG) v Defendant's name*.

The Legal Profession

The English legal profession is divided into two branches, barristers and solicitors. Traditionally, barristers were viewed as professional advocates and solicitors were viewed as general practitioners dealing with a wide variety of legal matters. However, that is not the case today. There are over 130,400 practising solicitors working in the UK (Solicitors Regulation Authority statistics, July 2014). Solicitors carry out a wide range of legal work including conveyancing, divorce, wills, corporate issues, and litigation although individual solicitors often specialise in one area of law. They have had the right to represent clients in the lower courts, i.e. the Magistrates' Courts and County Courts, for many years; however, since the 1990s solicitors have the right to appear in the higher courts provided they have certain additional qualifications.

There are approximately 15,500 self-employed barristers (The General Council of the Bar for England and Wales, Bar Barometer Trends in the Profile of the Bar, 2014). Their work includes advocacy in all courts and giving written opinions on legal issues. Prior to 1990, a barrister could only take instructions from a solicitor; however now for many cases the public access scheme allows anyone to go directly to a barrister for advice, representation, and drafting although there are some situations where a solicitor will still need to be instructed as well as a barrister. A lawyer cannot practise as a solicitor and barrister at the same time although it is possible to transfer from one profession to the other. Historically, judges, apart from those in the lower courts, were only drawn from the ranks of barristers. Although that changed in 1990 allowing for the appointment of former solicitors as judges at all levels depending on qualifications, the majority of higher court judges at present are former barristers.

Basic Terminology

For an online flashcard glossary visit the Online Resource Centre

Act of Parliament Statute, law made by Parliament.

Appellant The name given to the person bringing an appeal against a decision of a lower court.

Case law Law developed in the higher courts through a series of judge-made decisions.

Claimant The name used for a person who commences a civil action.

Common law Generally means law developed by judges through decisions in courts as opposed to laws created by Parliament.

Defendant In civil cases, it is the name given to the person who is being sued by the claimant. In criminal cases, it is the name given to the person who is being prosecuted for the crime.

Plaintiff The name used for a person who commenced a civil action prior to 2000. (The word used now is claimant.)

Precedent A decision of an earlier court case used as authority for deciding a later case with similar facts.

Respondent The name given in an appeal case to the party who has not brought the appeal case.

Statute Law that is set down in an Act of Parliament.

Summary

For an online printable version visit the Online Resource Centre

After studying this chapter students should be able to:

Explain what is meant by law

- Laws are rules and regulations which govern the activities of persons within a country.
- Some laws prohibit actions, other laws state conditions that must be fulfilled or complied with.

Outline the historical development and characteristics of English law

- In England and Wales, laws are composed of three main elements: legislation which is created through Parliament, common law, and directly enforceable EU law.
- Since the 11th century, English common law has developed partly through the decision of judges and it is accepted that judges do make and change the law.

- English law is uncodified, which means that unlike other European countries, the laws have not been systemised into code.
- The usual type of procedure in English courts is described as adversarial.
- The doctrine of binding precedent means that, in deciding a case, a judge is bound to apply the law decided by earlier cases heard in courts of superior status (and sometimes one of equal status).

Understand the difference between Public and Private Law and the difference between Civil and Criminal Law

- Public Law concerns the relationship between individuals and the state and is concerned with the decisions by, and control of, government bodies.
- Private Law is concerned with the rights and duties between individuals.
- In Civil Law an aggrieved person, the claimant, commences court action against the defendant and must prove his case on the balance of probabilities.
- In Criminal Law, action is usually taken by the state (CPS). A prosecutor must prove the defendant is guilty beyond reasonable doubt. The defendant does not have to prove his innocence.
- The purpose of a civil action is to provide a remedy for a civil wrong.
- The purpose of a criminal case is to punish the offender.

Questions

1. Consider the following cases and decide whether criminal or civil proceedings would result, and make a note of the parties in the action.

   a) Ali is being prosecuted for careless driving.
   b) Joe returns a faulty stereo to the shop where he bought it but the shop manager refuses to give him a refund.
   c) Kurt drives his car at 70 mph through town one Saturday night. He fails to see Gita on a zebra crossing and knocks her down.
   d) Sally is being sued by her landlord for non-payment of rent for three months.
   e) Jane is an alcoholic. She is pregnant and continues to drink heavily throughout her pregnancy and as a result her child is born with foetal alcohol syndrome.

2. Explain what is meant by the term 'common law'.

For outline answers visit the Online Resource Centre

Further Reading

Cownie, Bradney, and Burton, *English Legal System in Context*, 6th edn (Oxford University Press, 2013) Chapter 1.

Elliot and Quinn, *The English Legal System*, 15th edn (Pearson, 2014) Chapter 1.

Slapper and Kelly, *The English Legal System*, 15th edn (Routledge, 2014) Chapter 1.

Wilson, Rutherford, Storey and Wortley, *English Legal System*, 1st edn (Oxford University Press, 2014) Chapters 1 and 2.

Online Resource Centre

Test your knowledge by trying this chapter's **Multiple Choice Questions**. Visit:

www.oup.com/uk/orc/law/company/
jonesibl3e/01student/mcqs/ch01/

For more information, updates, and multiple choice questions, please visit the online resource centre at:

www.oup.com/uk/orc/law/company/
jonesibl3e/

The Court System and Alternative Dispute Resolution

Introduction

The English court system is fairly complex. There is a hierarchy of criminal and civil courts with the Supreme Court at the apex. The Supreme Court hears criminal and civil matters which are of constitutional or public importance on appeal from other courts. The court system is only one method of resolving disputes between parties. Sometimes other means of resolving conflicts which are less antagonistic may be more appropriate, particularly where businesses or other parties have had a close relationship and may seek to work together in the future. The oldest alternative dispute resolution procedure is arbitration. This is where the parties refer the dispute to an arbitrator to resolve, rather than use the court system. Alternatively, parties in dispute may prefer to use mediation or conciliation. Mediation is where a third party acts as an intermediary through which the parties negotiate in an attempt to reach a resolution; conciliation takes mediation a step further by giving the mediator the power to suggest solutions. In addition to the court system, a large number of tribunals have been set up, under various Acts of Parliament, to hear particular types of cases and deal with a range of issues such as immigration, employment, and social security.

Learning Objectives

After studying this chapter you should be able to:

- Demonstrate an understanding of the court system in England and Wales.
- Explain in which courts civil actions commence, criminal trials are heard, and appeal cases are dealt with.
- Show an understanding of criminal trials.
- Be familiar with a basic outline of civil procedure.
- Describe alternative methods of resolving disputes other than through the court system.

The English Court System

Basic Levels of the English Court System

The English court structure has four basic levels: the Supreme Court, the Court of Appeal, the High Court and Crown Court, and finally the County Court and Magistrates' Court. Within this structure there is no complete separation of criminal and civil courts or courts that hear cases in full for the first time, known as *courts of first instance* (or courts of **original jurisdiction**), and courts which hear cases on appeal from other courts, known as *appellate courts*. Some courts only hear civil cases and some courts are only appeal courts but other courts have more than one function; for example, the High Court hears original claims and appeal cases, and deals with civil, and to a limited extent criminal, matters.

Court hierarchy

The courts in England and Wales form a **system of hierarchy**, which means that certain courts are superior to other courts. At the lowest level are the Magistrates' Courts and the County Courts, which deal with the less serious criminal and civil cases respectively. In the next tier are the Crown Court, dealing mainly with criminal issues, and the High Court, dealing mainly with civil issues. These are followed by the Court of Appeal, which has a criminal and a civil division. At the apex of the hierarchy is the Supreme Court which is the ultimate appeal court for both criminal and civil cases in England, Wales, and Northern Ireland (in Scotland it is the final court of appeal for all civil cases). The Magistrates' Courts and the County Courts are known as inferior courts and all courts above them are known as superior courts (see Figure 2.1).

Civil and criminal courts

The two courts that hear criminal cases at first instance (courts that hear cases in full for the first time) are the Magistrates' Court and the Crown Court. The two main civil courts of first

Figure 2.1 An outline of the English court system

Supreme Court

Court of Appeal

High Court   Crown Court

County Court   Magistrates' Court

instance are the County Court and the High Court. Both the Crown Court and the High Court also hear cases on appeal, as do the Court of Appeal and Supreme Court.

The Judiciary

Judges are central to every legal system. In most European countries there is normally a career judiciary which is often viewed as part of the civil service. Lawyers decide to become judges at an early stage in their career and are specially trained as judges. They commence work in the lower courts before moving up to higher courts to deal with the more serious cases. In the UK, judges are appointed from the ranks of the legal profession and are usually experienced practising lawyers. Historically, only barristers could become senior judges; however today judicial appointments are open to all lawyers with the relevant legal qualifications provided they are citizens of the UK, Ireland, or a Commonwealth country. At present, the majority of judges previously practised as barristers.

Head of the judiciary

The Lord Chief Justice is the most senior member of the judiciary and President of the Courts of England and Wales. He is responsible for the training, guidance, and deployment of judges, and for expressing the views of the judiciary to Parliament and the government, but he is not a member of the government. The Lord Chief Justice is the head of the criminal division of the Court of Appeal. The head of the civil division of the Court of Appeal is the Master of the Rolls (see Figure 2.2).

Hierarchy of the judiciary

The most senior judges are the 12 *Justices of the Supreme Court* (at present 11 men and one woman). These judges hear cases in the Supreme Court and Privy Council.

Next in line are the *Lords Justices of Appeal* and *Lady Justices of Appeal* (there are seven Lady Justices and 30 Lords Justices). These judges sit in the Court of Appeal and the Employment Appeal Tribunal; they occasionally sit in other courts.

Next in order of seniority are *High Court Judges* sometimes called '*puisne* judges' (pronounced puny). There are approximately 110 High Court Judges. These judges hear cases in the High Court and the most serious criminal cases in the Crown Court. They may also sit with the Lord (or Lady) Justices of Appeal in the Court of Appeal.

Below the High Court Judges are the *Circuit Judges* who sit in the Crown Court and the County Court. There are currently just over 650 circuit judges. They are assisted by *Recorders*, who sit as judges on a part-time basis.

Finally, there are approximately 450 *District Judges* who sit in the County Courts, and approximately 140 *District Judges (Magistrates' Court)*, who sit in the Magistrates' Court. Until August 2000 these District Judges (Magistrates' Court) were known as Stipendiary Magistrates, but were renamed in order to recognise them as members of the professional judiciary. Assisting are part-time Deputy District Judges (approximately 750) and Deputy District Judges (Magistrates' Court) (approximately 145).

Figure 2.2 Senior judges

In addition to the legally qualified judiciary, there are approximately 23,000 lay magistrates who hear cases in the Magistrates' Courts. Magistrates (also called *Justices of the Peace*) are not legally qualified and do not receive a salary. They sit in the Magistrates' Court part-time, usually two or three times a month (see Figure 2.3).

Figure 2.3 Basic structure of where judges sit within the court system

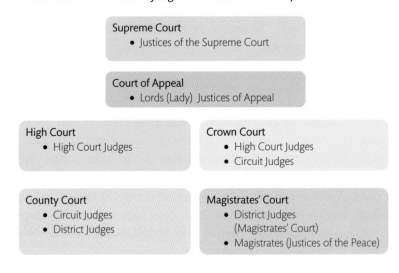

Key Concept Criminal trials are heard in the Magistrates' Courts and the Crown Court. Civil cases are commenced in the County Court or the High Court. The Court of Appeal and the Supreme Court hear cases on appeal from the lower courts.

The Magistrates' Court

There are 330 Magistrates' Courts throughout England and Wales. These courts are a key part of the criminal justice system and 95 per cent of criminal cases are completed there. Cases in the Magistrates' Courts are usually heard by three lay magistrates (Justices of the Peace). Magistrates come from all walks of life and do not usually have any legal qualifications but they do undergo a training programme. In a court hearing, a legally qualified Magistrates' Court clerk advises them on the law, sentencing, and procedure.

Where a case is being heard by a *District Judge (Magistrates' Court)*, the District Judge will sit alone. District Judges (Magistrates' Court) are located in the busiest Magistrates' Courts and generally deal with more complex or sensitive cases.

Classification of criminal offence

Whether an offence is triable in a Magistrates' Court or the Crown Court depends upon the seriousness of the offence. There are three categories of criminal offences:

- *Indictable offences:* Prosecution of these offences must be in the Crown Court. They are the most serious offences such as murder, manslaughter, rape, robbery.

- *Summary offences:* Prosecution of these offences must be in the Magistrates' Court. These are relatively minor offences and have all been created by statute, and cover crimes such as driving without insurance, careless driving, using threatening abusive or insulting words and behaviour.

- *Offences triable either way* (Offences triable either as summary offences or as indictable offences): Prosecution of these offences may either be in a Magistrates' Court or the Crown Court. These are the mid-range offences such as theft, burglary, assault occasioning actual bodily harm. The seriousness of a case will depend on its facts, for example, the offence of theft may be committed by theft of £500,000 from an employer where the employee held a position of trust or may be relatively minor where an individual stole a £30 jacket from a large shop.

Criminal jurisdiction of Magistrates' Courts

Magistrates have jurisdiction to hear all summary offences and offences triable either way. They also hear bail applications, requests by the police for arrest and search warrants, and legal aid applications.

If an offence is triable either way it is first brought before the Magistrates' Court, which will decide which is the most suitable venue for the trial of the case. If the magistrates decide that the case before them is serious and that the sentence that they have the power to impose would not be sufficiently severe, they can send the case for trial at the Crown Court. The defendant has no option but to go to the Crown Court for trial. However, if the magistrates are of the opinion that the case should be heard as a summary offence (in the Magistrates' Court) the defendant has the right to insist on trial in the Crown Court. Trials in Magistrates' Courts are called summary trials and trials in the Crown Court are called indictable trials.

The maximum sentence that Magistrates can normally impose on individuals for an offence is 6 months (12 months in total if the defendant is convicted of more than one either-way offence) and/or fines not exceeding £5,000. Businesses may be fined up to £20,000 for certain offences. (Although not yet in force, there is power in the Legal Aid, Sentencing and Punishment of Offenders Act 2012 to impose unlimited fines for some offences). Magistrates can impose other sentences such as community payback orders and probation orders. If a defendant is found guilty by the magistrates of a 'triable either way' offence, the magistrates may send him to the Crown Court for sentencing if a more severe sentence than they have the power to impose is thought necessary.

Youth Courts

Magistrates and District Judges (Magistrates' Court) sit in Youth Courts, which are special courts exercising jurisdiction over some offences committed by youths between 10 and 17 years. Procedure in the Youth Courts is less formal than that in adult courts and these courts are not open to members of the general public. Where a young person is accused of a very serious offence, such as rape or murder, the trial will be held in the Crown Court.

Appeals from Magistrates' Courts following summary trials

Less than one per cent of decisions of Magistrates' Courts are subject to an appeal; however, there are two different courts that an appeal can be made to (see Figure 2.4).

A defendant found guilty in a Magistrates' Court may appeal to the Crown Court against his conviction (if he pleaded not guilty) on points of fact or points of law or against sentence. The court may allow the appeal, reduce the sentence, or impose a higher sentence up to a maximum that could have been imposed by the magistrates.

Alternatively, either the defendant or the prosecution can appeal to the High Court (Divisional Court of the Queen's Bench Division). The appeal must be on a point of law or a claim that the magistrates have acted beyond their powers. These appeals are called 'appeals by way of case stated' because magistrates must state the case to be decided by the High Court.

If the defendant appeals by way of case stated, he cannot later take a further appeal to the Crown Court. If an appeal has been heard in the Crown Court, a further appeal by the prosecution or the defendant lies on a point of law or jurisdiction 'by way of case stated' from the Crown Court to the High Court.

If an appeal has been heard in the High Court, then a further appeal may be taken by either party to the Supreme Court provided the High Court certifies that the case involves

Figure 2.4 Appeals from summary trials in the Magistrates' Court

```
                        ┌─────────────────┐
                        │  Supreme Court  │
                        └─────────────────┘
                                 ▲
                   Appeal on points of law of general
                   public importance

┌──────────────────┐                              ┌──────────────────────┐
│   Crown Court     │   Appeal by D or P by        │  High Court:         │
│   Retrial of case │   'way of case stated'   ──▶ │  Divisional Court of │
└──────────────────┘                              │  Queen's Bench       │
         ▲                                         │  Division            │
                                                   └──────────────────────┘
   Appeal by defendant          Appeal by defendant or prosecution by      ▲
   against conviction           'way of case stated'
   and/or sentence

┌──────────────────┐
│ Magistrates' Court│
│ Summary trial of  │
│ summary offences  │
│ and offences      │
│ triable either    │
│ way               │
└──────────────────┘
```

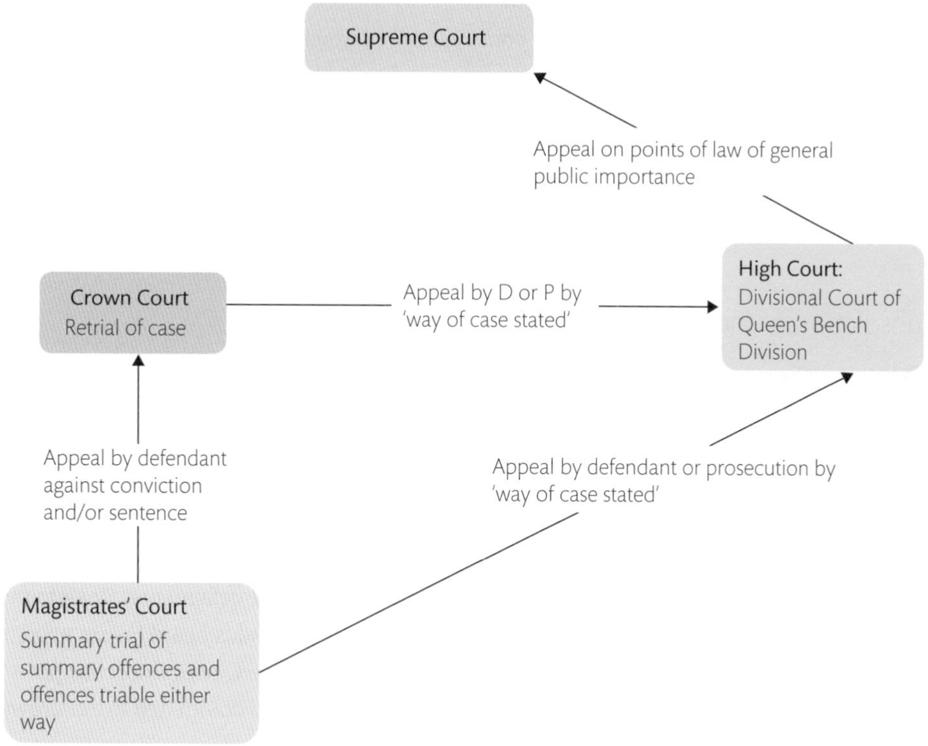

a point of law of general public importance and the High Court or the Supreme Court gives permission to appeal.

Civil jurisdiction of Magistrates' Court

Magistrates' Courts also have some **civil jurisdiction**. They hear family proceedings including orders for protection against violence, and proceedings concerning the welfare of children. In addition they have powers to licence betting shops and casinos and enforce council tax demands.

Key Concept Where a criminal trial takes place in the Magistrates' Court, the defendant may appeal to the Crown Court against conviction and/or sentence. The prosecution and the defendant may appeal to the High Court on a point of law.

Crown Court

The Crown Court is regarded as a single court, sittings of which may be held anywhere at any time. Currently there are 77 Crown Court centres in England and Wales. When sitting in the City of London, the Crown Court is known as the Central Criminal Court (Old Bailey). Judges that hear cases in the Crown Court are High Court Judges, Circuit Judges, and Recorders. High Court Judges hear the very serious crimes, e.g. murder, rape. Magistrates sit with a judge if the case is an appeal from a Magistrates' Court.

Jurisdiction of the Crown Court

The Crown Court has **criminal jurisdiction** to hear prosecutions of all indictable offences and offences triable either way sent from the Magistrates' Court. The trial is usually heard by a judge and jury of 12 ordinary people. The judge advises the jury on the law and the jury decide whether the defendant is guilty or not guilty. A majority verdict of 10–2 is sufficient to convict a defendant. Under the provisions of the Criminal Justice Act 2003 it is possible for a complex fraud case or a case where there is a risk of jury tampering to be tried by a judge alone.

The Crown Court has **appellate jurisdiction** to hear appeals by defendants convicted in the Magistrates' Court. The appeal takes the form of a new trial and is heard before a judge and two, three, or four lay magistrates. There is no jury present. The Crown Court has power to impose sentences on persons convicted in Magistrates' Court and committed to the Crown Court for sentencing. Applications for bail and legal aid can be heard in the Crown Court.

Business Insight

The Corporate Manslaughter and Corporate Homicide Act 2007 is an important development in corporate criminal liability. Prior to the new legislation, prosecutions of companies for gross negligence manslaughter were rare, and convictions of large organisations virtually impossible; for example, manslaughter charges had to be dismissed against a large company-operated rail service, where four passengers died and 102 were injured, despite the judge stating that it was 'the worst example of sustained, industrial negligence in a high-risk industry' he had ever seen. Under the Act, a company can be found guilty of corporate manslaughter if the way in which its activities are managed or organised causes a death and amounts to a gross breach of a duty to take reasonable care for a person's safety. On conviction, a company will face an unlimited fine which should seldom be less than £500,000 and may run into millions. In 2011 Cotswold Geotechnical Holdings became the first company in the UK to be convicted of corporate manslaughter under the Act. The company had not followed safety guidelines and an engineer died when a trench collapsed and buried him in mud.

Appeals from the Crown Court following trials on indictment

A defendant can appeal against conviction and sentence to the Court of Appeal (Criminal Division) with permission from the trial judge or the Court of Appeal. The prosecution have no right of appeal. A further appeal lies to the Supreme Court from either the defendant or the prosecution if the Court of Appeal certifies the case involves a point of law of general public importance and the Court of Appeal or the Supreme Court gives permission to appeal (see Figure 2.5).

The prosecution cannot appeal against a conviction or sentence given in the Crown Court; however, under s 36 of the Criminal Justice Act 1972, the Attorney General (government lawyer) can refer a case which has resulted in an acquittal to the Court of Appeal (Criminal Division). The acquittal of the defendant is not affected by the decision of the Court of Appeal but the law in issue is clarified for later cases.

If the Attorney General considers that a sentence given by the Crown Court is unduly lenient then, under s 36 of the Criminal Justice Act 1988, he may refer the case to the Court of Appeal to review the sentence and the Court can impose a harsher sentence.

Figure 2.5 Criminal appeals from the Crown Court

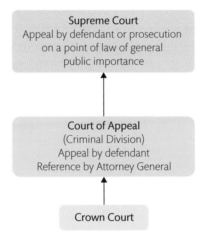

Supreme Court
Appeal by defendant or prosecution
on a point of law of general
public importance

Court of Appeal
(Criminal Division)
Appeal by defendant
Reference by Attorney General

Crown Court

Key Concept Where a defendant is convicted in a Crown Court he can appeal against conviction and sentence to the Court of Appeal and then on to the Supreme Court. The prosecution cannot appeal, but the Attorney General may refer the case to the Court of Appeal to review the sentence if he considers it too lenient.

County Courts

County Courts deal with the majority of civil cases in England and Wales. County Courts were first set up under the County Courts Act 1846 and, although they are called 'County' Courts, they do not follow county boundaries. There are 218 County Courts in England and Wales and each County Court has at least one Circuit Judge and one District Judge assigned to it. Circuit Judges are more senior than District Judges and can hear all types of cases, although they usually hear the most complex cases. District Judges preside over the 'small claims procedure' where the limit is £10,000 and hear fast-track and less complex multi-track cases and deal with pre-trial issues. The manner in which each case is dealt with depends on the value of the claim, so that the time and cost spent on the case is appropriate to its value.

Jurisdiction of the County Court

The County Courts deal with a wide range of civil cases including matters involving contract, tort, landlord and tenant, mortgages, wills, trusts, bankruptcies, insolvency, and divorce. Civil cases can either be commenced in the County Court or the High Court. The decision on which court to start civil proceedings is determined by the value of the case, the complexity of facts and issues involved, whether points of law of general public importance are raised, and the procedures and remedies available (some remedies are only available in the High Court). Generally non-personal injury claims worth up to £25,000 and personal injury claims where the claimant expects to receive compensation of less than £50,000 must be tried in the County Court. Cases that have been commenced in the County Court can be transferred to the High Court and vice versa. The transfer may be at the request of one of the parties or at the discretion of the judge.

Appeals in civil cases

Usually an appeal can only be made if permission to appeal is given either by the court that heard the case or the court to which the appeal is being made. Permission to appeal should only be given if the appeal has a real prospect of success or there is some compelling reason why the appeal should be heard. Where a case has been heard by a District Judge in the County Court, an appeal may be made to a Circuit Judge sitting in the County Court. Where a case has been heard by a Circuit Judge in the County Court, then an appeal may be made to the High Court unless it is an appeal from a final decision in a multi-track case, in which case the appeal is to the Court of Appeal. Where a case has been heard by the High Court, an appeal may be made to the Court of Appeal. Occasionally appeals from the High Court 'leapfrog' (see later) the Court of Appeal and go straight to the Supreme Court. Decisions from the Court of Appeal can be appealed to the Supreme Court.

High Court of Justice

The High Court sits at the Royal Courts of Justice in the Strand, London, but for the convenience of litigants and their solicitors it also sits at some major centres in provincial cities and towns in England and Wales. The work of the court is mainly civil and is handled by three divisions: the Chancery Division, the Queen's Bench Division, and the Family Division. Each division has a senior judge at its head and a number of High Court '*puisne*' Judges. Each of the Divisions hears cases at first instance (i.e. the case is commenced in the High Court); however each Division has a Divisional Court which hears cases on appeal from other courts and tribunals.

Key Concept The decision to make a claim in the County Court or the High Court depends on a number of factors including the value and complexity of the case and whether the issues involved raise points of law of general public importance.

Chancery Division

The Chancery Division deals with matters relating to trusts, mortgages, finance, administration of estates of deceased persons, company law, partnerships, and bankruptcies. There are two specialist courts within the Chancery Division: the Patents Court and the Companies Court.

Queen's Bench Division

The major part of the work of the Queen's Bench Division (QBD) is dealing with contract and tort cases that are unsuitable to be heard in the County Court. Most cases are heard by a judge sitting alone but occasionally (in approximately one per cent of cases) a civil jury of 12 ordinary people will sit, for example, in an action for defamation. Within the QBD there is a Commercial Court and an Admiralty Court.

Family Division

This division deals with difficult matrimonial and family issues such as legitimacy, adoption, defended divorces (where one of the parties seeks to prevent the marriage being dissolved), and other aspects of family law, e.g. proceedings under the Child Abduction and Custody Act 1985 and the Human Fertilisation and Embryology Act 1990.

Divisional Courts of the High Court

Each of the three divisions of the High Court has a Divisional Court where either one or more judges sit to hear cases (see Figure 2.6).

Divisional Court of Queen's Bench Division

The Divisional Court of Queen's Bench Division hears appeals on points of law by way of case stated directly from the Magistrates' Court or via the Crown Court. It also hears applications for judicial review of decisions which have been made by public authorities, government bodies, inferior courts or tribunals, and where the applicant is alleging that the body making the decision has acted unlawfully, without authority, or contrary to the Human Rights Act 1998.

Divisional Court of Chancery Division

The Divisional Court of Chancery Division hears appeals from General or Special Commissioners on taxation matters, appeals from the Adjudicator to HM Land Registry on land registration issues, and appeals from County Courts on insolvency matters.

Divisional Court of Family Division

The Divisional Court of Family Division hears appeals from the Magistrates' Courts on family issues, such as financial orders and orders under the Children Act 1989.

Figure 2.6 The Divisions of the High Court

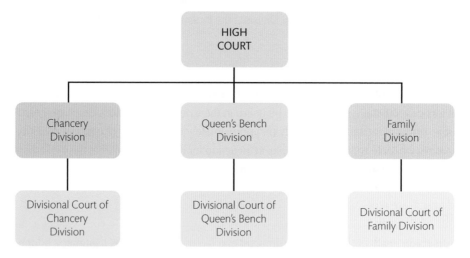

Court of Appeal

The Court of Appeal is located in the Royal Courts of Justice, in the Strand, London. It has two divisions: the Civil Division which is presided over by the Master of the Rolls and the Criminal Division which is presided over by the Lord Chief Justice.

Jurisdiction of the Court of Appeal

The Civil Division hears civil cases on appeal either from High Court or County Court. The Criminal Division hears criminal cases on appeal from the Crown Court. Cases are usually heard before three judges, although five judges may sit on very important cases. Decisions are by majority. If judges in the minority disagree then they will give dissenting judgments. The appeal is a re-hearing of the case through the media of the trial judge's notes, statements, and listening to counsel. Witnesses are not heard and new evidence is not examined. If new evidence comes to light in a criminal appeal, then in certain circumstances a retrial can be ordered.

Supreme Court

The Supreme Court is the highest appeal court in England and Wales and plays an important role in the development of English law. It was established by the Constitutional Reform Act 2005 and came into being on 1 October 2009. Prior to the setting up of the Supreme Court, the highest court of appeal was the Judicial Committee of the House of Lords, made up of 12 judges who sat in the judicial committee of the House of Lords and as such were Members of Parliament. In the UK, there are two Houses of Parliament: the House of Commons and the House of Lords. The House of Commons is an elected body. The House of Lords is an appointed body composed of life peers and hereditary peers. When the Supreme Court was set up, the judges who sat in the House of Lords became the first Justices of the Supreme Court.

The Supreme Court sits in London, in the former Middlesex Guildhall. Cases must be heard by at least three judges, but in practice five judges usually sit together to hear an appeal. Exceptionally, if the case involves particularly difficult or important issues, more than five judges can sit. For example, nine Supreme Court Judges sat in the case of *Radmacher v Granatino* (2010) to decide what weight should be given to pre-nuptial agreements.

Each judge may give his own judgment, setting out reasons for reaching the decision, although often only one or two judges set out their reasons and the others concur. Dissenting judgments are reported but the majority view prevails. The appeal is not a retrial and no oral evidence is given by witnesses. The judges read the documents in the case and listen to the barristers for each of the parties.

Jurisdiction of the Supreme Court

The Supreme Court is the final court of appeal of all civil and criminal matters in England and Wales and Northern Ireland, and for all civil matters in Scotland. The final court for criminal appeals in Scotland is the High Court of Justiciary. The Supreme Court mainly hears appeals from the Court of Appeal. Permission to appeal to the Supreme Court must usually be given by the court which handed down the last judgment, or may be given by the Supreme Court. Cases heard by the Supreme Court involve points of law of public or constitutional importance.

Leapfrog

Exceptionally, cases may bypass the Court of Appeal and 'leapfrog' from the High Court to the Supreme Court. About 10 cases a year use this procedure. The 'leapfrog' procedure was introduced by the Administration of Justice Act 1969. In order for this procedure to be used:

(a) all the parties must consent to it;

(b) the High Court Judge who heard the original case must certify that the case involves a point of law of general public importance which relates wholly or mainly to the construction of a statute or a statutory instrument, or the judge is bound by a previous decision of the Court of Appeal or Supreme Court;

(c) the Supreme Court must grant permission to use the leapfrog procedure. (See Figure 2.7.)

Figure 2.7 Civil Court system

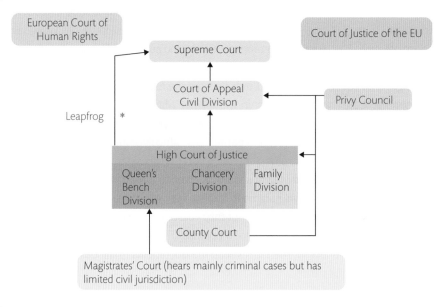

Key Concept The Court of Appeal and the Supreme Court hear both criminal and civil appeal cases from lower courts. The Supreme Court is the highest appeal court in England and Wales and plays an important role in the development of English law.

The Court of Justice of the European Union

The Court of Justice (CJ) is the Court of the European Union (EU). It sits in Luxembourg and consists of one judge from each Member State. The judge is appointed by the government of each state from judges holding high judicial office in that state. The function of the CJ is to ensure that EU law is interpreted and applied in the same way in each Member State, to ensure Member States carry out their treaty obligations, and to ensure that the institutions of the EU act legally. If a Member State breaks its treaty obligations, that Member State can be brought before the Court. The decision of the Court must be accepted by the Member States.

The CJ is not part of the English legal system and applicants cannot appeal from English courts to the CJ. However, if a case before an English court requires interpretation of EU law because the EU law is unclear, then the English court can (and must if it is the Supreme Court) request an interpretation of the EU law issue from the CJ. This interpretation of the EU law issue is binding on all English courts in future cases.

Judicial Committee of Privy Council

The Judicial Committee of the Privy Council sits in London. It is staffed by Lords of Appeal in Ordinary and lawyers from certain Commonwealth countries who have held high judicial office. It is the final court of appeal for civil and criminal issues from some Commonwealth countries such as the Channel Islands, Jamaica, Bermuda, and Trinidad and Tobago. Although decisions on points of law made by the Privy Council are influential, they are not binding and do not have to be followed by English courts. The Privy Council also hears appeals from some professional tribunals.

European Court of Human Rights

The European Court of Human Rights (ECtHR) was set up by the Council of Europe to ensure that states which signed the European Convention on Human Rights and Fundamental Freedoms 1950 adhered to their treaty obligations. The Convention lays down a list of civil and political rights and freedoms which each contracting party agrees to protect within their state. The Convention is an international treaty to which the UK has subscribed together with 46 other countries. The treaty is not an EU treaty although all 28 members of the EU have also signed the Convention. Countries not in the EU are also signatories. The ECtHR sits in Strasbourg and comprises 47 judges who are elected by the Council of Europe for a term of six years. Judges do not represent their country but sit as independent judges. Decisions are usually made by a committee of three judges or a chamber of seven judges, although occasionally they are made by a grand chamber of 17 judges.

Applications to the European Court of Human Rights

If a contracting state breaches one or more Convention rights, then another contracting state may make a complaint to the ECtHR. In 1976, the Republic of Ireland took the UK to the ECtHR alleging breach of Article 3—torture and inhuman treatment of some of its citizens resident in Northern Ireland. An individual may lodge an application to the ECtHR claiming to be a victim of a violation of the Convention by a state; however, the individual must first exhaust all his domestic remedies. This means that an individual from the UK must have first taken his case through the English court system before he can bring an action to the ECtHR. In 2002, Diane Pretty took the UK to the ECtHR alleging breaches of a number of Convention Articles including Article 2, the right to life; however, before she made her application to the ECtHR, she had already unsuccessfully taken her case through the English courts up to the House of Lords. All judgments of the ECtHR are binding on the states concerned. The Court can order compensation to be awarded to the victim if a state has violated his Convention rights. It is up to the Council of Europe to ensure that a judgment of the ECtHR is carried out and, if a state refuses to comply, it can be suspended or expelled from the Council.

Key Concept   The Court of Justice (CJ) is the Court of the European Union (EU) and deals with EU law. The European Court of Human Rights (ECtHR) deals with allegations of state breaches of the European Convention on Human Rights.

Civil Disputes

Civil disputes arise in every area of business. There are various methods of resolving disputes without recourse to the civil court system. A dispute may be resolved through discussion and negotiation with or without a solicitor or more formally through the process of arbitration, mediation, or conciliation. Only a small proportion of civil disputes reaches the stage of litigation and, where civil court proceedings are commenced, the cases are often settled before the final court hearing.

Civil Court Proceedings

In 1999, major changes in civil litigation procedure were introduced following recommendations in a report, 'Access to Justice 1996' by Lord Woolf, who was at the time Master of the Rolls (Head of the Civil Division of the Court of Appeal). These changes are commonly referred to as the Woolf Reforms. The major changes were brought into law by the Civil Procedure Act 1997 and the Civil Procedure Rules 1998 (CPRs). These rules applied to all civil courts and were designed to lead to quicker and less confrontational settlements, thereby reducing the amount of cost and delay. Simplified terminology was introduced to make courts more user friendly; for example, the term for the party bringing a civil court action was changed from 'plaintiff' to 'claimant', and the term for the form to start the claim was changed from 'originating summons' or 'writ' to 'claim form'. There are also *Practice Directions* (official guidance statements) which provide fine detail for the CPRs, telling parties how they should operate, what documents have to be filed with the court, and what can happen if they do not do something properly.

The ultimate goal of the reforms was to change the litigation culture, with the overriding objective that the rules should enable the courts to deal with cases justly and that litigation was to be used as a last resort. Under the CPRs, the judge is the case manager and is under an obligation to actively manage cases. This includes encouraging the parties to cooperate with each other, identifying issues in dispute early on, fixing timetables and controlling the process of the case, and seeing if the benefits of a particular method of hearing the case justify its costs.

There are various powers given to judges to encourage early settlement of cases wherever possible, and penalties can be imposed on parties acting unreasonably or breaching the CPRs.

Pre-action protocols

Before a civil case is commenced, the claimant must send a letter before claim setting out the allegations and the defendant must reply within a reasonable time. In some types of cases there are also pre-action protocols which must be observed. These are written guidelines of best practice. They are intended to encourage parties to exchange information and settle disputes fairly, or at least discover all information and carry out investigations before going to court. There are different protocols for different types of cases. If parties are unable to settle the dispute without going to court (although over 80 per cent of civil disputes are settled before reaching court) the parties will be asked if they followed the relevant pre-action protocol and, if they have not, they can be penalised by the judge.

Claim form

If the parties fail to settle the issue, the person bringing the action, the claimant, fills in a claim form and particulars of claim setting out the details of the claim, including the amount and a concise statement of the facts which the claimant relies upon. The form is submitted to the court, which processes it and serves a copy of it, usually by post, on the defendant.

Admission, defence, counterclaim

On receipt of a claim form with the particulars of a claim, a defendant must acknowledge receipt of it within 14 days and either admit the claim or put in a defence within 28 days. The defence must state which of the allegations in the particulars of the claim the defendant denies, giving reasons, and which allegations the defendant admits. If the defendant disputes the value that the claimant has put on the claim, he must state his reasons and if possible put an alternative value. The defendant may also make a counterclaim if he wants to defend the action and claim for loss that he has suffered at the hands of the claimant. Should a defendant receive a claim form and ignore it, after 14 days the claimant can enter judgment against the defendant for the sum specified in the claim form.

Allocation to track

When a defence has been received the court will allocate the case to one of three tracks.

- *Small claims track* is for claims of £10,000 or less. The hearing in these cases will be relatively informal before a District Judge. Although most hearings are open to the public, they generally take place in a room as opposed to a court. If parties agree and in the judge's opinion the case is appropriate, there can be a 'paper hearing' where the parties do not attend but send in written evidence. Legal costs of employing a solicitor or barrister are not recoverable from the party that loses the case.

- *Fast track* is generally for claims between £10,000 and £25,000. There is a standard streamlined procedure for handling these cases so that the legal costs remain proportionate to the claim. The trial is limited to a maximum of five hours and normally only written evidence is given at trial. The costs allowed for the trial are fixed depending on the level of advocate.

- *Multi track* is for claims over £25,000 (or lower in very complex cases). There is a range of procedures for handling these cases depending on the nature of the case. The judge will manage the progress of the case through case management conferences where issues are decided, such as whether the claim is sufficiently clear to the other party, which documents need to be shown to the other party, what expert evidence should be sought and disclosed, and whether it would save costs to have a separate trial on a particular issue. The principle of setting an early date for trial is paramount.

Settlement before trial

The CPRs provide an incentive for parties to settle their disputes before trial because the court takes notice of any pre-trial offer to settle. If an offer is made and the claimant refuses it, but later, despite winning the case, is awarded less by the court than the sum offered to settle pre-trial, he will not be able to recover all his court costs from the defendant. A judge will not be told of the offer before the trial.

Figure 2.8 Simple outline of civil claim procedure

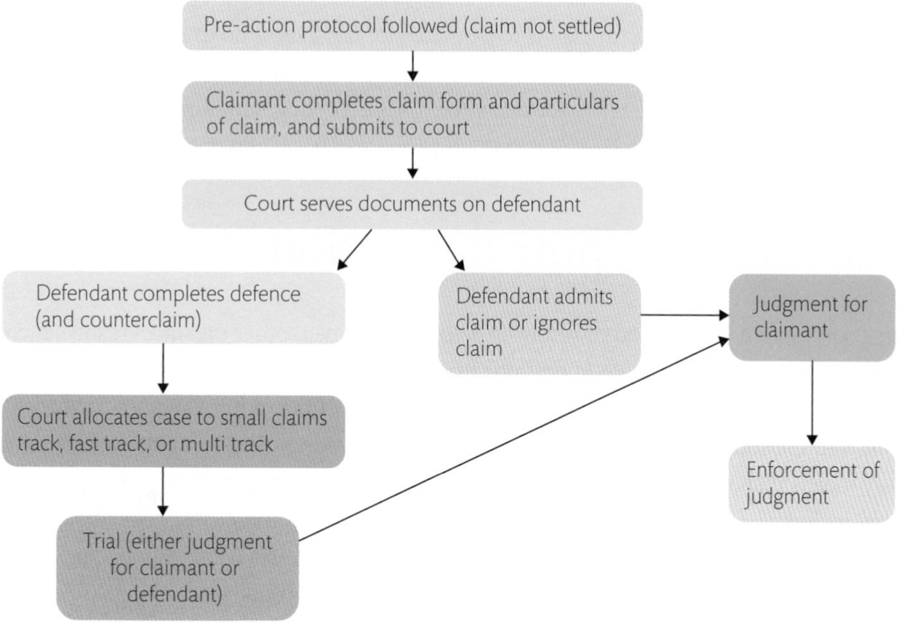

```
┌─────────────────────────────────────────────┐
│ Pre-action protocol followed (claim not settled) │
└─────────────────────────────────────────────┘
                        │
                        ▼
┌─────────────────────────────────────────────┐
│ Claimant completes claim form and particulars │
│ of claim, and submits to court                │
└─────────────────────────────────────────────┘
                        │
                        ▼
┌─────────────────────────────────────────────┐
│ Court serves documents on defendant          │
└─────────────────────────────────────────────┘
              │                    │
              ▼                    ▼
┌─────────────────────┐   ┌──────────────────┐   ┌──────────────────┐
│ Defendant completes │   │ Defendant admits │   │ Judgment for     │
│ defence             │   │ claim or ignores │──▶│ claimant         │
│ (and counterclaim)  │   │ claim            │   └──────────────────┘
└─────────────────────┘   └──────────────────┘            │
              │                                            ▼
              ▼                                   ┌──────────────────┐
┌─────────────────────┐                           │ Enforcement of   │
│ Court allocates case│                           │ judgment         │
│ to small claims     │                           └──────────────────┘
│ track, fast track,  │
│ or multi track      │
└─────────────────────┘
              │
              ▼
┌─────────────────────┐
│ Trial (either       │
│ judgment for        │
│ claimant or         │
│ defendant)          │
└─────────────────────┘
```

The trial

A civil case is heard in open court before a judge. Evidence is either by written documents which both sides have seen or by witnesses giving oral evidence and being cross-examined. The judge will have read the papers beforehand and need only deal with matters in dispute. The claimant or his solicitor or barrister speak first and have to prove the case on a balance of probabilities.

Enforcement of judgment

Winning a case in the civil courts and obtaining judgment for a sum of money is only the first step. If the defendant does not pay the money due, the claimant will have to take steps to enforce the judgment. Judgment may be enforced by a number of different methods. A *warrant of control* may be issued requesting an enforcement agent to take the defendant's goods to raise money to pay the debt. A *third party debt order* may be used to freeze money in bank or building society accounts held by the debtor and the judge will then decide if the money in the account should be used to pay the creditor. An *attachment of earnings order* may be made if the defendant is working. The court can order that the claimant is paid directly out of the defendant's salary. A *charging order* can be made, imposing a charge on the defendant's property (house, land, shares, trust funds, etc) and the property cannot be sold without paying off the debt. Alternatively, the claimant can seek a *bankruptcy order* against the defendant or, if the defendant is a company, seek to have the company wound up (see Figure 2.8).

Money claim online (MCOL)

An MCOL allows County Court claims to be issued for fixed sums up to £100,000 by individuals and organisations over the internet. The defendant may file a defence online but often claims are undefended. The claimant can apply online for judgment and enforcement. This service, available since 2002, has proved to be very popular with creditors.

Alternative Dispute Resolution

The court system is a method of resolving disputes; however, other means of resolving conflicts may be more appropriate in certain circumstances. For example, building contractors may have a dispute on the terms of one contract with a supplier but, because they wish to work with the supplier in future, they may wish to resolve the matter through more conciliatory means than a court action. There are a number of alternative methods of dispute resolution including arbitration, mediation, and conciliation. In some cases, disputes are dealt with by tribunals rather than courts. The UK government promotes ADR, encouraging people to resolve their issues out of court, using simpler, more informal, and less stressful procedures where possible.

Arbitration

Arbitration is the procedure by which the parties refer their disputes to a third party or parties for resolving, rather than taking their dispute to a Court. The parties agree to be bound by the decision of the arbitrator, who decides the dispute according to the law but outside the confines of the court and normal court procedure. In the commercial world, multinational corporations and other businesses will often prefer to refer a dispute to arbitration rather than take court action, not only because of the convenience, speed, and cost of arbitration procedure but also to ensure a continuing relationship with each other. There is a degree of interdependency between businesses and good relationships may be damaged through the adversarial nature of the court process. It is common practice for commercial contracts to contain express clauses referring any future disputes to arbitration. Alternatively, the parties may agree to arbitration after a dispute has arisen.

Principles of arbitration

The Arbitration Act 1996 sets out the following three general principles on arbitration:

- The object of arbitration is to obtain the fair resolution of disputes by an impartial tribunal without unnecessary delay or expense.

- The parties should be free to agree how their disputes are resolved, subject only to such safeguards as are necessary in the public interest.

- In matters governed by the Arbitration Act, the court should not intervene except as provided by the Act.

Arbitration procedure

If there is an arbitration agreement between parties, the agreement may state who should be appointed as an arbitrator. If there is no contractual agreement or the agreement is silent and the parties in dispute are members of a Trade Association, they may refer the dispute to the Association; alternatively, there are specialist arbitration bodies. An arbitrator may be, but does not have to be, legally qualified; often an arbitrator will be an expert in the field in dispute. Most of the powers set out in the Arbitration Act are not compulsory and it is up to the parties to decide which procedures they will adopt. The mandatory parts of the Act only take effect if parties do not reach an agreement. Parties can agree that the dispute should be decided on grounds of commercial fairness rather than on strict legal grounds. Under the Act, the arbitrator has the general duty to act fairly and impartially between the parties, giving each an opportunity to state their case, and to adopt suitable procedures to avoid unnecessary delay and expense. Any award given in arbitration is enforceable through the court system without having to argue the case again in court.

An appeal to court against the decision of an arbitrator is very limited. An appeal may be made if the arbitrator did not have jurisdiction to hear the case (but this ground may be lost if the parties took part in the arbitration without complaining about the lack of jurisdiction), or there was a serious irregularity affecting the operation of the tribunal such as failing to conduct the tribunal as agreed between the parties, or uncertainty of the award made to one of the parties.

If a party starts court proceedings contrary to a valid arbitration agreement, the other party can apply to court to have the court action discontinued.

Business Insight

There are a number of arbitration bodies in London including the London Court of International Arbitration (LCIA) and the London Maritime Arbitrators Association (LMAA). The majority of cases dealt with by LCIA are international and cover a diverse range of issues including agreements relating to aircraft, oil exploration, and the sale and purchase of commodities. Approximately 16 per cent of cases concern disputes of $20 million plus. The LMAA deals with maritime disputes, and reports that a greater number of maritime disputes are referred to arbitration in London than to any other place where arbitration services are offered.

Advantages of arbitration

Generally, the cost of arbitration is less expensive than court proceedings; however, arbitrators can command high fees. The proceedings are held in private, and the public, including rival companies, do not get access to potentially sensitive information. Therefore, parties to arbitration do not run the risk of any damaging publicity arising out of the proceedings. An arbitrator has specialist knowledge in the particular area and can ensure that his decision is in line with accepted practice of the business area. Proceedings are less formal than court proceedings and can be scheduled to fit in with businesses. Arbitration is generally much quicker than taking the case through the courts.

Mediation

Mediation is conducted in private at a time and place to suit the parties. The mediator is appointed by the parties and is trained as a mediator. He may or may not be legally qualified. The mediator acts like a facilitator through which the disputing parties can communicate and negotiate. Mediators can move between the parties without the parties meeting—they just communicate through the mediator. Alternatively, the mediator can operate in the presence of the parties.

The discussions with the parties are on a 'without prejudice' basis, which means that, if the parties fail to reach agreement at the end of the mediation process, the matters discussed at mediation cannot be used in later court proceedings. The emphasis is on getting the parties themselves to work out a shared agreement as to how best to settle the dispute.

If a dispute is successfully resolved through mediation, the parties themselves will have determined their own solution and therefore may be committed to and satisfied with the outcome. The dispute may be resolved with a compromise, with both parties partly achieving their aim rather than having a 'winner' and a 'loser'. If the parties agree, the agreement can be written down and is legally binding.

However, not all mediation is successful and, if mediation fails, the issue will remain unresolved at the end of the process, and court proceedings may then have to be issued to resolve the dispute.

Conciliation

Conciliation is less formal than mediation. The conciliator assists the parties to explore all possible solutions for settling the dispute and points out the positive and negative consequences of the different solutions. In mediation, it is the parties themselves who determine their own solution; however, in conciliation, the conciliator can suggest different options to the parties. If conciliation fails the parties may bring their dispute before a court.

An example of conciliation is the statutory scheme run by ACAS (the Advisory, Conciliation and Arbitration Service). Before an unfair dismissal case is taken to an employment tribunal, a conciliation officer from ACAS may contact the parties and discuss the case with the aim of settling the dispute. If the attempt at settlement fails and the case does go before an employment tribunal, any information revealed by either of the parties during the conciliation process cannot be brought before the tribunal without that party's consent.

Key Concept Instead of taking court proceedings parties may use a number of alternative methods of dispute resolution. These include arbitration, mediation, and conciliation.

Administrative Tribunals

The majority of legal and quasi legal decisions are not taken by the courts but by tribunals. Tribunals provide a specialist forum to deal with cases relating to disputes between private citizens and central government departments, and disputes requiring the application of special knowledge or expertise. Tribunals underwent a major reform under the Tribunals, Courts and Enforcement Act 2007. The Act created two new generic tribunals: the First-tier Tribunal and the Upper Tribunal. Generally, appeals from the First-tier Tribunal go to the Upper Tribunal. Within the two tribunals there are chambers so that jurisdictions can be grouped together. The chambers in the First-tier Tribunal include the Tax Chamber, the Social Entitlement Chamber, and the Health, Education and Social Care Chamber. The Upper Tribunal chambers include the Lands Chamber, the Tax and Chancery Chamber, and the Administrative Appeals Chamber.

Some tribunals, such as the employment tribunals and the Employment Appeal Tribunal, operate outside the two-tribunal system because of their specialist nature. Unlike most tribunals which are hearing applications of citizen against the state, employment tribunals are concerned with issues between private parties. There is a unified set of rules of procedure for tribunals produced by the Tribunal Procedure Committee. Tribunals are usually made up of three people; one is the chairperson who is legally qualified, and the other two are lay members but have specialist knowledge.

Advantages of tribunals

Tribunals are less expensive to run than courts and the waiting period for a hearing before a tribunal is generally much shorter than for a court hearing. The procedure is more informal and flexible than court procedure. Tribunals have their own policies based on justice, expediency, and social policy. Persons sitting on tribunals have expert knowledge in the subject area.

Disadvantages of tribunals

Technical experts sitting on tribunals may not be as impartial as judges. Decisions of tribunals receive little publicity, and therefore individuals are unaware of the outcome of cases similar to their own case. Legal aid is generally not available for tribunals and, although the proceedings may not be as formal as a court, an applicant may be facing an opponent who is an experienced government official or a lawyer paid for by an employer.

Ombudsman System

As the state impinges upon and sometimes conflicts with a citizen, there is a need for a system whereby a citizen can complain about the state authorities acting wrongly, even though the actions of the state are not necessarily illegal. The Parliamentary Commissioner for Administration (Ombudsman), set up by the Parliamentary Commissioner Act 1967, investigates complaints made by citizens about government departments which have fallen below acceptable standards. If, on investigation, the complaint is found to be justified, the Ombudsman will, if appropriate, make a recommendation to the department that compensation should be paid to the citizen.

Other Ombudsmen have been set up to administer complaints about government services such as local government, prisons, and the health service. There are also Ombudsmen overseeing the operation of non-government bodies, such as the Banking Ombudsman and the Legal Ombudsman.

Basic Terminology

For an online flashcard glossary visit the Online Resource Centre

Appellate jurisdiction Courts which have the authority to hear cases that have previously been heard in a lower court.

Civil jurisdiction Cases which are concerned with disputes between private citizens or citizens and the state.

Criminal jurisdiction Cases concerned with accusations against persons who have broken the criminal law.

Original jurisdiction Courts which have the authority to hear cases for the first time where no previous decision in that particular case has been made.

System of hierarchy The courts have greater authority than those lower down the structure.

Summary

After studying this chapter students should be able to:

Demonstrate an understanding of the court system in England and Wales

- The courts in England and Wales form a hierarchy.
- At the lowest level are the Magistrates' Courts and the County Courts, then the Crown Court and High Court, then the Court of Appeal, and finally the Supreme Court.

Explain in which courts civil actions commence, criminal trials are heard, and appeal cases are dealt with

- Criminal trials are heard in the Magistrates' Court and the Crown Court.
- Criminal appeals are heard in the Court of Appeal (Criminal Division) and the Supreme Court.
- Some criminal appeals on a point of law from the Magistrates' Court may be heard by the High Court.
- Civil cases are commenced in the County Court or High Court.
- Civil appeals are heard in the Court of Appeal (Civil Division) and the Supreme Court.

Show an understanding of criminal trials

- Trials in the Magistrates' Court are heard by three lay magistrates or a District Judge (Magistrates' Court).
- In a Magistrates' Court the judge or magistrates decide on the guilt of the defendant and on sentence.
- Trials in the Crown Court are heard by a judge and jury (a few exceptions).
- In the Crown Court the jury decide on guilt and the judge on sentence.

Be familiar with a basic outline of civil procedure

- Before a civil case is commenced the pre-action protocol should be followed.
- To commence an action, a claimant completes a claim form and it is served on the defendant, who may admit the claim or deny it and submit a defence.
- A case is allocated to one of three tracks depending on its nature and seriousness.
- A civil trial is held in open court before a judge.

Describe alternative methods of resolving disputes other than through the court system

- There are a number of alternative methods of dispute resolution, including arbitration, mediation, and conciliation.
- In addition to courts a large number of disputes are dealt with by tribunals.
- The Tribunals, Courts and Enforcement Act 2007 created two generic tribunals, the First-tier Tribunal and the Upper Tribunal.
- The employment tribunals and the Employment Appeal Tribunal operate outside the two-tribunal system because of their specialist nature.

For an online printable version visit the Online Resource Centre

Questions

1. Outline the advantages and disadvantages of tribunals over the court system.

2. Explain what is meant by arbitration, mediation, and conciliation.

3. Raj steals Asha's car, drives it to a remote part of town and sets it on fire. Raj is caught by the police and prosecuted for theft of the car. Asha wants to sue Raj for compensation for the damage to her car. Advise Raj in which court or courts he may have to face trial and explain to Asha how to commence a civil claim.

For outline answers visit the Online Resource Centre

4. Explain clearly which court would deal with the following matters:

   a) Ace plc is suing Fox plc for £20 million. The case involves complex commercial law issues.

   b) Virju is suing Beejal for £800 and his case is due to be heard by a District Judge.

   c) Southland Bank plc is suing Useless Ltd for £14,000 and the case is to be heard by a Circuit Judge.

   d) Adam is being prosecuted for manslaughter (an indictable offence).

   e) Kevin is being prosecuted for careless driving (a summary offence).

Further Reading

Cownie, Bradney, and Burton *English Legal System in Context*, 6th edn (Oxford University Press, 2013) Chapters 3, 4, 10, and 11.

Elliot and Quinn, *The English Legal System*, 15th edn (Pearson, 2014) Chapter 25.

Slapper and Kelly, *The English Legal System*, 15th edn (Routledge, 2014) Chapters 4, 6, and 12.

Wilson, Rutherford, Storey, and Wortley, *English Legal System*, 1st edn (Oxford University Press, 2014) Chapters 13, 15, and 17.

Courts and Tribunals Service: http://www.justice.gov.uk/.

Supreme Court: http://www.supremecourt.gov.uk/.

Online Resource Centre

Test your knowledge by trying this chapter's **Multiple Choice Questions**. Visit:

www.oup.com/uk/orc/law/company/ jonesibl3e/01student/mcqs/ch02/

For more information, updates, and multiple choice questions, please visit the Online Resource Centre at:

www.oup.com/uk/orc/law/company/ jonesibl3e/

Sources of English Law

Introduction

English law comes into existence from a variety of sources. Historically, much of English law derived from decisions made by judges in cases which were followed by judges in later cases. However, Parliament is the supreme law maker in the UK, as under the UK Constitution it has the power to enact or revoke any laws. Parliament can and does delegate its powers to pass laws to other bodies which pass secondary or **delegated legislation**. Since the UK joined the European Union (EU), an increasingly important source of law is EU law which can take precedence over conflicting English law. One of the EU's important achievements for business is creating a single market whereby goods, services, and money, as well as people can move around freely within the EU's internal frontiers. The Human Rights Act 1998 incorporates the European Convention on Human Rights (an international treaty) into UK law. Under the provisions of this Act, courts are instructed to interpret English law as far as possible so that it complies with the rights set down in the Convention.

Learning Objectives

After studying this chapter you should be able to:

- Identify the sources of English law.
- Explain how Acts of Parliament and delegated legislation are created.
- Be familiar with the doctrine of judicial precedent.
- Identify the rules and presumptions judges use to interpret statutes.
- Explain the impact of membership of the EU on the English legal system.
- Explain the impact of the Human Rights Act 1998 on the English legal system.

Meaning of Sources of Law

A source of law means the process by which law comes into existence. English law is derived from a number of different sources: the most important of these today are legislation (both Acts of Parliament and delegated legislation), case law, and European Union law. Custom is no longer an important source of law. Although much of the early **common law** developed through the courts applying existing custom in deciding cases, custom is generally considered to be a minor source of law today (see Figure 3.1).

Figure 3.1 Sources of law

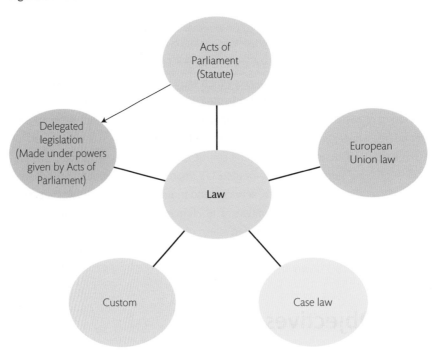

Legislation

The predominant method of law making in the UK today is through legislation. This can be divided into primary legislation and secondary legislation. Acts of Parliament (also called statutes) are primary legislation. Secondary legislation, also known as delegated legislation, is law made by persons or bodies to whom Parliament has given law-making powers through an enabling statute.

Parliament consists of the House of Commons, the House of Lords, and the monarch, Queen Elizabeth II. The House of Commons is an elected chamber with 700 members. A general election must be held at least every five years. The House of Lords is composed of approximately 650 peers appointed for life, 92 hereditary peers remaining under the provisions of the House of Lords Act 1999, and 26 senior bishops of the Church of England. Law Lords also sit in the House of Lords once they have retired as judges.

Parliamentary Sovereignty

The UK has no written constitution and, under British Constitutional Law, Parliament is sovereign. The traditional interpretation of **Parliamentary sovereignty** is that Parliament is the supreme law-making body in the UK and, as such, it has the power to make any statutes on any subject matter, and that British courts are bound to enforce the laws that Parliament has made and cannot question their validity. Even if Parliament passes a statute taking away citizens' civil rights and imprisoning citizens without trial, the courts cannot rule that the statute is illegal (although since the Human Rights Act 1998 the courts may declare that such a statute is 'incompatible' with the European Convention on Human Rights). In reality, Parliament is constrained as to laws it will pass by practical issues such as political expedience and enforceability of draconian laws.

In countries where there is a written constitution, usually the courts have the power to overrule laws that are 'unconstitutional' and there is a special legal procedure to change the contents of the written constitution. However, in the UK Parliament is sovereign and can change any laws, including laws relating to the British Constitution. All laws are subject to repeal and there are no laws that cannot be changed by an ordinary Act of Parliament.

Since the UK joined the EU in 1973, the doctrine of Parliamentary sovereignty has to be considered in the light of EU law. Membership of the EU requires that EU law overrides any inconsistent national law. If an English Act of Parliament is in conflict with an EU law, English courts are required to enforce the EU law. Of course, the UK together with other Member States is responsible for passing EU laws. In signing the treaty joining the EU, the UK agreed that EU law would become part of UK law, and Parliament passed the European Communities Act 1972 (in force on 1 January 1973) giving effect to this. Legally, Parliament could repeal the European Communities Act 1972, the UK could leave the EU and an Act of Parliament would once again be the highest form of law in the UK.

Key Concept The UK does not have a written constitutional document. Laws relating to the British Constitution can be changed by an ordinary Act of Parliament.

Acts of Parliament

An Act of Parliament creates new laws or changes or repeals old laws. An Act must pass through various stages in Parliament before it becomes law. While an Act is progressing through Parliament, it is known as a **bill**. In order to become an Act, a bill must usually go through various stages in the House of Commons and the House of Lords, and then receive Royal Assent from the Queen. Prior to a bill being tabled in Parliament, there may be a Green Paper and a White Paper issued by the government. A Green Paper is a consultation document in which the government sets out a range of legislative options and invites comments from interested parties. Once the Green Paper has received comments, a White Paper is produced which sets out the government's revised proposals in detail, and the intended aim of the proposed legislation. A bill is then written which will normally be introduced firstly into the House of Commons and, if passed by the House of Commons, it will go through the same procedures in the House of Lords. However, some bills, usually less controversial ones, are first introduced into the House of Lords and, if passed by the Lords, then proceed to the House of Commons.

The majority of bills are Public bills which affect all citizens and apply throughout England and Wales. Public bills are usually introduced into the House of Commons by a government minister. Provided the government has a majority of seats in the House of Commons, these bills usually become law. Some bills are introduced into Parliament by Members of Parliament (MPs) who are not ministers, and these bills are called Private Members' bills. Parliamentary time reserved for the introduction of Private Members' bills is very limited and these bills usually fail to become law unless backed by the government. Occasionally, a Private bill may be introduced into Parliament. This is a bill that only affects certain local areas or relates to the interests of particular organisations (see Figure 3.2).

Procedure for passing Public Acts of Parliament

Before a bill can become an Act it must pass through five stages in both Houses of Parliament. Usually a bill will commence in the House of Commons (although some bills can start in the House of Lords) and undergoes the following procedure (see Figure 3.3):

- *First Reading*
  The title of the bill is read out in the Main Chamber of the House of Commons. This acts as a notification to MPs, and interested MPs can get copies of the bill.

- *Second Reading*
  The government minister (or MP in charge of the bill if it is a Private Members' bill) explains it to the House, and the principles of the bill are debated by the House. At the end of the debate a vote is taken as to whether the bill should proceed and, provided the majority of MPs are in favour of the bill, it proceeds to the next stage.

Figure 3.2 Example of bills before Parliament 2014–15

```
                    ┌────────────────────┐
                    │   Three bills before│
                    │   Parliament 2014–15│
                    └────────────────────┘
        ┌───────────────────┼───────────────────┐
┌───────────────┐  ┌───────────────┐  ┌───────────────────────┐
│ Modern Slavery │  │ Zero Hours    │  │ Buckinghamshire County│
│ bill           │  │ Contracts     │  │ Council               │
│ (Consolidates  │  │ bill (Limits  │  │ (Filming on Highways) │
│ the current    │  │ the use of    │  │ bill                  │
│ offences       │  │ zero-hours    │  │ (Confers powers on    │
│ relating to    │  │ contracts.)   │  │ Buckinghamshire       │
│ trafficking    │  │               │  │ County Council in     │
│ and slavery.)  │  │               │  │ relation to filming   │
│                │  │               │  │ on highways.)         │
└───────────────┘  └───────────────┘  └───────────────────────┘
        │                  │                    │
┌───────────────┐  ┌───────────────┐  ┌───────────────────────┐
│               │  │               │  │                       │
│  Public bill  │  │ Private       │  │     Private bill      │
│               │  │ Members' bill │  │                       │
└───────────────┘  └───────────────┘  └───────────────────────┘
```

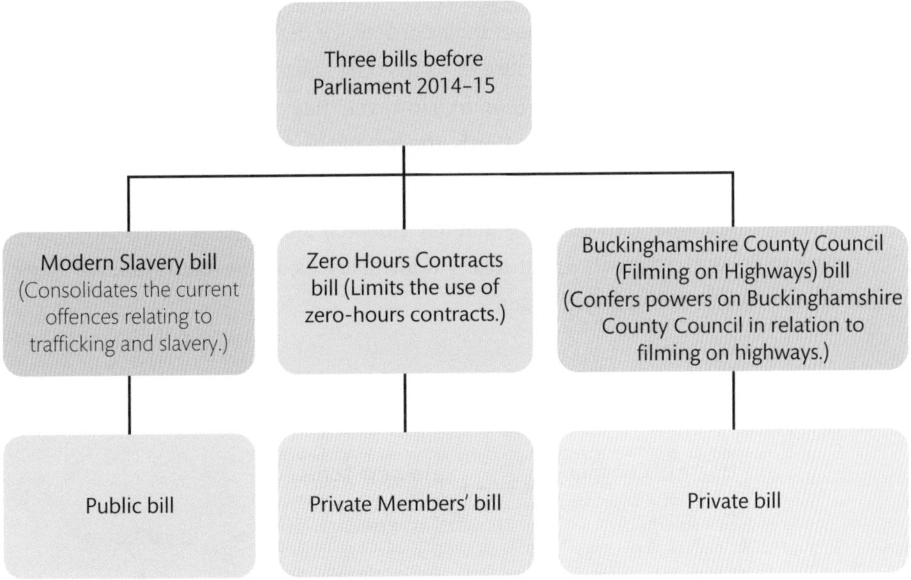

- *Committee Stage*

  The bill is examined and discussed in detail by a committee of the House of Commons. The Committee meets in a separate room in the Palace of Westminster and the members of the Committee are weighted to reflect the relative strengths of the political parties in the House. Therefore, the government, with the majority of MPs in the House, will have the majority of MPs on the committee. It is during this stage that amendments to the bill may be proposed and drafted. Occasionally a bill does not go to a committee but is considered by the whole House, in which case there is no report stage.

- *Report Stage*

  The committee reports back to the House and any proposed amendments are debated and voted upon.

- *Third Reading*

  The bill is re-presented to the House. There may be a short debate and minor amendments may be made. A vote is taken whether to pass the bill or not.

- *Transfer of the bill to the House of Lords*

  The bill is then transferred to the House of Lords and undergoes a similar procedure in the Lords. If the House of Lords amends the bill, it goes back to the House of Commons for further consideration and approval of the amendments. If the House of Commons does not agree the amendments, the bill will go back to the Lords and then passes between the two Houses until agreement on the exact wording of the bill is reached. Ultimately, if the House of Lords refuses to accept a bill passed by the Commons, it can be passed without their consent. Under the provisions of the Parliament Acts 1911 and 1949, the House of Lords only has the power to delay bills for up to a year (and a money bill for a month). However, only seven bills to date have been passed without the consent of the Lords, the last bill being the Hunting Act 2004.

- *Royal Assent*
  British Constitutional Law provides that the monarch must give her consent to all bills before they can become law, but this is a formality as, under constitutional rules, a monarch cannot refuse Royal Assent.

Figure 3.3 Stages of bill

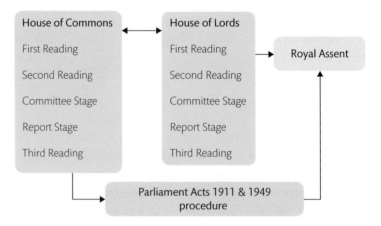

Commencement of an Act of Parliament

An Act of Parliament does not necessarily come into force on the day it receives Royal Assent. The Act itself may state the date it comes into force, which may or may not be the date it receives Royal Assent, or the Act may state that it will come into force on a 'date to be specified'. If the Act is silent about the commencement date, it will come into force when it receives Royal Assent. Each part of an Act is called a section (abbreviation 's'), and sections of an Act can come into force at different times.

Purposes of an Act of Parliament

An Act of Parliament may be passed for one or more of the following reasons.

- *To create new law*
  Parliament may pass statutes on subjects that have not previously been regulated by law.

- *To amend or repeal existing Acts of Parliament*
  Where Parliament wishes to change the law stated in a statute, it usually passes a later statute expressly amending or repealing the earlier statute. Under the provisions of the Human Rights Act 1998, if an Act of Parliament has been declared by a court to be 'incompatible' with the European Convention on Human Rights the offending Act may be changed by delegated legislation.

- *To consolidate the law*
  A consolidating Act of Parliament is one which brings together the law into one statute which was previously contained in a number of different statutes. The law is not generally changed but it is much easier to access. On occasion, some minor amendments are made to the law. For example, the Employment Rights Act 1996 brought together the provisions on employment which had previously been in several different statutes.

- *To codify the law*
  A codifying Act of Parliament is one which brings together all the existing legislation and case law into one statute. Examples include the Partnership Act 1890 and the Sale of Goods Act 1893 (now replaced by the Sale of Goods Act 1979).

- *Authorised taxation*
  A Finance Act is passed each year to levy taxes after the government has published its budget.

- *To give power to another body*
  An enabling Act of Parliament (sometimes called a 'Parent Act') is one where Parliament gives law-making powers to ministers, local authorities, and other bodies (see 'Delegated legislation').

Business Insight

The Companies Act 2006 consolidated and introduced some significant changes to company law. About a third of the sections re-state provisions in earlier Acts but the remainder introduce changes. The Act received Royal Assent on 8 November 2006 and is the longest statute ever enacted, having 1,300 sections and 16 schedules. Only a few of its provisions came into force on the day it was passed. The majority of the sections came into force at various times in the following three years.

Delegated Legislation

Parliament does not have the time or expertise to pass all the necessary detailed laws needed in a modern society and, therefore, it passes Acts of Parliament which lay down the basic framework of the law and delegate the power to create the detail to government depart-ments, local authorities, and other bodies. There are approximately 3,000 pieces of delegated legislation passed each year. Bodies given the power to pass delegated legislation can only pass laws within the limited power given to them under the enabling Act and if they pass laws outside these powers then the laws they make are said to be '*ultra vires*' (outside their powers) and can be declared invalid by the courts.

Types of delegated legislation

There are a number of different types of delegated legislation, including Orders in Council, statutory instruments, and byelaws. Orders in Council are laws drafted by the government and formally made by a committee of the Privy Council in the presence of the Queen. This form of delegated legislation is usually used in times of emergency. Statutory Instruments are the most common form of delegated legislation and are regulations made by various gov-ernment ministers. Byelaws are local laws made by local authorities and laws relating to particular functions made by other public bodies, for example parking restrictions made by an airport authority.

Business Insight

Health and safety at work offences can be found in Acts of Parliament and in delegated legisla-tion. London hotel owners were fined £4,000 by the City of London Magistrates' Court after the drive shaft of a lift used by staff at a London hotel sheared, causing the lift to fail and trapping a member of staff between floors. The owners were prosecuted for breach of the Health and Safety at Work Act 1974, s 2(1) (an Act of Parliament) for failing to provide a safe system of work, and for breach of regulation 9(3)(i)(a) of the Lifting Operations and Lifting Equipment Regulations 1998. These Regulations are delegated legislation and had been made by the Secretary of State for the Department of the Environment under the powers to make various Regulations given to him by Parliament in the Health and Safety at Work Act 1974.

Control of delegated legislation

There is general agreement about the necessity of having delegated legislation, but it is im-portant that there is control and supervision of it. Parliament does have some control as it de-fines and restricts the law-making powers it gives to other bodies. Once delegated legislation is drafted, in some instances it must be laid before Parliament, and positively approved by a majority of MPs before coming into force; in other cases, delegated legislation comes into force without a positive vote but it can be vetoed by Parliament within a limited time frame. In addition, Parliamentary Committees of both the House of Commons and the House of Lords examine certain delegated legislation (but not all of it) to see if Parliament's attention should be drawn to the contents.

The courts do have some control over delegated legislation, but only if a case is brought before them and one of the parties contends that a piece of delegated legislation is void on one of the recognised grounds. These grounds include where the delegated legislation has been made in excess of powers granted under the enabling Act, where the correct procedure for making the legislation has not been followed, and where the legislation made is irrational. The courts can also quash delegated legislation if its contents are incompatible with the European Convention on Human Rights, unless the terms of the enabling Act make the incompatibility unavoidable.

Key Concept Laws made directly by Parliament are Acts of Parliament (also known as statutes). Laws made under the authority of Parliament by other bodies such as ministers are referred to as delegated legislation. The courts have no power to quash Acts of Parliament but may under certain circumstances quash delegated legislation.

Advantages and disadvantages of delegated legislation

Advantages of passing laws through delegated legislation as opposed to Acts of Parliament include saving Parliament time, allowing laws to be enacted and repealed quickly, and enabling technical and detailed issues to be covered. Parliament does not have the time to consider and debate large numbers of very detailed laws and Parliamentary procedure can be very slow, whereas delegated legislation can be amended or repealed more easily which may be important if laws are needed in emergency situations, for example, an outbreak of the Ebola virus. Modern legislation often has to deal with meticulous technical issues such as building regulations or food hygiene matters, and MPs do not generally have the expert technical knowledge required in specific areas, and therefore it is more appropriate to delegate the power to make comprehensive regulations.

There are a number of disadvantages in using delegated legislation to make laws. Parliament is no longer in command and control of all legislation, and the government may be given very wide powers by the enabling Act to pass laws which have a major effect on citizens. As delegated legislation can be passed without the protracted Parliamentary procedure, issues may be insufficiently considered before becoming laws, and there is a tendency towards passing excessive amounts of very detailed delegated legislation which sometimes is not adequately publicised and yet is still enforceable (see Figure 3.4).

Figure 3.4 Advantages and disadvantages of delegated legislation

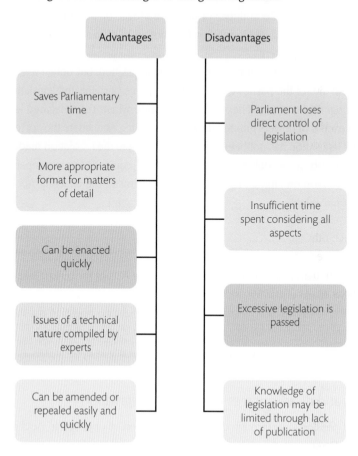

The Interpretation of Statutes

When judges make their decision in cases they sometimes state and develop common law principles; however, in other cases, in order to apply the law, judges interpret statutes made by Parliament. Statutes have to be written in such a way to ensure that they are flexible enough to cover different situations and they can be very complex, and sometimes ambiguous terms are used. In a dispute, a judge will have to determine the meaning of a particular word or section of a statute in a court case. This may have to be a creative process, because words sometimes have more than one meaning and their meanings sometimes change depending on their context. However, judges should only be interpreting legislation, not changing or modifying it, even if its application appears unjust. It is the function of Parliament to amend the law if it causes an unjust situation. As a general principle judges aim to give the disputed term the meaning that Parliament is thought to have intended.

There are two contrasting views of how judges should tackle interpreting legislation. One method is to take the *literal approach* where the judge looks primarily at the words in the legislation in order to construe their meaning; the other method is to take the *purposive approach* where the judge should, if necessary, look beyond the words and establish why the statute was enacted and interpret the statute in the light of that purpose. The purposive approach is used by the **Court of Justice of the European Union** interpreting EU legislation, as EU legislation tends to lay down the general principles, and the fine details of the legislation are left to judges to ascertain. English courts also sometimes use the purposive approach to interpret English legislation.

In order to assist judges in statutory interpretation, there are some rules and presumptions that have been evolved by the courts, although to some extent these rules and presumptions contradict each other. In addition, there may be definitions of terms in the statute itself, or in other sources. The approach which a court decides to adopt on statutory interpretation is up to the court, although as a general rule a court will use the approach that achieves justice in the case before it.

Key Concept In a dispute it is up to a judge to interpret the meaning of legislation and the judge may use the literal or purposive approach. When using the literal approach, the actual words of the legislation are examined. When using the purposive approach, the reasons why the legislation was passed are examined.

Rules of statutory interpretation

- *The literal rule*

  In using the literal rule, the intention of Parliament is found by examining the words in a statute, and giving them their ordinary, grammatical meaning. A dictionary may be consulted to ascertain the meaning of non-legal words. This rule cannot be applied if the words are ambiguous or have more than one meaning. Problems arise where giving words their ordinary meaning leads to absurd or illogical results making it questionable whether Parliament actually intended those results. However, the justification for using this approach is that it is up to Parliament, as opposed to the courts, to correct any unreasonable or inappropriate sections of statutes.

  The literal rule was used in the following two cases and led to the defendants being acquitted of criminal charges.

Whiteley v Chappell (1868–9)

Facts: A statute concerned with electoral malpractices made it an offence to impersonate 'any person entitled to vote' at an election. The defendant impersonated a dead person.

Decision: The defendant was acquitted because dead persons were not entitled to vote.

Fisher v Bell (1961)

Facts: Under a statute it was an offence to 'offer for sale' an offensive weapon. A shop displayed flick knives for sale in their window. Although a flick knife was an offensive weapon, under contract law principles displaying an article in a shop window is not an offer for sale but an 'invitation to treat' (a pre-offer).

Decision: The court used the literal contract meaning of 'offer for sale' and, as there was no legal offer, the accused was acquitted. (Parliament later changed the law to ensure such 'offers' were illegal.)

- *The golden rule*

  If the literal approach causes absurd or inconsistent results, the courts can use the golden rule which allows them to modify the literal meaning of the words in order to avoid the absurdity or inconsistency.

Adler v George (1964)

Facts: The defendant was charged under the Official Secrets Act 1920 with obstruction 'in the vicinity' of a prohibited area; she argued that she was not guilty of the offence as she was actually in the prohibited place rather than near it.

Decision: The court used the golden rule in interpretation of the statute stating that 'vicinity' included being inside the actual place.

On some occasions, such as in the following case, the literal interpretation is rejected and the golden rule used for public policy reasons.

R v Registrar General, ex parte Smith (1991)

Facts: The Adoption Act 1976 allowed persons to apply to the Registrar General for a copy of their birth certification. The question was, did the Act make it an absolute right or did the Registrar have a discretion to refuse an application?

Decision: The court interpreted the Act as giving the Registrar General the discretion, even though the literal wording of the Act did not give this discretion. It was believed the applicant, a convicted murderer, wished to harm his birth mother and the court decided that Parliament could not have intended to facilitate the carrying out of a crime.

- *The mischief rule*

  The mischief rule takes the purposive approach to interpretation of statutes. It is an old rule which was set out in *Heydon's case* (1584) and was used in the days when statutes set out their purpose, including what was intended to be remedied, in the preamble (the written introduction to the statute). Under this rule, the judge looked at what the common law was before the statute was passed, what was the problem or 'mischief' which the common law did not adequately deal with, and what remedy Parliament was trying to provide and the reasons for adopting that remedy.

Corkery v Carpenter (1950)

Facts: C was charged with being 'drunk on the highway in charge of a carriage'. He was in fact wheeling a bicycle. The question was, could a bicycle be a carriage?

Decision: The court looked to see what statute intended (to prevent people being drunk in charge of vehicles) and decided a 'carriage' could be interpreted as including a bicycle.

Statutes today are generally concerned with wider issues rather than just rectifying a simple 'mischief'. The purposeful approach is a broader concept, and, in order to determine the general purpose behind the statute, the court can look for Parliament's intention in the words in the Act and at extrinsic source material.

- *The contextual rule*

  The contextual rule is where the meaning of a word is taken from its surrounding text and from the context of the statute as a whole. A word is not examined on its own without reference to the surrounding words. In using this rule, words that may have vague or dual meanings on their own become much clearer if read in context. Where a statute uses specific words followed by a general word then the general word is given the same type of meaning as the specific words; for example, 'cat baskets, cat toys, cat litter trays, cat collars and other accessories' would only include other cat accessories. But if the Act only states specific words, and does not follow them by general words, only the specific words mentioned apply; for example, 'hamsters and gerbils' does not include rats and mice.

Statutory presumptions

The courts will assume that certain features are implied in all legislation. These presumptions include that the Act of Parliament in question:

- Applies to the whole of the UK.
- Does not breach any of the UK's international agreements.
- Does not alter the common law.
- Does not repeal earlier Acts of Parliament.
- Does not interfere with a person's liberty, private property, or other rights.
- Does not operate retrospectively, i.e. its provisions are not backdated to a date before the Act was passed.
- Provides that intention to commit the action must be present for criminal liability.
- Does not intend to remove any matters from the jurisdiction of the courts.

However, if a statute makes it clear that one or more presumptions are not applicable, then the courts must follow the law set down in the statute even if the law adversely affects the rights and liberties of citizens.

Intrinsic aids and extrinsic aids

In addition to the rules and presumptions, there are other tools that a judge can use to assist in the interpretation of statutes. Some are found in the statute itself and are known as intrinsic aids, and others are found outside the actual statute and are known as extrinsic aids.

Intrinsic aids

Intrinsic aids to interpretation are found in the statute itself and include the title of the statute. In older statutes there is an introductory paragraph, known as a preamble, which sets out the general purpose of the statute, and may assist in discovering its objective. Modern Acts of Parliament do not have a preamble but do have a long title which may help with interpretation. Acts sometimes contain interpretation clauses defining particular terms in the Act, for example, the Anti-Social Behaviour Act 2003, s 30 includes definitions of 'anti-social behaviour', 'public place', and 'relevant officer'.

Extrinsic aids

Judges can use the following extrinsic aids to assist in interpreting statutes:

* Interpretation Act 1978: This Act is not a comprehensive guide but contains a number of presumptions about the way words in statutes are to be defined. For example, where the word 'he' is used it includes 'she' and 'it'.

* Previous statutes on the same area of law.

* Oxford English Dictionary and relevant legal textbooks.

* Official Reports: If legislation is enacted following recommendations set out in a report of the Law Commission or other official body, the report can be examined to see if it indicates where and why changes in the law should be made.

* Explanatory Notes: Often important Acts will have explanatory notes written by the government department responsible for the Act. These notes are not part of the Act but provide background information about the Act and explain the meaning of various clauses.

* Hansard (official daily reports of Parliamentary debates): The speeches of ministers and other MPs introducing and discussing bills in Parliament are published in Hansard. Prior to 1993, courts were not allowed to examine Parliamentary speeches to ascertain the meaning of Acts of Parliament. However, in the case of *Pepper v Hart* (1993) the House of Lords decided that, in limited circumstances, speeches of the minister in charge of a bill could be consulted when trying to decide Parliament's intention.

Pepper v Hart (1993)

Facts: The meaning of a statute was unclear.

Decision: Reports and debates of what was said in Parliament can be consulted provided the legislation that the court was trying to interpret was ambiguous, obscure, or led to an absurdity, and the statements about the bill were clear and made by the minister or other MP responsible for the bill.

In *Three Rivers District Council v Bank of England (No 2)* (1996) the court stated that it is also permissible to consult Hansard if an Act was passed in order to enact the provisions of an EU directive.

Human Rights Act 1998

The Human Rights Act 1998 requires all UK courts to interpret Acts of Parliament, so far as possible, in a way which allows their provisions to be compatible with the rights set out in the European Convention on Human Rights.

Custom

Most customs that were part of the law in early centuries have become so established that they are recognised as part of the common law. Custom that is not part of the common law is relatively unimportant and a minor source of law. Some customs relate to a particular area, and others relate to a trade or commercial practice. For a local custom to be legally enforceable, it must be confined to a particular locality and have been in existence since 'time immemorial', which in law means since 1189. A trade custom may have come into existence after that time but all customs must be certain, clear, and reasonable and consistent with other customs of that area or trade. It must have existed continuously even if it has not been exercised continuously; for example, the right to hold an annual fair on certain land may be a custom although the fair has not been held for numerous years. The custom must have been exercised by persons peacefully, openly, and without the need for permission from anyone else. It must be considered binding by the people it affects. A custom cannot be contrary to an Act of Parliament.

Case Law

Case law is the law produced through a series of decisions made by judges in the higher courts. It is sometimes referred to as common law and is an important source of English law. Case law is usually concerned with the development and application of existing principles of law being applied to cases coming before the courts, rather than courts creating entirely new laws, which is a function that should be left to Parliament. Reliance mainly on case law for the introduction of new laws in today's society would be unfeasible because the development of the law in a particular area is quite slow and would depend upon cases being brought before the courts. The majority of new laws today are enacted by Parliament, or made through delegated legislation. However, it is up to the courts to interpret the meaning of Acts of Parliament and delegated legislation in any dispute.

Judicial Precedent

The reason for the importance of case law is because of the doctrine of binding precedent, also known as '*stare decisis*' (to stand by decisions). This means that, when a judge is determining a case, he must always look back to ascertain how previous judges have dealt with cases in that area of law that have similar facts to the case before him. The judge must then apply, and if necessary develop further, the legal principles from the earlier cases if the decisions are from higher courts or courts of the same level. On occasion, judges may distinguish a case on its facts, which means that the judge finds that the facts of the case before him are too different from the earlier cases for them to be binding on the present case. Case law has been gradually built up over the centuries, and there are now thousands of cases relating to all different areas of the law. In some areas of law there is only a body of case law, whereas in other areas the law is to be found in both statutes and cases.

Key Concept The doctrine of binding judicial precedent is part of English law. Where a case has established a principle of law, that principle must be followed by courts of the lower authority (and sometimes of the same authority) in deciding subsequent cases with similar issues. If a case establishes a very important legal principle or changes the law on an issue it is often known as a 'landmark case'.

Ratio Decidendi and Obiter Dicta

When a case comes before a court, a judge will listen to the evidence and the legal argument put forward by both parties. The judge will give a judgment, in which he states which party wins the case based on what he believes are the true facts of the case and the principles of law that apply to those facts. These legal reasons vital to the decision are known as the '**ratio decidendi**' (a Latin phrase meaning the 'reasons for deciding'). It is this part of the judgment that will bind future courts when deciding later cases with similar facts.

A judgment may also include comments on the law which are related, but not strictly relevant, to the case before the judge. These statements are called '**obiter dicta**' (a Latin phrase meaning 'things said by the way'). They may be hypothetical examples of what might have been the legal decision if the facts were different in some way. Judges in later cases may be influenced by *obiter dicta* statements but they are not bound to follow them. However, if a court of a high standing such as the Supreme Court states something *obiter dicta* it is often followed in later cases.

Reversing the Decision of a Lower Court

When a case has been decided in a lower court, the losing party may decide to appeal against the decision to a higher court. The higher court may decide the case was wrong in law and reverse the lower court's decision. The losing party in the lower court is now the winning party. For example in the case of *Hollier v Rambler Motors Ltd* (1972), Rambler Motors won the case when it was first heard in the High Court. Hollier appealed to the Court of Appeal and the Court of Appeal reversed the decision of the High Court and

Hollier won the case. Alternatively, the higher court may decide to refuse the appeal and uphold the decision of the lower court and the party who appealed, having lost in the first hearing, also loses his appeal.

Overruling the Law Set Down in a Court Decision

A case is said to be *overruled* where a principle of law set down by a lower court is over-turned by a higher court in a different later case. This makes no difference to the parties in the earlier case but the law is then changed for all later cases. Where the principle of law was set down in the Supreme Court (formerly the House of Lords) it can be overruled by a later decision in the Supreme Court. For example, in the case of *Robert Addie & Sons (Collieries) Ltd v Dumbreck* (1929) the House of Lords stated that an occupier of premises was not liable for any injury that occurred to a trespasser. In *British Railways Board v Herrington* (1972) the House of Lords overruled the earlier case, and stated that an occupier of premises may, in certain circumstances, be liable for injury that occurred to a trespasser. (The law relating to the liability towards trespassers has now been enacted in a statute, the Occupiers' Liability Act 1984.)

A principle of law set down in a case may also be overruled by a statute (Act of Parliament). Usually the statute only affects later cases, but Parliament has exceptionally made laws in statutes retrospective, which means that the outcome of the original case is altered by the statute.

Business Insight

The law relating to the liability of employers for mesothelioma caused by exposure to asbestos has been developed through cases and statute. In *Fairchild v Glenhaven Funeral Services Ltd* (2002) the claimants had been negligently exposed to asbestos during the course of employ-ment with more than one employer, and subsequently contracted mesothelioma, which can be caused by a single fibre of asbestos. It was very difficult for the claimants to prove which employment had caused the mesothelioma. The claimants could only show that each employer had subjected them to the risk of getting mesothelioma. The claimants lost their case in the High Court and their appeal to the Court of Appeal, but the House of Lords (highest court of appeal at the time) *reversed* the decision of the Court of Appeal and stated that each employer that had negligently exposed the claimants to asbestos dust could be held liable.

In the later case of *Barker v Corus plc* (2006) the House of Lords stated that an employer should only be liable to pay compensation for the portion of damages for which they were responsible. However, Parliament then passed the Compensation Act 2006 and section 3 of this Act *overruled* this element of the *Barker* case. The position in law today is that each employer who negligently allowed a worker to be exposed to asbestos is fully liable for the worker's losses if he contracts mesothelioma. (If a claimant only sues one employer that employer can seek a contribution from other employers.) The question of which of the employers' insurers should finally foot the bill was subject to further litigation and decided by the Supreme Court in *Durham v BAI (Run Off) Ltd* (2012).

Distinguishing One Court Decision from Another Court Decision

A new case may be *distinguished* from an earlier case and, therefore, not have to follow it. A case is distinguished because its facts are materially different from the earlier case, or because the point of law is not the same as the earlier case. The principle of distinguishing a new case from an earlier case is used by judges to avoid having to follow a particular precedent.

Advantages and Disadvantages of Precedent

There are advantages and disadvantages of having a system of precedent as opposed to having a legal system where courts are not bound to follow earlier case decisions. The disadvantages are often related to the advantages, for example, certainty is an advantage in the law, and a system of precedent brings certainty to the law because a later case follows the law set down in an earlier case. However, this may also be a disadvantage because it makes the law rigid, and may result in flawed legal principles being used in later cases.

The advantages of a system of judicial precedent include:

- *Consistency and certainty:* It is important that law is clear and stable, and individuals can rely on it not being subject to constant changes. The law is applied in the same manner in similar cases so that any personal views of individual judges are minimised, and lawyers can provide their clients with accurate advice.

- *Efficiency and time-saving:* As cases follow earlier cases, every issue that arises in the later cases need not be reconsidered again which saves court time and litigants money.

- *Precision:* It allows for judges to be able to develop the law to meet the needs of the case before them and results in very detailed law.

- *Flexibility:* Judges can distinguish cases on their facts or on points of law. A higher court can overrule principles of law set down in earlier cases.

- *Development:* The common law can be developed to deal with new situations or old situations where society's expectations have changed, without waiting for Parliament to legislate. In *R v R* (1992) the House of Lords stated that a man could be criminally liable for raping his wife, and that the old rule stating otherwise was no longer part of English law.

The disadvantages of a system of judicial precedent include:

- *Rigidity:* A judge is not free to depart from the legal principles set down in an earlier decision even if the law has been decided unfairly, or if the values of society have changed since that earlier case was decided. Justice is not necessarily served by following a bad decision simply in order to treat similar cases in the same manner.

- *Uncertainty:* The ability of higher courts to overrule decisions of lower courts and the Supreme Court's ability to overrule its own decisions means that the law relied upon may change without warning.

- *Complexity:* The ability of judges to subtly distinguish cases from earlier cases drawing very fine distinctions between cases means that the law can become convoluted and confusing.

- *Large number of case decisions:* There are thousands of cases and even an experienced solicitor or barrister may overlook an important relevant case when advising his client on a legal issue, and a judge may not be aware of a significant case when making a decision in court. However, since the introduction of electronic legal databases, the retrieval of relevant case authorities is less difficult.

- *Slow and random development of the law:* The development of the law depends on litigants taking their cases to the higher courts, which may not happen because of litigation expense, or because cases in that area of law have not arisen.

- *Difficulty of extracting principles of law:* When judges give judgments they do not state what the *ratio decidendi* of the case is, and it is sometimes difficult to clearly extract the *ratio* from their decisions, which may lead to vagueness in the law.

Law Reporting

In order for the doctrine of judicial precedent to operate successfully, there must be a comprehensive system of case reporting. The modern semi-official system of law reporting began in 1865 when a Council was established to publish court decisions; before that date there were numerous private sets of law reports published and the standard of reporting varied greatly. Today, there are the law reports published by the Incorporated Council of Law Reporting for England and Wales, in addition to a series of other reports, such as the All England Law Reports, the European Court Reports, and the Criminal Appeal Reports. A number of newspapers and legal journals also publish law reports. Many of the different series of law reports are available on electronic databases. Only cases heard in the higher courts are reported, and even then not all cases from those courts are reported. It is up to the law editors to decide which cases to publish in their reports. However, it is possible for lawyers to obtain transcripts of unreported cases, and since 1996 court judgments of the higher courts have been available from government sites on the internet.

Judicial Precedence in Individual Courts

In the English court system there is a system of precedence, with the lower courts being bound by the decisions of the higher courts. Courts outside the English court system may have an effect on case law (see Figure 3.6).

Court of Justice of the European Union

The Court of Justice (CJ) is the court of the European Union, and there is no appeal from English courts to the CJ. However, if an issue relating to EU law arises in an English case, the English judge may request an interpretation of EU law from the CJ. The judge then uses the interpretation received from the CJ to decide the case in the English court. Some types of cases commence directly in the CJ, and any decision that court makes about EU law is binding on English courts. The CJ is not bound by its own decisions made in earlier cases.

Supreme Court

Decisions of the Supreme Court bind all courts below it (and it in turn is bound by decisions of the CJ of the EU). A practice statement made in 1966 by Lord Gardiner, the Lord Chancellor at the time, stated that the House of Lords (now replaced by the Supreme Court) is not bound to follow its own previous decisions. However, although the Supreme Court can depart from previous decisions, it does so sparingly in cases where to follow previous decisions would cause injustice or prevent the proper development of the law, and the judges of the Supreme Court are always mindful of the need for certainty in the law.

Key Concept The Supreme Court is the highest court of appeal in England and Wales. Once a case has been decided by the Supreme Court, there is no further appeal to any other court.

Court of Appeal

Decisions of the Court of Appeal (Civil and Criminal Division) bind all courts below it and it in turn is bound by decisions of the CJ and the Supreme Court. (Note: references to the Supreme Court include the former House of Lords which was replaced by the Supreme Court in October 2009.) (See Figure 3.5.)

The Court of Appeal (Civil Division) is usually bound by its own decisions. In the case of *Young v Bristol Aeroplane Co Ltd* (1944) the House of Lords confirmed that the Court of Appeal (Civil Division) was bound by its own previous decisions except:

- Where there were two previous decisions of the Court of Appeal which conflicted with each other, then the Court of Appeal in the present case was free to follow either decision.

- Where an earlier Court of Appeal decision had been made in error because it was in conflict with a decision of the Supreme Court, the Court of Appeal should follow the Supreme Court decision and not its own earlier decision.

- Where the earlier Court of Appeal failed to consider a relevant statute or previous cases. (This is known as a decision that has been made as '*per incuriam*'.)

Since the UK joined the EU and Parliament passed the European Communities Act 1972, the Court of Appeal does not have to follow any of its previous cases that are contrary to EU law. Since October 2000, when the Human Rights Act 1998 came into force, the Court of Appeal

Figure 3.5 Decisions of the Court of Appeal

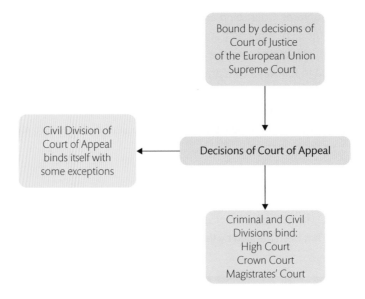

does not have to follow its earlier decisions if they conflict with the European Convention on Human Rights.

The Court of Appeal (Criminal Division) does not follow its own previously decided cases so rigidly because citizens' liberty is at stake, and if the court believes that the law in the earlier Court of Appeal decision has been misapplied or misunderstood then it may depart from following the case. However, the Court of Appeal (Criminal Division) cannot depart from an earlier decision of the Supreme Court even if it believes the law is unfair.

High Court

Precedent in the High Court depends on whether the decision has been made by the High Court where one judge sits alone, or in one of the Divisional Courts of the High Court where often more than one judge hears the case. The judges in the Divisional Courts of the High Court are bound by the decisions of the CJ, the Supreme Court, and the Court of Appeal, and decisions of the Divisional Court (subject to the same exceptions as the Court of Appeal, Civil Division). Divisional Court decisions bind High Court judges sitting alone and lower courts. Judges sitting in the High Court are bound by decisions of the CJ, the Supreme Court, the Court of Appeal, and decisions from their own Divisional Courts but not decisions of fellow judges sitting alone in the High Court. Precedents established in the High Court are binding on lower courts.

Crown Court, County Court, and Magistrates' Court

Decisions from these courts are seldom reported and are not binding on other courts. These courts are bound by the Supreme Court, the Court of Appeal, the High Court, and the CJ.

Privy Council

The judicial committee of the Privy Council is the final court of appeal for a number of Commonwealth countries and it also hears appeals from some domestic tribunals. Legal principles established in Privy Council decisions are not binding on English courts but they are strongly persuasive.

European Court of Human Rights

The Human Rights Act 1998, s 2 requires English courts and tribunals to take into account the jurisprudence of the **European Court of Human Rights** in so far as it may be relevant in the English courts. This means that judgments of the European Court of Human Rights are persuasive in English courts but not binding.

Figure 3.6 Outline of the doctrine of precedence in the court structure

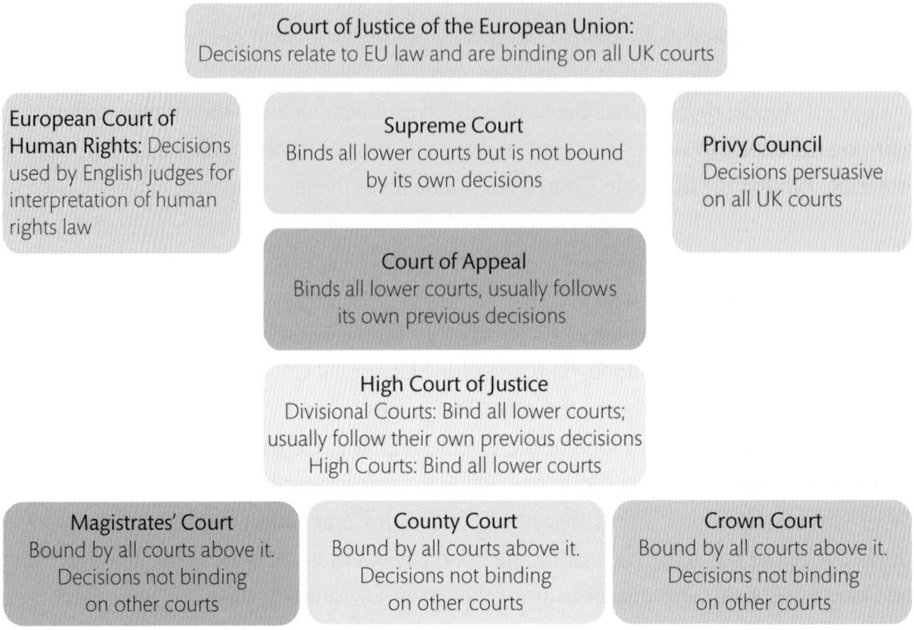

Court of Justice of the European Union:
Decisions relate to EU law and are binding on all UK courts

European Court of Human Rights: Decisions used by English judges for interpretation of human rights law

Supreme Court
Binds all lower courts but is not bound by its own decisions

Privy Council
Decisions persuasive on all UK courts

Court of Appeal
Binds all lower courts, usually follows its own previous decisions

High Court of Justice
Divisional Courts: Bind all lower courts; usually follow their own previous decisions
High Courts: Bind all lower courts

Magistrates' Court
Bound by all courts above it. Decisions not binding on other courts

County Court
Bound by all courts above it. Decisions not binding on other courts

Crown Court
Bound by all courts above it. Decisions not binding on other courts

European Union Law

The United Kingdom joined the European Union (formerly the European Economic Community) by the Treaty of Accession on 1 January 1973 and EU law has been a source of English law since that date. To enable EU law to become part of English law, Parliament passed the European Communities Act 1972 which came into force on 1 January 1973, and Parliament accepted that the UK would be bound by EU law. In the event of a conflict between EU law and English domestic law, EU law takes precedence. Since 1973 the UK has signed a number of other EU treaties, each of which has been brought into force in the UK by an Act of Parliament.

When the UK joined the EU it was then called the European Economic Community (EEC) and had six members: France, West Germany, Italy, Belgium, Luxembourg, and the Netherlands. It has since expanded to 28 members: the original six plus Ireland, UK, Denmark, Greece, Spain, Portugal, Sweden, Austria, Finland, Cyprus, Czech Republic, Estonia, Hungary, Latvia, Lithuania, Malta, Poland, Slovakia, Slovenia, Bulgaria, Romania, and Croatia.

The EU is not a federal state like the United States of America, and its Member States remain sovereign nations, but all Member States have given powers to the EU institutions allowing it to make decisions and rules affecting all Member States in specific areas.

The EEC was founded in 1957 by the Treaty of Rome, and its aim was to ensure closer economic ties between Member States. Since the Treaty of Rome was first signed, the role and scope of various Community institutions has developed considerably. The EEC took on responsibilities in additional areas such as social, financial, and environmental. To reflect its additional roles, the EEC was officially renamed the European Community (EC) by the Treaty on European Union 1992. Under this treaty, the governments of the Member States agreed to work together, not only as part of the EC, but also on two additional areas, namely 'foreign and security polices' and 'justice and home affairs'. The Treaty of Amsterdam 1997 sought to promote economic, monetary, and social progress and greater integration. In 1999, the euro was introduced, and today 18 states have adopted the euro as their currency. The Treaty of Lisbon 2007 entered into force on 1 December 2009, and aims to make the EU more democratic, transparent, efficient, and better able to address global problems, such as climate change. The treaty seeks to clarify which powers belong to the EU, which belong to EU Member States, and which are shared.

The treaty altered the structure of the EU institutions and provided for the treaty setting up the European Community to be renamed the Treaty on the Functioning of the European Union. One of the goals of the EU is to promote human rights both internally and around the world and the EU's Charter of Fundamental Rights sets out principles of human rights to be applied throughout the EU (although at present the Charter has no legal force).

Key Concept The United Kingdom became a member of the European Union on 1 January 1973. There are now 28 members of the EU. In a conflict between domestic law and EU law, all Member States must follow EU law.

Institutions of the EU

The five principal institutions of the EU are the European Council, the Council of the European Union, the European Parliament, the European Commission, and the Court of Justice of the European Union (see Figure 3.7). There are a number of other EU institutions that perform important functions such as the European Court of Auditors which is responsible for monitoring the expenditure of the EU, and the European Central Bank which manages the euro, the EU's single currency, and is responsible for framing and implementing the EU's economic and monetary policy.

European Council

The European Council is made up of the heads of state (presidents) or government (prime ministers) of each Member State plus the president of the European Commission. The

European Council is the highest policy-making body of the EU and meets about four times a year to review and agree overall policy. It was created in 1974 with the intention of creating an informal forum for discussion between heads of state or government.

Council of the European Union

The Council is the EU's main decision-making body and must be distinguished from the European Council (see earlier). Council meetings are usually held in Brussels, and are attended by a minister from each Member State. (Different ministers will attend meetings depending on the subject matter, for example, if it is an agriculture matter the Ministers for Agriculture from each of the Member States will attend the meeting.) The Presidency of the Council is rotated every six months. The Council has six key areas of responsibility. It is responsible for passing EU laws (in many areas jointly with the European Parliament), approving the EU's budget jointly with the European Parliament, concluding international agreements between the EU and other countries, coordinating broad economic policies of Member States, developing the EU's common foreign and security policy, and coordinating cooperation between national courts and police forces. Decisions of the Council are taken by vote and, generally, the bigger the population of a state, the more votes it has. In some sensitive areas such as immigration and taxation, the decisions of the Council have to be unanimous, although in most areas decisions are by qualified majority voting.

European Parliament

The European Parliament has 751 members who are directly elected every five years by citizens of the EU. Members of the Parliament do not sit in national blocks but in political groups. Parliamentary meetings take place in Strasbourg and sometimes in Brussels. The European Parliament has three main roles. Firstly, it passes the majority of European laws jointly with the Council. Secondly, it has the power to supervise other European institutions, in particular the Commission, which is politically accountable to Parliament. It approves all the appointments of Commission members and can pass a 'motion of censure' calling for the resignation of all Commissioners. Parliament regularly examines reports of the Commission and can require the Commission to answer any questions. It also monitors the work of the Council and can ask questions of the Council and its President. In addition, the European Parliament has some budgetary control, in that the EU's annual budget is decided jointly by Parliament and the Council. The budget is debated in Parliament and how the budget is spent is monitored by Parliament's Committee on Budgetary Control. However, it is important to note the powers of the European Parliament are not the same as the UK's Parliament and it is not the sole primary law-making body of the EU.

European Commission

There is one Commissioner from each Member State, who is appointed by the Member State for a period of five years. Its office is in Brussels but it also meets in Strasbourg. It is independent of national governments and its role is to represent the interests of the EU as a whole. It is the executive of the EU and is responsible for the administration of EU policies and the budget. It must ensure treaty obligations of Member States are met and can take a Member State before the CJ if the Member State fails to comply with a treaty obligation. It can impose fines on Member States that breach European competition law. The Commission proposes legislation to the European Parliament and the Council. It also negotiates international agreements on behalf of the EU. The Commission has a staff which is organised into departments.

Figure 3.7 5 key Institutions of the EU

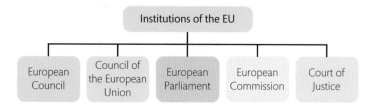

Court of Justice of the European Union

The Court of Justice (CJ) sits in Luxembourg, and its role is to ensure EU law is interpreted and applied in the same way in all EU states. Its decisions on Community matters must be accepted by national courts. At the present time, there are 28 judges, one from each Member State; however, all the judges rarely sit together. The Court sits as a Grand Chamber of 15 judges, or in chambers of three or five judges. The judges are judges in their own countries and are appointed by each Member State. The Court is assisted by nine Advocates General, one sitting in each case, who can question the parties and then give a reasoned opinion to the Court. Compared with English courts, a much greater emphasis is placed upon written submissions or pleadings rather than oral arguments. Decisions are by majority and usually only one judgment is given. There is no appeal from the CJ.

To assist the CJ with the large number of cases coming before it, a 'General Court' deals with cases brought forward by private individuals, companies, and some organisations, and cases relating to competition law. It is possible to appeal against a decision of the General Court to the CJ on a point of law.

Jurisdiction of the Court of Justice of the European Union

Direct actions

Cases that commence in the CJ (or the General Court) are known as direct actions. These may be one of the following types of cases:

- Actions brought against Member States, either by other Member States or by the Commission, on the ground that the treaty obligations or secondary EU law are not being adhered to. If the Court gives judgment against the Member State and the Member State does not comply with the court ruling within a time limit, the Court may impose a fine on the Member State.

- Actions brought by Member States, other bodies, or individuals against EU institutions for their failure to act in certain circumstances.

- Actions brought by any Member State or EU institution that believes an EU law is illegal, to request the court to annul the law.

- Actions brought by individuals, companies, or organisations against EU decisions or actions.

Preliminary rulings

As EU law has to be applied uniformly in all Member States, it is important that it is interpreted consistently by all domestic courts. Article 267 of the Treaty on the Functioning of the European Union provides for courts and tribunals of Member States to refer questions relating

Figure 3.8 Preliminary rulings

Case is before an English court

The English court requests preliminary ruling from the Court of Justice of the EU

The hearing is continued using the interpretation of EU law given by the Court of Justice of the EU

Court of Justice of the EU gives its ruling to the English court to the interpretation of EU law to the CJ for a preliminary ruling. Any domestic court may refer a matter to the CJ, but if it is the final court of appeal then it must refer the matter to the CJ. Therefore, in the UK the Supreme Court, as the final court of appeal, must refer a dispute on the validity or interpretation of EU law to the CJ. The CJ gives its ruling on the EU law, and the domestic court will decide issues of fact and then apply the law as stated by the CJ. If there is a conflict between EU law and English law, the courts must apply EU law (see Figure 3.8).

Business Insight

The Commission took the UK before the Court of Justice for failing to fully implement the Working Time Directive: *Commission of the European Communities v United Kingdom* (2006). The UK legislation implementing the directive did not state that employers must ensure workers have the minimum rest periods as stated in the directive. The Court found that the UK had failed to fulfil its obligations under the Working Time Directive. The UK changed its laws to comply fully with the directive.

Sources of European Union Law

There are a number of different sources of EU law. The primary sources are the treaties of the EU. Treaties are often written in broad terms and, in order to provide detail to European law, the European Council and Commission are empowered to issue regulations, directives, and decisions which can be classified as secondary or delegated EU legislation.

Treaties

Treaties are agreements between countries. The UK is party to numerous treaties both within the EU and outside it. Parts of treaties are called articles (in contrast to parts of Acts of Parliament which are called sections). Once a treaty is signed it does not automatically become part of UK law, and in order to do so it must be incorporated into an Act of Parliament. The primary source of EU law is the treaties made between Member States, which together create a wide framework of powers, duties, and rights. Important EU treaties include: Treaty of Rome 1957 (which set up the European Economic Community), Single European Act 1987, Treaty on European Union 1992, Treaty of Amsterdam 1997, Treaty of Nice 2001 (which prepared the EU for enlargement by reforming the EU institutions so that an enlarged EU could function efficiently), and Treaty of Lisbon 2007.

Regulations

The objective of regulations is to attain uniformity of law throughout the EU. They are binding on all Member States and legally enforceable from their creation. They apply to and within Member States without the Member States having to pass their own laws bringing them into force.

Directives

Directives are statements of policy that require Member States to alter their national laws so that they conform to the directive within a specified time limit. This is the most usual form of EU law and its intention is to ensure certain laws within Member States are similar, although not necessarily identical. A directive instructs all Member States to accomplish a certain goal but allows the government of each Member State to choose how that goal is to be achieved in their country. For example, the EU passed the Unfair Terms in Consumer Contracts Directive in 1993 and each Member State passed its own laws bringing the aims of the directive into force. In the UK, the objectives set out in the directive were brought into English law by delegated legislation, the Unfair Terms in Consumer Contracts Regulations 1994.

If a Member State fails to implement a directive within the time limit, an individual may be able to cite and rely on the directive in their dealings with the state (but not another individual) in court proceedings, provided that the directive is sufficiently precise and clearly worded. If an individual suffers loss through a Member State's failure to implement a directive, the individual may be awarded damages (monetary compensation) against the state. In the following case Miss Marshall was successful in her claim despite the fact the directive had not been implemented because she was taking action against the state as opposed to a private body.

Marshall v Southampton and South West Hampshire Area Health Authority (1986)

Facts: Miss Marshall was employed by West Hampshire Health Authority (a health authority is a public body and part of the state). Marshall was compulsorily retired at aged 60 but male workers employed by the Health Authority could continue working until aged 65. This type of discrimination potentially violated the Equal Treatment Directive which had been made by the EU, but had not been implemented into English law. Marshall sued her employer, the West Hampshire Health Authority.

Decision: Marshall was successful in her claim as she could rely on the Equal Treatment Directive, because she was employed by the state. (If Marshall had been working for a private company she would not have been able to rely on the directive until it had been made part of English law.)

Decisions

An issue may be brought before the European Council or Commission for consideration. The decisions of these institutions are binding on the state, persons, or companies to whom they are addressed but the decisions do not have general binding force on other states, persons, or companies.

Key Concept Treaties signed and ratified by Member States are the primary source of EU law. EU regulations, directives, and decisions are secondary sources of EU law.

The European Convention on Human Rights and Fundamental Freedoms and the Human Rights Act 1998

The European Convention on Human Rights and Fundamental Freedoms 1950

The UK belongs to two separate treaty organisations that bind it to other European states. It is a member of the EU (and has been since 1973) and it is also a member of a separate non-EU body, the Council of Europe, which was founded in the aftermath of the Second World War with the aim of furthering the ideals of political democracy, the rule of law, and the protection of fundamental human rights. There are 47 states in the Council of Europe. An important aspect of the work of the Council relates to the European Convention on Human Rights and Fundamental Freedoms which came into force in 1953.

A **convention** (or **treaty**) is an international agreement between states. Under English law, international treaty obligations entered into by the government are not part of the law unless and until they are specifically incorporated by an Act of Parliament. The European Convention on Human Rights and Fundamental Freedoms was not brought into effect in English law until the Human Rights Act 1998 came into force, despite the UK signing the Convention in 1953. Before the Human Rights Act 1998 came into force, an individual could not argue in an English court that a statute or an action of a public body was unlawful merely because it contravened the European Convention on Human Rights. Human rights were protected in other ways in English law, and English courts could use the Convention as an aid to statutory interpretation. Where a statute was ambiguous, the court would presume that Parliament did not intend to breach its international obligations under the Convention.

The Council of Europe (a non EU body) set up the European Court of Human Rights as a guardian of the Convention, and signatory states agreed to give their citizens the right to petition this Court if their human rights, protected under the Convention, were violated by the state. (The European Court of Human Rights is entirely separate from the Court of Justice of the EU.) The European Court of Human Rights sits in Strasbourg and hears cases where there has been an alleged breach by a member state of the European Convention on Human Rights. Cases can be brought by individuals or other states. Before an individual can bring his case before the European Court of Human Rights, he must first exhaust all his domestic remedies. This means that an individual must first try and get a remedy for breach of his human rights from his own country's courts before he will be allowed to take the matter before the European Court of Human Rights. If an applicant is successful in their case before the European Court of Human Rights and the Court declares that a state has breached the Convention, the Court can order that compensation is paid by the state to the applicant.

Rights protected under the European Convention on Human Rights

The Convention is a living instrument, which means that the rights protected have to be interpreted in the light of changing social conditions. It gives protection to everyone within a state's jurisdiction, and therefore includes non-citizens as well as citizens. Some of the rights set out in the Convention are absolute and without qualification, which means that there are no exceptions allowed. The prohibition of torture, Article 3, is an absolute right and there are no circumstances in which a state can sanction torture even in times of war or terrorist attacks. Other rights allow the state to impose restrictions, but only restrictions which are stated in the Convention itself. For example, Article 5 (the right to liberty) provides that liberty may be restricted by the state after conviction of an offence by a competent court. The third category of rights gives people qualified rights, which means that rights may be curtailed by the state, provided the restrictions imposed are no greater than necessary in a democratic society in the interests of the public for reasons such as national security, public safety, and prevention of disorder and crime.

The following is an outline of the rights protected by the Convention and enacted into English law by the Human Rights Act 1998.

- *Article 2:* Right to life. It is not a violation of Article 2 if the loss of life is caused by reasonable use of force in self-defence or the use of necessary force to carry out a lawful arrest or quell civil unrest.

- *Article 3:* Prohibition of torture, inhuman or degrading treatment, or punishment.

- *Article 4:* Prohibition of slavery and forced labour. Forced and compulsory labour does not include any work or service required to be done by prisoners, the military, in cases of emergency where the life or well-being of the community is threatened, or as part of normal civic duty.

- *Article 5:* Right to liberty and security of the person. This right protects a person from unlawful arrest and detention. Where persons are arrested lawfully they have the right to be informed of the reason for their arrest and to be brought promptly before a judge.

- *Article 6:* Right to a fair trial. In both civil and criminal cases everyone is entitled to a fair and public hearing within a reasonable time by an independent and impartial court or tribunal. Persons charged with a criminal offence are to be presumed innocent until proved guilty and given certain minimum rights, such as being informed promptly of the charge, given time to prepare a defence, and allowed an interpreter if necessary.

- *Article 7:* No one shall be punished for an offence which was not a recognised offence at the time it was committed.

- *Article 8:* Right to respect for family and private life. Everyone has the right to respect for his private and family life, his home, and correspondence. However, the state may interfere with this right in the interests of the public for reasons such as national security, public safety, the prevention of disorder or crime, or the protection of rights and freedoms of others.

- *Article 9:* Freedom of thought, conscience, and religion. Freedom to manifest one's religion or beliefs may be curtailed by the state on various grounds including public safety, the protection of health or morals, or the protection of rights and freedoms of others.

- *Article 10:* Freedom of expression. This includes freedom to hold opinions and receive and impart information and ideas without interference by public authorities. The exercise of this freedom may be subject to conditions and restrictions that are in the public interest for various reasons, including national security, public safety, for the prevention of disorder or crime, protection of the reputation or rights of others, and for preventing the disclosure of information received in confidence.

- *Article 11:* Freedom of assembly and association. Everyone has the right to meet and form groups, including the right to form and join trade unions. The state may place restrictions on this freedom in the interests of national security, public safety, prevention of disorder or crime, protection of health or morals, or the protection of rights and freedoms of others.

- *Article 12:* Right to marry and have a family.

- *Article 14:* The rights in the Convention apply without any discrimination on grounds of sex, race, colour, gender, etc.

- *Article 15:* Derogation in times of emergency. In times of war and other public emergencies threatening the life of the nation, a state can depart from some of the provisions of the Convention provided the state infringes no more rights than absolutely necessary to manage the situation. The state can never derogate from Article 3.

- *Protocols:* There are a number of protocols (additional extra rights) which states may sign up to. Protocol 1 and Protocol 6 have been incorporated into UK law by the Human Rights Act 1998. Protocol 1 relates to the protection of property, right to education, and the right to free elections. Protocol 6 prohibits the death penalty.

Business Insight

Article 11 includes a person's right to join a trade union for the protection of his interests. In *Wilson v UK* (2002) the European Court of Human Rights stated that there had been a breach of Article 11 where employers offered financial incentives to employees if they agreed to give up trade union protection.

Human Rights Act 1998

In 1998 Parliament incorporated most of the European Convention on Human Rights into English law by passing the Human Rights Act 1998 (HRA 1998) which came into effect on 2 October 2000. The HRA 1998 has had an impact on the development of many areas of English law. The Act binds public authorities and affects legislation and common law.

Public bodies

It is unlawful for public bodies to act in a way that is incompatible with the Convention (HRA 1998, s 6). The definition of public bodies is very wide and includes government departments, prisons, local authorities and courts, and other bodies carrying out public functions. A private company may be subject to the HRA 1998 if it carries out a public function; for example, a company that runs a private prison will be carrying out a public function in relation to the prisoners and can be taken to court if it breaches the Act. Parliament is not included in the definition of a public body.

Where a public body breaches an individual's Convention rights, that individual can take the public body before an English court, and if the court finds that there has been a breach it can award the victim the remedy it considers to be 'just and appropriate'. Remedies include damages (compensation) and injunctions (court orders preventing the state from carrying out actions). However, if the public body is acting in accordance with primary legislation (Acts of Parliament) then the court cannot give a remedy, but can make a declaration of incompatibility (see later). The person taking the action must be the victim of the breach (or representative if the victim is dead). An individual who loses his case before the English courts, and has no further right of appeal in the English court system, may take their case before the European Court of Human Rights. In the following case, having failed to achieve a remedy in the English courts, Diane Pretty was entitled to take a case before the European Court of Human Rights.

Regina (Pretty) v Director of Public Prosecutions (Secretary of State for the Home Department Intervening) (2002)

Facts: Diane Pretty alleged the state breached a number of her Convention rights, including Article 2 (the right to life), by not agreeing that her husband would not be prosecuted if he assisted in her suicide. The original case was heard in the High Court, appealed to the Court of Appeal, and then to the House of Lords.

Decision: The House of Lords (final court of appeal in England, now the Supreme Court) found no breach of Convention rights. (Diane Pretty then took her case to the European Court of Human Rights, where she was also unsuccessful: *Pretty v UK* (2002).)

An individual cannot take a direct action for breach of Convention rights against another individual or a private company (not exercising public functions). However, a court is a public body and it is bound by the HRA 1998 to adhere to the Convention, and may interpret and develop the law so that the Convention is not breached.

Interpretation of legislation

Since the HRA 1998 came into force, English courts may take previous decisions of the European Court of Human Rights into account when interpreting the Convention (HRA 1998, s 2), although they are not bound by them. All English legislation must be read, 'as far as possible' in such a way that it is compatible with the Convention (HRA 1998, s 3). This means that old legislation may have to be reinterpreted by the courts in order that it can be read so as to be compatible with the Convention. In the following case, the phrase 'husband and wife' set out in the Rent Act 1977 was interpreted in the light of the HRA 1998 to include same-sex couples.

Ghaidan v Godin-Mendoza (2004)

Facts: A question came before the court on succession rights and the court had to interpret what was meant in the Rent Act 1977 by 'surviving spouses and those who lived together as husband and wife'.

Decision: The Rent Act was to be interpreted to comply with the European Convention on Human Rights and therefore the term in question included same-sex couples.

A court cannot overrule an Act of Parliament. If it is impossible to interpret an Act of Parliament so that it is compatible with the Convention, then the higher courts (High Court and above) must grant a 'Declaration of Incompatibility' (HRA 1998, s 4). It is then up to Parliament to change the statute.

Bellinger v Bellinger (2003)

Facts: B, a transsexual woman who went through a ceremony of marriage with a man, asked the courts to recognise the validity of her marriage.

Decision: English law (the Matrimonial Causes Act 1973, s 11(c)) prevented transsexuals from entering into a valid marriage with a person of the transsexual's original sex. The Act was incompatible with the European Convention on Human Rights and the Court made a Declaration of Incompatibility. (Parliament later passed the Gender Recognition Act 2004 amending the law in this area.)

There is a fast-track procedure provided for under section 10 of the HRA 1998 whereby, if there has been a declaration of incompatibility by a court, a minister can make delegated legislation amending the offending Act of Parliament subject to Parliament's approval.

Key Concept The European Convention on Human Rights and Fundamental Freedoms 1950 is a treaty which the UK signed. The terms of the treaty could not be enforced in English courts until the treaty was made part of English law by the Human Rights Act 1998.

Legislation enacted after the Human Rights Act 1998

Although it would be very unusual, Parliament does have the power to pass legislation that breaches the European Convention on Human Rights. However, when a new Public bill is going through Parliament, the minister in charge of the bill must either state that the bill conforms to the Convention or, if such a statement cannot be made, the reasons why the government wishes to proceed with the bill (HRA 1998, s 19).

Basic Terminology

Bill A document of proposed law to be discussed by Parliament which if passed is called an Act.

Common law Generally means law developed by judges through decisions in courts as opposed to laws created by Parliament.

Convention/Treaty An international agreement between states.

Court of Justice of the European Union The Court of the European Union, dealing with interpretation and breaches of European Union law.

Delegated legislation Laws made by a body other than Parliament, under powers given by Parliament.

European Court of Human Rights The Court set up as the guardian of the European Convention on Human Rights, dealing with breaches of fundamental human rights.

Obiter dicta Part of the judgment of a case giving comments on the law but not with reference to the actual facts of the case. Persuasive statements of the law.

Parliamentary sovereignty The doctrine which states that laws made by Parliament are the highest form of laws in the UK and must be obeyed by the courts. This has been modified by membership of the EU.

Ratio decidendi Part of the judgment of a case giving the legal reasons for the decision. These are binding statements of the law.

For an online flashcard glossary visit the Online Resource Centre

Summary

After studying this chapter students should be able to:

Identify the sources of English law

- A source of law means the process by which law comes into existence.
- English law is mainly derived from legislation (both Acts of Parliament and delegated legislation), case law, and European Union law. Custom is a minor source of law.

Explain how Acts of Parliament and delegated legislation are created

- An Act of Parliament is created by a bill being passed through various stages in the House of Commons and the House of Lords and receiving Royal Assent.
- Parliament may pass an enabling Act giving powers to ministers, local authorities, and other bodies to make delegated legislation.
- If bodies pass delegated legislation outside their authority the courts have power to quash the legislation.

For an online printable version visit the Online Resource Centre

- Courts have no power to quash Acts of Parliament. An Act must generally be repealed by another Act.

Identify the rules and presumptions judges use to interpret statutes

- Judges interpret statutes made by Parliament and, as a general principle, judges aim to give the disputed term the meaning that Parliament is thought to have intended.
- To ascertain Parliament's intention, judges take the literal approach looking primarily at the words in the legislation, or the purposive approach where the judge establishes why the statute was enacted and interprets it in the light of that purpose.
- In order to assist judges in statutory interpretation, some rules and presumptions have been evolved by the courts. The main rules are the literal rule, the golden rule, and the mischief rule.

Be familiar with the doctrine of judicial precedence

- Judicial precedence is part of English law and means that, where a case has established a principle of law, that principle must be followed by courts of lower authority (and sometimes of the same authority) in deciding subsequent cases with similar issues.
- The doctrine of judicial precedence provides certainty, flexibility, and detail to laws but it can mean the law becomes rigid, complex, and cumbersome.

Explain the sources of European Union law and impact of membership of the EU on the English legal system

- The UK became a member of the European Union from 1 January 1973.
- Treaties signed and ratified by Member States are the primary source of EU law. EU regulations, directives, and decisions are secondary sources of EU law.
- Some EU laws are directly effective in the UK; other EU laws have to be implemented by the UK.
- EU law prevails over conflicting English law.

Explain the impact of the Human Rights Act 1998 on the English legal system

- The Human Rights Act 1998 incorporates the European Convention on Human Rights into English law and makes the Convention part of English law.
- It is unlawful for public bodies to act in a way which is incompatible with the Convention.
- UK courts are bound, as far as possible, to interpret all legislation in a way which is compatible with the Convention.
- If a statute conflicts with the Convention, the courts must make a declaration of incompatibility.

Questions

For outline answers visit the Online Resource Centre

1. What are the three main sources of law in England in the 21st century? Which do you think is the most important and why?

2. Explain the concept of judicial precedent in the English legal system. In England and Wales, both statute and common law exist together: which of these is a more superior form of law? Explain your answer.

3. Parliament passes the Safety at Work Act 2015 (fictitious) giving the power to the Secretary of State to pass regulations (delegated legislation) relating to workplace safety. The Act was passed to comply with an EU law directive. The Secretary of State passes a regulation making it an offence for businesses employing more than six people not to have a trained first aid officer on the premises during working hours. Explain the meaning of 'Act', 'delegated legislation', and 'directive', and discuss the relationship between them.

4. Jamie has just opened a new themed 1970s wine bar and reads in the paper about the new 'Alcoholic Drinks Bill' which appears to forbid the sale of alcohol in certain public outlets. The bill has had a First Reading in the House of Commons. Explain to Jamie the stages the new bill will have to go through before it becomes an Act of Parliament and, if the Act is made, how its sections will be interpreted by a court.

Further Reading

Cownie, Bradney, and Burton, *English Legal System in Context*, 6th edn (Oxford University Press, 2013) Chapters 5 and 6.

Elliot and Quinn, *The English Legal System*, 15th edn (Pearson, 2014) Part 1.

Slapper and Kelly, *The English Legal System*, 15th edn (Routledge, 2014) Chapter 3.

Wilson, Rutherford Storey, and Wortley, *English Legal System*, 1st edn (Oxford University Press, 2014) Chapters 3, 4, 5, and 6.

Parliament: http://www.parliament.uk/

European Union: http://europa.eu/index_en.htm

Council of Europe: http://hub.coe.int/.

Online Resource Centre

Test your knowledge by trying this chapter's **Multiple Choice Questions.** Visit:

www.oup.com/uk/orc/law/company/ jonesibl3e/01student/mcqs/ch03/

For more information, updates, and multiple choice questions, please visit the Online Resource Centre at:

http://www.oup.com/uk/orc/law/company/ jonesibl3e/

PART 2

CONTRACT LAW

The Nature of the Agreement: Offer and Acceptance

Introduction

A contract is an agreement made between two or more parties which is legally binding on them. Contractual relationships are fundamental to business. Most people will envisage a contract as a signed document such as a contract for a mobile phone or the hire of a car. However, contracts may be made orally or even inferred from the conduct of parties. Persons often make simple contracts every day without considering they are entering into legal relations, for example getting a bus, buying a newspaper, getting a plumber to install a shower, and putting money into a machine in a pay and display car park. Often ordinary citizens act without the knowledge that a contract is being made, and it is only when things go wrong and a remedy is sought that they realise the importance of whether a contract exists and the terms of that contract. Businesses also enter into contracts without being fully aware of the consequences and only examine the fine detail of the contractual terms in a dispute.

Terms of a contract must be clear, and terms agreed which are very vague will not be binding on the parties. Additional terms not mentioned by the parties may be part of the contract; for example the Sale of Goods Act 1979 implies terms such as 'the goods must be of satisfactory quality and fit for the purpose for which they are sold', into all consumer sales contracts.

Not all agreements between parties are legally enforceable. Generally, the law will only enforce agreements where the parties intended to be legally bound and where the agreement involves some type of exchange. The law of contract is concerned with ascertaining whether there is a legally binding agreement between the parties, and ensuring that there is a remedy if the agreement is not carried out according to its terms. The court does not usually force a party to carry out a contract. Generally, if there is a breach of contract the court will provide the other party with a remedy (usually compensation, called 'damages').

The sources of contract law are case law and legislation. Although case law relating to agreements has existed for several centuries, the development of modern contract law commenced in the 19th century with the expansion of trade and industry. The dominant economic philosophy at the time was called the *laissez-faire* doctrine which advocated that citizens were the best judge of their own interests and should, as far as possible, be left to pursue those interests without intervention of the state. This included making contracts on any terms they chose. In other words they had 'freedom of contract'. The law was used to uphold the agreements made by the parties and provide remedies if the agreements were broken, but not to decide on whether the content of the agreements was fair. No account was taken of the fact that one party may be in a much weaker commercial position and the other party may be able to dictate the terms of the agreement in a 'take it or leave it' manner. The general principles of contract law are based on these foundations and certain cases decided in the 1800s and 1900s are still valid today, although the common law has developed and legislation has been passed giving protection, particularly to consumers. Other branches of law such as employment law, partnership law, and agency law are based primarily on contract law.

Learning Objectives

After studying this chapter you should be able to:

- Explain the nature of contracts.
- Outline the essential elements of a valid contract.
- Understand the distinction between an invitation to treat and an offer.
- Demonstrate knowledge of the principal rules relating to offers.
- Demonstrate knowledge of the principal rules relating to acceptance.

Essentials of a Contract

Definition of a Contract

A contract is an agreement between two or more persons which is legally binding. Not all agreements between persons are contracts. An agreement between friends to meet at the cinema carries no legal sanctions if one of the friends fails to turn up (see Figure 4.1).

Freedom to Contract

The essence of a contract is a bargain, and in theory parties are free to make their own bargains and decide on the terms of the contract themselves; however, in practice there are some restrictions.

Figure 4.1 Importance of contracts to business

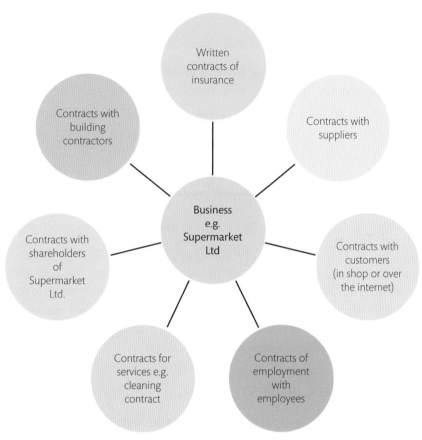

Standard Form Contract

This is a type of contract used by many large businesses. The terms of the contract are set out on a standard written document prepared by the organisation, and a person wishing to contract with the organisation can accept the terms as stated or refuse the contract but cannot negotiate different terms. A contract to fly economy class with an airline is set out in a standard form, as is the contract for the purchase of electricity from an electricity supplier. The customer is not in a position to negotiate with the airline or the electricity supplier for amended terms.

A number of Acts of Parliament, such as the Consumer Credit Act 1974 and the Unfair Contract Terms Act 1977, regulate some of the contents of **standard form contracts**.

> ## Chart 4.1 Standard form sample
>
> A standard form contract for coach travel may include terms such as:
>
> 1. Single fares are valid for a one way journey between two points on the same coach route; a journey cannot be broken using the same ticket.
> 2. The customer retains the risk of loss of, or damage to, the luggage at all times. The Company will not accept responsibility for any loss or damage to luggage however caused.
> 3. Passengers are not permitted to consume any form of hot food whilst travelling on board any coach.

Implied Terms

Terms are sometimes implied into contracts by statute or common law. The contractual parties are bound by these terms even though they did not agree to them. Terms as to fitness for the purpose for which goods are sold and the quality of goods are implied into contracts for the sale of goods by the Sale of Goods Act 1979. Certain common law duties of an employer and an employee are implied into contracts of employment.

Unenforceable Clauses

Certain statutes prohibit some types of contractual clauses and if such clauses are included in a contract document they will have no legal effect. The Unfair Contract Terms Act 1977 states that clauses in contracts which seek to exclude a party's liability for death or personal injury through negligence are ineffective. A coach company would not be able to escape legal liability for injury caused to passengers through the carelessness of its staff, even if tickets contained a clause stating 'this company accepts no legal responsibility for injury to passengers caused through the inexperience and carelessness of the driver'.

Issues in Contract Law

Contract law is concerned with three basic issues. Firstly, is there a contract? In answering this question, one must have regard to the rules relating to the formation of a contract. In order to be legally binding, a contract must have five elements present: an agreement (a valid offer and an acceptance), the intention of the parties to create a legal agreement, **consideration** (a promise to give or do something in return for a similar promise), legal capacity to make a contract (there are some restrictions on persons such as the mentally ill and minors entering into contracts), and form (some types of contracts must be in writing or by **deed**). Secondly, is the agreement one which the law recognises? Some contracts may be wholly or partly invalid because of factors such as mistake, misrepresentation, or undue influence. Thirdly, when do the obligations of the parties to the contract come to an end and what remedies are there if one of the parties breaks some or all of the terms of the contract? Some contracts will be for a fixed term while others may continue until an event has occurred. The usual remedy for breach of contract is damages (monetary compensation) but there are other remedies which a court may award.

Essential Elements of a Contract

For a contract to be binding in English law it must satisfy a number of criteria.

The following elements are essential to the formation of a valid contract.

- Agreement (offer and acceptance of definite terms).

- Consideration (a promise to give, do, or refrain from doing something in return for a similar promise).

- An intention to create legal relations (usually presumed in a business transaction).

- Compliance with required formalities where applicable (although some contracts can be made orally, others must be in writing or by deed to be legally enforceable).

- Capacity to contract (there are special laws relating to minors, drunks, mentally disabled persons, and corporations).

In addition, a contract must be legal. A contract will not be legally binding if its terms are contrary to statute, European Union law, or common law. The Competition Act 1998 restricts anti-competitive agreements and, therefore, a contract in which two competing businesses fix prices is illegal. A contract may not be enforceable if one of the parties did not genuinely consent to the terms of the contract. One of the parties may have been mistaken about the terms apparently agreed or even mistaken as to the identity of the other party. Alternatively, one party may put commercial pressure on the other party to accept unfavourable terms.

Key Concept   The essential elements of a valid contract are:

Agreement

Consideration

An intention to create legal relations

Compliance with required formalities where applicable

Capacity to contract

Void, Voidable, and Unenforceable Contracts

If one or more of the essential elements are not present then the contract may be void, voidable, or unenforceable.

- **Void contract:** It is not a contract and so has no legal effect. If a contract is void, this means that there is no contract and never has been a contract. A contract purporting to transfer ownership of goods from party Z to party Y that is void will mean that the ownership of goods never passed, and any further contract purporting to pass the goods on from party Y to party X will also be void.

- **Voidable contract:** It is a contract that is binding on one party but the other party has the option to have it set aside. Until the contract is set aside, it is treated as a valid contract and goods can be legally transferred under it.

For example, Ali owns a computer system. Tim purchases Ali's computer system with a forged cheque for £6,000 (contract 1). Later that day Tim sells the computer system to Brenda for £5,000 (contract 2). Tim disappears with Brenda's £5,000. Ali tries to recover his computer system from Brenda.

Either Ali or Brenda will lose out as there is only one computer system. If the contract between Ali and Tim (contract 1) is void, then ownership of the computer system cannot pass to Tim and therefore contract 2 will also be void. Ali will be able to recover the computer system which still legally belongs to him (see Figure 4.2).

Figure 4.2 Ownership does not pass in void contracts

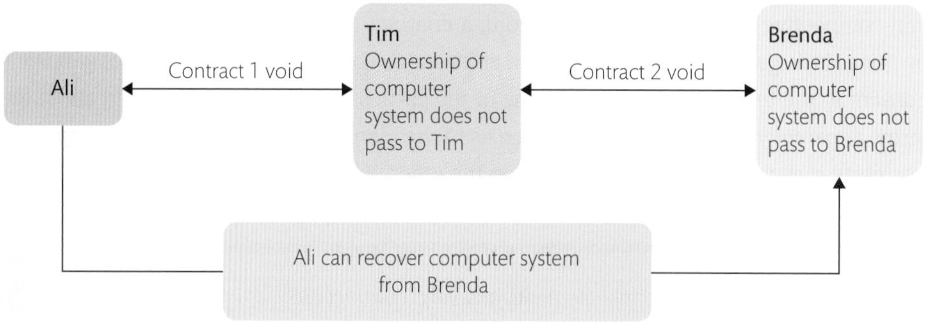

If the contract between Ali and Tim (contract 1) is voidable, then ownership of the computer system passes to Tim until the contract is avoided by Ali (which in the following example has not happened) and, therefore, the contract between Tim and Brenda is valid and ownership of the computer system belongs to Brenda (see Figure 4.3).

Figure 4.3 Ownership may pass in voidable contracts

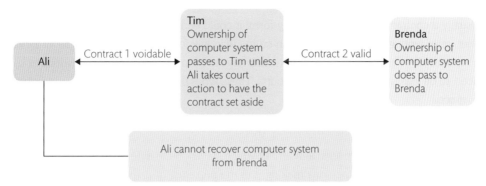

- **Unenforceable contract:** It is a valid contract that the parties are at liberty to carry out, but if one of the parties refuses to carry out their side of the contract the courts will not enforce it. An unenforceable contract only causes problems if it is breached. A contract for the sale of land which is not in writing is unenforceable.

Bilateral and Unilateral Contracts

A contract may be bilateral or unilateral. Most contracts are bilateral, which means that each party takes on some sort of obligation, usually promising to do something in return for a promise to do something from the other party. Ashwina promises to sell her car to Bejal for £2,000 and Bejal promises to give Ashwina £2,000 is a **bilateral contract**.

A **unilateral contract** is where one party promises to do something, usually in return for completion of a specified act, but occasionally for refraining to act. The other party does not have to promise to carry out the act. Carl offers to pay a reward of £500 if his lost pet python is returned to him is a unilateral offer. If anyone returns the python, then Carl is obliged to pay the reward (a unilateral contract is formed). However, no one need undertake to look for the python and return it.

Key Concepts The majority of contracts are bilateral. This is where a promise by one party is given in exchange for a promise by the other party. In a bilateral contract to build a garage, the builder promises to carry out works and the customer promises to pay the price agreed.

Form of a Contract

Usually a contract may be made in any form; it could be made by word of mouth, by conduct, or in writing. Contracts which can be made in any form are known as *simple* or *parol* contracts. However, certain types of contracts have to be in a particular form, in writing or by deed, to be legally enforceable by the courts. These types of contracts are known as *specialty contracts*.

Contracts required to be made by deed

A deed is a type of written legal agreement which states on the agreement that it is a deed. It must be signed by the persons making it in the presence of a witness. (Prior to 1991 a deed also had to be sealed with sealing wax or a paper seal.) The parties agree to carry out the action stated in the deed. All transfers conveying land (land includes houses, castles, and other buildings on the land, as well as minerals under the land) and leases of land for more than three years must be made by deed. A transfer is the actual assignment of the land from the previous owner to the new owner as opposed to an agreement to sell land in the future. An agreement to sell land does not have to be made by deed but must be in writing to be legally enforceable. If a person promises a gift to another person without anything in return, the promise of the gift can only be legally enforced if a contract is made by deed.

Contracts required to be made in writing

In order to be enforceable in the courts, certain transactions must be in writing. This means the contract containing the contractual terms must be in a written document and signed by one or both parties. The transfer of shares in limited companies and contracts for the sale of land in the future must be in writing.

Contracts required to be evidenced in writing

Certain types of contract can only be enforced by the courts if there is at least some written evidence of their terms and, although they are legal if they are made orally, they will not be enforceable. A promise made to a creditor to pay another person's debt if he fails to pay must be evidenced in writing to be enforceable in the courts. The person who makes this type of promise is called a guarantor.

 Key Concept The general rule is that contracts can be in any form (orally, in writing or through conduct) but there are exceptions and certain types of contracts have to be in a particular form.

The Offer

In order for a contract to exist, there must be an agreement between the parties. Generally, an agreement is shown to exist through the presence of offer and acceptance. One party makes an offer setting out the terms of the contract and the other party accepts the offer, indicating that he is willing to be bound by the terms of the contract. A valid offer contains what the party intends to do and what the other party agrees to do in return.

The person who makes the offer is called the **offeror**. The person who accepts the offer is called the **offeree**. (A person making a promise can be referred to as a **promisor**, and a person to whom the promise is made, a **promisee**.)

An offer may be made to one particular person: Jon offers his car to Gita. It may be made to a group of persons: Camilla offers to sell her pony to members of the Windsor Pony Club. Alternatively, an offeror may make his offer open to the general public: £1,000 reward for return of lost boxer dog, Pixie.

Parties may argue that they did not intend a statement made by them to be taken as an offer, but were merely opening up negotiations with another party to see if a contract could be reached. In order to decide whether an offer has been made, a court will consider the intentions of the parties, ascertaining them from the circumstances of the case. The fact that the parties may refer to a statement as an 'offer' does not mean that it is considered to be an offer in law. An advertisement in a newspaper stating 'special offer Levi 501 jeans £20' is not usually considered to be an offer in law. The supplier advertising the jeans will have a limited number of jeans and would not have intended to be contractually bound to everyone who requests a pair.

There are a number of common law rules (derived from case decisions) which must be applied in deciding whether a statement made by one party is an offer.

An Offer Must be Clear

An offer is a proposal made on certain terms by the offeror with a promise to be bound by that proposal if the offeree accepts the terms, i.e. the terms of the offer must not be too vague. In the following case the court decided that the terms of the purported offer were too vague to be open to acceptance.

Gurthing v Lynn (1831)

Facts: The claimant agreed to purchase a horse from the defendant for £63 and agreed to pay a further £5 'if the horse was lucky'.

Decision: The promise to pay a further £5 'if the horse was lucky' was too vague.

On occasion, if an offer is incomplete or vague then relevant details may be inferred making the terms definite enough to be an enforceable contract. Terms which are imprecise may be ascertained from previous dealings between the parties and trade custom.

Hillas v Arcas (1932)

Facts: A contract for the supply of wood made between the claimant buyer and the defendant seller had an option in it that permitted the buyer to buy additional wood the following year. The option did not specify what type or quality of wood was to be supplied.
Decision: The details of the option offered could be obtained from previous dealings and the custom and practice in the timber trade.

Key Concept   The terms of an offer must be clear and certain.

An Offer Must be Distinguished from an Invitation to Treat, a Statement Giving Information or Expressing an Intention, or a Mere Puff or Boast

An invitation to treat

An **invitation to treat** is not an offer that is capable of being accepted by the other party. It is a pre-offer whereby party A is asking party B if they would like to make an offer which party A may accept or refuse. The party making the first statement envisages further negotiations before a contract is formed.

Gibson v Manchester City Council (1979)

Facts: The City Council adopted a policy of selling council houses to tenants. The claimant, Gibson, applied to the Council for details of the scheme and received a letter back stating the Council 'may be prepared to sell the house to you at the purchase price of £2725 less 20%' and 'if you would like to make a formal application to buy … please complete the enclosed application form'. Gibson filled in the form and returned it to the Council. Before the Council replied to Gibson, there was a local election and the political makeup of the Council changed. The policy of selling council houses was reversed and the Council were only prepared to go ahead with sales where there was already a valid offer and acceptance. The Council refused to sell Gibson the house.

Decision: The statements made in the Council's letter 'may be prepared to sell …' and 'to make a formal application to buy' were an invitation to treat and not an offer. Gibson made the offer by sending in the application form. There was no acceptance by the Council and therefore no contract had been made.

Goods displayed in shops are generally invitations to treat and a shopkeeper is not contractually bound to sell an item in a shop that a customer wishes to purchase (although the display of misleading prices may be a criminal offence under the Consumer Protection Act 1987). The exception to this general rule is where a shop displays a notice stating in clear terms an offer to sell certain goods in return for an action by a customer, e.g. 'iPod shuffle for the first 50 customers to present £10 cash at the main cash desk on 10 June before 10 am'.

The following two cases demonstrate that goods displayed in shop windows or on shelves are not offers of sale but invitations to prospective customers to offer to buy the goods.

Pharmaceutical Society of Great Britain v Boots Cash Chemists (Southern) Ltd (1953)

Facts: Boots operated a self-service system, whereby customers selected items from the shelves and put them in their baskets and paid for them at the cash desk where there was a registered pharmacist. Under the Pharmacy and Poisons Act 1933, s 18, it was an offence to sell drugs without the presence of a pharmacist. If the sale of the drugs took place when the customers selected the drugs and put them in their baskets then Boots would have committed an offence under the Act as a pharmacist was not present; however, if the sale of the drugs took place when the customers paid for the drugs Boots would not be liable.

Decision: A display of goods on supermarket shelves is an invitation to treat. The fact that a customer picks up an item from the shelves does not amount to an acceptance of an offer. The customer makes an offer to buy goods at the cash desk and the contract is completed when the cashier accepts that offer. Boots had not committed an offence.

Fisher v Bell (1961)

Facts: A flick knife was on display in a shop window with a ticket behind it stating 'Ejector Knife—4s'. The shopkeeper was charged with the offence of offering to sell a flick knife contrary to the Restriction of Offensive Weapons Act 1959, s 1.

Decision: The display of goods in a shop window was an invitation to treat and not an offer for sale; therefore, no offence had been committed.

Generally, advertisements placed in newspapers, magazines, or posted on websites are invitations to treat even if they are headed 'offer for sale'. The customer makes the offer to buy the goods or services and the business or private person advertising may accept or reject the offer.

Partridge v Crittenden (1968)

Facts: Mr Partridge placed an advertisement in a magazine for the sale of Bramblefinch cocks and Bramblefinch hens (wild birds). He was charged with unlawfully offering for sale a wild live bird contrary to the Protection of Birds Act 1954.

Decision: The advertisement was an invitation to treat and not an offer for sale and, therefore, no offence had been committed.

This would appear to be logical where there is a limited supply of an item and the advertisement is open to the general public. If the advertisement was an offer, then acceptance would be by the customers replying to the advertisement and the supplier would be contractually bound to supply goods of which he may only have a limited number. Although normally an advertisement is an invitation to treat, there have been occasions when the courts have decided that an advertisement is a definite offer.

Carlill v Carbolic Smoke Ball Company (1893)

Facts: The defendants advertised a medicinal smoke ball claiming that it would prevent influenza, and in the advertisement they stated that they would pay £100 reward to anyone who caught influenza after using one of their smoke balls three times daily for two weeks according to the printed directions supplied with each ball. The advertisement also stated that as evidence of the defendants' sincerity they had deposited £1,000 with the Alliance Bank. Mrs Carlill bought one of the smoke balls at a chemist and used it according to the instructions and contracted influenza. She claimed £100 from the defendants.

Decision: The advertisement was a unilateral offer to the world at large. It was a promise by one party in return for an act by the other party. For a unilateral contract to be valid, communication of acceptance was not necessary (only performance of the action) unless expressly stated otherwise. In a unilateral contract, the completion of the requested action is both acceptance and consideration (for further information on consideration see Chapter 5). The deposit of £1,000 showed that the defendants had an intention to pay claims.

Applications inviting tenders and catalogues and prospectuses are invitations to treat. A **tender** is where a person seeking to have work carried out issues a statement inviting interested parties to submit the terms on which they are willing to carry out the work. The statement inviting tenders is an invitation to treat. The person making the tender is the offeror and the other party can accept or reject the offer made. If a tender is accepted then a binding contract comes into existence.

Business Insight eTendering

eTendering is the use of secure, web-based, collaborative tools by buyers and suppliers to conduct the tendering process online. It is used by both public and private bodies usually for higher value contracts for goods, works, and services. Businesses can register online to be alerted when a tendering opportunity arises.

In certain circumstances the statement requesting tenders is additionally construed as an offer to consider any tenders submitted. In this situation each tender submitted must be considered, although not necessarily accepted.

Blackpool & Fylde Aero Flying Club Ltd v Blackpool Borough Council (1990)

Facts: The claimant, B & F Aero Flying Club Ltd and six other parties, were invited by the defendant Council to tender for a concession to provide pleasure flights. The tenders had to be submitted in the envelope provided by noon on 17 March 1983. The claimant delivered the tender before the deadline but, due to an oversight by the Council, it was not noticed until after the deadline and therefore it was not considered.

Decision: Where tenders had been sought from specific parties and there were absolute conditions governing their submission, then the invitation to tender was an offer to consider all tenders received that conformed to the conditions. The Council was in breach of contract for failing to consider the tender submitted by the claimant.

Share prospectuses are invitations to treat. A public company may send out prospectuses to potential shareholders inviting them to apply for shares in the company. The application for shares by a potential shareholder is an offer to purchase shares and the company may accept or reject this offer (see Chapter 16).

Items in catalogues are invitations to treat; for example, at an auction for the sale of paintings, the items due to be sold are listed in a catalogue. This constitutes an invitation to potential buyers to make offers. During the auction when a painting comes up to be sold the auctioneer will ask for bids. This request for bids is an invitation to treat. The bids made by persons at the auction constitute offers. In the process of the auction there may be several offers made, each higher than the first. When the final offer is made, the auctioneer bangs his hammer on the table signifying the offer has been accepted. If an item up for auction has a reserve price and the bids do not reach that reserve price, then the auctioneer can refuse to sell the item, but if an item has no reserve price then the auctioneer is obliged to sell the item to the highest bidder, as the auctioneers are making an offer to the public at large that the item being auctioned will be sold to the highest bidder.

Barry v Davies (2000)

Facts: The claimant attended an auction and his bid of £200 each for two new engine analysers was the highest bid. The market value of the analysers was £14,000 each. The auctioneer refused to accept the bid and withdrew the analysers from the sale.

Decision: There was a contract between the auctioneer and the bidder that an item without a reserve price would be sold to the highest bidder. The auctioneer had breached the contract and the claimant was awarded £27,600 damages (the market value of the machines less the amount he bid).

Statements giving information or expressing an intention

An offer must be distinguished from a statement made by a party which is merely giving information to the other party or expressing an intention to do something in the future. A statement that one party intends to sell an item at a future date is not an offer to sell that item, and merely stating the price of an item will not constitute an offer to sell it for that price.

Harvey v Facey (1893)

Facts: The following telegraphs were exchanged between the prospective purchaser, the claimants, and the owner, the defendants. The telegraphs related to the purchase of land known as Bumper Hall Pen in Jamaica. The defendants had not advertised the land for sale but the claimants were asking about it. The claimants sent the first telegraph to the defendants stating, 'Will you sell us Bumper Hall Pen? Telegraph lowest cash price'. The second telegraph was sent by the defendants who replied, 'Lowest price for Bumper Hall Pen, £900'. The claimants then telegraphed the defendants stating, 'We agree to buy Bumper Hall Pen for £900 asked by you'. The defendants did not reply and the claimants sought a court order to force the sale of Bumper Hall Pen to them for £900.

Decision: The second telegraph was not an offer but was a statement of the minimum price the defendants may have been willing to sell the property for. The final telegraph by the claimants was an offer to buy Bumper Hall Pen but this offer was not accepted by the defendants. (See Figure 4.4.)

Figure 4.4 Request for information, *Harvey v Facey*

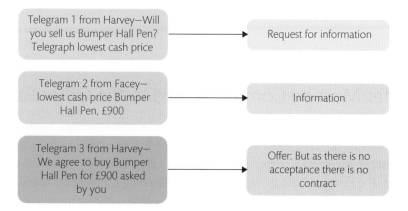

A 'mere puff or boast'

An offer must be distinguished from a mere puff or boast. For example, 'X washing powder washes whiter than any other powder'. This is a boast and not an offer. Sometimes it is quite obvious that a statement is a boast and not meant to be taken as a contractual promise, whereas at other times there is a fine line between a mere boast and a promise which a reasonable man would take seriously. In *Carlill v Carbolic Smoke Ball Company* (1893), see earlier, the court decided that the claim made by the Carbolic Smoke Ball Company, that using their smoke ball would prevent influenza, was part of an offer and not just a mere boast by the company (see Figure 4.5).

Figure 4.5 Nature of statements

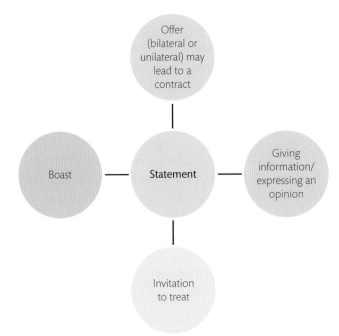

Offer (bilateral or unilateral) may lead to a contract

Boast — Statement — Giving information/ expressing an opinion

Invitation to treat

An Offer Must be Communicated to the Other Party

The communication of an offer may be written, spoken, or by conduct, but a person cannot accept an offer he does not know about. This situation has occurred in a few cases where a reward has been offered for information and a party gives information before learning of the reward. The reason for giving the information is irrelevant; if a party has knowledge of a reward when they gave the information, then they are contractually entitled to the reward.

Bloom v American Swiss Watch Co (1915)

Facts: The claimant gave information concerning a jewel thief but he did not know at the time there was a reward for information. He later learnt of the reward and tried to claim it.

Decision: A party cannot accept an offer of which he has no knowledge. The defendant was not legally obliged to pay the claimant the reward monies.

Key Concept An offer can be made to one or more persons or to the world at large. It can only be accepted if it has been communicated.

Offers in Unilateral Contracts

A unilateral contract is one where the offeror promises to do something, usually to pay money, in return for an act by the offeree, e.g. '£100 reward for return of fluffy black cat called Harris'. In a unilateral contract, an offer may be made to the world at large and a contract will be completed with any persons who fulfil the obligations set out in the offer. The court decided in *Carlill v Carbolic Smoke Ball Company* (1893), see earlier, there was an offer made to the world at large which was accepted by Mrs Carlill in purchasing and using the smoke ball.

In the following case the court decided that there was a unilateral contract between ABTA and a customer who had accepted an offer made by ABTA to the world at large.

Bowerman v Association of British Travel Agents Ltd (1996)

Facts: A tour operator who was ABTA-protected became insolvent and the claimant, who had booked with the tour operator, tried to claim all his loss from ABTA. When booking his holiday the claimant had seen a notice in the tour operator's offices describing the ABTA scheme of protection.

Decision: The notice was an offer to the public at large and the offer was accepted when the holiday was booked. The claimant could legally enforce the promises made by ABTA.

Termination of the Offer

An offer may be accepted by the offeree or alternatively the offer may be brought to an end in a number of different ways.

Termination by revocation

Revocation of an offer means that the offer to make a contract is withdrawn. A person making an offer may, at some stage, wish to withdraw his offer. If a business has made an offer to sell its consignment of goods to Company X and the offer is not readily accepted, it may be in the interest of the business to withdraw their offer and sell the goods elsewhere. An offer may be revoked at any time up until it is accepted, even if the offeror has informed the offeree he will keep it open for a period of time.

Routledge v Grant (1828)

Facts: The defendant offered to buy the claimant's house and gave the claimant six weeks to accept the offer. The defendant then withdrew his offer before the six weeks was up.

Decision: The defendant was entitled to withdraw his offer at any time before acceptance.

However, if the offeror has promised to keep his offer open and the offeree has given him something in return (this is called consideration in law, see Chapter 5), then the offeror is contractually bound by his promise.

Take the following example: on Monday Asha offers to sell Brian her car for £2,000. Brian informs Asha that he is interested in buying the car and will let her know by Saturday if he definitely wants it. Asha promises not to sell the car to anyone else before Saturday and in return for this promise Brian pays her £100. On Tuesday Asha sells her car to Corrie and informs Brian her offer is no longer open. Asha is in breach of contract: she promised to keep the offer open in return for £100 paid by Brian.

The withdrawal of the offer must be communicated to the offeree. Until the offeree is notified that an offer has been revoked, the offer remains open and is capable of being accepted.

Byrne v Van Tienhoven (1880)

Facts: 1 October, the defendants in Cardiff wrote to the claimants in New York offering to sell them 1,000 boxes of tinplates.

8 October, the defendants posted a letter revoking their offer.
11 October, the claimants received the defendants' letter offering to sell the tinplates.
11 October, the claimants accepted the offer by telegram.
15 October, the claimants confirmed their acceptance by letter.
20 October, the claimants received the defendants' letter of revocation.

Decision: A withdrawal of an offer is only effective when it is received. The revocation was not received until 20 October. A contract binding on both parties was entered into on 11 October.

Revocation of an offer does not have to be communicated to the offeree by the offeror. It is effective if it has been communicated by a reliable third party.

Dickinson v Dodds (1876)

Facts: The defendant, Dodds, offered to sell his house to the claimant, Dickinson. Before the claimant accepted the offer, he was informed by Berry that the defendant had sold his house to Allan.

Decision: An offer can be withdrawn at any time before acceptance, and information that the offer has been withdrawn can be communicated by a reliable third party.

Key Concept An offer can be terminated by revocation communicated to the offeree by the offeror or a reliable third party. The revocation must be received by the offeree.

Withdrawal of offers in unilateral contracts

A unilateral contract is one where there is a promise to do something in return for an action. Generally, where an offer has been made unilaterally, and the offeree has started performance, there is an implied obligation on the offeror not to withdraw the offer. The offeree should be given a reasonable time to complete the contract once performance has begun. In the following case, part performance of a unilateral contract prevented the offer from being withdrawn.

Errington v Errington and Woods (1952)

Facts: A father bought a house with a mortgage for his son and daughter-in-law to live in. He paid a deposit on the house and his son and daughter-in-law paid the mortgage instalments. He promised the house should belong to the couple as soon as they had paid off the mortgage. However, when the father died he left the house to his widow who claimed possession of the property.

Decision: The father's promise for the house in return for paying the instalments was a unilateral contract. It could not be revoked once the couple entered into performance of the act. The couple had paid the mortgage during the father's lifetime, and provided they continued to do so until the mortgage was paid off, they would be entitled to have the property transferred to them.

If an offer has been made to the world at large, it may be impossible to notify everyone who was aware of the offer that the offeror wishes to withdraw the offer. There is no English case on this issue but an American case (which is persuasive in English law) suggests that it is enough to give the same publicity to the revocation of an offer as was given to the offer. If an offer was advertised in three newspapers then revocation of the offer will be effective by placing advertisements in the same three newspapers.

Termination by lapse of time

Sometimes an offer has a time limit and the offer will expire at the end of that time limit. If there is no time limit stated, then the offer will expire at the end of a reasonable time. What constitutes a reasonable time depends on the circumstances of the case.

Ramsgate Victoria Hotel v Montefiore (1866)

Facts: The defendant, an investor, offered to buy shares in the claimant company in June. He heard nothing from the company until November when the company attempted to accept his offer and allocated him shares. The defendant no longer wanted the shares.
Decision: There had been an unreasonable delay in acceptance of the offer to purchase the shares. The defendant's offer made in June had expired and he did not have to buy the shares.

Termination by death

Death of the offeree terminates an offer, as an offeree who is dead is unable to accept an offer. If it is the person who made the offer that dies, then the offer terminates if the offeree knows of the death, or the contract requires personal performance by the offeror, such as designing a wedding dress. The law is uncertain whether an offer is terminated when the offeror dies and the offeree does not know of the death.

Termination by rejection and counter offer

Once an offer is rejected, it ceases to exist and a person cannot later purport to accept it. A statement attempting to accept an offer that has previously been refused will be seen in law as a new offer which the other party may accept or not. A **counter offer** is usually an offer made in reply to an offer, where one party makes an offer and the other party suggests different terms. It acts like a rejection and destroys the original offer which can no longer be accepted.

Hyde v Wrench (1840)

Facts: The defendant offered to sell his farm to the claimant for £1,000. The claimant replied offering to buy the farm for £950. The defendant refused to accept the £950. The claimant then attempted to buy the farm for £1,000.

Decision: The offer made by the defendant to sell the farm for £1,000 was no longer open. The offer, made by the claimant, to pay £950 for the farm was a counter offer, which had the effect of a rejection of the original offer.

If an offer is rejected by a counter offer, a new offer can be made again on exactly the same terms. The more recent case considered next follows the law set out in the previous decision. In this case the first two offers were made by the same party. It was the third offer made by the defendant on the same terms as the first offer that was accepted by the claimant (see Figure 4.6).

Pickfords Ltd v Celestica Ltd (2003)

Facts: The defendant hired the claimant to move his office equipment. On 13 September the claimant faxed an offer to carry out the move for a fixed price: £890 per load plus VAT and insurance. He estimated it would take 96 loads to complete the move, making a total cost of approximately £100,000. On 27 September the claimant sent a second offer on different terms for a fixed price of £98,760 plus VAT and insurance. On 15 October the defendant faxed confirmation of first offer price stating that the cost was not to exceed £100,000. The claimant carried out the move and claimed £98,760 plus VAT and insurance but the defendant failed to pay the total sum requested.

Decision: The claimant's second offer made on 27 September revoked the first offer made on 13 September and, therefore, the first offer could not have been accepted by the defendant. However, the defendant's fax of 15 October was a new offer which had been accepted by the claimant through their conduct in carrying out the move.

A request for information about an offer is not a counter offer. If a statement made by the offeree is interpreted as asking for further information about the offer as opposed to trying to vary the terms of the offer, then it is not a counter offer and does not terminate the offer.

Figure 4.6 Counter offer, *Pickfords Ltd v Celestica Ltd*

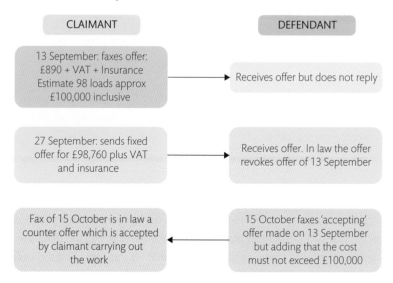

Stevenson v Mclean (1880)

Facts: The defendant offered to sell iron to the claimant at £2 cash per ton. The claimant telegraphed the defendant asking if delivery and payment of the iron could be made over two months. The claimant received no reply from the defendant and telegraphed accepting the original offer. Meanwhile the defendant had sold the iron to a third party.

Decision: The defendant was in breach of contract as the claimant's question was 'a request for information' as opposed to a counter offer and his second telegraph was acceptance of the offer.

Business Insight E-mails can be sufficient to evidence a contract—whether in fact they do, depend on the facts of the case

In *University of Plymouth v European Language Centre Ltd* (2009)—the Court of Appeal ruled that there was no contract between the University of Plymouth and the European Language Centre (ELC) for the supply of accommodation. For a number of years the ELC had rented accommodation from the University on a series of annual contracts. On 24 May 2005 the University sent the ELC an e-mail stating that there would be fewer beds available in 2006 and that 'it looks at the moment that there will only be 200 beds available for you to sell'. ELC did not reply to the e-mail. The University e-mailed on 13 September stating 'I am at present involved in finding out availability of accommodation for 2006 and will let you know what we will have available to let in due course'. A series of e-mails followed with the University stating the maximum number of beds they could offer was 100. ELC claimed the reduction in beds was not acceptable and the University was in breach of contract.

The Court of Appeal, reversing the decision of the County Court judge, stated that the e-mail of 24 May had not been a binding offer and the fact that ELC did not respond to it showed that they did not regard it as such. There was no contract between the parties. However, it is clear that, provided the terms are clearly expressed, contracts can be made via a series of e-mails.

Acceptance

Acceptance of an offer is the unconditional agreement to all the terms of the offer. Acceptance may be made orally, in writing, indicated by the conduct of the offeree, or the fall of a hammer in an auction. An example of acceptance by conduct is when an offeree delivers goods to the offeror after an offer to purchase them has been made. The courts will only infer acceptance through conduct if it appears reasonable to conclude that the actions of the offeree showed an intention to accept the offer.

Brogden v Metropolitan Railway Company (1877)

Facts: Mr Brogden supplied the Railway Company with coal for several years without a written contract. The parties decided to have a formal agreement. The Company sent Mr Brogden a draft contract. Mr Brogden altered the draft contract, signed it, and returned it approved. The draft contract was filed and Mr Brogden continued to supply coal. Some years later a dispute arose and Mr Brogden denied there was a contract between the parties, as he had altered the document, and therefore it became a counter offer which had not been accepted orally or in writing.

Decision: In returning the draft contract altered, it had become a counter offer but its terms were accepted by the Company's conduct in ordering and taking delivery of the coal.

Acceptance Must be Unconditional

The offeree must agree to the exact terms set out in the offer made by the offeror. Any introduction of new terms will be construed as a counter offer. If parties are in lengthy negotiation about the contents of a contract, it may be difficult to state exactly when offer and acceptance was made. The courts will have to consider all the correspondence and communications between the parties, to decide if a contract has been made and what terms were agreed. This can be particularly difficult when both parties send each other their own standard form contracts. Businesses often contract with other parties using a pre-printed form which the other party accepts or rejects. However, sometimes business A will send out a standard form to business B stating that the contract is to be on their standard terms and business B replies sending their own standard terms and stating that the contract is on their terms. There may be several exchanges of forms before the contract is made. This is known as the **'battle of the forms'**. The general rule is that each standard form is treated as a counter offer, and it is the last form to be sent out that becomes the offer, which is then accepted by the other party carrying out the obligations under the contract.

Butler Machine Tool Ltd v Ex-Cell-O Corp Ltd (1979)

Facts: The claimant sent a standard form contract to the defendant offering to sell tools for a named price, but stating that the price could fluctuate. The defendant sent back an order with a fixed price for tools and requested that the claimant sign and return a tear-off slip agreeing to the terms. The claimant signed and returned the slip. When the claimant delivered the tools he requested additional sums from the defendant.

Decision: The defendant was entitled to the goods at the fixed price stated in the order. The defendant's order was really a counter offer which the claimant accepted when he returned the tear-off slip. (See Figure 4.7.)

In *Tekdata Communications Ltd v Amphenol Ltd* (2010) the Court of Appeal confirmed that the general rule is still that of 'last shot wins', unless there is clear evidence of contrary intention to incorporate terms and conditions different to those referred to in the final counter offer.

Key Concept Acceptance is the agreement to the exact terms of the offer. Introduction of new terms will be treated as a counter offer.

Communication of Acceptance

The normal rule is that acceptance must be communicated to the offeror and received by him or at his place of business. (But be aware of the exceptions to this rule: see unilateral contracts and the postal rules.) If a contract is being made orally, face-to-face, it is relatively easy

Figure 4.7 Introduction of new terms, *Butler Machine Tools Ltd v Ex-Cell-O Corp Ltd*

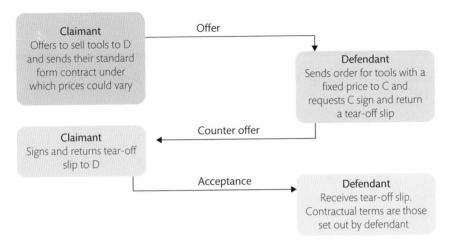

to ascertain if communication of acceptance has been received by the offeror. Problems may arise if an oral contract is being made over the telephone when there could be interference on the line, and the offeree is unaware that the offeror has not heard his acceptance. The courts will look at all the circumstances of the case and consider the usual business practice, but the general rule is that acceptance must be received.

Entores v Miles Far East Corporation (1955)

Facts: The claimant in London made an offer to the defendant in Amsterdam by telex. The defendant in Amsterdam accepted the offer by telexing the claimant in London. The issue in the case was whether the contract was made in England or Holland.

Decision: Where there is instantaneous communications between the parties the contract is completed when the acceptance is received by the offeror. Therefore the contract was made in England where the telex was received.

This case was approved by the House of Lords in the following decision.

Brinkibon Ltd v Stahag Stahl (1983)

Facts: A telex acceptance was sent from London to Vienna.

Decision: The contract had been made in Vienna where acceptance was received.

In the following case (which was not about acceptance of a contract), where a telex was sent out of office hours it was deemed to be received when the office next opened for business.

Mondial Shipping and Chartering BV v Astarte Shipping Ltd (1995)

Facts: The owners of a ship called 'Pamela' sent a telex notice to withdraw the ship from the charters for non-payment of hire charges. The telex was sent at 23.41 hours on Friday 2 December. Under the contract, payment could be made up until 24.00 hours on 2 December and, therefore, the telex notice could only be valid if it was received after that time.

Decision: The notice was communicated at the start of business the next working day, namely Monday 5 December at 9am.

In the modern business world faxes and e-mails, in addition to letters and telephones, are used as a means of communication but there are no specific cases regarding receipt of acceptance by fax, answerphone, or e-mail. A sender of a fax or e-mail may know immediately if they have not got through to the address, as the fax machine will inform the sender the message has not been sent, and an e-mail will usually bounce back to the sender. However, merely because an e-mail or fax has been sent successfully does not mean it has been received. It is suggested that if an offeree leaves a message of acceptance on the offeror's answerphone, or sends a fax or e-mail of acceptance, it is received when it is reasonable for the offeror to check his answerphone messages or access his fax or e-mail. In a business situation it might be considered reasonable to check answerphones, faxes, and e-mails during normal office hours.

Acceptance must be communicated by the offeree or his authorised agent. It is not effective if it is an ordinary third party that informs the offeror that the offeree is accepting the offer made.

Powell v Lee (1908)

Facts: The claimant applied for a post as headmaster. He was called for an interview and later informed by one of the managers, who had no authorisation from the Board of Managers, that he was successful. The Board later decided to re-open the matter and gave the post to someone else. The claimant sued for breach of contract.

Decision: There was no contract between the Board and the claimant as the communication of acceptance was not by an authorised agent.

> **Key Concept** Although revocation of an offer may be communicated by the offeror or a reliable third party, acceptance of an offer must be communicated by the offeree himself or his agent. Unilateral contracts and the postal rules are an exception.

Methods of Acceptance

If the offeror does not state a particular method of acceptance, then the court will usually accept any reasonable method used by the offeree. What constitutes a reasonable method of acceptance may depend upon the nature of the contract. If the offer is made by e-mail and an immediate reply is required, then response by posting a letter by second-class post may not be reasonable.

If an offeror states that his offer should be accepted by a particular method, for example by first-class post, then acceptance will only be valid if it is communicated in that way or an equally effective manner. To be equally effective, the communication method must not be slower or less advantageous to the offeror.

It makes no difference if the method of communication is less advantageous to the offeree. In the following case a letter sent by recorded or registered post was for the benefit of the offeree to ensure it was received and, therefore, using the ordinary post did not disadvantage the offeror.

Yates Building Co Ltd v Pulleyn & Sons (York) Ltd (1975)

Facts: The defendant offered the claimants an option to buy building plots for £18,900 exercisable by notice in writing between 6 April and 6 May 1973 to be sent by registered or recorded delivery post to the defendant or their solicitors. The claimants sent a letter accepting the offer on 30 April by ordinary post which reached the defendant before 6 May.
Decision: The acceptance was valid as the requirement of registered or recorded delivery was for the benefit of the offeree.

Although the offeror may specify how acceptance is to be made, he cannot stipulate that no reply from the offeree will amount to acceptance.

Felthouse v Bindley (1862)

Facts: The claimant and his nephew were negotiating for the sale of a horse. The claimant wrote to his nephew and said 'If I hear no more about it I consider the horse is mine for £30 15s'. The nephew did not reply. The horse was sold at auction and the claimant sued the auctioneer.

Decision: There had been no communication by the nephew of his intention to accept his uncle's offer to purchase the horse and he had not done anything to bind himself. Contractual liability cannot be imposed on a party by the offeror stating that silence will be construed as acceptance of the contract. There was no contract between the nephew and uncle.

There must be some positive act of acceptance. In a bilateral contract, the silence of the offeree cannot be imposed as acceptance. In a unilateral contract, performance of certain acts may amount to acceptance, but will only do so if the offeree is aware of the terms of the offer.

Exceptions to the Rule that Acceptance Must be Communicated

There are two exceptions to the rule that, in order to be valid, acceptance of an offer must be communicated to the offeror by the offeree or his authorised agent: unilateral contracts and contracts made where the postal rules apply.

Unilateral contracts

When a person makes an offer to enter into a unilateral contract, he impliedly indicates that he does not require notification of acceptance of the offer. A person who offers £100 for the return of their lost dog does not expect every person who may find the dog to first contact the offeror to inform him of their intention to return the dog if they find it. In *Carlill v Carbolic Smoke Ball Company* (1893), see earlier, Mrs Carlill was not required to inform the Carbolic Smoke Ball Company that she was accepting their offer before using the smoke ball.

Postal acceptances

The general rule regarding acceptance made by letter through the post is that a letter of acceptance correctly addressed and stamped is effective when it is put in the post box. The letter must be put in the postal system, not just handed to a messenger to post.

Adams v Lindsell (1818)

Facts: On 2 September the defendants wrote to the claimants offering to sell them certain fleeces of wool and requiring an answer in the course of the post (expecting the answer by 7 September). The defendants misdirected the letter which arrived on 5 September. On the same day, the claimants posted their acceptance which was received by the defendants on 9 September. However, on 8 September the defendants sold the fleeces elsewhere.

Decision: The acceptance was valid on the day of posting, 5 September; the delay in notifying the acceptance was as a result of the defendants' mistake. The defendants were in breach of contract.

Even if the letter never arrives, it is still valid acceptance provided it is not the fault of the sender because the letter was not addressed correctly or adequately stamped.

Household Fire and Carriage Accident Insurance Company Ltd v Grant (1879)

Facts: The defendant applied for shares in a company. The company posted a letter to the defendant allotting shares to him (acceptance). However, the letter never arrived. The company went into liquidation and the defendant was called upon to pay the amount still outstanding (the shares were only part paid).

Decision: Acceptance was complete when acceptance (letter of allotment) was posted even though it never arrived. The defendant had to pay for the shares.

Parties can exclude postal rules in their contract if they wish to do so. In today's business world, the postal rules are usually excluded as most offers require acceptance to be received. Even if the offer does not expressly state that the postal rules do not apply, they may be excluded if the wording of the contract is inconsistent with the rules.

Holwell Securities v Hughes (1974)

Facts: The defendant granted the claimant an option to purchase land (offer). The option had to be exercised by giving 'notice in writing' to the defendant within six months. The claimant wrote to the defendant giving notice of the exercise of the option (acceptance) but the letter did not arrive.

Decision: The letter accepting the offer had to actually be received because the offer had required communication, 'notice in writing'.

The postal rules only apply to acceptance of an offer and do not apply to a posted offer or a posted revocation.

Key Concept The postal rules state that, where the post is a valid method of acceptance, then acceptance occurs when it is posted, provided it is properly stamped and addressed.

Contracts made Electronically

The internet is increasingly being used to order goods and services; therefore, it is important to understand when a contract made over the internet is formed. Websites are usually considered to be shop windows and, therefore, invitations to treat. The offer is made by the customer who orders goods or services on the website usually entering his name, address, and credit or debit card details. The seller then has the option of whether to accept the offer or not. The timing of acceptance depends upon the wording given on the website. Acceptance may take place when a message is sent back acknowledging the order or when the goods are dispatched.

The Electronic Commerce (EC Directive) Regulations 2002 set out some formalities that have to be complied with when making a contract over the internet. There is a requirement that sellers give a clear and comprehensible account of the steps that have to be followed, allowing for full and informed consent by the customer before an offer is made. Receipts for orders placed electronically must be provided without delay.

If negotiations for a contract are conducted through e-mail, the postal rules do not apply but general legal principles of offer and acceptance are relevant. Communication of an acceptance must be received. Documents that are required to be in writing and signed in order to be legally binding may be completed electronically in some circumstances as the Electronic Communications Act 2000 allows the use of electronic signatures.

Business Insight Pricing errors on websites

In 2002 Kodak advertised a digital camera on its website for £100 in error (normal cost £330). Over 5,000 people placed orders and were sent an automated e-mail which confirmed the model and price. The e-mail was the seller's acceptance of the offer and Kodak was bound by the contract.

In 2006 Amazon mistakenly offered pocket computers on its website at £7.32 instead of £274.99. However, on its website Amazon specifically had stated that a contract was formed only when the goods were dispatched, in order to prevent being contractually bound by an automated e-mail, so Amazon did not have to honour the lower price. In 2014 Screwfix.com, a DIY retailer, suffered a technical glitch that reduced the price of everything (including products that cost over £1,000) on its website to £34.99. The terms and conditions on the website were carefully drafted and orders for items that had not been delivered or collected could be cancelled by the company.

Basic Terminology

'Battle of the forms' The correspondence between businesses in which each business seeks to impose its own standard terms as the terms of the contract.

Bilateral contract One where each party takes on some sort of obligation, usually promising to do something in return for a promise to do something from the other party.

Consideration A promise by one party to give, do or refrain from doing something in return for similar by the other party.

Counter offer An offer made in reply to an offer which has the effect of terminating the first offer.

Deed A written legal agreement which states on the agreement that it is a deed. It must be signed by the persons making it in the presence of a witness.

Invitation to treat This is a pre-offer whereby one party is asking the other party if they would like to make an offer.

Offeree A person who accepts an offer.

Offeror A person who makes an offer.

Promisee A person to whom a promise is made.

Promisor A person who makes a promise.

Revocation Withdrawal.

Standard form contract A contract where the terms are set out on a standard written document.

Tender A statement inviting interested parties to submit the terms on which they are willing to carry out the work required.

Unilateral contract A promise made by one party to do something, usually in return for completion of a specified act but sometimes for refraining to act.

Void contract One that has no legal effect.

Voidable contract A contract that is binding on one party but the other party has the option to have it set aside. Until set aside the contract has full legal effect.

For an online flashcard glossary visit the Online Resource Centre

Summary

After studying this chapter students should be able to:

Explain the nature of contracts

- A contract is a bargain, made between two or more persons, which is legally binding.
- Essentially parties are free to make their own contracts but there are some legal restrictions.
- Courts and statutes may imply terms into contracts.
- Businesses often use standard form contracts. When businesses attempt to impose their own standard forms on each other this will lead to the 'battle of the forms'.
- Contracts may be bilateral or unilateral.

Outline the essential elements of a valid contract

- Agreement (offer and acceptance of definite terms).
- Consideration (a promise to give, do, or refrain from doing something in return for a similar promise).
- An intention to create legal relations (usually presumed in a business transaction).
- Compliance with required formalities where applicable.
- Capacity to contract.

Understand the distinction between an invitation to treat and an offer

- An invitation to treat is a pre-offer.
- Displays of goods in shops and shop windows are invitations to treat.

For an online printable version visit the Online Resource Centre

- Advertisements are usually invitations to treat but may be unilateral offers.
- Applications inviting tenders, catalogues, and prospectuses are invitations to treat.

Demonstrate knowledge of the principal rules relating to offers

- An offer must be clear and the terms of the offer certain.
- An offer must be distinguished from an invitation to treat, a statement giving information or expressing an intention, or a mere puff or boast.
- An offer must be communicated to the other party by the offeror or a reliable third party.
- An offer may be terminated by revocation, lapse of time, death, counter offer, rejection.
- A unilateral contract cannot usually be revoked by the offeror once the act by the offeree is commenced.

Demonstrate knowledge of the principal rules relating to acceptance

- Acceptance is the unconditional assent to all the terms of the offer.
- Acceptance in a bilateral contract must be communicated to the offeror by the offeree or his authorised agent.
- If a particular method of acceptance is required, acceptance will only be valid if it is communicated in that way or an equally effective manner.
- Acceptance in a unilateral contract does not have to be communicated.
- Where the postal rules apply, a letter of acceptance is effective when it is put in the post box provided the letter is correctly stamped and addressed.
- The general rule that acceptance must be communicated to the offeror applies to contracts made on the internet.

Questions

For outline
answers visit the
Online Resource
Centre

1. Consider whether a valid contract has been formed in the following circumstances.

   a) Iraj sees the following advertisement in his local newspaper: 'For Sale: Rose Bushes only £12.99 for five. Hurry—limited supplies. Send cheque to Beautiful Gardens Ltd., PO box 123'. Iraj sends a cheque but is told the bushes are sold out.

   b) Dave writes to Peter, 'You mentioned that you would like to buy my red sports car. You can have it for £5,000. If you want it let me know by the end of the week.' The following day Dave sells his car to Jane. Peter learns of the sale and immediately tells Dave he accepts his offer.

   c) Mary sent out a circular to all interested businesses in her area offering for sale her fleet of company cars for which tenders were invited. Jane's tender turned out to be the highest but Mary has refused to sell her the cars.

   d) Strait and Co, a manufacturer of vitamin pills, states in an advertisement that the regular use of its 'Vito' pills will increase a user's energy levels in two weeks. Slouch takes 'Vito' pills every day for two weeks but notices no improvement in his energy.

   e) Penelope writes to Quentin offering to buy his car for £2,000 and says that if she has not heard from him within a week she will assume that he has accepted. A week elapses and Penelope has heard nothing from Quentin.

   f) On Monday Teresa sends a fax to Ursula offering to sell her diamond necklace at a knock down price of £10,000 for a quick sale. Ursula sends a letter back the same day accepting the offer. On Tuesday, before Ursula's letter arrives, Teresa agrees to sell the necklace to another person.

g) James offers to sell his laptop to David for £750. David offers to pay £500. James refuses to accept £500. David agrees to pay £750.

h) Paul sees a lawn mower in a shop window with a price tag of £100. He says that he will buy the lawn mower but the shop assistant says that the price tag should read £200 and refuses to sell it to him for £100.

i) Lin books a train to Exeter using Simplerail's internet service. Although she put in her credit card details when she booked the train, she has had no confirmation of her booking.

2. Andrea decides to sell her car and puts a notice on the back windscreen of the car. The notice reads, 'This car is for sale, excellent condition, low mileage, bargain at £2,000. Please phone Brighton 678123 or call in at 8 Hove Street.'

On Monday morning Bob telephones Andrea and offers to buy the car for £1,500. Andrea refuses to accept his offer. Later that day Bob changes his mind about the car and telephones Andrea. She is out so he leaves a message on her answerphone saying, 'I agree to give you the full asking price of £2,000 for your car and will be round to collect it tomorrow'.

On Tuesday morning, Carl sees Andrea's car and writes a letter of acceptance to Andrea enclosing a cheque for £2,000. He immediately puts the letter in the post box. On Tuesday afternoon Debs calls at 8 Hove Street but Andrea is out, so she puts a note through the letterbox stating, 'I have had a good look at your car—it is just what I want—I enclose a cheque for the full asking price of £2,000'.

Explain to Bob, Carl, and Debs if they have a valid contract to purchase Andrea's car, giving full reasons with case illustrations.

3. Fully explain the difference between 'an offer' and 'an invitation to treat'. In contract law, is an advertisement in a newspaper treated as 'an offer' or 'an invitation to treat'?

4. 'Acceptance must be communicated to the offeror by the offeree'. Discuss what this phrase means and consider any exceptions to the rule.

Further Reading

Poole, *Contract Law*, 12th edn (Oxford University Press, 2014) Chapters 1, 2, and 3.

Richards, *The Law of Contract*, 11th edn (Pearson, 2013) Chapters 1 and 2.

Taylor & Taylor, *Contract Law Directions*, 4th edn (Oxford University Press, 2013) Chapters 1 and 2.

Turner, *Unlocking Contract Law*, 4th edn (Routledge, 2013) Chapters 1 and 2.

Online Resource Centre

Test your knowledge by trying this chapter's **Multiple Choice Questions**. Visit:

www.oup.com/uk/orc/law/company/ jonesibl3e/01student/mcqs/ch04/

For more information, updates, and multiple choice questions, please visit the Online Resource Centre at:

www.oup.com/uk/orc/law/company/ jonesibl3e/

5 Intention, Capacity, Consideration, and Privity

Introduction

This chapter examines issues relating to the formation of contracts. A contract will only be formed if both parties are deemed to intend the agreement to be legally binding. At the time of making an agreement, parties often do not consider whether they intend the contract to have binding force, and it is only in a dispute that one party argues that their intention was that the agreement should be legally binding whereas the other party disagrees. The courts, through case law, have developed guidelines to determine objectively whether the parties intended to create legal relations. An objective approach is one which involves finding the parties' intention from the context of the agreement and the manner in which the parties behaved towards each other, as opposed to what the parties actually intended.

Consideration is essential to a contract, as under English law gratuitous promises are unenforceable unless made by deed. The law will only support agreements where there is something to be gained by both parties. There are a number of legal rules relating to what constitutes consideration. In order to make a valid contract, the parties have to be legally capable of entering into the binding agreement. There are some persons, including minors and drunks, whose ability to make contracts is limited by law. Companies may also have limited capacity to enter into certain types of contract. The doctrine of privity of contract states that any person who is not one of the parties to a contract cannot take legal action under the contract, nor can legal action be taken against him by one of the other parties. Therefore, even if a contract is made for the benefit of a person, that person cannot usually enforce it if he is not one of the parties. However, there are some exceptions to this rule (see Figure 5.1).

Learning Objectives

After studying this chapter you should be able to:

- Identify elements of an intention to create legal relations and explain the presumptions relating to commercial and domestic agreements.
- Outline the law relating to capacity to contract.
- Understand the meaning of consideration and explain what constitutes consideration.
- Outline the doctrine of privity of contract and be familiar with the exceptions to the doctrine.

Figure 5.1 Essentials for a legally enforceable contract

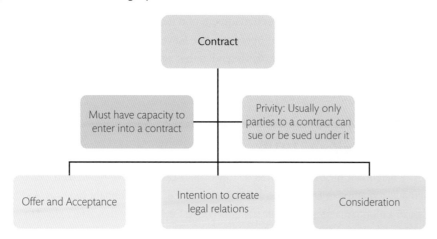

Intention to Create Legal Relations

In order for an agreement to be legally binding, the parties must intend that the agreement should impose legal rights and obligations on them. When making an agreement, parties often do not actually state whether they intend the agreement to be legally enforceable. One party might have thought the agreement was to be legally enforceable whereas the other party may have intended the opposite. In the event of a dispute over the agreement, a court will have to decide if there was an **intention to create legal relations** or not. The court will consider whether a reasonable person, observing the words and conduct of the parties objectively and considering the nature and context of the agreement, would conclude there was an intention to create legal relations. In assessing parties' intentions, the courts start from different positions depending upon whether the agreement was made in a commercial setting or a domestic or social environment. If the agreement was made in a commercial setting, then the courts presume the parties intend to create legal relations, whereas in a domestic or social context the courts presume the parties do not intend to create legal relations. However both these presumptions can be rebutted (not applied) by evidence to the contrary.

Key Concept For a contract to be legally binding, the parties to the contract must have an intention to create legal relations. If the parties disagree whether there was such an intention, the issue will be decided by the court.

Social, domestic, and family arrangements

Where an agreement is made between members of a family or within a social or domestic context the courts generally do not intervene, but leave the parties to sort out their own arrangements, presuming that the parties intended that agreements between them would not be legally binding.

Balfour v Balfour (1919)

Facts: The defendant husband returned to Ceylon (Sri Lanka) where he worked and his wife, the claimant, remained in England on her doctor's advice. The defendant orally agreed to pay his wife £30 a month maintenance until she returned to Ceylon. After they later agreed to remain apart, the claimant sued her husband for the maintenance that he had not paid.
Decision: The agreement was a domestic agreement between a husband and a wife and was never intended to be legally enforceable.

Jones v Padavatton (1969)

Facts: The claimant, Mrs Jones, offered to give a monthly allowance to her daughter, Mrs Padavatton, if she moved to England to train as a barrister. Mrs Padavatton, the defendant, came to England and began her training. Mrs Jones paid her daughter's fees and gave her an allowance. Later Mrs Jones purchased a house and agreed that her daughter should move into the house and have rents from tenants instead of an allowance. Several years later, the daughter had still not passed her barristers' examinations and, after an argument between the parties, Mrs Jones sought possession of the house and her daughter sued for non-payment of her allowance.

Decision: This was a domestic situation and there was no clear evidence of an intention that the promises should be legally binding. There was no binding contract as there was no intention to create legal relations.

These cases concern family members: husband and wife, daughter and mother. However, the presumption does not only apply to family agreements but also covers parties such as friends and work colleagues.

Hadley v Kemp (1999)

Facts: The claimants, three members of a former pop group Spandau Ballet, claimed they had entered into an oral agreement in 1980/81 with a fourth member of the group, the defendant, in which they had agreed he would share his publishing income with them. After the defendant ceased making payments they sued him.

Decision: For an oral agreement to be effective it must have been spoken with an intention to create legal relations. The parties had been friends since their schooldays and the relationship was not simply one of business. There was no evidence to show the defendant had made a statement about sharing his publishing income with the intention of creating legal relations.

Rebutting the presumption the parties did not intend to create legal relations

The presumption that parties do not intend to create legal relations can be rebutted by clear evidence of a contrary intention. The court will consider the apparent intentions of the parties, taking into account the content of the agreement and all the circumstances surrounding the case. In the following two cases, disputes arose where one party won a prize and there had been an agreement to share winnings with others.

Simpkins v Pays (1955)

Facts: Every week the defendant, her granddaughter, and her lodger (the claimant) entered into competitions in the newspaper. All parties shared the cost of entry and agreed to share the prizes. An entry form completed in the defendant's name was successful and the defendant won £750. The lodger claimed one third share of the prize money, but the defendant refused to pay her on the grounds that they had not intended their agreement to be legally binding.

Decision: There was a binding contract between the parties as they had all contributed to the competition with the expectation that the prize would be shared equally.

Robertson v Anderson (2003)

Facts: The claimant and defendant were friends who entered into an agreement to share their bingo prizes. The claimant won a substantial bingo prize (£108,000), but claimed that the agreement to share it was not legally enforceable.

Decision: Where an agreement was made in a purely social context it would not usually be considered to be legally binding; however, from the facts of this particular case, the court concluded that the parties had intended the agreement to be enforceable.

The facts of this case can be contrasted with *Wilson v Burnett* (2007) where on the facts the court decided that although the friends had discussed sharing winnings over £10 at the beginning of the evening there was insufficient evidence to show that there was an intention to create a legally enforceable agreement.

Business Insight National Lottery syndicates

Almost a quarter of National Lottery jackpot prizes are won by syndicates and disputes over winnings have occurred on a number of occasions. In one dispute, a person claimed to have dissolved the syndicate four days before buying the ticket because other members were in arrears with their contributions. In another dispute, a woman entered into a syndicate at a birthday party agreeing to buy 19 Lucky Dip tickets for a Saturday night draw of the National Lottery. The group won £20 and the group alleged she agreed to use the money to purchase tickets for the Wednesday draw. The woman disagreed and stated she bought the winning ticket (over £105,500) with her own money. Legal action was then taken against her by other members of the party. To prevent disputes arising after money has been won, it is advisable to enter into written legal contracts beforehand.

Where an agreement is between family members who put their financial security at risk, the court will usually find that the parties did intend to create a legally binding agreement.

Parker v Clarke (1960)

Facts: A young couple were persuaded by elderly relatives to sell their own house and move in with the elderly couple, who promised them a share in their home when they died. The couples fell out and the elderly couple asked the young couple to leave.

Decision: The presumption, usually applied to domestic agreements, was rebutted as the young couple would not have sold their own home if the agreement between the parties had been unenforceable.

The presumption that agreements between husbands and wives are made without the intention to create legal relations does not apply if the agreement itself is of a commercial nature, such as a partnership agreement, or if the parties are separated. In *Merritt v Merritt* (1970) the written maintenance agreement made by the parties after they were separated was legally binding. The presumption that there is no intention to create legal relations in an agreement between a husband and wife did not apply after separation.

Key Concept Where an agreement is made in a social or domestic setting, the courts presume the parties did not intend the agreement to be legally binding; however, this presumption can be rebutted by evidence to the contrary.

Commercial or Business Agreements

It is presumed that parties entering into commercial or business agreements intend to create legal relations. When 'free gifts' are offered in a commercial setting to promote a business, or prizes are offered in return for entering a competition, it is presumed the parties intended to enter into a legal relationship.

Esso Petroleum Ltd v Commissioners of Customs and Excise (1976)

Facts: Esso had a sales promotion whereby garage owners offered a 'free' World Cup coin with every four gallons of petrol. Customs and Excise wanted to claim purchase tax on the 'sale' of the coins. In order to succeed with their claim, they had to show there was a contractual agreement to supply a coin in consideration for purchasing four gallons of petrol, and there was an intention to create legal relations.

Decision: The House of Lords decided that, as Esso were using the promotion to gain more business, there was an intention to create legal relations. (However Esso was not liable to pay tax as the coins were not being 'sold'.)

Rebutting the presumption the parties intended to create legal relations

The presumption that there is an intention to create a legal relationship in commercial and business agreements can be rebutted from the facts of the case, or by the use of an **'honour clause'** in the agreement. An honour clause is one that specifically states the agreement is not legally binding on the parties.

Rose and Frank v Crompton Bros Ltd (1925)

Facts: The defendant appointed the claimant as sole distributor of his paper tissues in the USA. The agreement made between the parties stated that the agreement was not legally binding, and not subject to the legal jurisdiction of courts in England or the United States, and that each party 'honourably pledge' themselves that they will carry out the agreement. The defendant ended the agreement without notice, and refused to accept orders made under the terms of the agreement.

Decision: There was no binding legally enforceable contract between the parties.

A similar decision was taken in the following case, where football pool coupons contained conditions stating there was no legal relationship between the sender of the coupons and the pools company.

Jones v Vernon's Pools (1938)

Facts: The claimant contended that he had sent in his football pool coupons to the defendant collector. The defendant denied receiving them. The conditions on the pools coupons stated that the sending in of the coupons did not give rise to any legal relationship, rights, duties, or consequences and was not legally enforceable.

Decision: The conditions on the coupons made it clear there was no legal liability and the coupons were binding in honour only.

Key Concept Where an agreement is made in a commercial or business setting, the courts presume the parties did intend the agreement to be legally binding, but this presumption can be rebutted by evidence to the contrary.

Comfort letters

If a company or other person has an interest in a business, they may write what is known as a **'comfort letter'** to a lender encouraging the lender to extend credit to the business by stating the business has the ability to pay its debts. It is presumed that comfort letters are not legally binding (although there may be circumstances where a letter of comfort does amount to an offer).

Kleinwort Benson Ltd v Malaysia Mining Corporation (1989)

Facts: The claimant bank lent £10 million to Metals Ltd, which was a subsidiary company of the defendant company. During negotiations for the loan, the defendant company sent the claimant a comfort letter stating that its policy was to ensure that Metals Ltd was in a position at all times to meet its liabilities. Metals Ltd went into liquidation and the claimant sought to recover the loan from the defendant company.

Decision: The words of the comfort letter amounted to a policy statement and did not express a contractual promise. Therefore, the defendant company was not legally obliged to pay off the loan.

Ambiguities in business and commercial contracts

If a business agreement is ambiguous as to whether there is an intention to create legal relations, then the courts presume that the parties did intend the agreement to be binding. It is up to the party seeking to show that the agreement is not legally binding to prove, on the balance of probabilities, that there was no intention to create a legal relationship. If they are unable to do so then the agreement can be enforced against them (see Figure 5.2).

Edwards v Skyways (1964)

Facts: The claimant was employed by the defendant and, as part of his redundancy package, the defendant agreed to additionally pay him an *ex gratia* (give as a favour) payment in return for the claimant withdrawing his contributions from the pension fund and not claiming his full pension rights. The defendant later refused to make the *ex gratia* payment contending that the words '*ex gratia*' showed there was no intention to create legal relations.

Decision: Although the term *ex gratia* may sometimes show no intention to create legal relations, in this case, as it was a commercial agreement, there was a presumption that the parties intended to create legal relations. The term here could be interpreted to mean that the employers were not admitting they had a pre-existing liability to pay the claimant, as opposed to not intending the agreement to be legally binding.

Figure 5.2   Intention to create legal relations

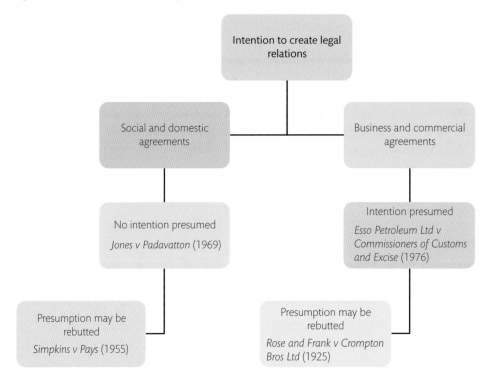

Contractual Capacity

There are some persons who do not have the legal power to make contracts or their power to make contracts is limited. Persons who may lack **contractual capacity** include drunks, persons with mental disorders, minors, and corporations (see Figure 5.4).

Minors

A minor is a person under the age of 18. The law governing minors' contracts is found in the Minors' Contracts Act 1987 and the common law. The laws relating to contracts made with minors are primarily designed to protect the minor from entering into unfavourable contracts with businesses and other persons. Although there are some exceptions, such as contracts for necessaries or education, generally a minor will not be bound by a contract he enters into. The other party is bound by the contract and it is legally enforceable unless the minor wishes it to be set aside.

Contracts for necessaries

A contract with a minor for **necessaries** is binding on the minor, provided it does not contain harsh terms which are detrimental to the minor. What are considered to be necessaries in law are more than just the basic essentials, and include goods and services which are regarded as appropriate to the minor's social standing and required by the minor at the time the contract is made.

Nash v Inman (1908)

Facts: A minor, who was a Cambridge student, was supplied with clothes including 11 fancy waistcoats from a Savile Row tailor. When he failed to pay for them the tailor sued him.
Decision: The clothes were suitable for a minor in his position but he already had a sufficient wardrobe of clothes and the waistcoats were not actually needed; therefore, the contract was not binding.

The definition of necessary goods is now in the Sale of Goods Act 1979 which defines necessaries as 'goods suitable to the condition in life of the minor … and to his actual requirements at the time of the sale'. Section 3 states that, if a minor accepts delivery of goods, then he is bound to pay a reasonable price for them. This may not be the contract price, if the price in the contract is considered to be unreasonable. If having promised to buy goods, the minor decides he no longer wants the goods ordered, there is no obligation to accept delivery of them and pay for them. The Sale of Goods Act only relates to goods but under common law a minor must also pay a reasonable price for services provided.

Necessaries can cover a wide range of goods, but if the contract contains harsh or onerous terms it will not be enforceable against a minor even if it is for necessaries.

Fawcett v Smethurst (1914)

Facts: A minor hired a car under a contract which included a term making him liable for damage to the car whether or not the damage was his fault.

Decision: Although the car was a necessary item, the term in the contract making the minor liable for all damage was too onerous; therefore, the contract was not enforceable against the minor.

Beneficial service contracts

A contract for training, education, apprenticeship, or employment is binding on a minor provided it is, on the whole, for his benefit. A court will examine all the terms of the contract and, even if some terms are to the detriment of the minor, provided the majority of terms are in his favour, it will be binding on him.

Doyle v White City Stadium (1935)

Facts: One of the clauses in an agreement between a minor (a professional boxer) and the British Boxing Board of Control stated that the minor would lose his payment for a fight if he were disqualified.

Decision: Although the clause allowed for non-payment for a fight, which could be considered detrimental, the agreement was binding on the minor as it encouraged clean fighting and protected young inexperienced boxers.

If the contract is predominately detrimental towards the minor, the courts will not enforce it.

De Francesco v Barnum (1890)

Facts: A 14-year-old girl entered into a seven year apprenticeship contract with De Francesco to be taught dancing. Under the contract her pay was very low, she could accept no professional engagements, or marry without De Francesco's permission, and De Francesco could terminate the contract at any time.

Decision: The terms of the contract were unfair and detrimental to the minor; therefore, it was unenforceable against her.

Key Concept Only contracts for necessaries and contracts for beneficial service are binding on minors. Other contracts made with minors cannot be legally enforced against them.

Contracts voidable by minors

Certain types of **contracts are voidable** by a minor, which means the minor can have them set aside before, or within a reasonable time after, reaching the age of 18. These contracts include partnership agreements, leases of property, and contracts to buy shares in a company. These types of contracts are of a continuous nature, and may be onerous; therefore, it is considered to be fair to allow a minor to repudiate them. A minor will be liable for any obligations that arose under the contract whilst it was still subsisting, such as rent or a call for payment of shares.

Proform Sports Management Ltd v (1) Proactive Sports Management Ltd (2007)

Facts: Wayne Rooney entered into a management and agency agreement with Proform Sports Management Ltd when he was 15. Two years later, he was persuaded to break the contract by Proactive Sports Management Ltd. Proform sued Proactive.

Decision: The contract between Rooney and Proform was not for necessaries or comparable to a contract of apprenticeship, education, or service (looking at all the terms of the contract as a whole it was not for the benefit of Rooney) and therefore was voidable by Rooney at any time. No action could be taken against him or the person who induced him to break the contract.

If a contract is voidable, then a minor is not obliged to have it set aside and on reaching 18 he may decide to **ratify** the agreement and continue with it.

Unenforceable contracts with minors

Contracts with minors that are not for necessaries or beneficial service and do not fall within the category of voidable contracts are unenforceable against minors. These contracts include contracts for non-necessary goods and services, and loans to minors. However, on reaching 18 a minor may ratify such contracts. To ratify a contract means to confirm that one intends to be legally bound by it. If a minor does not ratify such an agreement, it is not enforceable against him.

However, a minor will not be able to enjoy complete immunity from the law for contracts he signs; under the Minors' Contracts Act 1987, s 3, if a court considers it fair and just, it may require a minor to return goods or proceeds from the sale of goods which he has received under an unenforceable contract (see Figure 5.3).

Loans to minors

A loan to a minor is unenforceable and, therefore, if a minor wishes to obtain a loan he is usually required to provide someone who will guarantee it in the event of him failing to repay it. The Minors' Contracts Act 1987, s 2 states that the guarantor for a loan to a minor is bound by the contract. Therefore, although the lender could not pursue the minor for the recovery of the loan, he would be entitled to enforce the loan against the guarantor. On reaching 18, a minor may ratify a contract for a loan, in which case the contract will become binding on the minor.

Figure 5.3 Validity of contracts made with minors

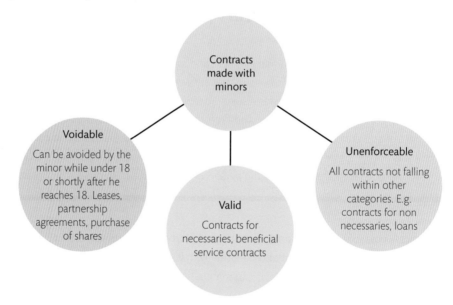

Intoxication

Persons who make contracts whilst under the influence of alcohol or drugs are presumed to know what they are doing and are usually bound by the terms of the contracts they enter into. A contract will be valid if one party is intoxicated at the time of making it, and the other party does not know this. However, if at the time of making a contract, a person is so intoxicated that he does not know the nature of the transaction he is entering into, and the other party realises this, then the contract will be unenforceable, unless the contract is for necessary goods that have been sold and delivered. If the contract is for necessary goods, the intoxicated person must pay a reasonable price for them: Sale of Goods Act 1979, s 3.

Mental Incapacity

The law provides some protection to mentally disabled persons who make contracts. The affairs of a person lacking mental capacity may be under the control of the court under the provisions set out in the Mental Capacity Act 2005. In these cases, the court takes control of a person's power to make contracts and any contracts purported to be made with the person personally are not valid. A contract made with a person who is not under the control of the court but has some form of mental incapacity is valid, unless it can be shown that, at the time of making the contract, the mentally disordered person did not know the nature of the transaction and the other party knew or should have known of the mental incapacity.

However, if the contract is for necessaries (goods or services actually needed at the time and suitable for the person's position in life) the Mental Capacity Act 2005, s 7 provides that, provided the services or goods are supplied, then a reasonable price must be paid for them.

Corporations

A corporation is a legal entity with its own legal personality. They include private and public companies, bodies set up by statute such as local authorities, and bodies set up by Royal Charter such as charities and some universities. Corporations do not have the same unlimited capacity to enter into contracts as mentally able people aged over 18. Where bodies have been set up by statute or Royal Charter, their capacity to act is stated in the statute or charter. Companies have constitutions, and capacity to act may be restricted by their constitution. A company or other body acting outside its powers is said to be acting '*ultra vires*' (beyond the powers). If a body acts *ultra vires*, then its actions may be invalid. In order to protect innocent parties contracting with companies, the Companies Act 2006 removes the effect of the *ultra vires* rule and, therefore, contracts made in good faith with a company are enforceable against the company even if they are outside the company's capacity (see Figure 5.4).

Key Concept A company is a legal entity and has the capacity to enter into contracts and sue and be sued for breach of contract.

Figure 5.4 Contractual capacity may be limited

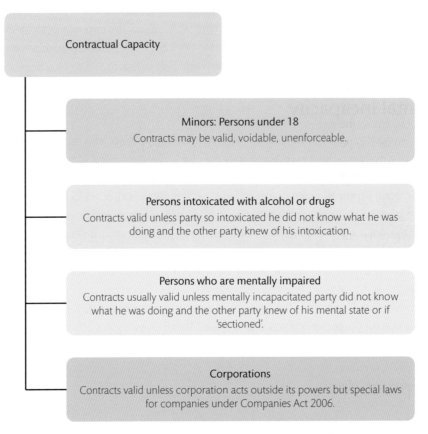

Contractual Capacity

Minors: Persons under 18
Contracts may be valid, voidable, unenforceable.

Persons intoxicated with alcohol or drugs
Contracts valid unless party so intoxicated he did not know what he was
doing and the other party knew of his intoxication.

Persons who are mentally impaired
Contracts usually valid unless mentally incapacitated party did not know
what he was doing and the other party knew of his mental state or if
'sectioned'.

Corporations
Contracts valid unless corporation acts outside its powers but special laws
for companies under Companies Act 2006.

Consideration

Consideration is an essential element of a binding contract. English law does not enforce gratuitous promises, unless made under deed. This means that a promise to give or do something without anything in return will not be legally binding. If Paul promises to give £5,000 to Save the Seagulls Ltd and later changes his mind, Save the Seagulls Ltd cannot sue him for breach of contract. If Paul had made the gift under deed (a legal agreement which is signed and witnessed) and then failed to give the donation, Save the Seagulls Ltd could sue him for the donation.

For a contract to be legally binding, there must be consideration by both parties. A party to an agreement must promise to give, do something, or refrain from doing something, in return for a similar promise or action by the other party. In a contract for the sale of goods, a seller promises to supply the goods and a buyer promises to pay for them.

Definition of Consideration

Consideration is sometimes difficult to define. In *Currie v Misa* (1875) the court stated that valuable consideration was 'some right, interest, profit or benefit accruing to one party, or some forbearance, detriment, loss or responsibility, given suffered or undertaken by the other party'. In other words, consideration was the giving of a benefit or the suffering of a loss.

The House of Lords, in *Dunlop Pneumatic Tyre Co Ltd v Selfridge & Co Ltd* (1915), defined consideration as the price that one contracting party bought the promise or the act of the other contracting party.

Key Concept   English law will only enforce a promise if it is supported by consideration or if the contract has been made by deed. Consideration is the 'element' given by each party to the contract.

Exchange of Consideration

There must be an exchange of consideration. One party to a contract must do something, omit to do something, or promise to do or omit to do something, in exchange for another party doing, omitting, or promising something.

In a contract, often promises are exchanged so that both parties are promisors (persons who make a promise) and both parties are promisees (persons who receive a promise).

For example, in a contract between Ali and Boris for the sale of a computer, Boris promises to pay Ali £1,000 (Boris is the promisor and Ali the promisee). Ali promises to give Boris a computer (Ali is the promisor and Boris is the promisee).

Executory or Executed Consideration

Executory consideration is where there is a promise to do something in the future. The promisor has agreed to do something but has not yet carried out the action. **Executed consideration** is consideration that has already been completed.

Take the following examples:

- Joe sends an order for 1,000 boxes of photocopying paper to Stationery Ltd and promises to pay £2,000. Stationery Ltd promises to deliver 1,000 boxes of photocopying paper within 14 days. It is at this point a contract is made. Both parties have made promises in the future and, therefore, the consideration given by Joe and the consideration given by Stationery Ltd is executory.

- Joe sends an order for 1,000 boxes of photocopying paper together with a cheque for £2,000 to Stationery Ltd who accept the order. It is at this point the contract is made: as Joe has already sent the £2,000 when the contract was made then his consideration is executed. Stationery Ltd still have to send the paper at the time the contract was made and, therefore, their consideration is executory.

In unilateral contracts, the offer is made by one party in return for an act by the other party. The contract is completed when the act is completed and, therefore, the consideration by the party who completes the act is said to be executed consideration. Terry offers £500 to all persons who swim across the Channel in December. Susie accepts the contract by swimming across the Channel. Susie's consideration (the swim) is executed at the time the contract is completed.

Past Consideration

If a promise is made after an act has been done, it is called past consideration and is not usually accepted as consideration in the eyes of the law.

Paul falls off the pier into the sea. Heather dives in and saves him. Paul promises to give Heather £5,000. This is not a binding promise because the promise to pay the £5,000 came after Heather's action.

The following case demonstrates the doctrine that past consideration is not sufficient for a binding contract.

Re McArdle (1951)

Facts: Mr McArdle died and left his house to his wife and then to his four children in equal shares. While Mrs McArdle was alive, one son and his wife moved into the house. The daughter-in-law made a number of home improvements costing £488. After she had completed the improvements, all the children signed an agreement stating that the daughter-in-law would be reimbursed when Mrs McArdle died. On Mrs McArdle's death, the children who inherited the house refused to reimburse her daughter-in-law.

Decision: The work was completed before the agreement to pay £488; therefore, the work was past consideration and the agreement was legally unenforceable.

Key Concept   Consideration given before the contract is completed (past consideration) is not adequate for a binding contract.

A request with an implied promise to pay

When a request is made for a service and the request implies a promise to pay for it, then completing the service is consideration (even though it is performed before any express agreement to pay for it). Rather than being seen as past consideration, it is recognised that there is an implied promise to pay before the act is completed, for example, hiring a taxi. In order for this rule to apply, the following three conditions must be present.

- The act must have been carried out at the request of the promisor.

- Both parties must contemplate that payment is going to be made for the service.

- If the payment had been promised before the act then the contract would have been legally enforceable.

Stewart v Casey (Re Casey's Patents) (1892)

Facts: Stewart was the joint owner of patent rights of an invention for a special type of container which could be used for carrying and storing inflammable liquids. Stewart asked Casey to promote the invention and, after two years of promoting it, Stewart wrote to Casey offering to pay him a third share of the profits for his work. When Stewart died, his executors refused to pay a third share of the profits to Casey.

Decision: The initial request to Casey implied a promise that he would be paid a reasonable sum for his work. The letter two years later merely fixed the amount he was to be paid.

The following case is a more recent example, where the Privy Council decided that a request not to act implied a promise to pay for that non-action.

Pao On v Lau Yiu Long (1980)

Facts: The defendants asked the claimants to promise that for a year the claimants would not sell their shares in a company of which the defendants were a major shareholder. If the claimants put their shares on the market, the defendants were concerned that the price of shares would fall. Later the defendants gave the claimants a guarantee stating that they would reimburse the claimants for any losses they suffered from retaining their shares for a year. During the year the shares fell in value but the defendants refused to reimburse the claimants, as they stated the guarantee came after the promise to retain the shares.

Decision: The claimants could recover their losses. Although the guarantee was given after the claimants had made the promise not to sell the shares, the claimants' promise had been made at the request of the defendants on the understanding that the claimants were to receive some sort of protection for a fall in value of the shares.

 Key Concept Where a request to act, made by a promisor, implies a promise to pay for that act at a later date, then completing the act is good consideration for the later payment.

Consideration must be provided by the promisee

The common law rule is that, in order for a promise to be enforceable, a person must have provided some consideration. However, under the Contracts (Rights of Third Parties) Act 1999, a party who has not provided any consideration can in certain circumstances enforce a contract. But if the circumstances necessary for the statute to be effective are not present, then the common law rule applies. For example, Alan services Bob's car in return for Bob's promise to pay Colin £100. Bob later refuses to give Colin £100. Colin has provided no consideration and therefore cannot sue Bob for breach of contract.

 Tweddle v Atkinson **(1861)**

Facts: Tweddle and Guy agreed that Guy would give £200 and Tweddle would give £100 to Tweddle's son, the claimant, after his marriage to Guy's daughter. Guy died before the £200 was paid and the claimant sued Guy's estate for the money.
Decision: The claimant had not provided any consideration for Guy's promise to pay £200 and therefore he could not take legal action under the contract.

The rule that someone can only enforce a contract if they have provided consideration is linked with privity of contract.

Consideration Need Not Be of Adequate Value

Provided that the consideration has some value in the eyes of the law, however small that value might be, it can constitute consideration. The courts allow parties freedom to make their own contracts and are not concerned if one party makes a good or a bad bargain. An agreement may be binding if some consideration has been given or promised. A contract to sell an iPod for 1p would be valid in respect of adequacy of consideration despite the fact that the value of an iPod is much greater than 1p.

Thomas v Thomas (1842)

Facts: An owner of a house promised that the widow of the previous owner could occupy the house for life in return for £1 per year and keeping the house in good repair. Later the owner tried to recover the house from the widow.

Decision: The promise to pay £1 per year and keep the house in good repair was sufficient consideration.

Even items which are disposed of by one of the parties as having no value may represent valuable legal consideration. In the following case, chocolate wrappers were adequate consideration.

Chappell v Nestle Co Ltd (1959)

Facts: The defendants, Nestle, offered records of a song 'Rockin' Shoes' to the public for 1s 6d (7.5p) plus three of the wrappers from their 6d (2.5p) chocolate bars. Issues arose under the Copyright Act 1956 and it was necessary for the court to assess whether the chocolate wrappers formed part of the consideration.

Decision: Chocolate wrappers were part of the consideration even though Nestle threw them away, because they benefited from the sales of chocolate which they may not otherwise have sold.

Consideration Must Be Sufficient

It must be 'sufficient' in the sense that the law recognises it as consideration. This means that what is promised must have some measurable and material value: it must be real, legal, and certain. A party cannot claim that they have provided consideration for giving up something that they do not have the right to do in any event, or for doing something when they already have a public or contractual duty to act.

White v Bluett (1853)

Facts: A promise by a son to stop complaining that he had been disinherited was not good consideration to release him from a promissory note for money that his father had lent him. When the father died his executors sued for the money due under the promissory note.

Decision: The son had no legal right to complain and, therefore, was not giving up anything of material value. He had given no consideration in return for the release from the debt.

Key Concept Consideration must be 'sufficient' but need not be 'adequate': consideration must have some value but its value need not be equivalent to the consideration received in return. The law will not intervene if a party makes a poor bargain in a contract.

Performance of a public duty—a duty imposed by law

A person who has a public duty to complete an act cannot use that act as good consideration in a contract. In the following case, Collins had a legal duty to act as a witness and therefore he could not use 'acting as a witness' as consideration in a contract.

Collins v Godefroy (1831)

Facts: Collins was a witness in a trial and was legally bound, under a court order, to give evidence at that trial. Godefroy promised to pay Collins six guineas if he attended court and gave evidence.

Decision: Godefroy's promise to pay was unenforceable as Collins had a legal duty to give evidence in court and, therefore, Collins had provided no consideration for the promised payment.

Where a person has a legal duty to perform an action but goes beyond that legal duty, then that extra act can amount to consideration, and the promisor will be bound by the promise they made.

Glasbrook Bros v Glamorgan County Council (1925)

Facts: During a miners' strike the pit owners wanted additional police officers to guard the mines. The owners agreed to pay the local authority for additional policing but later refused to do so, stating that the police had only carried out their existing public duty.

Decision: The local authority had provided more police officers than the police considered necessary for maintaining law and order. Therefore, there was consideration and the promise to pay for the additional police officers was binding.

Business Insight: Cost of policing at football matches

In *Harris v Sheffield United Football Club Ltd* (1987) the police presence that had been requested at a football match had to be paid for because a 'special police service' had been requested by the club. Although the provision of police services is now regulated by the Police Act 1996 the law reflects the common law position and the police can only charge for 'special police services'. In *Chief Constable of the Greater Manchester Police v Wigan Athletic AFC Ltd* (2009), the Court of Appeal stated that the football club did not have to pay for extra policing. The club had refused to accept the Chief Constable's suggestion that the level of policing should be increased because their team had been promoted, but the Chief Constable had gone ahead and provided a higher level of policing then sued the club when they refused to pay for it. In *Leeds United Football Club Ltd v Chief Constable of West Yorkshire* (2014) the court decided that the Club were not responsible for paying for the cost of policing and crowd control outside the immediate vicinity of the club premises on land not owned or controlled by the club.

Performance of a contractual duty owed to a party under a separate contract

The same consideration can be used by a party in more than one contract provided the contracts are with different parties (see Figure 5.5). The following case, where the stevedores used the same consideration in two contracts, demonstrates this principle.

New Zealand Shipping Co Ltd v A M Satterthwaite & Co Ltd (The Eurymedon) (1975)

Facts: O agreed with stevedores (S) (persons who unload boats) that S would not be liable for damage caused to machinery when S was unloading it. Consideration by S was the unloading of the machinery. In a second contract between S and C, S agreed to unload the machinery for payment.

Decision: S could use the unloading of the machinery as consideration in contract 1 even though they were contractually bound in contract 2 to unload the machinery.

Figure 5.5 The same consideration can be used by a party in more than one contract provided the contracts are with different parties

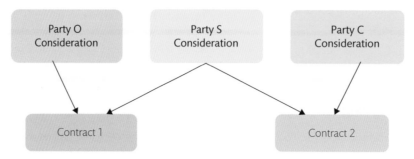

Performance of an existing contractual duty to a party in a contract

The law in this area was modified by *Williams v Roffey Bros & Nicholls (Contractors) Ltd* (1990). In the past, it was clear that an obligation owed to a party in an existing contract could not be used as consideration for a new promise with the same party. In *Stilk v Myrick* (1809), the seamen had promised to sail a ship home in return for a set wage, and they could not use their consideration, of sailing the ship home, in return for a promise of an additional sum.

Stilk v Myrick (1809)

Facts: When a ship was at a foreign port two seamen deserted. The captain of the ship could not find any replacements and promised the rest of the crew that the wages of the two deserters would be shared out between them if they sailed the ship back to London. The crew complied, but on reaching London the ship owners refused to share out the wages of the two deserters.
Decision: In completing the voyage the crew were performing their existing contractual duties, and had given no additional consideration in return for the promise to pay a share of the deserters' wages. The promise made by the captain was not legally binding.

The Court in *Stilk v Myrick* may have had public policy reasons for deciding that the seamen were not entitled to the extra payment, as to have enforced the promise may have been seen to risk exposing a ship's captain to blackmail from a crew refusing to sail a ship home without additional payment, knowing that new crew would be difficult to find.

If a party to a contract takes on additional duties that are beyond those in his original contract, then that is consideration for a further promise. *Stilk v Myrick* can be contrasted with *Hartley v Ponsonby* where the seamen promised to do over and above what they had previously promised.

Hartley v Ponsonby (1857)

Facts: Almost half the crew of a ship deserted and the master induced the remaining seamen to sail the ship home by promising to pay them a sum of money in addition to their wages. The crew performed the rest of the voyage with the diminished number, but at the end of the voyage the master refused to pay the additional sums.

Decision: The crew were entitled to the additional money as they had done more than their contractual duty. They had completed the voyage on a ship that was much more hazardous as it was so short of crew. This was good consideration for the additional sum promised.

The principle set out in *Stilk v Myrick*, was not overruled (set aside) by *Williams v Roffey Bros & Nicholls (Contractors) Ltd* (1990) (next), but the court did enforce a promise made by the defendant, Roffey Bros, to pay the claimant, Williams, an extra sum of money for work which the claimant was already under a contractual duty to perform for the defendant. The court's reasoning for enforcing the promise was that Roffey Bros gained a practical benefit because they were able to avoid a penalty in another contract, and they did not have to meet the expense of engaging other contractors to finish Williams' work, and the payment scheme agreed with Williams was changed so that Williams was paid per complete flat. Even though Williams was only doing what he had originally contracted to do, Roffey Bros received an extra benefit, and there had been no economic duress or fraud by Williams.

Williams v Roffey Bros & Nicholls (Contractors) Ltd (1990)

Facts: The defendant, building contractors, entered into a contract (contract A) with the owners, to refurbish a block of flats. In contract A there was a clause that stated that if the flats were not refurbished in time then a sum of money was payable to the owners. The defendant then entered into a second contract (contract B) with the claimant to carry out the carpentry work on the flats for £20,000. The claimant underestimated the cost of doing the carpentry work and got into financial trouble. The defendant was aware of the claimant's difficulties and knew the job had been underpriced. The defendant changed the working arrangements so that one flat was finished at a time and promised to pay the claimant a further sum for each completed flat. This amounted to £10,300. The defendant paid the claimant £1,500 but refused to pay him any further sums, claiming that the agreement was unenforceable as it was not supported by consideration.

Decision: Although the claimant was not doing any more than he originally agreed under contract B, the defendant had received a benefit from the claimant continuing with the work. The defendant would avoid paying damages for failing to complete contract A, and also benefited from the altered working arrangements and from not incurring the cost and inconvenience of having to find another carpenter. The promise that the defendant had made was enforceable against them.

Figure 5.6 Contracts in *Williams v Roffey Bros*

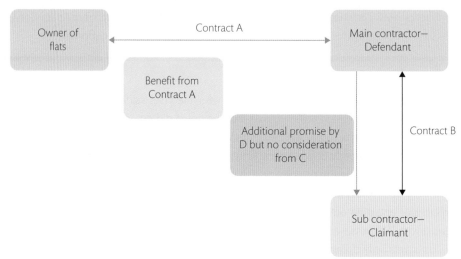

The decision in *Williams v Roffey Bros & Nicholls (Contractors) Ltd* may be applied in cases that meet the following criteria (see Figure 5.6):

- The subject matter of the new agreement was to make an extra payment for an originally agreed amount of work.
- The parties intended that the new promise would be legally binding.
- The party agreeing to pay the extra sum (promisor) gained some benefit from the agreement even if the other party (promisee) suffered no detriment.
- There was no evidence of duress by the party (promisee) receiving the extra payment.

Key Concept The performance of existing contractual duties can amount to consideration in circumstances where the promisor gains some benefit, and there is no duress or fraud by the promisee.

Part-payment of Debts

Where a debtor owes money to a creditor and cannot pay the full amount, he may offer to pay a smaller amount to the creditor, and the creditor may agree to accept the lesser sum as full settlement of the debt. However, it has been long established in law that this type of agreement is not usually binding, and the creditor can later demand the debtor pays the debt in full. The rule in *Pinnel's Case* (1602) states that a promise by a creditor to accept part-payment of a debt, when the whole debt is due, does not discharge the debtor from the whole debt.

Pinnel's Case (1602)

Facts: Pinnel sued Cole for the recovery of a debt. Cole stated that he had paid part of the debt and that Pinnel had accepted the part-payment in full satisfaction for the whole debt.

Decision: The court stated that payment of a lesser sum on the date the debt is due to be paid cannot be settlement for the whole debt. The court added that if payment were made on an earlier date or some other item was given, even if the item was worth financially less than the debt, this would be good consideration for the whole debt.

This legal principle was confirmed in *Foakes v Beer* (1884), where the court made it clear that a promise to accept payment of a smaller sum of money than owed is not enforceable, unless the party to whom the promise is made provides some additional consideration.

Foakes v Beer (1884)

Facts: Mrs Beer obtained a high court judgment for a debt of £2,090 19s owed by Dr Foakes. She agreed in writing with Foakes that she would not take further court action if Foakes paid off the debt by instalments. Nothing was mentioned of the interest which had accrued on the debt. Foakes paid the debt off in accordance with the agreement but then Beer sued him for the interest on the debt.

Decision: Beer was legally entitled to the interest on the debt because Foakes had not provided any consideration for her promise to accept less than due to her.

A debt will be discharged by part-payment if, in return for the creditor's promise to accept a lesser sum, the debtor gives some further consideration. The additional consideration must be accepted by the creditor. Good consideration is where the creditor requests either one of the following:

- Part-payment of the debt at an earlier date than it is due. A debt of £5,000 is due to be paid by 1 July and the creditor requests and accepts payment of £4,000 on 1 May; the creditor will not be able to pursue the debtor for the balance of the debt.

- Some goods or other material benefit to accompany the part-payment (these do not have to be of an equivalent value of the debt owed). A creditor requests and accepts £400 plus a ticket to see Robbie Williams, costing £120, in satisfaction of a debt of £2,000; the creditor will not be able to pursue the debtor for the balance of the debt.

Foakes v Beer (1884) was decided before *Williams v Roffey Bros & Nicholls (Contractors) Ltd* (1990), but in *Re Selectmove Ltd* (1995), heard in the Court of Appeal, the court made it clear that situations similar to *Williams v Roffey Bros* only applied to the supply of goods and services. Where the facts related to payment of a debt, then the law as stated by the House of Lords in *Foakes v Beer* must be followed.

Re Selectmove Ltd (1995)

Facts: A company which owed the Inland Revenue a considerable sum of money agreed with the collector of taxes to pay the money owed by instalments. The company then received a demand for the full amount owed and, when the company did not pay the full amount, the Inland Revenue petitioned the court to have the company wound up. The company objected on the grounds that an agreement to pay by instalments had been made with the Inland Revenue. **Decision:** The collector of taxes did not have authority to bind the Inland Revenue, but even if he had authority it was settled law that a promise to pay a sum which a debtor was already bound by law to pay was not good consideration. The principle set out in *Williams v Roffey Bros & Nicholls (Contractors) Ltd*, that a promise to perform an existing duty could amount to good consideration provided that there were practical benefits to the promisee, only applied where the duty involved a supply of goods or services.

The law at present is that one party's promise to perform an existing contractual duty for the supply of goods or services can amount to consideration if the other party receives a practical benefit and there is no duress or fraud. But in relation to debts this is not enough and there usually must be some additional benefit to the creditor.

Key Concept A promise by a creditor to accept a smaller sum (part-payment) than owed is not usually enforceable by the debtor unless the debtor provides some additional consideration.

There are some exceptions to the general principle that part-payment of a debt is not sufficient consideration to discharge the whole debt. These exceptions include:

- Composition agreement. This is a legal agreement and is made between a group of creditors and a debtor where the debtor owes monies to them all. Each creditor agrees to accept a portion of their debt in the composition agreement and a creditor cannot sue the debtor for any outstanding balance owed.

- Payment of a debt by a third party. This is where a part-payment of a debt has been made by a third party and the creditor promises not to pursue the original debtor for the balance (see Figure 5.7).

Figure 5.7 **Part-payment of a debt by a third party is good consideration to discharge the whole debt**

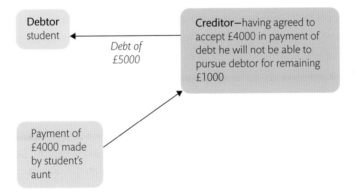

In addition, a debtor may be able to use the equitable defence of **promissory estoppel** to prevent a lender reneging on his promise.

Promissory Estoppel

As stated previously, a promise to accept part-payment of a debt is not generally enforceable unless the debtor has agreed to do something additional to what was required in the original contract. However, if a debtor is being sued for the remainder of a debt, where a lender had previously promised not to pursue him, the debtor can ask the court to use its equitable powers to prevent the lender going back on his promise. Equity is a system of fairness and, where an equitable remedy is sought, the courts have discretion on whether or not to grant it. The courts will only allow a debtor to use the principle of promissory estoppel if the debtor has acted fairly himself.

The rule of promissory estoppel, preventing a promisor from going back on his word where there has been no consideration by the promisee, was developed in the following case.

Central London Property Trust v High Trees House Ltd (1947)

Facts: In 1937 the defendants leased a block of flats from the claimant for £2,500 rent per year. The defendants intended to sublet the flats. During the war (1939–45) it became very difficult to find tenants, and the claimant agreed to reduce the rent to £1,250 per year. By 1945, when the war had ended, the flats were all sublet again and the claimant wanted the rent returned to its former amount of £2,500 and also requested six months' back rent.

Decision: The claimant was entitled to recover back rent for the last six months and to have the rent returned to £2,500 per year as, once the conditions under which the agreement to reduce the rent had been made no longer applied, the rent automatically returned to the full amount. The judges stated that the claimant would not have been successful if it had sought to recover the full rent for all the war years, when many of the flats were not sublet, because of the doctrine of promissory estoppel. The defendants had relied on the claimant's promise to reduce the rent and it was inequitable (unfair) to allow the claimant to break its promise.

The judge's statement relating to promissory estoppel preventing the claimant seeking the back rent was *obiter dicta* and, therefore, only persuasive in English law (the claimant was not actually seeking back rent for the war years). However, although the doctrine of promissory estoppel is not used very often, it has been applied in later cases.

The rules relating to promissory estoppel are as follows:

- It arises in an existing contractual agreement from a promise made by one party to the other party, where the other party has given no consideration in return.

- It varies rights within a contract.

- It cannot be used to create new rights but only to prevent the enforcement of rights already held. If a promisee is being sued by the promisor, then he can use promissory estoppel as a defence in court. He cannot use it to start an action in court. In the *High Trees* case, the defendants could use the claimant's promise to accept a lesser rent as a defence if sued for the full rent.

- Normally suspends rights for a period of time rather than extinguishing them altogether. Unless the promisor makes it clear that he is permanently giving up his rights, he can give notice that he wishes to return to the original position.

- Promissory estoppel is an equitable principle and the courts will only allow a defendant to use it if it is just to do so in all the circumstances. The promise relied upon must have been given voluntarily and, if the defendant has acted dishonourably, then the courts will not award him a remedy.

Tool Metal Manufacturing v Tungsten Electric Co Ltd (1955)

Facts: The claimants, owners of a patent, licensed the defendants to produce a certain number of items using the patent. Compensation was payable if the defendants produced more items than agreed. In 1942 the claimants agreed to forgo their compensation payments in the national interest. Later the claimants sought to have the compensation payments reinstated and to claim back compensation.

Decision: The promise to forgo compensation payments was binding but it did not destroy the right which could be revived with notice to the defendants.

D & C Builders v Rees (1965)

Facts: The claimant company, D & C Builders were a small company and were owed £482.75 by the defendants. The defendants knew the claimants were in real financial difficulty and offered £300 in settlement of the debt and said if the claimants did not accept it then they would get nothing. The claimants reluctantly accepted a cheque for £300 'on completion of the account'. The claimants later sued for the remaining £182.75.

Decision: Following the rule in *Pinnel's Case* there was no further consideration and, therefore, agreement to accept a lesser sum did not cancel the debt. Although promissory estoppel may have applied, it would be inequitable (unfair) to apply it in this case because the defendants had deliberately taken advantage of the claimants' financial problems using economic duress to persuade them to take less. The defendants had to pay the builders the remaining £182.75.

Key Concept Usually a debtor will be liable to repay the whole of his debt even if the creditor has agreed to accept a smaller sum than owed. However, promissory estoppel, a rule of equity, prevents a party to a contract from going back on a promise. If this applies, the creditor, who has agreed to accept less than the sum owed, may be prevented from going back on his word. There are special rules that govern when promissory estoppel can be applied.

Privity of Contract

A contract is a binding agreement between the offeror and the offeree. Privity of contract means that persons who are not party to the agreement cannot be bound by its contractual terms or take action if its terms are broken. Persons who have not contributed to the consideration of a contract cannot sue if the contract is breached, and the burden of a contract cannot be enforced against persons to whom no consideration has been promised. Under common law, only a person who is party to a contract has enforceable rights and obligations under it (see Figure 5.8).

Figure 5.8 Privity of contract

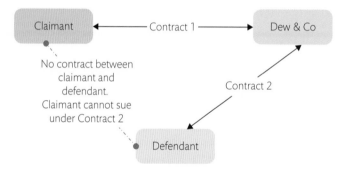

Dunlop Pneumatic Tyre Co Ltd v Selfridge & Co Ltd (1915)

Facts: The claimant supplied tyres to Dew & Co under a contractual agreement (contract 1) which stated that Dew would not resell the tyres for less than the price prescribed by the claimant. The contract also stated that, if Dew sold the tyres to wholesalers, then he would impose similar restrictions in his contract with the wholesaler. Dew sold tyres to the defendant, a wholesaler, under a contract (contract 2) which stated the defendant would pay the claimant £5 for every tyre sold below the list price. The defendant sold two tyres below the list price and the claimant brought an action against the defendant.

Decision: The claimant could not recover damages (compensation) under the contract made between the defendant and Dew (contract 2), as only a person who is party to a contract can claim under it.

> **Key Concept** Under the privity of contract rule, only persons who are party to a contract can sue or be sued on a contract. There are a number of exceptions to this rule, the most important one being the Contracts (Rights of Third Parties) Act 1999.

Exceptions to the Rule of Privity of Contract

The privity rule could cause injustice and, through case law, the courts developed a number of exceptions allowing persons not party to a contract to benefit from it. There are also a number of statutory exceptions relating to insurance policies, restrictive covenants relating to land, and bills of exchange. A major statutory change occurred with the introduction of the Contracts (Rights of Third Parties) Act 1999 which enables third parties, who have given no consideration in a contract, to enforce the terms of the contract in certain circumstances.

Contracts made for the benefit of a group of persons

Where a contract is made by one person but is for the benefit of a group of persons, only the person who made the contract is entitled to sue on it. However that person will be able to sue for his own losses and those of the group.

> ### *Jackson v Horizon Holidays Ltd* (1975)
>
> **Facts:** The claimant booked a family holiday in a hotel in Ceylon (Sri Lanka) with the defendant, a travel agency. The claimant told the defendant that he wanted everything at the hotel to be of the highest standard, and that there must be adjoining doors between the two bedrooms. Although the brochure stated that the hotel facilities included mini-golf, swimming pool, beauty salon and hairdresser, in fact it had none of these. The bedrooms were dirty and there was no connecting door, the bathrooms were inadequate, and the food distasteful. The claimant sued the defendant for breach of contract claiming damages (compensation) for loss of the holiday for himself, his wife, and their children.
>
> **Decision:** Where a person had entered into a contract for the benefit of himself and others, who were not parties to the contract, he could sue on the contract for the loss suffered not only by him but also by the others.

Contracts where the benefit is held in trust for a third party

A trust is where property is passed by one party to a second party (the trustee), stating that it is to be held by the trustee for the benefit of third parties (beneficiaries). If the trustee does not comply with conditions set out in the trust, then the beneficiary can apply to the court to enforce the terms of the trust.

Contractual rights assigned to a third party

It is possible to assign the rights of a contract to a third party without the permission of the other party to the contract. If one party has a right to be paid under contract (for example, for carrying out electrical work) then that right to be paid can be sold to a third party, who can then sue for payment. Where a small electrical business is owed money from a number of its customers, it may choose to sell those debts to a debt recovery firm. The customers can then be sued by the debt recovery firm. It is not possible to assign the burden of a contract; the customers who owed money to the electrical firm cannot assign their debt to a third party.

Contracts made between one party and an agent

If a contract is made between a party and an agent who is acting on behalf of a principal, then that contract is binding on, and can be enforced by, the principal.

Collateral contracts

Where a person enters into a contract with another person, relying on a promise made by a third party who is not party to the contract, the courts may infer a contract (a collateral contract) between the first person and the third party.

Shanklin Pier v Detel Products Ltd (1951)

Facts: The claimants owned a pier that needed repainting. The defendants, Detel, were paint manufacturers and promised the claimants that their paint was durable and weather resistant and would last for 7–10 years. The claimants employed contractors to paint the pier and specified in the contract that the contractors were to use Detel's paint. Three months after the pier had been painted, the paintwork began to deteriorate. There was a contract between the claimants and the contractors to paint the pier for an agreed sum. There was a contract between the contractors and Detel for the purchase and supply of paint. However, the claimants sued Detel.

Decision: There was a collateral contract between Detel and the claimants. Detel had promised the paint would be of a certain quality and the claimants' request that the contractors should use Detel's paint was consideration.

Contracts of insurance, covenants relating to land, and bills of exchange

A number of statutes provide for persons who are not party to an insurance contract to claim under it. For example, under the Road Traffic Act 1988, motorists are required to have insurance against damage and injury to other road users. In certain circumstances, an injured road user can claim compensation directly from the other party's insurance company. The Law of Property Act 1925 states that privity of contract does not apply to restrictive covenants on land. A restrictive covenant is an agreement between two parties not to do something with land (e.g. build a theme park). The covenant remains enforceable even if the buyer of the land sells the land to a third party. Under the Bills of Exchange Act 1882, where a bill of exchange (e.g. a cheque) is made payable to one party but that party endorses it (signs it) making it payable to a third party, then that third party can sue on it, if monies are not paid out.

Contracts (Rights of Third Parties) Act 1999

The Act applies to contracts entered into after 11 May 2000. The Act does not abolish all the privity rules or remove any existing rights and remedies available to third parties, but it does allow a third party rights in contracts which have been made for his benefit, in certain circumstances. Obligations cannot be imposed on third parties, only benefits. Persons who are not parties to a contract can sue for their rights under the contract in two situations:

- Where the contract expressly permits enforcement by third parties.

- Where the purpose of the contract is to benefit the third party, unless it is clear that the contract did not intend to create rights for third parties.

In these circumstances, third parties can enforce a contract even though they have provided no consideration.

Section 1 states that a person who is not party to a contract may enforce a term of the contract in their own right. The third party has the remedies for breach of contract that would have been available to him if he had been a party to the contract. The third party must be identified by name, as a member of a class of persons or as answering a particular description. A third party need not have been in existence at the time the contract is made; therefore, contracts can be made for the benefit of children not yet born or limited companies not yet registered.

Section 2 states that the parties who made the contract cannot cancel it or vary its terms without the third party's consent where the third party has communicated agreement to the terms or relied on the terms, and the parties knew this or ought reasonably to have known it. Contracting parties can opt out of this provision by expressly stating in the contract that it may be cancelled or varied without the consent of the third party.

Section 5 states that, where the promisee has recovered damages (compensation) for a third party's losses, then the third party is not entitled to a duplicate sum. In other words, the promisor only has to meet the cost of failing to fulfil his promise once and any payment made to the promisee reduces payments that can be claimed by the third party.

Section 6 contains a list of contracts where the Act does not apply, including contracts of employment and contracts for the carriage of goods by sea.

Basic Terminology

For an online flashcard glossary visit the Online Resource Centre

Comfort letter Statement made by one business to a lender encouraging the lender to extend credit to another business, by stating the business has the ability to pay its debts.

Consideration A promise by one party to give, do or refrain from doing something in return for similar by the other party.

Contractual capacity Legal power to make contracts.

Executed consideration Consideration that has already been completed.

Executory consideration A promise to do something in the future.

Honour clause A clause in an agreement that specifically states the agreement is not legally binding on the parties.

Intention to create legal relations An intention by the parties that the agreement should impose legal rights and obligations on them.

Necessaries Goods and services appropriate to a person's social standing and required at the time.

Promissory estoppel An equitable principle of law which prevents a promisor going back on his word.

Ratify To authorise or approve an agreement after it has been made.

Voidable contract A contract that is binding on one party but the other party has the option to have it set aside. Until set aside, the contract has full legal effect.

Summary

For an online printable version visit the Online Resource Centre

After studying this chapter students should be able to:

Identify elements of an intention to create legal relations and explain the presumptions relating to commercial and domestic agreements

- In order for an agreement to be legally binding, the parties must intend that the agreement should impose legal rights and obligations on them.
- Where agreements are made within a social or domestic context, it is presumed that the parties did not intend to create legal relations.
- Where commercial or business agreements are made, it is presumed that the parties did intend to create legal relations.
- These presumptions can be rebutted by clear evidence of a contrary intention.

Outline the law relating to capacity to contract

- Minors, persons with mental disabilities, intoxicated persons, and corporations may lack contractual capacity to enter into certain types of contracts.
- Contracts made with minors are usually voidable by the minor, but contracts made for necessaries, training, or education, are binding on the minor, provided they do not contain harsh terms which are detrimental to the minor.
- The contractual capacity of a company is stated in its constitution. Contracts made in good faith with a company are enforceable against the company even if they are outside the company's capacity.

Understand the meaning of consideration and explain what constitutes consideration

- Consideration by both parties is necessary for a legally binding contract.
- Past consideration is not accepted as consideration.
- Consideration must be something measurable and of material value.
- An existing legal duty to perform an action is not good consideration.
- An obligation owed to a party in an existing contract cannot usually be used as consideration for a new promise with the same party. However, this principle has been qualified by *Williams v Roffey Bros & Nicholls (Contractors) Ltd* (1990), where a promise to perform a duty already imposed in a contract can be good consideration if there have been renegotiations, provided there has been no fraud or duress and practical benefits have been gained by the promisor.
- A promise by a creditor to accept part-payment of a debt when the whole debt is due does not usually discharge the debtor from the whole debt unless the debtor gives some further consideration.

Outline the doctrine of privity of contract and be familiar with the exceptions to the doctrine

- Privity of contract means that persons who are not party to an agreement cannot be bound by its contractual terms. This rule has been changed by the Contracts (Rights of Third Parties) Act 1999 which enables third parties, who have given no consideration in a contract, to enforce the terms of the contract, where the contract expressly permits enforcement by third parties, or where the purpose of the contract is to benefit the third party.

Questions

1. **a)** Every week, Amy and Jim and their daughter, Sophie, enter the National Lottery, each contributing £1 for 3 lucky dip numbers. Sophie always fills in the form, pays over the money to the newsagent, and keeps the ticket. Last week five of their numbers came up and the ticket paid out £5,000. Sophie refuses to share the £5,000. Advise Amy and Jim.

   b) Discovering the kitchen on fire, Bella telephoned the fire brigade. On their arrival she told Sam, the officer in charge, that she would give each fireman £50 if they prevented the fire from damaging her living room which contained valuable antiques. The firemen extinguished the fire and confined its effects to the kitchen. Bella has refused to pay. Advise the fire brigade.

   c) Alice is travelling to Oxford when her car gets a puncture. The driver of a passing van stops and offers to change the wheel of Alice's car. When he has finished he says 'That will be £100 please. I'm part of the Blue Flag rescue service. I have a garage just down the road.' Explain to Alice if she is legally obliged to pay the £100.

   d) While Paul is away on holiday his neighbour, Jim, mends Paul's garden fence. When Paul returns he is so pleased he promises to give Jim a case of French wine. This was two weeks ago and Jim has still not received any wine. Has a contract been made between Paul and Jim?

For outline answers visit the Online Resource Centre

2. Anthony entered into a contract with Bruce to refurbish a block of 100 flats; the work was to be completed in three months. The contract stated that late completion would be charged at £5,000 per day. Anthony sub-contracted with Clive to install the fitted kitchens and bathrooms in each of the flats for a fixed price of £100,000. After a month it became obvious to both Anthony and Clive that Clive had grossly underpriced the cost of the materials and he would be in financial difficulties if he completed the job. Consequently, Anthony offered to pay Clive an additional £300 per flat provided they were finished before the completion date. Clive carried on with the contract and completed the work in time. Anthony is now refusing to pay him the additional money. Advise Clive.

3. In social and domestic agreements what presumption is made with regard to intention to create legal relations? How does this differ from the approach to intention in business agreements? Give examples from case law.

4. Explain what is understood in contract law by the statement 'Consideration must be sufficient but need not be adequate'.

Further Reading

Macdonald and Atkins, *Koffman & Macdonald's Law of Contract*, 8th edn (Oxford University Press, 2014) Chapters 4, 5, 6, and 18.

Poole, *Contract Law*, 12th edn (Oxford University Press, 2014) Chapters 4, 5, and 11.

Richards, *The Law of Contract*, 11th edn (Pearson, 2013) Chapters 3, 4, 5, and 19.

Taylor and Taylor, *Contract Law Directions*, 4th edn (Oxford University Press, 2013) Chapters 3, 4, and 13.

Turner, *Unlocking Contract Law*, 4th edn (Routledge, 2013) Chapters 3, 4, 13, and 14.

Online Resource Centre

Test your knowledge by trying this chapter's **Multiple Choice Questions.** Visit:

www.oup.com/uk/orc/law/company/
jonesibl3e/01student/mcqs/ch05/

For more information, updates, and multiple choice questions, please visit the Online Resource Centre at:

www.oup.com/uk/orc/law/company/
jonesibl3e/

The Terms of
a Contract

Introduction

The **terms** of a contract are the contents of the contract, and state the parties' legal duties and obligations to each other. Terms may be written, oral, or even implied into a contract. Although terms are usually the result of express agreement between the parties, some terms are implied into a contract by the courts, statute, or custom. Other terms, although expressly stated in the contract, are made ineffective by law. All parties to a contract will have obligations to each other under the terms of the contract. If one party fails to comply with an obligation of the contract, the other party will be entitled to claim damages and, depending upon what type of obligation was breached, may also be able to treat the contract as ended.

Learning Objectives

After studying this chapter you should be able to:

- Explain the difference between a term of a contract and a representation.

- Appreciate the necessity for certainty of contractual terms and explain the difference between express and implied terms.

- Distinguish between conditions, warranties, and innominate terms and explain the different legal consequences that result from breach of them.

- Describe the nature of exemption clauses and explain the methods used by the courts to restrict the use of such clauses.

- Explain the effects on exemption clauses of the Unfair Contract Terms Act 1977 and Unfair Terms in Consumer Contracts Regulations 1999.

- Demonstrate an understanding of contracts in restraint of trade.

Pre-contractual Statements

In order to determine the terms of a contract it is essential to establish what the parties said or wrote. However, when parties are in the process of negotiating a contract, promises and statements are often made over a period of time. Not all these statements will be deemed to be terms of the contract (see Figure 6.1).

A statement might be:

- Trader's hype or puff. This is a mere boast, often a gimmick used to advertise a product. Buyers are not expected to take such statements as literally true. Examples of trader's hype include: a computer package is 'incredible value', or a washing powder 'washes whiter than white'.
- A representation. This is a pre-contractual statement.
- A term of the contract. This is a statement that forms part of a contract.

If a statement made during negotiations becomes a term of a contract, and it is later found to be untrue, then the misled party has remedies for breach of contract (see Chapter 8). A statement made during negotiations which does not become a term of the contract is at most a mere **representation**, and, if the statement is later found to be untrue, the misled party will be limited to the remedies for **misrepresentation**. The misled party will not have a remedy for breach of contract but may make a claim for misrepresentation under the Misrepresentation Act 1967 (see Chapter 7).

Figure 6.1 Distinction between pre-contractual and contractual statements

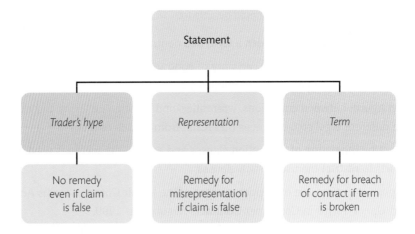

Factors Taken into Account in Distinguishing a Contractual Term from a Representation

Whether a statement is a term or a representation depends upon the intention of the parties. However, the test to decide the intention of the parties is objective, i.e. what a reasonable person would consider to be the intention of the parties when looking at all the circumstances in which the statement was made. There are a number of factors a court will consider in deciding whether a statement is part of a contract. These factors include the importance of the statement to the parties, the interval of time between the statement and contract, whether the statement is oral and the contract is written, and the knowledge and skill of the party making the statement.

The importance of the statement to the parties

If the statement is of major importance to either party and that party would not have entered the agreement without it, the statement will be a term of the contract.

Bannerman v White (1861)

Facts: The defendant purchaser wished to buy hops for brewing purposes and during negotiations he asked the claimant seller if the hops had been treated with sulphur. The seller assured him that the hops had not been treated with sulphur, and the defendant agreed to buy them. Later the defendant discovered the hops had been treated with sulphur, and he refused to accept delivery of them. The claimant seller sued for breach of contract, claiming that the statement relating to sulphur was a preliminary statement and not a term of the contract.

Decision: The claimant's statement regarding the sulphur was a fundamental term of the contract and, since it was not true, the defendant could terminate the contract.

The interval of time between the statement and contract

Where there is a lengthy time gap between the statement and the contract, the statement is usually a representation.

Oral statements and written contracts

Where the statement is oral and the contract is written, the oral statement is usually a representation. If the oral statement is put in writing after it was made, then it is more likely to be a contractual term.

The knowledge and skill of the party making the statement

A statement made by one party who has specialist skills or knowledge, to a party who is relying on those specialist skills, is more likely to be treated as a term of the contract. If the statement is made by a party without any specialist knowledge, this statement is less likely to be construed as a term of the contract, particularly if it is made to a person with expertise.

Compare the following two cases. In *Dick Bentley Productions Ltd v Harold Smith* the statement in question was made by a car dealer, who was expected to have specialist knowledge, to a customer, whereas in *Oscar Chess Ltd v Williams* the statement in question was made by an ordinary customer to a car dealer.

Dick Bentley Productions Ltd v Harold Smith (1965)

Facts: The claimant, a businessman, asked the defendants, car dealers, to find him a Bentley car in good condition. The defendants found a car and stated that it had only done 20,000 miles since a new engine and gear box had been fitted. In fact, the car had done 100,000 miles since the replacement parts were fitted.

Decision: The statement had influenced the claimant when making a decision to purchase the car. It was made by a specialist in the car trade and was a term of the contract.

Oscar Chess Ltd v Williams (1957)

Facts: The defendant seller traded in his car when buying another car from the claimants, who were car dealers. The defendant informed the claimants that the car he was trading in was a 1948 model (as stated in the registration document). The claimants valued the car at £280. It was later discovered to be a 1939 model and worth only £175. The registration documents had been altered by a previous owner.

Decision: The statement was not a term of the contract. The defendant had no specialist knowledge, and had made the statement to car specialists who were in a better position than the defendant to discover the truth.

Key Concept   Terms and representations: it is important to distinguish if a statement (either oral or written) is a mere representation inducing a party to enter into a contract or a term of the contract. A representation which is untrue is known as a misrepresentation.

Contractual Terms

Terms of a Contract Must be Certain

In order for an agreement to be a binding contract, there must be **certainty of terms**. This means that the terms agreed by the parties must not be too vague or incomplete. In deciding whether the terms of a contract are certain, the court will have regard to what a reasonable person would think, as opposed to the subjective views of the parties.

Scammel v Ouston (1941)

Facts: The defendant agreed to buy a van on hire purchase over two years but no detailed terms were agreed.

Decision: There are many different types of hire purchase agreements, and it was not clear what type of agreement was envisaged in this case. Therefore, there was no contract for purchase of the van.

However, in certain circumstances, although a contract may appear to be incomplete or vague, relevant details may be inferred making the terms definite enough to be an enforceable contract. In some cases, terms left out of contracts may be implied into the contract by statute. The Sale of Goods Act 1979, s 8, states that the buyer of goods must pay a reasonable price for the goods if no price is mentioned in the contract. On other occasions, details may be inferred from previous dealings between the parties and trade custom.

Hillas v Arcas (1932)

Facts: A contract for the supply of wood, made between the claimant buyer and the defendant seller, had an option that permitted the buyer to buy additional wood in the following year. The option did not specify what type or quality of wood was to be supplied.

Decision: The option was binding, as the details could be obtained from previous dealings and the custom and practice in the timber trade.

The court may find that there is provision in the contract itself for overcoming vague terms. In the following case, the parties left out essential details but the contract itself expressly stated how the details were going to be ascertained in the event of a dispute.

Foley v Classique Coaches (1934)

Facts: The claimant was an owner of a petrol station and the defendants ran a coach business. The claimant sold some land to the defendants, on condition that the defendants bought all their petrol for their coaches from him 'at a price to be agreed by the parties in writing from time to time'. The contract also had a clause which stated that disagreements between the parties should be referred to arbitration.

Decision: The contractual terms were sufficiently certain to be binding because there was an implied term that the petrol should be sold at a reasonable price, and the contract provided a course of action for the parties to take in the event of a dispute over the price (agreeing that an arbitrator set a fair price).

In the recent case discussed next the Court of Appeal decided that a clause in a contract between a low cost airline and an airport operator was not too vague to give rise to legal obligations.

Jet2.com Limited v Blackpool Airport Limited (2012)

Facts: The claimant, Jet2.com Ltd, contracted with the defendant Airport company to operate out of Blackpool airport. The agreement included a clause stating that the parties would cooperate and use their best endeavours to promote the claimant's services from the airport and facilitate the claimant's low-cost pricing. The defendant later informed the claimant that it would not accept departures or arrivals scheduled outside normal opening hours and the claimant sued for breach of contract.

Decision: The obligation to use 'best endeavours to promote the claimant's business' was not too uncertain to give rise to a legally binding obligation. It obliged the defendant to do all that it reasonably could have done to enable that business to succeed and grow.

Key Concept The law requires certainty in contracts. An agreement will not be a binding contract if its fundamental terms are vague or incomplete unless certainty can be inferred through law or previous dealings and trade custom.

Express and Implied Terms

Terms of a contract may be expressed or implied. **Express terms** are those actually stated, either orally or in writing, by one of the parties making the contract. However, a term may be deemed to be part of a contract even though it is not expressly mentioned by either party because terms can be implied into a contract by statute, the courts, or custom (see Figure 6.2).

Statute

Terms implied into a contract by statute are often ones that are aimed at protecting the party with the weaker bargaining power. For example, under the Sale of Goods Act 1979 (as amended by the Sale and Supply of Goods Act 1994) certain terms concerning the quality and suitability of goods are implied into contracts. The seller of goods will be in breach of contract if the goods do not meet certain standards, even though no mention of these standards was made in the express contractual agreement. In certain circumstances a statute will allow the parties to contract out of statutory **implied terms**, but where one of the parties is a consumer and the other is a trader, the statutory implied terms are usually compulsory.

Trade custom

Parties to a contract may be bound by terms implied into a contract through the custom of their trade.

However, trade custom cannot override an express term. Any term expressly stated in a contract will prevail over an implied trade custom.

Hutton v Warren (1836)

Facts: A landlord gave his tenant farmer notice to quit his tenancy, but insisted he farmed the land during the period of notice. The tenant requested an allowance for seed and his labour as he would have left the farm before harvest. There was no mention of an allowance in the tenancy contract.

Decision: The court implied into the tenancy contract the trade custom relating to seed and labour. This stated that, when a tenant is given notice to quit, he is bound to work the land during his notice period but trade custom permits him to claim a fair allowance for seed and labour.

The courts

In some circumstances, the courts will imply terms into a contract as a matter of fact or as a matter of law. Terms are implied as a matter of fact if the court concludes that the parties would have intended the terms to apply had they considered the issues at the time of making the contract. Terms may be implied into a contract where the parties have failed to cover a particular matter which, if not remedied, would make the contract unworkable and it makes commercial sense to imply the term into the contract. It may be that the parties have overlooked something which, if they had thought about it, they would have obviously included as a term of the contract and it is necessary to imply the term to give the contract 'business efficacy'.

The Moorcock (1889)

Facts: The defendant owner of a wharf agreed with the claimant to provide docking space for the claimant's ship to unload. The ship was damaged when it hit a ridge of rock at low tide.

Decision: The court stated that there was an implied term in the contract that the moorings provided by the defendant would be reasonably safe for the ship.

In *Attorney General of Belize v Belize Telecom* (2009) the court considered implied terms at length and confirmed a court had no power to improve upon a contract (for example to make it fairer) but that a term may be implied if it was necessary or to spell out what the contract was reasonably to be understood to mean.

The courts may imply a term into a contract as a matter of law. These are terms that are generally present in certain types of contract. In the following case, an implied term that the landlord should keep the common parts of a block of flats in a reasonable state of repair was implied into the tenancy agreement.

Liverpool City Council v Irwin (1977)

Facts: The defendants were tenants of the claimant council. The tenancy agreement did not state the obligations of the Council as regards maintenance of the building. The defendants withheld their rent because they argued that the lifts to their flat did not work and the stairs were unlit and unsafe.

Decision: There was a duty on the landlord to take reasonable care to keep the common areas of the building in reasonable condition for use by the tenants. A term, requiring the landlord to maintain and repair the lift and stairs, was implied into the tenancy agreement (although on the facts the court concluded that the council had not breached the implied term).

Figure 6.2 Terms may be express or implied

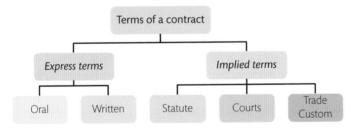

Types of Contractual Terms: Conditions, Warranties, and Innominate Terms

A term of a contract is usually classified by its importance to the contract. Traditionally a term was either classified a **condition**, a fundamental term of the contract, or a **warranty**, a minor term of the contract. (The legal terminology 'warranty' should not be confused with the expression 'warranty' in consumer/commercial practice meaning a manufacturer's guarantee in respect of goods.) However, there are instances where it is difficult to assign a term as either a condition or a warranty, until the effect of the breach of the term is established. Terms which cannot be assigned into either category are referred to as **innominate** or *intermediate* terms.

In negotiating the terms of a contract, the parties themselves may expressly agree that a term is to be designated a condition or a warranty. This is usually a good indication of the nature of the term, but sometimes in drawing up contracts parties do not use the right terminology and may state a term is a condition of a contract when on interpretation of the contract it is clearly a warranty or an innominate term. Alternatively, the parties may state a term is a warranty but, if the term goes to the root of the contract, it is a condition.

Where there is a dispute between the parties, a court will decide on the classification of the disputed term. The court will take into account the circumstances existing at the time the parties made the contract, and whether the parties regarded the term as fundamental and going to the root of the contract, or whether they regarded the term as less important to the main purpose of the contract.

Some statutes define particular clauses as conditions, for example the Sale of Goods Act 1979, s 12, provides that there is an implied condition in a contract for the sale of goods that the seller has or will have the right to sell the goods at the time when the ownership in the goods passes to the buyer.

Distinction between warranties and conditions

Conditions are vital terms that go to the root of the contract. If a condition is broken, the innocent party may treat the breach of contract as a substantial failure to perform a basic element of the contract and claim damages (compensation). The innocent party may also regard the contract as discharged, and, therefore, he is free from any further contractual duties, or he may elect to continue with the contract.

Warranties are minor terms of a contract which are incidental to the main purpose of the contract, and failure to observe warranties will not result in the collapse of the whole contract. If a warranty is broken, the innocent party can claim damages for loss suffered but must continue with the contract. If the innocent party refuses to continue with a contract, where only a warranty has been broken, then that innocent party will be in breach of contract.

The distinction between conditions and warranties is illustrated by the following cases (see Figure 6.3). In *Poussard v Spiers* the term of the contract that was breached was held to be a condition and, therefore, the injured party was entitled to treat the contract as at an end, but in *Bettini v Gye* the term of the contract that was breached was held to be a warranty, and, therefore, the injured party could only claim damages and would be in breach of contract himself if he purported to end the contract.

Poussard v Spiers (1876)

Facts: Poussard was employed to play a leading role in an operetta. She was ill and not available for the first week of the show. The producer hired a substitute and when Poussard recovered he refused to accept Poussard's services for the remaining performances.

Decision: The producer was entitled to terminate the contract as the opening night of the operetta was of utmost importance and failure to perform on that night was a breach of a condition of the contract.

Bettini v Gye (1876)

Facts: Bettini, an opera singer, was contracted by Gye to give a series of performances over three months and attend six days of rehearsals beforehand. Bettini arrived three days late for rehearsals and Gye refused to accept his services.

Decision: The term relating to rehearsals was a less important term of the contract, and failure to appear for rehearsals was a breach of warranty for which Gye could sue for damages, but he could not terminate the contract. In refusing to accept Bettini's services, Gye himself was in breach of contract.

> **Key Concept** If a condition of a contract is broken, the innocent party can treat the contract as at an end and claim damages, or he can decide to continue with the contract and claim damages. A warranty is a less important term of a contract and, if it is broken, the innocent party must continue with the contract, but can claim damages for breach of warranty.

Innominate terms

Not all terms can be clearly identified as conditions or warranties. Sometimes a term is worded broadly to cover a number of potential breaches, and it is not possible to decide whether a breach of the term would have important or trivial consequences. These terms have been described by the courts as innominate terms or intermediate terms. An injured party will only be entitled to damages for a breach of an innominate term if the consequences of the breach are relatively minor. However, if the injured party has been deprived of most of the benefit of the contract he can treat the contract as repudiated. For example, a term stating that a 'ship must be seaworthy' may be breached in a number of different ways, some of which would have a major impact on the contract, such as a large hole in the side of the ship incapable of being successfully repaired for months, whereas other breaches would have minor consequences, such as minor engine trouble which could be fixed in a number of hours.

Figure 6.3 **The difference between conditions, warranties, and innominate terms**

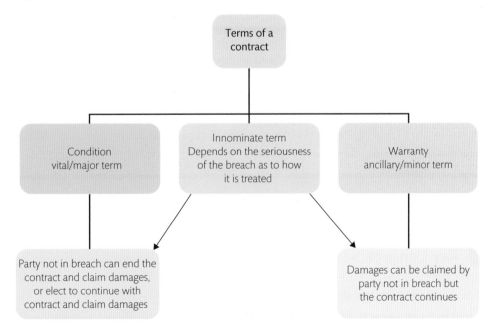

The following two cases illustrate examples of where the courts have held a term of a contract to be an innominate term.

Hong Kong Fir Shipping Co Ltd v Kawasaki Kisan Kaisha Ltd (1962)

Facts: The defendants chartered a ship from the claimants for 24 months. The contract stated the ship would be 'in every way fitted for cargo service'. Because of the age of the ship's engine and the incompetence of some of the crew provided by the claimants, the ship's first voyage was delayed for five weeks and additional repairs to the ship were required at the end of the voyage. The defendants purported to terminate the contract on the grounds that the claimants had breached a condition of the contract.

Decision: The term in question was an innominate term. The breach of the term relating to the ship's fitness for cargo service was not sufficiently serious to justify the defendants terminating the contract. The ship was still available for 17 months out of the 24 months' hire period and, therefore, the defendants were not entitled to treat the breach as a breach of a condition.

Cehave NV v Bremer Handelsgesellschaft (The Hansa Nord) (1975)

Facts: A contract for the sale of citrus pulp pellets provided that the pellets were to be delivered in good condition. The pellets were damaged and the buyers rejected them. The buyers later bought the pellets for a much reduced price and used them for the original purpose.

Decision: The term of the contract stating that 'the shipment to be in good condition' was not a condition or a warranty but was an innominate term. In this case the breach of the term was not so serious that it could not be dealt with by an award of damages; therefore, the buyers had not been justified in refusing delivery of the goods.

Key Concept A term of a contract may be classed as an innominate or intermediate term where it is not possible to decide the seriousness of the breach and whether a party had been deprived of substantially the whole benefit of a contract until the breach occurred.

Exemption Clauses

A contract may contain express clauses that attempt to exclude or limit one of the party's liabilities to the other party. These clauses may be referred to as exemption clauses as they seek to exempt one of the parties from certain liabilities for breach of contract. An exemption clause may attempt to exclude all legal liability and, therefore, may be referred to as an **exclusion clause**. For example, there may be an exclusion clause in a contract for car parking, excluding all legal liability for damage or theft from cars using the car park. Alternatively, an exemption clause may seek to limit legal liability and may, therefore, be referred to as a **limitation clause**. For example, in a contract for air travel there may be a limitation clause limiting a claim for loss or damage to baggage to £50.

Such exemption clauses may be good business practice, and where the parties to a contract have equal bargaining powers, it may be fair to allow the parties to decide the content of the contract. However, exemption clauses are commonly found in standard term contracts, where one of the parties has not had the opportunity to negotiate the terms of the contract. These types of contract are frequently used in business and require the same form, i.e. standard form, to be used for all customers. Although exclusion and limitation clauses are permissible, it has been recognised that, particularly where bargaining powers are unequal, the weaker party should be given some legal protection. Both Parliament, through legislation, and the courts, through the development of common law, have protected weaker parties such as ordinary consumers from stronger parties such as trading companies, by imposing restrictions on the effect of exclusion and limitation clauses.

Viewpoint Dan Hawes, Marketing Director, Graduate Recruitment Bureau

Working within a legal framework in my recruitment business is essential for compliance, risk management, a level of professionalism, and for peace of mind. With regard to contract law we have an established relationship with our business bank and their employment law division. Since our inception in 1997 they have provided the latest employee contract templates, amendments, guidelines, and advice which has helped greatly over the years employing in excess of 100 staff. Contract law is equally important when entering agreements to supply graduates to our recruiting clients. Our terms and conditions were formulated through consultation with the Recruitment and Employment Confederation (REC), the official association for the recruitment industry. Before supplying graduates our consultants have to have our terms and conditions agreed with the client. One of the main reasons recruitment agencies need this in writing is not only to agree fees, payment terms, and rebate periods but to avoid any dispute on when a candidate was introduced. The date the terms and conditions are agreed then essentially 'date stamps' any candidate introductions. This then covers the agency in the event of the candidate being introduced by other agencies or making a direct application. Disputes rarely happen, however having contracts agreed ensures each party is clear of their obligation which is essential in any business to build trust and long term, mutually beneficial business relationships.

Key Concept Contracts may include clauses which seek to limit or exclude the liabilities of one of the parties for breach of contract. The effect of exemption clauses is restricted by law.

Validity of Exemption Clauses

In order for an exemption clause to be effective, it must satisfy the following criteria:

- The exemption clause must be incorporated into the contract and not added after the contract has been made.
- The exemption clause must be clear and unambiguous. Exemption clauses are interpreted strictly and any vagueness will be construed against the party seeking to enforce the clause.
- The exemption clause must comply with the statutory rules set out in the Unfair Contract Terms Act 1977 and the Unfair Terms in Consumer Contracts Regulations 1999.

The Exemption Clause Must be Incorporated into the Contract

In order for a term to be part of a contract, the party to be bound by it must have sufficient notice of it. However, if a document is signed by a party, then that party is usually treated as having agreed to the terms of the contract.

Signed documents

Parties usually have constructive notice of the contents of any contractual document which they sign, even if the document has not been read and one of the parties is unaware of the existence of an exemption clause.

L'Estrange v Graucob (1934)

Facts: The claimant purchased a cigarette vending machine for her café. She signed a contract without reading it. The contract excluded various rights.

Decision: The claimant was bound by the exclusion clause regardless of the fact that she had not read the document as she had signed it.

The party who signed the agreement cannot complain that he did not understand the exclusion or limitation clause, unless the other party or his agent has incorrectly explained the meaning of the exclusion clause. In the following case, the agent of the defendant incorrectly explained the meaning of the exclusion clause and, therefore, the defendant could not rely on the wording of the exclusion clause as written into the contract.

Curtis v Chemical Cleaning & Dyeing Co (1951)

Facts: The claimant took her wedding dress to the defendant cleaning company and was asked to sign a paper which excluded the cleaners from liability for any damage to the article. The claimant asked the assistant what the paper was for and the assistant said that it excluded liability if beads or sequins were damaged in the cleaning process. The dress was returned to the claimant badly stained. The cleaning company tried to rely on the exclusion clause.

Decision: The defendant cleaning company could not rely on the exclusion clause as written because its scope had been misrepresented to the claimant. The defendant was bound by the statement their assistant made.

Unsigned documents and notices

A party to a contract may be bound by an exemption clause even if they have not signed a contractual document, provided reasonable steps are taken to bring the exemption clause to their attention. If exemption clauses are written on a document that is given to one of the parties, the document must be the sort of document that a reasonable man would regard as a contractual document and, therefore, one that may contain exemption clauses. If a reasonable man would regard a document as a mere receipt or a voucher, he will not be bound by any terms written on it.

Chapelton v Barry Urban District Council (1940)

Facts: The claimant took two deckchairs from a pile of chairs beside which there was a notice stating that payment should be made to the beach attendant. The claimant paid the beach attendant and was handed two tickets which he put into his pocket unread. Each ticket contained a clause exempting the defendant Council from liability for any accident or damage arising from the hire of the chair. The canvas on one of the chairs was defective and the claimant was injured when the deckchair collapsed. The claimant sought compensation from the defendant Council, but the Council tried to rely on the exclusion clause.

Decision: The court stated that a reasonable man would assume the tickets given to the claimant were mere receipts and not contractual documents which might contain conditions. Therefore the defendant Council could not rely on the exclusion clause to exclude their liability.

If the document is considered to be a contractual document, in order for the exemption clause to be valid, reasonable steps must be taken to bring it to the notice of the other party; for example, on the front of a ticket the words 'see back' would be sufficient to alert the party to conditions on the back of the ticket. But the reasonable notice test is objective, so if the recipient is illiterate and could not have read the clause, he is still bound by it, unless his disability was known to the other party.

Thompson v LMS Railway (1930)

Facts: The claimant, who was illiterate, was handed a railway excursion ticket which stated 'Excursion: For conditions see back'. On the back of the ticket it stated that the ticket was subject to conditions displayed in the company's timetables, which excluded liability for injury. The claimant was injured on her journey.

Decision: The company was not liable as reasonable notice of the exemption clause had been brought to the claimant's attention. The fact that she could not read did not alter the position. (Note: a similar exclusion clause would be invalid today because of the provisions of the Unfair Contract Terms Act 1977.)

What are considered to be reasonable steps to bring an exemption clause to the notice of the other party may change, depending on the nature of the exemption clause. If one party wishes to rely on a particularly onerous or unusual term, which would not generally be known to the other party, a greater degree of notice is needed in order to satisfy the reasonable notice test. Often, in these circumstances, the onerous term has to be specially drawn to the attention of the other party otherwise it will not become incorporated into the contract.

The following case relates to a penalty clause as opposed to an exemption clause, but the principle is the same.

Interphoto Picture Library v Stiletto Visual Programmes (1988)

Facts: A contract for the hire of photographic transparencies included a clause stating that, if the transparencies were not returned on time, there was a penalty payable of £5 for each transparency per day. The claimants were 14 days late returning 47 transparencies.

Decision: Reasonable steps had not been taken to bring the onerous nature of this term to the other side's attention and, consequently, the term was not part of the contract. The court awarded damages of £3.50 per week on a quantum meruit basis (as much as is merited in the circumstances) and would not apply the excessive charge of £5 per day per transparency.

In order for a term to be part of a contract it cannot be inserted after the contract has already been made. If an exemption clause is written on a notice or contained in a document, that notice or document must be displayed or given to the other party before or at the time of entering into the contract. In the following case, the exclusion clause was displayed after the contract had been made, so it was too late to be included as one of the terms of the contract.

Olley v Marlborough Court Ltd (1949)

Facts: The claimant guests, Mr and Mrs Olley, arranged to stay at the defendants' hotel, and on arrival paid in advance at the reception desk for their accommodation. The claimants went upstairs to their room where there was a notice stating, 'The proprietors will not hold themselves responsible for articles lost or stolen unless handed to the manageress for safe custody'. After unpacking, the claimants went out, locking the door and leaving the key at reception. Whilst they were out, Mrs Olley's furs were stolen from the room, and she sued the hotel owners who claimed the protection of the exclusion clause.

Decision: The defendants could not rely on the exclusion clause displayed in the hotel bedroom because the contract was made at the reception desk before the claimants had notice of the clause. Contractual terms notified after a contract is made are not effective; therefore, the defendants were liable for the loss.

It is clear, therefore, that notice of an exemption clause must be given before or when a contract is being made, but problems as to exactly when a contract is being made may arise in situations where one of the parties is dealing with a machine, such as a vending machine or a ticket machine. In the following case, the court decided that when dealing with a machine, once one party was bound by their decision to make a contract, for example placing money into a machine, then it was too late for the other party to attempt to impose an exemption clause.

Thornton v Shoe Lane Parking (1971)

Facts: The claimant parked his car in the defendant's car park. There was an automatic ticket barrier at the entrance to the car park. After the claimant placed his money in the machine, a ticket was issued that purported to exclude liability for injury. When the claimant collected his car there was an accident in which he was injured.

Decision: Where there is an automatic ticket barrier the contract is completed when the customer places his money in the slot. The contract was made before the ticket was issued, and any terms and conditions expressly referred to on the ticket came too late and were not part of the contract. Therefore, the defendant proprietor of the car park could not rely on the exclusion clause.

There is one exception to the rule that there must be prior notice of the exemption clause in a contract, and this is where the parties have had consistent previous dealings with each other. Where there have been consistent previous dealings between the parties, the courts presume that the parties are aware of the existence of the exemption clause and have accepted to be bound by it, even though on that particular occasion the exemption clause had not been brought to their attention before the contract was made.

Spurling v Bradshaw (1956)

Facts: The defendant, having dealt with the claimant company for many years, delivered eight barrels of orange juice to the claimant's warehouse for storage. A few days later the defendant received a document which acknowledged receipt of the barrels and contained an exemption clause excluding liability for damage caused by negligence. When the defendant collected the barrels they were empty.

Decision: The defendant was bound by the exemption clause because there had been regular dealings between the same parties on the same conditions for a number of years.

If the parties have had previous dealings but not on a consistent basis, then a party will only be bound by an exclusion clause if he is sufficiently aware of it when making the latest contract. It is a question of fact as to what amounts to consistent dealings, but in the following case the court was not prepared to accept that dealing with the same garage three or four times in five years constituted persistent dealing.

Hollier v Rambler Motors Ltd (1972)

Facts: Over a period of five years, the claimant car owner took his car to the defendant garage three or four times for repair and servicing. In the past, on at least two occasions, the claimant had been asked to sign a form excluding the company's liability for damage caused by fire to customers' cars on the premises. However, on this occasion the claimant was not asked to sign a form and, while his car was in the garage, it was damaged in a fire caused by the defendant's negligence.

Decision: The claimant was not bound by the exclusion clause as it had not been incorporated into the oral contract for the repair of his car. The three or four transactions that had taken place in the past between the claimant and the defendant did not amount to regular dealings.

The Exemption Clause must be Clear and Unambiguous

In order for an exemption clause to be valid, whether it is part of a signed document or an unsigned document or notice, it must be written in a clear and unambiguous manner. If there is any doubt about the meaning or extent of the clause, the court will construe it against the party seeking to rely on it. This is known as the '*contra proferentem* rule' (against the party who offered it). If a clause fails to clearly deal with a particular matter, the court will interpret the clause so that it does not cover the matter in question. For example, if a contract contains a clause excluding 'all liability for theft' then such a clause would not exclude liability for accidental loss.

In the following case, the court decided that, as the wording of the exclusion clause only stated implied terms, it did not apply to express terms.

Andrews Bros Ltd v Singer & Co (1934)

Facts: A contract was made for the sale and purchase of new Singer cars. The contract expressly stated that new Singer cars would be supplied. The contract also contained a clause excluding 'all conditions, warranties and liabilities implied by statute, common law or otherwise'. One of the cars delivered was technically a used car and was rejected by the purchaser. The seller tried to rely on the exemption clause.

> **Decision:** The exemption clause only excluded liability for implied terms, and the term relating to the car being a new car was an express term as it had been expressly stated in the contract and, therefore, the exclusion did not cover this term.

If a party wishes to exclude damage caused through their negligence, this has to be expressly stated in the exclusion clause. In *Hollier v Rambler Motors Ltd* (see earlier), the exclusion clause in question could have been interpreted to either apply to all accidental damage or to accidental damage other than caused through their negligence. In interpreting the exclusion clause, the court used the latter narrow interpretation and stated that if a party wished to exclude damage caused through their negligence, it had to be expressly stated in the exclusion clause.

Liability for Fundamental Breach

An exclusion clause may purport to exclude liability for a fundamental breach of contract, i.e. one party attempts to exclude liability even though he has failed to do basically what he promised to do under the contract. There was previously judicial disagreement regarding the effectiveness of such exclusion clauses; however, the House of Lords confirmed that there was no law by which exclusion clauses were automatically invalid if they excluded liability for a fundamental breach of contract. In each case it was a question of construction of the contract as to whether the clause covered the breach in question. Although there was a presumption that exclusion clauses were not intended to apply to very serious breaches of contract, this presumption could be rebutted if the clause was drafted so widely that it did cover fundamental breaches of contract. The following case demonstrates that the court will allow an exclusion clause to operate even though it applies to a serious breach of contract, but note this was a commercial contract and in a consumer transaction it is likely that a clause similar to the one used by Securicor would be regarded as unreasonable and unenforceable under the Unfair Contract Terms Act 1977.

Photo Production v Securicor Transport (1980)

Facts: The defendants, Securicor, entered into a contract with the claimants to guard their factory. In the contract there was an exclusion clause which was drafted so widely that it exempted Securicor from liability even if one of Securicor's employees damaged the factory. One of Securicor's guards deliberately set fire to the factory.

Decision: The clause covered the events that had happened and it was a valid term of the contract. Securicor were not liable for the damage caused to the factory.

Key Concept Exemption clauses must be clearly expressed and part of the contract. In order to be valid, an exemption clause which is not part of a signed document must be brought to the other party's attention at the time or before the contract was entered into. If there is any doubt about the meaning or extent of the clause, the court will construe it against the party seeking to rely on it.

Business Insight Reform of consumer law

The Consumer Contracts (Information, Cancellation and Additional Charges) Regulations apply to contracts made after 13 June 2014 and are part of extensive reform of consumer law currently being undertaken by the UK. Key changes brought in by the Regulations include giving consumers the right to cancel distance or off-premises contracts (e.g. made online) without having to give any reason within 14 days. A trader cannot charge for additional items by adding a pre-ticked box—consumers must give express consent before a trader can take any additional payments from them. A trader must provide a basic rate telephone number—if a consumer is ringing to make a complaint, enquire about or cancel an order, the trader cannot use a premium rate number. Further reform of consumer rights is in the Consumer Rights Bill 2014 which seeks to codify consumer law into one Act and to update the law in certain areas in particular in relation to the supply of digital content. It also introduces new statutory rights and remedies for consumers.

Unfair Contract Terms Act 1977

In order for an exemption clause to be enforceable, it must comply with statutory law. Both the Unfair Contract Terms Act 1977 (UCTA) and the Unfair Terms in Consumer Contracts Regulations 1999 have an effect on the validity of exemption clauses.

UCTA is of great importance in relation to the control of exemption clauses (see Figure 6.4). The title of the Act, 'Unfair Contract Terms', can be misleading as it does not relate to all unfair terms in contracts but is mainly concerned with controlling the use of exclusion and limitation clauses inserted into agreements by commercial enterprises and businesses. UCTA uses two methods of controlling exemption clauses: it either prevents an exemption clause from being of any effect in any circumstances, or it prevents an exemption clause from being of any effect unless it satisfies the test of reasonableness. The exemption clauses that are rendered ineffective by UCTA do not apply even if they have been expressly written into a contract and the parties have signed the contract agreeing to the clauses. Certain types of contract are specifically excluded from the Act, such as contracts of insurance and contracts relating to the creation, transfer, or termination of rights and interests in land or intellectual property.

Non-contractual Notices

The Act relates to all types of exemption clauses. It deals with exemption clauses in contracts, and it also deals with exemption clauses in situations where there is no contract between the parties. For example, there may be a notice in a car park excluding liability for theft from parked cars. If a person has paid to park, the notice may be part of the contract; if it is a free car park, there is no contract but UCTA still applies to the notice.

Business Liability and Dealing as a Consumer (UCTA, s 1(3))

The Act only applies to business liability. This means it only applies to actions arising in the course of business or through the occupation of business premises and, therefore, the Act does not apply to transactions between private persons. The greatest protection under the Act is given to persons who deal as consumers. A consumer is a party who is not acting (or pretending to act) in the course of a business. For the purposes of UCTA, companies can be consumers; for example, an airline company that purchases a car for its managing director will be dealing as a consumer for the purchase of the car, but would be dealing in the course of business when it purchases aeroplanes. UCTA also gives some protection to non-consumers where one party deals on the other's standard terms.

Liability for Negligence (UCTA, s 2)

Negligence includes any express or implied term of a contract to take reasonable care, and the common law duty in the tort of negligence to take reasonable care (see Chapter 11). A person acting in the course of a business cannot exclude liability for negligently causing death or personal injury at all, either in a contract or in a non-contractual notice. Liability for causing other loss or damage through negligence, for example to property or goods, can be excluded but only if the exclusion or limitation is reasonable (s 2(2)).

Smith v Bush (1989)

Facts: The claimant bought a house relying on the valuation report prepared on the instructions of her building society by the defendant surveyor. The report included a clause excluding liability for negligence. The surveyor had negligently overlooked some serious defects. The chimney of the house collapsed and expensive structural repairs had to be carried out. The claimant sued the defendant surveyor, who attempted to rely on the exclusion clause.

Decision: The damage that occurred was caused by the defendant's negligence and so s 2(2) of UCTA applied. The clause was ineffective because it failed the test of reasonableness.

Liability for Breaches of Contract other than Through Negligence

Where a business uses a standard form contract, it cannot exclude or vary liability for its own breach of contract unless the exemption is reasonable. The same applies whenever a business deals with a consumer, whether or not on standard terms.

Liability for Breaches of Contract Involving the Sale or Hire of Goods

In contracts relating to the sale and supply of goods (Sale of Goods Act 1979 and Supply of Goods and Services Act 1982), certain conditions are implied into the contract to protect the purchaser of the goods or services. These implied terms relate to title to goods (the supplier or seller has rights of ownership), description (the goods match their description), quality and suitability (the goods are of satisfactory quality and suitable for their purpose), and sample (the goods correspond to any sample that has been supplied to the purchaser). UCTA states that these terms cannot be excluded or restricted in a consumer contract, and in a non-consumer contract the implied term relating to good title cannot be excluded, and the exclusion or limitation of the other implied terms must be reasonable.

Key Concept Under the provisions of the Unfair Contract Terms Act 1977, when acting in the course of a business, exemption clauses purporting to exclude liability for negligently causing death or personal injury are void. Exemption clauses for all other loss through negligence must be reasonable.

Excluding Liability for Misrepresentation

A term excluding or restricting any liability or remedy for misrepresentation is not effective unless it is fair and reasonable.

The Test of Reasonableness

Under UCTA, the burden of proving whether an exemption clause is reasonable is on the party seeking to rely on it. In order to be regarded as reasonable, the term must be fair and reasonable taking into account the circumstances that were known, or ought reasonably to have been known or in the contemplation of the parties when the contract was made. The courts have also taken into account factors such as insurance and whether the party should have sought independent advice. In *Smith v Bush* (see earlier) it was reasonable for the purchasers to rely on the report of the building society's surveyor rather than seek their own advice. In the following cases, the court took into account the possibility of insurance.

George Mitchell v Finney Lock Seeds (1983)

Facts: The defendants were seed merchants and contracted with the claimants, who were farmers, to supply 30 lbs of Dutch winter cabbage seed for £201. The seed was defective and the claimants lost crops worth over £60,000. The defendants sought to rely on a limitation clause in the contract which limited their liability to replacing the seed or the purchase price of the seed.
Decision: The limitation clause was not reasonable and therefore ineffective. The breach of contract was as a result of the defendants' negligence and the defendants could have insured against crop failure without significantly increasing the cost of the seed.

St Albans City and District Council v International Computers Ltd (1996)

Facts: The claimant Council entered into a contract with the defendant company for the supply of computer software to administer their collection of the Community Charge. The software contained an error which led to the loss of £1.3 million for the Council. The defendant company sought to rely on a limitation clause limiting liability to £100,000.
Decision: The limitation clause was unreasonable as the sum stated in the limitation clause was very low, and the defendant had indemnity insurance of £50 million.

Where a contract is negotiated between businesses of equal bargaining strength, the court will not usually interfere with an exemption clause.

179

Watford Electronics Ltd v Sanderson (2001)

Facts: A contract for supply of computer hardware and software contained a limitation clause limiting liability for direct loss to the price paid under contract namely £104,596. The goods did not perform as required and the claimant lost £5.5 million.

Decision: The court stated that, as the contract had been negotiated between experienced businessmen with equal bargaining powers, unless the limitation clause was so unreasonable so as not to have been understood, it should not interfere. The court decided that the clause was not that unreasonable and, therefore, it was valid.

In the following case the Court of Appeal (overturning the decision of the lower court) decided that the clause excluding liability for loss of business and loss of profits in a standard term contract was reasonable.

Regus (UK) Ltd v Epcot Solutions Ltd (2008)

Facts: Regus provided serviced office accommodation to Epcot, who complained that the air conditioning was faulty. After negotiations broke down, Epcot withheld fees and when Regus sued, Epcot counterclaimed for approximately £626 million and stated that the exclusion clause in the contract was unreasonable under the UCTA.

Decision: The clause was reasonable. There was no inequality of bargaining power between the two businesses, and Regus had advised Epcot to protect themselves by insurance for business losses. It was generally more economical for the person who sustained the loss to take out insurance.

Business Insight Exclusion clauses interpreted in accordance with business common sense

Great care is needed in drafting exclusion clauses. Parties seeking to exclude liability need to be very clear in the drafting of clauses and if they wish to exclude a claim for loss of profits due to non-performance of the contract then a clause should be very clear. Inadequate drafting can cost a company millions. In *Kudos Catering (UK) Ltd v Manchester Central Convention* (2013) Kudos claimed £1.3 million for loss of profits. The Court of Appeal (overturning the earlier court decision) refused to allow Manchester Central to rely on their exclusion clause because it did not make business sense to interpret it literally to exclude all liability including non-performance of the contract. If the parties intended to exclude liability for non-performance of the contract it would have be very clearly spelt out in the contract.

Guidelines in Schedule 2

UCTA, Schedule 2, sets out guidelines to ascertain what is meant by reasonableness in the context of contracts for the sale or transfer (hire or exchange) of goods. Although these guidelines relate specifically to contracts for the sale and transfer of goods, similar considerations may be used in ascertaining the reasonableness of clauses in all consumer transactions. The guidelines cover the following issues:

- Relative bargaining strengths of the parties, taking into account issues such as whether there are alternative means of supplying the purchaser's requirements. If one party is in a strong position as regards bargaining power, and the other party is in a weak position, the stronger party may not be allowed to rely on an exemption clause.

- Whether the purchaser received an inducement to agree to the term (such as a price reduction), or in accepting the exemption clause the purchaser had the opportunity to make a similar contract with other parties lacking such a term.

- Whether the purchaser knew, or ought to have known, of the existence and extent of the exclusion clause, having regard to trade custom and previous course of dealing.

- Where the term excludes or restricts liability if a condition is not complied with, whether it was reasonable at the time of making the contract to expect the customer to comply with the condition.

- Whether the goods were manufactured, processed, or adapted to the special order of the purchaser. If the seller has been required by the purchaser to adapt goods in a certain way, then it might be reasonable and fair to allow an exclusion clause in respect of faults due to the design the purchaser insisted upon.

The Unfair Terms in Consumer Contracts Regulations 1999

The Unfair Terms in Consumer Contracts Regulations implement the European Unfair Contract Terms Directive (93/13/EEC). The Regulations operate side by side with UCTA, and a party to a contract wishing to rely on a particular term must ensure that it satisfies the requirements of both the Regulations and UCTA. Some terms will be invalid under the

Regulations and the Act, while other terms may be valid under one but not under the other. The Regulations apply to most consumer contracts, although there are a number of contracts that are specially excluded, such as contracts relating to employment, family law rights, and the incorporation of companies. Unlike UCTA, the Regulations only apply to contractual terms and not to notices that do not form part of any contract.

The Regulations apply to any terms in a contract that have not been individually negotiated, made between a seller or supplier of goods or services and a consumer. A consumer is a natural person (not a company) making a contract for non-business purposes. The Regulations cover all terms of a contract and not just exclusion clauses, so in some respects they are wider than UCTA. The Regulations provide that a term which is deemed to be unfair, according to the criteria laid down in the Regulations, is not binding on a consumer. Provided the contract is viable without the unfair term then, although the unfair term will not be enforceable, the parties will be bound by all the other terms in the contract.

Requirement of Good Faith

Regulation 5 states that a term is unfair if 'contrary to the requirements of good faith, it causes a significant imbalance in the parties' rights and obligations arising under the contract to the detriment of the consumer'. In assessing whether the contract meets the requirement of good faith, a court must have regard to all the relevant circumstances. The Regulations set out various matters to be taken into account. These include:

- The bargaining strength of the parties.
- Whether the consumer had an inducement to agree to the terms (the goods were cheaper because the term was included).
- Whether the goods or services were sold or supplied as a special order of the consumer (the goods had been specially adapted to the consumer's specifications).
- The extent to which supplier or seller dealt fairly and equitably with the consumer.

Terms that may be Regarded as Unfair

Schedule 2 gives an indicative and non-exhaustive list of terms which may be regarded as unfair. This means that a term is not necessarily unfair merely because it is of the type included in the list, and a term may be unfair even if it is not included in the list. The list includes such terms as:

- A term that excludes or limits the liability of a seller or a supplier for the death or personal injury of the consumer resulting from an act or omission of that seller or supplier.
- A term enabling the seller or supplier to alter the contract unilaterally without a valid reason which is specified in the contract.

- A term requiring a consumer, who fails to fulfil his obligations, to pay a disproportionately high sum in compensation to the seller or supplier.

- A term making the contract binding on the consumer, but allowing the seller or supplier to totally or partially avoid performing the contract.

- A term which allows the seller or supplier to keep a deposit if the consumer cancels the contract.

Office of Fair Trading v Ashbourne Management Services Ltd (2011)

Facts: OFT brought proceedings against Ashbourne alleging that terms in the standard form agreements which Ashbourne used for membership of gym and health clubs specifying minimum membership periods of 12 to 36 months were unfair under the Unfair Terms in Consumer Contracts Regulations 1999.

Decision: The court stated that the terms were unfair since they were designed to take advantage of the naivety and inexperience of the average consumer in overestimating his use of the gym facilities.

Business Insight   A warning to online operations

Cochrane (C) opened an account online with S, a spread betting bookmaker. C entered a password and clicked on 'Agree' to signify agreement to S's terms and conditions. One of the terms stated 'You will be deemed to have authorised all trading under your account number'. C was watched by his partner's 5-year-old son while he was using his computer to trade. When C was away for a couple of days the boy, without his knowledge, made numerous trades on his account incurring losses of £50,000. S sued C for payment. The court, *Spreadex Ltd v Cochrane* (2012) decided that the agreement was not a contract because it lacked consideration by S, and even if there was a contract the way in which S had made C aware of the clause was inadequate. The clause was unfair and void under the Unfair Terms in Consumer Contracts Regulations 1999. C was not liable for the trades made on his account without his authorisation.

It is clear from the Regulations that the assessment of the fairness of a term does not relate to the adequacy of the price for the goods or services. In other words whether the goods or services provided are 'value for money' is not relevant. In the following case the Supreme Court concluded that bank charges were part of the price for banking services.

Office of Fair Trading v Abbey National plc (2009)

Facts: OFT wanted to investigate the fairness of bank charges under the Unfair Terms in Consumer Contracts Regulations 1999. Members of the public had complained that the size of charges levied on customers taking unauthorised overdrafts from banks was unfair and disproportionate.
Decision: The Supreme Court stated that, as bank customers agreed to pay overdraft charges as part of the price of having a current account and that the agreement was in plain intelligible language, the charges fell outside the scope of the 1999 Regulations. The Regulations specifically state that the assessment of fairness of a term does not relate to the price paid for the goods or services.

It is up to the consumer to prove that the term is unfair and, merely because a term is not beneficial to a consumer, it does not necessarily mean that it is unfair or a breach of good faith.

Terms Must be in Plain Language

The Regulations require all contractual terms to be made in plain intelligible language. If there is any doubt as to the meaning of a term, it is to be interpreted in favour of the consumer. (Note: this is similar to the common law *contra proferentem* rule.)

Key Concept The Unfair Terms in Consumer Contracts Regulations 1999 (see Figure 6.5) provide that if a term in a contract with a consumer is unfair and the consumer can prove its unfairness, the term will not be binding on the consumer.

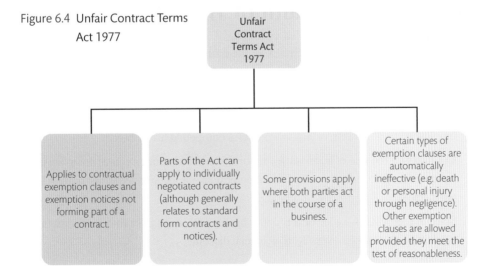

Figure 6.4 Unfair Contract Terms Act 1977

Unfair Contract Terms Act 1977

Applies to contractual exemption clauses and exemption notices not forming part of a contract.

Parts of the Act can apply to individually negotiated contracts (although generally relates to standard form contracts and notices).

Some provisions apply where both parties act in the course of a business.

Certain types of exemption clauses are automatically ineffective (e.g. death or personal injury through negligence). Other exemption clauses are allowed provided they meet the test of reasonableness.

Figure 6.5 Unfair Terms in Consumer Contracts Regulations 1999

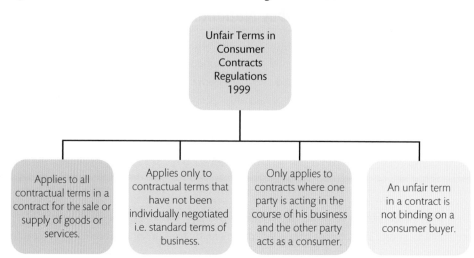

Competition and Markets Authority

Under the Regulations, the Competition and Markets Authority (CMA) (prior to 2014, the Office of Fair Trading) has the duty to investigate complaints that contracts which have been drawn up for general use are unfair. A similar duty is imposed on certain 'qualifying bodies' such as the Rail Regulator and the Gas and Electricity Markets Authority. If the CMA or a qualifying body finds that the term is unfair, the CMA or other body may apply to the court for an injunction to prevent the use of the unfair term.

Contracts in Restraint of Trade

Some contracts contain clauses which restrict the future freedom of one of the parties to a contract to carry on his business, trade, or profession. Restraint clauses are commonly found in the following types of contracts:

- Contracts of employment. Employees are required to give undertakings not to reveal employers' trade secrets, or not to work for a competing firm when they leave.

- Contracts for the sale of business. A vendor (seller) of a business agrees not to set up in competition with the purchaser. The same principle applies to a partner retiring from partnership.

- Solus agreements. A seller of a product agrees with a supplier that he will obtain a product solely from him usually for a special discount.

Such clauses in contracts are prima facie (initially) void because it is not in the public interest to impede competition or freedom of movement. However, such clauses may be valid if the person seeking to enforce them can show that, in their particular circumstances, the restraint is reasonable. In deciding whether a restraint is reasonable, the three relevant points to consider are:

- Whether the business interest is one which can be legally protected such as goodwill or trade secrets.
- The length of time the restraint lasts.
- The width of the geographical area that the restraint covers.

Contracts of Employment

A restraint clause may restrict an employee's freedom to contract both during his period of employment and after the termination of his employment. The courts determine reasonableness in the way most likely to produce a fair outcome for both parties, recognising the unequal bargaining strength of the employer and the employee. A restraint will only be reasonable if it is no wider than needed to protect the employer's legitimate interests, such as trade secrets or confidential information, and does not place unreasonable restraints on the employee.

Forster & Sons Ltd v Suggett (1918)

Facts: The defendant, whilst employed by manufacturers of glass and glass bottles, gained technical knowledge of making glass bottles. The defendant's contract of employment stated that when he left his employment he would not carry on or have an interest in the manufacture of glass bottles for five years in the UK or in any business connected with glass-making similar to that of his employer.

Decision: The restraint clause was reasonable, and it was enforceable as it protected the employer's secret manufacturing process.

However, a distinction must be made between trade secrets and skills acquired during the term of employment. An employer has no right to restrain an employee from applying personal knowledge and skill acquired during his period of employment to another employment.

Morris (Herbert) Ltd v Saxelby (1916)

Facts: Saxelby commenced work for Morris Ltd as an apprentice and eventually became head of a department. He had limited knowledge of his employer's technical secrets but had become a skilled draftsman in engineering design work. The restraint clause in his contract prevented him from working in a similar business in the UK for seven years.

Decision: The restraint was on Saxelby's own skill and knowledge and the employer had no right to be protected from competition from a former employee using his own skill. The restraint clause was not valid.

If an employer wishes to protect his connection with customers by preventing employees from enticing customers away, he must show that the employee had personal contact with customers and some influence over them.

Home Counties Dairies v Skilton (1970)

Facts: Skilton was employed as a milkman and his contract of employment stated that, on leaving his employment, Skilton was prohibited from selling milk or dairy produce to any persons who had been customers of his employer in the last six months. The restraint was for 12 months.

Decision: The purpose of the clause was to prevent the dairy's loss of customers from Skilton's old milk round and not to prevent Skilton selling dairy produce in places such as shops. The court decided that the exclusion clause was excessive as regards selling of any dairy produce but was valid in relation to working as a milkman.

However, the connection with customers must be more than a routine connection with them and a restraint clause will be invalid if the employee does not have influence over the customer.

S W Strange v Mann (1965)

Facts: A bookmaker employed Mann to conduct business mainly by using the telephone. The restraint of trade clause was not to engage in a similar business within a 12-mile radius on termination of his employment.

Decision: The restraint clause was invalid as Mann did not have face-to-face contact with his customers and, therefore, had no real influence on them.

The employer must show that the restraint is reasonable, i.e. no more than is necessary to protect his interests. In the following case Proactive were unable to show that the restraint of trade clause in their contract with Wayne Rooney was reasonable in the circumstances.

Proactive Sports Management Ltd v Rooney (2012)

Facts: Wayne Rooney (R) entered into a contract with Proactive (P) when he was 17 giving P 20% of all profits from use of his image worldwide for eight years.

Decision: The restraint of trade clause was unreasonable on the facts. It imposed very substantial restraints upon R's freedom to exploit his earning capacity over a lengthy period of time. R was only 17 years old when the agreement was made and he had not taken independent legal advice. The burden of proof was on the party seeking to enforce the contract and P had failed to show that the restrictions were reasonable.

Restraints on Sellers of Businesses

A purchaser of the goodwill of a business can protect what he has bought by imposing restrictions on the seller in the contract for the purchase of the business. To be valid, the restraints must protect the business that has been sold, and must not be excessive. A purchaser of a business will wish to protect himself against the seller, who may take the customers with them to a newly set up similar business. However, goodwill must actually exist, and the courts will not enforce a clause that merely restrains competition.

Vancouver Malt & Sake Brewing Co Ltd v Vancouver Breweries Ltd (1934)

Facts: The sellers were licensed to brew beer but in fact only produced sake. The business was sold and, in the contract for sale, there was a restraint clause preventing the sellers from brewing beer for 15 years. The sellers then started to brew beer, and the purchaser sought to enforce the restraint clause.

Decision: At the time of the sale, the sellers did not produce beer; therefore, there was no goodwill relating to the brewing of beer to sell. The restraint clause was not enforceable.

Solus Agreements

A solus agreement is a contract where one party agrees to buy goods only from one supplier, usually in return for a trade discount. Garages selling petrol commonly make such agreements with one of the oil companies. In the following case, the courts found one solus agreement valid but the other unreasonable.

Esso Petroleum v Harper's Garage (1968)

Facts: Two solus agreements were made between Harpers and Esso. In one agreement, Harpers undertook to buy all the petrol for one garage for four and half years in return for a discount on the price of the petrol. In the second agreement, in return for a mortgage loan of £7,000 from Esso for another garage, Harpers agreed to purchase Esso petrol for 21 years (the period of time for the loan repayment).

Decision: The first agreement was reasonable but the second agreement was for an unreasonable length of time. It was longer than necessary to allow Esso to protect their business interests, and it was irrelevant that the length of time had been agreed in relation to a mortgage.

The Effect of an Invalid Restraint Clause

If a restraint clause is too wide, the whole clause is usually void as the courts will not rewrite a restraint clause so that it is reasonable. However, in some cases severance of the offending part of the clause is possible, allowing the rest of the clause to continue. In the following case, the unreasonable parts of the restraint clause could be crossed out without affecting the remaining reasonable parts of the clause.

Goldsoll v Goldman (1915)

Facts: The defendant seller sold his imitation jewellery business to the claimant. The business was located in London but much of its business was conducted through mail order in the UK. In the contract for the sale of his business, the defendant seller undertook that he would not participate in the sale of real or imitation jewellery anywhere in the UK, France, Russia, the USA, or within 25 miles of Berlin or Vienna.

Decision: The restraint clause was too wide in respect of geographic area and business interest to be reasonable. However, it was possible to sever the reference to 'real jewellery' and the reference to certain geographical areas, leaving the clause to read 'sale of imitation jewellery anywhere in the UK'.

Key Concept Restraint of trade clauses restrict the future freedom of one of the parties to the contract to carry on his business, trade, or profession and will only be valid if the person seeking to enforce them can show that in the particular circumstances the restraint is reasonable.

Basic Terminology

Certainty of terms Terms agreed by the parties must not be too vague or incomplete.

Condition A fundamental term that goes to the root of the contract.

Exclusion clause A clause which excludes the liability of one party.

Express term Term stated either orally or in writing by one of the parties making the contract.

Implied term A term in a contract which is not expressly agreed by the parties to the contract.

Innominate term Broadly worded term where it is not possible to decide whether a breach

of the term would have important or minor consequences.

Limitation clause A clause which limits liability of one party to a certain sum.

Misrepresentation A false statement of fact which may induce a party to enter in to a contract.

Representation A pre-contractual statement that induces the making of the contract.

Term A statement that is part of the contract.

Warranty A minor term of a contract which is incidental to the main purpose of the contract.

For an online flashcard glossary visit the Online Resource Centre

Summary

After studying this chapter students should be able to:

Explain the difference between a term of a contract and a representation

- A representation is a pre-contractual statement.
- Whether a statement is a term or a representation depends on the intention of the parties.

Appreciate the necessity for certainty of contractual terms and explain the difference between express and implied terms

- Terms of a contract must not be too vague or incomplete, and if they are, the agreement will usually not be a binding contract.
- Terms can be express, or implied into contracts by statute, trade custom, or the courts.

Distinguish between conditions, warranties, and innominate terms and explain the different legal consequences that result from breach of them

- Conditions are fundamental terms of a contract. If a condition is broken, the innocent party can treat the contract as discharged and claim damages, or can continue with the contract and claim damages.

For an online printable version visit the Online Resource Centre

- Warranties are minor terms of the contract. If a warranty is broken, damages can be claimed.
- Innominate terms are ones where the seriousness of the breach can only be ascertained after it has occurred.

Describe the nature of exclusion/limitation clauses and explain the methods used by the courts to restrict the use of such clauses

- Exemption clauses are contractual terms which attempt to exclude or limit one party's liability to the other party.
- An exemption clause must be incorporated into the contract.
- Where an exemption clause is contained in an unsigned notice, then reasonable steps must be taken to bring the clause to the attention of the other party.
- Once a contract is completed, it is too late to add an exemption clause, unless there have been consistent previous dealings between the parties.
- If there is any doubt as to the meaning of an exemption clause, then the courts will construe it against the party seeking to rely on it.

Explain the effects of the Unfair Contract Terms Act 1977 and Unfair Terms in Consumer Contracts Regulations 1999, on exemption clauses

- Exemption clauses must comply with the Unfair Contract Terms Act 1977.
- A person acting in the course of a business cannot exclude liability for negligently causing death or personal injury. Liability for other loss or damage through negligence can be excluded, but only as far as it meets the requirement of reasonableness.
- The Unfair Terms in Consumer Contracts Regulations 1999 apply to any non-negotiated term in a contract made between a seller or supplier of goods or services and a consumer.
- A term which is deemed to be unfair according to the criteria laid down in the Regulations is not binding on the consumer.
- The Competition and Markets Authority has the duty to investigate complaints that contracts that have been drawn up for general use are unfair.

Demonstrate an understanding of contracts in restraint of trade

- A restraint of trade clause restricts the future freedom of one of the parties to the contract to carry on his business, trade, or profession.
- Restraint of trade clauses are usually invalid unless the party seeking to enforce them can show that in the particular circumstances the restraint is reasonable.
- In deciding whether a restraint is reasonable, the courts will consider if the business interest is one that can be legally protected, and the reasonableness of the length of time imposed and the geographical area covered.

Questions

For outline answers visit the Online Resource Centre

1. Dr Know, a well-known academic, is due to speak at the Annual Brighton Small Business Conference. She arrives early and books into the Ship Hotel, owned by Leisure Ltd. She has stayed there on a number of occasions in previous years. Her room is not ready so she asks the receptionist if she can leave her overnight bag with him. He takes her bag and gives her a cloakroom ticket, which she stuffs into her pocket without reading. The back of the cloakroom ticket reads 'All items left at reception at owner's risk.' When Dr Know returns to the hotel she is informed that her bag has gone missing but will be returned to her as soon as it is found.

Dr Know goes up to her bedroom and sees a large notice which states: 'Leisure Ltd accepts no responsibility for loss of property or injury to persons, howsoever caused'. Dr Know decides to carry her laptop computer to dinner in case it is stolen from the hotel room. Unfortunately, on her way to dinner, Dr Know catches her shoe in a large hole in the stair carpet, and falls down the stairs breaking her arm and damaging her laptop.

Advise Dr Know whether she can claim, in law of contract, for the loss of her overnight bag (which has never been found), the damage to her laptop, and for the injury caused to her arm.

2. **a)** Hari took a lease for 10 years of a garage from British Petrol plc. The lease stated that Hari could only sell petrol provided by British Petrol plc. Hari has now discovered he could buy Ecco petrol cheaper. Advise Hari if he is bound by the solus agreement with British Petrol plc.

    b) Gerald is employed by Dairy Ltd and has learnt their trade secret of making chocolate that does not melt in temperatures below 40°C. His contract states that if he leaves Dairy Ltd he must not be involved in the manufacture of chocolate or any other confectionery in the UK or the rest of the world for five years.

    Discuss whether this restraint clause is lawful.

3. Distinguish between:

    a) A puff, a representation, and a term.

    b) A condition, a warranty, and an innominate term.

4. Explain the effects of the Unfair Contract Terms Act 1977 and the Unfair Terms in Consumer Contracts Regulations 1999 in relation to exclusion clauses.

Further Reading

Poole, *Contract Law*, 12th edn (Oxford University Press, 2014) Chapters 6 and 7.

Richards, *The Law of Contract*, 11th edn (Pearson, 2013) Chapters 7 and 8.

Taylor and Taylor, *Contract Law Directions*, 4th edn (Oxford University Press, 2013) Chapters 5 and 6.

Turner, *Unlocking Contract Law*, 4th edn (Routledge, 2013) Chapter 6.

Competition and Markets Authority: https://www.gov.uk/government/organisations/competition-and-markets-authority

Trading Standards Institute: http://www.tradingstandards.gov.uk/.

Online Resource Centre

Test your knowledge by trying this chapter's **Multiple Choice Questions.** Visit:

  www.oup.com/uk/orc/law/company/ jonesibl3e/01student/mcqs/ch06/

For more information, updates, and multiple choice questions, please visit the Online Resource Centre at:

  www.oup.com/uk/orc/law/company/ jonesibl3e/

7

Vitiating Factors

Introduction

A contract may meet the necessary formation requirements of offer and acceptance, consideration, and intention to create legal relations, but still not be binding because it lacks other necessary factors. There may have been no genuine consent between the parties to the contract, or the contract may be illegal, or contrary to public policy. These invalidating factors are sometimes referred to as **'vitiating factors'** and comprise **misrepresentation**, mistake, **duress**, **undue influence**, and illegality (see Figure 7.1). The lack of genuine consent to a contract will usually mean that the contract is void or voidable. If the contract is declared void, there never was a contract and neither party can enforce it. If the contract is declared voidable, the innocent party can chose whether to end the contract or to continue with it. A contract is voidable if it was entered into under duress (coercion), undue influence, or after a misrepresentation. A contract is usually void if one party or both parties are mistaken about some aspect of the contract, and the mistake is in respect of an issue which is of fundamental importance to the contract. If the mistake is not of fundamental importance to the contract, then the contract will be valid even though a mistake has been made. A contract may be void if its terms, purpose, or performance are contrary to statute or common law.

Learning Objectives

After studying this chapter you should be able to:

- Define statements that constitute actionable misrepresentations.
- Distinguish between fraudulent, negligent, and innocent misrepresentation and be aware of the remedies available for each type of misrepresentation.
- Explain types of mistake and their effect on a contract.
- Describe how duress and undue influence may arise and their effect on contracts.
- Outline the types of contract that are illegal.

Figure 7.1 Factors that can invalidate a contract

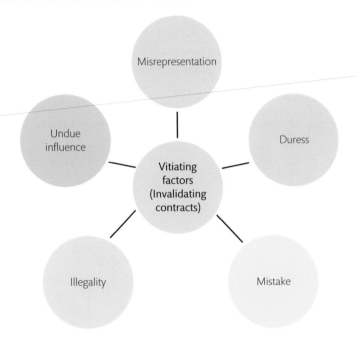

Misrepresentation

During negotiations, before a contract is completed, parties frequently make all sorts of statements. A statement made during negotiations may become a term of a contract (see Chapter 6). If this is the case, and the statement is untrue, then there will be a breach of contract and the innocent party can pursue remedies for breach of contract (see Chapter 8). If the statement is not a term of the contract it may, nevertheless, have been very influential in persuading the other party to enter into the contract. Where such a statement is untrue, the innocent party may be able to take action in court against the other party, for misrepresentation (see Figure 7.2).

A contract made after a misrepresentation is voidable. Therefore, it is a valid contract unless and until the party who entered the contract as a result of reliance upon a misleading statement applies to have the contract set aside.

Key Concept A party may be able to have a contract set aside and/or claim compensation if there has been misrepresentation, and the innocent party has entered into the contract on reliance of an untrue statement made by the other party to the contract.

Definition of Misrepresentation

In order for a claim for misrepresentation in court to be successful, before or at the time of the making of a contract one party must have made an unambiguous false statement of fact which induced the other party to enter into the contract.

Figure 7.2 An untrue statement may lead to a claim for misrepresentation

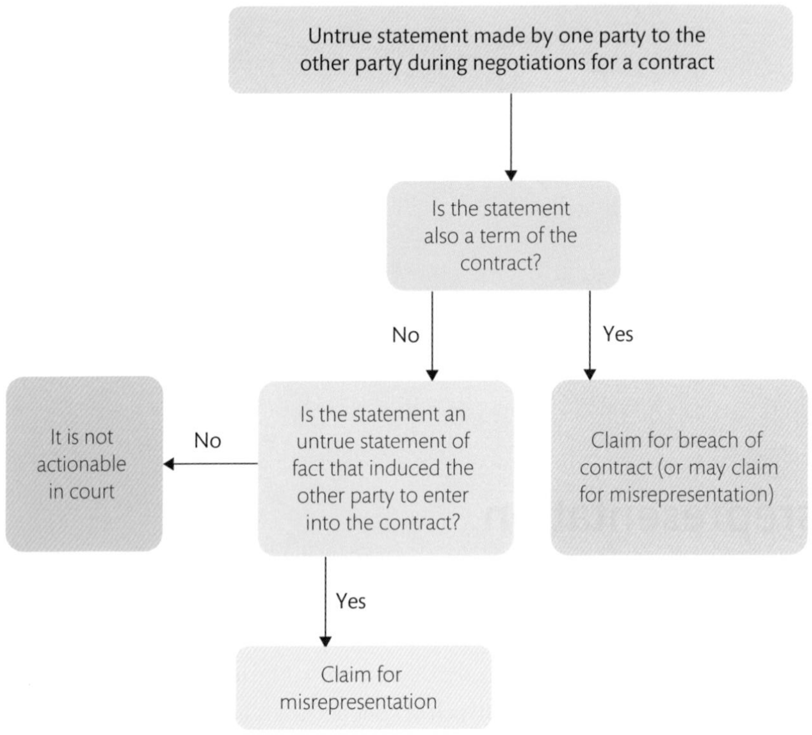

The statement may be oral, written, or by conduct

There must be a statement made during negotiations for a contract. Silence will not usually amount to a false statement. Generally, in English law there is no duty to disclose information, unless the contract is one of the utmost good faith, or a special relationship of trust exists between the parties, for example between solicitors and clients or between cohabiting partners. Contracts of utmost good faith include insurance contracts where parties are obliged to disclose all material facts to each other. If a person enters into a car insurance contract and does not disclose all the material facts, such as a recent car crash, the insurer is entitled to have the contract set aside.

Usually there is no obligation to disclose information to the other party. It is up to each party to seek out any information they require. When a house is being sold, the buyer's solicitor asks a series of questions about the house, known as 'preliminary enquiries', before a contract is signed and the seller must answer these questions but he is not required to give additional information.

Sykes v Taylor-Rose (2004)

Facts: In negotiations for the sale of a house, one of the questions asked in the preliminary enquiries to the seller was 'Is there any other information which you think the buyer may have a right to know?' The seller replied 'No' and did not reveal that a gruesome murder had been committed in the house several years beforehand.

Decision: The answer 'No' was not a misrepresentation because it was the answer to the question asked; the seller honestly believed the buyer had no right to be told about the murder.

A statement in negotiations is usually spoken or put in writing but a statement may be made through conduct. A party may make a misrepresentation by answering a question with a nod or a shake of the head. In the following case, attending a photo shoot together with express assurances of commitment amounted to a misrepresentation.

Spice Girls Ltd v Aprilia World Service BV (2002)

Facts: Aprilia, a motor scooter manufacturer, entered into negotiations with Spice Girls Ltd (a company owned by the Spice Girls) under which Spice Girls Ltd agreed that the group, currently comprising five members, would promote Aprilia motor scooters in return for sponsorship. Before the agreement was signed, Ginger Spice (Geri Halliwell) informed the group that she intended to leave in six months' time. The group then participated in a photo shoot and other promotional material for the scooters. The sponsorship agreement was signed, and three weeks later Geri left the group. Aprilia refused to make any further sponsorship payments and, when sued by Spice Girls Ltd, Aprilia counterclaimed for damages for misrepresentation, on the grounds that Spice Girls Ltd knew Geri intended to leave before the contract was signed, and if they had been informed they would not have entered into the contract.

Decision: The group and management knew Geri intended to leave, and the group taking part in the promotion amounted to a misrepresentation by conduct, and Aprilia were entitled to recover all their losses under the sponsorship contract.

The statement must be false

The statement made must be false. It can be written, orally expressed, or inferred through conduct. The party making the statement may know that the statement is untrue, but a statement may still be a misrepresentation if the party making it does not realise that it is untrue at the time.

If a statement is true when it is made but before the contract is completed, it becomes false, the party who made the original statement must disclose the new position, and if he does not he will be liable for misrepresentation.

With v O'Flanagan (1936)

Facts: In January 1934, negotiations were entered into for the sale of a medical practice. The doctor selling the practice correctly said it had an income of £2,000 per year. However, the doctor became ill, and by the time the contract for the sale of the practice was made in May, its income had fallen drastically. This fact was not disclosed to the purchaser.

Decision: The failure to tell the purchaser of the fall in value of the practice was a misrepresentation. The representation that the practice had an income of £2,000 per year was treated as a continuing representation until the contract was signed. Once the doctor knew the representation had become false, there was a misrepresentation if he failed to correct the statement.

If a party makes a statement which itself is true but misleads the other party because of what is left unsaid, it may amount to a misrepresentation. In the following case, land described as occupied by tenants was true but, as they were about to leave, the statement was a misrepresentation.

Dimmock v Hallett (1866)

Facts: Farm land for sale was described by the seller as being occupied by certain tenants. Although the land was let out to tenants, the tenants had given notice to quit and were about to leave.

Decision: The statement was misleading as one would assume that the tenants had not given notice to quit. The statement was a misrepresentation.

Key Concept Misrepresentation covers false statements and half-truths. A statement which is true when it is made, but becomes false before the contract is completed, may be a misrepresentation. Statements which mislead the other party because of what is not disclosed may also be misrepresentations.

The statement must be fact

The statement made must be more than a mere opinion of one of the parties. An opinion which is genuinely believed by the party making it cannot amount to a misrepresentation, even though the opinion was incorrect. Sometimes it is difficult to tell the difference between a statement of fact and a statement of opinion. The statement of opinion must be uninformed as opposed to an informed opinion. It must not be in contradiction to other facts known to the party giving the opinion. A statement is more likely to be regarded as merely an opinion if it is made by a person who is in no better position to know its truth than the recipient, and the recipient is aware of this.

Bissett v Wilkinson (1927)

Facts: The seller of land told the prospective purchaser that he believed the land would support 2,000 sheep. The land had never been used as a sheep farm before and the purchaser was aware of this fact.

Decision: The seller's statement was an expression of his opinion, and not a statement of fact, as both parties were aware that the land had never been used as a sheep farm.

If the facts are not equally known by the parties, a statement made by a party who should know the situation may be treated by the courts as a statement of fact rather than an expression of opinion.

Smith v Land & House Property Corporation (1884)

Facts: The claimants put their hotel up for sale and described it as 'let to Mr Frederick Fleck (a most desirable tenant) at a rent of £400 per year'. In fact, Mr Fleck was in arrears with his rent and had been threatened with court action for non-payment of rent. In an action for breach of contract, the claimants alleged their statement was just an opinion.

> **Decision:** The statement made by the claimants was one of fact, asserting that nothing had occurred in the relations between the claimants and the tenant which would make the tenant an unsatisfactory one. It was a statement of fact implying that the tenant was desirable.

Where the party making the statement is, or professes to be, an expert, he is under a duty to take reasonable care and skill to ensure the advice and information he gives is accurate, and any statements he makes are likely to be construed as a fact.

Esso Petroleum Ltd v Mardon (1976)

Facts: Esso's sales representative, who had many years experience, wrongly advised Mardon that the new garage development would be able to sell about 200,000 gallons of petrol a year. Relying on this statement, Mardon signed a three-year tenancy agreement. In fact, petrol sales were less than half that estimated by the sales representative.

Decision: A party, having or professing to have special knowledge or skill, who makes a representation to another with the intention of inducing him to enter into a contract, is under a duty to use reasonable care to ensure the statement is correct. The estimate of the forecast sales of petrol was incorrect and a misrepresentation.

A statement of fact does not include exaggerated advertising or vague boasts (sometimes referred to as 'mere puffs') about the subject matter of a contract, which are not intended to be relied on. The court will judge the statement objectively and, although the person making it may declare that they did not intend it to be taken seriously, the court may decide that a reasonable person would take the statement seriously.

Fordy v Harwood (1999)

Facts: The defendant advertised a replica kit car he had constructed as 'absolutely mint. All the right bits and does it go.' Although the car was roadworthy, the wheels were not properly aligned. The judge at the first hearing decided that 'absolutely mint' was a mere puff referring to the appearance of the car.

Decision: The Court of Appeal reversed the decision of the trial judge and stated that 'absolutely mint' was a representation and included the mechanical condition of the car. As this was defective, the statement was a misrepresentation.

A statement of future intention to do something is not generally a statement of fact, unless the person making the statement had no intention at the time of carrying out the expressed intention. He is actually making a false statement of fact by saying he had an intention to carry something out, when in fact he had no such intention.

Edgington v Fitzmaurice (1885)

Facts: The claimant lent money to a company partly on the basis of a statement in the company prospectus saying that the loans would be used to improve the company's buildings and expand the business. In fact, at the time of making the statement, the directors intended to use the loans to pay off company debts.

Decision: The directors of the company were liable—their statement of intention was a statement of fact.

Where a statement of law relates to how the law can be applied to certain facts, the statement will usually be actionable as a misrepresentation if it is incorrect. In the following case, the law as it applied to a car park occupier was incorrectly stated. The incorrect statement was a misrepresentation.

Pankhania v Hackney London Borough Council (2002)

Facts: In negotiations for the sale of property, part of which was used as a car park, the seller stated that the occupier of the car park, National Car Parks Ltd, could have their lease terminated on three months' notice. This was incorrect as the occupier was a protected business tenant under the Landlord and Tenant Act 1954.

Decision: The seller had incorrectly stated the law as it applied to the occupier of the car park, and the purchaser of the property was entitled to a remedy for misrepresentation.

The statement must have induced the other party to enter into the contract

Once it has been established that a representation is a false statement of fact, the innocent party must show that he relied on the statement and it was one of the reasons why he entered into the contract. If the innocent party did not know about the false statement, or knew about it and either knew it was false or did not take it into account, he cannot have relied on it; therefore, it is not misrepresentation for which action can be taken in court.

If a false statement of fact has been made by one of the parties during the negotiations for the contract, but the innocent party had sought their own expert advice on the subject rather than relying on the statement, it is not an actionable misrepresentation.

Attwood v Small (1838)

Facts: The seller of a mine made exaggerated claims about the mine's potential to prospective purchasers. In order to check on the seller's statements, the purchasers appointed their own expert to examine the mine. Their own expert reported that the mine had a similar potential to that which the seller had ascertained.

Decision: The purchaser had relied on their own expert and not on the seller's statements. It was not an actionable misrepresentation, and the fact that their expert was wrong did not make the seller liable.

The false statement does not have to be the only factor relied upon. It may be one of a number of reasons that persuaded the innocent party to enter into a contract. In *Edgington v Fitzmaurice* (1885) (see earlier), the claimants lent money to the company partly because of the misleading statement in the prospectus, and partly because of their own mistaken belief about the terms of the loan. The claimants were successful in their claim for misrepresentation because the false statement was one of the reasons for making the loan.

If a party knows that the statement made by the other party is untrue, he cannot be said to have relied on it. If he believes it to be true, it may be a misrepresentation even if he could have easily discovered the statement was false.

Redgrave v Hurd (1881)

Facts: An elderly solicitor, who wished to sell his share of the practice to a prospective partner, gave the partner information about the income of the practice and told him the figures could be checked from a bundle of documents. The prospective partner chose not to inspect the documents, but relied on the statement made by the elderly solicitor.

Decision: The statement was a misrepresentation, and failure to take the opportunity to examine the documents did not alter the effect of the misrepresentation.

If a misrepresentation would have induced a reasonable person to enter into a contract a court will presume that the claimant was misled (unless it can be shown otherwise). Where a reasonable person would not have been misled, the claimant may still be successful if he can prove he actually relied on the misrepresentation.

Museprime Properties Ltd v Adhill Properties Ltd (1990)

Facts: Inaccurate statements about three properties sold in the auction were contained in auction particulars and repeated by the auctioneer. The inaccurate statements related to rent reviews, and the defendants argued that it was unreasonable for anyone to allow themselves to be influenced by the statements.

Decision: It was immaterial whether a reasonable person would have been induced by the misrepresentation to enter into the contract; the question was whether the claimant had been induced to enter into the contract. The claimant had been induced by the statement; therefore, it was an actionable misrepresentation.

Key Concept In order for a misrepresentation to be actionable in the courts it must be untrue, it must be a statement of fact (not uninformed opinion), and it must have induced the other party to enter into the contract. A misrepresentation may have been made fraudulently, negligently, or innocently.

Types of Misrepresentation

A misrepresentation can be classified as fraudulent, negligent, or wholly innocent and the remedies available depend upon which type of misrepresentation has been made.

Business Insight Warning to sales teams who make unrealistic promises to win contracts

In January 2010, BSkyB won a protracted High Court battle against IT supplier Electronic Data Systems (EDS) (now a part of Hewlett-Packard) for fraudulent and negligent misrepresentations made to BSkyB about EDS's ability to design and implement a new Customer Relationship Management system within a certain timescale. In 2000 EDS had successfully bid against competing IT suppliers for a contract worth approximately £48 m. However, the sales team of EDS, particularly the Bid Team Leader, had made various representations, some of which proved to be fraudulent. Although there was a clause limiting liability to £30 million, this was not effective against fraudulent misrepresentation. The amount of compensation payable was agreed by the parties out of court. It was reported that BSkyB was paid a total of £318 million in full and final settlement of their claim.

Fraudulent misrepresentation

Fraudulent misrepresentation is where a party makes a false statement that they do not believe is true. In the case of *Derry v Peek* (1889) the court stated that to establish fraudulent misrepresentation the innocent party must prove that the false statement was made '(i) knowingly, or (ii) without belief in its truth, or (iii) recklessly as to whether it is true or false'. It can be very difficult to prove that someone is being reckless or dishonest as opposed to negligent.

Negligent misrepresentation

A false statement made by a person, who believes that the statement is true but has no reasonable grounds for that belief, is negligent misrepresentation. A victim of negligent misrepresentation can take court action either under the Misrepresentation Act 1967 or under common law. Provided that the misrepresentation made by one party induced the other party to enter into a contract with him, the usual court action taken would be under the Misrepresentation Act 1967 because the burden of proving that the statement was made negligently does not fall on the injured party. Under the Act, all misrepresentations are presumed to be fraudulent unless the maker of the statement can prove they were innocent.

Section 2(1) of the Misrepresentation Act 1967 states that, where a person has entered into a contract after a misrepresentation has been made to him by another party and as a result he has suffered loss, he will be able to claim damages even though the misrepresentation had not been made fraudulently, unless the party making the statement proves that he had reasonable grounds to believe and did believe, up to the time the contract was made, that the facts represented were true.

This means that, under s 2(1), once it is established that a false statement has been made, the burden of proof transfers to the person who made the false statement to establish that he had reasonable grounds for believing the statement was true.

Howard Marine and Dredging Co Ltd v A Ogden and Sons (Excavations) Ltd (1978)

Facts: The defendants needed to cost the depositing of excavated earth at sea and asked the claimants for the precise capacity of their barges. The claimants' Marine Manager gave a figure of 1,600 tonnes based on insurance documents, rather than checking the actual shipping documents which would have shown the correct figure of 1,055 tonnes. The defendants hired the barges but refused to pay for them and, when sued, claimed misrepresentation under the Misrepresentation Act 1967, s 2(1).

Decision: There was insufficient evidence to prove that the claimants had reasonable grounds to believe the information given was true. The Manager had not checked the actual shipping register.

Since the House of Lords decision in *Hedley Byrne & Co Ltd v Heller & Partners Ltd* (1964) (see further Chapter 11), court action under the law of **torts** may be taken in common law for negligent misstatements, where there has been financial loss. However, to take an action in common law, the claimant must prove that the other party made the false statement negligently and that there was a special relationship between the parties.

If a contract between the parties is made following a misrepresentation, action is usually taken under the Misrepresentation Act 1967. However, a claimant will have to take court action in common law where there is no resulting contract between the parties, for example, the misrepresentation is discovered before the contract is entered into, or if the misrepresentation is made by a third person who is not party to the contract.

Innocent misrepresentation

Innocent misrepresentation is where a false statement is made by a person who has an honest and reasonable belief in its truth. This belief must be present when the statement is made and right up until the time the contract is entered into.

Key Concept Where a party sues another for a misrepresentation under the Misrepresentation Act 1967, it is up to the party who made the misrepresentation to prove (on the balance of probabilities) that it was made innocently.

Remedies for Misrepresentation

The two possible remedies available for misrepresentation are rescission and damages.

Rescission

Rescission sets the contract aside, and puts the parties back into the same position they would have been in if the contract had never been entered into. The court can order that any money that has been paid or property that has been exchanged between the parties is returned to the original party. It is an equitable remedy, and this means that it is up to the court to decide whether it is fair in all the circumstances to allow the contract to be rescinded. A court will not usually set a contract aside if an innocent third party has acquired rights under the contract, or it is impossible to restore the parties to their pre-contractual position, for example, where goods bought under a contract have been sold to a third party, lost, or consumed. A contract will not be rescinded if the innocent party, being aware of the misrepresentation, indicates in writing, orally, or through conduct that he intends to continue with the contract.

Damages

Damages are a financial payment made to compensate the innocent party. Damages for misrepresentation aim to put the innocent party back in the position they would have been in, had the misrepresentation not occurred. Therefore, the innocent party cannot claim for loss of profits that would have been made under the contract if the representation had been true. This is different from the award of damages for breach of contract because, where there is a breach, the damages are calculated to put the parties in the position they would have been in if the contract had been performed as agreed, so any profits due to be made under the contract could be claimed (see Chapter 8).

The remedies awarded by the court depend upon which type of misrepresentation had been made.

Remedies for fraudulent misrepresentation

The innocent party is entitled to damages for all losses he has suffered. The damages are based on the tort of deceit, and are assessed to meet all losses that have directly resulted as a consequence of having entered into the contract, whether or not they were foreseeable at the time the misrepresentation was made.

Smith New Court Securities v Scrimgeour Vickers (1996)

Facts: As a result of a fraudulent misrepresentation, the claimants were induced into buying shares in Ferranti at 82.25p per share, amounting to a total of over £23 million. At the time of the misrepresentation, the market value of the shares was 78p per share. After the fraud was discovered, the share price in the company had fallen considerably and the claimants sold their shares at prices ranging from 30–49p, making a loss of over £11 million.

Decision: The losses were as a direct result of the fraud; therefore, the claimants were entitled to all their losses, not just the difference between the price paid, 82.25p, and the market value at the time, 78p.

In addition, the innocent party can claim rescission of the contract. Alternatively, the innocent party may elect to continue with the contract and only claim damages.

Remedies for negligent misrepresentation

Where there has been negligent misrepresentation, the innocent party is entitled to damages for any loss suffered under the provisions of s 2(1) of the Misrepresentation Act 1967. The

Court of Appeal stated in *Royscot Trust Ltd v Rogerson* (1991) that damages under s 2(1) should be assessed in the same way as damages for fraudulent misrepresentation. Therefore, an innocent party can recover all losses incurred as a result of the misrepresentation even though the other party was not acting fraudulently. The Court of Appeal reached their decision by using the express literal words of the statute (see Chapter 3 on interpretation of statutes).

The innocent party can also claim rescission of the contract. However, under the provisions of s 2(2) of the Misrepresentation Act 1967, the court can award damages instead of rescission if it is more equitable (fairer) to do so in the circumstances. This allows the court to take into account the effects that rescission might have on both parties to the contract. The amount of damages awarded is less than under s 2(1) and will generally be the difference in value between what the claimant believed he was acquiring and the value of what in fact he received. If the misrepresentation had a relatively minor impact on the contract, it may be fairer to allow the contract to survive.

Where a party has taken action in *common law* then rescission (if a contract has been entered into with the party responsible for making the negligent misrepresentation) and/or damages for the tort of negligence can be claimed. Damages for the tort of negligence are limited to losses that were reasonably foreseeable.

Remedies for innocent misrepresentation

Where there has been innocent misrepresentation, the innocent party can claim rescission. However under the provisions of s 2(2) of the Misrepresentation Act 1967, a court can award damages instead of rescission if it is more equitable to do so in the circumstances. Where the misrepresentation did not have a major effect on the subsequent contract, it may be fairer to award damages instead of rescission.

Exclusion Clauses

A contract may contain a clause excluding or limiting liability for negligent or innocent misrepresentations. However, s 3 of the Misrepresentation Act 1967, amended by the Unfair Contract Terms Act 1977, states that clauses attempting to exclude or restrict liability for misrepresentations are only valid if reasonable and it is for those claiming that a term is reasonable to show this. The guidelines for what is reasonable are set out in the Unfair Contract Terms Act 1977.

Key Concept Where there has been misrepresentation, the contract is voidable, i.e. it may be set aside. Where there has been an operative (fundamental) mistake, the contract is void, i.e. treated as though it never existed.

Mistake

Where one party or both parties are mistaken about an aspect of the contract they have entered into, the contract is usually still valid. However, there are certain circumstances where the mistake is so fundamental to the contract that the courts will regard it as an **'operative' mistake** which renders the contract void. The contract is treated as though it never existed. The parties are returned to their pre-contractual condition and no rights can pass under the contract. Mistake can be divided into three categories: common mistake, mutual mistake, and unilateral mistake. But whichever category the mistake falls into, the general rule that mistake does not usually affect a contract still applies. For a mistake to be operative in common law, it must go to the root of the contract.

Common Mistake

A common mistake is where both parties make the same mistake. In order to make the contract void, the mistake must be fundamental to the contract itself. If at the time of making the contract, the subject matter does not exist or the subject matter already belongs to the buyer, the contract may be void for common mistake.

Common mistake as to existence of the subject matter

If at the time of making the contract the subject matter did not exist, then the contract is likely to be void for an operative mistake, as neither party would contract for something that is non-existent.

Couturier v Hastie (1856)

Facts: A contract for the sale and purchase of a cargo of corn was made whilst the corn was in transit. Unknown to either party, the corn had been sold by the ship's captain, because it had begun to deteriorate.

Decision: The contract was for specific goods and, at the time it was made, the subject matter of the contract no longer existed. The contract was therefore void. This provision can now be found in s 6 of the Sale of Goods Act 1979, which provides 'where there is a contract for specific goods, and the goods without the knowledge of the seller have perished at the time when the contract is made, the contract is void'.

In the following case, the contract was for the sale of a life assurance policy, but the contract was void for mistake because, unknown to both parties, the subject of the policy was no longer in existence.

Scott v Coulson (1903)

Facts: A contract was made for the sale of a life policy which was assured on the life of Mr Alfred Death. At the time of the contract both parties mistakenly believed Mr Death was alive.

Decision: As at the time of making the contract, unknown to both parties, the assured man was dead, the contract was void for mistake.

The following case is a more modern example of where both parties shared the same mistaken belief that the subject matter of a contract existed.

Associated Japanese Bank v Credit du Nord (1988)

Facts: The claimant bank bought some machines from its client, Bennett, and then leased them back to him under a guarantee from the defendants. Bennett went bankrupt and the claimant sued the defendants on the guarantee. In fact, the machines did not exist and had not done so at the time of the contract. The scheme had been a fraud by Bennett.

Decision: The machines were security for the guarantee and, as they did not exist, and both parties to the contract were unaware of their non-existence, the contract was void for mistake.

Where the subject matter of a contract does not exist, but it was the responsibility of one of the parties to ensure its existence, the contract may be valid. The court may decide that, rather than there being an operative mistake, there is an implied term in the contract that one of the parties will provide a certain item and, if he is unable to do so because the item does not exist, the contract is breached.

McRae v Commonwealth Disposals (1952)

Facts: The claimants entered into a contract with the defendant, which gave the claimants the right to salvage a wrecked oil tanker which the defendant stated contained oil and was lying at a particular location. After spending a considerable sum in attempting to locate the wreck, it became apparent that the wreck never existed.

Decision: The claimants had bought the salvage rights on the implied condition in the contract that the wreck existed. The contract was valid, it had been breached by the defendant, and the claimants were entitled to damages.

Common mistake as to ownership of the subject matter

If a party enters into a contract for the sale of goods as the purchaser, when in fact, unknown to either party, he already owns the goods, the contract will be void for mistake.

Cooper v Phibbs (1867)

Facts: The claimant contracted to lease a salmon fishery from the defendant. At the time, both parties thought the defendant owned the property but it was later discovered that, at the time of the contract, the claimant already had rights to the fishery.

Decision: The contract for the lease was set aside for mistake. As the defendant had spent money on the fishery he was allowed to recover this under the rules of equity (fairness).

Common mistake as to quality

Common mistakes as to quality occur when both parties make an identical mistake on a fact relating to the quality of the subject matter. In most cases, mistakes as to the quality of the subject matter do not make a contract void. However, occasionally a mistake as to quality will make a contract void if the mistake relates to an essential or vital part of the subject matter. The leading case is *Bell v Lever Bros* (1932), where Lord Atkin stated that a mistake as to quality or value should not be regarded as an operative mistake unless 'it is a mistake of both parties and is as to the existence of some quality which makes the thing without the quality essentially different from the thing as it was believed to be'. Circumstances in which a contract will be essentially different will be rare.

In the following case there was no mistake about the subject matter of the sale and the contract was not void for mistake.

Leaf v International Galleries (1950)

Facts: The claimants bought a painting of Salisbury Cathedral for £85 from the defendants who told them it was by Constable (a famous English landscape painter). The claimants discovered this was untrue when they tried to sell the painting five years later.

Decision: The contract was not void for mistake. The contract was for the sale of a painting and the mistake was as to the quality of the painting.

In *Great Peace Shipping v Tsavliris Salvage* (2003), considered next, the Court of Appeal had to consider if the services that the ship, the Great Peace, was in a position to provide were essentially different to those the parties had agreed to in their contract. The court decided that it was still possible for the ship to provide rescue services. The court also stated that there were no separate rules in equity on common mistake.

Great Peace Shipping v Tsavliris Salvage (2003)

Facts: The owners of a ship, damaged in the Indian Ocean, engaged the defendants to assist in its recovery. The defendants hired a vessel, the Great Peace, which both parties believed to be very near the damaged ship, from the claimants. In fact, it was 410 miles away and, when the defendants discovered this, they looked and found another ship which was much closer, and then sought to cancel the contract with the claimants for common mistake, i.e. that the contract was based on the common incorrect assumption that the two ships were closer together.

Decision: It was not an operative mistake. The subject matter of the contract, the Great Peace, existed, although the parties were genuinely mistaken as to its whereabouts. The ship could have arrived in time to provide some assistance and the contract had not been cancelled until the defendants had found a closer ship. The contract for the hire of Great Peace was valid.

Mutual Mistake

A mutual mistake occurs when the parties are at cross purposes and, therefore, never really agree. They have two different understandings of the facts. In such cases the court will provide an objective test, and try to identify the main substance of the contract. If this can be done, the contract continues on the terms that the court believes represents the intention of the parties. However, on occasion it is impossible to reconcile the two differences and the contract will be void for mistake.

Raffles v Wichelhaus (1864)

Facts: A cargo of cotton was described as being on SS Peerless from Bombay. Unknown to the parties, there were two ships of that name leaving Bombay. The seller intended the cotton to go on the second ship and the buyer expected the cotton to go on the first ship.

Decision: There was no possibility of finding a common intention between the parties. The contract was void for mistake.

Unilateral Mistake

A unilateral mistake is where only one of the parties to the contract is mistaken and the other party is aware of the mistake. The mistake may concern the terms of the contract or the identity of the other party to the contract. In order for the mistake to be operative it must be essential to the contract. A unilateral mistake as to quality will have no effect on the contract.

Unilateral mistake as to the terms of a contract

If one of the parties is genuinely mistaken as to a fundamental term of a contract, through no fault of their own, and the other party is aware of the mistake, the contract may be void for mistake.

Hartog v Colin & Shields (1939)

Facts: The defendant offered to sell the claimants 30,000 hare skins at 10¼ pence a pound (there are about three hare skins to the pound). The trade custom was to sell by the individual skin and 10¼ pence was about the market value per skin. The claimants accepted the offer and tried to enforce the contract. The defendant argued that the offer was wrongly stated and that the claimants knew this.

Decision: The claimants clearly must have realised that a clerical error had been made in the offer, and were not entitled to take advantage of it. It was a material mistake and therefore the contract was void.

If the other party is unaware of the mistake, the contract will be binding even if there is a genuine mistake.

Centrovincial Estates plc v Merchant Investors Assurance Co Ltd (1983)

Facts: A landlord offered to renew his tenant's lease for £65,000 a year. The tenant accepted the lease, not realising there was a mistake in the terms. The landlord had made a mistake and had intended to offer a renewal of the lease for £126,000 a year.

Decision: The contract was valid. It was not void for mistake as the tenant had not known of the mistake when he entered into the contract.

Unilateral mistake as to the identity of the other party to the contract

Where there has been a genuine mistake as to the actual identity of one of the parties to the contract, and that party's identity is one of fundamental importance, the contract will be void for mistake. However, if the mistake concerns the other person's attributes as opposed to their identity, the contract will not be void for mistake, but may be voidable for fraudulent misrepresentation.

The general scenario in these cases is that a rogue (crook) pretends to be someone else and goods are sold to him on credit. The rogue then sells the goods on to an innocent third party, who buys in good faith, not realising that he is purchasing goods from a rogue. If the initial contract is void for mistake, no title (right of ownership) to the goods passes in the contract between the seller and the rogue. Therefore, the rogue has no title to the goods that he can pass on to the eventual buyer. The original seller can reclaim his goods. If the contract between the seller and the rogue is not void for mistake, it may be voidable for fraudulent misrepresentation, in which case title to the goods passes. The original seller may seek court action to have the original contract set aside, but the courts will not set aside a voidable contract where goods have already been bought in good faith by a third party. The original seller can attempt to find and sue the rogue, but rogues can be difficult to locate and, if they are found, they often do not have the financial means to settle a claim (see Figure 7.3).

Figure 7.3 **Ownership does not pass in a void contract but may pass in a voidable contract**

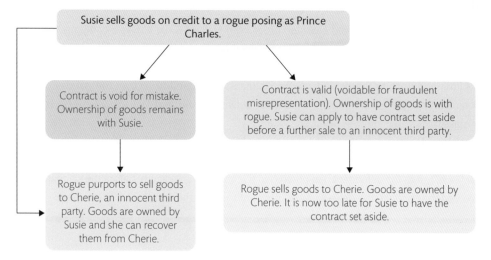

Where the parties make a contract at a distance from each other, for example, by post, fax, e-mail, or telephone, it is easier to establish that the identity of the person placing the order is of fundamental importance to the contract, and that the innocent party intended only to deal with the person they believed the other party to be.

Cundy v Lindsay (1878)

Facts: Blenkarn ordered linen by post from Lindsay, signing his name to look like 'Blenkiron & Co' which was a highly respected, well-known firm with an address in the same street. Lindsay sent the linen on to Blenkarn on credit. Cundy purchased the linen from Blenkarn, in good faith.

Decision: The contract between Blenkarn and Lindsay was void for mistake as Lindsay had intended to deal with 'Blenkiron & Co' and not the crook, Blenkarn. As the contract was void for mistake, the ownership of the goods had not passed to Blenkarn and, therefore, no ownership could pass on to Cundy who had to return the linen to Lindsay.

The innocent party cannot claim to have intended to contract with a party that does not exist. In the following case the company purporting to order the goods did not exist. The claimants had intended to deal with the writer of the letter. They thought the writer had certain attributes, namely creditworthiness and respectability, when in fact he was a dishonest crook.

King's Norton Metal Co Ltd v Edridge, Merrett & Co Ltd (1897)

Facts: The claimants received a written order from Hallam & Co. It was a company they had not heard of, but the letterhead described Hallam & Co as a large firm. In fact it did not exist, but was an alias for a crook, Wallis. The claimants sent goods to Hallam & Co on credit. Wallis sold the goods on to the defendant. The claimants attempted to recover the goods from the defendant on the grounds that the contract between them and Hallam & Co was void for mistake.

Decision: The claimants had not made a mistake as to identity because they had intended to contract with the writer of the letter. It was not an operative mistake. The contract was voidable for fraud, but as the defendant had purchased the goods in good faith, before the claimants had avoided the contract, the defendant had the right to retain the goods.

Where a contract is made face-to-face, it is presumed that the parties intended to deal with the person physically present. Most cases on mistaken identity relate to the credit status of a buyer. The seller is prepared to give credit to the buyer in the belief that he is someone else who is creditworthy. In these cases, although the contract may be voidable for fraudulent misrepresentation, it is not usually void for mistake.

Phillips v Brooks (1919)

Facts: North purchased jewellery in a shop and wrote a cheque for £3,000 misrepresenting himself as Sir George Bullough. After finding Sir George Bullough's address in the directory, the jeweller agreed that he could take the ring worth £450 and collect the rest of the jewellery when the cheque cleared. The cheque bounced. The jeweller found the ring in a pawn shop, and attempted to recover it from the pawnbroker on the grounds that the contract between North and the jeweller was void for mistake.

Decision: The jeweller had intended to contract with the person in front of him, who was North. The contract was not void for mistake and the pawnbroker gained good title to the ring as he had purchased it in good faith.

In the following case, the court came to a similar conclusion when a rogue pretended he was a television actor.

Lewis v Averay (1972)

Facts: Lewis advertised his car for sale and the man, a rogue, who came to purchase it, said he was Richard Greene (an actor who played Robin Hood in a TV series which was running at the time). The rogue showed Lewis his forged studio card, which was in the name of Greene, and Lewis allowed him to take the car in return for a cheque for £450 signed R.A. Greene. The cheque was dishonoured. The rogue sold the car for £200 to Averay. Lewis attempted to recover the car from Averay, on the grounds that the contract between him and the rogue was void for mistake.

Decision: Lewis could not recover the car from Averay, as the contract between Lewis and the rogue was not void, because there was no operative mistake in the contract. Lewis had contracted to sell the car to the man in front of him.

On occasion, the courts have found that, even though a contract is conducted 'face-to-face', on the evidence there is an operative mistake as to the identity of one of the parties, making the contract void.

Ingram v Little (1961)

Facts: Three elderly sisters negotiated with a rogue for the sale of their car. The rogue said his name was Hutchinson. They were reluctant to allow him to pay by cheque, but agreed after checking his name and address against a telephone directory entry. The rogue sold the car to the defendant, a car dealer who bought the car in good faith.

Decision: On the evidence presented, the court accepted that the sisters had only intended to contract with Mr Hutchinson and not with the person pretending to be him. The contract between the claimants and the rogue was void for mistake and, therefore, the claimants could recover the car from the defendant.

Ingram v Little is difficult to reconcile with the earlier case of *Phillips v Brooks* and the later case of *Lewis v Averay.* However, the court may have been persuaded on policy reasons to decide in favour of the claimants as the defendant who purchased the car was a car dealer and the claimants were the more vulnerable party.

The issue of mistaken identity was considered by the House of Lords in *Shogun Finance Ltd v Hudson* (2004) (see Figure 7.4). The majority of the Lords stated that, where there is an oral contract and the parties are 'face-to-face', there is a presumption that the contract is intended to be made between the parties physically present. However, where the contract is conducted via written correspondence, then the mistaken party may rely on the terms of the contract. If an essential term of the contract contains a fundamental mistake, such as the identity of one of the parties, then the contract will be void.

Shogun Finance Ltd v Hudson (2004)

Facts: A customer pretending he was a Mr Patel completed hire purchase forms for the purchase of a car worth £22,250. He produced a stolen driving licence in the name of Durlabh Patel to confirm his identity. The car dealer faxed the claimant, a finance company, a copy of the licence and the HP agreement. The finance company checked Mr Patel's address and credit rating and then agreed to buy the car from the dealer and sell it to Mr Patel on hire purchase terms. The customer paid a 10 per cent deposit and drove the car away. Shortly afterwards, he sold it to the defendant, Mr Hudson, for £17,000 and disappeared. The claimant finance company sued Mr Hudson for the recovery of the car.

Decision: The case depended upon whether the hire purchase agreement between the customer and the claimant finance company was valid. The contract had not been carried out 'face-to-face' but had been completed by fax. The car dealers were not agents for the claimant but intermediaries. (If the dealer had been an agent of the claimant then the contract would have been face-to-face.) The identity of the customer was crucial to the contract, and at all times the claimant intended to contract with the real Mr Durlabh Patel. The contract between the claimant and the customer was void for unilateral mistake. The claimant was entitled to recover the car from Mr Hudson.

Mistake in signing a written document

If a person signs a document he is usually bound by its contents, even if he has not read or understood them. However, if a person is under a complete misapprehension as to the type of document he is signing, or as to its contents, then he may be able to plead '*non est factum*' ('it is not my deed'). The rules are subject to strict requirements. The person claiming *non est factum* must prove he was unaware of the true meaning of the document and that he had taken all reasonable care. The standard of care is that of the actual person, and the courts will take into account the age, literacy, and physical and mental capacities of the person.

Figure 7.4 In *Shogun Finance Ltd v Hudson*, the car could be recovered by the finance company as the contract between the company and rogue was void for mistake

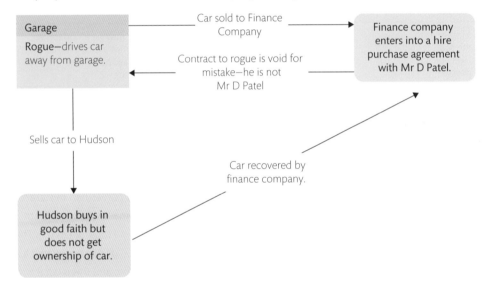

Saunders v Anglia Building Society (1970)

Facts: Mrs Gallie aged 78 signed a document without reading it as her reading glasses were broken. She had been told by Lee it was a deed of gift of her house to her nephew, when in fact it was a deed assigning the house to Lee for £3,000. Lee mortgaged the house to the building society but did not repay the instalments due. The building society sought possession of the house and Mrs Gallie sought to have the assignment set aside on the basis of *non est factum*. By the time the case reached the House of Lords, Mrs Gallie had died but her executrix continued the action against the building society.

Decision: There was no fundamental mistake in the type of document that Mrs Gallie had signed and the one she thought she had signed. Both were documents transferring ownership of the house. In addition, she had not taken sufficient care in signing the document. She should have waited until her glasses were repaired or asked someone to read the document to her.

Table 7.1 Types of mistake

Common mistake	Mutual mistake	Unilateral mistake
Both parties make the same mistake.	Both parties make different mistakes.	One of the parties is genuinely mistaken and the other party is aware of the mistake.
Existence or ownership of the subject matter may be an operative mistake.	The mistake will only be operative if impossible to reconcile the differences.	Mistake as to terms may be an operative mistake.
Mistake as to quality of the subject matter will rarely be an operative mistake.		Mistake as to identity may be an operative mistake, but if the parties are face-to-face it is presumed they intended to contract with the person in their presence.

Business Insight Keeping Quiet—a costly mistake

In a recent case, *Daventry District Council v Daventry & District Housing Limited* (2012), the Court of Appeal reversed the decision of the lower court and decided that both parties had mistakenly believed the terms of the contract reflected the terms of the initial agreement. Daventry District Council (C) had agreed to transfer housing and staff to Daventry & District Housing Ltd (H). The staff pension scheme had a deficit of approximately £2.4 m and the parties initially negotiated for H to pay the £2.4 m. In error, one e-mail stated that C would pay the £2.4 m and this is what was written in the contract. H's lead negotiator realised there was a misunderstanding between C and H but chose to keep quiet. In allowing the contract to be rectified to reflect the original intention the court was influenced by the fact that H's negotiator had failed to point out the error to H.

Duress and Undue Influence

A contract which is entered into after one party exercised duress or undue influence on the other party is voidable by the innocent party. This means the contract is valid after it has been made, but the innocent party may apply to a court to have the contract set aside. Duress has developed as a principle of common law and means that one party has threatened physical violence or serious economic coercion on the other. Undue influence has developed through equity, and covers situations where excessive persuasion has been applied by one party to the other. Undue influence may be presumed if there is a special relationship existing between the parties, such as solicitor and client, parent and child, and trustee and beneficiary.

Duress

Duress is where threats of actual unlawful violence or unlawful imprisonment are made to a party in order to induce them to enter into a contract. The unlawful actions must be one of the reasons for entering into the contract but need not be the only reason.

Barton v Armstrong (1976)

Facts: Armstrong was the chairman of an Australian company and Barton was the company's Managing Director. Armstrong threatened to have Barton killed if he did not buy out Armstrong's interest in the company on very favourable terms.
Decision: Armstrong's threats had contributed to Barton's decision to buy Armstrong's interest in the company, although there may have been other factors influencing Barton. The contract was voidable for duress.

Business Insight Is it tough commercial bargaining or is it economic duress?

Before many business agreements are made the parties usually negotiate and hammer out the details of the contract. The success of many businesses may depend on their ability to negotiate or renegotiate contracts. However the exertion of undue pressure in the course of negotiations by one powerful party may amount to economic duress and result in the contract being voidable by the victim of the duress.

Economic duress is a relatively new development in the law of duress. It arises where a contract has been agreed to after extortion by one of the parties. To establish economic duress, the innocent party must show that an illegitimate threat or pressure was applied by the other party, the threat or pressure was significant in inducing them to agree to the contract, and they had no practical choice but to agree. It is an objective test, therefore the courts must be satisfied that a reasonable person would have acted in the same manner as the innocent party and signed the contract. The innocent party must also have protested at the time, or shortly after the contract was made.

Atlas Express Ltd v Kafco (Importers and Distributors Ltd) (1989)

Facts: The defendants were a small company which imported and sold basketware to retailers. The defendants contracted to supply basketware to 800 Woolworths' stores. The defendants entered into a contract with the claimant, a delivery company, to deliver the goods to the stores for a set price. The claimant then sent a revised price list and informed the defendants that, unless they agreed to revise the contract with the new price, no more loads would be carried. The defendants were committed to Woolworths and, as this was the run up to Christmas period, they could not find another carrier and, therefore, signed the new agreement. Later the defendants refused to pay the new price agreed.

Decision: The defendants were forced to renegotiate the terms of the contract against their will. They had no alternative but to accept the new terms; therefore, the contract was set aside for economic duress.

Kolmar Group AG v Traxpo Enterprises Pvt Ltd (2010)

Facts: K agreed to buy a set amount of methanol from T for a specified price within a specified timeframe. K needed it to sell on to an important client. T informed K he would not be able to comply with the agreement but would only supply less methanol at a higher cost 'take it or leave it'. K had no option but to agree to pay the higher price.

Decision: K had no practical choice but to agree to pay an increased price for the methanol it did receive and K's agreement was as a result of illegitimate pressure amounting to economic duress on the part of T. K was entitled to recover $1.4 million which was the payment actually made, less the price due under the original agreement.

Although the economic coercion applied by one of the parties does not have to be unlawful, it must be greater than normal commercial pressure. In the following case the action of the defendants was not economic coercion.

CTN Cash and Carry v Gallaher (1994)

Facts: The defendants had a monopoly on supplying the most well-known brands of cigarettes. They supplied cigarettes to the claimants on credit terms. One of the orders made by the claimants was delivered to the wrong warehouse. The claimants complained about this to the defendants, but before redelivery could be arranged the consignment was stolen. The defendants charged the claimants for the stolen consignment. The claimants reluctantly agreed to pay for it, after the defendants stated they would withdraw the credit facilities if they did not. The claimants later argued that the agreement to pay for the stolen consignment was obtained by duress.

Decision: The withdrawal of credit facilities was not unlawful. The defendants had not threatened to breach the contract, only to alter the terms on which they supplied goods. There was no economic duress.

Undue Influence

The doctrine of undue influence was developed by equity and makes the contract voidable. As it is an equitable doctrine, the court has discretion on whether to set the contract aside. Undue influence covers situations where some form of improper pressure has been put on a person to enter into a contract. The victim is often emotionally or physically vulnerable, and they have only agreed to a contract because excessive pressure has been applied by the other party or by a third party with the knowledge of the other party. Undue influence can be divided into actual and presumed.

Actual undue influence

To establish actual undue influence, the victim must prove that he entered into the contract as a result of genuine intimidation. The dominance over the victim must be to such an extent that the victim is unable to act independently of this influence. It is a subjective test as to whether the victim was under the dominance of the other party and was unable to exercise his own free will. A **subjective test** means that the courts will take into account what the actual victim genuinely believes, as opposed to an **objective test** where the court takes into account what the reasonable person in the victim's position would believe. Unlike economic duress, the victim does not have to prove that there is no practical alternative other than entering into the contract, but must clearly prove that he would not have entered into the contract without the undue influence.

Bank of Credit and Commerce International SA v Aboody (1990)

Facts: Mrs Aboody did not understand business matters, and her husband bullied her into signing a number of charges on her property as security for business loans on a business owned by Mr and Mrs Aboody. On one occasion, when she was receiving advice about the implications of signing the charge from an independent solicitor, her husband came into the room and shouted at her to sign, reducing her to tears.

Decision: There had been actual undue influence on Mrs Aboody by her husband and the bank was aware of this (although in this case the transactions were not set aside by the court for other legal reasons).

In the case of actual undue influence, the victim does not have to show that the transaction entered into was disadvantageous to them, only that there was actual undue influence and that the other party knew or is legally presumed to have known of it.

CIBC Mortgages plc v Pitt (1994)

Facts: The defendant was induced by her husband to agree to a second mortgage to CIBC on the matrimonial home as security for a loan. She had not wanted to agree but eventually did so after actual undue influence by her husband.

Decision: Where there is proof of actual undue influence, the party who proves the undue influence does not have to additionally prove the transaction is to their disadvantage. However, in this case the court did not set aside the agreement as CIBC had no knowledge of the undue influence.

Presumed Undue Influence

Where there is a relationship of trust and confidence with the party against whom the undue influence is alleged, then it is presumed that undue influence has occurred. The victim need only prove the relationship existed and the transactions entered into were clearly disadvantageous to him. It is up to the dominant party to prove that he has not exerted undue influence and abused the relationship of trust. In order to prove this, the dominant party will have to show that the other party entered into the contract with full knowledge of the nature and effect of the transaction. This is usually shown by evidence that the victim had the benefit of independent, impartial advice before they entered into the transaction.

Influence will be presumed where there is a special relationship of confidence between the two parties entering into the contract. Such a relationship of trust is known as a **fiduciary relationship**. If a relationship falls into one of several categories, then it is automatically presumed to be a fiduciary relationship. The categories include solicitor and client, doctor and patient, religious advisor and disciple, guardian and ward, trustee and beneficiary.

In the following case, a fiduciary relationship was presumed as the relationship was between a religious advisor and a disciple, but because the claimant had waited six years before commencing a legal action, the court refused to give her a remedy.

Allcard v Skinner (1887)

Facts: In 1868 the claimant joined a Protestant convent. She took her vows of poverty, chastity, and obedience in 1871 and gave her property to the value of £7,000 to the religious order. In 1878 she left the order to become a Roman Catholic and sued for the return of her property.

Decision: Taking into account the submissive nature of the vows and the fact that under the rules of the sisterhood she was prevented from seeking outside advice, undue influence was presumed. However, she did not commence her court claim for six years after leaving the order and, therefore, her claim was refused due to delay.

Where a fiduciary relationship is not automatically presumed, the court may be prepared to find that one existed from the facts of the case.

Re Craig (1971)

Facts: After the death of his wife, Mr Craig, aged 84, employed a companion/secretary, Mrs Middleton. Over six years he gave her gifts amounting to £30,000. On his death, the executors of his estate sought to recover the gifts.

Decision: The court set aside the gifts because the circumstances showed that a fiduciary relationship existed, raising the presumption of undue influence, which Mrs Middleton failed to rebut.

Generally the courts do not find there is a fiduciary relationship between husbands and wives or cohabiting partners, even if the transaction entered into is for the benefit of the dominant party. A wife may provide security for her husband's business debts for reasons of love and affection as opposed to undue influence, but it depends on the facts of each case. There have been a number of cases in recent years, where a wife has claimed that her husband has used undue influence to coerce her to sign her interest in the matrimonial home to a bank or other creditor, in order to secure a loan for her husband's business debts. When the business fails and the bank seeks to recover the property, the wife then attempts to avoid the bank gaining the property by showing the agreement she signed was as a result of undue influence by the husband. The bank will not be able to enforce the agreement if it had actual or **constructive notice** of undue influence. Constructive notice means that the bank does not actually know there has been undue influence by the dominant party, but it is legally deemed to know this.

Barclays Bank plc v O'Brien (1994)

Facts: Mr O'Brien persuaded his wife to sign a guarantee for an overdraft for his company using the jointly-owned matrimonial home as security. He told her the overdraft was limited to £60,000 and would only last three weeks, when in fact the overdraft was for £120,000. The bank had not ensured that Mrs O'Brien was fully aware of the nature of the transaction and had received independent advice. Mr O'Brien's business collapsed and Mrs O'Brien sought to have the guarantee she had signed set aside.

Decision: The bank had constructive notice of the undue influence. The bank should have made sure that the transaction had been fully explained and understood by the wife.

Provided a bank advises the parties to a contract to take independent legal advice, the bank will have discharged its liability and will not be deemed to have constructive notice of undue influence. It is not up to the bank to check that the advice given is delivered competently. In *Royal Bank of Scotland v Etridge (No 2)* (2001) the House of Lords stated that a bank is 'put on enquiry' whenever a wife (or other partner) offers to stand as **surety (guarantor)** of her husband's debts. Once a bank has been 'put on enquiry' then it must take reasonable steps to satisfy itself that the wife understands the nature and basic elements of the transaction she is intending to enter into. This can be satisfied if a solicitor advising the wife, separately from her husband, confirms to the bank that appropriate advice has been given.

Royal Bank of Scotland v Etridge (No 2) (2001)

Facts: A wife agreed to a charge, to the bank, on her joint interest in the family home as security for her husband's business debts. She later claimed undue influence because she had not been given independent advice. She had been advised by a solicitor, but she argued that she regarded the solicitor as working for her husband. On the facts, the wife was unsuccessful in her claim but the House of Lords set out guidelines relating to undue influence where a wife (or other partner in a relationship) stood as surety (guarantor) for her husband's debts.

Decision: A bank is automatically put on enquiry whenever a wife (husband or non-married partner) acts as surety for her husband's debts. The bank should take reasonable steps to satisfy itself that the wife had been fully informed of the implications of the proposed transaction. The bank can rely on confirmation from a solicitor, acting for the wife, that he had advised her appropriately. If the bank does not take reasonable steps to inform the wife of the risks she is taking, then the bank will be deemed to have notice of any undue influence exerted on her.

Key Concept Duress is where a party has entered into a contract after the other party has threatened physical violence or serious economic coercion. Undue influence is where a party has entered into a contract after excessive persuasion has been applied by the other party. Undue influence is presumed where there is a relationship of trust and confidence.

The presence of duress or undue influence will make a contract voidable.

Illegality

An agreement may possess the necessary elements of a valid contract but neither party will be able to enforce the contract because it is illegal. A contract may be illegal because its purpose is illegal, or because the manner in which the contract is to be performed is illegal. A contract which does not actually break the law but is against public interest may also be illegal. An illegal contract is void and unenforceable. A party, who at the time of making a contract knows that it is for an illegal purpose, may not be able to recover any monies paid or property exchanged under the contract. If Trevor pays a contract killer £50,000 to shoot his business partner dead and the contract killer fails to do so, Trevor cannot ask the court to assist in the recovery of his money. A contract may be illegal at common law or under statutory legislation.

Contracts which are Illegal under Statute

Some types of contracts are expressly or impliedly illegal by legislation. An Act of Parliament may expressly prohibit certain types of agreement. The Act may state that such agreements are contrary to the criminal law, or alternatively prohibit the making of such contracts, rendering them void but not criminal. The Competition Act 1998 prohibits price fixing agreements and other anti-competitive practices. Under the Competition Act, agreements between manufactures and retailers under which the retailer agrees not to sell items below list prices are, in certain circumstances, illegal. If this is the case and a retailer breaks a price fixing agreement selling goods below the list price, the manufacturer would not be able to sue him in court for breach of contract.

Business Insight Rewards for information about cartels

Illegal agreements (cartels) between businesses to fix prices and share markets cause considerable damage to other businesses and are detrimental to consumers. The Competition and Markets Authority offers financial rewards of up to £100,000 (in exceptional circumstances) for information about cartel activity. Companies found guilty of cartel activities can be fined up to 10 per cent of their turnover. Individuals can face up to five years' imprisonment and an unlimited fine if found to have been involved in cartel activities and to have acted dishonestly.

A statute may impliedly render a contract void. The statute does not expressly state a certain type of contract is illegal, but the provisions of the statute may affect a contract making it illegal. For example, where a statute provides that a trader is required to have a certain type of licence to practise, if a trader practises without a licence, contracts he enters into may be void, particularly where the purpose of requiring the licence is to protect the public.

Cope v Rowlands (1836)

Facts: Under the provisions of a statute, it was illegal for a stockbroker to trade without a licence. The claimant set up a business without a licence. He did some work for the defendant which the defendant failed to pay for. The claimant sued the defendant.
Decision: The claimant's lack of a licence made the contract between him and the defendant illegal and unenforceable.

Contracts which are Illegal under Common Law

Contracts that are illegal under common law may be illegal because the parties agree to do something which is against the law, or for public policy reasons. Public policy is difficult to define. A contract contrary to public policy is one that is against the interests of society generally. Public policy changes over time, and what was viewed as contrary to public policy

100 years ago may have changed in the light of the development of society. In 1867 the hire of a hall for a meeting of atheists was held to be illegal, but in 1917 a court decided that a contract for a similar purpose was not contrary to public policy and not illegal.

The following are examples of contracts illegal under common law.

Contracts to commit a crime or a tort

A contract involving the commission of a criminal offence, or a civil wrong is illegal.

Everet v Williams (1725)

Facts: Two highwaymen decided to rob a stagecoach and agreed to share the proceeds of their crime. When one of the highwaymen refused to share the loot the other sued him.
Decision: The contract was illegal and the court would not enforce it. (The court ordered the barristers to pay the legal costs, fined the solicitors £50, and ordered the highwaymen to be hanged).

Contracts damaging the country's safety

Contracts made with the enemy during a war are illegal. If the contract is made before a war starts, and one of the parties becomes an enemy, all existing rights and obligations are suspended until the end of the war.

Contracts damaging a country's foreign relations

A contract is illegal if it is to perform an action in a friendly foreign state which is contrary to the laws of that state. A contract to smuggle whisky into the United States during the prohibition period, when alcohol was banned, was illegal. In the following case, a contract to export goods to a country where exportation was banned was illegal.

Regazzoni v KC Sethia (1958)

Facts: Indian law prohibited the sale of goods to South Africa. The claimant agreed to buy the defendant's jute from India, with the intention that it would first be exported to Europe, and later from Europe to South Africa. The defendant failed to deliver the jute and the claimant sued.
Decision: It was the common intention of both parties to breach the law of India and, since this would endanger friendly relations with India, the contract was illegal as contrary to public policy.

Contracts to promote corruption in public life

A contract is illegal if its purpose is the corruption of officials by bribes or payments for favours.

Parkinson v College Ambulance Ltd and Harrison (1925)

Facts: The claimant gave a charity £3,000 on the understanding that the secretary of the charity could secure him a knighthood. The claimant failed to get a knighthood and sought the return of his £3,000.

Decision: It was a corrupt practice and illegal as against public policy. The claimant could not recover the £3,000.

Contracts to defraud the Inland Revenue

Any attempt to defraud the Inland Revenue is illegal, and the courts will not enforce any agreement which includes tax evasion.

Napier v The National Business Agency (1951)

Facts: The claimant entered into an employment contract under which the defendant employer agreed to pay the claimant a low salary plus £6 expenses, when in fact his expenses were no more than £1. Expenses were not subject to income tax so the purpose of the agreement was to avoid paying tax on £5. After the claimant was dismissed, he sued for unpaid wages and expenses.

Decision: The whole agreement was contrary to public policy and therefore unenforceable.

Key Concept   A contract may be illegal because: (a) it has an illegal purpose, (b) it is to be performed in an illegal manner, (c) it is against public interest. An illegal contract is void and unenforceable.

Contracts in Restraint of Trade

A contract which restrains free competition or movement of labour is generally regarded as against the public interest and, therefore, not enforceable, although there are exceptions if the restraint is reasonable. This topic is considered in detail in Chapter 6.

Basic Terminology

Constructive notice Where knowledge of a fact is presumed by the law.

Damages Monetary compensation.

Duress A threat of physical violence or serious economic coercion.

Fiduciary relationship Relationship of confidence and trust between two parties.

Guarantor A person who is legally bound to pay another person's debts if the latter fails to do so.

Misrepresentation A false statement of fact which induces a party to enter into a contract.

Objective test What the reasonable person would believe.

Operative mistake Where the mistake is so fundamental to the contract that the courts will regard the contract as void.

Rescission Remedy granted by the courts which sets the contract aside and puts parties back into the same position they would have been in if the contract had never been entered into.

Subjective test Judging the defendant by his own capabilities.

Surety A person who is legally bound to meet another person's obligations if the latter fails to do so.

Tort A civil wrong for which a remedy, usually compensation, may be awarded to the wronged person.

Undue influence Where some form of improper pressure has been put on a person to enter into a transaction.

Vitiating factors Invalidating reasons.

For an online flashcard glossary visit the Online Resource Centre

Summary

After studying this chapter students should be able to:

Define statements that constitute actionable misrepresentations

- A misrepresentation is a false statement of fact, made before or at the time of making a contract, by one party to the other, which induced the other party to enter into the contract.
- The statement may be written, oral, or by conduct and must be more than an opinion.

Distinguish between fraudulent, negligent, and innocent misrepresentation and be aware of the remedies available for each type of misrepresentation

- Fraudulent misrepresentation is where a party makes a false statement that he does not believe is true. The innocent party is entitled to damages for all losses he has suffered, and rescission of the contract.
- Negligent misrepresentation is a false statement made by a person who believes that the statement is true, but has no reasonable grounds for that belief. The innocent party is entitled to damages and rescission, or, if fairer, only damages.
- Innocent misrepresentation is a false statement made by a person who has an honest and reasonable belief in its truth. The innocent party is entitled to rescission or damages.

Explain the types of mistake and their effect on a contract

- Only where a mistake is fundamental to the contract will the courts regard it as an 'operative' mistake, making the contract void.
- A common mistake is where both parties make the same mistake.
- A mutual mistake is where the parties are at cross purposes.
- A unilateral mistake is where only one of the parties to the contract is mistaken and the other party is aware of the mistake.

For an online printable version visit the Online Resource Centre

Describe how duress and undue influence may arise and their effect on contracts

- Duress is where a party has entered into a contract after the other party has threatened physical violence or serious economic coercion.
- Undue influence is where a party has entered into a contract after excessive persuasion has been applied by the other party. It is presumed where there is a relationship of trust and confidence.
- The presence of duress or undue influence will make a contract voidable.

Outline the types of contract that are illegal

- A contract may be illegal because of the type of contract, its purpose, or because of the manner in which the contract is to be performed.
- A contract which does not actually break the law but is against public interest may also be illegal.
- An illegal contract is void and unenforceable.

Questions

For outline answers visit the Online Resource Centre

1. In October, Atomic Kat Ltd begins negotiations with Alcopops plc for sponsorship for Atomic Kat, a famous pop group. In November, Natasha from Atomic Kat informs the rest of the members of the group that she is thinking of going solo. In December, Atomic Kat Ltd sign the sponsorship contract with Alcopops plc under which Atomic Kat Ltd agrees to promote Alcopops in return for sponsorship of £50,000 in Atomic Kat's forthcoming six-week Christmas tour. At the end of the first week on tour, Natasha announces publicly she is leaving the group.

Advise Alcopops plc who have stated they would not have entered into the contract if they had known Natasha was leaving.

2. Lulu owns a luxury watch and jewellery store in Brighthelm. She receives an e-mail order for two top-of-the-range watches, costing £2,000 each, from Terry who claims to be from Anex Design, an interior decorating company which requires the watches quickly as retirement presents for two of their long-serving employees. Lulu has the watches in stock and she agrees to sell them on receipt of a company cheque. The cheque arrives the next day and Lulu sends the watches to Anex Design.

The following day Heather comes into the store and wishes to buy a diamond ring, priced £1,000. Heather writes out a cheque, but Lulu explains that the store does not take personal cheques. Heather replies 'You must know my face—I'm the famous actress Heather Miles. I live here in Brighthelm' and shows Lulu her equity card which contains a photo and the name 'Heather Miles'. Lulu looks up the phone book and sees that a Heather Miles lives in Brighthelm. She accepts Heather's cheque and lets her take the ring away.

The cheques from Anex Design and Heather Miles are dishonoured. Lulu has now discovered that Anex Design does not exist and the watches have been sold on to Chris and Barbara, and that the diamond ring has been sold on to Kia. Advise Lulu.

3. Discuss what is meant by common mistake, mutual mistake, and unilateral mistake in the law of contract and explain the effect mistake will have on a contract.

4. A contract entered into where there is undue influence or duress is voidable but what constitutes: (a) duress, and (b) undue influence?

Further Reading

Poole, *Contract Law*, 12th edn (Oxford University Press, 2014) Part 4.

Richards, *The Law of Contract*, 11th edn (Pearson, 2013) Chapters 9, 10, 11, and 12.

Taylor and Taylor, *Contract Law Directions*, 4th edn (Oxford University Press, 2013) Chapters 7, 8, and 9.

Turner, *Unlocking Contract Law*, 4th edn (Routledge, 2013) Chapters 8, 9, 10, 11, and 12.

Online Resource Centre

Test your knowledge by trying this chapter's **Multiple Choice Questions.** Visit:

www.oup.com/uk/orc/law/company/ jonesibl3e/01student/mcqs/ch07/

For more information, updates, and multiple choice questions, please visit the Online Resource Centre at:

www.oup.com/uk/orc/law/company/ jonesibl3e/

Discharge of Contract and Contractual Remedies

Introduction

Discharge of a contract means that the obligations of the contract come to an end. When discharge occurs, all duties which arose under the contract are terminated. There are four main ways in which a contract may be discharged. These are: by agreement, performance of the contract, frustration (for example, where the contract becomes impossible to perform), and breach of contract by one of the parties. In addition some statutes give consumers the right to cancel contracts within a short time limit. For example the Consumer Contracts (Information, Cancellation and Additional Charges) Regulations 2013 give consumers the right to cancel certain contracts for goods or services within 14 days where the contract was made in someone's home or workplace. Where a contract has been breached, the innocent party may seek a remedy from the court. There are two common law remedies: damages, and an action for price, and if the court is satisfied that there has been a breach of contract, a party is entitled to an appropriate common law remedy. However, the innocent party may ask the court to grant an equitable remedy, such as specific performance (where a party is ordered to carry out the terms of the contract). Where a party seeks an equitable remedy, the court has a discretion whether to award it or not and will not award it unless the legal remedy is inadequate and it is not unfair to do so.

Learning Objectives

After studying this chapter you should be able to:

- Explain how a contract can be discharged through agreement between the parties.
- Outline the elements necessary for a contract to be discharged by performance.
- Describe the meaning and effect of frustration of a contract.
- Explain the meaning of breach of contract and understand its consequences.
- Demonstrate knowledge of the remedies for breach of contract.

Discharge of a Contract

When a contract comes to an end it is said to be discharged (see Figure 8.1). All obligations under the contract finish and the parties are no longer bound in law. There are four methods of terminating a contract. The most satisfactory conclusion is where both parties fully perform their contractual duties, but a contract may also be terminated by the parties' agreement or by an event making it impossible to complete the contract. Where one party breaches a fundamental term of a contract, the other party may elect to discontinue with the contract.

Figure 8.1 Discharge of a contract

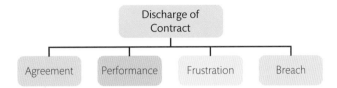

Discharge by Agreement

The parties to a contract may agree to bring a contract to an end before all the obligations under it have been completed. This is discharge by agreement (see Figure 8.2). The agreement to end a contract before it is completed is actually a second contract between the parties, and this second contract is binding on the parties provided all the necessary elements of a contract are present. The discharge may be bilateral or unilateral.

Bilateral agreement to discharge

This is where neither party has completed all their obligations under the contract. They both agree to release each other from completing the contract, each receiving a benefit from the discharge. There is consideration as they have both given something up in releasing each other from the obligations under the contract.

Unilateral agreement to discharge

This is where one party has performed all their obligations under the contract, and the other party has not, but wishes to be released from their obligations to do so. An agreement to release the party who has not performed all their obligations will only be binding if that party provides some consideration for the release, or the agreement is made by deed. (A deed is a legal agreement which has been signed and witnessed.) Where consideration is provided for the release, the agreement is called an *accord* and the supply of consideration is called *satisfaction*. Therefore, the arrangement made between the parties can be referred to as *accord and satisfaction*.

Figure 8.2 Discharge of contract by agreement

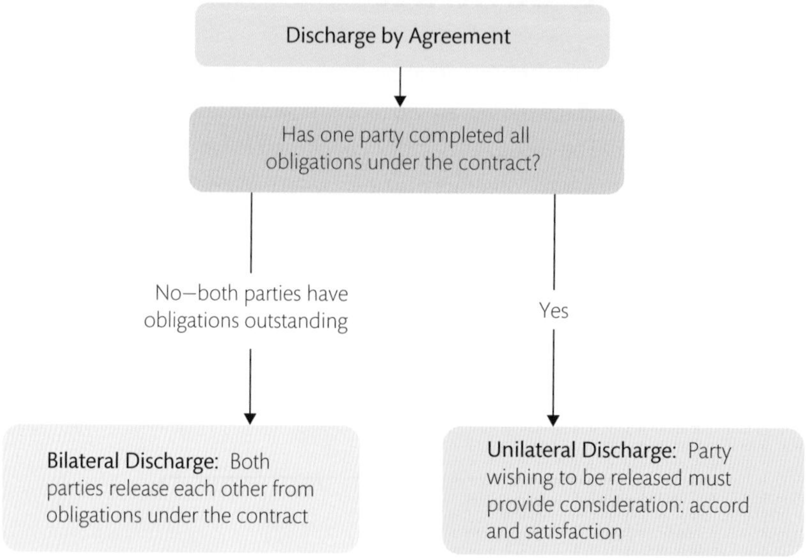

Discharge by Agreement

Has one party completed all obligations under the contract?

No—both parties have obligations outstanding

Yes

Bilateral Discharge: Both parties release each other from obligations under the contract

Unilateral Discharge: Party wishing to be released must provide consideration: accord and satisfaction

Discharge by Performance

The ideal method of discharge of a contract is that each party does precisely and exactly what they promised to do, so that the contract ends because all the obligations under the contract have been performed (see Figure 8.3). The general rule is that performance must exactly match what was agreed by the parties. It must not be something less than agreed. A party who does not totally complete his side of the contract cannot generally sue on it. The strict interpretation of this rule sometimes leads to unjust results, as can be seen in the following classic case.

Cutter v Powell (1795)

Facts: Cutter contracted to act as second mate on a ship from Jamaica to Liverpool. It was agreed he would be paid £30 guineas provided he completed the journey. He completed most of the journey but died a few weeks before the ship reached Liverpool. His widow sued the ship owners for his wages up until his death.

Decision: The contract required entire performance, and payment was agreed on completion of the voyage and not on a weekly or daily basis. Cutter had not completed the voyage; therefore, his widow was not entitled to any payment.

Where the obligations under a contract are seen as a single transaction that cannot be broken down in any way, it is an entire contract and, unless the parties agree otherwise, the contract is to complete the entire obligation. In *Cutter v Powell* the widow had claimed for wages to be paid on a *quantum meruit* basis, which means 'as much as he has earned', but the payment was refused because the contractual terms required completion of the voyage. As the general rule relating to entire performance can have harsh results, the courts allow four exceptions, which are: substantial performance, divisible contracts, partial performance, and prevention of complete performance. It depends on the circumstances and facts of the case whether the court will allow recovery of some payment under one of the exceptions.

Key Concept Discharge of a contract by performance

The general rule is that performance must exactly match what was agreed by the parties and it must not be something less than agreed. There are four exceptions whereby a contract is partly enforceable even though performance has not been fully completed.

Substantial performance

Where a contractual obligation is regarded as an entire requirement, a party may be entitled to payment for the work they have carried out if they have almost or very nearly completed the whole contractual obligation. If the court decides that a party to a contract has substantially carried out the terms of the contract, it will allow him to recover costs for the work he has done, less an amount to cover the obligations that he has not completed. In the following case, less than 10 per cent of the work was outstanding and the court allowed the claimant to recover costs for substantially completing the contract.

Hoenig v Isaacs (1952)

Facts: The defendant contracted with the claimant to decorate and furnish his flat for £750. The defendant paid £400 while the work was being carried out, but he refused to pay the remaining £350 because of defects in a bookcase and wardrobe (which it was established would cost £55 to correct). **Decision:** The contract was substantially performed and only in some minor details did it differ from the terms agreed. The claimant was entitled to the contract price less the cost of correcting the defects.

Whether the contractual obligations have been substantially carried out or not, is a matter of fact to be decided by the court. In the following case, the court took a different view to *Hoenig v Isaacs* and decided that substantial performance had not taken place.

Bolton v Mahadeva (1972)

Facts: The claimant entered into a contract with the defendant to install a central heating system for £560. The central heating was defective and required substantial work to repair the defects, which cost £174.

Decision: The cost to repair the central heating was too great a proportion of the original cost to accept the contract had been substantially performed. Therefore the claimant could not recover any payment for the work he had done.

Divisible contracts

Some contracts are divisible into parts, and payment becomes due at various stages of performance as opposed to at the completion of all the obligations. Most contracts of employment are divisible. Employees are paid weekly or monthly as opposed to when they leave their employment, even when they have entered into a fixed term contract of employment. A contract to build a house is generally divisible into three parts with payment due at each stage reached: foundation, roof, and completion. Whether a contract is an entire contract as in *Cutter v Powell* or a divisible contract as in *Ritchie v Atkinson*, considered next, depends on the intentions of the parties and the express and implied terms of the contract.

Ritchie v Atkinson (1808)

Facts: A ship owner contracted with owners of a cargo of hemp to transport the hemp at £5 a ton. The ship owner only transported part of the load. The owners claimed they were not bound to pay any transportation costs as the ship owner had not transported all the hemp.

Decision: The obligation to carry the hemp was divisible, and the ship owner could claim for each ton of cargo that had been carried.

Acceptance of partial performance

Where a contract is not divisible and is an entire contract, it may be possible to show that the other party has voluntarily accepted partial performance. Where a party accepts partial performance of a contract, then he must pay an appropriate price for the work completed. For example, Mick enters into a contract with Booze Bros for the purchase and delivery of 24 cases of Australian 2010 wine for £900 and Booze Bros delivers 20 cases of Australian 2010 wine. Mick can either reject all the cases or accept the 20 cases of wine, in which case he will have to pay for them. The parties are in fact abandoning their original contract, both giving up their obligations under it and making a second contract on different terms.

The party accepting partial performance of the other party's obligations must have a genuine choice whether to accept or reject the goods or work done. In *Sumpter v Hedges*, the claimants failed in their claim for payment for partial performance because the defendants had no option but to accept the incomplete work. However, the defendants did have a choice as to whether or not to use materials left behind by the claimants and so had to pay a reasonable sum for them.

Sumpter v Hedges (1898)

Facts: The claimant, a builder, contracted with the defendant to construct two houses and a stable on the defendant's land for £565. After completing some of the work, the claimant abandoned the site. The defendant completed the work himself using the materials left by the claimant. The claimant sued for the cost of his materials and for the work done (valued at £333). **Decision:** The work had not been substantially completed. The defendant had not voluntarily accepted partial performance by the claimant. He had been given no choice because the claimant had just left; therefore, the claimant was not entitled to any payment on a *quantum meruit* basis. However, the defendant had chosen to use the materials left by the claimant and was liable to pay for them.

Prevention of complete performance

A party is entitled to recover the costs of partially completing a contract if he is prevented from completing all the work he has agreed to undertake due to the fault of the other party. The party who prevents performance is in effect in breach of contract for preventing the contract being completed and the other party can sue for damages for breach of contract. Alternatively, the other party can sue for the work he has done to date and be paid on a *quantum meruit* basis.

Planche v Colburn (1831)

Facts: An author agreed to write a book, as part of a series of books on a particular theme, for payment of £100 on completion of the book. After the author had started researching and writing his book, the publisher decided to stop publishing the series of books, and informed the author that his book was no longer required.

> **Decision:** The author was entitled to part-payment of £50 on a *quantum meruit* basis, for preparation of a book which he had been prevented from finishing.

Figure 8.3 Discharge of a contract by performance

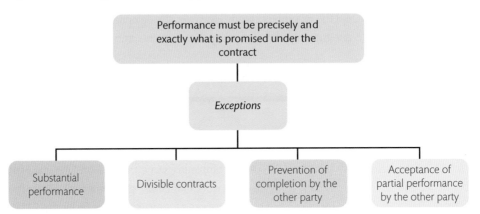

Discharge of a Contract by Frustration

After a contract has been formed but before all the obligations under the contract have been completed, an event may occur which causes the contract to be frustrated. In order for the event to terminate the contract, it must occur through no fault of either of the parties, and must make performance of the contract impossible, illegal, or radically different from what had been agreed. Where a contract is frustrated, both parties are discharged from carrying out any further obligations imposed by the contract (see Figure 8.4). The courts are reluctant to accept anything but the most fundamental changes as frustrating events. Examples of events where contracts have been held to be frustrated include: destruction of the subject matter of the contract, illness of one of the parties, non-occurrence of a central event, subsequent illegality of the contract, and government intervention.

Situations leading to frustration of a contract

There are a number of situations which are so fundamental to the contract that, if present, would result in the contract being frustrated. These include the following.

The destruction of the subject matter of the contract

A contract will be frustrated where the object of the contract becomes impossible, after the contract has been made, because the subject matter of the contract has been destroyed or it is not possible to use it.

Taylor v Caldwell (1863)

Facts: Caldwell agreed to rent a music hall for a series of concerts over 4 days from Taylor. After the contract was agreed, but before the concerts had taken place, the music hall was destroyed by fire. **Decision:** Performance of the contract was impossible; therefore, the contract was frustrated, and both parties were released from their obligations under it.

In the following case the Spanish Authorities had banned the use of the venue.

Gamerco SA v ICM/Fair Warning (Agency) Ltd (1995)

Facts: The claimant agreed to promote a rock concert for Guns N' Roses in a stadium in Madrid (the home of Atletico Madrid). The Spanish authorities declared the stadium unsafe and banned its use until further tests. There was no other venue available. **Decision:** The contract was frustrated because the use of the stadium was banned.

Personal incapacity of one of the parties

A personal contract, such as a contract of employment, is ended by frustration if one of the parties to the contract dies. Illness will not usually frustrate a contract, particularly if it is relatively short term. But if a party becomes permanently incapable of performing the contract through illness, it will be frustrated.

Condor v Barron Knights (1966)

Facts: Condor contracted to be drummer in the Barron Knights. The contract stated that he must be available to perform seven nights a week, if required. Condor became ill and was advised by the doctor to rest and work not more than four nights a week. **Decision:** The contract was frustrated by Condor's health preventing him from performing his duties.

If a contract requires the presence of a particular person, the contract may be frustrated even if they are not dead or seriously ill, if there is a good reason for their unavailability, such as imprisonment or conscription into the army.

Morgan v Manser (1948)

Facts: A contract for 10 years commencing in 1938 was made between a music hall artiste and his manager. The artiste was unavailable for work between 1940 and 1946 because he was conscripted into the army.

Decision: The artiste's presence was central to the contract; as he was unavailable the contract was frustrated, and both parties were released from their obligations.

Non-occurrence of event central to the purpose of a contract

A contract may be frustrated if the parties have based the whole purpose of the contract on some forthcoming event which is cancelled. The parties must have made the contract on the understanding that an event will happen, and the cancellation of the event must make the contract radically different from what the parties contemplated. The non-occurrence of the event must be the fault of neither of the parties. The following two cases resulted from the cancellation of King Edward VII's coronation, and demonstrate the difference between a contract where the only purpose for the hire of a flat related to the coronation of the King, and a contract where part of the purpose of the contract could still be carried out.

Krell v Henry (1903)

Facts: The coronation of Edward VII had been planned for June 1902 and processions were due to take place on 26 and 27 June. On 20 June the defendant, Henry, hired a flat for 26 and 27 June in order to watch the processions. In the contract there was no specific mention of the purpose of the hire but it was clear to both parties that it was to watch the processions. Edward VII was ill and the coronation was cancelled. The defendant refused to pay for the flat.

Decision: Watching the procession was the sole purpose of hiring the flat; therefore, the foundation of the contract had been destroyed. The contract was frustrated, and the defendant was not liable to pay for the flat.

In order for a contract to be frustrated, all commercial purposes of the contract must be destroyed. If there is still some purpose in a contract it will subsist, even though one of the reasons for the contract no longer exists. In the following case, the contract was not frustrated despite the cancellation of the naval review because the sole basis of the contract did not relate to that event.

Herne Bay Steam Boat Co v Hutton (1903)

Facts: As part of the coronation celebrations there was to be a naval review by Edward VII. The defendant hired a boat for the day to see King Edward's naval review, and to have a cruise around the Solent to see the fleet all together in port. When the naval review was cancelled due to King Edward's illness, the defendant claimed the contract for the hire of the boat was frustrated.

Decision: The contract for the hire of the boat was not frustrated because, although one of the purposes of the contract had gone, the main purpose was the cruise and the defendant could still use the boat to see the fleet. The commercial value of the contract had not been destroyed.

Subsequent illegality

If a contract is legal when it is made but afterwards there are changes in the law, or circumstances alter making the fulfilling of the obligations under the contract illegal, the contract will be frustrated. Where obligations under a contract have become illegal, the contract itself cannot be legally enforceable. A contract made with a foreign national before a war will become illegal if the foreign state is occupied by an enemy.

Fibrosa Spolka Akcyjna v Fairbairn Lawson Combe Barbour Ltd (1943)

Facts: A contract was made in July 1939 under which an English company agreed to supply machinery for £4,800 to a Polish company. In September 1939, before the machinery was delivered, Germany invaded and occupied Poland.

Decision: The contract was frustrated because it is illegal to trade with an enemy-occupied country.

Where legislation is passed making the purpose of a contract illegal, the contract will be discharged for frustration.

Denny, Mott & Dickson Ltd v James B Fraser & Co Ltd (1944)

Facts: A contract was made for the sale and purchase of timber. Under the terms of the contract, there was an option to purchase timber for a number of years. In 1939 legislation was passed making it illegal to sell timber.

Decision: The contract for the sale of timber was frustrated.

Government intervention

During national emergencies and times of war the government may, acting in the public interest, requisition goods or property. If this happens then relevant contracts relating to the goods or property will be frustrated.

Re Shipton, Anderson & Co and Harrison Bros Arbitration (1915)

Facts: A contract was made for the sale of wheat stored in a Liverpool warehouse; before the wheat was delivered to the buyer, the government requisitioned it.

Decision: Delivery of the wheat was impossible as the wheat had been legally requisitioned; therefore, the contract was frustrated.

Figure 8.4 Discharge through frustration

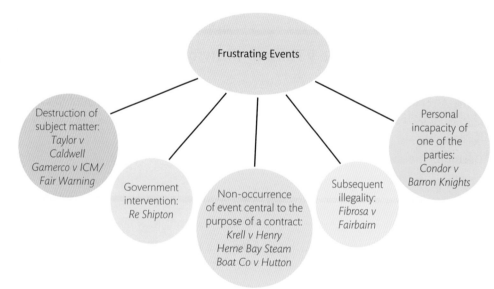

Limits of the doctrine of frustration

The courts are reluctant to allow parties to escape their contractual obligations and, therefore, there are limitations to the doctrine of frustration. These limitations include the following.

The event must occur after the contract has been entered into

The frustrating event must occur after the contract is made, but before it has been completed. If the event occurs before the contract is made, the contract may be void for mistake. For example, in *Taylor v Caldwell* (1863) the music hall burnt down after the contract was made, but before the concerts had taken place, and, therefore, the contract was discharged by frustration. Had the music hall burnt down before the contract was made, without the knowledge of the parties, then the contract would be void for mistake (see Chapter 7).

There must be no commercial purpose left in the contract

In order for a contract to be frustrated, all commercial purposes of the contract must be destroyed. It is clear from *Herne Bay Steam Boat Co v Hutton* (1903) that if there is some purpose in a contract, it will subsist even though one of the reasons for the contract no longer exists.

The parties must not have foreseen the event

A contract will not be frustrated if at the time it was made the parties foresaw, or should have foreseen, the risk of the frustrating event occurring. The courts assume the parties made the contract with the knowledge of what could happen and so agreed the terms of the contract accordingly. The exception to this is war, where, even if the parties could have reasonably foreseen the likelihood of war, contracts made with the enemy are still frustrated.

Business Insight Cost of repair exceeds market value: Is the contract frustrated?

In *Bunge SA v Kyla Shipping Company Ltd* (2012) the court reversed the decision of an arbitrator that a contract was frustrated when the likely cost of the repair ($9 million) to a ship was greater that its market value ($5.75 million). The ship which had been hired to a charterer by the owners was damaged in a collision. The owners informed the charterers that the contract was frustrated and sold the ship for scrap (the loss to the charterers was around $4 million). There was a clause in the contract stating that the owners would insure the vessel up to the value of $16 million. The judge stated that there is no general principle of law that such a contract would be discharged where the cost of repair exceeded the value of the vessel. In each case the contract between the parties had to be examined to see if it had provided for the event or allocated the risk of the event to one of the parties. As the owners had agreed to insure the vessel up to $16 million the contract was not frustrated.

The frustration must not be self-induced by one of the parties

The doctrine of frustration requires the frustrating event to be outside the control of either party. If one of the parties has caused the supervening event or it is within their control, the contract will not be discharged for frustration. In the following case, the contract was not frustrated because one of the parties had a choice on which to act.

Maritime National Fish Ltd v Ocean Trawlers Ltd (1935)

Facts: The defendants were a fishing company and owned four trawlers. They hired a fifth trawler from the claimants. In order to use the trawlers the defendants needed licences. They applied to the government for five licences but were only awarded three, which they used for their own boats. They then claimed that lack of a licence for the hired boat frustrated the contract. The claimants sued for payment.

Decision: The contract for the hire of the boat from the claimants was not frustrated, as the defendants had chosen to license their own boats and could have chosen to use one of the licences for the boat hired from the claimants.

There is no frustration if the parties have provided for the frustrating event in the contract

Parties cannot claim frustration if, when making the contract, they contemplated the frustrating event, and included a clause in the contract to cover such a situation. These clauses are called *force majeure* clauses. The clauses state the rights of the parties in the event of specified frustrating incidences outside the parties' control. By including a *force majeure* clause, parties may prevent a contract being discharged through frustration of an event that has been contemplated. In addition, the parties can specify in the contract who should bear losses. A *force majeure* clause will only prevent frustration of a contract if the actual frustrating event is one that has been contemplated and provided for by the parties.

Metropolitan Water Board v Dick Kerr & Co (1918)

Facts: In 1914 a contract was made for the construction of a reservoir to be completed within six years. The contract contained a clause allowing the time limit to be extended in the event of 'difficulties, impediments or obstructions howsoever caused'. In 1916 the government ordered the halt of the work.

Decision: The contract ceased to be operative due to frustration. The parties could not have contemplated the lengthy delays enforced by government intervention at the time of making the contract.

A contract that becomes more onerous is not frustrated

A contract is not frustrated because, as a result of an intervening event, it becomes more difficult or expensive to perform. A contract that can still be performed, but becomes less lucrative for one of the parties, is not discharged for frustration.

Davis Contractors Ltd v Fareham UDC (1956)

Facts: A building contractor agreed to build 78 houses for a local authority in eight months for £92,425. Due to poor weather, a shortage of materials, and labour shortages, the houses took 22 months to complete, and cost the builders a further £17,651. The builders claimed the original contract was frustrated.

Decision: The events that caused the delays could reasonably be expected to happen in a building contract, and did not make the contract fundamentally different from the one contemplated by the parties. The fact that a contract was more difficult or expensive to perform did not change the nature of it. The builders had contracted to build houses and their obligation had not changed. The contract was not frustrated.

A number of cases, where performance of a contract became more expensive than originally anticipated when the contract was made, arose from the Suez Canal crisis in 1956. The Suez Canal was closed, which meant that ships sailing to and from Asia to Europe could no longer use the Suez Canal but had to sail round the Cape of Good Hope in Africa, making the journey for delivery of goods much longer and more expensive.

Tsakiroglou v Noblee Thorl GmbH (1962)

Facts: A seller contracted for the sale and delivery of groundnuts to the buyer. Both parties assumed the shipment would be made via the Suez Canal. Due to hostilities, the Suez Canal was closed. The goods could have been shipped by the Cape of Good Hope but it was a longer journey and more costly. The seller claimed the contract had been frustrated.

Decision: The contract was not frustrated by the closure of the canal. The seller should have used the alternative route which was not substantially different from the envisaged route. The fact that it was more expensive was irrelevant to the issue.

Key Concept A contract will end through frustration where an event occurs, through no fault of either party, which makes performance of the contract impossible, illegal, or radically different from what was agreed.

The consequences of frustration

When a contract is discharged through frustration, then the contract automatically terminates at the point that the frustrating event occurs. Both parties are released from any further obligations under the contract. Although a contract terminates, the parties might have already incurred expenses and one of the parties might have paid a deposit. The consequences of a contract being frustrated are governed by the Law Reform (Frustrated Contracts) Act 1943.

Law Reform (Frustrated Contracts) Act 1943

The Law Reform (Frustrated Contracts) Act 1943 covers situations when a contract has been frustrated and the parties have not made their own provisions in the contract for the consequences of such an event.

The Act makes the following provisions for contracts that are discharged by frustration:

- Money owed under the contract

All money still owing under the contract ceases to be payable: s 1(2).

- Money paid in advance

Money paid in advance of performance of the contract is recoverable: s 1(2).

- Recovery of expenses incurred

The court has discretion to allow a party to retain some of the money paid, or to recover some of the money due, to cover expenses incurred in performing the contract up until the frustrating event. The court will award a sum of money which it believes to be fair in all the circumstances of the case, although this amount might not cover all the expenses actually incurred. The amount of money recoverable for expenses cannot exceed the amount of money already paid or due to be paid at the time of the frustrating event: s 1(2).

- Recovery of a sum for a value benefit

If a party has received a benefit from the other party (other than the payment of money) before the contract was frustrated, the court may order payment to be made by the party receiving the benefit. The amount awarded is what the court considers to be just in all the circumstances, but cannot be more than the value of the benefit received by the other party: s 1(3).

Gamerco SA v ICM/Fair Warning Agency (1995)

Facts: A contract was made between the claimant, a concert promoter, and the defendant, a rock group, to promote a rock concert, the contract was frustrated. The claimant had paid the defendant $412,500 in advance and both parties had incurred expenses in preparing for the concert.

Decision: It was up to the judge's discretion to award a party any expenses and there need not be an equal division of loss. The judge allowed the claimant to recover the $412,500 and, taking into account the circumstances of the case, did not allow any deduction for expenses.

BP Exploration Co (Libya Ltd) v Hunt (No 2) (1982)

Facts: Hunt had a concession from the Libyan Government to explore and drill for oil in Libya. Under a contract between BP and Hunt, BP agreed to finance the project in return for a half share in the oil concession. The agreement provided that, when oil was discovered in commercial quantities, the operating expenses were to be shared. Oil was discovered, and some extracted. The Libyan Government then withdrew the concession, and claimed all rights in the oil field. The contract between BP and Hunt was frustrated. BP had spent $87 million on development and had only recovered a proportion of its expenses. BP claimed that Hunt had obtained a value benefit under the contract before it was frustrated.

Decision: Any sum awarded should be based on the benefit that Hunt had obtained, as opposed to the sum BP had spent financing the project. The sum of $35 million was awarded to BP as this did not exceed the value of the benefit gained by Hunt.

The development of the law on the effects of frustration

Prior to the Law Reform (Frustrated Contracts) Act 1943, any rights that arose prior to the frustrating event were retained by the party who received them. This meant that, if one party received property before the frustrating event, he was entitled to keep it, and, if payment for the property was not due until after the frustrating event, he was not obliged to pay it. This is encapsulated in the phrase 'the loss lies where it falls'. When a frustrating event occurred, the result for the parties depended upon the point reached in the contract, and the same event could have different effects in different contracts. *Chandler v Webster* (1904) arose out of the events of the cancellation of the coronation of Edward VII. The facts were similar to *Krell v Henry* (1903) but, in this case, payment had been made in advance for a room to watch the coronation and, therefore, could not be recovered when the coronation was cancelled. The rule relating to non-recovery of property and advance payments was clearly unjust, and the House of Lords modified the harshness created by this principle in *Fibrosa Spalka Akeyjna v Fairbairn Lawson Combe Barbour Ltd* (1943), which allowed for the recovery of advance payments where there had been a total failure of consideration. If one party had performed none of their obligations under the contract, then advance monies paid by the other party had to be returned. Although the *Fibrosa* case reduced the injustice, it did not cover situations where some consideration had been given in return for large advance payments. In order to regulate the consequences of frustration, Parliament passed the Law Reform (Frustrated Contracts) Act 1943. The Act did not change the common law as to when contractual frustration occurs, but now governs the rights of the parties after the event.

 Key Concept When a contract is discharged through frustration, the contract automatically terminates at the point that the frustrating event occurs. Under the provisions of the Law Reform (Frustrated Contracts) Act 1943, any money owed under the contract ceases to be owed and any money already paid is recoverable. The court has discretion to award sums for expenses incurred and any benefits already received.

Discharge of a Contract by Breach

A contract is breached if one of the parties breaks one or more of the terms of the contract, or indicates in advance that he does not intend to perform the contract. Where a term of a contract is broken, the breach will only discharge the contract if the term is a condition of the contract or an innominate term where the breach deprives the party not in default of substantially the whole benefit of the contract. If the term is a warranty, the contract is not discharged.

Breach of conditions

Conditions are vital terms that go to the root of the contract. A breach of condition covers situations where there has been a failure to perform the contract at all, or where performance is so inadequate that the contract is almost meaningless. If a condition is broken, the innocent party may treat the breach of contract as a substantial failure to perform a basic element of the contract. He may then either claim damages (compensation) and regard the contract as discharged, meaning that he is free from any further contractual duties; alternatively, the innocent party may decide to just claim damages and choose to continue with the contract. As soon as the innocent party is aware that the other party does not intend to carry out their obligations under the contract, he can bring the contract to an end.

Breach of warranties

Warranties are minor terms of a contract which are incidental to the main purpose of the contract. Failure to observe warranties will not result in the collapse of the whole contract. If a warranty is broken, the innocent party can claim damages for loss suffered but must continue with the contract. Where only a warranty has been broken, the innocent party will be in breach of contract if he refuses to continue with the contract.

Breach of innominate terms

Where a term is worded broadly to cover a number of potential breaches it may not be possible to decide whether a breach of the term would have important or trivial consequences. These types of terms are called innominate terms. An injured party will be entitled to damages for a breach of an innominate term and, if he has been deprived of substantially the whole benefit of the contract, he can treat the contract as repudiated. (For further information on conditions, warranties, and innominate terms see Chapter 6.)

Actual breach of contract

An actual breach of contract takes place when performance of a contract is due and one party fails to carry out his obligations, or carries out his obligations so ineptly that the main purpose of the contract is destroyed (see Figure 8.5).

Anticipatory breach

An anticipatory breach of a contract arises where one party, prior to the actual date of performance, expressly informs the other party that they do not intend to perform some or all of their contractual obligations, or from their conduct it is clear that they do not intend to do this. The innocent party is entitled to treat the contract as at an end as soon as the other party indicates their intention not to complete the contract. The innocent party is entitled to recover damages for the loss of any benefit that they would have received if the contract had been performed.

Hochster v De La Tour (1853)

Facts: The defendant agreed to employ the claimant to act as a courier starting on 1 June. On 11 May, the defendant wrote to the claimant cancelling the contract by informing him that his services were no longer required. The claimant immediately commenced an action for breach of contract.

Decision: There was no requirement for a claimant to wait until a contract was actually breached. The claimant could bring a court action as soon as he was aware the contract was going to be breached by the defendant.

When the innocent party is aware there will be a breach of contract by the other party they do not have to sue straight away. The innocent party has a choice whether to sue as soon as they know the other party intends to breach the contract, or they can wait until the date of performance is passed and sue after the contract has actually been breached. The innocent party does not have to formally communicate acceptance of an anticipatory breach, i.e. they do not have to expressly inform the other party they are going to treat the contract as breached, but the other party must be aware of the innocent party's intention to treat the contract as at an end. The awareness may come from the conduct of the innocent party, or information received from an authorised third party. In the following case, the court had to decide if one of the parties, through their conduct, had treated a contract as ended. The court looked to see if a reasonable person would conclude that the innocent party was electing to treat the contract as ended.

Vitol SA v Norelf (1996)

Facts: V ordered goods from N, which were to be loaded and arrive by ship. Worried about delay V sent a telex to N rejecting the goods. This rejection of the goods was in breach of contract. On receipt of the telex N did not communicate with V and did not send V a bill of lading, which is usual trade practice when a cargo has been loaded. N sold the goods at a reduced price to a third party and sued V for breach of contract.

Decision: The court stated that if a party accepts a contract has ended he does not have to specially inform the other side, provided his conduct shows he is treating the contract as at an end. The issue was, would a reasonable person conclude that N was accepting the repudiation of the contract. Through their conduct, in not sending a bill of lading, N had indicated that they intended to treat the contract as ended by V's breach.

It may be advantageous for the party to wait, as the other party may change their mind and perform the contract. However, if the party does wait until the time for performance is passed, they take the risk of the contract being ended for some other reason; for example, a frustrating event intervenes and the contract is discharged through frustration.

Avery v Bowden (1856)

Facts: The defendant agreed to load a cargo onto the claimant's ship in the Russian port of Odessa within 45 days, but shortly afterwards the defendant informed the claimant that no cargo would be available. The claimant chose to wait until the end of the 45 days for a cargo. Before the end of the 45 days, war broke out between Russia and the UK and it became illegal to load a cargo at an enemy port.

Decision: The contract was frustrated. No damages could be claimed for anticipatory breach of contract, because the claimant had chosen to affirm the contract.

Once a contract is actually breached, an innocent party must take steps to **mitigate losses**. This means that a party cannot recover any losses which he could have avoided by taking reasonable steps. For example, if Asher breaches a contract with Bernice by refusing to accept delivery and pay for 100 kilograms of oranges he ordered, Bernice must mitigate his loss by trying to sell the oranges elsewhere, even if it is for a lesser sum than had been agreed with Asher, rather than let the oranges rot in a warehouse.

However, where a breach is anticipated but has not yet happened, a party has no legal obligation to accept the breach. Until a breach of contract is accepted, there is no duty to mitigate loss. Where there is an anticipatory breach, the innocent party may decide to treat the contract as continuing and perform his part, waiting until the actual time for performance before taking action, even if his loss is increased when he finally sues for damages. This principle can have unfair results as seen in the following case.

White and Carter Ltd v McGregor (1961)

Facts: The claimants were advertising agents who supplied litter bins on which they displayed adverts. The defendant contracted with the claimants to advertise his garage for three years, but later the same day he cancelled the agreement. The claimants refused to accept the cancellation, carried out their part of the contract, and claimed the agreed payment from the defendant.

Decision: Repudiation of a contract does not bring the contract to an end, but gives the innocent party the choice to accept or reject the repudiation. The claimants did not have to accept the defendant's anticipatory breach but were entitled to complete the contract. There was no duty to mitigate the loss until the breach was accepted.

The principle in *White and Carter Ltd v McGregor* is restricted to cases where no cooperation for performance is required from the other party to the contract, and where the innocent party has a genuine reason for continuing with the contract.

Clea Shipping Corp v Bulk Oil International Ltd (The Alaskan Trader) (No 2) (1984)

Facts: A contract was made for the hire of an old ship. Before the hire date, the charter party informed the ship owners they no longer wanted to hire the ship. The owners then spent £800,000 repairing the ship and keeping a full crew ready during the hire period. After the hire period the owners sent the ship for scrap, but sued the charter party for full costs.

Decision: The owners had no legitimate interest in continuing to perform the contract, and had acted wholly unreasonably, and, therefore, could not recover all sums spent.

Isabella Shipowner SA v Shagang Shipping Co Ltd (2012)

Facts: S chartered a boat from O for 61 months. S attempted to redeliver the boat 3 months before the finish date. O refused to accept the breach (and mitigate their loss) until the finish date.

Decision: No cooperation was needed from S to keep the contract alive and O had a legitimate interest in holding S to the contract. There was nothing unreasonable or perverse in O's decision. O was entitled to claim all the hire due.

Figure 8.5 Actual and anticipatory breach of contract

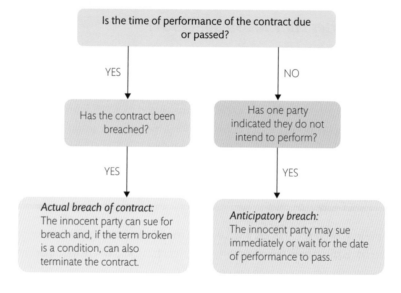

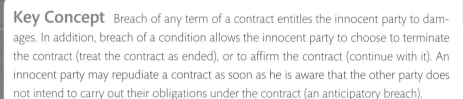

Key Concept Breach of any term of a contract entitles the innocent party to damages. In addition, breach of a condition allows the innocent party to choose to terminate the contract (treat the contract as ended), or to affirm the contract (continue with it). An innocent party may repudiate a contract as soon as he is aware that the other party does not intend to carry out their obligations under the contract (an anticipatory breach).

Remedies for Breach of Contract

If a contract is breached, the innocent party will be entitled to take court action and claim one or more of the following remedies:

- **Damages**: this is monetary compensation aimed to put the parties in the position they would have been in, if the breach had not occurred.

- Action for agreed contract price: this is an amount agreed in the contract. In some circumstances a party may sue for non-payment of the price agreed rather than damages.

- *Quantum meruit*: 'as much as he has earned'. Where performance of a contract is not completed because it has been prevented by the other party, a claim for work actually completed may be made.

- **Specific performance**: a court order requiring the parties to complete the obligations under the contract.

- **Injunction**: this prevents a party breaking their contractual obligations.

- **Repudiation**: treating the contract as ended so that further performance of the contract is not required.

Business Insight Additional statutory remedies for breach of contract where payment is by credit card

Where a customer pays for goods or services (costing between £100 and £30,000) using a UK credit card, and the provider of the goods or services breaches the contract, the customer can claim against either the provider or the credit card company (Consumer Credit Act 1974, s 75). This includes buying goods when abroad and ordering goods from overseas by telephone, mail order, or via the internet to be delivered to a UK address. There is a misconception that this provision can only be used if action against the provider fails (for example, the company providing the goods goes into liquidation before the goods are dispatched) but this is incorrect, and a customer can choose to first pursue the credit card company. The amount that can be claimed from the credit card company is not limited to the payment made. All losses incurred from the breach of contract can be claimed even if only a deposit was paid by credit card.

Damages

Damages are the most commonly sought remedy and their purpose is to compensate the innocent party. They are governed by common law rules, and a party entitled to damages for breach of contract must be awarded damages by the court. However, it is up to the court to decide the amount of damages to grant, unless the parties themselves have pre-estimated the amount of damages and stated the amount in the contract. Where the innocent party has suffered no real loss, then damages awarded will be nominal. There are rules governing how far the liability of the defendant extends (remoteness) as well as how much (measure) he must pay. The aim of damages is not to punish the party who has broken the contract, but to restore the innocent party to the same financial position he would have been in if the contract had been performed.

Remoteness of damage

When a contract has been breached, the innocent party may not be able to claim for every loss that he has incurred as a result of the breach. The court will decide how far the liability of the defendant extends. Claims for damages are restricted to the recovery of losses that are not too remote. The test for determining remoteness of damage is in two parts and was laid down in *Hadley v Baxendale*.

Hadley v Baxendale (1854)

Facts: A shaft broke in a mill. The owner ordered a new mill shaft and contracted with a carrier to deliver the new shaft. The carrier did not know that the mill owner did not have a spare shaft. The carrier was late with the delivery of the shaft, and the owner was unable to use the mill without a shaft. The owner sued the carrier claiming for loss of profits because the delivery was late.

Decision: Damages could arise from losses reasonably anticipated by the parties at the time of entering into the contract or from the parties' specific knowledge of the potential losses. The carriers were not liable because they were not aware of the importance of the delivery of the shaft.

Hadley v Baxendale established that damages will only be awarded:

- *For losses that arise naturally as a normal consequence of the breach of contract.*

This is an objective test and it means losses that a reasonable person would expect to arise from the breach of contract.

- *For losses which both parties may have reasonably contemplated when the contract was made as being a probable result of its breach.*

This is a subjective test and depends on the actual or implied knowledge of the parties at the time the contract was made. It relates to non-usual or special losses which both parties did or should have contemplated when they made the contract.

In *Victoria Laundry v Newman Industries* the claimants were only entitled to claim for losses which arose as a normal consequence of the breach, as the other party was unaware of the circumstances relating to the special losses.

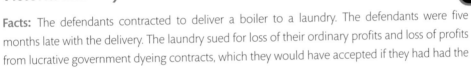

Victoria Laundry v Newman Industries (1949)

Facts: The defendants contracted to deliver a boiler to a laundry. The defendants were five months late with the delivery. The laundry sued for loss of their ordinary profits and loss of profits from lucrative government dyeing contracts, which they would have accepted if they had had the new boiler.

Decision: The defendants were liable for loss of the ordinary profits that the claimants would have made but were not liable for the loss of profits on a lucrative dyeing contract of which they had no knowledge.

In *Heron II* the loss of profits was within the reasonable contemplation of the parties and, therefore, was recoverable.

Koufos v C Czarnikow Ltd (The Heron II) (1969)

Facts: The ship owners contracted to deliver a cargo of sugar to the claimants. The ship owners knew the claimants were sugar brokers and intended to sell the sugar on arrival. The delivery was delayed, and when it was delivered the market price of sugar had fallen.

Decision: The loss of profits could be recovered because the place of delivery was a trade centre, and the ship owners knew there was a market for sugar and should have expected the buyers would have wanted to sell the sugar on. The loss was not too remote: it was within the reasonable contemplation of the parties.

Where consequences of a breach of contract are reasonably contemplated by both parties, then a party may be liable for losses even though those losses are more serious than expected.

H Parsons (Livestock) Ltd v Uttley Ingham (1978)

Facts: The claimants, who were pig farmers, entered into a contract with the defendants for purchase and installation of a food hopper. The defendants erected the hopper, but failed to unseal the ventilator. As a result the pig food went mouldy and the pigs contracted a rare intestinal disease and 254 of them died.

Decision: The defendants were liable for loss of the pigs. The food was affected by bad storage, illness was a natural consequence, and death was not too remote.

In *The Achilleas* case, in deciding whether or not a loss is recoverable, three of the judges considered that it was important to ask not only whether the defendant reasonably contemplated the loss but also whether the defendant assumed responsibility for the type of loss that actually occurred. The other two judges hearing the case took the view that the loss was within the reasonable contemplation of the parties.

Transfield Shipping Inc v Mercator Shipping Inc (The Achilleas) (2008)

Facts: A charterer of a ship (The Achilleas) redelivered the ship late. As a result, the owners of the ship had to agree a reduced rate of hire for the follow-on charter. There was an unusual 'extremely volatile market' at the time, and the market rate for hire of ships had fallen. The owners claimed that their loss was $8,000 per day for the duration of the follow-on charter and they claimed $1,364,584. The charterers argued that their liability was limited to $158,301 which was the difference between the market rate and the charter rate for the overrun period.

Decision: There had been no assumption of responsibility. The charterers were only liable for the difference in the charter rate and the market rate during the overrun period.

In the later case of *Sylvia Shipping Co Ltd v Progress Bulk Carriers* (2010) the judge stated that the standard test, whether the loss was within the reasonable contemplation of the parties at the time the contract was made, should be used in the majority of cases. Consideration of 'assumption of responsibility' would only be applied in unusual cases where using the standard test might lead to unpredictable or disproportionate liability or where such a liability would be contrary to market understanding and expectations.

Business Insight   Foreseeable losses due to the recession

In *Rubenstein v HSBC Bank plc* (2012) the Court of Appeal decided that an investor's loss of capital from market movements was foreseeable by the bank and not too remote for a claim in contract. In *John Grimes Partnership Ltd v Gubbins* (2013) the Court of Appeal allowed a property developer to claim up to £400,000 for loss in value in land as the fall in property prices at the start of the recession was reasonably foreseeable.

Measure of Damages

The purpose of damages in contract law is to put the claimant (as far as money can) in the position he would have been in if the contract had been satisfactorily performed by the defendant. When it has been established that a party is entitled to damages, the court must calculate the amount that compensates the claimant. The award of damages is not to punish the party in breach; therefore, the amount recovered should not put the innocent party in a better financial position than he would have been in if the contractual obligations had been carried out. If a party has suffered no loss, he will only be entitled to nominal damages. Any money recovered by the claimant through mitigation will be taken into account when the court assesses the claimant's loss.

Assessing the loss

The general principle is to compensate for actual financial loss. Where the contract is for the sale of goods, damages are usually assessed according to the market rule. This means that the court will look to see what the goods would have cost on the open market. If the seller fails to deliver the goods, damages are assessed on what similar goods will cost the buyer on the open market. Alternatively, if the buyer refuses to accept the goods, the seller is entitled to damages of the contract price less the amount he would gain from selling the goods on the open market. If the goods have increased in value then the seller would not have incurred any losses, but if the goods have decreased in value the seller can claim for his losses.

It must be possible to assess a claimant's loss in financial terms, although the court's inability to evaluate a claimant's loss with mathematical accuracy is not a sufficient reason for refusing to grant any compensation. The loss of an opportunity is recoverable if the lost chance can be quantified.

Joyce v Bowman Law Ltd (2010)

Facts: When acting for a buyer of a house, the licensed conveyancer negligently failed to include a buyer's option to purchase additional adjoining land for £20,000. The buyer claimed for loss of profit he could have made by redeveloping the land.

Decision: The buyer was entitled to damages of £37,700 that reflected the chance lost by him to redevelop the property.

Where a building contract is breached, the usual measure of damages will be the cost of correcting the defect. But the courts may decide that the cost of remedying the defects is totally disproportionate to the difference in value of what was supplied and what was ordered. Instead of awarding damages to repair the defects, the court will award damages to reflect the loss of value.

Ruxley Electronics and Construction Ltd v Forsyth (1995)

Facts: A contract to build a swimming pool specified that the pool would be 7 foot 6 inches deep at one end. In breach of contract, the pool was built 6 foot 9 inches deep (9 inches too shallow). The cost of reconstructing the pool was over £20,000.

Decision: No damages were awarded for the cost of reconstruction of the pool as there was no difference in value between the pool contracted for and the pool built. Only damages of £2,500 were awarded for loss of amenity.

In is clear from case authority that damages may be claimed for distress and disappointment in certain circumstances.

Jarvis v Swan Tours (1973)

Facts: The claimant booked a two-week winter sports holiday which was advertised as a 'house party'. The brochure stated there would be a welcome party, afternoon tea and cakes, and a yodelling evening. There was no welcome party, the tea consisted of crisps, and the yodeller turned up in his work clothes, did a couple of songs and left. The house party consisted of 13 people the first week, and in the second week the claimant was the only guest.

Decision: The claimant was entitled to recover damages not only for the difference in value of the holiday he had contracted for, and the one he got, but could also claim damages for disappointment and mental distress.

The scope of damages for distress and disappointment was further examined in the following case.

Farley v Skinner (No 2) (2001)

Facts: The claimant was thinking of buying a house 15 miles from Gatwick Airport. He instructed a surveyor to look at the property and specifically instructed him to assess the impact of aircraft noise on the property. The surveyor inaccurately stated that the property would be unlikely to suffer from aircraft noise. In fact the property was badly affected. The claimant sought damages for loss of amenity caused by aircraft noise.

Decision: The subject of the contract did not have to be entirely to ensure pleasure, relaxation, or peace of mind; it was sufficient if it was a major and important objective of the contract. The claimant had specifically asked for a report on aircraft noise and was entitled to damages of £10,000 for loss of amenity.

However the Court of Appeal made it clear in *Milner v Carnival Plc (t/a Cunard)* (2010) that damages awarded by the courts for ruined holidays must be consistent with awards in other fields and that distress in holiday cases 'does not equate with bereavement'. The court reduced the sum awarded for distress and inconvenience when the Milners' holiday of a lifetime cruise was ruined to £4,500 for Mrs Milner and £4,000 to Mr Milner.

Key Concept Damages are aimed at restoring the innocent party to the same financial position he would have been in if the contract had been performed, as opposed to putting the parties in their pre-contractual position.

The Duty to Mitigate

The claimant must take steps to reduce his losses. He cannot claim damages for losses which he could reasonably have avoided. The burden of proving the claimant did not mitigate his loss is on the defendant.

Brace v Calder (1895)

Facts: The claimant's fixed term contract of employment had two years to run but ended when the defendants' partnership was dissolved. The claimant was offered a new contract on similar terms with a new partnership, but refused to accept it and sued the old partnership for loss of two years' wages.

Decision: The claimant had a duty to mitigate his loss. He should have taken the new contract offered.

The innocent party is not required to take any risky measures, or to go to extraordinary lengths, to mitigate his loss. The claimant is only expected to take reasonable action.

Pilkington v Wood (1953)

Facts: The claimant purchased a house with a defective title. His solicitor had negligently failed to notice the defect when acting for the claimant in the purchase of the house. The claimant sued the solicitor. The solicitor argued that the claimant could have mitigated his loss by bringing an action against the seller of the house.

Decision: It was unreasonable to expect the claimant to take legal action against the seller.

Liquidated Damages and Penalties

If a contract does not state the amount of damages that have to be paid in advance then the damages are *unliquidated damages*, and it will be up to the court to assess how much should be paid. However, a contract itself may state a sum to be paid in the event of breach of contract. The sum stated is known as **liquidated damages**, and, provided the sum agreed in the contract represents a genuine pre-estimate of the loss, that sum will be awarded by the courts. Where damages are liquidated and the sum is less than the actual loss incurred, the innocent party cannot claim any additional damages, but if it is greater than the loss suffered, the innocent party can retain the additional amount.

If the sum stated in the contract is not a genuine pre-estimate of the loss, but is in fact a penalty payment, the courts will not enforce it. A penalty sum is one that is larger than necessary to compensate the innocent party, and is there as a punitive measure to intimidate the other party into performing their part of the contract, or to punish the party for breaching the contract. If the wording of a contract states a sum is liquidated damages, when in fact it is a **penalty clause**, the court will not enforce it, but will decide what is the correct amount of damages. Where the sum of liquidated damages is the same for different types of breaches, some more serious than others, it is likely to be regarded by the court as a penalty. If an accurate pre-estimation of the loss is almost impossible to ascertain, provided the parties have made a genuine attempt to make a reasonably accurate assessment of losses, the court will accept the sum as liquidated damages.

Dunlop Pneumatic Tyre Co Ltd v New Garage & Motor Ltd (1915)

Facts: Dunlop supplied tyres to New Garage at a trade discount and in return New Garage agreed not to sell the tyres at less than list price. Under the contract New Garage was liable to pay £5 liquidated damages for every tyre sold below list price. New Garage sold tyres at less than the list price.

Decision: It was impossible to forecast the exact loss which would be incurred by Dunlop if tyres were sold at less than list price. However, £5 was not an extravagant amount and was a genuine attempt by the parties to estimate the loss. The £5 damages per tyre sold was liquidated damages and enforceable.

Action for Agreed Contract Price

In certain circumstances, a party may sue for non-payment of the price agreed in the contract rather than damages. The amount claimed is the amount stated in the contract and, as it is an action for price and not damages, the rules relating to remoteness and mitigation are not relevant. Usually a party can only sue for the contract price if he has completed his own obligations under the contract.

Specific Performance

Specific performance is a court order given to the party in breach of contract, to perform his obligations under the contract. It is an equitable remedy, which means that it is subject to the court's discretion. This is different from an award of damages, which is a common law remedy, and must be awarded provided a breach of contract is established. If a party claims specific performance, it is up to the court to decide whether to grant the award. The court will only grant an equitable remedy if in all the circumstances, it is just to do so in respect of both parties.

The following rules are limitations to an order of specific performance

- Specific performance will not be granted where damages would be an adequate remedy. Therefore, it is not usually available for breach of contracts concerning the sale of goods as similar goods can usually be obtained elsewhere, unless the goods are a unique item such as a famous painting. Specific performance is used most commonly for the sale of land.

- Specific performance is never available for contracts of employment. The courts will not insist one party works for another.

- Specific performance will not be granted where the court cannot supervise the performance of the contract. Therefore, it is not usually granted where the obligations are of a continuing nature.

- The party seeking specific performance must not have acted oppressively or unfairly. He must have acted equitably and honestly.

Co-operative Insurance Society Ltd v Argyll Stores (Holdings) Ltd (1997)

Facts: The claimants were owners of a shopping centre. They granted a 35-year lease to the defendant for a supermarket in the centre. In the lease, the defendant agreed to keep the supermarket open during usual trading hours. Six years later, the defendant closed the store and the claimants sought specific performance.

Decision: It was unjust to insist an unprofitable business remains open, and an order for specific performance was impracticable as it would require constant supervision by the court. Damages were the appropriate remedy.

Key Concept A court order of specific performance directs the party in breach of contract to perform his obligations. As it is an equitable remedy, it will only be granted at the court's discretion if it is fair in all the circumstances.

Injunction

An injunction is a court order directing a person not to take an action which breaks their contract. It is also an equitable remedy and will only be granted at the court's discretion if it is fair in all the circumstances.

The following rules are limitations to an order for an injunction to prevent a breach of contract

- An injunction will not be granted where damages would be an adequate remedy.

- An injunction will only be granted to enforce a negative stipulation in a contract. It will not be granted to enforce a positive obligation. The negative requirement may be either expressed or implied, unless it is a contract of employment, in which case it must be expressed. The courts will not enforce a term of a contract that compels a party to employ someone or to work for another. However, where a contract contains a restraint of trade clause (see Chapter 6) the court may grant an injunction preventing a person taking up certain employment. The order must not amount to a compulsion to work for the original employer; therefore, there must be an option of taking up employment.

Warner Bros v Nelson (1937)

Facts: The film star, Bette Davis, contracted with Warner Bros not to act on stage or screen for anyone other than Warner Bros for a year. Bette Davis breached the contract and entered into a contract with a UK company to star in a film.

Decision: Warner Bros were awarded an injunction to prevent her working for the UK company. They would not be granted specific performance to force her to work for them, but could have an injunction to prevent her working for a UK film company, on the grounds that the injunction did not force her to work for Warner Bros as she could do some other type of work.

In later cases the courts have taken the view that an injunction should not be granted in an employment contract unless the employee can take up reasonable employment elsewhere, and have not required an employee to change their profession.

The courts will not grant an injunction if it has the effect of forcing a party to employ another.

Page One Records v Britton (1969)

Facts: The Troggs, a pop group, were contracted to employ the claimant as their manager indefinitely. The contract stated that they would not employ anyone else as their manager. When the Troggs attempted to appoint a new manager, the claimant sought an injunction to enforce the contract.

Decision: The court stated that the Troggs were simple persons with no business experience and could not survive without a manager. The court refused to grant an injunction as it would have the effect of forcing the Troggs to employ the claimant as their manager indefinitely.

Key Concept A court has the power to award an injunction, which is an order directing a person not to take an action which breaks their contract. As it is an equitable remedy, it will only be granted at the court's discretion if it is fair in all the circumstances.

Repudiation

This means treating the contract as ended so that further performance of the contract by the innocent party is not required. Where there is a breach of condition in a contract, the party who is not in breach may treat the contract as repudiated and no longer has to carry out his obligations under the contract.

Restitution

Restitution is not a remedy for breach of contract but it means giving back a benefit that has been obtained. The general principle on which restitution is based is that one party should not be unjustly enriched at the expense of another. Where no contract exists or where there is no longer an obligation to perform a contract, a party may reclaim money that has been paid to the other side or may have to pay for benefits received.

Quantum meruit

The term *quantum meruit* means a party should be awarded a sum representing 'as much as he has earned'. Claims may be paid on a *quantum meruit* basis for work completed so far by one party, if total performance of a contract is prevented by the other party. The claimant in *Planche v Colburn* (1831) (see earlier) was able to claim payment for research work carried out before the contract was terminated by the defendants. Where parties have entered into a contract, but have not set a price for performance of contractual obligations, the courts will award a reasonable sum on a *quantum meruit* basis.

Basic Terminology

For an online
flashcard glossary
visit the Online
Resource Centre

Damages Monetary compensation.

Discharge of a contract Contractual obligation came to an end.

Injunction A court order preventing a person carrying out or ceasing an action.

Liquidated damages A genuine pre-estimation of loss.

Mitigate losses Take reasonable steps to reduce losses.

Penalty clause A punitive clause used to prevent a party breaching a contract.

Quantum meruit As much as he has earned.

Repudiation Treating the contract as at an end.

Specific performance A court order to carry out the terms of a contract.

Summary

After studying this chapter students should be able to:

For an online printable version visit the Online Resource Centre

Explain how a contract can be discharged through agreement between the parties

- The parties to a contract may agree to bring a contract to an end before all the obligations under it have been completed.
- The agreement may be bilateral, where both parties have not completed all their obligations and have agreed to release each other.
- A unilateral agreement, where one party has performed all their obligations but the other has not, will only be binding if there is consideration or the agreement is by deed.

Outline the elements necessary for a contract to be discharged by performance

- The general rule is that performance must exactly match what was agreed by the parties.
- There are some exceptions to the rule: substantial performance, divisible contracts, partial performance accepted by the other party, and prevention of complete performance.

Describe the meaning and effect of frustration of a contract

- A contract will be frustrated if an event occurs, through no fault of either of the parties, that makes performance of the contract impossible, illegal, or radically different from what had been agreed.
- There must be no commercial purpose left in the contract; the parties must not have actually foreseen or should have foreseen the event.
- There is no frustration if the parties have provided for the frustrating event in the contract through a *force majeure* clause.

Explain the meaning of a breach of contract and understand the consequences of breach of contract

- A contract is breached if one of the parties breaks one or more of the terms of the contract, or indicates in advance that he does not intend to perform the contract.
- Where the term broken is a condition, the innocent party can claim damages and elect to repudiate the contract.
- Where the term broken is a warranty, the innocent party can claim damages but must continue with the contract.
- An anticipatory breach arises where one party, prior to the actual date of performance, expressly or impliedly informs the other party that they do not intend to perform their contractual obligations.
- When a breach of contract occurs the other party has a duty to mitigate his loss.

Demonstrate knowledge of the remedies for breach of contract

- Damages may be liquidated or unliquidated.
- The aim of damages is to restore the party not in breach to the position he would have been in if the breach had not occurred.
- Assessment of damages is made using the rules relating to remoteness, how far the liability of the defendant extends, and measure, how much (measure) he must pay.

- An action for the agreed contract price may be brought in certain circumstances.
- Specific performance is an equitable court order obliging the party in breach of contract to perform his obligation.
- An injunction is an equitable court order directing a person not to take an action which breaks their contract.
- Claims may be paid on a *quantum meruit* basis.

Questions

For outline answers visit the Online Resource Centre

1. Sally used to be the owner of a prosperous dating agency in Brighton. Three years ago she made a contract with Speedy Ltd to advertise her agency on four of their buses for a period of one year. Soon after she had made this contract, Sally decided to terminate her dating agency and become an accountant. She asked Speedy Ltd not to go ahead with the advertisements, but Speedy refused to cancel the agreement, and for the last year has been carrying out its side of the bargain. Last week Sally received a bill from Speedy Ltd for £7,000. Advise Sally.

2. Sebastian is the owner of a famous fish restaurant 'Poissons'. He has just engaged a top chef, Pierre, who has contracted to work solely for him during the next six months, and not to work in any other restaurant within a mile during that time. 'Poissons' has a large tank full of a variety of live fish from which customers choose their dinner. In breach of contract, the fish food suppliers, Shark Ltd, supply poisonous fish food on Friday morning, and by Friday evening all the fish are dead. As a result, Sebastian closes the restaurant both Friday and Saturday evening losing one hundred bookings each night. A few days later, Pierre argues with Sebastian, walks out, and goes to work in the restaurant next door. Advise Sebastian:

   a) In a claim for damages against Shark Ltd.

   b) Of any remedies he may have against Pierre.

3. Explain the meaning of 'Remoteness of damage' and 'Measure of damages'.

4. In what circumstances may a contract be discharged because of frustration?

Further Reading

Poole, *Contract Law*, 12th edn (Oxford University Press, 2014) Part 3.

Richards, *The Law of Contract Law*, 11th edn (Pearson, 2013) Parts 4 and 5.

Taylor and Taylor, *Contract Law Directions*, 4th edn (Oxford University Press, 2013) Chapters 10, 11, and 12.

Turner, *Unlocking Contract Law*, 4th edn (Routledge, 2013) Chapters 15 and 16.

Financial Ombudsman Service: http://www.financial-ombudsman.org.uk/

Online Resource Centre

Test your knowledge by trying this chapter's **Multiple Choice Questions**. Visit:

www.oup.com/uk/orc/law/company/ jonesibl3e/01student/mcqs/ch08/

For more information, updates, and multiple choice questions, please visit the Online Resource Centre at:

www.oup.com/uk/orc/law/company/ jonesibl3e/

The Law of Agency

Introduction

In the business world the law of agency is important because there are many situations where one party, known as the principal, authorises another party, known as the **agent**, to act on their behalf. Businesses would not be able to operate effectively unless transactions were carried out by agents, who may be employees of the business, or independent contractors. Generally, where a contract has been made between an agent and a **third party**, the agent has no personal rights or liabilities in the contract. The rights and duties in the contract are between the principal and the third party, although where an agent acts negligently, or contrary to instructions given by his principal, the agent may be liable to the principal. The law imposes duties on agents, whether or not an agent is paid by a principal, and gives agents certain rights (see Figure 9.4). Normally an agent discloses to a third party that he is acting on behalf of a principal, but there may be situations where an agency relationship is created where the existence of a principal is undisclosed. An agency may be terminated by the parties themselves or by operation of the law.

Learning Objectives

After studying this chapter you should be able to:

- Define agency.
- Describe the different methods by which an agency relationship may be created.
- Explain the authority of an agent.
- Identify the rights and duties of an agent.
- Understand the relationship between agent, principal, and third party.
- Explain how an agency relationship may be terminated.
- Be aware of different types of agencies.

Definition of Agency

An agency is the relationship which exists between two persons (natural or legal): the agent and the principal. The agent's purpose is to form a contract between his principal and a third party. 'Third parties' are everyone with whom the agent deals on behalf of the principal (see Figure 9.1). An agent may be an employee of the principal. A person on the checkout till at a supermarket is acting as an agent for the supermarket company in making contracts with customers for the sale of goods. Although the transaction is handled by the checkout person, the contract for the sale of goods is between the customer and the supermarket company. An agent may be an independent contractor used for his particular expertise, representing the principal in certain business transactions, for example, an insurance broker or a stockbroker. Where there is a partnership, the partners act as agents of the firm and their fellow partners. In a company, the company directors act as agents of their company. An agent may act solely for one principal or may be an agent for several principals. An estate agent will act as agent for numerous sellers (who are all principals of the estate agent) at the same time. An agent may be authorised to act in just one transaction, or more commonly in business, an agent may act regularly for a principal carrying out a range of business transactions. Usually an agency relationship is a commercial or business arrangement, but there are circumstances where an agency relationship arises where a friend or relative agrees to handle the affairs of another.

⊛ Key Concept An agent represents the principal, and creates a legal relationship between the principal and a third party.

Figure 9.1 The agent negotiates on behalf of the principal but the contract is between the principal and third party

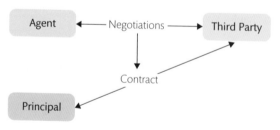

It is always important to establish whether an agency relationship has been created. Where a third party reaches an agreement with a person believing him to be acting for a principal, when in fact there is no agency relationship, the third party will not be able to pursue a legal action against the person he believed to be a principal (although he can take action against the purported agent).

The Creation of Agency

An agent must have legal authority to act on behalf of a principal in order for a contract with a third party to be binding by or against the principal. The authority to act arises when an agency relationship is created (see Figure 9.2). It is usually created by express agreement between the parties, although the agreement may be an informal one. However, it is possible for an agency relationship to be created without express consent, if circumstances exist whereby it would be unfair to a third party or agent to deny an agency relationship exists. It is also possible for a principal to **ratify** a contract so that transactions entered into by an agent without authority become legally enforceable by and against the principal.

Express Agreement

The most common method of creating an agency relationship is by an express agreement made between the principal and the agent. The principal appoints the agent and gives him actual authority to act on his behalf, either for a specific transaction, or for a variety of functions. Although there are no legal requirements to appoint an agent in writing, and an appointment may be made orally, it is usual to appoint an agent by a written contract. A seller of a house may appoint an estate agent to act on his behalf. A contract is made between the seller and the estate agent whereby the seller agrees to pay a commission to the estate agent, if the house is sold to a purchaser introduced by the agent.

In certain circumstances an agent must be appointed by deed. A deed is a formal written agreement which is signed by the parties and their signatures are witnessed by independent persons. If the principal requires the agent to execute deeds on his behalf, he must appoint the agent by deed, which gives the agent 'power of attorney'. An agent would have to be appointed by deed if the principal required the agent to transfer the principal's house to a third party, because any transfer involving land or buildings has to be executed by deed.

It is possible for an agency agreement not to be a legally binding contract because the agent is acting **gratuitously**, receiving no payment for his services. A person who agrees to collect the rent from a friend's property when he is abroad for no payment will be a gratuitous agent. In the following case, a friend who undertook to find a suitable car was held to be an agent and therefore the duties of an agent were imposed upon him.

Figure 9.2 Creation of an agency relationship

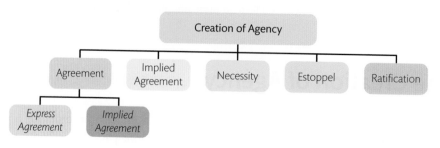

Chaudhry v Prabhakar (1988)

Facts: The claimant, who knew nothing about cars, asked her friend, the defendant, who claimed to have knowledge of cars, to find her a suitable second-hand car. She stipulated that the car should not have been involved in an accident. The defendant found a car on which he noticed the bonnet had been crumpled and straightened or replaced, but thought it was in good condition, and recommended she purchased it for £4,500. A few months later it became apparent that the car had been involved in a serious road accident, repaired badly, and was unroadworthy.

Decision: The defendant had acted as a gratuitous agent offering to find a second-hand car for the claimant. He had not shown the care and skill expected from a person with the expertise he claimed. He was in breach of his duties as an agent and was liable to the claimant.

Implied Agreement

The relationship that the parties have with each other may give rise to an implied agency agreement. It is assumed that the principal has given the agent authority to act on his behalf because of the particular position held by the agent. This type of agency often arises in an employer–employee relationship. Depending on the job, an employee has authority to contract on behalf of his employer. In company law, a company secretary has, by virtue of his position, implied authority to act on behalf of the company on administrative matters.

Necessity

An agency relationship is created through necessity, where an emergency arises which requires a person to take a particular action to protect the interests of another. There is no agreement made between the parties to act, but usually the agent is in possession of the principal's goods and an unexpected situation occurs. In order to protect the principal's interest, the agent must take action. If an agency of necessity arises, the agent can claim back his expenses from the principal. If the agent sells goods belonging to the principal, he will be assumed to have authority to deal with the goods and any third party purchasing the goods will get good title (ownership) to them.

In order for agency of necessity to arise, all the following conditions must be satisfied:

- The agent must be in control of the principal's property, and a genuine emergency must have arisen requiring the agent to take particular action to protect the interests of the principal.

- It must be impossible for the person acting as agent to get the principal's instructions. (This is unusual today in the light of electronic communications.)

- The agent must act in good faith in the best interests of the principal.

- There must be an emergency.

Usually in cases involving necessity, the person acting as agent is in possession of goods or other assets belonging to the principal and it is in relation to those goods that the emergency arises. In the following case, the railway company had to make a decision on what to do with livestock where it was impossible to get instructions from the owner, and, therefore, an agency of necessity arose.

Great Northern Railway v Swaffield (1874)

Facts: The defendant owner sent his horse by rail from Kings Cross to Sandy station. When the horse arrived at Sandy station there was no one to collect it and no one at the station knew the name or address of the owner. The claimant railway company arranged for the horse to be fed and stabled. When the defendant collected his horse, he refused to reimburse the railway company for their expenses in having the horse stabled.

Decision: The claimant had acted in the best interests of the defendant in arranging to have the horse stabled. An agency of necessity had arisen and the defendant was bound to pay for the cost of stabling the horse.

This case can be contrasted with the next case, where no agency of necessity arose because it would have been possible for the railway company to seek instructions from the owners of the tomatoes (who in court stated they would have sent up a lorry to collect the goods in the event of a rail strike).

Springer v Great Western Railway (1921)

Facts: A cargo of tomatoes arrived at Weymouth station. The defendant railway company was contracted by the claimants to deliver the tomatoes to Covent Garden. There was a railway strike, and the railway company, noticing that the cargo of tomatoes were in poor condition, sold them locally. **Decision:** It would have been possible for the railway company to seek the instructions of the owners of the tomatoes by sending a telegram. They had been contracted to carry, not to sell, the tomatoes. To give them the right to sell, circumstances must exist which put them in the position of agents of necessity for the owners. As the railway company could have communicated with the owners, there was no agency of necessity.

An agency of necessity does not arise merely because someone no longer wishes to retain another person's goods for them.

Sachs v Miklos (1948)

Facts: The defendant agreed in 1941 to store some of the claimant's furniture without charge. By 1944 the defendant had lost touch with the claimant and letters written to his previous known address were returned. In order to gain some space, the defendant sold the claimant's furniture. When the claimant later returned, he sued and the defendant claimed an agency of necessity had arisen. **Decision:** There was no agency of necessity as no emergency had arisen when the furniture had been sold. It was not as though the house that the furniture was stored in had been destroyed and the furniture left exposed to thieves and the weather. The house was available for storage of the furniture.

Agency by Estoppel

An agency by **estoppel** is created where the principal's words or actions give the impression that he has consented to a person acting as his agent. The principal is then prevented or stopped from denying this later. The third party making the contract with the agent can presume that the agent has authority to act because of representations made by the principal. The representation as to the authority of the agent must have been made by the conduct of the principal, and the third party must have relied on the representation. The third party must believe that the agent has authority to act, and from the circumstances would not be expected to know the truth. The principal will not be able to reject an agreement made with a third party on the grounds that the person who was apparently acting as his agent was in fact not his agent. The agent does not have actual authority to act on behalf of the principal, but he has apparent authority and, therefore, binds the principal to the agreement.

In the following case a director was held out by a company as being the managing director with authority to enter into contracts. The company was estopped (prevented by law) from denying this, when a third party entered into a contract in good faith on reliance on this representation.

Freeman & Lockyer v Buckhurst Park Properties Ltd (1964)

Facts: The defendant company had four directors but in practice one director made all the contracts as if he were the managing director. However, he was never actually appointed as a managing director and, therefore, had no actual authority to bind the company. The other directors knew and acquiesced to this. The company refused to pay out on one of the contracts entered into by the unauthorised director.

Decision: The company was liable on the contract as they had held out the director as having the necessary authority. An agency by estoppel had been created.

Ratification

This is where an agency relationship is made retrospectively. At the time of the agreement, there is no agency relationship because the person purporting to be acting as an agent enters into an agreement with a third party, without any authority from the principal, or exceeds his authority. At this stage the principal will not be bound by the agreement, which will actually be between the third party and the person purporting to be acting as the agent. However, the principal may ratify the agreement provided certain conditions are in place. The principal will then be bound by its terms. Ratify means to authorise or approve an agreement after it has been made. It is up to a principal whether he wishes to ratify an agreement and there is no obligation on the principal to do so. The ratification may be expressed or inferred through conduct.

In order for an agreement to be ratified the following conditions must be met:

- The agent must have purported to be acting as an agent and either named the principal or, if not actually named, the principal must be capable of being identified by the third party. A principal that cannot be identified by the third party cannot subsequently ratify an agreement. In the following case the defendant understood that the person they were making the contract with was acting as an agent for a named principal.

Borvigilant (Owners) v Owners of the Romina G (2003)

Facts: The claimant's tug and the defendant's tanker collided and the tug sank. At the time, the tug had been chartered by NIOC, a company which had entered into an agreement with the defendant. The claimant wanted to rely on various terms in the agreement made between NIOC and the defendant, and purported to ratify it.

Decision: The defendant was aware of the claimant's existence and it was clear from the agreement that the defendant understood NIOC to be the agent of the claimant. The claimant could ratify the agreement.

Ratification is not applicable unless the person making the contract professes to act as an agent. A court will not allow an agreement to be ratified when, at the time of making the contract, the other party believes he is actually contracting with the agent and is unaware of the existence of a principal.

- The ratification must take place within a reasonable time of the contract being made. How long is a reasonable time depends on all the circumstances. If, before ratification, a third party acquires rights which would be adversely affected by ratification then the possibility of ratification may be lost.

- The principal must adopt the whole contract with full knowledge of what it entails. He cannot pick and chose the parts of the contract that suit him and reject other parts of the contract.

- The principal must have had legal capacity to make the contract when the agent made it and when it was ratified. If the principal was not in existence at the time the agent entered into the contract, he will not be able to ratify it later. A company does not come into existence until it is registered at Companies House and, therefore, persons intending to form a company cannot act as its agents beforehand. A company will not be able to ratify any agreement entered into before its existence. The persons who made the agreement will be personally liable.

Kelner v Baxter (1866)

Facts: Baxter, Calisher, and Dales, intending to form a company at a later date, contracted to buy wine for £900 from the claimant. When the company was formed it purported to ratify the contract. The wine was consumed and the company went into liquidation before paying the claimant's bill for £900.

Decision: The ratification was not effective because the company was not in existence at the time the contract for the wine was made; therefore, the company did not have capacity to enter into contracts. Baxter, Calisher, and Dales were personally liable.

Where an agreement is ratified by a principal, the arrangement is the same as if the agent had actual authority at the time of making the agreement. This means that, if a contract was entered into on Monday by someone purporting to be acting as an agent, but not ratified by the principal until Friday, the contract is effective from the Monday. The following case concerns an offer which was accepted without authorisation. The third party later attempted to withdraw the offer; however, the principal then ratified the contract. As the acceptance predated the attempted withdrawal, the contract was valid.

Bolton Partners v Lambert (1889)

Facts: The defendant wrote to S, who was the acting managing director of the claimants' company, offering to purchase Lavenham Sugar Works. The offer was accepted by S on behalf of the claimants. Although S was the agent of the claimants, he was not authorised to make any contract for sale. A few days later, the defendant stated he was withdrawing his offer; however, the claimants then ratified the acceptance made by the acting managing director.

Decision: The ratification by the claimants made the contract valid from acceptance; therefore, there was a binding contract between the claimants and the defendant.

Although this may seem unfair to third parties, it has to be remembered that a contract has to be ratified within a reasonable time and at the time of making the contract the third party believed they were contracting with an agent and expected to be bound by the contract. The ratification is usually communicated in writing or orally, but it may be inferred through conduct if the principal demonstrates that he is accepting the contract made by the purported agent, for example, by retaining and using goods delivered.

A void contract can never be ratified. There is no binding agreement between the agent and the third party to be validated by ratification.

If an agreement is not ratified by the person named as principal and there is no agency arrangement in place, the contract is between the purported agent and the third party. Any action for breach of contract will be between the third party and purported agent. The third party will not be able to take any action against the alleged principal.

Authority of an Agent

A contract made by an agent with a third party is binding on the principal only where the agent was acting within his authority. The authority of an agent may be actual authority, expressed or implied, or it could be apparent (ostensible) authority. It is important to understand that an agent may still be acting within his authority even where he has not been given express instructions to act on behalf of the principal. Actions by an agent which are unauthorised and outside the agent's authority will not be binding on the principal, unless the principal ratifies the contract, thereby creating an agency by ratification. A third party who deals with an agent who has no authority to act will only be able to take action against the agent.

Express Actual Authority

This is authority which is expressly given by the principal. An agent appointed expressly is not usually given authority to act in all matters but is instructed to carry out particular tasks, and given the necessary power and authority to perform those tasks. If the agent acts outside the limits of his express authority, then he may still be acting within his implied or apparent authority.

Implied Actual Authority

Implied actual authority is where the authority to act on behalf of the principal is inferred from the conduct of the parties and the circumstances of the case. It is usually authority which the agent has in excess of his express authority, expanding the powers of the agent from those that have actually been expressed by the principal. Sometimes an agent's authority may be entirely implied. Where an agent is appointed to a particular position, the principal will have impliedly agreed that the agent should have all the powers that are normally given to a person holding that position. An agent who is employed in a particular trade or business will have implied authority to act in accordance with the powers usually associated with that trade or business. In the following case, the chairman had implied actual authority to bind the company because the company had agreed through its conduct that the chairman should have the same powers as if he had been appointed managing director.

Hely-Hutchinson v Brayhead Ltd (1968)

Facts: The Board of Directors of Brayhead (B Ltd) allowed the company chairman to act as though he had been appointed as managing director of the company, although he had not been appointed to this position and, therefore, had no power to enter into certain transactions on behalf of the company. The chairman agreed, in the name of B Ltd, to provide a guarantee for a debt for Company A. When Company A defaulted on the debt, B Ltd was asked to honour its guarantee. The Board of Directors claimed the guarantee was invalid as the chairman had no authority to bind B Ltd.

Decision: B Ltd was bound by the guarantee because the chairman had implied authority to bind the company. Financial contracts that he had entered into on behalf of the company in the past had not been challenged by the Board. He had acquired implied authority to act for the company.

Usual Authority

Sometimes in law, cases are difficult to fit in with established principles. In the following case, the court decided that there was an agency agreement because an agent had acted within the usual authority of a person in his position even though there was no actual or apparent authority, in fact he had been told not to carry out the transaction. The court stated that the principal was bound by his agent who had exceeded his authority, because the principal had allowed the agent to hold himself out as being the proprietor of the business, and the agent had acted within the usual scope of authority that an agent would have had in his position.

Watteau v Fenwick (1893)

Facts: H was employed by F as a manager of a pub. H had previously been the owner of the pub and his name still appeared above the doorway. F expressly instructed H not to purchase cigars and other articles on credit. H ordered cigars on credit from W. F refused to accept the contract and W sued.

Decision: H had no actual authority to act as agent for F in ordering the cigars but he was acting within the usual authority of a pub manager and, therefore, F was bound by the contract.

There was no actual authority because the manager of the pub had been expressly prohibited from buying cigars. There was no apparent authority because the principal had never represented to the third party that the manager had authority to act. The principal was bound by the contract entered into by the agent because the agent acted within the usual authority of an agent holding that position.

Apparent (Ostensible) Authority

Apparent authority, sometimes referred to as ostensible authority, arises from a representation (either expressed or through conduct) made by a principal to a third party, that an agent has authority to act on his behalf, when in fact he does not. If the third party relies on the representation, the principal will be bound by the actions of the agent, even though the agent has acted without actual authority.

Apparent authority may arise where a principal has previously told a third party that an agent has authority to act and has since revoked that authority but not informed the third party, or when the agent has never been given authority. See *Freeman & Lockyer v Buckhurst Park Properties Ltd* (1964) and the following, more recent, case.

Racing UK Ltd v Doncaster Racecourse Ltd and Doncaster Metropolitan Borough Council (2005)

Facts: Doncaster racecourse was managed by Doncaster Racecourse Ltd (DR Ltd) but owned by Doncaster Council. Without informing the Council, Mr Sanderson, chief executive of DR Ltd, purporting to act as the Council's agent entered into an agreement with Racing UK Ltd giving Racing UK Ltd television rights over the course. The Council claimed that DR Ltd did not have authority to enter into such an agreement on their behalf.

Decision: The contract was binding on the Council. Although Mr Sanderson, acting for DR Ltd, did not have actual authority he had apparent authority. In recent years, negotiations for contracts for Doncaster Racecourse had all been conducted through Mr Sanderson. Racing UK Ltd believed that DR Ltd was an agent of the Council and there was no reason why they would think that Mr Sanderson and DR Ltd would not have authority to enter into media rights agreements.

Rights and Duties

All agency relationships are fiduciary ones, which means that they are based upon faith and trust. As a result, the law imposes various fiduciary duties on an agent, such as requiring an agent to act honestly in good faith, to avoid conflicts of interest, and not to make secret profits or take bribes. The agent is given certain rights by law of agency. Often there is also a contractual relationship between an agent and a principal, and contractual rights and duties of each of the parties are expressed or implied in the contract made between them. Gratuitous agents (agents who provide their services without remuneration and, therefore, are not contractual agents as there is no consideration) are still bound in law to comply with their fiduciary duties.

A principal's duties and rights to an agent largely reflect the agent's rights and duties to the principal. For example, an agent's right to claim **indemnity for expenses** reflects the principal's duty to reimburse the agent for expenses incurred in carrying out his functions as an agent.

Key Concept An agency relationship is based on trust. All agents owe fiduciary duties to their principals.

Duties of an Agent

Duty to perform agreed tasks and follow instructions

A contractual agent must carry out all the lawful tasks he has agreed to do for the principal, and has a duty to act in accordance with his principal's instructions. In some agency agreements, an agent may be given a wide discretion when to act; in others, a principal will give his agent particular instructions, such as when to sell property and a minimum price to accept. The agent must follow these instructions, even if he believes it might be in the principal's best interest to disobey them (see Figure 9.3).

Bertram, Armstrong & Co v Godfrey (1830)

Facts: The principal instructed his agent to sell stock when the stock reached £85 per unit. The agent delayed selling hoping the price would rise. In fact the price fell, and the agent sold the stock for under £85 a share.

Decision: The agent was liable for the loss as he had not acted in accordance with the principal's instructions.

An unpaid agent will have no duty to act as no consideration has been provided by the principal but, if he does act, he must do so in accordance with the instructions set out by the principal.

Viewpoint Seán O'Flynn, European Trader, London

Having completed my MBA in Finance in 2008 I moved to London to begin work as a trader. My first role entailed acting as an outsourced trader, primarily for hedge funds. I executed buy and sell orders in European stocks for the portfolio managers of these funds.

Our clients can give various types of instructions for the execution of their orders which place obligations upon us. Some instructions are strict and require careful adherence to price limits and volume restrictions while others are more lenient and allow a certain degree of discretion. For example a client may want to buy all of their stock at a certain price. If the stock trades at that level, we need to be involved and if we miss that opportunity to buy and subsequently the stock trades higher we may be responsible for compensating the client for the difference.

Duty to personally perform agreed tasks

Generally, an agent is required to perform his duties himself and is not permitted to delegate his tasks to others to perform, although there are a number of exceptions to this rule. A principal may expressly permit delegation of some or all of an agent's tasks, or a power to delegate may be implied as customary from trade practice. Delegation is also allowed where necessary due to unforeseen circumstances, or where the tasks delegated require little skill, such as form filling.

Duty to exercise care and skill

All agents must carry out their duties with reasonable care and skill. An agent with professional or trade skills will be expected to maintain the standard of skill and care of a person in that profession or trade. An estate agent will be liable to his principal if he does not carry out his duties with the same degree of skill as a reasonably competent estate agent.

Keppel v Wheeler (1927)

Facts: An estate agent who had obtained an offer from a purchaser to buy his principal's property, subject to contract, subsequently received an offer from another person to buy at a higher price. The agent failed to inform the principal of the higher offer and the sale was completed at the lower price.

Decision: The agent had committed a breach of duty and was liable in damages to his principal.

Even a gratuitous, non-professional agent will be liable to his principal if he fails to exercise the reasonable care and skill that a reasonable person would apply to his own affairs. If an agent claims to have a particular expertise, then he will be expected to act with the skill of a person with that expertise. In *Chaudhry v Prabhakar* (1988) the defendant, who was acting as a gratuitous agent, was liable for breach of duty when he had not shown care and skill expected from a person with the expertise he claimed to have.

Duty to account

An agent must provide full information of the transactions carried out on behalf of his principal, and account for all money and any other financial benefits arising from performance of his duties. The agent should keep his own property separate from that of the principal's property. If he does muddle them up, the principal may be entitled to all the property, unless the agent can prove which property is clearly his own. Records should be kept of dealings made on behalf of the principal, which the principal will be entitled to inspect.

Duty to avoid a conflict of interest

An agent owes a duty to his principal not to put himself in a position where a conflict of interest may arise, without informing the principal of that possibility. If the possibility of a conflict of interest has been disclosed, the principal can decide whether to allow the agent to proceed with the transaction or not. If an agent is acting for a principal in the purchase of property or shares, the agent must not sell his own property or shares to the principal without disclosure even if the sale price is fair.

Armstrong v Jackson (1917)

Facts: A principal asked his agent to purchase 600 shares in a company. The agent sold the principal shares in the company which he pretended he had bought on the open market but in fact had belonged to the agent.
Decision: The principal was entitled to have the agreement for the purchase of the shares set aside.

An agent can only act for two principals with conflicting interests where both principals agreed or where the principal must have appreciated that the nature of the agent's business was to act for numerous principals, for example an estate agent.

Rossetti Marketing Ltd v Diamond Sofa Co Ltd (2012)

Facts: A was a Thai manufacturer of leather furniture and R was a company which helped Asian furniture manufacturers to penetrate the UK market. A knew that R was acting for two of its competitors but had been led to believe that their products did not clash with its own.
Decision: R could not act for principals other than A in so far as their product ranges clashed.

Duty not to make a secret profit

An agent must not use his position as agent to secure a financial advantage for himself, unless it is done with the knowledge and authority of the principal. A secret profit includes profit that arises from the use of the principal's property or from knowledge or information which the agent has acquired through acting for the principal. This duty is enforced strictly by the courts and applies even if the principal gains from the agent's actions.

Boardman v Phipps (1967)

Facts: The agent was a solicitor to a trust that had a substantial holding of shares in a company. The agent solicitor advised the trust to buy additional shares in the company. The trust did not do so and the solicitor bought some shares himself. The company shares increased in value. The trust claimed the profits the solicitor had made on his own behalf.

Decision: The solicitor had used knowledge he had acquired while acting as agent for the trust; therefore, he had to account to the trust for the profit he had made on the shares.

Duty not to take a bribe

A bribe is where an agent accepts a secret commission or other inducement given by a third party in return for completing contracts between the third party and the principal. A bribe may include circumstances where an agent buyer is given financial or other inducements to favour a particular supplier.

Boston Deep Sea Fishing and Ice Co Ltd v Ansell (1888)

Facts: Ansell was the managing director (agent) of the claimant company. Ansell accepted commission and bonuses to purchase items from a particular supplier.

Decision: Ansell was in breach of his fiduciary duty as an agent for accepting bribes in return for orders.

A principal who discovers that his agent has been accepting bribes may dismiss the agent, recover the amount of the bribes from him, refuse to pay the agent his fees, and recover any fees paid to him. The principal may also be able to claim for any losses that he has sustained.

Business Insight 'The Law imposes on agents high standards. Footballer's agents are not exempt from this.' Lord Justice Jacob in *Imageview Management Ltd v Kelvin Jack* (2009)

If a player does not know and approve of payments made to his agent in connection with his transfer, his agent will be in breach of duty. The player will be entitled to recover payments made to his agent, and he can cancel the agency agreement. Berry (whose company, Imageview Ltd was the agent for Kelvin Jack, Trinidad and Tobago's international goalkeeper) had not told his client, Jack that, when he was going to negotiate with Dundee United to sign Jack up, he was also going to make a deal for himself. Jack had agreed to pay Imageview 10 per cent of his monthly salary if he got him signed up. Berry negotiated the deal with Dundee United and Dundee United paid Imageview £3,000 to get Jack a work permit (which he needed as he was a non-EU citizen). In real terms, the cost of getting the permit was about £750. About a year later, when Jack found out about the work permit agreement, he refused to pay any further agency fees. In the resulting court case, the court stated that Imageview had breached its fiduciary duty not to make a secret profit; therefore, Jack did not have to pay any further agency fees and was entitled to repayment of all the agency fees paid by him.

Duty to maintain confidentiality

An agent owes his principal a duty of confidentiality in respect of information he has acquired as a result of being an agent. The duty to keep the principal's business confidential can continue even after the agency relationship has expired.

Rights of an Agent

Right to remuneration

There is no automatic right of an agent to be paid for acting as an agent. However, when an agent is appointed in a contractual agreement it is usual for the amount of payment to be stated either as wages or commission, or both. Sometimes an agent will only be entitled to payment on completing a particular task. Exactly when and if payment is due depends on the agreement between the parties. Consider the following two cases. In the first case, commission was payable on the actual sale of the cinemas, and in the second case, commission was payable on completion of a contract for sale of the property.

Figure 9.3 Duties of an agent

Luxor (Eastbourne) v Cooper (1941)

Facts: The contract between the estate agent and the seller of two cinemas stated that the agent would be paid on completion of the sale. The agent introduced a purchaser who was willing and able to buy the cinemas but the seller refused to go ahead with the sale.

Decision: The sale had not taken place and, therefore, the agent was not entitled to commission.

Scheggia v Gradwell (1963)

Facts: The contract between the estate agent and the seller of premises stated that the agent would be paid commission, if within three months any person introduced by the agents entered into a legally binding contract to purchase the business and property. The agents introduced a buyer who entered into an agreement to purchase the property and business, paid a deposit, but later withdrew, and the sale did not go ahead.

Decision: The estate agent was entitled to the commission; he had fulfilled his agency duties.

Where there is a commercial agency relationship and the amount of payment is not stated, provided the agreement between the parties does not expressly exclude payment, a court will generally imply an intention to pay remuneration at a reasonable rate or the customary rate of that trade or profession. A gratuitous agent is not entitled to any payment for services carried out.

Business Insight Agent gets 6 million euros for an introduction

Where there has been an agreement to pay commission even though it is not in writing and the amount is not fixed, an agent will be entitled to some payment. In *Berezovsky & another v Edmiston & Co Ltd & another* (2011), Berezovsky (B), a wealthy Russian businessman, wished to sell a yacht he was having built for him, and asked a yacht broker, Edmiston (E), to find a buyer. E told B that F, a businessman in the United Arab Emirates, was a potential purchaser. F did not want to deal through a broker and negotiated directly with B and eventually bought the yacht for 240 million euros. B alleged that E was not entitled to commission as he had not negotiated the contract of sale. The court decided that, even though the usual course of business would be for a broker to negotiate the terms of sale, as E had introduced the purchaser and was then prevented from dealing with the negotiations, he was still entitled to commission. This was set at 3 per cent by the High Court but reduced to 2.5 per cent (6 million euros) on appeal.

Right to a lien over the principal's property

A **lien** is a legal claim over someone's property as security for a debt. An agent, who is in possession of goods belonging to his principal, has the legal right to keep them, until the debts connected to those goods are paid. The lien of an agent is a particular lien as opposed to a general lien. This means that the lien is over the particular goods which are connected to the agreement or a related transaction, rather than a general lien over the entirety of the principal's property in his possession. An agent who is appointed to purchase cases of wine, on behalf of a principal in return for commission, will be entitled to a lien over the cases of wine in the agent's possession, if the principal does not pay the commission owed.

Right to claim indemnity

Both contractual and gratuitous agents have a right to claim indemnity for expenses and losses incurred in carrying out their authorised duties as agents. In order to be entitled to reclaim expenses, the agent must have been acting within the course of his agency. If the agent acts negligently or exceeds his authority, he may not be entitled to recover his costs.

Figure 9.4 Rights of an agent

Relationship between Agent, Principal, and Third Party

The general rule is that, once an agent has created a contract between a third party and a principal, the agent has no further responsibility. The only persons that can sue and be sued on the contract are the third party and principal, even if the agent has been responsible for the breach of contract.

Where a person purports to be acting as an agent, but in fact the principal does not exist, the agent is liable on the contract made with a third party. If a principal exists but the agent acts outside his authority, representing to the third party that he has authority to act, the agent will be liable for breach of warranty of authority. The third party can claim damages (compensation) for breach of warranty. The amount of damages awarded is calculated so as to put the third party back in the position he would have been in had the warranty not been breached. The agent will not be liable if the third party knew, or should have known, that the agent had no authority, or if the principal later ratifies the agreement.

Key Concept Once an agent has created a contract between a third party and principal, the agent usually has no further responsibility, and the only persons that can sue and be sued on the contract are the third party and principal.

There are some circumstances where the agent may be personally liable on the contract even though he acts within his authority. Different rules apply depending upon whether the third party knows the agent is acting as an agent (the principal is **disclosed**), and when the third party believes the agent is acting on his own behalf (the principal is **undisclosed**) (see Figure 9.5).

Disclosed Agency

A disclosed agency is where an agent indicates expressly, or through conduct, that he is acting as an agent. The actual name of the principal does not have to be disclosed to the third party. The third party should be aware that an agent does not intend to be personally liable and that any contract made will be binding on the principal party and not the agent. Therefore, where a principal is disclosed, the agent will incur no liability unless the agent has expressly accepted liability at the time of making a contract, or the principal does not actually exist.

Figure 9.5 Liability of agent where the principal is disclosed or undisclosed

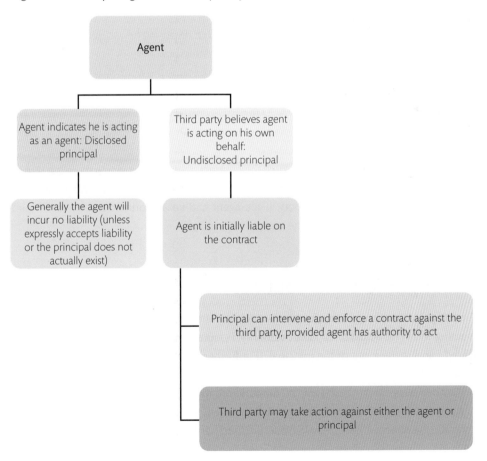

Undisclosed Agency

An undisclosed agency is where a third party is not told of the principal's existence, and believes that the agent is acting on his own behalf. When this occurs, the third party and agent can initially sue and be sued on the contract. However, provided the agent has authority to act, the principal will usually be able to intervene and enforce the contract against the third party. There are a few circumstances where an undisclosed principal will not be able to intervene, even if the agent had authority to act, such as where the third party can show he would have refused the contract if he had been aware it was with the undisclosed principal, or the agent denied he was acting for an undisclosed principal. Alternatively, the contract itself may include a term that either expressly excludes agency or is inconsistent with the existence of the agency.

Humble v Hunter (1848)

Facts: An agent chartered out his principal's ship without disclosing he was acting as an agent. He signed a contract describing himself as the owner of the ship.

Decision: The principal could not enforce the contract because the word 'owner' in the contract itself was inconsistent with an agency relationship.

If it is the third party that wishes to enforce the contract, then on discovering there is a principal, he can choose to take action against either the agent or the principal, provided the agent had actual authority or usual authority. If the agent had no authority to act, then the third party can only take action against the agent.

Liability in Tort and Contract

A principal is vicariously liable for tortious acts committed by his agent provided the agent is acting within his actual or apparent authority. Persons against whom torts have been committed can sue the agent or the principal. (For further information on vicarious liability, see Chapter 12.)

Provided an agent is acting within his authority, contracts made with third parties on behalf of a principal are binding on the principal. If the agent is responsible for causing a breach of contract, the principal will still be liable to the third party.

Termination of Agency

An agency relationship may be terminated by operation of the law or by the parties themselves. A principal, subject to certain limitations, can withdraw his authority to act at any time, although, if the principal does not inform a third party that he has withdrawn his authority, the agent may have apparent authority and still be able to bind the principal.

Operation of the law

Death or bankruptcy of either party

An agency relationship is one of trust and good faith; therefore, if one of the parties dies, the relationship is automatically cancelled. A problem may arise if an agent is not aware that his principal has died and continues to act, because in these circumstances the agent will be personally liable on any contract completed. If either the principal or the agent becomes bankrupt, the agency relationship is usually terminated.

Mental incapacity

Mental incapacity of the agent always terminates the agency relationship. Mental incapacity of the principal will discharge the agency relationship, unless the agent has been given a Lasting Power of Attorney under the Mental Capacity Act 2005. This type of authority to act has to be registered with the Office of the Public Guardian and allows the agent to act even when the principal becomes mentally incapacitated.

Frustration of the agency agreement

An agency agreement will be frustrated for the same reasons other contracts are frustrated, for example, performance of the contract becomes impossible, or something occurs that makes the contract illegal.

Termination by Parties

Completion of fixed term or task

Some agencies are expressly made for a definite period of time and will end on expiry of that fixed term; others have a fixed purpose and terminate when that purpose has been performed.

Agreement

Both parties may mutually agree to end the relationship by giving a reasonable amount of notice.

Revocation by one party

One party may revoke the agreement by giving the other notice, even though the other wishes to continue the relationship. However, unless the principal informs third parties that he has withdrawn his authority, the agent may have apparent authority to bind the principal in subsequent contracts. A unilateral termination may amount to a breach of contract, in which case the aggrieved party can claim damages. If an agent is an employee, unilateral termination by his principal may amount to unfair dismissal. In some circumstances the principal may be justified in terminating the agent's contract, for example, if the agent has committed a breach of his duties by accepting a bribe.

Irrevocable agreements

In some situations it is not possible to revoke an agency agreement. A Lasting Power of Attorney cannot be revoked once it is registered with the Office of the Public Guardian and the person no longer has their mental capacity. Where the agent has 'authority coupled with an interest' (usually a debt owed by the principal to the agent), then the agency cannot be revoked by the principal until the interest is satisfied (the debt has been paid).

Types of Agents

There are a number of different types of agents. Some agents are general agents who have authority to act for a principal generally in the ordinary course of their business, such as partners acting on behalf of the partnership. Others are special agents who only have authority to act in particular transactions. The law of agency applies to all agents. However, additional rights and duties have been created by statute where an agent is a commercial agent as defined by the Commercial Agents (Council Directive) Regulations 1993.

Distribution Agent

This is an agent who is appointed by a supplier of goods to arrange for the distribution of the goods within a particular geographical area. The agent does not buy goods himself, he makes contracts on behalf of the supplier and receives commission on sales.

Factors

A factor is a mercantile agent who is defined in the Factors Act 1889 as an agent who has authority to sell goods, to consign goods for the purpose of sale, to buy goods, or raise money on security of goods. Factors are in physical possession of their principal's goods and have authority to deal with the goods, including using them as security to raise money.

Commercial Agents

Commercial agents are self-employed intermediaries who have continuing authority to negotiate the sale or purchase of goods on behalf of a principal. The Commercial Agents (Council Directive) Regulations 1993 were introduced to conform with a European Union directive. The Regulations apply to all oral and written agreements that have been made after 1 January 1994 and set out certain rights and obligations which are binding on both the principal and the agent and cannot be excluded.

- An agent is entitled to a written contract with a set minimum period of notice.

- An agent is entitled to commission within a specified time. If the amount of commission is not specified in the written agreement, the agent is entitled to reasonable commission.

- An agent and principal must act dutifully and in good faith to each other, and give each other the necessary information and documents to perform their obligations and duties.

Basic Terminology

Agent Someone who has the authority to represent another party (the principal) and create a legal relationship between the principal and a third party.

Disclosed agency Where an agent indicates expressly or through conduct that he is acting as agent.

Estoppel To be prevented or stopped from denying something.

Gratuitously Receiving no payment.

Indemnity for expenses To reclaim money spent.

Lien A legal claim over someone's property as security for a debt.

Ratify To authorise or approve an agreement after it has been made.

Third party Someone with whom the agent deals on behalf of the principal.

Undisclosed agency Where a third party is not told of a principal's existence and believes that the agent is acting on his own behalf.

For an online flashcard glossary visit the Online Resource Centre

Summary

For an online printable version visit the Online Resource Centre

After studying this chapter students should be able to:

Define agency

- An agency is the relationship which exists between two persons (natural or legal): the agent and the principal. The agent creates a legal relationship between his principal and a third party.

Describe the different methods by which an agency relationship may be created

- Express agreement or implied agreement.
- Necessity.
- Estoppel: where the principal's words or actions give the impression that he has consented to a person acting as his agent.
- Ratification: the principal may only ratify the agreement if certain conditions are in place.

Explain the authority of an agent

- Express actual authority.
- Implied actual authority: authority to act is inferred from the conduct of the parties and the circumstances of the case.
- Usual authority: the agent has the usual authority of a person in that position.
- Apparent (ostensible) authority: a representation has been made by a principal to a third party that an agent has authority to act when in fact he does not.

Identify the rights and duties of an agent

- The duties of an agent are: to perform agreed tasks, to exercise care and skill, to account, to avoid a conflict of interest, not to make a secret profit, not to take a bribe, to maintain confidentiality.
- Rights of an agent are: to remuneration, to a lien over the principal's property, and to claim indemnity for expenses and losses incurred in carrying out their authorised duties as agents.

Understand the relationship between agent, principal, and third party

- Usually once an agent has created a contract between a third party and a principal, the agent has no further responsibility and only the third party and principal can enforce the contract.
- Where the principal is disclosed, the agent will usually incur no liability.
- Where the principal is undisclosed, the agent is initially liable on the contract but the principal may intervene and enforce a contract provided the agent has authority to act.
- A principal is vicariously liable for tortious acts committed by his agent acting within his actual or apparent authority.

Explain how an agency relationship may be terminated

- Operation of the law: death, bankruptcy, or mental incapacity (unless agent has lasting power of attorney), or frustration of the agency agreement.
- Termination by parties: completion of fixed term or task, mutual agreement, unilateral revocation by one party.
- Some agency agreements are irrevocable.

Be aware of different types of agencies

- General agents have authority to act for a principal in the ordinary course of their business.
- Special agents have authority to act in particular transactions.
- Commercial agents are self-employed intermediaries who have continuing authority to negotiate the sale or purchase of goods on behalf of a principal.

Questions

For outline answers visit the Online Resource Centre

1. Jenny authorises Sam, her agent, to sell Jenny's antique diamond ring for not less than £3,000 and to purchase twenty plasma screens for Jenny's business for up to £6,000. Sam buys the ring herself for £3,000 using a nominee and then sells it on to a dealer for £4,000. Sam keeps the £1,000 she has made. Sam, who is well known at Dixons plc as an agent for Jenny, contracts to buy ten plasma screens from them for £7,500. Advise Jenny.

2. Harry appoints Lin, as an agent, to sell his microlight aeroplane and agrees to pay her 5 per cent commission. Lin sells the aeroplane to Paul for £50,000 and Harry pays her £2,500 commission. As Paul has got the plane cheaply, he gives Lin a commission of £1,000. Lin does not disclose this to Harry.

   Harry appoints Alice as his agent to sell two paintings. He tells her to sell the paintings for at least £10,000 each. Alice sells one painting to Kiri for £8,000. Unknown to Harry, Alice buys the other painting herself for £13,000, and sells it on to Prad for £18,000.

   Advise Harry, who has now learnt of the £1,000 Lin received from Paul, and of Alice's dealings on the paintings.

3. Explain the different methods by which an agency relationship may be established.

4. Discuss the rights and duties of an agent.

Further Reading

Chuah and Furmston, *Commercial and Consumer Law*, 2nd edn (Pearson, 2013) Chapter 3.

Dobson and Stokes, *Commercial Law Textbook*, 8th edn (Sweet and Maxwell, 2012) Part 4.

Munday, *Agency: Law and Principles*, 2nd edn (Oxford University Press, 2013).

Online Resource Centre

Test your knowledge by trying this chapter's **Multiple Choice Questions**. Visit:

http://www.oup.com/uk/orc/law/company/jonesibl3e/01student/mcqs/ch09/

For more information, updates, and multiple choice questions, please visit the Online Resource Centre at:

http://www.oup.com/uk/orc/law/company/jonesibl3e/

10 The Sale of Goods and Supply of Services

Introduction

Transactions entered into by businesses and individuals often involve the sale and supply of goods and services. The general principles of contract law such as offer and acceptance, consideration, and intention to create legal relations apply to contracts for the sale of goods. However, in addition to these general principles, other laws specifically focused on the sale of goods have developed since the 19th century. Much of the law evolved to protect consumers in their contracts with businesses and to ensure that buyers were treated fairly. Today the law on the sale of goods is found in the Sale of Goods Act 1979 as amended by later legislation, in particular the Sale and Supply of Goods Act 1994.

The Sale of Goods Act 1979 focuses on terms governing the nature and quality of the goods sold, and the transfer of ownership from one party to another. Certain terms are implied by this statute into contracts for the sale of goods and, where the sale is by a business to a consumer, then these terms cannot be excluded by the seller. It is essential that businesses, especially those involved in retail, are aware of the provisions of the Sale of Goods Act 1979. The Act only applies to the sale of goods in return for money and does not apply where goods are installed, such as a fitted kitchen, or hired, as in a hired car. There are other Acts that imply terms into contracts other than contracts for the sale of goods. The Supply of Goods and Services Act 1982 implies terms into contracts for the supply of services, the supply of goods, and hire contracts; and the Supply of Goods (Implied Terms) Act 1973 implies terms into hire purchase contracts. The terms implied are similar to those found in the Sale of Goods Act 1979.

Further information and practical advice for businesses concerning the sale of goods can be found on the government website <https://www.gov.uk/> (click on businesses and self-employed).

Learning Objectives

After studying this chapter you should be able to:

- Explain what is meant by a contract for the sale of goods.
- Identify terms that are implied into contracts for the sale of goods.
- Distinguish between the right to ownership of goods and the right to possession of goods, and explain when rights may be transferred from a seller to a buyer.
- Identify the rules relating to delivery of goods.
- Outline the duties of a seller and buyer and the remedies available for breach of a sale of goods contract.
- Identify terms that are implied into contracts for the supply of goods and services, contracts for the hire of goods, and hire purchase contracts.

The Sale of Goods

Definition of a Contract for the Sale of Goods

A contract for the sale of goods is defined in s 2(1) of the Sale of Goods Act 1979 (SOGA) as: 'a contract by which the seller transfers, or agrees to transfer, the property in goods to the buyer for a money consideration called the price'.

This means that the seller transfers or agrees to transfer (at a later date) ownership (property) of goods to the buyer for money. A contract for the sale of goods may be in any form, oral, written, or through conduct (see Figure 10.1).

Contract of sale

A contract for sale is where ownership (sometimes referred to as 'title' or 'property') of goods is transferred immediately the contract is made, for example, buying a bottle of beer in a shop. The goods (bottle of beer) already exist and are in the possession of the seller and, therefore, ownership can be transferred immediately to the buyer.

Agreements to sell

The SOGA also applies to agreements to transfer ownership of goods. An agreement to sell is a binding contract which only becomes a contract of sale once the specified goods exist. For example, Smith decides to buy a fleet of ten vans for his business. He looks at the vans in a showroom and then orders ten new white Citroen vans from the salesman. The exact vans

Smith is buying are not in the possession of the salesman but are together with 100 vans in the Citroen warehouse, and therefore it is an agreement to sell.

There are two examples of an agreement to sell:

- Future goods which have not yet been manufactured or acquired by the seller.

- Goods that are *unascertained* (not specified), e.g. an order for 100 Christmas trees will be unascertained if they are in a warehouse containing 1,000 trees. The goods will become specific when the seller selects the 100 trees specifically for this order. Goods advertised in catalogues are often unascertained until earmarked for a particular buyer.

> **★ Key Concept** The Sale of Goods Act 1979 applies to contracts where ownership of goods is to be transferred immediately from the seller to the buyer and to contracts where the seller agrees to transfer ownership at some later date.

Meaning of 'goods'

The SOGA, s 61(1), defines 'goods' as all personal chattels (this means property that is tangible, such as cars, telephones, furniture), crops, and other things attached to land which are agreed to be severed from the land before sale or under a contract of sale. The SOGA does not cover land, money, services, or 'things in action'. A thing in action is an intangible asset such as a guarantee, trademark, or copyright.

If, unknown to the seller, the goods have already perished when the contract is made, then the contract is void: SOGA s 6.

Meaning of 'price'

For a transaction to fall within the SOGA, the consideration given by the buyer for the goods must consist of money. The money can be paid by any means such as cash, credit, or debit card, and a contract will still be valid even if the exact price is not specified. The SOGA, s 8, provides that, where a price is not specified, then the buyer must pay a reasonable price. What is considered a 'reasonable price' depends on the factual circumstances of each case. A contract will not be covered by the SOGA where a 'free gift' is passed to a consumer and no money is due, or where goods are exchanged for other goods and no money changes hands. Where goods are exchanged for goods plus money, it is less clear whether it is a contract of exchange or a contract of sale. It may depend upon the intention of the parties and whether the money was a substantial part of the consideration. However, for businesses this is of little importance as similar terms are implied into contracts for exchange.

Figure 10.1 Contracts for the sale of goods

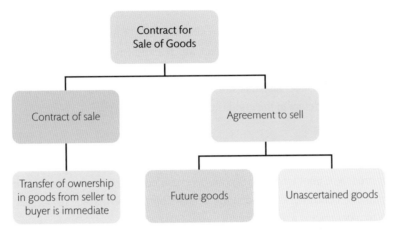

Terms Implied into Contracts by the Sale of Goods Act 1979

The SOGA implies certain terms into contracts for the 'sale of goods'. These terms include:

- The seller has the lawful right to sell the goods and transfer ownership of them (s 12).
- If the goods are sold by description, the goods will match their description (s 13).
- If sold in course of a business, the goods will be of satisfactory quality (s 14(2)).
- If sold in course of a business, the goods will be reasonably fit for their specified purpose (s 14(3)).
- If sold by sample, the goods will match the sample, and be free from any defect of quality not apparent on a reasonable examination of the sample (s 15) (see Figure 10.2).

Sections 12, 13, and 15 apply to all contracts for the sale of goods but ss 14(2) and 14(3) only apply where the goods are sold by a seller acting in the course of a business (see Table 10.1).

Meaning of 'in the course of a business'

The courts have confirmed that 'in the course of a business' includes goods that are not necessarily integral to the business, i.e. part of their stock-in-trade. In *Stevenson v Rogers* (1999) a fisherman, whose business was the selling of fish, sold his fishing boat and the court decided that the sale of the fishing boat was, for the purposes of SOGA, s 14, 'in the course of a business' as it was connected to his business.

Implied terms are conditions

The SOGA states that the implied terms are all conditions of the contract. A condition of a contract is a fundamental term of the contract which, if broken, allows the innocent party to treat the contract as at an end within a reasonable time and to claim damages for any losses they have incurred. The seller also has strict liability. This means that the seller will be liable even if unaware of the defect in the goods sold.

Meaning of 'consumer contracts'

Liability for breach of implied terms cannot be excluded or limited in consumer contracts. The definition of a consumer is found in the Unfair Contract Terms Act 1977. This provides that a party to a contract is a 'consumer' if:

- He does not make the contract in the course of a business or hold himself out to be acting in the course of a business.
- The other party does act in the course of a business.
- The goods are the type ordinarily supplied for private use or consumption.

Figure 10.2 Implied terms in a consumer contract for the sale of a raincoat

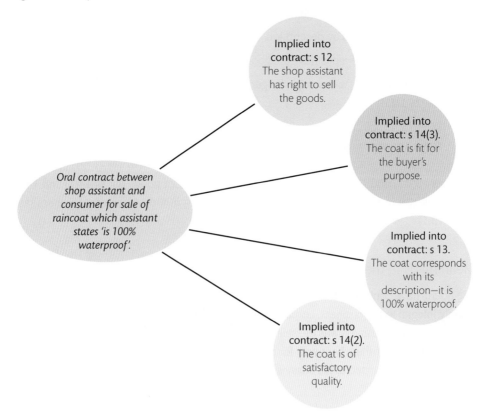

Key Concept The Sale of Goods Act 1979 implies certain terms into sale of goods contracts, relating to title, description, quality, fitness for purpose, and (if sale by sample) that the sample matches the rest of the goods. Terms relating to quality and fitness for purpose are only implied into contracts where the seller acts in the course of a business.

Table 10.1 Implied terms in contracts for the sale of goods

Implied term	Section number	Applies to goods sold in the course of a business	Applies to private sales
Title (right to sell)	12	Yes	Yes
Match their description	13	Yes	Yes
Satisfactory quality	14(2)	Yes	No
Reasonably fit for purpose	14(3)	Yes	No
Match the sample	15	Yes	Yes

The Right to Sell (Title): Section 12

A condition is implied into all contracts for the sale of goods that the seller has the right to sell the goods, or in the case of an agreement to sell that he will have the right at the time when the property is to pass to the buyer. In legal terminology this is known as the right to transfer **title** in the goods to the buyer.

This term is implied into all sale of goods contracts, including private sales.

The seller will break this term if it transpires that the goods are stolen, because the seller will not have good title to the goods. The true owners of the goods will not have given their permission to sell the goods.

Rowland v Divall (1923)

Facts: A thief stole a car and sold it to the defendant who did not realise the car was stolen. The claimant bought the car from the defendant for £334. Four months later, the police found the car and returned it to its original owner. The claimant sued the defendant for the £334.

Decision: The claimant was entitled to all his money back. There was no reduction for four months' use. The defendant never had the right to sell the car and, therefore, had no right to an allowance for the use of the car. (See Figure 10.3.)

Figure 10.3 Ownership of stolen goods does not pass, *Rowland v Divall*

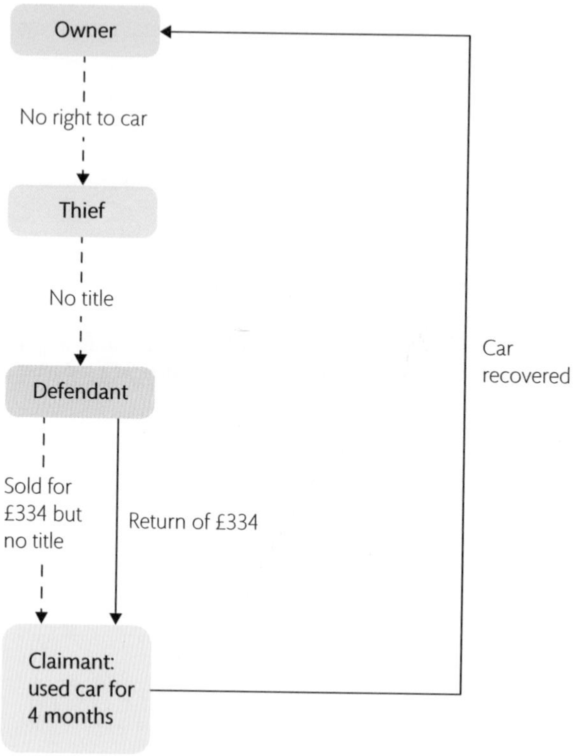

Sale by Description: Section 13

Where there is a contract for the sale of goods by description, there is an implied term of the contract that the goods will correspond with the description. A 'sale by description' is a sale where there is reliance on a description. This covers sales where the goods are described but not seen. Therefore, a sale of *future goods* or *unascertained goods* will usually be a sale by description, e.g. goods ordered from the Argos catalogue or the Next Directory. However, it can also include goods which have been examined or selected by the buyer provided the buyer relied on a description given of the goods.

The description may be given orally; for example, a butcher might inform his customer that 'the beef is organic'. Alternatively, the description may be in writing; for example, a label on a dress stating '100% cotton'. The seller is responsible even if he did not attach the description to the goods, for example, if it was put there by the manufacturer (printed on an attached label or even on the packaging). In practice, sale by description covers most transactions as items are usually labelled or described in some way, such as 'cashmere cardigan', 'plasma 42 inch TV', 'wooden shelves half an inch thick'.

Sample and description

In some situations a sale is by **sample** and description. For example, Alice enters into a carpet shop and chooses a purple carpet from a sample which is labelled '100% wool'. She orders the carpet from the shop. The sale is by description ('100% wool') and sample (she chose the carpet after examining the sample). The seller will be in breach of s 13 if it does not match the description even if the goods match the sample.

Description and quality

Quality and description may overlap. Stating the age or mileage of a car may be a description and a reference to quality. This is particularly important in a private sale, where s 14 (quality) is not implied into the contract but s 13 (description) is implied.

In the following case the defendant was a private seller and the incorrect description he gave was an implied term of the contract.

Beale v Taylor (1967)

Facts: A car was described by a private seller as a 1961 Triumph Herald. In fact it was two halves of two different cars welded together and only the rear half was a Triumph Herald. The seller was unaware of this.

Decision: The seller was liable for breach of s 13. The car did not match its description. The seller was not liable for breach of s 14, relating to the car's quality, as it was not a business sale.

In *Beale v Taylor* the car was defective, but goods can be rejected even though they are not defective and are of satisfactory quality, if they do not meet the description given to them and the buyer relied on that description.

Arcos v Ronaasen (1933)

Facts: Wooden staves were described by the seller as 'half an inch thick'. When the staves were delivered they varied from between half an inch to nine sixteenths of an inch in thickness.

Decision: The buyer could reject the staves as they did not match their description.

Minor incorrect descriptions in non-consumer contracts

Since *Arcos v Ronaasen* was decided, the law has changed with regard to non-consumer contracts. Section 15A of the SOGA provides that the term relating to the description is not a condition where the breach is so slight that it would be unreasonable to allow the buyer to reject the goods and treat the contract as ended. This means that in non-consumer sales, where the breach is minor, the term is treated as a warranty and only damages can be claimed. Therefore, if the *Arcos* case were decided today (as it was a non-consumer sale), the buyer would not be able to reject staves that were only one sixteenth of an inch (approx 2 mm) thicker than those ordered.

Reliance on description

Where goods are 'sold as seen', this indicates that the goods are not sold under any description within the meaning of s 13. In these cases it is up to the buyer to examine the goods carefully. If the buyer did not know of the description or did not rely on it, then the sale is not by description. Where a buyer with expert knowledge of the goods buys from a seller who is not an expert, the court may decide that the buyer has not relied on the seller's description. This was the position in the following case.

Harlingdon & Leinster Enterprises Ltd v Christopher Hull Fine Art Ltd (1991)

Facts: The seller offered a painting which he claimed to be by the German expressionist Munter, but he made it clear that he was not an expert on German paintings, and informed the buyer that he should examine the painting for himself. The buyer inspected the painting and bought it. The painting turned out to be a forgery.

Decision: The buyer could not recover the purchase price from the seller, because he had not relied on the description in making a purchase; it was therefore not a 'sale by description'.

Key Concept In a sale by description the buyer must have relied on the description given by the seller. It is not a sale by description where goods are 'sold as seen'.

The Goods are of Satisfactory Quality: Section 14(2)

There is an implied condition for goods sold in the course of a business that the goods are of **satisfactory quality**. This term is not implied into private sales; therefore, a buyer purchasing goods privately will not be able to complain under s 14(2) if the goods are of poor quality. For businesses this is an important section because all products sold, whether new or second-hand, must be of satisfactory quality. The law imposes strict liability on the seller, which means the buyer only needs to show that the goods are not of satisfactory quality, and does not have to prove the seller was to blame or how the goods came to be defective. However, if the seller is found liable he may be able to recover his losses from the manufacturer, distributor, or supplier, see *Godley v Perry* (1960) later in the chapter. Goods include their packaging and instructions.

The term 'satisfactory quality' came into force on 3 January 1995 as a result of an amendment to the SOGA by s 7 of the Sale and Supply of Goods Act 1994. It replaced the implied term of 'merchantable quality'.

The 'satisfactory quality' standard

The requirement of 'satisfactory quality' means satisfactory in the eyes of the reasonable buyer. Perfection cannot always be expected and what is considered to be satisfactory quality can vary between goods depending upon age, price, and other factors. Section 14(2A) states that goods must meet the standard that a reasonable person would consider satisfactory, taking into account all relevant circumstances including price and description. Section 14(2B) of the SOGA sets out some of the relevant circumstances which may be taken into account when deciding quality. These are:

- the goods supplied are fit for all the purposes that goods of that type are usually supplied;
- appearance and finish;
- freedom from minor defects;
- safety; and
- durability.

It is clear that goods that are broken or dangerous cannot meet the requirement of satisfactory quality. However, where products are second-hand or cheap, the reasonable buyer may expect some minor defects. Where products are expensive then higher standards can be expected.

Clegg v Andersson (2003)

Facts: The Cleggs bought a new yacht from Andersson (A) for £236,000 with a shoal draught keel 'in accordance with the manufacturer's standard specification'. Upon delivery, A informed the Cleggs that the yacht's keel was substantially heavier than the manufacturer's specification. After discussion of possible means of remedying the defect the Cleggs rejected the yacht.

Decision: On the basis of all the evidence a reasonable person would consider that the yacht as delivered was not of satisfactory quality because of the overweight keel, the adverse effect it had on rig safety, and the need for more than remedial work. There was a breach of condition under the SOGA, s 14(2) and the Cleggs were entitled to reject the yacht.

In the following case the judge preferred the evidence of the defendant's witnesses and the claimant was unsuccessful in his claim for breach of s 14(2).

Egan v Motor Services (Bath) Ltd (2007)

Facts: The claimant bought a new car from the defendant, car dealers, for £32,300. After the car had been supplied, the claimant alleged that the car veered to the left when being driven at speed. Various tests and inspections were carried out. However, the claimant was not satisfied and claimed breach of the SOGA, s 14(2).

Decision: The judge, on hearing evidence from witnesses of both the claimant and defendant, preferred the evidence of the defendant's witnesses that the car handled normally and in accordance with the manufacturer's specification. There was no breach of s 14(2).

In recent cases, a software package was found to be of unsatisfactory quality and not reasonably fit for the purpose for which it was sold and a luxury yacht that exploded 15 minutes after delivery was also of unsatisfactory quality.

Kingsway Hall Hotel Ltd v Red Sky IT (Hounslow) Ltd (2010)

Facts: The claimants, owners of a hotel, purchased a computer software package to manage reservations. The software had flaws such as inaccuracies in advance bookings, and despite attempts the defendants were unable to sort the problems out. After six months the claimants rejected the software and claimed damages.

Decision: The software was not fit for the purpose for which it was sold, and it did not meet the standard that a reasonable person would regard as satisfactory, taking into account any description of the goods, the price, and all other circumstances. The claimants were entitled to reject the goods and were entitled to damages for loss of profits and goodwill.

Ward v MGM Marine Ltd (2012)

Facts: The claimant purchased a luxury motor yacht from the defendant boat dealers. Very shortly after taking delivery of the yacht, the claimant and a passenger heard an unusual noise and saw that blue smoke was coming from the port exhaust. The claimant and passenger managed to escape on a lifeboat when the yacht burst into flames.

Decision: There was no evidence that the fire occurred other than as a result of engine defects present when the yacht was sold. The yacht was not of satisfactory quality.

Public statements

Further protection is given to consumers under the provisions of s 14(2D) of the SOGA (added by the Sale and Supply of Goods to Consumers Regulations 2002). In a consumer sale, when deciding if goods are satisfactory, the court can take into account public statements by the producer or his representatives about the specific characteristics of the product, particularly advertising or labelling. However, a public statement will not be relevant if the seller can show that he did not know about the statement, or was not reasonably aware of it, or if, before the contract was made, the statement had been publicly retracted or corrected. In addition, the statement will not be relevant if the seller can prove that the buyer's decision to buy the goods was not based on or influenced by the public statement.

Liability may arise from goods which are of satisfactory quality themselves, but are contaminated by something else which should not have been present in the goods.

Hazlewood Grocery Ltd v Lion Foods Ltd (2007)

Facts: Chilli powder provided by Lion to Hazlewood contained a minute quantity of an industrial dye that was not a permitted additive in food. That powder was subsequently incorporated by Hazlewood into food manufactured by them.

Decision: The chilli powder contaminated with industrial dye breached the fitness for purpose requirement in s 14(2) and s 14(3) of the SOGA.

Knowledge and examination

There are a number of circumstances where a buyer will not have the protection of s 14(2) even though the goods are of unsatisfactory quality. This is because the buyer has either had the defect pointed out to him or he has examined the goods and should have noticed it. The SOGA, s 14(2C), states that the implied term of satisfactory quality does not apply in the following circumstances:

- If the defect making the goods of unsatisfactory quality is specifically drawn to the buyer's attention before the contract. Only defects pointed out will be covered; for example, a buyer will not be able to complain about a broken zip if she purchased a designer dress with a label on it stating 'broken zip' but could complain if the seams came apart on first wearing it.

- Where before the contract is made, the buyer examines the goods and that examination revealed or ought to have revealed the defect. A buyer is under no obligation to examine goods but, if he chooses to do so and fails to spot an obvious defect, the seller will not be liable.

- If it is a sale by sample and the defect would have been apparent on reasonable examination of the sample.

Instructions and precautions

The buyer is expected to follow instructions supplied with the goods. If the buyer fails to follow instructions, the seller will not be liable for the resulting damage. The buyer is also expected to take normal precautions when using the relevant type of goods. In the following case, it was common public knowledge that pork should be thoroughly cooked before eating.

Heil v Hedges (1951)

Facts: Heil (C) bought two pork chops infested with trichinella which caused C to become ill. If the chops had been properly cooked the trichinella would have been killed. It was common knowledge among the general public that pork should be cooked substantially longer than other meat.

Decision: The chop was of satisfactory quality (and reasonably fit for the purpose of human consumption). C failed to cook it correctly.

However, a buyer is not expected to take special precautions unless specially instructed to do so by the seller.

Grant v Australian Knitting Mills (1936)

Facts: Grant bought a pair of woollen underpants. The underpants contained an excess of sulphite, a chemical used in their manufacture. This should have been eliminated before the product was finished. After wearing the pants, Grant developed a rash which turned out to be dermatitis and spent many months in hospital. He would not have developed dermatitis if he had washed the pants before wearing them.

Decision: The pants were not of satisfactory quality. It is not usual practice to wash underwear before wearing it. The claimant had normal skin.

If the goods are mishandled by the buyer the resulting damage will not be due to their unsatisfactory quality.

Aswan Engineering Establishment Co v Lupdine Ltd (1986)

Facts: The sellers supplied the buyers with a waterproofing compound in plastic pails. The pails were stacked in five containers and sent by ship to Kuwait. The containers were unloaded but the buyers left them on the quayside for several days and the temperature inside reached 70°C. The plastic pails melted and the compound was lost.

Decision: The plastic pails were of satisfactory quality for exporting the compound, and the sellers were not in breach of s 14 if the pails collapsed under extreme climatic conditions.

The Goods are Reasonably Fit for their Purpose: Section 14(3)

Where the seller sells goods in the course of business, and the buyer expressly or by implication makes known to the seller any particular purpose for which the goods are being bought, there is an implied term that the goods are reasonably fit for that purpose, even if it is not a purpose for which such goods are commonly supplied.

This term only applies to the sale of goods made in the course of business and, therefore, is similar to s 14(2). It does not apply to private sales. In many cases there may be an overlap between goods being suitable for purpose and of satisfactory quality, but there may be cases where only s 14(3) will assist an aggrieved consumer. For example, goods might be of satisfactory quality but not fit for the particular purpose to which the buyer wishes to put them.

A consumer buying goods for their normal purpose will not have to inform the seller of how he intends to use the goods, as it will be implied that he had made this known to the seller and that he relied on the seller's skill and judgement to supply goods which are fit for that purpose. A consumer wishing to use goods for unusual purposes must expressly inform the seller.

The seller can avoid liability if he can prove that the buyer did not rely on the seller's skill or judgement or that, although the buyer did rely on the seller's skill and judgement, it was unreasonable for the buyer to do so.

Section 14(3) only requires the goods to be reasonably fit for their purpose. If the buyer has special requirements and does not inform the seller, then the buyer will fail in a claim.

Griffiths v Peter Conway (1939)

Facts: The buyer of a Harris Tweed coat suffered an allergic reaction. The buyer had abnormally sensitive skin, and there was nothing in the cloth which would have affected the skin of a normal person. The buyer had not told the seller about her skin.

Decision: The abnormality was one that no seller would assume to exist. The coat was fit for purpose.

In the following case, Jewsons proved that the developer had not relied on their skill and judgement.

Jewson Ltd v Kelly (2003)

Facts: The defendant, a property developer, purchased 12 boilers from the claimant, Jewson Ltd, for flats he was converting. He failed to pay for them claiming that, as the boilers had a high energy rating, they were not fit for purpose. Jewson sued.

Decision: The defendant had not relied on the skill and judgement of the claimant because, although he informed the claimant that he had wanted to buy the boilers to instal them in flats, he had not given the claimant any information about the nature of the building and asked whether the boilers were suitable for those particular flats.

Key Concept The implied terms, that goods are of satisfactory quality and reasonably fit for their purpose, are only implied into contracts where the seller acts in the course of a business. They are not implied into private sales.

Business Insight Car traders prosecuted after posing as private sellers

In 2014 two rogue car traders in Wales were convicted of fraud for posing as private individuals when placing advertisements on Gumtree, the online classified ads website. Purchasers of the cars believed that they were entering into a private sale rather than dealing with a trader. Purchasers were misled into believing they did not have protection if the car turned out to be of unsatisfactory quality or not fit for purpose.

Sale of Goods by Sample: Section 15

Many businesses buy goods after having looked at a sample. A retailer may examine a sample of a toy and then make a large order from the wholesaler. Other goods commonly sold to consumers by sample include carpets and furnishing fabrics. Where there is a sale by sample there is an implied condition that:

- The bulk (remainder of the goods) will correspond with the sample in quality, and

- The goods will be free from any defect, making their quality unsatisfactory, which would not be apparent on reasonable examination of the sample.

This condition is implied into all sales by sample, whether in the course of a business or a private sale. It is possible for goods to be sold by sample and by description; in such cases, the goods must correspond with both the sample and description. When goods are sold by sample there is an obligation for the buyer to examine the sample. The buyer will not be able to claim the bulk of the goods are of unsatisfactory quality if this could have been discovered by making a reasonable examination of the sample. However, if it would not have been possible to discover the defect on reasonable examination of the sample, then s 15 will apply.

Godley v Perry (1960)

Facts: The claimant, a boy, bought a catapult from Perry, a newsagent who sold toys. The boy used the catapult to fire a stone, the catapult broke, and he lost his left eye. It was found that the catapults were made of cheap material and likely to fracture. Perry had purchased a box of catapults from a wholesaler after testing a sample. Perry had pulled back the elastic of the sample catapult and no defect had been detected.

Decision: Perry was in breach of s 14 because the catapult was not of satisfactory quality or fit for the purpose. The wholesalers were liable under s 15, despite the fact that the retailer had examined the sample, as the defect was not apparent by a reasonable examination.

The buyer will not be considered to have accepted the goods until he has had an opportunity to check that the goods match the sample, and will be able to reject the goods even though they have been delivered, if they do not correspond with the sample. Once goods have been accepted, then a buyer will no longer have the right to reject the goods but he may still be able to claim damages for any defects in the goods.

Exclusion of Implied Terms

The Unfair Contract Terms Act 1977 provides that liability for breach of all implied terms cannot be excluded or limited in consumer contracts. Where the buyer is dealing as a consumer and the seller is selling in the course of a business, the terms are always implied into the contract. Where both the seller and the buyer are acting in the course of a business, then terms relating to quality, fitness for purpose, description, or correspondence with sample may be excluded but only if it is reasonable to do so. Implied terms relating to title in the property (ownership of goods) cannot be excluded in any contracts. A buyer is allowed a reasonable amount of time to check that the goods comply with the implied terms.

Passing of Property (Title) in Goods from Seller to Buyer

It is important to ascertain when property (ownership) in goods passes from the seller to the buyer. This does not necessarily take place when possession of the goods passes or payment for the goods is made. Disputes between who has property in goods may arise in various circumstances, such as in contracts between businesses when goods are lost or destroyed in transit and there is no agreement as to which party to the contract should bear the risk. Another example is when a buyer, who has possession of goods which have not been paid for, becomes insolvent and secured creditors attempt to take possession of these goods which the unsecured seller wishes to recover. The SOGA sets out rules governing when property (ownership) in goods passes from the seller to the buyer. Usually, when the property in goods passes from the seller to the buyer the risk of loss or destruction moves with it.

Passing of Risk

In a consumer contract, the risk only passes on delivery of the goods to the consumer. In non-consumer contracts, unless otherwise agreed between the parties, the risk generally passes at the same time as property in the goods passes (property means ownership of the goods not possession of the goods). Once ownership has been passed to the buyer, he is responsible for any loss or damage to the goods irrespective of whether the goods are in his possession: SOGA, s 20.

Specific and Unascertained Goods

The moment of passing of ownership in non-consumer contracts depends upon whether the goods are 'specific' or 'unascertained'. **Specific goods** are those that are identified at the time the contract of sale is made, for example, the purchase of a second-hand car or products in a self-service shop. **Unascertained goods** are products that have not yet been manufactured or acquired by the seller, or are unidentified, such as 1,000 kilos of oranges where the seller has not identified which oranges are the subject of the contract.

Passing of property in specific goods

The first point to consider is the intention of the parties. Section 17 of the SOGA provides that the property in specific or ascertained goods passes when the parties intend it to be transferred. The parties' intention is established by looking at the terms in the contract, the conduct of the parties, the custom of the particular trade the contract relates to, and any relevant circumstances of the case. Where no intention is evident, then the four rules set down in s 18 are used (see Figure 10.4).

Section 18: Rule 1

In an unconditional contract for the sale of specific goods in a deliverable state, the property passes to the buyer when the contract is made.

'Unconditional' means that the contract does not contain terms under which the passing of the property is delayed for various reasons. The goods must be in a deliverable state, which means they must be ready and capable to be passed to the buyer. In the following case, the machinery was not deliverable as it was embedded in the seller's floor.

Underwood Ltd v Burgh Castle Brick and Cement Syndicate (1922)

Facts: The claimant contracted to sell an engine to the defendant, to be delivered 'free on rail' (loaded on a train). The engine was embedded in the claimant's concrete floor and had to be dismantled and loaded on to the train for delivery. It was damaged while being loaded.
Decision: Property (ownership) had not passed to the buyer at the time the contract was made because the engine was not in a deliverable state, i.e. 'free on rail'.

Section 18: Rule 2

In a contract for the sale of specific goods where the seller has agreed to do something to the goods to put them in a deliverable state, the property does not pass until the thing is done and the buyer is notified.

In *Underwood Ltd v Burgh Castle Sand and Cement Syndicate* (just discussed), the engine was not in a deliverable state until it had been loaded on to the train. Therefore, as it was damaged before it was loaded, property (ownership) and, consequently, risk remained with the seller.

Section 18: Rule 3

Where the seller is to weigh, measure, or test the goods to find the price, property does not pass until this is completed and the buyer has been notified.

In order for Rule 3 to apply, the weighing, measuring, or testing must be due to be carried out by the seller and it must be in order to establish a contract price; for example, Concrete Ltd agrees to buy a shipment of sand from PO Ltd at £500 a tonne and that PO Ltd will weigh the sand and charge Concrete Ltd accordingly. Ownership of the sand does not pass until it has been weighed and Concrete Ltd has been informed that this has been done.

Section 18: Rule 4

If goods are delivered on approval, sale or return, or other similar terms, ownership passes when the buyer:

- Signifies approval, or
- Takes some action which assumes ownership (for example, the buyer consumes the goods or sells them on), or
- Keeps the goods longer than the time limit stated in the contract, or
- If no time limit is stated, keeps the goods for more than a reasonable time.

Poole v Smith's Car Sales (Balham) Ltd (1962)

Facts: At the end of August a car dealer supplied another car dealer with a second-hand car 'on sale or return'. The car was not sold or returned despite repeated telephone calls and letters over the next three months.
Decision: Title had passed to the second dealer because a reasonable time had expired without the car being returned.

Key Concept Ownership of goods does not always pass when physical possession passes to the buyer. Ownership of specific goods passes in accordance with the intention of the parties to the contract or, if no intention is evident, according to the rules set out in the Sale of Goods Act 1979, s 18.

Passing of property in unascertained goods

Section 16 of the SOGA states that, where there is a contract for the sale of unascertained goods, the property (ownership) of the goods is not passed to the buyer unless and until the goods are ascertained. Goods are ascertained when the goods that are the subject of sale are identified; for example, the seller sets aside 100 kilos of specific oranges for the buyer. Once this happens, s 17 of the SOGA applies. Property (ownership) passes when the parties intend ownership to pass. If no intention is evident, then s 18 Rule 5 of the SOGA is used.

Section 18: Rule 5

Ownership of unascertained goods passes when the goods matching the contract description are in a deliverable state and are unconditionally appropriated to the contract. The unconditional appropriation must be done by the seller with the buyer's agreement or by the buyer with the seller's agreement.

In order for goods to be 'unconditionally appropriated' to the contract, it must have been decided which actual goods are to be the subject of the contract and these goods must be irrevocably earmarked. The seller will no longer be able to substitute other goods of a similar nature. One way of proving that goods have been unconditionally appropriated is to deliver them to the correct address. Even if goods are ready for delivery, if the seller still has an opportunity to stop shipment and substitute the goods then it will not be an unconditional appropriation.

Figure 10.4 Passing of property in goods in non-consumer contracts

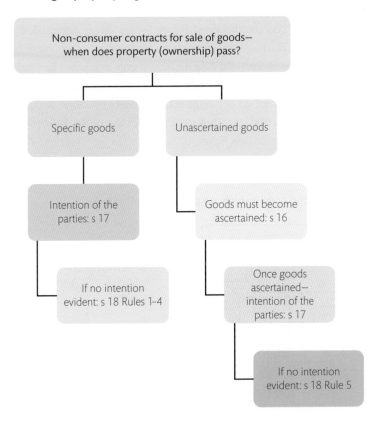

Carlos Federspiel & Co SA v Charles Twigg & Co Ltd (1957)

Facts: The buyer ordered and part paid for bicycles from the seller. The seller made the bikes and packed them in containers with the buyer's name and address on them. Before delivery the seller became insolvent. The question was, had ownership of the bikes passed to the buyer.

Decision: Ownership had not passed. The seller could have changed his mind and sent the bicycles elsewhere and used other bicycles to fulfil this order. As property in the goods had not passed, the buyer (who had part paid for the goods) was treated as an ordinary unsecured creditor.

Unascertained goods which are part of identified bulk

Where goods are unascertained in that they have not been irrevocably set aside for a particular buyer, but the contract for sale is for a specified quantity of goods which form part of an identified bulk, and the buyer has paid for some or all of the goods, then the buyer becomes a co-owner of the bulk (unless agreed otherwise): SOGA s 20A. This gives protection to the buyer because, if the seller becomes insolvent before the goods are delivered, the buyer will be able to claim his goods. The bulk may be made up of the goods of a number of buyers, all of whom may be co-owners of the bulk. Alternatively, if only one buyer has made payment for goods, he is the co-owner of the bulk with the seller. Co-ownership of a bulk of goods would arise if a plane carries a cargo of mangoes belonging to the seller, and a buyer agrees to buy one tonne of mangoes from the cargo and pays for them. The buyer becomes a co-owner of the cargo with the seller (see Figure 10.5).

Figure 10.5 Unascertained goods which are part of identified bulk

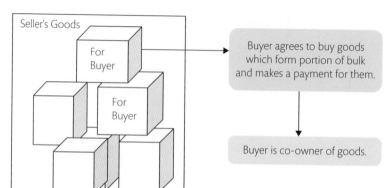

A second situation, where property in unascertained goods is transferred to a buyer, is where there is a specified bulk of goods subject to a number of contracts for sale, and the buyer's contract is the last one to be fulfilled. Goods are taken from the bulk to complete various contracts and, when there are only enough goods left to complete one final contract, the goods will belong to that contract. For example, Buyer A agrees to buy one tonne of mangoes from Seller X's ten tonne stored cargo of mangoes. Once Seller X has sold nine of the tonnes to other customers, property in the remaining one tonne of mangoes passes to Buyer A.

Key Concept Ownership of unascertained goods (not part of a specified bulk) passes according to the intention of the parties, but only after the goods have been irrevocably set aside for a buyer.

Reservation of Title Clauses

In the commercial world, goods are often supplied on credit, and a seller supplying goods on credit terms may be concerned that he will not be paid. In recent years there has been an increase in business practice of incorporating **reservation of title** clauses into contracts. The seller protects himself by adding a clause to the contract of sale retaining title of the goods until payment has been made. Where such a clause is used, the buyer obtains possession and use of the goods but will not obtain ownership until the goods are paid for. The seller will be able to recover the goods if the buyer fails to pay for them. Should the buyer become bankrupt or, in the case of a buyer company, go into liquidation, the goods are not part of the bankrupt/liquidated buyer's assets and can be recovered by the seller. Without a reservation of title clause, ownership would have passed to the buyer and the seller would rank alongside other unsecured creditors in attempting to recover payment from a bankrupt person or a liquidated company. The SOGA, s 19, envisages reservation of title clauses in contracts, stating that the seller may, by the terms of the contract, reserve the right of disposal of the goods until certain conditions are fulfilled, and ownership of the goods will not pass to the buyer until that condition is fulfilled. The condition would be that the goods are paid for. The reservation of title clause will only be effective if it is a term of the contract.

Simple reservation clause

Some reservation of title clauses provide that title in particular goods will not pass until those goods are paid for. Other reservation of title clauses may cover all debts owed by the buyer, with the clause stating that title in goods will not pass until money due for the goods in question and other goods supplied under different contracts is paid.

Armour v Thyssen Edelstahlwerke AG (1990)

Facts: The sellers, Thyssen, sold and supplied quantities of steel to C Ltd. The contracts of sale stated that the property in the steel would not pass to C Ltd until Thyssen had been paid all the money due to them. C Ltd went into liquidation and the steel was claimed by C Ltd's creditors. **Decision:** The reservation of title clause, covering all debts owed by C Ltd, was valid and Thyssen were entitled to recover the steel. The steel did not form part of C Ltd's assets that could be claimed by ordinary creditors.

A basic or simple reservation of title clause will only cover situations where the goods in question can be identified and have not been converted into other products or mixed with other goods.

Complex reservation clause ('Romalpa' clause)

Some reservations of title are more complex when the seller attempts to insert a clause giving him rights in the goods even after they have been sold on to a third party, by the buyer, or where they have been used in a manufacturing process. These complex reservation of title clauses are sometimes called **Romalpa clauses** after the case in which the validity of such clauses was upheld by the court. When the buyer became insolvent without paying for goods sold under a contract containing a reservation of title clause, the seller was able to recover not only the remaining goods but also money received from the sale of some of those goods.

Aluminium Industrie Vaassen BV v Romalpa Aluminium Ltd (1976)

Facts: AIV sold large quantities of aluminium foil to Romalpa. The contract of sale stated that ownership of the foil was not to pass to Romalpa until full payment had been made, and if the foil were mixed with other items during manufacturing AIV would become owners of the finished products until payment. The foil and completed items containing the foil were to be stored separately from other goods. Romalpa became insolvent and AIV claimed the return of all the foil which remained at AIV's warehouse and the proceeds of sale from unmixed foil. **Decision:** The claimants were successful in recovering foil supplied together with the proceeds of sale of goods containing the unmixed foil.

In the *Romalpa* case, the seller only claimed unmixed goods and proceeds of sale of unmixed goods. The goods sold were identifiable after the manufacturing process. The seller did not attempt to claim the goods that had been mixed with other goods. Difficulties may arise where materials obtained from more than one seller are mixed in one product or where the goods have become altered into something else.

Borden v Scottish Timber Products Ltd (1981)

Facts: The seller supplied resin to the buyers, who used it to manufacture chipboard. The contract contained a reservation of title clause. The buyers became insolvent owing the seller £318,321.
Decision: The clause did not protect the seller once the goods (resin) had been mixed with the other products as they had lost their identity as an independent commodity.

In the following case the goods had been manufactured into another product and title in the goods had passed to the buyer. As the buyer had not paid for the goods, the seller had a charge over the new products (and their proceeds of sale), but in order for a charge over the assets of a company to be enforceable it must be registered with the Registrar of Companies.

Re: Peachdart (1983)

Facts: The seller sold leather to the buyer, a company which manufactured handbags. The contract contained a reservation of title clause in respect of unworked leather, handbags made from the leather, and proceeds of sale of the handbags. The company became insolvent and the seller claimed the leather, the handbags, and the proceeds of sale.
Decision: The seller had the right to the unworked leather, but once the leather was made into handbags it was no longer the property of the seller and a charge arose over the handbags and their proceeds of sale. The charge was void because it had not been registered against the company.

Reservation of title clauses must be part of the contract of sale. It is not enough to include the clause on an invoice, because the contract has been made by this time and an invoice cannot introduce new terms.

Sale of Goods by Non-owner

The general rule is that only the owner, or his agent acting with his authority, can transfer ownership of goods to the buyer. The rule is sometimes expressed in Latin as *nemo dat quod non habet* which translated means 'no one can give what he does not have'. A seller who does not own goods will not be able to transfer ownership (title) of the goods to a buyer. In every sale of goods contract, there is an implied term that the seller has the right to transfer title in the goods, and if the seller does not have this right he will be in breach of contract. Generally, where goods are sold by someone who does not have the right to sell the goods, ownership will not pass to the buyer. The true owner will be able to claim the goods back from the buyer. The person who sold the goods will be liable to return the purchase monies to the buyer, but often that person is a crook and disappears before action can be taken against him. Although the general rule is that ownership will not pass if the sale is by a non-owner, there are some exceptions to this rule where the innocent buyer does acquire ownership of goods even though the seller did not have the right to sell them, as in the exceptions which follow.

Agency

The law of agency applies to the sale of goods. If an agent sells goods with the authority of his principal, then ownership of the goods will pass to the buyer. If the agent acts outside his actual authority, ownership of the goods may pass if the agent acts within his apparent authority, and the buyer is unaware of the agent's lack of actual authority.

Special rules apply if an agent is an independent mercantile agent (sometimes called a factor). This is a professional type of agent whose business is buying and selling people's goods. When dealing with goods, the factor acts in his own name rather than that of the buyer or seller. Laws relating to factors can be found in the Factors Act 1889. Under the provisions of this Act, a buyer who buys goods from a factor will get good title to the goods even though the factor did not have the seller's authority to sell the goods, provided the following conditions are met:

- The goods were in possession of the factor with the consent of the owner.
- The factor acted in the ordinary course of business in selling the goods.
- The buyer was unaware of the factor's lack of authority to sell the goods.

Estoppel (stopped from denying)

Where the owner of the goods knowingly allows an innocent buyer to believe that the seller has authority to sell the owner's goods, the owner will be prevented (estopped) from later denying this: SOGA, s 21. Ownership of the goods will pass to the buyer.

Estoppel only applies in a contract of sale where the goods are 'sold' to the buyer and does not apply to an agreement to sell.

Sale by a person with voidable title

Where a person obtains goods under a voidable contract, for example, where there has been a misrepresentation, then he obtains voidable ownership of the goods. This means that the contract under which he obtained the goods may be set aside and the goods returned to the original owner. However, if the goods are resold to an innocent buyer before the contract is set aside, ownership of the goods passes to the innocent buyer. The original owner may avoid the voidable contract before the sale to the innocent buyer, and reclaim the goods, but he will need to act quickly (see Figure 10.6).

Figure 10.6 Sale of goods by a person with a voidable title

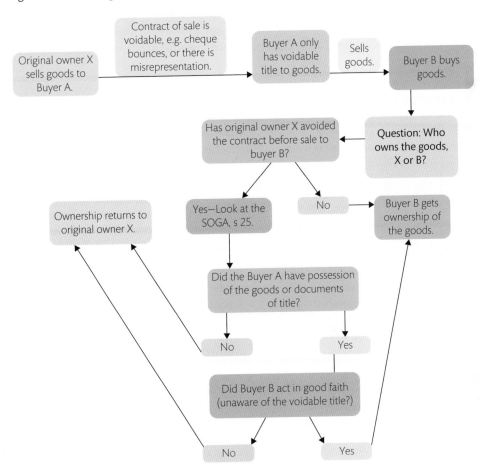

Usually, a contract can be avoided by informing the other party to the contract that it is to be set aside or, if there has been fraud and the other party has disappeared, then informing the police may suffice to avoid the contract. In *Car & Universal Finance v Caldwell* (1964) a rogue bought a car with a false cheque and sold the car on to another. The court decided that, when the original owner informed the police, this was sufficient to avoid the contract between the original owner and the rogue. However, an innocent party who purchases goods from a person who has possession of the goods or documents of title to the goods with the owner's consent, may gain good title to the goods under the SOGA, s 25.

Resale by a buyer in possession

Section 25 of the SOGA applies where a buyer agrees to buy goods from a seller and obtains possession of them with the consent of the seller, and then resells the goods before acquiring ownership. Possession and ownership do not have to pass together; in business, a seller may often deliver goods to a buyer but retains ownership until the goods have been paid for. Where a buyer, without ownership but with possession of goods or documents proving ownership, resells the goods to a second buyer, that second buyer will gain ownership. The second buyer must act in good faith and be unaware that the buyer selling the goods did not have ownership of them.

Newtons of Wembley Ltd v Williams (1964)

Facts: The claimants sold a car to R who took possession of the car. R paid for the car by cheque but the cheque bounced. The claimants took immediate steps to avoid the contract of sale by informing the police. Before the car could be recovered R sold the car to X who bought the car in good faith unaware of R's lack of ownership.
Decision: Ownership of the car passed to X under statute.

The first buyer must have obtained the goods with the consent of the seller and, therefore, if the goods are stolen s 25 will not apply. In the previous case, the car was not stolen because the rogue had taken it away with the consent of the owner, albeit with a cheque that was dishonoured; therefore, ownership passed. But in the next case, the van was originally stolen; therefore, ownership did not pass under s 25.

National Employers Mutual General Insurance Association Ltd v Jones (1988)

Facts: A thief stole a car from the claimants and sold it to X. The car was sold several times before it was eventually sold to Jones who bought the car in good faith unaware it was stolen.

Decision: Under the SOGA, s 25, ownership of the car could not pass to Jones as the thief was not in possession of the car with the consent of the owner.

Sale by a seller in possession

Section 24 of the SOGA applies where a seller has already sold goods to a first buyer, but keeps possession of them or of documents proving ownership of them, and then sells the goods to a second buyer. Provided the second buyer takes possession of the goods or the documents, and acts in good faith being unaware that the goods have already been sold, then ownership passes to the second buyer (see Figure 10.7). For example, a seller sells an Elvis Guitar to buyer 1, who pays full price for the guitar, but before buyer 1 collects the guitar the seller sells it again to buyer 2, who takes immediate possession of the guitar. Ownership of the guitar passes to buyer 2 and buyer 1 will not be able to claim the guitar but could sue the seller for breach of contract.

Figure 10.7 Sale by a seller in possession of buyer's goods

Key Concept The general rule is that only the owner of goods or his agent, acting with his authority, can transfer ownership of goods to the buyer. There are some exceptions to this rule covered by agency, estoppel, sale with a voidable title, resale by buyer in possession, and sale by seller in possession.

Duties of the Parties of Contract for Sale of Goods

The SOGA imposes duties on both the seller and the buyer in a sale of goods contract. It also sets out remedies if these duties are broken. Section 27 of the SOGA states 'it is the duty of the seller to deliver goods, and of the buyer to accept and pay for them, in accordance with the terms of the contract of sale'. Payment and delivery of goods does not have to take place simultaneously but if there is no agreement to the contrary then it will take place concurrently: SOGA, s 28.

Duties of Seller: To Deliver the Goods

The seller has a duty to deliver the goods to the buyer, but delivery is not used in the popular sense of the word and does not mean the seller has to physically dispatch or send the goods to the buyer. The legal meaning of **'delivery'** is the 'voluntary transfer of possession from one person to another'. It is the seller's duty to ensure the goods are in a state to be dispatched to the buyer but not to actually do the sending, unless that is what is agreed in the contract. Delivery is the transfer of possession of goods not of ownership. In some cases the buyer already has physical possession of the goods because he has had the goods on hire from the seller. The seller and the buyer may agree that the buyer has to collect the goods from the seller's warehouse or may agree that the seller will transport the goods to the buyer's place of work or residence. If the seller and buyer make no arrangements for delivery of goods and the place of delivery is not stated in the contract, then the rules set out in s 29 apply.

- Delivery is at the seller's place of business, unless the contract for sale is for specific goods and at the time the contract is made those goods, to the knowledge of the parties, are at some other place, in which case delivery is at that other place.

- If the goods are in possession of a third party, delivery does not take place until the third party acknowledges to the buyer that he is holding the goods on the buyer's behalf.

Date and time of delivery

If it is agreed that the goods are to be sent by the seller but no time is stated in the contract, then the goods must be sent within a reasonable time at a reasonable hour of the day. What is reasonable depends on the circumstances. Late delivery of goods is a breach of contract but whether the buyer can treat the contract as at an end depends if delivery is of the essence to the contract. This means that the term of the contract relating to delivery was so important that it is treated as a condition of the contract. Whether delivery is of the essence to the contract depends upon the intention of the parties, which may be expressed or implied into contracts. For example, the delivery date of a marquee for a 21st birthday party, where the date of the party is known to the seller, will be implied as being of the essence to the contract. In commercial contracts, where a delivery date is a fixed day then it is presumed that the date is of the essence.

If a delivery date is fixed and a condition of the contract but the seller asks the buyer for an extension, the buyer may agree to a later fixed date or agree without fixing a new date. If the latter happens, the buyer is entitled to give the seller reasonable notice that he will not accept the goods after a certain date. Alternatively, the buyer can refuse to grant the extension and repudiate the contract.

Quantity of goods: SOGA, s 30

If goods are delivered in the wrong quantity (too many or too few) the buyer can reject all the goods (subject to s 30A), accept all the goods delivered, or if too many are delivered just accept the quantity contracted for. If goods are accepted, they must be paid for at the contract price. Section 30A states that a buyer does not have the right to reject goods in a non-consumer contract where the shortfall or excess delivered is so slight that it would be unreasonable to reject.

The nature and quality of goods

The goods delivered must be those specified in the contract and comply with the express and implied terms of the contract. If the goods do not comply with the terms of the contract, the buyer may reject the goods. If the wrong goods (as opposed to the wrong quantity of the right goods) are supplied, the buyer can only accept the goods if the seller agrees to sell them.

Delivery by instalments: SOGA s 31

Unless otherwise agreed, a buyer does not have to accept delivery by instalments. Where the contract does provide for goods to be delivered and paid for by instalments, and delivery of some of the instalments is defective, the question is whether the buyer can treat the whole contract as at an end. This will depend on the terms of the contract and the circumstances of the case. Where the breach is small and unlikely to be repeated, usually the buyer will only be allowed to claim damages and the contract continues.

Duties of Buyer: Accept Delivery and Pay for Goods

The buyer has a duty to accept delivery of the goods and pay for them: SOGA, s 27. The general rule is that the buyer takes delivery from the seller's place of business and the seller should have the goods ready for collection. If the buyer fails to collect the goods at the specified time where time is of the essence, or within a reasonable time, then the buyer is in breach of contract. The buyer will be liable for the seller's losses including the seller's reasonable charge for storage and care of the goods.

The SOGA, s 35, provides that acceptance by a buyer takes place:

- When he informs the seller that he has accepted the goods, or
- When he does something to the goods, once they have been delivered to him, which is inconsistent with the ownership of the seller (for example, he sells the goods to another person or he consumes the goods).
- When he retains the goods for a reasonable amount of time, without informing the seller that he has rejected them.

Where goods are delivered to a buyer who has not previously examined them, the buyer will not be considered to have accepted goods until he has had a reasonable opportunity of examining them and checking that the goods conform to the contract, or if it is a sale by sample checking that the bulk conforms with the sample.

What is considered to be a reasonable time depends upon the facts and circumstances of each case.

Rogers v Parish (1987)

Facts: The claimant sought to reject a £16,000 Range Rover car after seven months with 5,500 miles on the clock. The car had endless mechanical problems from the moment of delivery and spent most of the time in the garage undergoing unsuccessful repairs.

Decision: The car had not been 'accepted' under the SOGA, s 35, and the claimant was entitled to reject it.

However, in the following case the courts held that a reasonable time to reject the goods had expired.

Jones v Gallagher (2004)

Facts: The buyers complained to the sellers that the fitted kitchen they had bought had various defects, and the colour did not match existing kitchen furniture. However, it was several months later that the buyers rejected the contract, mainly on the grounds of colour.

Decision: A reasonable time had passed and the right to reject the contract had been lost. The colour of the kitchen would have been evident on initial examination. The buyers could receive damages but not the whole contract price.

Where defective goods are delivered to a buyer, the buyer is not considered to have accepted goods merely because he asks for or agrees to goods being repaired by the seller. In a consumer contract this right cannot be excluded and, therefore, gives protection to a consumer who does not initially realise that they have the right to reject faulty goods and instead had agreed that the seller could repair the goods.

In *J & H Ritchie Ltd v Lloyd Ltd* the House of Lords stated that, where goods are repaired, the buyer must be given enough information to make a 'properly informed choice' whether to accept the repaired goods or not.

J & H Ritchie Ltd v Lloyd Ltd (2007)

Facts: The claimants, farmers, bought a combination seed drill and power harrow from the defendant manufacturer. After a few days use, the claimants noticed the harrow was vibrating very badly and returned it to the defendants. The defendants informed the claimants that the harrow had been repaired to 'factory gate specifications' and was ready for collection. The harrow had been missing two bearings but, despite requests, the defendants would not tell the claimants what the problem had been. Eventually the claimants discovered that the bearings had been missing, and rejected the harrow believing that the missing bearings may have caused damage to other parts of the machinery.

Decision: The claimants were entitled to reject the harrow. They were not deemed to have accepted the harrow merely because they had agreed to have it repaired, and were entitled to the information requested so they could make an informed decision whether to accept the repaired harrow or not.

Buyer's duty to pay for the goods

The purchase price of the goods is usually such an important point that the amount to be paid for goods is usually fixed in the contract. If it is not fixed then the buyer must pay a reasonable price. The time that the payment for the goods is to be made may be fixed by the parties, but if it is not fixed the buyer has the duty to pay for the goods when he takes possession of them. In business contracts the seller sometimes demands payment in advance or, more usually, accepts credit and delivers the goods before payment.

Key Concept It is the duty of the seller to deliver goods, and the duty of the buyer to accept and pay for them, according to the terms set out in the contract of sale.

Remedies of the Buyer and Seller for Breach of Contract

Various remedies are available where one of the parties to the contract is in breach depending upon a number of factors, including whether the breach is a condition or warranty, and which party is in possession of the goods.

The Seller's Remedies

The seller has two types of remedy if the buyer breaches the contract of sale. The seller can take action against the buyer personally by suing him for the contract price or for damages for non-acceptance of the goods. Alternatively, the seller can take action that involves a claim on the goods (see Figure 10.8).

Claim for the price or for damages for non-acceptance: SOGA, s 50

The seller can sue the buyer for the contract price where the buyer has failed to pay for the goods and either ownership of the goods has passed to the buyer, or payment was due on a specific date and that date has passed. If it was an agreement to pay by a specific date then the ownership of the goods need not have passed to the buyer. The seller can sue for damages for non-acceptance of delivery of goods if the buyer fails to accept the goods. The seller can also recover damages for storing or insuring the goods, or arranging a resale of the goods.

Business Insight Dispute over oral agreement to sell

In *McCandless Aircraft v Payne and Eminence Aviation Ltd* (2010) the High Court had to decide which of the parties' evidence was the most credible, in an argument relating to the oral agreement to sell a helicopter for $265,000. The court accepted the evidence of the claimant, that at a meeting the parties had agreed that the claimant would sell a helicopter to the defendant but retain title to it until the defendant sold it on to a third party. During this time, the defendant would pay the interest on a loan that the claimant had on the helicopter. The resale was to take place within six months, and if it was not resold within that time the defendant was to pay $265,000 for it. Although the helicopter was delivered, and used by the third party for two years, the defendant failed to sell it or pay for it. Eventually the claimant successfully reclaimed the helicopter, sold it for $180,000, and sued the defendant for non-acceptance of goods under the Sale of Goods Act 1979, s 50. The claimant was entitled to interest on the loan and the difference between the contract price of $265,000 and the resale price of $180,000.

Action against the goods

The right of lien: SOGA, ss 41–43

Lien is the right of the seller to retain the goods until the contract price of the goods has been made in full. The seller has to be in possession of the goods and can only use this right against payment for the goods, and not for other expenses such as storage costs. This right exists if the goods have been sold and:

- The buyer has not paid for the goods, and there was no agreement for credit.
- The goods were bought on credit, and the credit period has expired.
- The buyer becomes insolvent (the buyer is unable to pay his debts as they become due).

The seller will lose his right of lien if the buyer pays for the goods or takes possession of them. The seller will also lose his right of lien if he hands the goods over to a carrier for transportation to the buyer and does not reserve the right to dispose of the goods or agrees to give up that right.

The right to stop the goods in transit: SOGA, ss 44 and 45

Where goods have been given to a carrier to deliver to a buyer, a seller may have the right to stop the goods in transit and retake possession of them if the buyer becomes insolvent. The seller retakes possession by taking physical control of the goods or by informing the carrier. The seller can only stop the goods in transit if they are not already in the possession of the buyer or his agent.

The right of resale: SOGA, s 48

Generally, the right of lien and stopping the goods in transit mean that the seller keeps or retakes possession of the goods but this does not generally give the seller the right to resell the goods. Section 48 of the SOGA allows the seller to resell goods that are perishable, provided the seller has either notified the buyer of his intention to resell and the buyer has not paid within a 'reasonable' time or the contract expressly allows for resale. If the goods are resold for less than the original contract price (the goods may no longer be in such good condition by the time they are resold) the seller will have the right to sue the original buyer for the shortfall.

The Buyer's Remedies

The buyer's primary remedy, for breach of contract by the seller, is to reject the goods and repudiate the contract. Alternatively, if the buyer does not have the right to reject the goods, he may claim damages. In limited circumstances the buyer may be able to claim specific performance. A consumer buyer has certain additional remedies under the SOGA, ss 48A–48F (see Figure 10.9).

Figure 10.8 Seller's remedies

Reject the goods

Where the seller has breached a condition of the contract, the buyer is entitled to repudiate the contract provided he has not already accepted the goods. If an electrical store sells a television that is not of satisfactory quality, the buyer is entitled to reject the television and reclaim the purchase price provided the buyer has not already 'accepted' it. The rules on what constitutes 'acceptance' are set out in the SOGA, s 35, and have been considered earlier under 'Duties of Buyer'. If a buyer has accepted goods, he will not be able to reject them later but he will have a claim for damages. If a buyer 'accepts' a television that is of unsatisfactory quality, then he will have lost his right to reject it. However, in a consumer sale, a buyer is not assumed to have accepted faulty goods just because he agrees to the goods being repaired. In a non-consumer sale, s 15A states that a buyer does not have the right to reject goods for breaches of sections 13–15 where the breach is so slight that it would be unreasonable for him to reject them.

Claim damages

The buyer may claim damages where an express or implied term of a contract for the sale of goods has been breached by the seller or the seller has failed to deliver the goods. The amount of damages the buyer is entitled to is governed by ordinary contract principles and the SOGA.

Damages for non-delivery of goods: SOGA, s 51

Where the seller wrongfully neglects or refuses to deliver goods, the buyer can sue for damages. The amount of damages is the estimated loss that arises in the ordinary course of events directly as a result of the breach. If there is a market price for the goods, the amount of damages is the difference between the contract price and the market price at the time the goods should have been delivered. Monies paid in advance for the goods can be reclaimed: s 54.

Damages for breach of a contractual term: SOGA, s 53

The buyer can sue for damages where the seller has breached a term of the contract for sale and either the term is a warranty, or the term is a condition, and the buyer elects or is compelled (e.g. has accepted the goods) to carry on with the contract and claim damages. The amount of damages is usually the difference between the contracted goods and the goods received. For example, the difference in price between 1,000 shirts which are 100 per cent silk (stated in the contract) and 1,000 shirts which are 75 per cent silk (delivered by the seller and accepted by the buyer).

Specific performance: SOGA, s 52

Where the seller refuses to deliver goods, the buyer can sue for specific performance. However, the court is unlikely to grant this remedy unless goods are unique or are unavailable elsewhere.

Additional remedies for consumers: SOGA, ss 48A–48F

The Sale and Supply of Goods to Consumers Regulations 2002 amended the Sale of Goods Act 1979, giving consumers additional remedies where goods do not conform to the contract at the time of delivery. The SOGA, s 48B, states that the buyer has the right to require the seller to repair or replace the goods within a reasonable time. The seller must pay for the repair or replacement and any transportation or postage costs. The right to repair or replacement is qualified in that the seller does not have to repair or replace the goods if it is impossible, or disproportionate in relation to other remedies. For example, the buyer demands repair of the goods, and a price reduction or rescission would be more than adequate. In considering if a remedy is disproportionate, account is taken of the difference in the goods supplied and the goods contracted for (their different values and qualities) and whether using a different remedy would cause significant inconvenience to the buyer.

Figure 10.9 Buyer's remedies

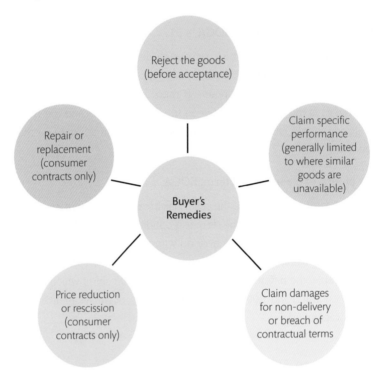

If the buyer cannot claim repair or replacement, or the seller fails to repair or replace the goods within a reasonable time, the buyer can rescind the contract (similar to **rejection of goods** in this context), or get a reduction in the price. But in these cases, the money the buyer gets back may be reduced to take account of the use he has had of the goods.

If the buyer is making a claim within six months of delivery of goods, it is assumed that the goods were defective at the date of delivery unless the seller proves otherwise.

Business Insight Reform of Consumer Law

Extensive reform of Consumer Law is currently being undertaken by the UK. The Consumer Rights bill consolidates, updates and clarifies the law on consumer rights and covers goods, services and digital content. It is expected to be passed by Parliament and come into force in October 2015. The Consumer Contracts (Information, Cancellation and Additional Charges) Regulations 2013 are in force and apply to contracts made after 13 June 2014. Key changes brought in by the Regulations include giving consumers the right to cancel, within 14 days, distance or off-premises contracts (e.g. contracts made online) without having to give any reason. A trader cannot take any additional payments from a consumer without their express consent. This means that a trader cannot charge for additional items by adding a pre-ticked box. Traders must provide a basic rate telephone number for consumers who may wish to make a complaint, enquire about or cancel an order rather than a premium rate number.

Terms Implied into Other Contracts

The implied terms set out in the SOGA do not apply to contracts that fall outside the definition of a sale of goods contract; however, similar terms are implied into contracts for the transfer or hire of goods, the provision of services, and hire purchase agreements. The same protection, in relation to public statements in the SOGA, is also given to consumers under these other contracts. Namely that public statements made about specific characteristics of products can be relevant circumstances for the purposes of deciding whether goods are of satisfactory quality.

Contracts for the Supply of Services and the Transfer of Goods

The Supply of Goods and Services Act 1982 (SOGASA) applies to contracts for the supply of services such as hairdressing, plumbing, and contracts under which the supplier agrees to supply goods and carry out a service, such as supply and fit a kitchen. The kitchen units and appliances are the goods, and the fitting of these items is the supply of a service. The Act also implies terms into barter contracts, which is where goods are transferred in return for other goods. In addition, the Act applies to contracts of hire (see later in the chapter).

The SOGASA implies similar terms as found in the SOGA in contracts for the supply of goods (with or without services). These terms are conditions of the contract, which if breached allow for the contract to be rescinded and damages claimed for any losses.

- Right to transfer the goods (title): s 2.
- The goods correspond with description: s 3.
- The goods are of satisfactory quality (where goods are supplied in the course of a business): s 4(2).

- The goods are fit for the buyer's purpose (where goods are supplied in the course of a business): s 4(5).
- The goods correspond with sample: s 5.

Where a service is supplied and the supplier is acting in the course of a business, the following two terms are implied into the contract.

- The supplier will carry out the service with reasonable care and skill: s 13.
- If no time is fixed, then the work will be carried out within a reasonable time: s 14.

In addition, implied into all contracts for the supply of a service, whether acting in the course of a business or not, is:

- If no price is fixed then the price charged will be reasonable: s 15.

Reasonable care and skill is an objective test and, for example, a plumber contracted to install a bathroom will be expected to carry out the work of a competent tradesman rather than an amateur. In the following case, the court considered the duty of a tour operator under s 13 to take reasonable care and skill.

Wilson v Best Travel Ltd (1993)

Facts: The claimant booked a hotel in Greece through the defendant, a tour operator. He suffered extensive injuries when he fell through glass patio doors at the hotel. The doors, at 5 mm thick, complied with Greek safety standards but not British safety standards. The claimant sued the tour operator for breach of s 13 of the SOGASA.

Decision: Under s 13 of the SOGASA, the tour operator owed a duty to exercise reasonable care to exclude accommodation where guests could not spend a holiday there in reasonable safety. This duty had been discharged as the hotel met Greek safety standards, and the absence of higher standards was not such that a reasonable holidaymaker might decline to take a holiday at the hotel.

What is considered to be a reasonable time or reasonable price is a question of fact and depends upon the circumstances. A customer taking his car to a garage for minor repair work can expect it to be completed in a few days and, if no mention is made of the cost of the repair, then a reasonable sum can be charged. If the car is not repaired for months then the garage will be in breach of s 14 and, if the charge is exorbitant, in breach of s 15.

The terms implied into contracts where services are to be supplied are innominate terms. This means that, unlike ss 2, 3, 4, and 5 (discussed earlier), they are not necessarily conditions of the contract but may be treated as conditions or warranties depending upon what was agreed between the parties and the seriousness of the breach. If the term is a warranty and it is breached by the supplier, the customer will be entitled to damages but will not be entitled to treat the contract as at an end.

Contract of Hire

In a contract of **hire**, ownership of goods does not pass but the customer has the right to possess and use goods for a limited time. Contracts of hire are common in business, particularly in the building and construction industry where equipment such as cranes, excavators, and scaffolding are often hired. Other common contracts of hire are for the hire of cars. The implied terms are similar to those for the supply of goods. There is also an implied right to transfer possession for the agreed period of hire. The terms relate to the state of the goods at the beginning of the hiring and for a reasonable time afterwards. It does not impose a duty on the supplier to maintain and repair the goods, but this may be provided for expressly in the hire contract.

The terms implied into contracts of hire are:

- Right to hire: s 7.

- The goods correspond with description: s 8.

- The goods are of satisfactory quality (where goods are supplied in the course of a business): s 9(2).

- The goods are fit for the buyer's purpose (where goods are supplied in the course of a business): s 9(5).

- The goods correspond with sample: s 10.

Hire Purchase Contracts

A hire purchase contract is where the hirer agrees to hire goods for a fixed period of time and is given the option to purchase the goods for a nominal sum at the end of that period of time. New cars are often purchased by consumers under a hire purchase agreement. The car that the customer desires is sold by the garage to a finance company. This company then enters into a hire purchase agreement with the customer. The car is in fact 'hired' by the customer for a number of years in return for a monthly payment. The final instalment is the nominal sum to purchase the car, and ownership of the car is then passed from the finance company to the customer. The Supply of Goods (Implied Terms) Act 1973 implies similar terms to those in the SOGA into contracts of hire purchase.

- Right to sell: s 8.
- The goods correspond with description: s 9.

- The goods are of satisfactory quality (where goods are supplied in the course of a business): s 10(2).

- The goods are fit for the buyer's purpose (where goods are supplied in the course of a business): s 10(3).

- The goods correspond with sample: s 11.

Transfer of ownership

The Hire Purchase Act 1964 protects a private purchaser who buys a car in good faith unaware that the seller does not own the car but has hired it under a hire purchase agreement. Ownership of the car will pass to the private purchaser. The hirer will have the registration documents of the car and the unsuspecting buyer will not know that the car is owned by the hire purchase company. The Act only protects private purchasers, because a trading garage will have access to information on cars subject to hire purchase agreements.

Exclusion of Implied Terms

The Unfair Contract Terms Act 1977 provides that liability for breach of all implied terms cannot be excluded or limited in any consumer contracts. These contracts could be ones not only for the sale of goods contracts but also for the supply of goods or hire of goods. Where both the seller and the buyer are acting in the course of a business, implied terms, other than those relating to title or right to hire, may be excluded but only if it is reasonable to do so.

Basic Terminology

For an online flashcard glossary visit the Online Resource Centre

Delivery (legal meaning) Voluntary transfer of possession from one person to another.

Express term Term stated either orally or in writing by one of the parties making the contract.

Hire Possession (but not ownership) of goods in return for payment.

Implied term A term in a contract which is not expressly agreed by the parties to the contract.

Lien A legal claim over someone's property as security for a debt.

Rejection of goods Refusal to accept goods.

Reservation of title clause A clause in a contract of sale retaining ownership of the goods until payment has been made.

Romalpa clause Complex reservation of title clause where the seller retains rights in the goods after they have been sold on to a third party, or where they have been used in a manufacturing process.

Sample A small quantity of goods to be examined by the buyer on the understanding that the bulk will conform to the sample.

Satisfactory quality Goods meet the standard that a reasonable person would regard as satisfactory, taking into account price, description, and other relevant factors.

Specific goods Goods identified at the time the contract of sale is made.

Title Ownership of goods.

Unascertained goods Goods that have not yet been manufactured, acquired by the seller, or are unidentified.

Summary

After studying this chapter students should be able to:

Explain what is meant by a contract for the sale of goods

- A contract for sale of goods is 'a contract by which the seller transfers, or agrees to transfer, the property in goods to the buyer for a money consideration called the price'.
- 'Goods' are defined as all personal property, crops, and other things attached to land which are agreed to be severed from the land before sale or under a contract of sale.
- The 'price' must consist of money. If the exact price is not specified the buyer must pay a reasonable price.

Identify terms that are implied into contracts for the sale of goods

- The seller has the lawful right to sell the goods and transfer ownership of them. This term can never be excluded from the contract for sale of goods.
- If the goods are sold by description, the goods will match their description.
- The goods will be of satisfactory quality (only applies where the seller is acting in the course of a business).
- The goods will be reasonably fit for their purpose (only applies where the seller is acting in the course of a business).
- If sold by sample, the goods will match the sample, and be free from any defect of quality not apparent on a reasonable examination of the sample.

Distinguish between the right to ownership of goods and the right to possession of goods and explain when these rights may be transferred from a seller to a buyer

- Title (ownership) in goods does not have to pass from the seller to the buyer at the same time as physical possession of the goods.
- Ownership of specific goods passes in accordance with the intention of the parties or if no intention is evident according to the rules set out in the Sale of Goods Act 1979, s 18.
- Ownership of unascertained goods passes when the goods matching the contract description are in a deliverable state and are unconditionally appropriated to the contract.
- Where a contract for the sale of goods contains a 'reservation of title clause', ownership of the goods will not pass to the buyer until payment is made by the buyer.
- The general rule on transfer of title is that only the owner or his agent acting with his authority can transfer ownership of goods to the buyer. There are a number of exceptions to this rule.

Identify the rules relating to delivery of goods

- Delivery is the 'voluntary transfer of possession from one person to another'. It is the transfer of possession of goods not of ownership.

For an online printable version scan here or visit the Online Resource Centre

- Unless agreed otherwise delivery is usually at the seller's place of business.
- If it is agreed that the goods are to be sent by the seller but no time is stated in the contract, the goods must be sent within a reasonable time at a reasonable hour of the day.
- The goods delivered must be those specified in the contract and comply with the express and implied terms.
- Unless otherwise agreed, a buyer does not have to accept delivery by instalments.

Outline the duties of a seller and buyer and the remedies available for breach of a sale of goods contract

- It is the duty of the seller to deliver goods, and of the buyer to accept and pay for them, according to the terms set out in the contract of sale.
- The seller has two types of remedy if the buyer breaches the contract of sale: action against the buyer personally, by suing him for the contract price or for damages for non-acceptance of the goods. Alternatively, the seller may have the right of lien, the right to stop the goods in transit, or the right of resale.

Identify terms that are implied into contracts for the supply of goods and services, contracts for the hire of goods, and hire purchase contracts

- Similar terms to those implied in the Sale of Goods Act 1979 are implied into contracts for the transfer or hire of goods, the provision of services, and hire purchase agreements by the Supply of Goods and Services Act 1982 and the Supply of Goods (Implied Terms) Act 1973.
- In addition, implied into contracts for service are terms relating to care and skill, time, and price.

Questions

For outline answers visit the Online Resource Centre

1. Cathy, the owner of a small business, is going on a skiing holiday. Before leaving she orders a grey carpet for the office from carpets2U Ltd's sample book. The back of the sample has a sticker on it which describes the carpet as 100 per cent wool. Cathy also treats herself to an expensive set of new skis from Alpine Ltd. The first time Cathy uses the skis they snap into pieces. On her return from holiday, Cathy discovers the office carpet that has been laid is pink and 100 per cent polypropylene. Advise Cathy if any of the terms which are implied into contracts under the Sale of Goods Act 1979 (as amended) may have been breached in the contract for the sale of the carpet and the contract for the sale of the skis.

2. Ali, a student, buys a new laptop computer for £400 from a local retailer 'IT Solutions'. When he pays, he signs a document (which he doesn't read) which is an acceptance note. In the first three months, the laptop has to be returned nine times to have minor defects remedied. In total, Ali only has use of the computer for two weeks within that three-month period. When the laptop malfunctions for the tenth time, Ali returns to 'IT Solutions' and demands his money back. The manager of the store points to a large sign behind the counter which says 'No Refunds—Only Repairs'. Advise Ali.

3. Explain the terms which are implied into contracts for the sale of goods by ss 13, 14(2), 14(3), and 15 of the Sale of Goods Act 1979.

4. 'Ownership of goods passes when the parties intend it to pass' but when does ownership pass if no intention of the parties is evident?

Further Reading

Adams and Macqueen, *Atiyah's Sale of Goods*, 12th edn (Pearson, 2013).

Chuah and Furmston, *Commercial and Consumer Law*, 2nd edn (Pearson, 2013) Chapter 4.

Dobson and Stokes, *Commercial Law Textbook*, 8th edn (Sweet and Maxwell, 2012) Part 2.

Consumer Rights Bill 2014/15: https://www.gov.uk/government/publications/consumer-rights-bill

Law Commission: http://lawcommission.justice.gov.uk/index.htm.

Competition and Markets Authority: https://www.gov.uk/government/organisations/competition-and-markets-authority

Online Resource Centre

Test your knowledge by trying this chapter's **Multiple Choice Questions**. Visit:

www.oup.com/uk/orc/law/company/ jonesibl3e/01student/mcqs/ch10/

For more information, updates, and multiple choice questions, please visit the Online Resource Centre at:

www.oup.com/uk/orc/law/company/ jonesibl2e/

PART 3

TORT LAW

The Tort of Negligence

Introduction

A **tort** is a civil wrong for which a remedy, usually compensation, is available to the wronged person in the civil courts. In the Law of Torts, duties are owed to persons in various circumstances, and liability for negligent or wrongful action is imposed by law. For example, a duty of care to other road users is imposed by law on all drivers. An occupier of property owes a duty of care to all visitors on his premises. This is different from obligations in a contract where the parties voluntarily agree to be bound. The occupier of property and the driver of a vehicle cannot escape liability for breaching their duties, although they may be able to cover losses through insurance. Where persons are insured, the insurance company usually 'steps into the shoes' of the insured and, in the event of a legal action, it is the insurance company that settles any claims.

The primary function of the Law of Torts is to provide remedies to claimants who have suffered harm, loss, or an infringement of rights. The harm includes physical injury to persons or property, damage to persons' reputations or financial interests, and interference with persons' use and enjoyment of their land. However, just suffering such a loss does not necessarily mean the law will provide a remedy; a claimant must show that the person committing the tort owed them a duty of care and that the tort caused the loss.

The Law of Torts covers a range of different civil wrongs including negligence, trespass, nuisance, and defamation. Each tort has its own rules about liability but most torts require an element of culpability, which means that liability is only imposed on a person who intentionally or negligently acts or fails to act in a particular manner. However, there are some torts, called **strict liability** torts, that impose liability on a person even though they have not been at fault in any way. In some situations, a person can be held strictly liable for torts committed by another person. This liability is called **'vicarious liability'** and it is particularly important in the business environment as employers may be vicariously liable for the torts of their employees.

Usually, to succeed in a tortious claim, a claimant must prove that the tortious act or omission caused some damage (although there are a few torts such as trespass where the claimant does not have to prove he suffered actual damage). There are various defences to an action in tort. Some are called general defences because they apply throughout the Law of Torts, and other defences are called specific defences because they only apply to a particular tort. Defences will be examined in Chapter 12.

The Law of Torts has largely been developed through case law from decisions of judges, although, in more recent times, new tortious duties have been created by statute. The enactment of the Human Rights Act 1998, which brought the European Convention on Human Rights into UK law, means that judges must now develop the common law and interpret torts to ensure compliance with the Convention.

Learning Objectives

After studying this chapter you should be able to:

- Outline the difference between the Law of Torts and Contract and Criminal Law.

- Explain the necessary ingredients of negligence.

- Explain how a duty of care may be established.

- Understand the special requirements for the recovery of pure economic loss and for loss as a result of psychiatric injuries.

- Describe the principle of breach of a duty of care.

- Explain the extent of damages resulting from breach of a duty of care.

Distinction between the Law of Torts and Criminal Law

Both the Law of Torts and Criminal Law are concerned with wrongs; however, the Law of Torts is primarily about providing a remedy for people for harm that they have suffered, and Criminal Law is primarily about punishing the people who have committed wrongs in the eyes of the state (see Figure 11.1). Sometimes an event can give rise to both criminal and tortious actions. If a driver of a car carelessly loses control of his car and knocks over a cyclist, the driver will be prosecuted for careless/dangerous driving in the criminal courts, and, if found guilty, will be punished by a sentence imposed by the court. At the same time, the cyclist can bring a civil action in the tort of negligence to recover compensation for his personal injuries and damage to his bicycle. If the defendant is found liable, he will have to pay compensation to the claimant.

Figure 11.1 Difference between a tort and a crime

Crime → Defendant is **prosecuted by the state** in the Magistrates' Court or Crown Court. → If found guilty, the defendant will be punished by imprisonment, fine, etc.

Tort → Defendant is **sued by the claimant** in the County Court or High Court. → If found liable, the defendant will have to pay compensation to the claimant.

Distinction between the Law of Torts and Contract Law

Both Contract Law and the Law of Torts are part of the Civil Law; however, in the Law of Contract, the obligations imposed in the contract have been agreed to by the parties when they entered into the contract. The parties have entered into legal relations voluntarily.

The Law of Torts concerns involuntary obligations that are imposed upon persons by the law. The cyclist who has been negligently knocked off his bike by a car driver can sue the driver. The liability of the driver is imposed by the law and he has no choice in the matter. In a contract, it is up to the parties to decide whether to enter into a contract, accepting liability for their contractual obligations. The Law of Torts is particularly important in the business world, and covers actions such as nuisance, brought against a business whose operations disturb the peace and quiet of their neighbours, and gives protection to consumers who may not have a contractual relationship with the manufacturer of defective goods. In some cases, a person may have the choice whether to sue in the Law of Contract or the Law of Torts. For example, where professional advice, which has been paid for, is given carelessly and as a result the client incurs a loss, he may be able to sue his advisor for breach of contract or in the tort of negligence. Which action he decides to take may depend on practical differences, such as legal time limits on bringing the action or how compensation is calculated. Under the Limitation Act 1980, the time limit for bringing a court action in the Law of Torts is either six years from the date of damage or, where the claim is based on certain torts such as negligence or nuisance, the time limit for bringing an action is three years. The time limit in contract cases is six years from the date of breach of contract. Both in the Law of Torts and Contract Law, an award of damages (compensation) is the usual remedy for a party who has suffered loss, although the method of calculation of loss may differ. If there is a contract between the parties, usually, an action for breach of contract is commenced.

Key Concept The Law of Torts covers a range of civil wrongs for which a remedy, usually compensation, may be awarded by the civil courts to the wronged person.

The Tort of Negligence

Negligence is an important tort that covers a wide range of situations where persons negligently cause harm to others. In order to succeed in an action for negligence, it is necessary for a claimant to establish the following three elements:

- The defendant owed the claimant a duty of care.
- The defendant breached that duty of care.
- Reasonably foreseeable damage was caused by the breach of duty.

Each of these elements needs to be examined and understood in turn, but it is important to note that these three elements sometimes overlap, and in a court case the issues are often looked at together rather than separately.

Element 1: Duty of Care

Prior to 1932 there was no general duty of care principle, and the courts had a very restrictive attitude to the recovery of loss suffered as a result of negligence. There were a small number of circumstances where the courts had held that a duty of care was owed, such as by road-users to other road-users, and occupiers of premises to visitors. In the landmark case of *Donoghue v Stevenson* (1932), a general principle called the 'neighbour principle' was set down to determine whether a duty of care was owed for negligently-inflicted loss.

Donoghue v Stevenson (1932)

Facts: The claimant, Mrs Donoghue, and her friend went to a café where the friend bought the claimant an ice cream and a bottle of ginger beer. The ginger beer was in an opaque bottle and was opened at the table. The café owner poured part of the ginger beer over the ice cream which the claimant consumed. The friend then poured the rest of the ginger beer into a glass and the remains of what appeared to be a decomposed snail came out of the bottle. The claimant argued that she suffered shock and gastroenteritis as a result of drinking the ginger beer on her ice cream and claimed £500 damages from the defendant, Stevenson, who was the manufacturer of the beer. The claimant could not sue the defendant in the law of contract as there was no contract between them.

Decision: Every person owed a duty of care to his neighbour, who was somebody that a person could reasonably foresee would be injured by his acts or omissions. The defendant could reasonably foresee that someone, other than the purchaser, would drink the ginger beer and, therefore, owed a duty of care to the ultimate consumer. The neighbour principle was laid down by Lord Atkin who said:

> You must take reasonable care to avoid acts or omissions which you can reasonably foresee would be likely to injure your neighbour. Who then is my neighbour? The answer seems to be persons who are so closely and directly affected by my act that I ought reasonably to have them in contemplation as being so affected when I am directing my mind to the acts or omissions which are called in question.

Although the neighbour principle had the potential of being applied in numerous circumstances, the development of the new tort of negligence was very cautious to begin with. However, in the 1970s and early 1980s the scope of the duty of care was expanded by the courts, and it appeared that a duty of care could be owed for any reasonably foreseeable negligently-inflicted loss, unless there were policy reasons against imposing a duty.

Policy reasons means that, when making a decision, a court should take into account the implications the decision will have for law in society. Factors that influence judges include:

- Which party is best able to afford the loss? Is one of the parties insured?
- Will there be a flood of claims? If a duty is imposed will the number of potential claimants be huge?
- Will imposing a duty encourage people to take more care in certain circumstances?
- Are there moral reasons for imposing a duty?

The Three-Stage Test

The rapid expansion of persons owing a duty of care to others came to an end in the late 1980s. Senior judges clearly became worried that the tort of negligence could get out of control and sought to check its growth. A more cautious approach to the development of the duty of care was taken. Unless a duty of care had already been firmly established by previous cases, such as a duty owed by manufacturers to consumers, vehicle-drivers to passengers, or employers to their employees, then a three-stage test had to be satisfied. The three-stage test to determine whether a duty of care exists was set out by the House of Lords in *Caparo v Dickman* (1990) (see Figure 11.2).

Caparo Industries v Dickman (1990)

Facts: The claimants, Caparo, owned shares in Fidelity plc. Caparo read and relied on the statutory audited accounts of Fidelity plc, prepared by the defendants, Dickman, when making their decision to purchase additional shares in Fidelity plc and then to mount a successful takeover bid. However, the accounts were inaccurate and showed a profit of £1.3 m instead of a loss of £465,000. Caparo sued Dickman for negligent misstatement.

Decision: The House of Lords stated that Dickman was not liable because auditors owed no duty to the public at large or to the individual shareholders who rely on the accounts to buy further shares. The purpose of a statutory audit was to enable shareholders to exercise proper control over a company and not to provide information for share dealings or takeovers. Lord Bridge outlined a new 'three-stage' test for determining the duty of care issue:

... What emerges is that, in addition to the foreseeability of damage, necessary ingredients in any situation giving rise to a duty of care are that there should exist between the party owing the duty and the party to whom it is owed a relationship characterised by the law as one of 'proximity' or 'neighbourhood' and that the situation should be one in which the court considers it fair, just and reasonable that the law should impose a duty of a given scope upon the one party for the benefit of the other.

Key Concept   The three-stage test for establishing whether a duty of care exists is:

- Was the harm or loss caused reasonably foreseeable?
- Was there a sufficient relationship of proximity between the claimant and the defendant for a duty to be imposed?
- In all circumstances is it fair, just, and reasonable that the law should impose a duty on the defendant?

Figure 11.2 Test for establishing whether a duty of care exists

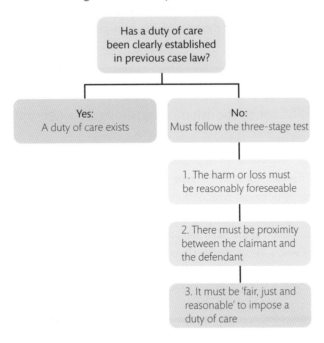

Today, in order to ascertain whether a claimant is owed a duty of care in a particular case, firstly it has to be established whether there is any existing legal authority for a duty of care in those circumstances. If there is a duty of care recognised by earlier cases, then the court can follow the earlier decision. But if there is no existing legal authority, then all the three requirements outlined in the *Caparo* three-stage test just described will have to be established if the court is to recognise a duty of care. These three elements are linked and claimants may be unsuccessful in proving an existence of a duty of care for more than one of the factors.

Was the harm or loss caused reasonably foreseeable?

In order for a duty of care to exist, the loss or harm caused to the claimant must have been reasonably foreseen at the time the defendant was negligent.

Home Office v Dorset Yacht Co (1970)

Facts: 'Borstal boys', who had been taken on a trip to Brownsea Island by officers from the borstal (who worked for the Home Office—a borstal was a type of youth custody centre), escaped one night and damaged the claimants' yacht.

Decision: The Home Office owed a duty of care to the claimants. Although usually one man is under no duty of controlling another to prevent injury to a third, in this case there was a special relationship between the boys and the officers. The damage caused to the claimants' property was reasonably foreseeable.

Was there a sufficient relationship of proximity between the claimant and the defendant?

Proximity does not necessarily mean physically nearby, but means legal closeness between the claimant and the defendant at the time of the cause of complaint. Legal closeness includes issues such as personal relationships between the parties, length of time between events, and whether goods may have been tampered with. In *Donoghue v Stevenson* the bottle of ginger beer was opened at the table and so could not have been tampered with by another party, whereas in *Evans v Triplex Safety Glass Co Ltd* (considered next) the windscreen could have shattered for reasons other than defective manufacturing.

Evans v Triplex Safety Glass Co Ltd (1936)

Facts: The claimant bought a car which had been fitted with a windscreen of 'Triplex Toughened Safety Glass'. The claimant was injured when the windscreen shattered while he was driving.
Decision: The manufacturers of the windscreen were not liable because too much time had elapsed between the manufacture of the windscreen and the incident. The windscreen had been in place for over a year. In addition it may have shattered for other reasons such as poor fitting by the car makers.

The level of proximity required differs from one situation to another, because certain types of damage or conduct require a more direct connection between the claimant and the defendant. In order to succeed in a claim for economic loss, a claimant will have to prove a much closer relationship with the defendant than the claimant would have to prove in a claim for physical damage to his property. Proximity is also of particular significance where the claimant suffers only psychiatric injury.

In the following case the Court of Appeal stated that there was not a sufficient degree of proximity between a football club and a doctor who negligently treated one of its players and it would not be fair, just, or reasonable to impose a duty on the doctor for financial loss to the club. There was no evidence to show that the doctor would have realised he was taking on this additional duty and if this duty had been imposed then it might have conflicted with his duty of care towards the patient (e.g. by treatment which would enable the patient to play football but cause him problems in later life).

West Bromwich Albion Football Club Ltd v El-Safty (2006)

Facts: West Bromwich Albion Football Club claimed £2 million for financial loss against a surgeon who negligently advised that one of their players, Michael Appleton, should undergo reconstructive surgery for a knee injury.

Decision: The court stated that the doctor did not owe a duty of care to the club for financial losses incurred from losing the player and having to replace him. Although it was reasonably foreseeable that the club would suffer financial loss, there was not a sufficient degree of proximity (special relationship) between the club and the doctor and it would not be fair, just, or reasonable to impose a duty.

When is it 'fair, just and reasonable' to impose a duty of care?

Even if the harm is reasonably foreseeable and there is proximity between the claimant and the defendant, a court may still find that there is no duty of care if it is not fair, just, or reasonable to impose a duty on the defendant. This is usually a matter of public policy, and is where the courts have to take pragmatic considerations into account and decide if it is in the public interest to impose a duty of care. This final factor covers a range of issues such as if the imposition of a duty of care would prevent the defendant from carrying out his job appropriately, or if the injured person is assisting in the commission of a crime.

Hill v Chief Constable of West Yorkshire (1989)

Facts: The claimant, mother of the last victim of the serial murderer Peter Sutcliffe (the 'Yorkshire Ripper') sued the police in negligence. She argued that the police had been negligent in investigating the earlier murders committed by Sutcliffe, and if they had not acted carelessly Sutcliffe would have been caught much earlier and her daughter's death prevented.

Decision: The House of Lords stated that police do not generally owe a duty of care to individual members of the public as to the way in which they carry out their functions of investigating and controlling crime. There was insufficient proximity between the police and the public for a duty of care to be imposed on the police to protect potential future victims. There were also public policy reasons for not imposing a duty of care on the police, because to do so might lead the police to act in a defensive manner and divert their attention from their primary functions of suppressing crime.

In the following case the judge stated that, for public policy reasons, the duty of care was not owed by one participant of a criminal enterprise to another.

Ashton v Turner (1981)

Facts: Three drunken men committed a burglary and then sought to escape in a car owned by one of them. The car crashed. The claimant, one of the passengers, was injured and sought to bring a claim for negligence against the driver.

Decision: For public policy reasons, the driver was not liable for persons involved with him in the commission of a crime.

Courts may decide that a duty of care should not extend to new situations where parties could be expected to protect their interests by taking their own precautions such as insurance. Where issues are covered by other areas of law, the court may decide not to impose a duty of care if this would result in additional obligations on a party.

CBS Songs Ltd v Amstrad Consumer Electrics Plc (1988)

Facts: The defendants manufactured twin deck tape recording machines which enabled music to be illegally copied, in breach of copyright. The owners of the copyright claimed the defendants owed them a duty of care to ensure copyright was not breached.

Decisions: The court refused to impose a duty of care, under the Law of Torts, on the defendants to prevent breach of copyright. Copyright legislation that had been passed by Parliament imposed liability only where copying was unauthorised. It did not impose a duty on manufacturers of recording machines to prevent others from breaking copyright law.

The courts are sometimes reluctant to expand the duty of care, where to do so might encourage a large number of similar claims. This is known as the floodgates argument.

Human Rights Act 1998

When considering whether to extend the duty of care in new situations concerning public bodies, a court must now take account of the Human Rights Act 1998, which states that public bodies must act in accordance with the provisions of the European Convention on Human Rights. In *Z v United Kingdom* (2001) the European Court of Human Rights found that the UK had breached the Convention when a local authority had not acted promptly enough in taking children into their care.

Failing to act

In English law there is generally no duty for failing to act even if another person suffers as a result. A person who sees someone struggling to swim in a pool has no duty to attempt to rescue them. A passer-by has no duty to prevent a child running in the road in front of a car. This is based on the principle that there is no liability for 'pure' omission. However, a person does owe a duty of care for failing to act if he has undertaken to carry out a specific duty to an individual person, or if a duty has been imposed upon him. A lifeguard will have a duty to act to help a person struggling in the swimming pool and parents are expected by law to care for their children.

Key Concept For a duty of care to exist the claimant must establish that there is earlier legal authority for a duty existing in the same circumstances or prove: (a) the harm or loss caused was reasonably foreseeable, and (b) there was proximity between the claimant and the defendant, and (c) it is fair, just, and reasonable in all the circumstances for the law to impose a duty on the defendant.

Pure Economic Loss

Where there has only been **pure economic loss**, recovery of losses incurred through the tort of negligence is very limited. If there is a contract between the parties, then damages can be claimed for 'pure economic loss', but where there is no contract, and no physical injury or damage to property, the law does not usually impose a duty of care, although there are some exceptions where there is a particularly close relationship between the parties.

It is important to be clear what is meant by 'pure economic loss'. A person may have suffered financial loss because his property is destroyed, but in law this is not classed as 'pure economic loss' because the financial loss is a consequence of physical damage to his property. If a car is written off in an accident, caused by the negligence of another, the owner of the car will be entitled to recover damages in the form of a financial payment. Equally, where a claimant suffers loss of profit because his property is negligently damaged, he will be able to recover his financial loss. Problems arise where a person suffers financial loss because of damage to someone else's property. For example a vet negligently injects cattle with a virus that kills them and the auctioneer at the annual cattle market suffers a loss of profits because there are no cattle to auction. The cattle do not belong to the auctioneer and, therefore, his loss of profits is categorised as 'pure economic loss'.

Weller v Foot and Mouth Research Institute (1966)

Facts: The defendants negligently allowed a cattle virus to escape from their laboratory. As a result, there was an outbreak of foot and mouth in cattle and legal restrictions were imposed on the movement of cattle. The claimants were auctioneers of livestock and lost a considerable sum of money as they could not hold any auctions during the outbreak.

Decision: The claimants' loss of profits was pure economic loss and, therefore, was not recoverable from the defendants.

Key Concept Recovery of pure economic loss, where financial loss is not connected to any physical injury to the claimant or damage to his property, is very limited in the tort of negligence.

In the following case the claimant was entitled to recover loss of profits on the product that had been damaged, but not for any potential profits that may have been made had the electricity supply continued.

Spartan Steel v Martin & Co Contractors Ltd (1973)

Facts: The claimant operated a stainless steel factory. The defendants, who were digging the road up outside the factory, negligently cut a power cable. The factory was without electricity for 14 hours. The loss of electricity caused damage to a number of 'melts' in the furnace at the time of the power cut and prevented four new melts, that would have been made, from being processed.

Decision: The claimant was entitled to compensation for the damaged melts and the loss of profits on those melts (i.e. the physical damage and financial loss which flowed from it) but was not entitled to the loss of profit on the melts which did not take place (i.e. the pure economic loss).

If a negligent statement results in physical injury then a claimant will be entitled to recover damages for his loss or injury.

Clay v Crump (1963)

Facts: An architect on a demolition site stated that a wall could be left standing, as it was safe. Later the wall collapsed injuring the claimant.
Decision: The architect was liable to the claimant for his injuries.

Pure economic loss stemming from ownership of defective structures and products

Generally, there is no duty of care for pure financial loss stemming from ownership of a building or a product that turns out to be defective. At one time it was thought that the courts might allow a duty of care to extend to the construction of property; however, it is clear from case authority that the law does not impose liability in negligence for pure economic loss on persons approving, designing, or constructing buildings. A duty of care is not owed to an owner of a building who has suffered pure economic loss without any physical damage to the property.

Murphy v Brentwood District Council (1990)

Facts: The claimants bought a new house in 1970. In 1986, after discovering that the foundations of the house were defective, the claimants sold the house for £35,000 less than it would have been worth in sound condition. As the District Council had been responsible for checking the foundations when the house was being built, the claimants sued the Council.
Decision: The House of Lords agreed that the house was defective, but stated that the Council were not liable as this was pure economic loss, and the claimants had not suffered any personal injury nor had their property been damaged.

Special cases of pure economic loss

There are some exceptions where the courts have stated that a duty of care is owed to a claimant even though that claimant has only incurred pure economic loss. These exceptions fall in circumstances where the courts have decided there is a particularly close proximity between the claimant and the defendant. The claimant is someone that the defendant would contemplate as being closely and directly affected by his actions. An example of an exceptionally close relationship is that of a solicitor and a beneficiary under a will. If the solicitor is negligent in preparing the will to such an extent that the intended beneficiary is unable to inherit, then that beneficiary may be successful in his claim even though he has only suffered pure economic loss.

Ross v Caunters (1980)

Facts: Solicitors sent a testator his will to sign but failed to inform him that the will should not be witnessed by the spouse of an intended beneficiary. The will was returned signed and witnessed. The solicitors did not notice that the will had been witnessed by a beneficiary's spouse. When the testator died, the intended beneficiary was unable to claim under the will and sued the solicitors.
Decision: The claimant was a named beneficiary and a foreseeable victim. A duty of care was owed to the claimant by the defendant solicitors.

In the following case, the House of Lords decided there was a duty of care owed by solicitors to a potential beneficiary because the solicitors had assumed responsibility and there was a relationship of trust.

White v Jones (1995)

Facts: A father made a will disinheriting his two daughters after a family quarrel. He later became reconciled with them and asked his solicitors to prepare a new will. The solicitors negligently delayed making the will and the father died before the new will was completed. The daughters lost £9,000 each which they would have got under the new will.
Decision: The solicitors owed a duty of care to the daughters as potential beneficiaries. By agreeing to amend the father's will, the solicitors had assumed responsibility for ensuring the will was made promptly. Responsibility was to the person making the will and the intended beneficiaries. The financial loss to the claimants was reasonably foreseeable.

Pure economic loss as a result of negligent statements

In special circumstances it is possible to succeed in a claim for pure economic loss caused through a defendant's negligent statement. Prior to 1964 the only action available for pure financial loss caused by a false statement was in the tort of deceit, where, in order to succeed, the claimant had to prove the defendant had acted dishonestly. However, in 1964, in *Hedley Byrne & Co Ltd v Heller* (1964) the House of Lords accepted that, in some special circumstances, there could be a duty owed in the tort of negligence for financial loss caused through a defendant's negligent statement. For such a claim to succeed, it was not enough to show that the loss suffered by the claimant was 'reasonably foreseeable', the test set out in *Donoghue v Stevenson* (1932), but in addition there had to be a 'special relationship of proximity' between the parties. A duty of care would only arise where the defendant, either expressly or impliedly, undertook the responsibility to exercise care in making the statement. The defendant must possess special skill and judgement which the claimant relied on, and it must be reasonable in the circumstances for the claimant to rely on the statement. The defendant must also know, or should reasonably have known, that the claimant would rely on the statement. In *Hedley Byrne* a financial reference was sent by the defendants and relied on by the claimants.

Hedley Byrne & Co Ltd v Heller & Partners Ltd (1964)

Facts: The defendants, Heller & Partners, were bankers and the claimants, Hedley Byrne, were advertising agents. The claimants were considering running an advertising programme for Easipower Ltd, which involved giving Easipower credit. The claimants asked their bank to find out the financial position of Easipower. The claimants' bank asked Easipower's bank, Heller & Partners, which replied that Easipower was '... a respectably constituted company, considered good for ordinary business engagements'. Easipower went into liquidation and the claimants lost £17,000 and sued Heller for negligent misstatement.

Decision: The House of Lords stated that, in certain circumstances where there was a 'special relationship' between the parties, there could be a duty of care for financial loss caused by a negligent misstatement. However, in this case there was a valid disclaimer as the advice given by Heller was headed 'without responsibility' and, therefore, the defendants were not liable.

The requirement of a special relationship restricts liability to within reasonable grounds, limiting the number of claims that may be made against a defendant who makes a negligent statement which could potentially affect thousands of people.

Key Concept A claim for pure economic loss caused by a negligent statement may be successful if there is proximity between the parties, i.e. a *'special relationship'* between the parties.

To ensure that persons making statements would not be under a duty of care to potentially large numbers of people whom they might foresee would rely on their statements, the House of Lords restricted the principles set out in *Hedley Byrne* in the later case of *Caparo Industries v Dickman* (1990). The number of potential claimants that fell within the necessary proximity (i.e. a special relationship) was further restricted.

The court decided that, in order for there to be a special relationship between the defendant and the claimant, it was essential that:

- The defendant knew that the statement would be communicated to the claimant (either a named or unnamed individual or an identifiable group of persons).

- The advice was given specifically in connection with an identifiable transaction or transactions of a particular kind.

- The defendant reasonably anticipated that the claimant was likely to rely on the statement for the purpose of the transaction without seeking further independent advice.

Caparo Industries v Dickman (1990)

Facts: The claimants, Caparo, owned shares in Fidelity plc. Caparo read and relied on the statutory audited accounts of Fidelity plc, prepared by the defendants, Dickman, when making their decision to purchase additional shares in Fidelity plc and then to mount a successful takeover bid. However the accounts were inaccurate and showed a profit of £1.3 m instead of a loss of £465,000. Caparo sued Dickman for negligent misstatement.

Decision: The House of Lords stated that the defendants did not owe a duty of care to the claimants as there was not a sufficient degree of proximity between them. The accounts had not been prepared specifically for the claimants to rely on when deciding to purchase additional shares.

In the following decision, no duty of care was owed by the defendant accountants because they did not know the claimants would rely on their draft accounts and it was reasonable in the circumstances to assume the claimants would seek independent advice (see Figure 11.3).

Figure 11.3 Factors necessary to establish duty of care for negligent misstatements

Defendant knew identity of claimant.

Advice was in connection with specific or particular type of transaction.

Duty of Care Negligent Misstatements

Defendant could reasonably anticipate claimant would rely on statement.

It was reasonable for the claimant to rely on the misstatement without seeking independent advice.

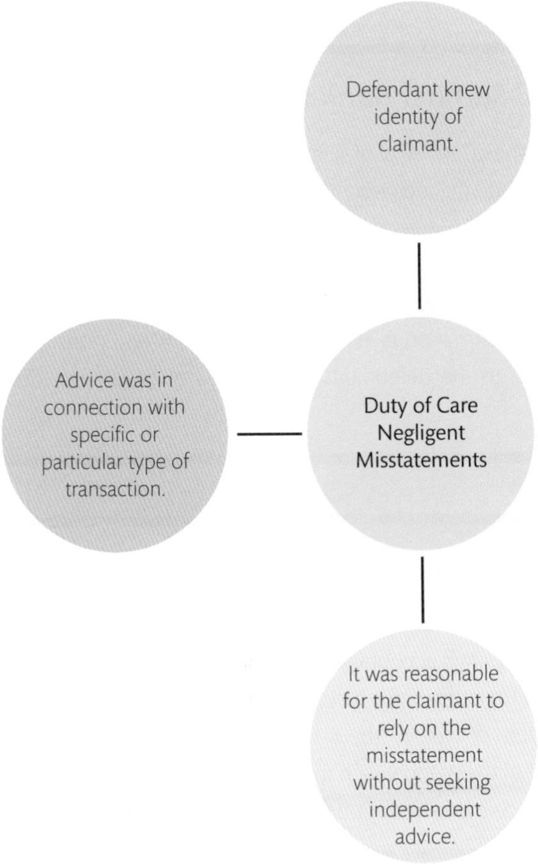

James McNaughton v Hicks (1991)

Facts: The defendants were accountants to 'MK Papers' which was the subject of an agreed takeover bid by the claimants. At the request of MK, the defendants prepared some draft accounts to assist the negotiations. Subsequently it was discovered that the accounts were inaccurate and the claimants suffered economic loss.

Decision: The defendants did not owe a duty of care because there was no evidence that the defendants were aware that the claimants would rely on the accounts for a takeover. The accounts were only in draft and it was reasonable to assume that the claimants would seek independent advice.

In the following two decisions, a duty of care was owed by the defendants because they were aware of the particular claimants, and it was reasonable to assume that the claimants would rely on the accounts given in connection with a particular transaction and not seek independent advice.

Morgan Crucible v Hill Samuel Bank (1991)

Facts: The defendants were the financial advisers of a company targeted for a takeover by the claimants. During the takeover bid, the defendants made inaccurate statements about the accounts and financial prospects of the company. The claimants increased their bid and subsequently suffered loss on taking over the company.

Decision: The defendants were liable as they knew of the claimants' bid, and had intended the claimants to rely on the financial information given, and the claimants had done so. Much of the information was only available to the defendants and could not have been obtained independently by the claimants.

Yorkshire Enterprise Ltd v Robson Rhodes (1998)

Facts: The claimants invested £250,000 in the company which went into liquidation shortly afterwards. The claimants sued the company's accountants, stating they had relied on negligent misstatements in audited accounts, and in letters written by the accountants sent to the claimants.

Decision: The defendants owed a duty of care to the claimants as they were aware that the claimants were potential investors and of the use to which the accounts would be put. Also, in the circumstances, it was reasonable for the claimants to rely on the information without further enquiry.

Where a statement is made in a purely social setting, or given as a quick response to a question, it may not be reasonable to rely on it even if it is made by someone with expertise. However, in exceptional circumstances, where it is clear that careful, considered advice is being sought, a statement made by a friend may give rise to a duty of care.

Chaudhry v Prabhaker (1988)

Facts: The claimant asked a friend who was knowledgeable about cars to find her a second-hand car. She emphatically said she did not want one that had been involved in an accident. The defendant recommended a car, which the claimant purchased. Subsequently, it was discovered the car had been involved in a road accident and was not roadworthy.

Decision: The defendant owed the claimant a duty of care because he had claimed to have knowledge of cars.

Key Concept Negligent statements

In order to establish a duty of care for pure economic loss through a negligent statement, not only must the loss caused be reasonably foreseeable, and fair, just, and reasonable in the circumstances that the law should impose a duty on the defendant, but in addition there must be a 'special relationship' of proximity between the defendant and the claimant which means the claimant must prove:

(a) The defendant knew that the statement would be communicated to the claimant.

(b) The advice was given specifically in connection with an identifiable transaction or transactions of a particular kind.

(c) The defendant reasonably anticipated that the claimant was likely to rely on the statement for the purpose of the transaction without seeking further independent advice.

Disclaimer of responsibility

A disclaimer of responsibility by the defendant for any negligent statements may be sufficient to exclude the duty of care. In *Hedley Byrne & Co Ltd v Heller* (1964) the disclaimer, by the bank, prevented the bank being liable for their negligent reference. The Unfair Contract Terms Act 1977 applies not only to contracts but also to tortious situations and this Act states that liability for causing death or personal injuries through negligence can never be excluded. Liability for other damage or loss can only be excluded if it is reasonable to do so. In *Smith v Eric Bush* (1989) a negligent report, prepared by the defendant, had a disclaimer of liability but the court stated that the disclaimer was unreasonable, and, therefore, invalid under the Unfair Contract Terms Act 1977.

Psychiatric Injury (Nervous Shock)

Psychiatric injury, which is sometimes referred to as **'nervous shock'**, is a form of personal injury but it is more problematical to claim for than physical injury. There must be evidence that the claimant has suffered a serious psychiatric illness such as post-traumatic stress disorder. Ordinary grief, anxiety, or fright, without any physical injury, is not enough as it does not amount to a psychiatric illness. The courts have always been cautious in recognising a duty of care in relation to psychiatric injury, for a number of reasons. It is more difficult to diagnose psychiatric injury than physical injury and, therefore, is easier to make fake claims. It may open the floodgates of litigation with a rush of claims being made, and psychiatric injury may be difficult to quantify in terms of compensation.

The problem only arises in claims for 'pure' psychiatric injuries. This means where the claimant suffers only psychiatric injuries and is not physically harmed. There has never been a problem of establishing a duty of care where a claimant suffers psychiatric injuries as a result of a negligently inflicted physical injury. A claimant can even be compensated for emotional distress and anguish as a result of physical injury. The general principles of negligence are used where a claimant suffers a psychiatric injury and physical harm. However, where a claimant suffers only psychiatric injuries, additional requirements have to be met for a successful claim. In cases of pure psychiatric injuries a distinction must be made between a **primary victim** who is involved in the incident, and a **secondary victim** who merely witnesses the incident or arrives shortly after it has happened. Stricter rules limit the defendant's liability towards secondary victims. It would not be fair, just, or reasonable for the defendant to be responsible for all persons who only witness the defendant's negligent actions or happen upon them shortly afterwards but are not directly involved in the actions.

Primary victims

A primary victim is a person who was under actual threat of bodily harm or reasonably believed themselves to be so, as a result of the negligent event. For example, Sanjay is involved in a car crash caused by Leon's negligence. Although Sanjay suffers no physical harm in the car crash, he does subsequently develop a psychiatric illness as a result of his experience. Provided that Sanjay was under actual threat of bodily injury, or reasonably believed himself to be so, at the time of the crash, he will be considered a primary victim.

Dulieu v White (1901)

Facts: The claimant, a pregnant woman, worked behind the bar at a pub. The defendant's employee drove a horse and cart through the window of the pub causing the claimant to fear for her safety, suffer nervous shock, and miscarry her baby.

Decision: The claimant could recover damages for nervous shock as it had been caused by a real and immediate fear for her safety.

In *Page v Smith* (1995) the House of Lords stated that a primary victim would be owed a duty of care for pure psychiatric injury if it was reasonably foreseeable that a person of 'reasonable fortitude' would have suffered some form of personal injury (either physical or psychiatric) as a result of the defendant's negligence.

Page v Smith (1995)

Facts: The claimant was involved in a car crash caused by the defendant's negligence. Minor damage was caused to the cars and the claimant suffered no physical injuries; however, the claimant did suffer from a reoccurrence of ME (myalgic encephalomyelitis) which was classed as a psychiatric illness.

Decision: A duty of care was owed to a primary victim if some personal injury, either physical or psychiatric, was foreseeable as a result of the negligent action. In this case, physical injury to the claimant was foreseeable; therefore, the defendant owed him a duty of care. It was of no consequence that the injury that developed was psychiatric rather than physical.

The House of Lords, in the following case was not prepared to extend the principle in *Page v Smith* to a psychiatric illness caused by worry of the possibility of an illness developing.

Grieves v F T Everard & Sons Ltd (2007)

Facts: G had been negligently exposed to asbestos at work and developed pleural plaques. These did not interfere with his health and would not cause damage but were an indication that asbestos had entered his body. G worried so much about the risk of future illness that he developed a psychiatric injury.

Decision: The presence of pleural plaques did not constitute an injury for which you could claim damages. There was no evidence that a person of reasonable fortitude would become mentally ill as a result of worrying about the possibility of a future illness. What was foreseeable was that G would contract an asbestos related disease which had not occurred. His injury was caused by his worry that it might occur which was not the same.

Business Insight Stress at work

Psychiatric injury does not have to arise from being involved in or witnessing an accident. Liability has been imposed on employers where the likelihood of psychiatric injury to an employee's health, caused by stress at work, is reasonably foreseeable. In 2012, a Union reported that a six-figure, out-of-court settlement had been made to an employee who suffered a stress-related psychiatric injury after their employer refused to respond to the employee's concerns of an excessive workload. However it is not an 'easy' claim to make as the claimant has to have suffered a recognised psychiatric injury and the employer has to be aware of the likelihood of the injury occurring and fail to take reasonable steps to protect the employee.

Rescuers

Prior to 1999 it was understood that, in law, rescuers were automatically to be treated as primary victims and a duty of care was owed to a rescuer who suffered mental trauma as a result of helping out in an accident.

Chadwick v British Rail (1967)

Facts: The claimant was a volunteer rescuer at the scene of a rail disaster where 90 people died. He later suffered from a psychiatric illness as a result of the horrific nature of what he had experienced.

Decision: A duty of care was owed to the claimant as it was reasonably foreseeable that volunteers would assist at the scene and suffer mental illness as a result.

However, in *White v Chief Constable of South Yorkshire* (1999) the House of Lords made it clear that a rescuer could only be classed as a primary victim if the rescuer was, or reasonably believed himself to be, in danger of physical injury. The court recognised that *Chadwick*, just considered, was correctly decided because the rescuer in that case was in physical danger from the collapse of the wreckage, but the rescuers in *White* were not at risk and could not claim as primary victims.

White v Chief Constable of South Yorkshire (1999)

Facts: As a result of the negligent failure of the police to control admission to the Hillsborough football stadium in Sheffield, numerous fans were crushed against railings and barricades. Ninety-five people were killed and hundreds injured. The claimants were police officers who took part in the rescue operation and suffered post-traumatic stress disorder (a psychiatric illness) as a result of the horrific scenes they encountered. They sued the Chief Constable of South Yorkshire Police.

Decision: No duty of care was owed by the Chief Constable to the claimants as primary victims because the claimants were not actually at risk themselves. They had not been exposed to danger or fear of danger.

Secondary victims

A secondary victim is a person who suffers a psychiatric illness as a result of witnessing an accident or its 'immediate aftermath'. The person himself is in no danger but suffers shock as a result of either seeing another person injured, reasonably believing that another person is injured, or coming to the scene immediately afterwards. In addition, the secondary victim must have a close tie of love and affection for the victim of the accident (see Figure 11.4).

Figure 11.4 Claims for psychiatric injury by primary and secondary victims

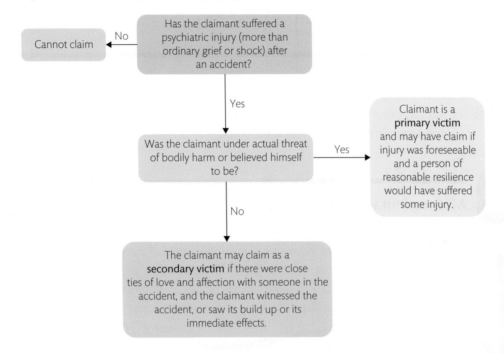

Cannot claim ←— No —— Has the claimant suffered a psychiatric injury (more than ordinary grief or shock) after an accident?

Yes

Was the claimant under actual threat of bodily harm or believed himself to be? —— Yes —→ Claimant is a **primary victim** and may have claim if injury was foreseeable and a person of reasonable resilience would have suffered some injury.

No

The claimant may claim as a **secondary victim** if there were close ties of love and affection with someone in the accident, and the claimant witnessed the accident, or saw its build up or its immediate effects.

Hinz v Berry (1970)

Facts: The claimant and her husband and children were travelling in a van when they stopped in a lay-by. The claimant went across the road with one child to pick flowers, when a car drove into the van. The claimant saw the accident in which her husband died and several of her children were injured. The claimant suffered psychiatric illness.

Decision: The claimant was entitled to damages for psychiatric illness caused by witnessing the accident.

In *Hinz v Berry* the claimant had actually witnessed the accident, but it is possible to succeed in an action where psychiatric illness is attributable to the actual perception of an accident and the real and immediate fear for the safety of the victim, provided there is a close personal relationship with the victim.

Hambrook v Stokes Bros (1925)

Facts: The claimant suffered psychiatric illness, after she saw the defendant's out-of-control lorry and heard a collision, which led her to reasonably fear for the safety of her children whom she had just left at the bottom of the hill outside school.

Decision: The claimant was entitled to damages for psychiatric illness caused by the real and immediate fear for the safety of her family.

In the following case, the claimant did not witness or perceive the accident as it was happening, but was successful because she suffered mental illness after seeing what was described as the 'immediate aftermath' on arriving at the hospital.

McLoughlin v O'Brian (1982)

Facts: The claimant's husband and her three children were in a car accident which was caused by the defendant's negligence. The claimant was two miles away but she reached the hospital within an hour, where she was told her three-year-old child was dead, and she saw, through a window in the corridor, another of her children covered in blood and oil and could hear a third child shouting and screaming. Subsequently the claimant suffered mental illness and sued the defendant.

Decision: The court awarded the claimant damages since her loss was reasonably foreseeable and the scene that greeted the claimant when she arrived at the hospital constituted the 'immediate aftermath'.

For public policy reasons, it is important to make certain that the duty of care, imposed on defendants, for psychiatric injury caused to secondary victims is restricted within reasonable confines. There are legal limitations on the claims of secondary victims. In the important case of *Alcock v Chief Constable of South Yorkshire Police* (1991) the House of Lords set out the criteria necessary for a defendant to be liable for psychiatric injury caused to a secondary victim.

The claimant must establish all of the following essential requirements:

- A close tie of love and affection with someone involved in the accident so that it is reasonably foreseeable that the claimant will suffer psychiatric illness. (A close tie of love and affection is presumed to exist between spouses, and parents and children, but other claimants must prove such a relationship exists.)

- A geographical proximity to the accident or its aftermath. The claimant must be either present at the scene of the accident, see the build up to the accident, or its immediate effects. The claimant must have seen or heard the accident or the immediate aftermath with his own unaided senses. (The claimant will not be successful if he has imagined the scene after being told of it by a third party or if he has seen the incident on television.)

- A medically-recognised psychiatric illness is suffered by the claimant as a result of the incident.

Alcock v Chief Constable of South Yorkshire (1991)

Facts: Ninety-five people were killed and numerous others were injured in the Hillsborough football ground when the defendants, South Yorkshire Police, negligently allowed too many supporters into the football ground and people at the front were crushed against the barriers. The scene was witnessed by the claimants, who were friends and relatives of the persons injured. Some claimants were at the ground while others saw the events on the television or heard them described on the radio. All the claimants suffered psychiatric illness.

Decision: In order to succeed in a claim for psychiatric illness, the relationship between the claimant and the primary victims had to be sufficiently proximate. There had to be close ties of love and affection. Two claimants who were in the ground were unsuccessful in their claim because they did not have a sufficiently close relationship with any of the victims. In addition, the claimants had to prove they were close to the accident in terms of time and distance. Claimants who saw the accident on television were not in the sight or hearing of the accident and the broadcasting code of ethics forbade any graphic depiction of suffering.

In *Taylor v A Novo (UK) Ltd* (2013) the court decided that the claimant could not claim for psychiatric harm suffered after she witnessed her mother's death. Her mother died three weeks after suffering severe injuries in an accident at work. The daughter had not witnessed the accident or its immediate aftermath. The court treated the death as a separate event and for policy reasons refused to extend the boundaries of secondary victims otherwise there could be many more claims where persons had died years after an accident.

Key Concept   The elements of the tort of negligence are:

The defendant owed the claimant a duty of care.
The defendant breached the duty of care owed.
Reasonably foreseeable damage was caused by the breach of duty of care.

Element 2: The Defendant Broke his Duty of Care

In order to succeed in a claim for negligence, the claimant must establish that the defendant owed him a duty of care, but this is only the first stage. The claimant must also establish that the defendant broke his duty of care. He must prove that the defendant did something that a reasonable man in the circumstances would not have done, or that the defendant failed to do something that a reasonable man in the circumstances would have done.

Standard of Care

The standard of care is an **objective test**. The defendant must act with the degree of care and skill expected from a reasonable person. It is no defence for the defendant to claim he is inept or unskilled. A learner driver owes the same objective standard of care to his passengers and other road users as every other driver. His lack of experience is not taken into account, and the standard of care he is judged by is the same as that of a competent driver.

Nettleship v Weston (1971)

Facts: The claimant agreed to teach the defendant to drive. On the third lesson the defendant hit a lamp post and the claimant was injured.

Decision: The duty of care that a learner driver owed to other passengers and the public was the same objective standard as any other driver. The claimant was liable regardless of the fact that she was an inexperienced driver.

The standard of care will be lower if the defendant is a child rather than an adult. Children are expected to take the same precautions as a reasonable child of their age.

Orchard v Lee (2009)

Facts: A lunchtime supervisor was seriously injured when a 13-year-old schoolboy collided with her whilst he was playing a game of tag in the playground.

Decision: The boy was not liable as no ordinarily prudent and reasonable 13-year-old boy would reasonably have foreseen the risk of injury through playing tag and he had not fallen below the standard that could reasonably be expected of a child of that age.

Standard of care owed by skilled defendants

The standard of care expected by professional persons is the standard that a reasonably competent person in that profession would show. If a defendant claims to have special skills, then he is expected to act to the same standard as a person with those skills.

Phillips v Whiteley Ltd (1938)

Facts: The claimant contracted a disease after having her ears pierced by the defendant.

Decision: The defendant was not liable because the standard of care required by the defendant was that of a skilled and competent ear piercer, not a medical practitioner. The defendant had met the standard required.

The defendant is judged on the level of qualification claimed, not on the amount of experience he has. A defendant who has just qualified and started in a job will be expected to show the same level of care as a competent person holding that post. In *Wilsher v Essex Area Health Authority* (1988) the House of Lords stated that a doctor should be judged by reference to the particular post he holds and the degree of experience in that particular post was irrelevant.

Where a professional person acts in accordance with accepted practice of persons in his profession, then he will not be negligent even if others would have taken different action. The claimant must prove the defendant has been negligent on the balance of probabilities, and, therefore, if there is proof that other professional persons would have acted in the same way, the defendant may not be negligent. A doctor who conforms with accepted medical procedure may not be negligent, despite the fact that some doctors disagree with the practice.

Bolam v Friern Hospital Management Committee (1957)

Facts: The claimant received ECT treatment. Before the treatment, the claimant was given relaxant drugs which caused the claimant to suffer fractures. Medical opinion was divided on whether relaxant drugs should be administered but the majority of opinion was against it. The claimant sued the hospital.

Decision: If a doctor acts in accordance with skilled medical opinion he will not be negligent even if other practitioners would have taken a contrary view. The hospital was not liable because its doctor had acted in accordance with accepted medical practice.

However, it was made clear by the House of Lords in *Bolitho v City and Hackney Health Authority* (1997) that, in order for a court to be satisfied that the action of a doctor was not negligent, it must be reasonable and logical in all the circumstances for the doctor to follow expert opinion. Before following an expert's opinion, a doctor must examine all the risks and benefits of the action and ensure that the expert's opinion stands up to logical analysis.

Factors to be Taken into Account

Most actions involve an element of risk to others. When there is a known risk involved in an activity, the question for a court to determine is, what precautions, if any, would the reasonable person have taken against the risk. The court will take into account a number of different factors when deciding whether a duty of care has been broken.

The factors which the court will take into account include:

- The probability of harm being caused to the claimant.

- The potential seriousness of the harm that is likely to be caused.

- The reasonableness/practicalities of taking precautions to prevent the harm occurring.

- The value to society/usefulness of what the defendant was attempting to achieve.

These factors interlink with each other and cases are decided on taking a balanced view of all the relevant circumstances (see Figure 11.5).

Figure 11.5 Factors relating to breach of duty of care

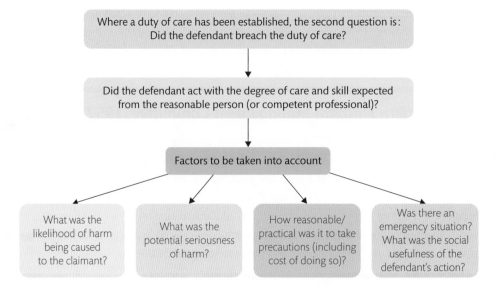

The probability of harm

Where it is highly probable that injury will be caused to someone by a defendant's actions, particularly if the injury caused may be serious, then it is likely that the defendant will have breached his duty of care. The more likely the harm, the more caution required to meet the standard of care necessary.

The following two cases both concern cricket balls being hit over a perimeter fence. In the first case, the defendant was not liable because the risk of harm was relatively small, whereas, in the second case, the defendant was liable because the risk of injury was sufficiently large to have expected the defendant to take greater precautions to prevent injury occurring.

Bolton v Stone (1951)

Facts: A batsman, playing in a cricket ground run by the defendant cricket club, hit a cricket ball over a 17-foot-high fence. The claimant, who was in the street outside the cricket ground, was hit by the ball. A ball had been hit outside the fence six times in 30 years; therefore, the risk of it happening was foreseeable but small.

Decision: The defendant club was not liable. They had taken reasonable precautions in maintaining a 17-foot fence and the risk of a ball going over the fence was so small that the club was entitled to ignore it.

Miller v Jackson (1977)

Facts: The claimant's house, which was close to a village cricket ground, was damaged by cricket balls. Balls were hit over the fence about eight or nine times a season, and the claimant's property had been damaged more than once.

Decision: The defendant cricket club was liable. The risk was sufficiently large to have expected more precautions from the cricket club.

The potential seriousness of the harm

In cases where the risk of injury to the claimant is small, but the gravity of the injury if it occurs is great, then it is more likely that a duty of care will be broken if precautions are not taken, provided that the injury, although perhaps unlikely, is foreseeable.

Paris v Stepney Borough Council (1951)

Facts: The claimant was blind in one eye and the defendant was aware of this disability. The claimant was working in the defendant's garage under a vehicle, when a piece of metal went into his good eye and blinded him. At the time it was not standard practice to issue safety goggles.

Decision: The potential severity of damage to the claimant was greater than other workers (i.e. the increased risk of total blindness) and, therefore, the defendant was liable for not providing him with goggles. The cost of providing the goggles was small.

The practicalities/cost

If it is simple to take precautions and the cost of avoiding the harm is not out of all proportion to the reduction of the risk, the defendant will have breached his duty of care if he fails to take action. However, if spending a large amount of money would only reduce the risk a little, then it may not be reasonable to spend it.

Haley v London Electricity Board (1965)

Facts: The claimant, a blind man, fell into a hole which had been dug in the pavement by the defendants. The defendants had taken the precaution of putting up a warning sign.

Decision: The precaution taken was sufficient for a sighted person but not for the blind. The presence of blind people walking along a street was foreseeable. This, combined with the ease of taking precautions against the risk and the potential severity of damage to a blind person who did fall down such a hole, meant that the defendants had breached the duty of care.

In the following case the court concluded that the practicalities and cost of reducing the risk further was not justified.

Latimer v AEC (1953)

Facts: Following a heavy downpour, the floor of the defendant's factory became very slippery. The defendant covered most of the floor with sawdust. The claimant slipped and was injured.

Decision: The defendant was not liable. The only remaining precaution that the defendant could have taken would have been to close down the factory. Given the size of the risk, this was not justified.

The value to society/usefulness of what the defendant was attempting to achieve

If a defendant is faced with an emergency or is doing something which socially is more useful, then more latitude is allowed. A defendant will not breach his duty of care if he takes reasonable risks because of an emergency situation.

Watt v Hertfordshire County Council (1954)

Facts: A woman was trapped under a lorry. The fire service transported a lifting jack on an ordinary lorry, because a specialised lorry was not available. En route, the jack slipped injuring the claimant, a fire officer. The claimant sued his employer.

Decision: The employer was not liable. The risk which the claimant had been exposed to was reasonable in the circumstances.

Compensation Act 2006

The Compensation Act 2006 does not change the law in respect of breach of a duty of care, but makes it clear that the courts should take into account whether the precautions required to meet the standard of care would have prevented a desirable activity being restricted or taking place at all. In addition, the court can look at whether the steps required would discourage people from participating in the carrying out of desirable activities. The Compensation Act 2006 was introduced partly to counteract the public perception of a compensation culture, whereby the organisation of activities could lead to liability in negligence if there was any risk of injury to any participants. For example, there is always a risk that a child may be injured if a school arranges outside activities, but the educational value of such activities may outweigh the risks involved. The Act was not intended to change the law but to codify the common law, and make it clear that an appropriate standard of care would be met where desirable activities were carried out without the need for extremely stringent measures.

Section 1 of the Compensation Act 2006 states that, when a court is considering a claim in negligence, it may, in determining whether a defendant should have taken particular steps to meet a standard of care (either by taking precautions against a risk or other action), have regard to whether a requirement to take those steps might:

(a) Prevent a desirable activity from being undertaken at all, to a particular extent, or in a particular way, or

(b) Discourage persons from undertaking functions in connection with a desirable activity.

Section 2 states that an apology, an offer of treatment, or other solution does not amount to an admission of negligence.

The Compensation Act 2006 applies to the standard of care to be applied in negligence cases and in cases where there may be a breach of statutory duty, such as that imposed by the Occupiers Liability Acts 1957 and 1984 (see Chapter 12).

Business Insight   No liability for freak accidents

In a recent case an outdoor pursuits company was not liable for injuries suffered (spinal injury resulting in permanent tetraplegia) by the claimant, when he fell and hit his head on the ground after throwing a wellington boot during a 'welly-wanging' event the company had organised. The judge stated that the law of tort should not stamp out socially desirable activities just because they carry some risk. The standard of care was an objective test of reasonableness which should take into account the circumstances and characteristics of the persons at risk. The risk which needed to be foreseen by the company was the risk of serious injury and not just the risk of any injury. There was no foreseeable real risk; it was a tragic and freak accident for which no blame could be established.

Proving the Breach of Duty of Care

As a claim for negligence is a civil claim, the claimant must prove on the balance of probabilities that the defendant breached the duty of care. In some cases, this can be difficult. There are two significant ways in which a claimant may be helped in establishing a breach of a duty of care. Firstly, the Civil Evidence Act 1968, s 11, provides that a conviction of a criminal offence shall be proof that the offence was committed. Therefore, a claimant may rely on a defendant's conviction for careless driving in a road accident to prove negligence in a civil claim for damages.

Secondly, a claimant may be able to rely on the doctrine of **'res ipsa loquitur'** (the thing speaks for itself). This doctrine can be used when, on the face of it, the evidence seems to clearly suggest that the defendant must have breached his duty of care for the injury to occur, despite the fact that the claimant cannot prove exactly how the injury was caused. If the court allows the claimant to rely on *res ipsa loquitur*, the burden of proof is reversed and, instead of the claimant having to prove that the defendant had breached his duty of care, the defendant will have to prove, on the balance of probabilities, he has not breached his duty of care.

The presumption that the accident was caused by the defendant's negligence applies when the following criteria are present:

- The defendant was in control of the thing or situation that caused the damage.
- The damage would not normally have occurred without carelessness by some person.
- The exact cause of the accident cannot be determined.

As the principle relies on the absence of knowledge of the exact facts, it will not apply if the facts of what actually happened are known or can be discovered.

Ward v Tesco Stores (1976)

Facts: The claimant slipped on some yoghurt spilled on the floor of the defendants' supermarket. The defendants would have breached their duty of care if steps had not been taken within a reasonable time to clear it away. The claimant could not prove how long the yoghurt had been on the floor, but in the absence of any explanation it was likely the defendants were at fault.
Decision: The defendants were liable, on the basis that the claimant had slipped and they could not positively establish that they had not been negligent.

In *George v Eagle Air Services Ltd* (2009) the court applied the doctrine of *res ipsa loquitur* to air crashes. Crashes do not normally occur without some failure by someone who flew, maintained, or designed the aircraft. The defendants were liable for the death of C's partner in a plane crash as they did not produce any evidence to show they had not been negligent.

Key Concept Where the evidence clearly suggests that the defendant must have breached his duty of care even though the claimant cannot prove exactly how the injury was caused, the burden of proof is reversed. The defendant will have to prove that, on the balance of probabilities, he has not breached his duty of care.

Element 3: The Claimant Suffered Loss or Damage as a Result of the Defendant's Breach of Duty

In order for a claimant to succeed in a negligence claim, he must not only show that the defendant owed him a duty of care and breached that duty of care, but he must additionally prove that the damage or loss he suffered was as a result of the defendant's breach. There are two factors necessary for this element. Firstly, the defendant must have caused the claimant's loss or damage. This is a factual matter which is usually assessed by the 'but for' test (immediately following). Secondly, the loss or damage suffered by the claimant must be of a type that was reasonably foreseeable, i.e. the damage must not be too remote.

Key Concept The three elements of the tort of negligence are:

The defendant owed the claimant a duty of care.

The defendant breached the duty of care owed.

Reasonably foreseeable damage was caused by the breach of duty of care.

The 'But For' Test: A Causal Link

In order to succeed in a claim, there must be a causal link between the breach of duty by the defendant, and the damage suffered by the claimant. The claimant must prove, on the balance of probabilities, that the defendant's negligence caused or materially contributed to the injury or loss sustained. This is known as the 'but for' test.

Barnett v Chelsea & Kensington Hospital Management Committee (1969)

Facts: A widow sued the hospital for negligence after her husband died having attended the hospital in the evening and been sent home by a doctor without being examined.

Decision: The hospital did owe a duty of care to examine the man and was in breach of duty by sending him home. However, his death was not as a result of the breach, because he had been poisoned with arsenic and, even if he had been correctly diagnosed and treated when he arrived at the hospital, he would have died anyway. There was no antidote to arsenic poisoning.

The question is, would the claimant have suffered the loss but for the defendant's negligence? The defendant will not be liable if the claimant would have suffered the injury in any event, even if the defendant had been negligent.

Multiple Causes

There are problems in establishing loss as a result of a defendant's breach, where the claimant's loss was not only because of the defendant's action but also because of the actions of others. The courts have stated that the 'but for' test can be disregarded where the defendant's breach had materially contributed to causing the claimant's injury by significantly increasing the risk of him contracting a disease.

McGhee v National Coal Board (1973)

Facts: The claimant was exposed to brick dust during the course of his employment. The employer did not provide washing facilities and after work the claimant cycled home covered in dust. The failure of the defendant employer to provide adequate washing facilities was a breach of his duty of care.

Decision: The House of Lords stated that a defendant may be liable in circumstances where a breach of duty 'materially increases the risk' of a particular harm to a claimant. The defendant was liable in negligence to the claimant.

Where there are a number of possible causes for a particular harm, the defendant will not be liable if the claimant is unable to prove that it was the action of the defendant which was a material cause of the injury.

Wilsher v Essex AHA (1988)

Facts: The claimant was a premature baby who contracted retrolental fibroplasia (RLF). Due to the defendant's negligence, the baby had received an excessive concentration of oxygen, which could have caused the RLF. However, there are also a number of other possible causes of RLF in premature babies.

Decision: The claimant had to prove, on the balance of probabilities, that the defendant's negligence was the cause of, or materially contributed to, the RLF. The claimant was unable to do this and, therefore, failed in the claim.

However, where the claimant can prove that his injury was caused by a particular factor, he may be successful in his claim against a defendant employer, even though he is unable to prove which actual employer exposed him to the factor that caused the harm. In the following case, mesothelioma was contracted from a single exposure from working with asbestos dust. The claimants had been exposed to asbestos dust in a number of different jobs and could not prove which employer had subjected them to the exposure that caused mesothelioma.

Fairchild v Glenhaven Funeral Services Ltd (2002)

Facts: The claimants had been negligently exposed to asbestos during the course of employment with more than one employer, and subsequently contracted mesothelioma. Unlike other asbestos-induced illnesses, mesothelioma may be caused by a single fibre, and once contracted, will not be exacerbated by further exposure. This made it very difficult for the claimants to establish, on the balance of probabilities, that any one of their defendant employers had actually caused or materially contributed to the mesothelioma. All that the claimants could prove was that each of their employers had negligently exposed them to the risk of contracting mesothelioma.

Decision: The House of Lords stated that common sense and justice demanded a relaxation of the traditional causation rules, and that the exposure of the claimants to the risk of mesothelioma by the defendants should be treated as actually having made a material contribution to their contracting the disease. Therefore, all of their negligent employers were liable. The claimants could sue any one of them. (However, any employer sued could then seek a contribution from other employers that had also negligently exposed the claimants to asbestos dust.)

Liability relating to mesothelioma is now covered in section 3 of the Compensation Act 2006 which states that where a defendant is responsible for negligently exposing a claimant to asbestos, and that person gets mesothelioma as a result, the defendant is liable for the whole of the damage caused. Where several parties have all negligently exposed the claimant to asbestos the defendant can claim a contribution from the others. However if the other parties have ceased trading then it will be the defendant (or usually his insurers) that have to meet the full cost of the claim.

In the following case the claimant had been exposed to asbestos by only one employer but the Supreme Court found that the exposure materially increased her risk of contracting mesothelioma.

Sienkiewicz v Greif (2011)

Facts: C was negligently exposed to a moderate amount of asbestos dust by her employer which increased her chance of getting mesothelioma by 18 per cent. C contracted the disease and died.

Decision: The increase in risk was not insignificant; the employer was liable to fully compensate for C's death.

Business Insight Insurance

Although cases appear to be between individuals in reality many of them are between the defendant and the claimant's insurers. Some areas of liability are required by statute to have compulsory insurance. For example, the Road Traffic Act 1988 requires motorists to be insured against damage to third parties and the Employers' Liability (Compulsory Insurance) Act 1969 requires employers to insure against liability for injury or disease sustained by their employees in the course of their employment.

Remoteness of Damage

The damage suffered by the claimant must not be too remote, which means that it must be reasonably foreseeable. This is an objective test, and the defendant is only responsible for the damage which a reasonable man would have foreseen as a likely consequence of his action.

Overseas Tankship (UK) Ltd v Morts Dock & Engineering Co Ltd (The Wagon Mound) (1961)

Facts: The defendants spilt oil from their ship the Wagon Mound in Sydney Harbour. The oil spread to a wharf where some welding was going on. The welding stopped until the defendants found that it would not ignite in the water. Three days later a bit of cotton waste was floating in the oil and it ignited from a spark from the welding. The claimant's wharf was destroyed.

Decision: Although the fire was as a direct result of the oil spillage, it was too remote, as no one knew oil could ignite in that way, i.e. it was not reasonably foreseeable.

The precise nature of the injury suffered need not be foreseeable, if the injury was of a kind that was foreseeable, even if the damage is more severe than anticipated.

Hughes v Lord Advocate (1963)

Facts: Post Office workers left a manhole open surrounded by paraffin lamps. Two boys climbed into the manhole. One of the boys took one of the paraffin lamps and dropped it into the manhole. The paraffin from the light vaporised and was ignited by the flame causing an explosion. Both boys suffered severe burns.

Decision: The defendant was liable, as the type of harm was foreseeable even if the exact way in which it occurred was not. The explosion was not foreseeable but burning was foreseeable.

Jolley v London Borough of Sutton (2000)

Facts: A small boat was abandoned on grounds near a block of flats owned by the Council. The boat became derelict and rotten. The Council was aware that children played on the boat, which they knew was dangerous. The claimant, aged 14, and a friend were injured when they tried to jack up the boat to repair it.

Decision: The Council was liable as some harm was foreseeable, even if the precise way the harm occurred could not be foreseen.

The Eggshell Skull Principle

The *Wagon Mound* case states that injury or damage must be reasonably foreseeable, but this does not displace the legal principle that the defendant must take his victim as he finds him. If a victim has a particular susceptibility or weakness (a thin skull or a weak heart, for example) and suffers a greater injury than a normal person, the defendant will be liable to the full extent of the claimant's injuries.

Smith v Leech Brain & Co Ltd (1962)

Facts: The claimant's husband was splashed on the lip with molten metal due to his employer's negligence. He suffered a minor burn but, because his lip was in a pre-cancerous condition, the burn activated cancer from which he later died.

Decision: Although the only foreseeable injury was the burn, the defendants were liable for the death because a normal person would have suffered some harm.

The same principle applies even when the harm caused is psychiatric injury which proves to be more serious because the claimant has a particular susceptibility to mental illness. It also has been applied to cases of economic loss.

Lagden v O'Connor (2003)

Facts: C's car was damaged in an accident caused by D. C was unemployed and could not afford to pay for a hire car and therefore hired a car on credit which was more expensive than normal hire.

Decision: D had to take C as he found him which included his financial situation.

Intervening Acts ('*Novus Actus Interveniens*')

The situation of an intervening act usually applies in circumstances where the negligence of the defendant has triggered a sequence of events leading to the harm suffered by the claimant. The intervening event may be the act of the claimant himself, or a third party over which the defendant had no control. The court has to decide whether the new act is sufficiently serious to be the cause of the damage rather than the original act. A defendant who injures a claimant who has already been injured will be liable only in so far as his act increases or exacerbates the pre-existing injury.

For example, Zac negligently crashes into the back of Yvonne's car. Yvonne, who is bruised and disorientated by the crash, steps out of her car without checking the traffic and is run over by a van being driven at a great speed in the opposite direction. As a result, Yvonne's legs are damaged. At the hospital the surgeon is negligent and Yvonne eventually has to have her legs amputated. Zac's initial negligence triggered the sequence of events, but the court will decide if the intervening actions of the van driver and doctor broke the chain of causation between Zac's original negligence and the final loss suffered by Yvonne.

In the following case it was the intervening actions of the claimant that broke the chain of causation.

McKew v Holland (1969)

Facts: The defendant negligently injured the claimant's leg. As a consequence, the claimant's leg was liable to give way. The claimant attempted, unassisted, to descend a steep flight of stairs without a banister. He fell and suffered additional injuries.

Decision: The defendant was not liable for additional injuries because the claimant had acted unreasonably, and this constituted a break in the chain of causation.

Where an intervening act breaks the chain of causation, the defendant will only be liable for injuries that occurred to the claimant prior to that event. The cause of the final loss suffered by the claimant is that intervening event, which if it is the act of a third party, may result in the claimant taking action against the third party.

Basic Terminology

Nervous shock A psychiatric illness or condition such as post-traumatic stress disorder.

Objective test Judging the defendant by the capabilities of the reasonable person.

Primary victim A person who is under actual threat of bodily harm or reasonably believes themselves to be so.

Proximity Legal closeness between the claimant and the defendant at the time of the cause of complaint. Legal closeness includes personal relationships between the parties and length of time between events.

Pure economic loss Where a claimant's financial loss is not connected to his physical injury or damage to his property.

***Res ipsa loquitur* (the thing speaks for itself)** The evidence clearly suggests that the defendant must have breached his duty of care. (The burden of proof is changed so that the defendant must show that he was not negligent.)

Secondary victim A person who suffers a psychiatric illness as a result of witnessing an accident or its 'immediate aftermath'.

Strict liability Liability which is imposed on a person without having to prove that the person was negligent or at fault.

Subjective test Judging the defendant by his own capabilities.

Tort A civil wrong for which a remedy, usually compensation, may be awarded to the wronged person.

Vicarious liability Liability which arises because of one person's relationship with another, such as employer and employee.

Summary

After studying this chapter students should be able to:

Outline the difference between the Law of Torts and Contract and Criminal Law

- A tort is a civil wrong and is primarily about providing a remedy for people for harm that they have suffered. The Law of Torts concerns involuntary obligations that are imposed upon persons by the law.
- Criminal Law is primarily about punishing the people who have committed wrongs in the eyes of the state.
- In the Law of Contract, the obligations imposed in the contract have been voluntarily agreed to by the parties when they entered into the contract.

Explain the necessary ingredients of negligence

- The three necessary ingredients to establish a duty of care are:
  - The defendant owed the claimant a duty of care;
  - The defendant breached that duty of care;
  - Reasonably foreseeable damage was caused by the breach of duty.
- The three elements sometimes overlap, and in a court case the issues are often looked at together rather than separately.

Explain how a duty of care may be established

- For a duty of care to exist, the claimant must establish that there is earlier legal authority for a duty existing in the same circumstances, or prove the three-stage test:
  - The harm or loss caused was reasonably foreseeable, and
  - There was proximity between the claimant and the defendant, and
  - It is fair, just, and reasonable in all the circumstances for the law to impose a duty on the defendant.

Understand the special requirements for the recovery of pure economic loss and for loss as a result of psychiatric injuries

- Pure economic loss is where the financial loss of the claimant is not connected to any physical injury of the claimant or damage to his property.
- Recovery of pure economic loss through the tort of negligence is very limited. A duty of care will only be imposed if there is a 'special relationship' between the parties.

Describe the principle of breach of a duty of care

- The claimant must establish that the defendant broke his duty of care by doing something that a reasonable man in the circumstances would not have done, or failing to do something that a reasonable man in the circumstances would have done.
- The standard of care is an objective test.
- In deciding a duty has been breached, the court will take into account the probability and potential seriousness of harm being caused to the claimant, the reasonableness/practicalities of taking precautions, and the usefulness to society of what the defendant was attempting to achieve.

Explain the extent of damages resulting from breach of a duty of care

- The claimant must prove, on the balance of probabilities, that the defendant's negligence caused or materially contributed to the injury or loss sustained.
- The loss or damage suffered by the claimant must be reasonably foreseeable.
- If a claimant has a particular weakness and, therefore, suffers a greater injury than a normal person, the defendant will be liable to the full extent of the claimant's injuries.
- The chain of events may be broken by an intervening event or act.
- The defendant is only liable for injury up until the intervening event.
- A defendant who injures a claimant who has already been injured will be liable only in so far as his act increases or exacerbates the pre-existing injury.

Questions

1. Ruby, who recently passed her driving test, decides to drive into town. On turning right at a junction, she negligently fails to see a car being driven by Sapphire and crashes into it. Sapphire was not wearing a seatbelt at the time of the accident, and was badly injured. Sapphire's husband, Tom, hears the crash and rushes to the scene of the accident; he is so shocked at seeing Sapphire's injuries that he shortly afterwards develops a psychiatric illness.

   Explain the essential ingredients of a negligence action and consider the legal liability of Ruby in the Law of Torts.

2. Fraud and Co, a firm of accountants and auditors, were employed to prepare the accounts and balance sheet of Apple plc, knowing the accounts were to be sent to Bill, a private investor, who was thinking of buying a majority shareholding in Apple plc. The accounts were negligently prepared and showed the company as financially stable, whereas in fact the opposite was true and the company had large debts outstanding. Bill showed the accounts to his friend Richard. Bill purchased £500,000 worth of shares and Richard purchased £200,000 worth of shares. Within six months, Apple plc went into liquidation and both Bill and Richard lost their investments.

   Advise Bill and Richard on the likelihood of them succeeding in their actions against Fraud and Co.

3. Discuss what is meant by 'a duty of care' in the tort of negligence.

For outline answers visit the Online Resource Centre

4. Explain the test which is applied in the tort of negligence to determine whether the defendant breached the legal duty of care owed to the claimant. What factors would a court take into account when determining how a reasonable person would act?

Further Reading

Bermingham and Brennan, *Tort Law Directions*, 4th edn (Oxford University Press, 2014) Chapters 3, 4, and 5.

Cooke, *Law of Torts*, 11th edn (Pearson, 2013) Part 2.

Horsey and Rackley, *Tort Law*, 3rd edn (Oxford University Press, 2013) Part 2.

Competition and Markets Authority:https://www.gov.uk/government/organisations/competition-and-markets-authority.

Trading Standards Institute: http://www.tradingstandards.gov.uk/.

Online Resource Centre

Test your knowledge by trying this chapter's **Multiple Choice Questions.** Visit:

www.oup.com/uk/orc/law/company/ jonesibl3e/01student/mcqs/ch11/

For more information, updates, and multiple choice questions, please visit the Online Resource Centre at:

www.oup.com/uk/orc/law/company/ jonesibl3e/

Product Liability, Defective Premises, Interference with Land, and Defences

Introduction

The tort of negligence is important in the business world, but there are other torts that all businesses need to be aware of, including a claim for defective products under the Consumer Protection Act 1987 and liability for defective premises. Almost all businesses own or occupy premises, and an occupier has a duty imposed upon him to ensure the safety of visitors on his premises and even owes a duty of care to trespassers to ensure harm does not befall them. In addition, there are a number of torts concerning interference with the use and enjoyment of land. Trespass on land occupied by another is a tort, and builders who use another's land for access to their building site without permission may be committing trespass. A business (or person) that interferes unreasonably with another's use or enjoyment of their land may be liable for private nuisance, and if they have endangered the health, property, or comfort of the general public they may be liable for public nuisance.

Learning Objectives

After studying this chapter you should be able to:

- Distinguish between an action for defective products taken in the tort of negligence and an action under the Consumer Protection Act 1987.
- Identify the elements necessary for a claim under the Consumer Protection Act 1987.
- Explain the liability of occupiers to visitors and trespassers.
- Outline liability for trespass to land.
- Describe private and public nuisance.
- Outline liability established by *Rylands v Fletcher*.

- Explain the defences of contributory negligence, consent, and illegality.
- Understand the meaning and extent of vicarious liability.

Liability for Defective Products

A Claim in the Tort of Negligence

If a person should suffer a loss as a consequence of a defective product, they may sue in the tort of negligence for breach of a common law duty as discussed in Chapter 11, or they may take action under the Consumer Protection Act 1987 for breach of a statutory duty. If there is a contract between the parties, the usual action for loss caused by a defective product will be in the Law of Contract. An action in the Law of Contract has certain advantages as liability is generally strict, and all losses which stem from the breach of contract, provided they are not too remote, are recoverable. However, sometimes a contractual remedy will not be available, for example, where the seller of the defective product has gone into liquidation, or where there is no contract between the seller of the defective product and the consumer who suffered the loss. The product may have been purchased by a friend and given to the consumer.

In the landmark case of *Donoghue v Stevenson* (1932) the House of Lords resolved that the manufacturer of products owes a duty of care to the ultimate consumer, where the manufacturer intends the products to reach the ultimate consumer without further examination. This is provided that the manufacturer knows that the absence of reasonable care in the preparation of the products will result in injury to the consumer. The definition of product is broad, and there have been cases concerning products such as hairdryers, lifts, underpants, cars, and tombstones. The ultimate consumer has been interpreted to include anyone who may foreseeably be affected by the defective product. The range of potential defendants has extended beyond manufacturers and includes persons who have repaired, assembled, or supplied goods.

In the following case, a repairer was liable in negligence.

Stennett v Hancock (1939)

Facts: The defendant garage negligently repaired the wheel on a lorry. Later, when the lorry was driven, part of the wheel came off and hit a pedestrian.

Decision: The garage owed a duty of care in negligence to the pedestrian and was liable for his injuries. The owner of the lorry was not liable as he had not been negligent.

In some situations more than one defendant may be liable, in which case they will be **jointly and severally liable**. This means that, if a product is defective, each defendant is liable individually and jointly with the other defendants. A claimant can choose to sue either one or more of the defendants.

The problem for a claimant consumer, taking action under the tort of negligence for a defective product, is that the claimant will have to prove the defendant is at fault. A defendant is not automatically liable for a defective product which causes harm to a claimant. He will only be liable if the claimant proves, on the balance of probabilities, that the defendant breached the duty of care. The defendant must be shown to have been negligent, in that he failed to take reasonable care to protect against reasonably foreseeable events. This includes taking into account the special needs of the ultimate consumer, and giving adequate advice and warnings about the use or dangers of a particular product.

A manufacturer of a product may escape liability if there has been interference by a third party or if warnings have not been heeded.

Holmes v Ashford (1950)

Facts: The claimant suffered dermatitis when hair dye was applied to her hair by a hairdresser. The claimant sued the manufacturer of the hair dye.

Decision: The defendant manufacturer was not liable because the hairdresser had failed to test the product, in accordance with the manufacturer's instructions, before using it on the claimant.

A manufacturer may escape liability if the product could have been tampered with between leaving the manufacturer and reaching the claimant, or the defect could have occurred for a reason other than the manufacturer's negligence.

Where a defendant is found liable in the tort of negligence for a defective product, usually a claimant will only be able to claim compensation for personal injury, death, or damage to property caused by the defective product, and financial loss as a result of the injury, death, or damage. A claimant cannot generally recover compensation for the defective product itself, nor can he claim compensation if a product poses a danger but has not actually caused an injury. General dissatisfaction with legal protection given to consumers for defective goods across the European Union led to the EU issuing a directive in 1985 (EC Directive 85/374/EEC) which instructed EU Member States to provide a certain level of consumer legal protection. To comply with the provisions of the directive, Parliament passed the Consumer Protection Act 1987.

Viewpoint Paul Edmondson, Regional Manager, Bladerunner Ltd

As a manager of Bladerunner Ltd (a corporate gym management company) I am required to understand and adhere to certain safety standards in the gyms that I operate. Bladerunner complies with ISO 9001 safety standards and outsources general health and safety to a contracting company.

Health and safety within the fitness environment is very high in priority, and from the outset Bladerunner agreed a joint responsibilities matrix with the company involved to identify who is responsible for different areas. For example, building asbestos risk management wouldn't be the responsibility of Bladerunner as we do not own the building; however, Bladerunner would require a copy of the risk assessment.

It is vitally important that I understand where liability would fall with regard to negligence, and it is my job to make sure that the liability of Bladerunner is covered. As a manager I continually complete checks to ensure we do our utmost to ensure facilities are safe and risks are reduced to a minimum. If these checks were not completed and signed off, Bladerunner as a company plus the Bladerunner staff and management would be held responsible for any negligence, and as such could be taken to court (depending on the nature of the incident), resulting in fines or potentially a custodial sentence. All equipment in a centre is checked on a daily basis to ensure there are no issues or breakdowns and these checks are signed off by a staff member; health and safety checks are also completed daily and signed off to ensure there are no issues.

Furthermore, before anyone can use one of our centres, they must undergo a medical questionnaire and have their blood pressure taken. These forms and blood pressure tests are repeated at minimum on an annual basis. Once they have passed the medical checks, all members would undergo a full induction with a fully qualified member of staff to ensure they use the correct training technique on all the equipment in the centre. Members then sign off a disclaimer to say they have undergone the induction and understand their responsibilities. From this point, misuse of the equipment falls on to the member.

A Claim under the Consumer Protection Act 1987

The Consumer Protection Act 1987 came into force on 1 March 1988 and applies to damage caused by defective goods circulated after that date. The protection provided by the Act does not replace the common law protection given through the tort of negligence but it provides an additional statutory remedy. The Act was designed to impose liability on businesses; therefore, the Act does not cover private individuals who are not acting in the course of a business.

Strict liability

The Consumer Protection Act 1987 places **strict liability** for defective products on a number of possible defendants. Where 'strict liability' is imposed, this means that a claimant does not need to prove any intention or negligence on the part of the defendant. This is unlike the tort of negligence, where the claimant must show fault by the defendant. It is unusual, in the Law of Torts, to impose liability on defendants who may not be at fault, and, therefore, where strict liability is imposed an Act will normally provide some statutory defences. There are a number of defences provided by the Consumer Protection Act. Where damage is caused wholly or partly by a defect in a product, the defendant is liable unless he can prove one or more of the defences stated in the Act. Section 7 states that liability cannot be limited or excluded by a notice or any other means.

Potential claimants

Any person who has been injured or whose private property has been damaged by a defective product is a potential claimant under the Consumer Protection Act 1987.

Potential defendants

There are a range of potential defendants set out in ss 1 and 2 of the Act. The potential defendants are as follows:

- Producer: This includes the manufacturer of the product, the manufacturer of a defective component of the product, the extractor of raw materials (such as electricity), and processor of agricultural produce: s 1(2).

- Own brander: Anyone who holds themselves out as a producer, and does not make it clear that the goods are produced for them by another manufacturer. Many supermarkets, for example, will be 'own branders' when they sell goods as their own brand and do not make it clear that the goods have been made for them by an independent producer: s 2(2)(b).

- Importer: Anyone who imports the product from outside the EU into a Member State in the course of business. The importer is the first person who imports the goods into the EU: s 2(2)(c).

- Supplier: A supplier of the goods is only liable if he does not identify the producer, own brander, importer, or the person who supplied him with the goods, within a reasonable time after receiving a request from the injured party. The injured party must request these details, from the supplier, within a reasonable time of the damage: s 2(3)(a)–(c).

If there is more than one of these potential defendants, then the defendants are jointly and severally liable. This means that a claimant can take action against all or any one of the defendants (see Figure 12.1).

Figure 12.1 Potential defendants for defective products under the Consumer Protection Act 1987

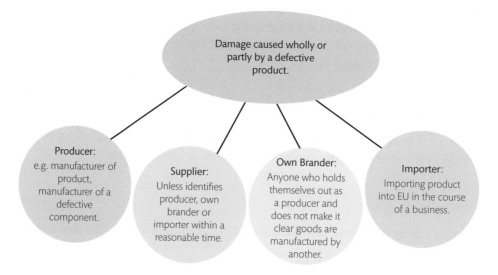

The product

The products covered by the Act encompass a wide range of goods, including ships, aircraft and other vehicles, electricity and water, and, unprocessed agricultural produce and game. A product also includes components of another product. Buildings are not included within the definition but building materials are included.

Supply of the product

The product must have been obtained from a supplier acting in the course of business. The product may have been purchased, hired, or bartered for, or alternatively may have been obtained as a gift or prize.

Human body products such as semen and blood, fall within the definition of 'product' in the Act.

A v National Blood Authority (2001)

Facts: The claimants contracted hepatitis B after receiving blood transfusions.

Decision: Blood and blood products were 'products' within the meaning of the Consumer Protection Act 1987, s 1.

The defect

The claimant must prove that there was a defect in the product. The Consumer Protection Act 1987, s 3, states that a product has a defect if the safety of the product is not such as persons generally are entitled to expect. The safety which persons are entitled to expect will depend on the circumstances of each case. The Act states that the circumstances which should be taken into account include:

- The manner and purposes for which the product has been marketed.

- Any instructions or warnings given with the product. A warning given on a potential hazardous product may make the product safe, but no or inadequate instructions on how to properly use a product may make the product dangerous.

- What might reasonably be expected to be done with or to the product. If a consumer is harmed by a product because he uses it for something outside its expected use, the producer will not be liable. However, a producer must take account of a potential consumer, and a toy produced for small children will require different safety standards to toys produced for teenagers.

- The time when the product was supplied by its producer to another. Time is an important factor, because if a product is perishable it may become unsafe after it has moved down the distribution chain. Alternatively, when the product was made it may have met the approved safety standards which later become more stringent.

Richardson v LRC Products Ltd (2000)

Facts: A condom failed during use and as a result the claimant became pregnant. The claimant sued the manufacturer of the condom for breach of the Consumer Protection Act 1987.

Decision: The defendant was not liable because the product did not have a 'defect', as people were not generally entitled to expect that a condom would be 100 per cent effective.

Abouzaid v Mothercare (2000)

Facts: The claimant, a 12-year-old, was struck in the eye by a metal buckle when he was trying to attach an elastic strap on a fleece-lined sleeping bag to his brother's pushchair.

Decision: The product was defective as there was a risk in using the product and no warning had been given.

Loss which is recoverable under the Act

A claimant can recover compensation for death or personal injury and damage to 'other' property over £275. The property must ordinarily have been intended for private use and intended by the claimant to be used for private use. Compensation is not recoverable for damage to the product itself, damage to 'other' property under £275, or any damage to 'business' property.

Causation

The claimant must prove on the balance of probabilities that the defective product wholly or partly caused the damage they suffered. If the claimant can show this, then the defendant will be liable despite the fact that he was not careless in any way, unless the defendant can prove he has a defence (see Table 12.1).

Defences

The claimant must establish on the balance of probabilities that the defective product wholly or partly caused the damage he suffered. If the claimant can show this, the defendant will be liable despite the fact that he was not careless in any way, unless he can prove that he has one of the defences set out in s 4 of the Act. These defences are:

- The defect is caused by complying with a requirement imposed by UK or EU legislation.

- The defendant did not supply the goods in the course of a business; for example, the goods were homemade biscuits supplied by a friend.

- The defect came about after the time of supply by the defendant. The defendant is not liable if, after supply, the defect occurred because of interference with the goods by a third party or the consumer himself.

- The state of scientific and technical knowledge at the relevant time was not such that a producer of products, of the same description as the product in question, might be expected to have discovered the defect if it had existed while the products were under his control. The 'relevant time' is the time that the defendant supplied the product. The effect of the defence is to exonerate the defendant from liability if the defendant can show that the defect was not known and was not foreseeable when the product was put into circulation.

The Act also provides that contributory negligence applies to actions under the Act and, therefore, if a claimant is partly to blame for his injuries then his compensation will be reduced.

Key Concept When making a claim under the Consumer Protection Act 1987, the claimant must prove the product was defective, and he suffered personal injury or damage to personal property as a result of the defective product. He does not have to prove that the producer was at fault when making or supplying the product.

Time limits

Under the provisions of the Limitation Act 1980, a claimant must take action against a defendant for a claim under the Consumer Protection Act 1987 within three years of discovering the defect, incurring the damage, or ascertaining the identity of 'the producer'. If the claimant has suffered personal injuries the court can allow an extension on the three-year limit but there is an absolute limitation period of ten years from the date the defendant supplied the defective product.

Table 12.1 The difference between an action in the tort of negligence and under the Consumer Protection Act 1987

	Negligence	**Consumer Protection Act 1987**
Claimant	Person injured or whose property is damaged.	Person injured or whose property is damaged.
Defendant	Must owe a duty of care to the claimant. May be a manufacturer, supplier, or servicer of goods.	Producer of product. May be a manufacturer, own brander, importer from outside EU, or supplier.
The claimant must prove	The defendant owed a duty of care.	The product was defective.
	The defendant broke the duty of care.	Damage was suffered as a result.
	The claimant suffered loss or damage as a result of the breach.	The claimant does NOT have to prove the defendant was at fault.
Claim	Any loss or damage provided it is not too remote. Generally excludes pure economic loss.	Death, personal injuries, or damage to property (other than business property) over the value of £275.

Occupiers' Liability

The liability of occupiers for injuries caused to others by the defective state of the occupiers' property is governed by two statutes, the Occupiers' Liability Act 1957 and the Occupiers' Liability Act 1984. These statutes impose duties on the occupiers of premises for the safety of the people who enter upon the land they occupy. If these duties are breached and harm is caused to someone on the premises, an action for damages may be brought against the occupier. The duties owed under these statutes only relate to harm caused by the state of the premises, and not activities carried out on the premises. Where injuries are caused by activities, as opposed to the state of the premises, then the general tort of negligence applies. In relation to the liability of occupiers, the law makes a distinction between the duty owed to **visitors** and the duty owed to **non-visitors** (such as trespassers).

Liability to Visitors

Liability of occupiers to visitors is governed by the Occupiers' Liability Act 1957. An occupier of land owes a common duty of care to all visitors on his premises. A claimant may bring a claim for death, personal injury, and damage to possessions. A visitor is a person who enters property with the express or implied permission of the occupier. The permission may be restricted in terms of time, place, and purpose. If the visitor does not comply with these restrictions, he will become a trespasser and will no longer be a visitor. If permission is given for a window cleaner to access a kitchen in the house to fill up a bucket of water, he will become a trespasser if he decides to go and have a look round upstairs. Section 2(6) of the Act provides that certain categories of people are deemed to be visitors. This includes firemen entering premises to put out a fire, and members of the public using public premises such as parks and libraries.

The occupier

The occupier is someone who has control over the premises. There may be more than one occupier of premises.

Wheat v E Lacon & Co Ltd (1966)

Facts: The defendant owned a pub which was run by a manager. The manager took in paying guests, who stayed in rooms on the first floor of the property. One of the paying guests fell down a staircase and was killed.

Decision: For the purposes of the Occupiers' Liability Act 1957, both the defendant and the manager were 'occupiers' of the premises as they had control over the premises (although neither were liable on the facts).

The premises

The term 'premises' is widely defined and includes not only buildings and land but also fixed or moveable structures such as ships in dry dock, vehicles, and aircraft.

The standard of care

The occupier must take such care as is reasonable, in all the circumstances of the case, to see that the visitor will be reasonably safe in using the premises for the purpose for which he is invited or permitted by the occupier to be there. The duty of care imposed on occupiers requires them to ensure that their visitors are reasonably safe. It is not to guarantee that the premises are reasonably safe.

In carrying out this duty, the occupier is entitled to take into account the behaviour that would reasonably be expected of the visitor.

Clare v Perry (2005)

Facts: The claimant, a guest at the defendant's hotel, chose to exit the hotel one evening by climbing over a perimeter wall rather than using a nearby official exit. As it was dark, the claimant had not realised there was a six-foot drop on the other side of the wall. The claimant suffered serious injuries and sued the defendant.

Decision: The key question was whether the defendant had breached the common duty of care. In deciding the case, the court took into account the behaviour which is reasonably expected of a visitor, and in this case the claimant had behaved in a foolish way that was not reasonable for the defendant to guard against. The defendant was not liable.

Business Insight   Visitors' behaviour and occupiers' responsibility

In 2005 a claim, under the Occupiers' Liability Act 1957, of a hotel guest who fell through a second floor open bedroom window was dismissed. If the claimant's argument had been successful, virtually every window in every building would have to have bars or restricted opening. The court stated that it was not reasonably foreseeable that an adult occupying a room would lean out of the window and fall. There was no duty of care on the hotel proprietor to restrict the opening of windows.

In 2011, an 18-year-old girl failed in her claim against her friend's parent after sustaining serious head injuries on diving into his private swimming pool. The girl had been invited for a 'midnight swim' by her friend while her parents were out. The court stated that the girl was an adult and had done something that carried an obvious risk.

The standard of care depends on the circumstances: some visitors, such as children, can be expected to be more vulnerable than others and a higher standard of care will be owed to them. Other visitors, such as contractors, can be expected to take precautions themselves, particularly if warnings have been given. The 1957 Act makes special provision in respect of the standard of care that should be showed to children and skilled visitors.

Children

An occupier must take account of the fact that children will be less careful than adults and consequently a higher standard of care is required to be exercised by the occupier.

B v JJB Sports (2006)

Facts: The claimant, a boy aged 10, slipped on a wet floor between indoor football pitches and sustained head injuries. The premises were owned by the defendant and the floor had recently been washed.

Decision: The defendant was liable under the Occupiers' Liability Act 1957, as it was foreseeable that the floor might be damp after cleaning and he had failed to allow for children being less careful than adults. An adult might be expected to see a sign warning of a wet floor but signs were insufficient to guard against enthusiastic children.

However, an occupier is not liable for all accidents that happen to children on his premises. In some circumstances it may be reasonable for an occupier to assume that a small child will be supervised by sensible parents.

Bourne Leisure Ltd v Marsden (2009)

Facts: The M family were staying at a caravan park owned by B. While Mrs M was talking to another camper Mrs M's 2-year-old son wandered off, fell into a nearby pond on the site, and drowned.

Decision: B was not liable. B did not have a duty to fence the pond or to give a precise location of it. All visitors had been given a map showing ponds, river, and beach. It would have been clear to any parent that it was dangerous to let a small unaccompanied child wander off on his own.

Skilled visitors

An occupier is entitled to expect that a person carrying out his job on their premises will appreciate and guard against any special risk arising from his job. Contractors should be aware of the risks that are ordinarily incidental to their occupation.

Roles v Nathan (1963)

Facts: The claimants were chimney sweeps who died from carbon-monoxide poisoning while cleaning a chimney.

Decision: The occupier of the property was not liable because it was reasonable to expect chimney sweeps to know about and guard against such a risk.

Business Insight   Common sense and the compensation culture

In April 2007 Mrs Cole broke her leg when she tripped over a hole in a village green where a maypole used to stand. She sued the British Legion who had organised the annual fete. The Court of Appeal decided that the British Legion had taken reasonable steps to make the green safe and if a higher standard was required then there could be a flood of claims for accidents that most people would consider as being no one's fault. The test set out under the Occupiers' Liability Act 1957, to 'take such care as in all the circumstances of the case is reasonable to see that the visitor will be reasonably safe', allows courts to consider public policy when deciding what is 'reasonable'. The Court took into account that the activity, of running a village fete, was being carried out for the 'greater good' and if it allowed the claim, then it may threaten village traditions that go back centuries.

Warning notices

A notice which warns visitors of a danger on premises may be enough to discharge the occupier's duty of common care, provided that the notice was enough to make the visitor reasonably safe in visiting the premises. Notices that go further than just warning of dangers but actually attempt to exclude liability may not be effective. Under the provisions of the Unfair Contract Terms Act 1977, a business cannot exclude liability if a visitor dies or is personally injured as a result of an occupier's failure to take reasonable care. Liability for damage to property may be excluded, provided it is reasonable to do so, taking into account all the circumstances. However, it is possible for private occupiers to exclude or restrict liability by agreement or notice.

Liability to Trespassers

An occupier of premises does not owe the same duty of common care to persons who he has not expressly or impliedly invited on his premises as he does to visitors. The majority of persons who are not lawful visitors are trespassers, although not all non-visitors are trespassers. Persons who have a legal right of way over an occupier's land are not trespassers, although they are only given the same legal protection as given to trespassers. A trespasser may be a burglar, or a child who has climbed over railings to play on a railway line, or a person who has inadvertently strayed on to a dangerous building site. An occupier's liability to non-visitors is governed by the Occupiers' Liability Act 1984. The definition of premises and occupiers is the same as in the Occupiers' Liability Act 1957. However, the 1984 Act only covers liability for death or personal injury whereas the 1957 Act covers liability for death, personal injury, and damage to personal property (possessions). The duty of care to a visitor is a positive one and requires an occupier to ensure visitors are reasonably safe, whereas the duty of an occupier to trespassers and other non-visitors is only to take reasonable steps to prevent them being harmed (see Figure 12.2).

Business Insight   Dismissal of occupier's liability claim

In *Driver v Dover Roman Painted House* (2014) the court dismissed a claim by a woman who suffered skull fractures after she fell over a three foot wall at a Roman site, landing in a dry moat. She had entered the car park of the site after midnight when looking for somewhere to urinate after an evening's drinking. The judge stated that any permission the claimant might have had to enter the area did not extend to going to the toilet and so she was a trespasser. Under the 1984 Act the question was whether there was danger due to the state of premises. The premises had not been dangerous, the wall being three-foot high and adequately lit even at night.

Duty of care owed to trespassers

A duty of care is not automatically owed to the trespasser. Section 1(3) of the Occupiers' Liability Act 1984 provides that a duty will be owed by an occupier to a trespasser who has suffered injury on his premises if:

- The occupier was aware of the danger on the premises or had reasonable grounds to believe that it existed; and

- The occupier knew or had reasonable grounds to believe that the trespasser was in the vicinity of the danger; and

- The risk was one against which, in all the circumstances of the case, the occupier could reasonably be expected to offer the trespasser some protection.

Ratcliff v McConnell (1998)

Facts: The claimant, a drunken student, decided to go swimming with friends in the early hours of the morning. They scaled the locked gate of their college's open-air swimming pool and the claimant dived into the shallow end of the pool, causing himself very serious injuries.
Decision: The defendants were not liable as the claimant had realised the risk of diving into water of an unknown depth.

The standard of care owed to trespassers

The occupier must take such care as is reasonable in all the circumstances of the case to ensure that the trespasser does not suffer injury on the premises because of the state of danger of the premises. What amounts to reasonable care will depend on the facts of the case. Depending on the circumstances it may be enough for an occupier to discharge his duty of care by putting up a warning sign. The court will take into account the age of the trespasser, the type of premises, the extent of the risk, and the practicality of taking precautions. If the likelihood of trespassers coming on to premises is very remote or the practicality of taking precautions is very difficult, the occupier will be able to discharge their duty without taking extreme precautions. However, if children are likely to trespass on property, the occupier will be expected to take steps to ensure no harm befalls them.

Tomlinson v Congleton (2003)

Facts: The claimant broke his neck when he dived into a lake at a country park owned, occupied, and managed by the defendants. There were notices by the lake which stated 'Dangerous Water. No Swimming'. The claimant sued the defendants for breach of the Occupiers' Liability Act 1984, accepting that he was a trespasser at the time of the accident.
Decision: No duty was owed to the claimant. The risk was obvious, the claimant was an adult, and this was not the sort of risk which an occupier would reasonably be expected to offer a trespasser protection against.

Key Concept An occupier's liability towards visitors is to take such care, as is reasonable in the circumstances, to see that the visitor will be reasonably safe. An occupier's liability towards trespassers is to take such care as is reasonable in the circumstances, to see that the trespasser does not suffer injury on the premises because of the state of danger of the premises.

Figure 12.2 Occupier's liability to visitors and trespassers

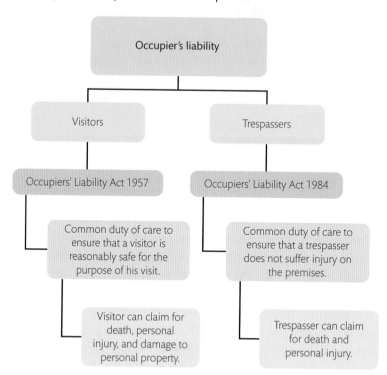

Trespass to Land

Trespass to land is the direct interference with a person's possession of land without lawful authority. It does not only apply to land in the sense of 'the ground' but also to anything permanently attached to its surface such as a house. It is a wrong done to the possessor of land, who is someone who either physically occupies the land or occupies the land through servants or agents. It is **'actionable per se'**, which means an action can be taken against a defendant without proof that loss has occurred.

Business Insight Squatting becomes a criminal offence

An example of trespass to land is when squatters occupy an empty property belonging to someone else. This is now not only a civil issue; the Legal Aid, Sentencing and Punishment of Offenders Act 2012 made squatting in a residential property a criminal offence.

Interference Must be Direct

The interference must be either by entering the land without lawful authority, or remaining on the land after permission has been withdrawn, or placing objects on the land. A common form of trespass is the dumping of rubbish, or parking vehicles on someone's land without permission.

League Against Cruel Sports v Scott (1986)

Facts: The claimants owned land on Exmoor which they maintained as a deer sanctuary. The hounds from the local hunt repeatedly got on to the claimants' land and disturbed the deer.
Decision: The Master of Hounds was liable for trespass if he deliberately encouraged the dogs to enter the land or if he negligently failed to prevent them entering the land.

Entry below the surface of land or into airspace may be trespass if that area is within the ordinary use of the land.

Kelsen v Imperial Tobacco Co (1957)

Facts: The defendant erected an advertising sign which projected into the claimant's airspace by eight inches.
Decision: The defendant was liable for trespass.

In the following case there was no trespass as the aircraft was so high above the land.

Bernstein v Skyviews & General Ltd (1978)

Facts: The defendant took aerial photographs without permission from the claimant landowners.
Decision: There was no trespass as the rights of landowners in airspace above their land was restricted to such height as is necessary for the ordinary use and enjoyment of the land and the structures upon it.

The Civil Aviation Act 1982, s 76, states that there is no liability for trespass or nuisance from aircraft flying at a reasonable height over any property. However, the owner of the aircraft is liable for damage caused by things falling from it.

Key Concept Trespass to land includes not only entering on to land without lawful authority but also leaving rubbish and vehicles on land.

Defences

There are some circumstances where a person has the right under statute to enter another's land. For example, the police have the right to enter premises for the purposes of making an arrest under the Police and Criminal Evidence Act 1984. The Countryside and Rights of Way Act 2000 provides a right to roam across certain land. There are some common law rights to enter land such as the right to use the foreshore for passing and repassing on foot or with boats. It is also a defence if the entry on the land was necessary because of a threat to life or property.

Rigby v CC Northamptonshire (1985)

Facts: The police fired CS gas into a gunsmith shop owned by the claimant in order to force a psychopath out. The gas canister started a fire and the claimant's shop burned down.
Decision: Necessity was a defence to trespass and therefore the police were not liable in trespass.

There is a defence of permission or licence. This is where the claimant expressly or impliedly consents to the defendant entering the land. A newspaper delivery boy will have an implied permission to enter property to deliver a paper. If the permission has been granted for a specific purpose, then the defendant will not be liable for trespass while he adheres to the terms of the permission.

Remedies

The key remedy available to a claimant is damages (compensation). The amount awarded is to put the claimant in the position he would have been in if the trespass had not been committed. Damages will cover costs of repairs and loss of profits. Even if the claimant has suffered no loss, nominal damages (a very small amount) may be awarded by the court. If a trespass is continuing then the court may award an **injunction**. This is an Order by the Court which requires a defendant to cease the trespass. Failure to obey a court order is a criminal offence.

Private Nuisance

Private nuisance is the unlawful interference with someone's use or enjoyment of their land. Only persons with some interest in the land, such as an owner or occupier, can sue in nuisance. Interfering with someone's use or enjoyment of their land does not automatically give rise to an action for private nuisance. The law has to strike a balance between the right of one land owner or occupier to do as they please on their own land, with the right of a neighbouring land owner or occupier not to have their use and enjoyment of land interfered with. Nuisance is important in business as most businesses are run from owned or tenanted premises, and nuisance covers issues such as emitting noxious fumes and unreasonable levels of noise.

When is Interference with Use and Enjoyment of Land Unlawful?

Unlawful interference broadly means that the interference must be unreasonable. However, what one person regards as reasonable his neighbour may regard as totally unreasonable. In deciding if an action is reasonable, the court will take into account a number of factors including locality, duration, and timing of the activity, the extent of the interference, the sensitivity of the claimant, and whether the defendant was acting through malice. The claimant must prove that the nuisance has caused some damage, although the damage does not have to be physical damage; it may be loss of sleep caused through noise or the inability to open windows due to fumes. Where there has been some physical damage, as opposed to inconvenience or disturbance, then generally the claimant will be successful in a claim for nuisance.

St Helens Smelting Co v Tipping (1865)

Facts: Fumes from the defendant's copper smelting works damaged trees and crops on the claimant's estate. The claimant's estate was in a manufacturing area.
Decision: The court stated that an occupier is entitled to protection from physical damage no matter where they live and, therefore, the defendant was liable in the tort of nuisance.

Key Concept A person may have a claim in private nuisance where there is an unreasonable interference with the use or enjoyment of his land.

Locality

Where the damage claimed is some loss of amenity, as opposed to physical damage (as in *St Helens Smelting Co v Tipping*), locality is an important consideration in deciding if the use of land is unreasonable. It is not reasonable to expect the same level of peace and quiet in commercial and industrial areas as may be expected in residential areas. In rural areas agricultural activities, involving smell or noise from farm machinery, may be reasonable.

Gillingham BC v Medway (Chatham Docks) Co Ltd (1992)

Facts: Having obtained planning permission from the Council, the defendant operated a commercial dock 24 hours a day. Heavy lorries passed through the adjacent district, causing substantial interference with the enjoyment of the affected properties.

Decision: There was no nuisance because of the character of the neighbourhood. It was a commercial area.

Duration and timing

For an activity to amount to a nuisance it usually has to be continuous or regular. Timing is also important. Loud noise at night is more likely to cause a nuisance than daytime noise.

Leeman v Montagu (1936)

Facts: The defendant, who had a poultry farm on the edge of a residential area, kept a flock of up to 750 cockerels in an orchard about 100 yards from the claimant's house. The claimant was kept awake each night from about 2am to 7am with the cockerels' crowing.

Decision: The defendant had committed a nuisance.

The claimant's sensitivity

Nuisance only protects the ordinary and reasonable use of the claimant's land. If the claimant is using the land for something particularly sensitive, then the defendant will not be liable in nuisance if the claimant's use is interfered with and damage results.

Robinson v Kilvert (1889)

Facts: The claimant occupied the ground floor of premises and used it to store brown paper. The basement was occupied by the defendants. The heat from the defendants' manufacturing process in the basement caused damage to the paper.

Decision: Ordinary use of the claimant's premises would not have caused any problems. The damage was due to sensitivity of paper. The defendants were not liable in nuisance.

If the defendant's activities would have caused loss to the claimant's ordinary use of land, then the claimant will be able to claim for loss for sensitive use provided it is reasonably foreseeable that damage would occur. Therefore, if the defendant's fumes cause damage to the claimant's ordinary crops in addition to his exotic crops, he will be able to claim for both.

McKinnon Industries v Walker (1951)

Facts: The defendant's factory emitted sulphur dioxide which damaged the claimant's commercially-grown orchids.
Decsion: The interference would have damaged non-sensitive plants. The defendant was liable and the claimant was able to recover the full extent of his loss.

Malice

If the defendant's motive is ill-will or antagonism towards the claimant, then the court may regard an activity, which might have been reasonable in some circumstances, as unreasonable.

Hollywood Silver Fox Farm v Emmett (1936)

Facts: The claimant bred silver foxes on his farm. After an argument with the claimant, the defendant, who owned the next door farm, ordered guns to be fired on his own land but close to the claimant's land. His intention was that noise would prevent foxes from breeding.
Decsion: The defendant's motive amounted to malice and he was liable in nuisance.

Who Can Sue?

Only persons with some interest in the land, such as an owner or occupier, can sue. A person with no interest in the land cannot make a claim for private nuisance.

Malone v Laskey (1907)

Facts: The claimant, who was the wife of the tenant, was injured by a lavatory cistern falling on her head because of vibrations from adjoining property owned by the defendant.

Decision: The defendant was not liable in nuisance because the claimant had no interest in the premises herself as she was not the tenant.

The House of Lords confirmed in *Hunter v Canary Wharf Ltd* (1997) that a person who had no right in affected land could not sue for private nuisance.

Hunter v Canary Wharf Ltd (1997)

Facts: Mr Hunter and others brought an action in nuisance against Canary Wharf Ltd, claiming that the newly-constructed Canary Wharf tower on the company's land interfered with their television reception.

Decision: The court stated that the mere fact that a building was in the way of television reception was not enough to amount to private nuisance and only persons with an interest in the land affected (e.g. tenant, owner) could bring an action.

Who Can be Sued for Nuisance?

In a private nuisance action, there may be more than one person liable. If there is more than one defendant, then the defendants are jointly and severally liable. Therefore, the claimant can sue all or one of them. Action can always be taken against the creator of the nuisance, whether or not he is the occupier of the premises. The occupier of the land from which the nuisance arises will also be liable if the nuisance is caused by the occupier's own actions or omissions, or caused by an employee of the occupier. In addition, the occupier may be liable if the nuisance is created by someone whom the occupier had control over when on his land, such as a lawful visitor.

   If the nuisance was created by a trespasser or arose by an act of nature, then the occupier will only be liable if he knew or should have known of the existence of the nuisance and he failed to take reasonable steps to prevent it.

Sedleigh Denfield v O'Callaghan (1940)

Facts: A local authority, without permission (therefore as a trespasser) installed a drainage pipe in a ditch on the defendant's land. A grating which was part of the work was installed incorrectly. The defendant was aware there was a danger of flooding and usually cleaned out the ditch. However, one year the drainage pipe became blocked and the claimant's land was flooded.

Decision: The defendant was liable in private nuisance. He had failed to take reasonable steps (e.g. install the grating) to prevent flooding the claimant's land.

In the following case, the nuisance was created by an act of nature but it was one which the occupier was aware of, and failed to take reasonable steps to prevent damage occurring to the claimant's property.

Leakey v National Trust (1980)

Facts: The defendant, the National Trust, owned land on which there stood a large mound of earth. They knew it was prone to subsidence. Following a dry summer, cracks appeared in the mound which gave way and slid on to the claimant's property.

Decision: Nuisance could be caused by the state of the land itself. The defendant knew of the risk of landslides and had failed to take reasonable steps to prevent it happening and, therefore, was liable in nuisance.

A landlord will not usually be liable for a nuisance arising from rented property unless the nuisance was present before the tenancy and the landlord knew about it or ought to have known about it or, as in the following case, the landlord authorised the nuisance.

Tetley v Chitty (1986)

Facts: The defendant let his land to a go-cart club. Local residents brought an action for nuisance against the defendant.

Decision: The defendant was liable, as noise nuisance was an ordinary and inevitable consequence of allowing the go-cart club to use the land.

Defence of Prescription

It is possible for a person to have a prescriptive right to carry on an activity which causes a nuisance if they have continuously carried on the activity for the last 20 years without action being taken against them. The 20 years starts to run when the claimant becomes aware that the activity is causing a nuisance.

Sturges v Bridgman (1879)

Facts: The claimant built a new consulting room at the end of his garden and then complained of noise from the defendant, his neighbour, who was operating a confectionery business next door. The defendant had been running his business for more than 20 years near the boundary wall where the noise was clearly audible.

Decision: It was the activity rather than the nuisance that had continued for more than 20 years. The nuisance only arose after the claimant built in the garden; therefore, it had not been actionable for over 20 years. The defendant was liable in private nuisance.

Defence of Statutory Authority

A defendant will not be liable in nuisance if it was committed in order to comply with a statutory obligation.

Allen v Gulf Oil Refining Ltd (1981)

Facts: The defendant was given a power, by statute, to compulsorily purchase land, and build an oil refinery and associated works. The claimant, who lived nearby, complained of nuisance caused by smell, noise, and vibration.

Decision: The defendant had a defence to nuisance because Parliament had intended that an oil refinery should be built and operated on the site, and the noise, smell, and vibrations were a consequence of the refinery.

Public Nuisance

A public nuisance is an act 'which materially affects the reasonable comfort and convenience of a life of a class of her majesty's subjects'. Public nuisance is primarily a crime designed to protect certain public rights, such as unobstructed and safe use of the highway. If a defendant commits a public nuisance, he may be prosecuted by the state. In addition, if a member of the public can show that they have suffered particular damage, over and above that suffered by others, they may be able to sue the defendant in tort. Many public nuisances arise through obstructing the highway; however, if the obstruction is temporary then generally it will only be regarded as a public nuisance if it is also unreasonable.

Special Damage

The claimant must show that they have suffered loss beyond that suffered by others affected by the public nuisance and that the loss suffered was particular to them and was direct and substantial.

Tate & Lyle v GLC (1983)

Facts: The claimant operated a jetty on the River Thames from which they loaded sugar on to boats. The defendant constructed two ferry terminals on the river which caused silting and obstructed access of vessels to the claimant's jetty. The claimant had to spend money on dredging the river.

Decision: The defendant was liable for the cost of dredging, as the interference with public right of navigation was a public nuisance and the cost of dredging was 'particular damage' suffered by the claimant.

The Rule in *Rylands v Fletcher*

The rule in *Rylands v Fletcher* has its roots in the tort of private nuisance, and it was developed to protect an occupier whose land is damaged by the escape of something that is 'non-natural' from another person's land where that other person has not been negligent. The definition of the tort was explained in the case of *Rylands v Fletcher* by Mr Justice Blackburn who stated: 'We think that the rule of law is, that the person who for his own purposes brings on his land and collects and keeps there anything likely to do mischief if it escapes, must keep it at his peril, and, if he does not do so, is … answerable for all the damage which is the natural consequence of its escape.'

Rylands v Fletcher (1866)

Facts: The defendants owned a mill and engaged a reputable independent contractor to build a reservoir on their land. Beneath the defendants' land were some disused mineshafts. The contractors negligently failed to block mineshafts which connected to the claimant's mines. When the reservoir was filled, the claimant's mines were flooded.

Decision: The defendants themselves had not been negligent, but because the water on their land had escaped they were liable for the damage it caused to the claimant's mines.

The rule in *Rylands v Fletcher* is one of strict liability, which means a defendant is liable even though he is not at fault. In order to establish a defendant's liability the claimant must show that the defendant:

- Brought something on to his land, or collects it and keeps it there.

- It must be a non-natural use of the land (i.e. not an ordinary use of the land). What is considered non-natural use may vary according to the circumstances. Water for domestic purposes carried in a service pipe may be an ordinary use of the land, but water accumulated on land in a reservoir may be a non-natural use.

- The thing must be likely to do mischief if it escapes (e.g. water, electricity, fire, chemicals, and explosives).

- The thing must escape.

The House of Lords confirmed the continued existence of the rule in *Rylands v Fletcher* in *Transco plc v Stockport MBC* (2004) and the rule was applied in the following case.

LMS International Ltd v Styrene Packaging & Insulation Ltd (2005)

Facts: The defendant made expanded polystyrene at its factory. Fire broke out when the defendant's employee was cutting expanded polystyrene blocks with a hot wire machine. The fire spread and caused extensive damage to the claimant's premises and their contents.

Decision: The defendant had brought things on to their premises that were likely to catch fire and the material was kept in such a way that, if ignited, the fire was likely to spread to the claimant's premises. The defendant's use of the land was a non-natural use. The defendant was liable under the rule in *Rylands v Fletcher.*

Key Concept The rule in *Rylands v Fletcher* states that a person who collects and keeps or brings something non-natural on to his land, which is likely to do mischief if it escapes, is liable for all the damage which is the natural consequence of its escape.

Special Defences

In addition to the general defences available in tort, the defendant may plead a number of special defences. The defendant can use the defence of 'act of a stranger' where the escape of the thing is caused by a person who the defendant has no control over, such as a trespasser, or the defence of force of nature (act of God), if the escape is caused by events such as a freak tornado or an earthquake. There is no liability if the escape is wholly the fault of the claimant, and a defendant may have a defence of statutory authority, for example, where a company is obliged to keep particular substances on land.

General Defences in Tort

Even though a claimant may be able to prove all the necessary requirements of a tort, he will be unsuccessful in his action or have his damages reduced if the defendant is successful in proving a defence. There are a number of general defences that apply to all torts. In addition to the general defences, there are some special defences that only apply to specific torts, for example, the defence of prescription to the tort of private nuisance. The burden of proving a defence is on the defendant (see Figure 12.3).

Contributory Negligence

The defence of contributory negligence is a partial defence. This means that it does not completely exonerate a defendant from liability, but operates so as to reduce the amount of damages payable to a claimant.

Originally in law, if a claimant had been negligent and contributed to his own injuries or loss, then he could not recover any damages from another, but this was changed by statute in 1945. The Law Reform (Contributory Negligence) Act 1945, s 1(1), states that, where any person suffers injury or loss partly through his own fault and partly of the fault of another person or persons, then damages (compensation) will be recoverable. However, those damages will be reduced to such an extent as the court thinks just and equitable, having regard to the claimant's share in the responsibility for the injury or loss.

This means that the court will take into account the extent to which the claimant was to blame for his loss or injuries and reduce the amount of compensation according to what is fair. To take advantage of this statutory defence, the defendant has to establish that the claimant did not take reasonable care, and contributed to his own loss. Often, contributory negligence will be pleaded on the ground that the claimant negligently contributed to the accident itself. However, to successfully plead the defence, the claimant's negligence does not have to contribute to the actual accident. It is enough that the claimant's negligence merely contributed to the damage caused as a consequence of the accident. For example, a claimant involved in a car accident, who was not wearing a seatbelt at the time of the accident, will not have contributed to the accident, but probably will have contributed to the injuries suffered.

In the following case, the claimant's negligent behaviour contributed to the accident and her damages were reduced according to her level of fault.

Sayers v Harlow UDC (1958)

Facts: The claimant went into a public lavatory owned by the defendant. When the door closed behind her she realised that she could not get out and having failed to attract anyone's attention to her plight she decided to attempt to climb over the door. She put one foot on the toilet roll holder and a hand on the top of the door but the toilet roll holder rotated and she fell and was injured. The claimant sued the defendant.

Decision: The claimant was successful in her claim against the defendant, but she had been guilty of some contributory negligence and the damages payable to her were reduced by 25 per cent.

In the following case the claimant did not contribute to the actual accident, but his negligence in failing to wear a seatbelt contributed to the level of injury caused.

Froom v Butcher (1976)

Facts: The claimant was injured in a car accident caused by the defendant's negligence. The claimant was not wearing a seatbelt at the time of the accident. The claimant's injuries would not have been so severe if he had been wearing a seatbelt.

Decision: The prudent man should guard against the possibility of negligence by others by wearing a seatbelt. The claimant's damages were reduced by 20 per cent.

The standard of care expected of a claimant is that of a reasonable person with the characteristics of the claimant such as age, infirmity, or pregnancy. A child will not be expected to take the same level of care of itself as an adult.

Apportionment of liability between the claimant and the defendant

Where it is proved that the claimant failed to take reasonable care of his own safety, damages are reduced according to the apportionment of blame. The court calculates the full amount of damages to which the claimant would have been entitled if he had not been contributorily negligent, and then calculates the amount by which the total sum should be reduced so as to reflect the degree to which the claimant is to blame for his own loss or injuries. The claimant can never be 100 per cent contributorily negligent.

Green v Bannister (2003)

Facts: The defendant reversed down a narrow road looking over her right shoulder, taking care not to hit parked cars. She failed to see the claimant, the son of her next-door neighbours, who had collapsed in the road extremely drunk, and drove over him.

Decision: If the defendant had looked in her mirror and over her left shoulder she would probably have seen the claimant and, therefore, was negligent. However, the claimant was 60 per cent to blame for the accident as he was lying in the road in a drunken stupor. His damages were reduced by 60 per cent.

Key Concept A claimant who is contributorily negligent may have either contributed to the accident or contributed to the level of injury caused. Damages will be reduced according to the claimant's level of blame.

Consent

The defence of consent is sometimes referred to as *volenti* or *volenti non fit injuria* (no wrong is done to one who consents). A defendant will not be liable for injury to a claimant where the claimant freely consents to take the risk involved. The defence is a complete defence; if the defendant successfully proves consent, then he will not be liable to the claimant for any damages. In order for consent to be a valid defence, the claimant must understand the risk involved and freely agree to the consequence of the risk. The agreement can be expressed or implied. The test is subjective, which means that the claimant himself must know of the risk and voluntarily accept it. If the claimant has no choice but to accept the risk, the defence will fail.

Smith v Baker (1891)

Facts: The claimant was drilling holes in a quarry. The defendant's crane moved rocks above him from time to time. The claimant was aware of the danger of rocks falling from the crane and had complained to the defendant. No warning was given when the crane was in use. The claimant was injured when the crane moved stones over his head and a stone fell on him.

Decision: The claimant was aware of the danger but there was no evidence that he had voluntarily consented to the risk of injury. The defence of consent failed.

The defence of consent may succeed in circumstances where a claimant is pursuing a dangerous method of work, through his own choice, without any regard for his own safety.

ICI v Shatwell (1965)

Facts: The claimant and his brother ignored safety precautions at work, and broke their statutory duty to observe certain safety regulations for testing detonators. The claimant was injured in an explosion. The claimant sued his employer.

Decision: The claimant had consented to the conduct that resulted in his injury and had voluntarily accepted the risk of injury.

The defendant must prove that the claimant knew of the risk and consented to it. Under the provisions of the Road Traffic Act 1988, consent is not a valid defence for drunken road drivers who injure their passengers, even if the passengers were aware of how drunk the driver was at the time of the accident. However, the passengers who get into a car with a drunk driver, who later causes an accident, may have their damages reduced through contributory negligence. The Road Traffic Act 1988 only applies to road drivers, and consent may apply to a person who accepts a ride in an aircraft with a very drunk pilot.

Morris v Murray (1990)

Facts: The claimant and his friend were drinking together and the claimant knew, when he accepted a ride in an aircraft driven by his friend, that his friend was very drunk.

Decision: The claimant had accepted the risk of riding in a plane with someone not in a fit state to pilot it and had voluntarily consented to the risk of injury.

Consent is implied by participants in sport except where the rules are not complied with.

Simm v Leigh Rugby Football Club (1969)

Facts: The claimant's leg was broken when he was tackled playing rugby league football, and thrown towards a concrete wall.

Decision: The tackle was within the rugby rules, and the claimant had voluntarily accepted the risks involved in playing the game.

A claimant who voluntarily attempts a rescue to save injury to others or damage to property is not usually considered to have voluntarily accepted the risk of injury to himself. The rescue must be necessary and the action taken reasonable in the circumstances.

Haynes v Harwood (1935)

Facts: The claimant was injured when he attempted to stop the defendant's horses bolting down a street where children were playing.

Decision: The defendant was liable as it was foreseeable that someone would attempt to stop the horses and the claimant had not consented to the risk of injury.

Illegality

In Contract Law it is clearly established that, if a contract is illegal, then the claimant will not be able to enforce it. In the Law of Torts there are certain situations where it would clearly be contrary to public policy to allow a claimant to recover damages for injury or loss while he was engaged in illegal actions. The defence of illegality is a complete defence and can be pleaded by a defendant if a claimant was harmed in the course of committing a criminal offence. Not all criminal conduct will give rise to the defence. It is not clear from case authority what are the exact limitations of the defence, but there has to be a firm link between the criminal conduct of the claimant and the loss he has suffered.

Ashton v Turner (1980)

Facts: The claimant, a burglar, sued the defendant, another burglar, for harm suffered in a high-speed getaway.

Decision: The court allowed the defence of illegality and the claimant could not recover damages in tort.

Revill v Newberry (1996)

Facts: The claimant attempted to break into the defendant's garden shed. The defendant, who was hiding inside the shed, fired a shotgun through the keyhole, causing the claimant serious injuries.

Decision: The defence of illegality was not accepted by the court because the defendant's actions were out of all proportion to the claimant's illegal conduct. (However, the court did reduce the claimant's damages by 66 per cent on grounds of contributory negligence.)

Clunis v Camden and Islington Health Authority (1998)

Facts: The claimant, who had suffered from a history of mental illness, stabbed another man to death and was convicted of manslaughter. The claimant sued his health authority for failing to properly assess his mental condition and allowing him to be released from a psychiatric hospital.

Decision: The health authority was successful in its defence of illegality. The court stated that the act of the claimant was essentially his own and he must have known that what he was doing was wrong.

Figure 12.3 Defences in tort

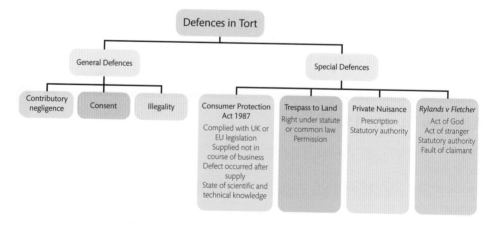

Vicarious Liability

Vicarious liability means being liable for the torts of others and it arises because there is a special relationship between the parties. The person who commits the tort is still liable, but where there is vicarious liability then another person is also liable. Vicarious liability commonly arises in employment situations, as an employer is vicariously liable for the torts committed by his employees during the course of their employment.

If an employee commits a tort, in the course of his employment, the employer and employee are jointly and severally liable. This means that the injured party can take action against the employee or alternatively sue the employer, who is vicariously liable for his employee's actions. The injured party is more likely to sue the employer, because the employer will usually be in a better financial position to pay compensation because he is insured. If a successful action is taken against the employer, then the employer can claim a contribution from his employee under the Civil Liability (Contribution) Act 1978. Alternatively, the employer can claim the costs from the employee by suing him for breach of contract, although in practice this rarely occurs.

In order for an employer to be liable for a tort committed by his employee, the employee's tort must be committed in the course of his employment.

Relationship of Employer and Employee

An employer is only vicariously liable for the torts of his employee and he is not liable for the torts of an independent contractor. Therefore, it is important to be able to distinguish between an employee and an independent contractor. A small company may employ a number of office staff who are employees, but the servicing of all the office equipment may be carried out by a specialist engineer who is an independent contractor. In some cases, it is quite straightforward to identify whether a worker is an employee or not, whereas in other situations it can be difficult to distinguish whether a worker is an independent contractor or an employee. Although a contract may expressly state that a worker is an independent contractor or is an employee, a court will look at the reality of the situation, examining the terms in the contract between the parties (these may be written or oral), and take into account a number of different factors depending on the case. The factors that a court will look at include issues such as whether the worker provides his own equipment, how far the worker is under the control of the person he is working for, whether he can substitute someone else to do his work, and how much financial risk he takes in carrying out the job. This approach of examining multiple factors was established in *Ready Mixed Concrete (South East) Ltd v MPNI* (1968) (see Chapter 13).

Sometimes an employer may temporarily lend out one of his employees to another employer. If the employee commits a tort, there may be a dispute as to who is the 'employer' for the purposes of vicarious liability. Usually the employer who lends the employee will be vicariously liable, unless it can be shown, on the facts, that the other employer had a certain level of control over the borrowed employee. Depending on the facts, sometimes both employers can be held vicariously liable for the employee's torts.

Key Concept In order to establish vicarious liability of an employer, there must be a relationship of employer and employee and the employee must be acting in the course of his employment.

Course of Employment

What constitutes the course of employment is a question of fact in each case, but it does encompass a wide range of actions by the employee. It appears, from the case law, that an employer will be liable for wrongful acts expressly or impliedly authorised by him, and for actions of employees that are wrongful ways of carrying out authorised acts.

An act carried out by an employee will be within the course of his employment if it is to help his employer.

Kay v ITW (1968)

Facts: An employee attempted to move a lorry belonging to another firm because it was blocking access to his employer's warehouse. He was driving the lorry out of the way in order to carry on with his work, but in doing so he ran over the claimant.
Decision: The employee had attempted to move the lorry in order to get on with his work and was acting in the course of his employment; therefore, the employer was vicariously liable for the claimant's injuries.

An employer will be vicariously liable for an employee who, although carrying out an authorised act, does so in a careless or unauthorised way, and as a result injures a third party or damages property belonging to a third party.

Century Insurance Co Ltd v Northern Ireland Road Transport Board (1942)

Facts: A tanker driver delivered petrol to a garage; while the storage tank was being filled, he lit a cigarette and threw away a lighted match. There was an explosion caused as a result of his actions.

Decision: The employer was liable for his employee. The driver was carrying out his job of delivering petrol and emptying his tanker, although he was doing so in a negligent manner.

If the action carried out by the employee is expressly prohibited by an employer it still may be considered to be in the course of employment if it was done while furthering the employer's business.

Rose v Plenty (1976)

Facts: A driver of a milk delivery van disobeyed his employer's orders by taking a 13-year-old boy round to help with deliveries. The boy was injured partly through the driver's negligence. The boy had one leg dangling over the van so that he could jump off quickly and his foot was crushed between the van and the curb.

Decision: The employer was vicariously liable because the milkman was acting in the course of employment as he was delivering milk.

However, if the purpose of the action is nothing to do with the employer's business, then it will be outside the course of employment. For example, if in the previous case, the milkman, instead of letting a child help deliver milk, had given a lift to a hitchhiker who was then injured, the employer would not be vicariously liable.

Warren v Henlys (1948)

Facts: A heated argument arose between an employee, a petrol pump attendant, and a customer who the employee mistakenly accused of trying to evade payment. The customer threatened to report him to the police and his manager. In response, the employee hit the customer.

Decision: The employer was not vicariously liable as the employee had not been acting in the course of his employment. The action of the employee in hitting the customer was one of personal vengeance.

Twine v Bean's Express (1946)

Facts: A van driver was expressly prohibited by his employer from giving lifts. The driver gave a lift to a man who was killed in an accident caused by the driver's negligence.

Decision: The employee was acting totally outside the scope of his employment in giving the lift; the employer was not vicariously liable.

In the following case the House of Lords reviewed the application of vicarious liability to criminal acts and established that for policy reasons an employer will be vicariously liable for torts of an employee if the connection between the assault and the employment is sufficiently close to make it fair and just to hold the employer vicariously liable.

Lister & Ors v Hesley Hall Ltd (2001)

Facts: The defendant ran a school for boys with behavioural difficulties. The claimants, boys at the school, were abused by the warden employed by the defendant. Criminal action was taken against the warden and a civil action was brought against the defendant for vicarious liability.

Decision: The key factor was the closeness of the connection between the employment and the commission of the torts of the warden. In this case, the torts were carried out on school premises at times when the defendant should have been caring for the boys. There was a risk of abuse, which the employer should have guarded against. Considering all the circumstances it was fair and just to hold the defendant vicariously liable.

It is possible for two or more defendants each to be vicariously liable.

Various Claimants v Institute of the Brothers of the Christian Schools (2012)

Facts: A Catholic brotherhood (D) supplied brother teachers to a residential school for boys managed by a Welfare Society. There were allegations of physical and sexual abuses perpetrated by some of the brother teachers on the boys at the school.

Decision: The Supreme Court looked at the close connection between the brothers and D and the brothers' employment in the school and the alleged abuse. The court ruled that D was vicariously responsible for the actions of the brothers and that legal responsibility should be shared between the Society which managed the school and D.

In the following case the Court of Appeal confirmed that vicarious liability will only be made where there is a sufficiently close connection between the wrongdoing and the employment so that it would be fair and just to hold the employer vicariously liable.

Mohamud v WM Morrison Supermarkets Plc (2014)

Facts: A customer entered a petrol station kiosk and asked K, an employee of D if he could print off some documents from a USB stick for him. K responded in abusive fashion and followed C onto the forecourt of the petrol station where he punched and kicked him.

Decision: There was not a sufficient connection between the wrongdoing and the employment. K's job was to interact with customers and did not involve any element of authority over them or responsibility for keeping order. D was not vicariously liable.

Where an employee does something completely outside his employment, then he is said to be 'on a frolic of his own' and his employer will not be responsible. An employee who leaves work unofficially and goes off for an unauthorised break will be acting outside the course of his employment.

Hilton v Thomas Burton (Rhodes) Ltd (1961)

Facts: A number of employees left their place of work and drove to a café about seven miles away. On the way back, the driver negligently crashed the van and one of the workmen was killed.

Decision: The driver was acting outside his employment. He was on a 'frolic of his own' and the employer was not vicariously liable for his actions.

Liability for Independent Contractors

A person who engages an independent contractor to carry out work for him will not be vicariously liable for the contractor's actions; however, he may be liable for damage caused by the contractor in certain circumstances. For example, a person will be liable if he authorises an independent contractor to commit a tort, or if he is under a legal duty where responsibility cannot be delegated to another person. An employer has a duty to provide a safe system of work and will be liable if he breaches that duty by engaging incompetent independent contractors.

Basic Terminology

For an online flashcard glossary visit the Online Resource Centre

'Actionable per se' An action can be taken against a defendant without proof that loss has occurred.

Injunction A court order preventing a person carrying out or ceasing an action.

Jointly and severally liable Liable both individually and together with others.

Non-visitor (including a trespasser) under the Occupiers' Liability Act 1984 A person who is on land or premises without the express or implied permission of the occupier or has exceeded the limits of their permission.

Strict liability Liability which is imposed on a person without having to prove that the person was negligent or at fault.

Vicarious liability Liability which arises because of one person's relationship with another such as employer and employee.

Visitor under the Occupiers' Liability Act 1957 A person who enters property (land or premises) with the express or implied permission of the occupier.

Summary

For an online printable version visit the Online Resource Centre

After studying this chapter students should be able to:

Distinguish between an action for defective products taken in the tort of negligence and an action under the Consumer Protection Act 1987

* In the tort of negligence, the claimant must prove the defendant owed a duty of care, the defendant broke the duty of care, and the claimant suffered loss or damage as a result of the breach.
* Under the Consumer Protection Act 1987, the claimant must show a causal link between the defendant's actions and any damage suffered wholly or partly by a defect in a product.

Identify the elements necessary for a claim under the Consumer Protection Act 1987

* A claim can be brought if a person has been injured or their private property has been damaged by a defective product.
* Liability is on the 'producer' of the defective product.
* The claimant must prove that there was a defect in the product.
* A claimant can recover compensation for death or personal injury and damage to other property over £275.
* Defences are provided by the Act.

Explain the liability of occupiers to visitors and trespassers

* Under the Occupiers' Liability Act 1957, an occupier must take such care as is reasonable, in all the circumstances of the case, to see that the visitor will be reasonably safe in using the premises for the purpose for which he is invited or permitted by the occupier to be there.
* The 1957 Act covers liability for death, personal injury, and property damage.
* Under the Occupiers' Liability Act 1984, an occupier's liability towards trespassers is to take such care as is reasonable in all the circumstances of the case to see that the trespasser does not suffer injury on the premises because of the state of danger of the premises.
* The 1984 Act covers liability for death or personal injury.

Outline liability for trespass to land

- Trespass to land is the direct interference with a person's possession of land without lawful authority.
- The interference must be either by entering or remaining on the land without lawful authority, or placing objects on the land.

Describe private and public nuisance

- Private nuisance is the unlawful interference with someone's use or enjoyment of their land.
- Public nuisance is primarily a crime designed to protect certain public rights. However, if a member of the public can show that they have suffered particular damage, over and above that suffered by others, they may be able to sue the defendant in tort.

Outline liability established by *Rylands v Fletcher*

- A person who for his own purposes brings on his land and collects and keeps there anything likely to do harm if it escapes, is liable for all the damage which is the natural consequence of its escape.

Explain the defences of contributory negligence, consent, and illegality

- Contributory negligence is a partial defence where a claimant has either contributed to the accident or contributed to the level of injury caused.
- Consent is a complete defence where the claimant freely consents to take the risk involved.
- Illegality is a complete defence. It may be available if the claimant was harmed in the course of committing a criminal offence.

Understand the meaning and extent of vicarious liability

- Vicarious liability means being liable for the torts of others and it arises because there is a special relationship between the parties.
- An employer is vicariously liable for the torts committed by his employee during the course of his employment.

Questions

1. Wayne decides to hold a party to celebrate England winning the World Cup. John, who has not been invited, enters via the back door and on seeing Wayne coming towards him, goes through a small door marked 'Dangerous Steps'. The door opens inwards and John falls down the steps into a cellar. He smashes his Rolex watch and breaks his wrist. Ric, aged four, wanders off from his parents, goes outside and falls into the swimming pool and drowns. Alex trips over badly laid flooring and falls into a bucket of bleach and seriously burns his hands and clothing. George decides to leave the party by climbing over the garden wall rather than using the door. He does not realize there is a 10-foot drop on the other side of the wall and breaks both his legs.

   Explain to Wayne the duties and standard of care owed by an occupier of premises and advise him of any claims John, Ric, Alex, and George may have under the Occupiers' Liabilities Acts 1957 and 1984.

2. Sam enters a competition run by his local newspaper, the Surrey Times. He wins second prize, an 'Excel washing machine', which has been manufactured by Excel Appliances Ltd. Sam used the machine for nine washes successfully but, while his tenth wash is on, the machine bursts into flames. Sam managed to put the fire out but the machine is beyond repair, and Sam's designer clothes worth £700 which were in the machine have been burnt, his mobile phone (provided by his employer) which was lying on top of the machine is damaged, and due to smoke damage Sam's kitchen needs redecorating. Advise Sam.

For outline answers visit the Online Resource Centre

3. To what extent is taking an action under the Consumer Protection Act 1987 an improvement on taking an action in the tort of negligence?

4. With reference to liability in the torts of trespass, private nuisance, and the rule in *Rylands v Fletcher*, explain the extent to which occupiers of land should ensure that the state of their property, and activities which take place on their property, do not interfere with the use and enjoyment of neighbouring properties.

Further Reading

Bermingham and Brennan, *Tort Law Directions*, 4th edn (Oxford University Press, 2014) Chapters 11, 12, 13, and 14.

Cooke, *Law of Torts*, 11th edn (Pearson, 2013) Chapters 10, 11, 13, 16, and 17.

Horsey and Rackley, *Tort Law*, 3rd edn (Oxford University Press, 2013) Parts II and IV.

Competition and Markets Authority: https://www.gov.uk/government/organisations/competition-and-markets-authority.

Trading Standards Institute: http://www.tradingstandards.gov.uk/.

Citizens Advice Bureau: http://www.adviceguide.org.uk/consumer_e.htm.

Online Resource Centre

Test your knowledge by trying this chapter's **Multiple Choice Questions.** Visit:

www.oup.com/uk/orc/law/company/ jonesibl3e/01student/mcqs/ch12/

For more information, updates, and multiple choice questions, please visit the Online Resource Centre at:

www.oup.com/uk/orc/law/company/ jonesibl3e/

PART 4

EMPLOYMENT LAW

The Contract of Employment and its Termination

Introduction

Employment law is the law that covers the workplace. In our current society, there have developed many different kinds of working relationship. There are full and part-time employees, contractors, people who work on short-term contracts, agency workers, and people who work at home. All of these in some way or other are covered by employment law. As an employment relationship is, therefore, not the only kind of relationship in the workplace, this section of the book might be better called 'work law' rather than employment law.

The main distinction is made between 'employees' and 'contractors', and all forms of working relationship will fit into one of these categories. Contractors are of two kinds: those that the law calls 'workers', and those that it calls 'self-employed'. An employment contract, however, can only be between an employer and employee.

Being able to tell who is an employee and who is not is important because employees have much more protection under the law than others such as protection from unfair dismissal and rights to redundancy payments. Workers still have some protection, and self-employed people have almost none, only what they agree in their contracts (which are ordinary contracts, not contracts of employment).

An employee works under a contract of employment which may or may not be in writing but exists when the employee and employer agree terms and conditions of employment. In addition to the terms agreed by the parties, the contract will also contain terms that have been implied by common law and statute. Although an employer may be entitled to bring an employment contract to an end it is important to ensure this is done correctly or certain consequences such as a claim for unfair dismissal by the former employee may follow.

The sources of law for employment law come from common law (much of employment law is about contracts between employers and employees), statutes, and directives from Europe that have then been brought into UK law by other statutes and regulations. There have been many changes to employment law in the past 20 years or so, and, therefore, there is a large amount of legislation that covers this area of law. However, the main statute that deals with most of what is discussed in this chapter is the Employment Rights Act 1996.

Although the sources of employment law are the same as most other types of law, it is different in that most employment cases start in the Employment Tribunal, with appeals to the Employment Appeal Tribunal (which is of the same level as the High Court), then to the Court of Appeal, and then to the Supreme Court. As we have seen earlier, courts at any level can make an application for the Court of Justice of the European Union to consider a point of law (see Figure 13.1).

Learning Objectives

After studying this chapter you should be able to:

- Explain the difference between an employee, a contractor, and a self-employed person.
- Outline the types of implied terms contained in a contract.
- Understand the difference between unfair, constructive, and wrongful dismissal.
- Set out the potentially fair and automatically unfair reasons for dismissal.
- Demonstrate knowledge of a redundancy situation.

Issues in Employment Law

There are a number of main issues that will be dealt with in this chapter. Firstly, is there an employment relationship? In other words, is the person an employee, and if so what rights does he have? Secondly, assuming there is a **contract of employment**, what are the terms of that contract? Thirdly, when looking at the **termination of an employment contract**, was that termination done for a fair reason and in a fair manner, and was the procedure appropriate?

Employment Status

There are several different kinds of relationships in the workplace, such as employees, employee shareholders, workers, and independent self-employed contractors. It is important to know the difference, because employees have more rights under the law and employers may be vicariously liable for harm caused to third parties by employees.

Figure 13.1 The structure of the court system as it relates to employment law

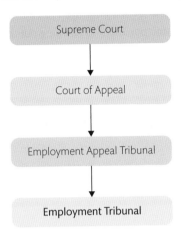

Most people are **employees**. This means that they have an employment contract with the **employer**, who can be a person, a partnership, or a company, and that they have the full protection of employment law. The Growth and Infrastructure Act 2013 introduced a new **'employee shareholder'** employment status. In this new type of contract employees give up some employment rights, such as their right to claim unfair dismissal (except for automatically unfair reasons) and the right to request flexible working, in exchange for shares in their employer's business. The majority of employee rights such as holiday pay, sick pay, and maternity and paternity rights are retained.

A person may be classified as a worker who, although not an employee, is entitled to some of the core employment rights such as the right to be paid the minimum wage. It is a broader category than 'employees' and includes persons who work on a casual basis such as agency workers or short-term casual workers. A worker is obliged to carry out his contractual duties in person and the person he works for must not be a client or customer.

An **independent contractor** is someone (who may be a company, a partnership, or a single self-employed individual) who contracts to provide services for a fee. A self-employed contractor may substitute someone to cover for him if necessary. Although independent contractors do not have employment rights as they are self-employed they do have some legal protection, for example, the client must ensure the premises on which the independent contractor is working meet health and safety standards.

The way that the distinction between employees and independent contractors is often referred to is the split between a **contract of service** and a **contract for services**. An employee works under a contract of service. This means that there is a master–servant relationship between the employer and the employee. The employer gives instructions to the employee and provided those instructions are reasonable and within the terms of the contract the employee is obliged to obey them. A self-employed person works under a contract for services and the relationship with the person he is carrying out the work for is that of client and contractor.

Key Concept An employee works under a contract *of* service. This means that there is a master–servant relationship between the employer and employee. An independent contractor works under a contract *for* services. There is no such master–servant employment relationship in these circumstances, rather the relationship is that of client and contractor.

In many cases there is no dispute whether someone is a worker/self-employed or an employee. Someone who is on the payroll and takes orders from a manager who has control of his work will generally be working under a contract of service. This would suggest that a person is working in a subordinate role, in which he is under the control of the employer.

A builder who spends several weeks at someone's home building an extension and is paid at the end of completing the job is working under a contract for services and is not an employee. The problem generally arises in the grey area between the two, for example, someone who is regarded as a contractor and is paid upon submitting an invoice, but who goes into the office every day and is subject to instructions from a manager. What would this person's employment status be? Would he be an employee, or an independent contractor?

Business Insight Zero-hours contracts

Zero-hours contracts (casual contracts) enable employers to hire staff with no guarantee of work. Most zero-hours contracts will give staff 'worker' employment status and sometimes the right to refuse work offered. Workers are entitled to the national minimum wage and annual leave but will not be paid for being available to work only for the work undertaken. These types of contracts are useful for employers because they give flexibility to only pay for work when it is available. In 2014 figures from the Office for National Statistics (based on a survey of employers), estimated that there were over 1.4 million zero-hours contracts. Critics have argued that the growth of zero-hours contracts illustrates the growing reliance of employers on insecure workers.

> ## Key Concept
>
> - An employee is entitled to all the available employee rights (including all the rights that workers have).
> - An employee shareholder is entitled to the majority of employee rights except for those given up (such as the right to claim unfair dismissal) in return for shares in the company.
> - A worker is entitled to some employment rights, such as equal pay, working time, minimum wage, basic health and safety rights, non-discrimination.
> - An independent self-employed contractor has almost no employment rights.

Employee

There is no proper definition in statute of what is an employee. In order to decide if someone is an employee, there are a number of tests that have been applied over the years by the courts, and which look at the nature of the relationship between the supposed employee and employer. These tests are:

- *The control test*. This was one of the earliest tests, and looks at the extent that a person is under the control of the employer, if he has to obey orders, etc.

- *The integration test*. Because the control test was not sufficient to deal with all situations, the integration test was formulated. This looks at how much the work is fully integrated into the core activities of the employing organisation. Is the work done as an integral part of the business? The more integrated a worker is the more likely he is to be considered to be an employee. Is the person entitled to any benefits that form part of the standard employee package, such as joining the occupational pension scheme? In short, how integrated is he within the organisation?

- *The economic reality test*. This looks at things from the opposite angle to the integration test. Instead of looking at the relationship between the employer and employee, it considers how far a person can be said to be 'in business on his own account'. In other words, it looks for evidence of self-employment rather than employment, and looks at issues such as does the person send invoices, does he use his own equipment, does he get paid holidays, is tax deducted from his pay, is he permitted to supply a substitute for himself if he is away, does he take any personal financial risks?

- *The mutuality of obligation test*. The courts then moved on to look at whether the employer is obliged to provide work for the employee, and the employee is obliged to accept it. If there is such an obligation, then there is a contract of employment. If not, then it is a contract for services. If, for example, a person is offered work and refuses it with no consequences, that can suggest that the person is a worker and not an employee. If, however, he turns down the work and as a result is not offered any in the future, then it is likely that there is mutuality of obligation and the person would be regarded as an employee.

Carmichael v National Power Plc (1999)

Facts: C worked as a tour guide at a power station. She had no fixed hours, but could be called at any time when a party of tourists was expected. Tax and national insurance was deducted from her pay, which was calculated on an hourly rate. When a collective union agreement increased pay generally at the site, her pay also increased following that agreement.

Decision: C was not an employee, because there was no mutuality of obligation. When she was called to work, that created a contract just for the duration of that day's work. She was not obliged to accept any particular day's work, and so she was not an employee.

O'Kelly v Trusthouse Forte plc (1983)

Facts: A group of wine waiters worked on a casual basis at a hotel. They were described as 'regular casuals'. They had no fixed hours of work, but were called in whenever needed. They were paid through the payroll, with tax and national insurance being deducted. They had to wear the uniform of the hotel, and worked a varying number of hours each week. When the men became active in the union, they were offered no further work.

Decision: In a controversial (and not very clear) decision, the Court of Appeal held that, although the tribunal was entitled to find that there were some elements that might point to a contract of employment, there was no mutuality of obligation and so no contract. This case did, however, make the point that even a short, one-day contract could be a contract of service, in other words an employment contract.

In the following case an employment relationship was deemed to continue between assignments so that a casual worker was in fact an employee and had built up enough continuity of service to claim unfair dismissal. (Employers need to be aware that an employment relationship may be deemed to occur when taking on casual staff.)

Drake v Ipsos Mori UK Ltd (2012)

Facts: D worked for Mori as a market researcher under a succession of individual assignments from 2005 to 2010. Although he was told he was not an employee he was given a handbook which stated that when he accepted a job it amounted to a verbal contract and he was expected to complete the job in the specified manner and in a certain timeframe. He also had to complete the job personally.

Decision: There was sufficient mutuality of obligation for an employment relationship to exist and there had been a series of successive employment contracts.

- *The multiple test.* This is the test that has been most often used in recent times, and in effect the court will look at all these tests and consider the whole situation before deciding if someone is an employee or not (see Figure 13.2).

Ready Mixed Concrete v Minister of Pensions and National Insurance (1968)

Facts: Ready Mixed Concrete hired drivers who used their own lorries to deliver the company's concrete and mixers to customers. The drivers had to wear company uniforms, and had to comply with reasonable orders from the company. The drivers had to maintain the vehicle at their own cost, and could decide which route to take. They could also pay for a substitute driver if absolutely necessary.

Decision: The drivers were each running a small business of their own, and as such were self-employed, not employees. This case set out the principles that:

- an employee cannot substitute another worker for himself;
- control is an important factor, but it is not the only factor;
- the contract as a whole had to be looked at to see if it was consistent with a contract of service, so factors such as who owned the assets, financial risk, and the opportunity to profit are not consistent with a contract of service.

Worker

Originally the only distinction was between an employee and a self-employed contractor. In recent years, however, an intermediate **'worker'** category has been established, of someone who is not an employee, but is not fully self-employed either. This has been as a result of the expansion of protection given to those who are not employees, coming from European law.

Figure 13.2 The multiple test

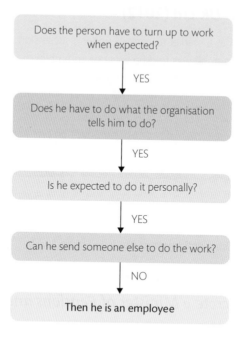

Does the person have to turn up to work when expected?

↓ YES

Does he have to do what the organisation tells him to do?

↓ YES

Is he expected to do it personally?

↓ YES

Can he send someone else to do the work?

↓ NO

Then he is an employee

Workers, therefore, have less protection than employees, in that they cannot, for example, bring a claim of unfair dismissal, but have more protection than genuinely self-employed independent contractors. Workers are, for example, subject to the working time rules and so should be given paid holiday, and are also entitled to the minimum wage. Examples of workers are those such as agency workers, or some casual and home workers. Under the Agency Workers Regulations 2011 all agency workers who have worked in the same job for 12 weeks are entitled to the same pay and basic working conditions as 'comparable workers' i.e. employees doing the same job in the same workplace.

In the following case, the Supreme Court decided that for the purpose of employment legislation members of Limited Liability Partnerships (LLPs) (see Chapter 15 for information on LLPs) were 'workers'.

Bates van Winkelhof v Clyde & Co LLP (2014)

Facts: B was a partner at Clyde and Co LLP, a law firm. After she disclosed a bribery allegation she was expelled from the partnership and brought a whistleblowing claim against them. In order to succeed she had to show she was at least a worker.

Decision: B was a worker. She was contracted to work personally for the LLP and was an integral part of their business. The LLP were not her client or customer.

Independent Self-Employed Contractor

An independent contractor will be someone who effectively works for himself. He will run his own business, and will do his work in his own way. He will also generally provide his own equipment and tools. Examples would be a plumber or a taxi driver.

Just because people call themselves self-employed does not mean that they are. For example, a building firm can use another person as a 'self-employed' contractor, but expect him to turn up every day and do exactly as the 'boss' tells him to. This person is at least a worker, if not an employee, and must be paid the minimum wage, have paid holidays, and be subject to the working time rules. The court will look at the true nature of the relationship between the parties. In the following case the Supreme Court upheld the Court of Appeal's decision that car valets, whose contracts stated that they were self-employed, were actually employees.

Autoclenz Limited v Belcher and others (2011)

Facts: The claimants were car valeters who worked for Autoclenz Ltd and had each signed contracts describing them as self-employed. They paid their own tax, purchased their own insurance, uniforms, and materials. Included in their contract was a clause stating that they could use substitutes to carry out their duties.

Decision: The Supreme Court confirmed that the claimants were employees. The court considered the true nature of the relationship between the parties. Despite the substitute clause in the written contract this was not what had been actually agreed between the parties which was that the claimants themselves would turn up to work each day and carry out the work when provided. They were fully integrated into Autoclenz's business and subject to its control.

Implied Terms

As we saw in Chapter 6, all contracts contain express terms and implied terms. Express terms are details of a contract that are specifically agreed by the two people making the contract, known as 'the parties' to the contract, which in an employment contract will be the employer and the employee. Express terms typically cover issues such as rates of pay, location of work, and holiday entitlement.

Implied terms are terms which the parties did not specifically comment on, but which are implied into the contract. There are two main ways that such terms can be implied.

The first is where the terms are so obvious that any other person would have agreed 'well, of course it is part of the contract!' These terms are implied by common law. Examples of such terms are:

- The duty of an employee to obey instructions: the employee has a duty to obey instructions which are lawful and reasonable. What amounts to reasonable instructions depends on all the circumstances of the case but clearly an employee is not expected to obey instructions which might endanger his personal safety.

- The duty of an employee to exercise reasonable care and skill: what amounts to a reasonable standard depends on the level of qualification and skill of the employee and his position in the business. Employees who are professionally qualified will be expected to show the care and skill that could be expected of someone in that profession.

Janata Bank v Ahmed (1981)

Facts: The defendant bank manager negligently lent money to customers who were in no financial position to repay it.

Decision: The employee was liable to pay damages to the bank as he had not exercised reasonable care when carrying out his job.

- The duty of an employer to provide work: an employer will have a duty to provide work in certain cases such as where the lack of work causes a reduction in income because for example the employee works on commission, or where work is needed to maintain an employee's reputation and skill.

- The duty of an employer to provide support: an employer must have sufficient and capable staff to enable an employee to carry out his work effectively.

- The duty of fidelity: this means that employees must not act in a way that is calculated to harm the interests of their employer or to enter into competition against their employer.

- The duty of mutual trust and confidence: both the employer and the employee owe each other this duty and because of the general nature of the duty it can be applied in many different situations such as telling off an inexperienced employee for his incompetence in front of his workmates, requiring an employee to undergo a medical examination without reasonable cause, telling a fellow employee that a personal assistant was 'an intolerable bitch on a Monday morning' within her hearing.

These implied duties go towards creating a harmonious working relationship.

For example, Lisa is upset because she is being bullied at work. She tells her manager on several occasions, but he does not take it seriously, and suggests simply letting the situation improve by itself. The manager, and, therefore, the employer, is in breach of the implied duty of an employer to provide support to its employees. It is probably also in breach of the duty of mutual trust and confidence, as Lisa might feel that she no longer has confidence in her employer if she is being subjected to such treatment with their knowledge and they take no action.

In *Courtaulds Northern Textiles v Andrew* (1979) the court stated that 'it was an implied term of the [employment] contract that the employers would not, without reasonable and proper cause, conduct themselves in a manner calculated or likely to destroy or seriously damage the relationship of confidence and trust between the parties'. In the following case the court stated that whether the manager intended to breach the duty of mutual respect and confidence was irrelevant. The question was whether his actions constituted a breach.

Parsons v Bristol Street Fourth Investments Ltd (2008)

Facts: L, the manager of the defendant company, was tactile with staff slapping them on the back, and punching them in the arm. P claimed L had physically and verbally assaulted him including grabbing him by the testicles, and referring to him as 'the old parsonage, old buzzard and old git'. L claimed that this was his manner with all staff and he did not intend any breach of trust.

Decision: L's intention was irrelevant. There had been a breach of trust and confidence.

The second main source of implied terms is statutes, which incorporate terms into all employment contracts. These are terms such as the duty on employers to pay at least the national minimum wage (National Minimum Wages Act 1998), and their duty not to breach the Working Time Regulations 1998.

Termination of Contract

An employment tribunal can deal with any area of employment law, from discrimination to working time to holiday pay. By far the most common dispute brought to tribunals, however, concerns the way that an employment contract has been terminated.

Statutory Notice Periods

If an employer wishes to dismiss an employee he will, in most cases, have to give the proper notice. Equally, if an employee wants to leave his job for whatever reason, he will usually have to give notice.

There are two situations, however, where no notice needs to be given. The first is when the employer believes that the employee is guilty of gross misconduct. In such a case the employee can be dismissed immediately, and this is known as **summary dismissal**. The second scenario is where there is a serious breach of contract by either employer or employee, which entitles the other to treat it as terminated. This is the case in constructive dismissal, where the employee is entitled to leave immediately and treat himself as unfairly dismissed because the employer has acted in such a way that the employee could not reasonably be expected to stay in his job. Gross misconduct and constructive dismissal are considered later in the chapter.

The amount of notice required will usually be agreed in the contract. However, if the employer and employee have not agreed a notice period in their contract, then the Employment Rights Act 1996 imposes a minimum amount of notice that has to be given (See Table 13.1).

Notice by an Employer

The minimum notice that an employer has to give to an employee is shown in Table 13.1.

Table 13.1 Minimum notice period required to be given by employer

Time in job	Minimum notice
Less than 1 month	No notice required
1 month to 2 years	1 week
2 years	2 weeks
3 years	3 weeks
4 years	4 weeks

This carries on with an extra one week's notice for each extra year in the job, until 12 years' service. Twelve weeks' notice is the maximum that the law goes up to, even if the person has been employed for longer than 12 years.

Notice by an Employee

An employee who has been employed for at least one month has to give one week's notice. This is the most he is required to give by statute. If he leaves before he has been employed for one month he only has to give 'reasonable notice'.

This is the minimum period of notice; the employer and employee can agree in their contract for a much longer period of notice on either side, but they cannot agree less.

The employer and employee can, however, decide that the employer can give the employee payment instead of notice. So, for example, if the employer is required to give the employee five weeks' notice, but wants him to leave straight away, then he can pay him five weeks' wages (with any other outstanding pay, such as holiday pay). This can only be done if the contract says so, or if the employee agrees.

Types of Dismissal Claim

There are three different types of dismissal claim that can be made in the employment tribunal. The three types are:

1. Wrongful dismissal.
2. Unfair dismissal.
3. Constructive dismissal.

Wrongful Dismissal

If an employer dismisses the employee without giving him the notice agreed in his contract, or dismisses him in breach of his contract in any other way, then this would be a **wrongful dismissal**.

An example of a dismissal in breach of contract might be if the correct notice is not given. Another example is if there are specific procedures on dismissal that are set out in the staff handbook, such as a requirement to give a verbal warning and a written warning before dismissal, but no warnings were given. This would be a dismissal in breach of contract and give the former employee the right to go to court or tribunal. (Note that this would not apply in the case of gross misconduct, where the employer is entitled to dismiss without warnings or notice.)

Another example is if the person is employed on an employment contract that is to last for a certain period of time (known as a 'fixed term contract'), say six months, but this contract is terminated after four. This would be a dismissal in breach of contract. If this happens the employee can go to court or tribunal and recover the money that he would have earned had he been given the proper amount of notice in his contract, or get damages for breach of contract.

Because wrongful dismissal is a breach of contract claim, not necessarily a specific employment case, the employee can take the case to a court or a tribunal, unlike most other employment cases, which have to be heard in the employment tribunal.

A claim of wrongful dismissal can be brought by any employee; he does not have to have a minimum amount of service.

Unfair Dismissal

Unfair dismissal relates to the reasons why an employee has been dismissed and the reasonableness of the employer in carrying out the dismissal.

Business Insight

The maximum compensation award for an unfair dismissal claim is at present £76,574, or 12 months gross pay whichever is lowest. (Unfair dismissals for whistleblowing or related to certain health and safety reasons are uncapped.) In 2013–14, the average award was £11,813 with the median figure being just £5,016.

Most tribunal cases are brought because people have lost their jobs. A person who believes he should not have been dismissed, or that it was done in an unfair way, may have been unfairly dismissed and can make a claim against his employer to an employment tribunal within three months of the dismissal. If the tribunal finds that it was unfair, then the former employee can be awarded compensation.

Claims for unfair dismissal are the most common type of claim to be brought before the employment tribunal. **Unfair dismissal** is covered by the Employment Rights Act 1996, s 98, and basically means that the reasons for the dismissal, or the way that it was handled by the employer, were unfair.

In order to bring a claim for unfair dismissal, the person has to have been a proper full or part-time employee, not a worker or self-employed independent contractor, and he has to have been employed by the employer for a full two years. The employee must prove that he has been dismissed. There are three ways in which dismissal may have taken place.

- The contract of employment is terminated by the employer (with or without notice).
- A fixed term contract has expired and not been renewed.
- The employee ends the contract due to constructive dismissal.

Key Concept   When considering if there has been an unfair dismissal, the questions to be asked are:

1. Has there been a dismissal?
2. What was the reason for the dismissal?
3. Did the employer handle the dismissal in a reasonable manner?

Potentially fair reasons for dismissal

Assuming that there is no dispute that there has been a dismissal (this generally only arises in cases of constructive dismissal), the next question to ask is: 'What was the reason for the dismissal?'

Not all dismissals are unfair. The law says that certain kinds of dismissal are *capable* of being fair. This does not mean that they are automatically fair, although two rare types of dismissal *are* in fact automatically fair (unofficial industrial action and national security), but it depends on the circumstances of the case. These potentially fair reasons for dismissal are:

- Capability.
- Conduct.
- Redundancy.
- Statutory bar.
- Taking part in official industrial action after 12 weeks of such action.
- Some other substantial reason.

Even if the employer has a reason for dismissal that comes within the list, he still has to look at all the circumstances, and consider if there is any other kind of action he can take, before the dismissal can be capable of being fair.

Capability

A person can be dismissed if he is not up to the job. This can relate to three kinds of issues:

1. *Qualifications:* does a person have the right qualifications for the job? The employer should, however, consider before dismissing whether such qualifications are actually needed for this job.

2. *Incompetence:* can the person actually do the job? It might be that he has made one major error, or a series of smaller ones, but the employer still has to consider whether the employee was given proper training, or given any warnings about his performance so that he has a chance to improve. If these actions were not taken, then any dismissal might still be unfair.

Davison v Kent Meters Ltd (1975)

Facts: 471 of 500 components assembled by D were faulty. She was dismissed.
Decision: D's dismissal was unfair because the supervisor should have instructed D and then checked her work after a small number of components had been assembled and she should have been warned.

3. *Health:* if an employee is off work frequently, and the employer has considered all the alternatives he could do to help, then this could be a fair reason for dismissal. It depends on the circumstances of the case, and the larger and better-funded an organisation,

the longer it is expected to wait before dismissing someone who is suffering from a long-term illness, because a larger organisation is able to cover for absence more easily than a small one (see also the section on 'Duty to make adjustments' in Chapter 14).

Key Concept In cases where an employer believes the employee is incompetent, ACAS advises the following procedure:

1. Carry out a full investigation to identify the problem.
2. Issue a warning to the employee stating what the consequences of a failure to improve will be.
3. The employee should be given a fair opportunity to improve.

This procedure can be adapted for most dismissals.

Conduct

There are two types of misconduct: ordinary misconduct and gross misconduct. For example, someone who is persistently late might be committing ordinary misconduct. Other examples might be not wearing the proper uniform, persistently looking scruffy for a front-of-house job, or persistently using the office phone when they knew the employer's policy was that this was not permitted. Gross misconduct is much more serious, and includes things like theft, physical violence or bullying, or serious incapability through drink or drugs. The contract of employment should set out what kinds of things are regarded by the employer as being gross misconduct, as this might be different from one employer to another, and is generally for employers to decide depending on their own particular circumstances.

Adegbola v Marks & Spencer Plc (2013)

Facts: A admitted she had purchased goods with her staff store discount card for resale contrary to the card's terms.

Decision: This was gross misconduct. The dismissal was fair.

The employer should investigate all matters of misconduct, and should only dismiss someone if he genuinely believes that the person has committed the misconduct. Even if it turns out that the belief was wrong, so long as the employer honestly believed it, then the dismissal can be fair.

The difference between the two types of misconduct is that, for gross misconduct, the employer can dismiss the employee without notice (although it is better to suspend on full pay while investigating, as then there will be no risk of unfairness). For ordinary misconduct it would not be reasonable to dismiss for a first offence, but rather a warning should be given, and the employee should only be dismissed after a second or (for larger employers) third breach of the rules.

Burchell v British Home Stores (1980)

Facts: BHS suspected, but could not prove, shoplifting by a member of staff in one of its stores.
Decision: The dismissal was fair. The test for whether a dismissal for gross misconduct was fair was:

- the employer believed the employee was guilty;
- he had reasonable grounds to believe this;
- he had carried out as much investigation as possible in the circumstances.

The employer has to investigate before reaching a decision about whether to dismiss someone. He does not have to do an exhaustive investigation, but just taking one person's word for it is probably not enough, if other people have some knowledge of the matter. In recent years there have been a number of misconduct cases relating to posting on social networking sites. *Gill v SAS Ground Services UK Limited* (2009) established that employers can use entries on websites such as Facebook and YouTube as evidence in disciplinary proceedings.

Gill v SAS Ground Services UK Limited (2009)

Facts: Mrs Gill took part in London Fashion Week while being on sick leave from her employment. On her Facebook page she posted that she had auditioned 300 models and was choreographing a fashion show. There was also YouTube video of an event at the fashion week, which showed her walking along a catwalk and presenting a bouquet of flowers to the fashion show's designer.
Decision: Gill's dismissal for gross misconduct was fair.

Derogatory remarks made about work on social media sites do not necessarily make a dismissal fair. It depends on the circumstances of each case and whether the action of the employer was a reasonable response.

Crisp v Apple Retail UK Limited (2011)

Facts: Crisp, an Apple employee posted derogatory comments about work and its products on Facebook. Crisp had received instructions and training from Apple relating to conduct outside of work including reference to social networking sites. Apple's disciplinary procedure also made clear that derogatory comments about Apple made online would constitute gross misconduct. Crisp was dismissed.

Decision: Dismissal of Crisp was fair. His postings had brought the company into disrepute in that they had attacked Apple's core value of protecting its image.

Redundancy

If the person's job is redundant, then the person can be fairly dismissed, if the correct procedures are followed. We shall look at this in more detail later.

Statutory bar

This is where the employer believes that it would be unlawful for him to employ the person, such as where his work permit has run out, or the person is a driver who has been disqualified from driving. The employer should check, however, whether he can, for example, give the driver other duties until his driving ban expires.

Taking part in official industrial action

After 12 weeks of striking or being part of some other industrial action, a person can be dismissed.

Some other substantial reason

This comes into play if the employer has been dismissed for a reason which does not come within the others in the list, but which is a fair one and is 'substantial', not just a whim of the employer. This is, therefore, effectively a mop-up section that allows employers to dismiss someone for other reasons.

Examples include where a business is being reorganised, but the reorganisation does not fit into the definition of redundancy that we will see later. Another example is where a major client of a small organisation states that they will take their business elsewhere if a particular employee is not dismissed (this would probably not be substantial if the client was a minor one, or the employer a large one).

Henderson v Connect (South Tyneside) Ltd (2009)

Facts: The employer provided transport services. Mr H was employed as a minibus driver, taking disabled children to school. The service was provided under a contract with the Council who had the right to object to the employment of particular individuals. The Council refused to allow H to drive the children. The employer dismissed H as he had no other role for him.

Decision: The dismissal was fair. Dismissal because of third-party pressure came within 'some other substantial reason'.

A further example, would be a breakdown in working relationships.

Ezsias v North Glamorgan NHS Trust (2011)

Facts: E was employed as a surgeon. He was very critical of several other surgeons and the department generally. E's complaints against his colleagues were 'excessively frequent, unacceptably detailed and unrelenting to an extreme degree'. His complaints led to serious difficulties in working relationships. He was dismissed.

Decision: A breakdown in working relationships was a fair dismissal and came within 'some other substantial reason'.

Retirement

Since October 2011 compulsory retirement is not allowed unless an employer can objectively justify setting a retirement age, in other words if he has a genuinely strong business reason for doing so. Justification for dismissal because an employee had reached a certain age would fall within the 'some other substantial reason'.

Automatically fair reasons for dismissal

In addition to the potentially fair reasons for dismissal, there are some reasons which are automatically fair reasons to dismiss someone. They are not very common. Such reasons are:

- If the employee had taken part in *unofficial* industrial action. If the trade union does not follow the proper procedures that are set out in the Trade Union and Labour Relations (Consolidation) Act 1992, and the action is, therefore, not an official one, then the employer can dismiss an employee who is taking part in such action, and it does not matter whether the employer's actions are reasonable or not.

- If the dismissal was for the purpose of protecting national security.

Automatically unfair reasons for dismissal

If an employer dismisses an employee for one of the following reasons, it will be automatically unfair, and the employee will be entitled to a remedy, even if the employer had good reasons for doing so. For automatically unfair dismissals, an employee can bring an action even if he has not worked for the employer for two years, unlike ordinary unfair dismissals.

Automatically unfair reasons include:

- Dismissal for a reason relating to pregnancy, maternity, parental leave, paternity leave.
- Dismissal for health and safety reasons, such as refusing to work in an unsafe situation.
- Dismissal for a trade union reason, such as being a member of a trade union.
- Dismissal in the first 12 weeks of an official industrial action.
- Dismissal just because someone is part-time or fixed-term.
- Dismissal for making protected disclosures (whistleblowing).
- Dismissal for asserting a statutory right, such as minimum wage or working time.
- Dismissal for a reason connected with a transfer of an undertaking (which is effectively when a whole business or section of business is transferred to a new owner), if there is no valid economic, technical, or organisational reason for the dismissal.

Consider the following scenario. Catherine is pregnant, and takes some time off for ante-natal appointments. The employer feels that she should be at work, as this is making his largely male workforce resentful. He dismisses her. This would be an automatically unfair dismissal, and would also be sex discrimination, as will be seen in Chapter 14.

As a further example, suppose Eva has been employed in a crèche for the past three months. She is paid £5.50 an hour, which is less than the minimum wage. She asks her employer to pay her at least the minimum wage. The employer refuses, saying that she cannot afford to do so, and dismisses Eva. This is an automatically unfair dismissal, because the reason was because Eva had asserted a statutory right. Eva can bring her case to a tribunal even if she has not been employed for at least two years, because her dismissal is automatically unfair.

The band of reasonable responses

The list of potentially fair reasons that was discussed earlier is only *potentially* fair. Each dismissal that comes within a reason on the list still has to be judged according to the **'band of reasonable responses'**.

Whether a dismissal is unfair or not depends on the facts of each case. A tribunal will look at whether the employer handled the dismissal in a reasonable manner. It is not just a question of whether the employer acted reasonably, however. The test used by the courts is the 'band of reasonable responses' test, and allows employers quite a lot of leeway. In effect, the tribunal will ask itself the following question:

'Is is possible to describe the employer's actions as being reasonable?'

If it is, then the dismissal will be fair. If not, the dismissal will be unfair and the employee entitled to a remedy. The important thing is for the tribunal not to decide what *it* would have done in the circumstances, but rather whether what the employer did is capable of being described as reasonable in the circumstances. What is reasonable can also depend on the size and resources of the employer.

There is no list of what is or is not reasonable, but by looking at the cases over the years, it is possible to identify three issues that tribunals generally look at. These are:

1. Procedure used.

2. The consistency of the employer.

3. Whether dismissal was an appropriate sanction in the circumstances.

Fair procedure

Polkey v Dayton (1987)

Facts: An employer wanted to make an employee redundant, but did not consult him as was required. He claimed unfair dismissal. The employer argued that consultation would have made no difference to his dismissal.

Decision: The employer's argument was irrelevant. A dismissal can be unfair purely because of a lack of procedure. The fact that consultation would have made no difference could reduce the amount of compensation awarded, but it made no difference in relation to the unfairness of the dismissal.

This is one of the most important cases in employment law. The House of Lords in *Polkey* said that, if a proper procedure was not used by the employer in making his decision whether to dismiss or not, the dismissal has to be found to be unfair. If the tribunal finds that the employee would have been dismissed anyway, then the compensation awarded to him could be reduced, but it would still be an unfair dismissal.

One of the ways that an employer can show that he followed a fair procedure is by following the ACAS Code of Practice.

ACAS is the Advisory, Conciliation and Arbitration Service. It is there to mediate between employers and employees, and one of its functions is to produce Codes of Practice. These are not legal codes; they do not lay down the law, and an employer is not obliged to follow them. They do, however, show what is good practice, and an employer would be well advised to follow a procedure which includes investigating misconduct, etc, giving warnings if appropriate, and allowing the employee to have a fair hearing at which he can be accompanied by a friend or representative if he wishes, and an appeal if necessary before making a final decision. The full 'Code of Practice on Disciplinary and Grievance Procedures' can be found on the ACAS website. If an employer unreasonably fails to comply with the Code, a tribunal can increase any compensation made to the former employee by up to 25 per cent.

Key Concept If an employer dismisses for a reason that is capable of being fair, he still has to show that the procedure that he used for the dismissal was a fair one.

Consistency

When deciding what action to take against an employee, the employer has to make sure that he acts consistently between his employees. He should not give a warning to one person yet dismiss another for the same reason in similar circumstances. For example, if one person is given a warning for misuse of the company internet policy, whereas another is dismissed, this would be inconsistency. It would not be inconsistent, however, if the first person was warned because he was constantly checking his personal email, whereas the second person was viewing child pornography, as these are not similar circumstances.

Appropriate sanction

This all depends on the particular facts of each case. The employer should look at all the options that he has, such as warnings or re-deployment, before coming to a decision and should take into account all the mitigating factors.

Who can bring an action for unfair dismissal?

In order to bring a complaint of unfair dismissal to an employment tribunal, the person complaining has to have been an employee. He also has to have been employed for at least two continuous years.

Workers and self-employed people cannot bring such a claim. Also, a few groups of employees do not have this right either, such as those in the police service and members of the armed forces. The claim must generally be started within three months of the dismissal. An employee can only bring a claim before a tribunal after going through a conciliation process (which has failed to resolve the issue) at ACAS.

Cost of bringing an action

In July 2013 the Government introduced fees for taking claims to the Employment Tribunal. An employee must pay a fee of £250 to take an unfair dismissal, equal pay or discrimination claim and a further £950 if a hearing takes place. Since the introduction of fees there have been approximately 80 per cent fewer claims lodged than in the preceding year. In September 2014 the trade union UNISON was given permission by the Court of Appeal to take Judicial Review proceedings to argue that the fees denied access to justice for workers treated unfairly by employers.

Remedies

A person who wins a case for unfair dismissal in an employment tribunal is entitled to a remedy. There are three main kinds of remedies that a tribunal can give, but only one of them is widely used. The three remedies are:

Reinstatement: an employee who is reinstated by a tribunal can go back to his previous job as if he had never been dismissed. For obvious reasons, this is very rarely awarded.

Re-engagement: a tribunal can order that an employee is re-engaged by the employer, but this is not necessarily into exactly the same job or on the same terms and conditions. The job has to be comparable to the old one, and suitable. Again, this is not very common.

Compensation: by far the most common outcome if unfair dismissal is found is compensation.

Compensation

This is divided into two parts. The first is called the basic award, and is calculated as follows:

- 1.5 weeks' pay for each completed year of service over the age of 41 (a week's pay is set at a maximum of £465, a figure which usually rises each year).
- 1 week's pay for each completed year of service between the ages of 22 and 41.
- 0.5 week's pay between 18 and 22.

This is subject to a maximum of 20 years' service, so the maximum basic award is £13,920 (2014–15 figure).

(The £465 per week and £13,920 are 2014–15 figures, which are raised each year.)

The second part is called the compensatory award, which compensates the successful claimant for financial losses arising because of the dismissal, and depends on his expenses in looking for work, his loss of earnings, etc. This is set at a maximum of £76,574 (2014–15 figure) or 52 weeks pay, whichever is the lower.

The compensatory award can be reduced because of the former employee's conduct, for example, if he is found to have contributed to some extent to his own dismissal, or in a '*Polkey*' situation considered earlier, where a proper procedure would have made no difference to the decision to dismiss.

If an employer does not comply with an order from a tribunal to re-engage or reinstate an employee, the tribunal may make an additional award of between 26 and 52 weeks' pay, subject to the £465 limit on a week's pay.

Constructive Dismissal

A **constructive dismissal** is where an employee is entitled to resign without giving any notice because of the employer's behaviour, and is set out in the Employment Rights Act 1996. Although the employee has resigned, he is entitled to apply for compensation for constructive dismissal from an employment tribunal, and this is calculated in the same way as previously described.

The test is not whether the behaviour of the employer was unreasonable. To amount to constructive dismissal, the employer must have acted in such a way as to breach the employee's contract in a fundamental way. This is usually by breaching the implied term of mutual trust and confidence that was discussed earlier in this chapter.

Western Excavations (ECC) Ltd v Sharp (1978)

This case set out the three conditions for deciding if a resignation can be a constructive dismissal:
- The employer must have done something which is in breach of contract (or going to be in breach of contract).
- The employee must decide to resign shortly after the breach.
- The employee must resign *because* of this breach.

The action of the employer does not have to amount to a single big incident—a series of smaller breaches can also lead to a 'last straw' for the employee, allowing him to leave and treat himself as constructively dismissed.

Some examples of an employer breaching the contract in a fundamental way can be:

- failing to pay wages;
- putting someone in a very difficult situation at work without supporting them;
- humiliation of an employee in front of colleagues;
- changing the employee's terms of employment without consultation;
- changing the employee's place of work at short notice.

Redundancy

Redundancy can be a fair reason for dismissal. There are two reasons why former employees bring redundancy cases to employment tribunals. The first is because they have not been paid the proper redundancy payment that they are entitled to. The second is because the manner or procedure of the redundancy process was such as to make it an unfair dismissal.

Redundancy Situations

The Employment Rights Act 1996 contains the definition of what a redundancy situation is. In effect, it is:

- when a business is closing;
- when a workplace is closing;
- where there is a diminishing need for employees to do particular kinds of work in an organisation.

In other words, if the business no longer needs a particular employee to do the particular job for which he is employed, and wishes to terminate his contract, then he will be redundant and will be entitled to a redundancy payment. If the dismissal is for another reason, such as a restructuring or reorganisation of the allocation of work, then this will not be a redundancy dismissal, and comes under 'some other substantial reason' that was discussed earlier in this chapter.

Murray v Foyle Meats (1999)

Facts: Foyle Meats were slaughterers. The claimants worked in the slaughter hall. There was a decline in business, and fewer employees were required to work in the slaughter hall. The claimants were made redundant, but claimed unfair dismissal.

Decision: As the business had less need for employees in the slaughter hall due to its decline in business, the employees were redundant. The courts set out a test to decide if someone has been made redundant:

1. Has the employee been dismissed?
2. Has there been a reduction in the need for employees to do a particular kind of work?
3. Is the dismissal wholly or mainly because of this reduction?

Redundancy Procedure

There is nothing in the statutes that says what procedure an employer should use when deciding who to make redundant. It is important, however, for employers to have a procedure, and it should contain two main elements—consultation and fair selection criteria. Some good guidance can be found in the ACAS guide on 'Redundancy Handling'. The procedure does not have to be fixed, and can vary depending on the size and situation of the employer.

Consultation

There is a difference between the legal obligations for employers who want to make only small numbers of employees redundant, and those who are contemplating larger numbers of redundancies.

For those who are proposing to dismiss 20 or more employees, the legal requirement is for 'collective' as well as 'individual' consultation. For employers making less than 20 people redundant, there is no specific legal requirement, but it is good practice to have a proper redundancy procedure, which would include individual consultation. If employers do not do this, they run the risk of the redundancy being found by a tribunal to be an unfair dismissal.

Consultation should include:

- the reason for the redundancy dismissals;
- why and how individuals have been selected;
- possible ways of avoiding redundancy;
- possible alternative work.

Selection

In practice, case law has developed a two-stage process for an employer who is deciding which of its employees to make redundant.

The first stage is to identify those who are at risk of redundancy. This is known as the 'pool' of employees. This is important because the employer can then consult the people in this pool, and comply with the consultation requirements. It also helps morale because the employer can tell the staff who is *not*, therefore, at risk.

The pool will usually consist of those who do a similar type of work in a particular department, or those whose work has ceased or diminished.

The second stage is then to select from that pool people who will actually be made redundant. There are three ways that an employer can generally do this:

- Last in, first out (LIFO);
- Points-based system;
- Selection-based system.

We shall look at these in turn.

Last in, first out (LIFO)

This used to be the most common method of selecting employees for redundancy, but no longer. One reason is that it is not always the best system, as good employees may end up being made redundant, whereas weaker ones who have been there longer keep their jobs. There is also an issue as to age discrimination, as it might be more favourable to older workers than younger ones. Age discrimination will be covered in Chapter 14.

Points-based system

This can be complicated, but basically the employer will decide on certain criteria, such as attendance, performance, skills, etc. The criteria that are chosen have to be objectively justifiable on business grounds, and not just because the employer felt like choosing them. The employer also has to make sure that the criteria are not discriminatory.

Selection-based system

This is very different to the other two approaches. If the employer chooses this, he should draw up the new organisational structure, and ask employees in the pool to apply for the jobs in the new structure. Those who do not have the required skills, etc will then be made redundant. Again, it is important that the requirements are fair and objective.

Redundancy payments

People often think of redundancy payments as a huge windfall, and assume that they are a large proportion of someone's salary. This is not the legal requirement, and in fact if someone does not have an agreement about redundancy in their employment contract, the maximum that can be awarded in 2014–15 is £13,920. This is calculated in the same way as described in the unfair dismissal 'remedies' section earlier.

The employer and employee are free, however, to agree a much more generous scheme in their contract of employment, and this is often the case.

If the employer is insolvent and therefore does not have the funds to make redundancy payments, then there is a scheme for statutory payments to be made by the Secretary of State from the national insurance fund.

Basic Terminology

For an online flashcard glossary visit the Online Resource Centre

ACAS The Advisory, Conciliation and Arbitration Service. This mediates between employers and employees, gives advice, and publishes guides ('Codes') which employers should follow if they want to be seen to be reasonable by a tribunal.

Band of reasonable responses The test used by tribunals to decide if the actions of the employer were fair or not, when deciding if an unfair dismissal had taken place.

Constructive dismissal When an employee who has at least two years' service feels he has no choice but to leave his employment because his employer has fundamentally breached his contract of employment.

Contract of employment A contract between an employer and an employee which sets out their relationship. It can be oral or written. It sets out the terms of their agreement, which can include pay, hours of work, etc.

Contract of service A contract of employment.

Contract for services A contract between a person or organisation and a worker or independent contractor.

Employee A person who is a party to an employment contract who is under the control of the employer and is obliged to follow his instructions.

Employee shareholder An employee who has given up some of their employment rights in exchange for shares in their employer's business.

Employer A person or organisation who provides work and who is party to an employment contract.

Implied term A term in a contract which is not expressly agreed by the parties to the contract.

Independent contractor Someone who is genuinely self-employed and in business on his own account.

Redundancy Where a person is dismissed because there is less work for him to do, or his organisation or workplace is closing.

Summary dismissal Dismissal of an employee without giving the proper amount of notice. This can usually only be done if an employee is guilty of gross misconduct.

Termination of an employment contract The bringing to an end of the contract.

Unfair dismissal Dismissal of an employee who has been employed for over two years by an employer either for an unfair reason or because of unfair dismissal procedures.

Worker A person who is not an employee but who provides his services to an organisation.

Wrongful dismissal Dismissal in breach of contract.

Summary

After studying this chapter students should be able to:

Explain the difference between an employee, a contractor, and a self-employed person

- An employee is employed under a contract of service.
- A worker or self-employed person works under a contract for services.
- There are a number of tests to determine the difference, the most recent being the multiple test, which looks at all the elements of control, integration, economic reality, and mutuality of obligation.

For an online printable version visit the Online Resource Centre

Outline the types of implied terms contained in a contract

- All contracts contain express terms and implied terms.
- Employment contracts contain terms implied both by statute and common law.
- Terms implied by common law are those such as fidelity, and mutual trust and confidence.
- Terms implied by statute are those such as an entitlement to at least the minimum wage and rights under the Working Time Regulations.

Understand the difference between unfair, constructive, and wrongful dismissal

- Unfair dismissal is the dismissal of an employee who has at least two years' service for an unfair reason and/or in an unfair manner or procedure.
- Constructive dismissal also applies to an employee who has at least two years' service, and who feels he has no choice but to leave because his employer has fundamentally breached his contract of employment.
- Wrongful dismissal can be brought by any employee even if he does not have two years' service. It is a complaint about a dismissal which is in breach of the contract of employment.

Set out the potentially fair and automatically unfair reasons for dismissal

- The Employment Rights Act 1996 sets out a number of potentially fair reasons for dismissal.
- These are capability, conduct, redundancy, statutory bar, industrial action after 12 weeks, some other substantial reason.
- There are a number of automatically unfair reasons which are also set out in the statute. Examples of these are any kind of dismissal for a reason related to pregnancy, or a health and safety issue.

Demonstrate knowledge of a redundancy situation

- A redundancy situation occurs when a business or workplace is closing, or there is a reduction in the need for employees to do particular kinds of work.
- A redundancy which is not carried out by means of a proper procedure can amount to an unfair dismissal.

Questions

1. Explain how an employer can show that the way he dismissed an employee was reasonable. What kinds of action can be reasonable?

2. Explain the difference between an employee and a self-employed contractor. Why is the difference important?

For outline answers visit the Online Resource Centre

3. A football manager is employed on a five-year contract. After three years, his team does extremely badly in the Premiership and is relegated. The club wishes to dismiss the manager. What issues are raised?

4. A lecturer is asked to teach on a course at a college of higher education. The course has already been written, and the lecturer is given lesson plans to follow. She only has to come to the college for two hours on a Tuesday to teach that particular course. She does not have a manager and is told that she is not an employee. The HR Department asks her to sign a form stating that she is a 'freelancer'. What is her employment status and why?

Further Reading

Emir, *Selwyn's Law of Employment*, 18th edn (Oxford University Press, 2014) Chapters 1–3, 10, 12, 13, and 15–19.

Sargeant and Lewis, *Employment Law*, 7th edn (Pearson, 2014) Chapters 2, 3, and 4.

Strevens and Welch, *Living Law: Employment Law* (Pearson, 2013) Chapters 2–6.

Taylor and Emir, *Employment Law: an Introduction*, 3rd edn (Oxford University Press, 2012) Chapters 2, 3, 12, and 13–17.

Online Resource Centre

Test your knowledge by trying this chapter's **Multiple Choice Questions**. Visit:

www.oup.com/uk/orc/law/company/ jonesibl3e/01student/mcqs/ch13/

For more information, updates, and multiple choice questions, please visit the Online Resource Centre at:

http://www.oup.com/uk/orc/law/company/ jonesibl2e/

Discrimination and Health and Safety

Introduction

In Chapter 13 we looked at the contract of employment and its termination. Here we will consider discrimination and Health and Safety Law. These areas of law can arise in recruitment, termination, or during the course of a working relationship. We shall only consider the employment law aspect of discrimination and health and safety. They do, of course, apply in other situations, but those are outside the scope of this book.

There has been some sort of discrimination law in the UK since the 1960s, when the first Race Relations Acts came into force. Before that there was no regulation, and incidents could freely occur such as the refusal of a hotel room in London to an international sports star simply because he was black, or the existence of the 'marriage bar', where employers were perfectly entitled to refuse to employ women once they were married.

Much has changed since then, and there has been a plethora of statutes and statutory instruments over the years, some originating in the UK, some in Europe, that purport to prevent discrimination. In 2010, these were all brought together under the umbrella of the **Equality Act 2010**. This aims to simplify discrimination law, and harmonise the various differences that arose when the law changed incrementally and piecemeal.

Under the 2010 Act the law has not been changed significantly but has simply been brought together and harmonised and therefore cases discussed in this chapter which were decided under the original statutes are still valid.

The law protects a number of different characteristics, such as race, sex, religion, age, disability, sexual orientation, etc. Within those categories it also prohibits different types of conduct, such as direct discrimination, indirect discrimination, harassment, and victimisation. This chapter also looks at another main area that is of importance to employers and their staff, that of health and safety. This is the way that the law tries to ensure the health and safety of both the buildings and working practices that people face in their daily working lives. It is divided into criminal law, where the state prosecutes employers who have breached the law, and civil law, which aims to provide compensation for those who have been injured in some way.

Learning Objectives

After studying this chapter you should be able to:

- Describe the difference between direct and indirect discrimination.
- Understand the difference between positive action and positive discrimination.
- Explain how the protected characteristics and prohibited conduct interact.
- Explain the difference between criminal and civil health and safety.

Discrimination Law

Discrimination law in the employment field applies in advertising for jobs, interviewing, and during a job for terms and conditions, training, and promotion, and when choosing whose contract of employment to terminate. It applies to applicants, employees, and contract workers.

The Equality and Human Rights Commission (EHRC) was set up under the Equality Act 2010 (replacing the Equal Opportunities Commission, the Commission for Racial Equality, and the Disability Rights Commission). The EHRC has responsibility for promoting equality and human rights and for ensuring compliance with the law. It can conduct enquiries, and can also bring cases against employers if it considers it necessary. It also undertakes formal investigations when it believes that an employer is persistently acting unlawfully in respect of discrimination law.

The majority of cases, however, are brought by individuals against their employers on a case-by-case basis. Compensation is unlimited in the Employment Tribunal, but obviously depends on the seriousness of the case.

Business Insight Unlimited damages for discrimination cases

In December 2011, a consultant physician was awarded compensation of almost £4.5 million by the Employment Tribunal after winning her claim for sex and racial discrimination. The tribunal heard how there had been a concerted campaign to bring the doctor's employment to an end while she was on maternity leave. Her treatment resulted in a psychiatric illness, and what was likely to be a permanent change in her personality. The tribunal concluded that she would never return to work as a doctor. The major part of the compensation was for loss of earnings and pension. This award was at the highest end of the scale, thought to be the highest award ever made (a major part of the compensation was for loss of earnings and pension).

Although damages are unlimited for cases of discrimination, there is guidance as to how much can be awarded in compensation. This was originally given by the case of *Vento v Chief Constable of West Yorkshire* (2003), and updated by another case, *Da'Bell v NSPCC* (2010):

- lower band (for minor and isolated one-off examples of unlawful discrimination) (£500–£6,000);
- middle band (for serious cases) (£6,000–£18,000);
- upper band (for the most serious cases such as a lengthy campaign of harassment) (£18,000–£30,000).

Protected Characteristics

Over the years, discrimination law has developed piecemeal, and gradually protected a number of characteristics. These each had their own legislation, and the conduct that was prohibited varied from one to the other. As well as harmonising the conduct for all the areas, the Equality Act has brought together all the **protected characteristics**. In alphabetical order, they are:

- age;
- disability;
- gender reassignment;
- marriage and civil partnership;
- pregnancy and maternity;
- race;
- religion or belief;
- sex;
- sexual orientation.

Age

Age discrimination has been seen as important because of the ageing population of the UK, and a desire to protect older workers. It does not just, however, protect people discriminated against because they are older. The legislation protects anyone discriminated against because of their *age* or *age group*, and that includes if they are younger. So, for example, if someone is not given a job because the employer thinks he is too young, that would be discrimination just as much as if the employer thinks the person is too old. This is because most protected categories are 'symmetrical', i.e. people are protected if they are older or younger, men or women, gay or straight, etc.

Thomas v Eight Members Club and Killip (2007)

Facts: T was 19 when she was dismissed from her job as a membership secretary at Eight Members Club. She had been told 'you're too young—if only you had come along a few years later.'

Decision: T had been unlawfully discriminated against on the grounds of her age.

In the following case the Employment Tribunal found there had been age discrimination by the BBC when an older presenter was replaced with younger presenters.

O'Reilly v BBC (2010)

Facts: M, aged 51, had been employed by the BBC on its *Countryfile* programme. The BBC informed M that she would no longer be required to appear on the show as they wanted to attract a significantly larger audience by 'refreshing' the existing presenter line-up. The new presenters were aged between 26 and 38.

Decision: The tribunal found that the evidence suggested that the BBC was essentially looking for younger people, that 'comparative youth' had been a significant factor in appointing the new presenters and M's age had been key factor in the decision not to consider her, M had been discriminated against because of her age.

The Equality Act 2010 makes it clear that age discrimination includes 'age group' so for example an employer cannot discriminate against persons who fall within 'the over 50s age group' or the '60–65' age group.

Homer v Chief Constable of West Yorkshire (2012)

Facts: When H joined the police as a legal advisor in 1995 a law degree was not essential but in 2005 the police changed their career structure and in order to progress to level 3 a law degree was needed. Because of H's age the earliest he could obtain a law degree was a year after the police's compulsory retirement age.

Decisions: The requirement to have a law degree put people in H's age group (60–65) at a particular disadvantage and unless justified was age discrimination.

Key Concept Age discrimination applies to people discriminated against because they are older as well as those discriminated against because they are younger.

Demographics are changing. With people living longer, and with less pension provision available, more and more people are having to work past 'retirement' age. In October 2011 the default retirement age was abolished and businesses that wish to set a compulsory retirement age for their employees must be able to justify it clearly.

Disability

A person has to be disabled before they can be protected under this characteristic. This is one of the few types of characteristics which is not symmetrical, and it is acceptable to treat a disabled person 'more favourably', in other words, better, than a person who is not disabled. That means that an employer can take steps to make things easier for a disabled person without worrying about complaints from someone who is not disabled. The law therefore tries to put disabled people on an equal footing with people who are not disabled.

Definition of disability

A person can be disabled for a large number of reasons. The **disability** can be mental or physical, and the person will be disabled if the impairment has 'a substantial and adverse long-term effect on the person's ability to carry out his normal day-to-day activities'. This means that the disability has to have quite an effect on someone's life, and has to have lasted, or is expected to last, at least 12 months. Day-to-day activities are things like walking down the street, reading a newspaper, or driving a car.

Quinlan v B & Q plc (1998)

Facts: Mr Quinlan was dismissed from his job at a garden centre after seven days because he refused to carry out the heavy lifting work that was required of him. He would not do this because he had had open heart surgery 10 years earlier, and had been told that lifting heavy weights might injure his health. He brought a case of disability discrimination.

Decision: The court decided that he was not disabled because lifting heavy weights was not found to constitute 'a normal day-to-day activity'. He could only have succeeded if his illness had not allowed him to lift everyday objects, such as when shopping, or moving a chair.

Later in this chapter we will look at direct and indirect discrimination, and all the other types of prohibited conduct. These cover disability, but there is also a specific type of prohibited conduct known as 'discrimination arising from disability'. This applies only to disabled people, and will be discussed later.

A further element of the disability section of the Equality Act is that employers will be prevented from asking candidates questions about their health that are unrelated to the job role. It will mean those with mental health issues, a medical condition or a disability will not be forced to disclose their condition prior to the offer of employment, unless it hinders their ability to do the job.

Duty to make adjustments

An employer has a duty to make reasonable adjustments for disabled people. This might have to be done in one of three ways.

1. The first is by changing the way things are done, such as changing a practice, for example, allowing a disabled person to arrive an hour later if she has difficulty with public transport in the rush hour.

2. The second involves making changes to the building or the environment, such as providing access to a building for a wheelchair user.

3. The third involves providing auxiliary aids, such as special voice-to-text software for visually impaired people, or a special chair or keyboard for people with various problems.

Such adjustments are only expected if they are reasonable, and take the employer's size and resources into account.

Gender Reassignment

The characteristic of **gender reassignment** relates to people who are transsexual. People are protected from discrimination if they have proposed, started, or completed a process to change their sex. This protects both women who intend to become male, and men who wish to become female. The person doesn't necessarily have to have had medical intervention; it is sufficient if they just have the intention to live as someone of the opposite sex.

Consider the following three examples:

1. A man wishes to change his sex medically and become a female. He discusses this with his employer, and starts to live as a woman, wearing female clothes and changing his name. He would be protected under the characteristic of gender reassignment.

2. A woman decides that she will start to live as a man. She does this for a number of years, but decides not to undergo any operation, as she feels she does not need it. She would also be protected under the characteristic of gender reassignment.

3. Jeremy is a man, and likes to dress up as a woman sometimes, but he lives his life as a man. He would not be protected, because he is a transvestite, not someone who has changed his gender.

P v S and Cornwall County Council (1996)

Facts: P was employed as a manager of an educational establishment as a man, but a year later decided to become female. She took sick leave for the initial operation, but was asked not to come back.

Decision: This case went all the way up to the European Court of Justice, because at the time it was not clear if gender reassignment discrimination was covered under UK law. It was held by that court that it was, and so the action taken against P was discriminatory.

Marriage and Civil Partnership

People who are married or who are civil partners are protected from discrimination. While most discrimination law is symmetrical, in that, for example, both men and women are protected under sex discrimination, this does not apply in this case, as single people are not protected. The original effect was to prevent situations such as the 'marriage bar' described previously from occurring. Civil partnerships were added when these became legal. It does not apply to people who are divorced, or who have had a civil partnership dissolved.

Consider the following three examples:

1. Mary and Maggie are civil partners. They apply for a job which requires a married couple to work as housekeeper and gardener in a stately home. They are refused because they are both homosexual. This would not be discrimination because they are civil partners, but because they are gay, and as such would be covered by sexual orientation discrimination (see later in the chapter).

2. Dave and Tara apply to be house wardens in an old people's home. They are refused because they are not married. This would not be discrimination, as the law is not symmetrical for this characteristic.

3. Maryam and Stuart apply for two jobs as teachers in an independent school. They are refused as the school feels that having a married couple working there would be disruptive for the staff and students. This would be discriminatory.

Pregnancy and Maternity

Pregnancy and maternity are further examples of a type of protected characteristic which is not symmetrical, as obviously men cannot become pregnant. A woman is protected in the workplace against any discrimination which takes place because she is pregnant, or has a pregnancy-related illness, or because she takes or tries to take maternity leave.

She is protected during her pregnancy and any statutory maternity leave to which she is entitled (the extent of such leave, etc, is outside the scope of this chapter).

Race

This was one of the first characteristics to be protected under UK discrimination law. The word 'race' also includes colour, nationality, national or ethnic origins, and caste.

The notes to the Equality Act 2010 give these examples:

- Colour includes being black or white.

- Nationality includes being a British, Australian, or Swiss citizen.

- Ethnic or national origins include being from a Roma background or of Chinese heritage.

- A racial group could be 'black Britons' which would encompass those people who are both black and who are British citizens.

To give an example, a woman is not given a job in a youth centre because she is white, and it is felt that the high proportion of black teenagers would prefer a black person. This would be discriminatory, as simply preferring someone to be of a particular race or colour is not an essential requirement for the job.

Likewise, a man is not given an interview for a job in Norfolk on the basis that he has stated on his CV that he comes from Poland and the employer wishes to promote employment of local people. This is race discrimination.

Religion or Belief

The protected categories under this characteristic are:

- religion;

- religious belief;

- philosophical belief;

- lack of belief.

This protected characteristic is, therefore, not just for those who follow an established religion, but those who have a belief, whether religious or philosophical. This includes a lack of belief, so atheists are also covered from being discriminated against.

There is nothing that specifically defines what a religion or philosophical belief is, but factors taken into account are whether there is a clear structure and belief system, and if the person has a profound belief affecting their way of life or view of the world. A religion can be anything from Christianity and Islam to Rastafarianism and Zoroastrianism. It can also include sects within religions, for example, Protestants or Catholics. The law has some caveats to ensure, for example, that cults which are involved in illegal activities are not covered. A philosophical belief does not usually cover purely political beliefs unless it could be considered a political philosophy.

Redfearn v Serco (2006)

Facts: Mr Redfearn, who was white and had been employed a bus driver, was dismissed after he was elected as a councillor for the British National Party (BNP). Membership did not require a certain philosophical belief so he brought a claim of racial discrimination.

Decision: R had not been dismissed on racial grounds but for a non-racial reason, namely membership of, and standing for election for, the BNP.

Mr Redfearn later made an application to the European Court of Human Rights which stated that the UK was under an obligation to protect employees from dismissal on the grounds of political opinion or affiliation. In 2013 the Employment Rights Act 1996 was changed and an employee may now claim unfair dismissal, even if he has not been employed for two years, where the sole or principal reason for dismissing him is his political belief. There is still a lack of protection for employees treated less favourably (other than by dismissal) for political beliefs.

Key Concept Some people can be covered by more than one characteristic. For example, Jewish people are a race, and so are protected from racial discrimination. Judaism is also a religion, and so they would also be protected from religious discrimination. The same applies to Sikhs, but not Muslims. Muslims come from very diverse backgrounds and do not form a single race, but are protected from religious discrimination.

Sex

This is one of the oldest types of protected category, and covers both men and women. For example, if a woman is not given a promotion because she is a woman, that would be discrimination. Equally, however, if a man is not given a job because a female employer likes to keep her business female, then unless there is an occupational requirement (which we will look at later), that will be sex discrimination against the man.

Sexual Orientation

This characteristic has been part of our law since 2003, after regulations deriving from Europe came into force in the UK. Gay and lesbian people are now protected in the same way as those with the other characteristics. People are also protected if they are bisexual or hetero-sexual—for example, if a heterosexual person is employed in a largely gay organisation, he will be protected from any discrimination because he is heterosexual.

For example, suppose Gina works for a large company as an administrator. The company holds an annual dinner to which employees can bring their partners. Gina is a lesbian, and wishes to bring her female partner. Her manager tells her that this is not appropriate, as it might make people uncomfortable. This would be sexual orientation discrimination.

In the following case the Supreme Court stated that civil partnership was akin to marriage and therefore it was unlawful to discriminate between couples who were married and couples who were in a civil partnership.

Bull and Bull v Hall and Preddy (2013)

Facts: Mr and Mrs Bull refused to allow Mr H & Mr P, civil partners, a double room in their hotel because on religious grounds they only allowed this type of room for heterosexual married couples.

Decision: Discriminating between married and civil partnered people (which was equivalent to marriage) was direct discrimination on grounds of sexual orientation.

Equal Pay

As well as harmonising the protected characteristics, the Equality Act 2010 also replaces the Equal Pay Act 1970, and makes a claim for equal pay more in line with sex discrimination. Contractual pay secrecy clauses in people's employment contracts will become unenforceable, making it easier for people to discover if they are being underpaid because of their sex. They will also be able to use hypothetical comparators (see later) and any difference in pay can be justified by the employer as being because of a 'material factor'.

Business Insight

According to the Office for National Statistics, although the gender pay gap has decreased markedly between 1997–2013 the gap between the highest earning males and females has not decreased as much as between lower earners. The gender pay gap in 2013 for all employees is 19.7 per cent. This is after over 40 years of equal pay legislation.

Prohibited Conduct

As well as a number of characteristics, the Equality Act 2010 also prohibits certain kinds of conduct. This is the behaviour that is seen as discriminatory by the law. This conduct can be by the employer himself, or it can be vicarious, in other words the conduct of his other employees, for example a manager.

The main types of such **prohibited conduct** are:

- Direct discrimination;
- Associative discrimination;
- Perceptive discrimination;
- Combined discrimination;
- Indirect discrimination;
- Harassment;
- Victimisation.

Direct Discrimination

Direct discrimination is what most people think of when they think of discrimination. They think of somebody deliberately being treated badly because, for example, they happen to be black or female.

In law, this is called **direct discrimination**, and is described as where a person A treats a person B less well than he would treat someone else, person C, because person B comes under one of the protected characteristics. The person C is called the **comparator**.

Direct discrimination applies to all the protected characteristics.

Comparator

In discrimination law, in most circumstances, there has to be a comparator. The person complaining of the discriminatory treatment has to compare him or herself with like in cases of direct, indirect, and dual discrimination (indirect and dual discrimination are looked at later in the chapter).

Consider the following example. Frank is a manager. He does not like people of Indian or Pakistani origin. Jamil (person B) is Asian and works on Frank's team, but is always passed over for training and interesting projects. These always go to Denise and Abigail, the other members of the team. If the reason that he is passed over is because he is of Pakistani origin, then Frank (person A) would be liable for discrimination, and either Denise or Abigail would be the comparator (person C).

The comparator can be either a real person or a hypothetical one, and has to be someone who does not have the same protected characteristic of the person claiming discrimination. So, in the case of a woman, the person who does not share her protected characteristic is a man (in other words, he is not of the same sex); in the case of a Buddhist claiming religious discrimination, the comparator is a person who is not a Buddhist; in the case of a person complaining of sexual orientation discrimination because he is homosexual, the comparator would be a person who is not homosexual.

For example, Ruth is Jewish, and feels she is being discriminated against because of her religion by not being promoted. She can bring a case to court comparing herself to someone in the same or similar job for the same employer who is not Jewish. The person can be real or hypothetical. The question is either how did the employer treat the other person, or how would they have treated them if they were hypothetical?

Irrelevance of alleged discriminator's characteristics

If a person is being discriminatory against another, it is not a defence for him to say that it does not matter because he himself has the same characteristic and so it should not count as discrimination.

Consider the following examples:

1. A female employer does not promote other females because she does not believe that they are as committed to their jobs as men are, and she does not want to risk her employees leaving to have a family. This would be discriminatory, and it is irrelevant that the employer herself is female.

2. A gay employer does not provide training to someone which would benefit that person, because he believes the employee is also gay, although he is not. This would be perceptive discrimination.

Justification of direct discrimination

Direct discrimination in most cases cannot be justified. That means that the employer or person who is being discriminatory cannot make an excuse to explain the reason for the discrimination. This is the case even when the excuse is one that comes from a good motive.

Amnesty International v Ahmed (2009)

Facts: A was of Sudanese origin and worked for Amnesty International but she was not given the position as Researcher for Sudan because Amnesty genuinely believed that there would be a conflict of interest and if she visited Sudan she would be at an increased risk of ill-treatment or violence.

Decision: This was direct discrimination on the ground of her ethnic origin.

When direct discrimination can be justified

In a few circumstances, however, the law allows for direct discrimination to be justified.

The Equality Act says that age discrimination can be justified if the employer can show the justification is 'a proportionate means of meeting a legitimate aim'. This means that if the employer has an objective reason for his actions, and this reason is reasonable, then he can justify what might otherwise appear to be discriminatory actions. The main use that an employer would have for this is if he wishes to set a retirement age for his employees.

Occupational requirements

The rule that direct discrimination cannot be justified for most characteristics (apart from those such as age) also does not apply where there is an **occupational requirement** for the job. That means that where being of a particular sex, race, disability, religion or belief, sexual orientation, or age, or *not* being a transsexual person, married, or a civil partner is an essential requirement for the work that is to be done. The requirement must be crucial to the post, and not merely one of several important factors. It also must not be a sham or pretext. In addition, applying the requirement must be 'proportionate so as to achieve a legitimate aim'.

There are a number of different reasons for such requirements. The examples given in the explanatory notes to the Equality Act are:

- The need for authenticity or realism might require someone of a particular race, sex, or age for acting roles (for example, a black man to play the part of Othello) or modelling jobs.

- Considerations of privacy or decency might require a public changing room or lavatory attendant to be of the same sex as those using the facilities.

- An organisation for deaf people might legitimately employ a deaf person who uses British Sign Language (BSL) to work as a counsellor to other deaf people whose first or preferred language is BSL.

- Unemployed Muslim women might not take advantage of the services of an outreach worker to help them find employment if they were provided by a man, so a woman would be required.

- A counsellor working with victims of rape might have to be a woman and not a transsexual person, even if she has a gender recognition certificate, in order to avoid causing them further distress.

- There are also specific exceptions for religions, but only if being of that religion or belief is a requirement for the work. For example, a Catholic priest can be required to be a man, but a requirement that a church accountant should not be gay would not be covered, as his sexuality is nothing to do with how he performs his job.

Associative Discrimination

The Equality Act allows for a person to bring an action if he has been discriminated against because of someone else that he is associated with. This is known as **associative discrimination**.

For example, suppose Rob is dismissed from his job because it is discovered that his wife is a Muslim, and his employer feels that he is unable to trust him because of this. This would be associative religious discrimination.

Coleman v Attridge Law (2009)

Facts: Mrs Coleman was a legal secretary working for the defendant law firm. She had a baby who was disabled, and she was the child's main carer. When she came back from maternity leave she was treated in a way that parents of non-disabled children would not have been, in that she had not been allowed to return to her existing job, was criticised when she sought time off to care for her child, and had been subjected to abusive and insulting comments about her and her child.

Decision: It was decided that this could be disability discrimination and compensation was agreed between the parties. This was the case which established that there can be discrimination by association, and this principle is now enshrined in the Equality Act 2010.

The principle of associative discrimination does not, however, apply in the case of marriage and civil partnership, so just because, for example, someone lives with a married couple, that does not provide him with grounds for complaint to a tribunal if he is discriminated against on that basis. It therefore has to be the 'victim' of the discrimination, not anyone else, who is the married person or civil partner.

Perceptive Discrimination

A person can also bring a case if he has been discriminated against because people *perceive*, or *believe* that he has the protected characteristic. This is sometimes known as **perceptive discrimination**. If, for example, a person is dismissed because his employer *thinks* he is gay, whereas he is in fact not gay, he can still bring an action for sexual orientation discrimination. This is something that was beginning to be established in case law for some areas of discrimination, but has now been enshrined in the Equality Act.

For example, suppose Craig acts in what his colleagues at work view as a very camp manner, and they decide that he must be gay, although he is in fact heterosexual. He is treated badly as a result. This would be sexual orientation discrimination.

Dual or Combined Discrimination

This is a new element in discrimination law, and means that a person can bring a claim on the basis that he or she has two or more protected characteristics and that is why he or she has been discriminated against. It is not yet known when the Government intend to implement this part of the Equality Act, if at all.

The protected characteristics that can be combined are:

- age;
- disability;
- gender reassignment;
- race;
- religion or belief;
- sex;
- sexual orientation.

The comparator for a person claiming dual discrimination is a person who does not share either of the protected characteristics.

An example given in the explanatory notes to the Equality Act 2010 is that of a black woman who has been passed over for promotion to work on reception. The reason is because her employer thinks black women do not perform well in customer service roles.

The employer has a white woman and a black man doing similar work in reception, and so the black woman cannot say that it is because of her sex or her race. The only option she has, therefore, is to claim combined discrimination on the basis that she is a black woman, because of her employer's prejudice against black women. The comparator would be someone who is not a black woman.

Indirect Discrimination

When most people think of discrimination what they are really thinking of is direct discrimination. They assume that discrimination consists of someone being deliberately badly treated because of a particular characteristic, such as sex or race.

Another major type of prohibited conduct, however, is that of **indirect discrimination**. This is where the employer may not even realise that he is discriminating, but is in fact doing something that makes it more difficult for one group of people to comply with than another. This is also a type of discrimination.

If, for example, the employer has a policy (which the law calls a 'provision, criterion or practice') that he applies equally to all his employees, but which makes it more difficult for women to comply with than men, then this would be discriminatory. Although what the employer might be doing is not a deliberate measure, then if it is an unjustifiable practice that stands in the way of women achieving equal opportunities with men, and it has a disproportionate impact on women, then it is discriminatory.

An example is if the employer requires his staff to work unsociable hours, as this would have a disparate impact on women, who have childcare commitments, or insisting that staff should not have beards, as this would impact disproportionately on Sikh men. Such policies would be discriminatory unless the employer has an objective justification for them.

A good way to describe indirect discrimination is 'disparate impact', as it shows that the discrimination lies in the impact that a particular practice has on one sex. 'Disparate impact' is what this kind of discrimination is known as in the United States.

Indirect discrimination applies to all the protected characteristics, apart from pregnancy and maternity. Instead of a single comparator, there is a **pool of comparison**. These are the other people to which the policy or practice applies.

London Underground v Edwards (1995)

Facts: Mrs Edwards was a single parent with a young child. She worked as an underground train driver. Her employer announced a new shift system, which made it very difficult for her because of her child.

Decision: The tribunal decided that this was indirect discrimination. They looked at the 'pool' of comparison, which was all the other underground drivers to whom the new rota applied. 100 per cent of men could comply, but only 95 per cent of women. This impacted more on women, and so the new rota was discriminatory.

One area in particular where there have been a number of cases of indirect discrimination has been cases concerning dress codes. Some of the most high profile cases have been those claiming religious discrimination. Most claimants complain of both direct and indirect discrimination.

Noah v Desrosiers t/a Wedge (2008)

Facts: Ms Noah was a Muslim who applied for a job as a hairstylist. The owner of the salon rejected her because she wore a headscarf. Noah claimed both direct and indirect religious discrimination.

Decision: The claim of direct discrimination failed because the employer would also have turned down a non-Muslim woman who wore a headscarf. The claim of indirect discrimination, however, was successful, because the only defence open to the employer was to justify the decision not to allow headscarves, which impacted more on Muslim women. The tribunal found that the purported justification of stylists displaying their own hair at work was not sufficient, and so the decision was indirect discrimination.

Eweida v British Airways (2010)

Facts: Ms Eweida was a British Airways check-in clerk who was not allowed to wear a crucifix around her neck, as it was general company policy that jewellery should be hidden.

Decision: The Court stated that this was not discriminatory. However in 2013 Ms Eweida succeeded in her claim before the European Court of Human Rights that the UK breached her right to manifest her religion under article 9 of the European Convention on Human Rights.

Discrimination Arising from Disability

Discrimination arising from disability covers the situation when a disabled person is treated unfavourably not because of the person's disability itself but because of something arising from, or in consequence of, their disability. An example of this could be the need to take a period of disability-related absence. It is the absence that is the problem, not the disability itself, but the need for absence has arisen because of the disability.

It is, however, possible to justify such treatment if it can be shown to be a proportionate means of achieving a legitimate aim. For this type of discrimination to occur, the employer or other person must know, or reasonably be expected to know, that the disabled person has a disability.

For example, suppose Andrew suffers from a visual impairment. It means that he cannot do as much work as his colleagues who are not disabled. He is dismissed because of the volume of his work. This would be discrimination arising from disability, unless the employer could justify it by showing that it was a 'proportionate means of achieving a legitimate aim', in other words that it had objective reasons that were proportionate, such as the fact that it is a small organisation and is losing money because of his lack of work, and that there was no other solution.

If, in the previous example, the impairment is not obvious, and the employer did not know, and could not reasonably have been expected to know, of Andrew's condition, for example, if he didn't tell them why he was so unproductive despite enquiries, then the employer would not be acting unlawfully.

Harassment

Harassment has been prohibited for some time, but the Equality Act has simplified and clarified it. There are now three types of harassment.

1. The first type applies to all the protected characteristics apart from pregnancy and maternity, and marriage and civil partnership. It consists of unwanted conduct which is related to a protected characteristic and has the purpose or effect of creating an intimidating, hostile, degrading, humiliating, or offensive environment for the complainant or violating his dignity.

   In other words, it is behaviour which is related to race, disability, etc, and makes the person hearing it feel intimidated, offended, or degraded. For example, it could include physical abuse, offensive language, racist, etc jokes, and banter.

   The notes to the Equality Act give the example of a white worker who sees a black colleague being subjected to racially abusive language and who could have a claim for harassment if the language also causes an offensive environment for her.

2. The second type is sexual harassment, which is unwanted conduct of a sexual nature where this has the same purpose or effect as the first type of harassment. This is effectively the same as the first type, but is specifically sexual harassment.

   The notes give the example of an employer who displayed any material of a sexual nature, such as a topless calendar. This could be harassing his employees if this makes the workplace an offensive place to work for any employee, whether female or male.

3. The third type is treating someone less favourably than someone else because he or she has either submitted to or rejected sexual harassment, or harassment related to sex or gender reassignment.

The notes give the example of a shopkeeper who propositions one of his shop assistants. She rejects his advances and is then turned down for promotion. She believes that she would have got the promotion if she had accepted her employer's advances. The shop assistant would have a claim of harassment.

Employers are vicariously liable for anything done by an employee in the course of his employment. An employer will have a defence if they took all reasonable steps to prevent the employee's unlawful behaviour. In the following case the employer was liable for the harassment because they had not taken all reasonable steps.

Martin v Parkam Foods Limited (2006)

Facts: M was a gay man employed by P. Homophobic graffiti with his name against it appeared on the toilet wall in his workplace. M complained about this and about homophobic remarks made to him. M's name was removed but not the graffiti. Notices were put up about graffiti vandalism but no mention was made of homophobia.

Decision: The steps taken by P were ineffective in ensuring that homophobic behaviour was not repeated. There should have been training, team briefings, notes in payslips, etc. P was vicariously liable for harassment.

Victimisation

If a person makes a complaint about discrimination, or supports someone else in their complaint, and does this 'in good faith', in other words not maliciously in relation to a false complaint, then they are protected from being victimised.

Suppose a man brings a complaint against his employer for religious discrimination. As a result of this complaint, he is denied promotion. This would be victimisation.

However, suppose a woman who has a grudge against her employer knowingly gives false evidence in an employment tribunal discrimination claim by a colleague. She is then dismissed because she supported the claim. The dismissal would not be victimisation because of her untrue and malicious evidence. Her evidence was not given in good faith.

The Equality Act has slightly changed the previous law on victimisation in that there is no longer any need for a comparator.

Positive Action

There is a difference between positive action and positive discrimination. **Positive action** is lawful, and has been for some time, and is included in the Equality Act. It allows employers to take measures to alleviate disadvantage experienced by people who have one of the protected characteristics. It allows measures to be targeted to particular groups, such as offering training courses that meet the needs of women or members of ethnic minorities who aspire to be managers, if there are very few women or ethnic minority managers in the organisation, and the employer wishes to encourage more.

Positive discrimination, however, is unlawful. This would be, for example, where an employer who employs few women, and wishes to employ more, advertises a job and says that it will consider only female applicants. That would be sex discrimination against men.

The only time an employer can take a protected characteristic into account is when deciding who to recruit or promote. If there are two people who are as qualified as each other, and one is a man and one is a woman, and women are under-represented in the organisation, the Equality Act will allow the employer to appoint the woman. The employer has to make this decision on a case-by-case basis, and cannot have an automatic policy that in such cases it will always appoint the woman.

To give a hypothetical example, Noisy Enterprises has interviewed a number of people for a job, and has shortlisted them down to two, one man and one woman. The man has more experience than the woman, and is slightly more qualified. The company wishes to increase its female staff, and so decides to appoint the woman. This would be discriminatory. If, however, they both had the same experience and qualifications then it would be lawful.

Health and Safety

The law covering health and safety in the workplace is divided into two parts: that which comes under criminal law, and that which comes under the civil jurisdiction. The two share the main principles, but the way that they are enforced is very different. The aim of the criminal law is to prevent workplace injuries and illnesses from occurring in the first place, and to punish those who don't take reasonable steps to prevent such injuries.

The aim of the civil law is different—it is to provide compensation to employees who have suffered injury because of the actions or inactions of their employers.

Criminal Law

The law makes it a criminal offence for an employer not to provide a safe and healthy working environment. That means that the employer can be prosecuted and punished if found guilty.

Health and Safety at Work Act 1974

The main statute that covers this area is the Health and Safety at Work Act 1974. It provides for inspectors to do checks on employers to make sure they have proper procedures, and allows for prosecution of the employers in the criminal courts. The main requirement on employers is to act reasonably when it comes to looking after the health and safety of their employees. If they do so, then they will be able to defend themselves if there is a prosecution in a case where there has been a serious injury to an employee.

There are also a large number of regulations that have been passed in relation to health and safety. Examples are duties on employers to have adequate first aid equipment, protecting employees' hearing when exposed to noise, regarding training in relation to hazardous substances, and many, many more. One well-known example is that of the smoking ban, which was introduced by the Health Act 2006 in England, and by regulations in Scotland, Wales, and Northern Ireland. Other regulations deal with issues such as training people in lifting techniques, allowing people regular breaks from computer screens, and assessment of work stations.

Viewpoint Lisa Williams, Manager, Lonstone

Working for Lonstone, a concrete products manufacturer, the use of heavy-duty machinery and forklift trucks is a daily necessity. As a result, Health and Safety Law is a critical issue for us. Even though we use an outsourced Health and Safety Specialist, it is vital that I understand the basics of the Health and Safety at Work Act 1974 and other related acts to protect our employees. There are constant implications for my day-to-day role in the company, including monitoring and ensuring procedures and records are maintained. Unless we follow these requirements we could be leaving not only our employees open to danger, but also Lonstone, as a company, at risk of potentially expensive law suits and down time in the event of an accident.

Health and Safety concerns are so numerous and wide ranging for us at Lonstone. At a basic level we must provide a whole range of safety ware, e.g. ear defenders, high visibility jackets, and steel toe cap shoes (all of which are now an integral part of my working wardrobe!). But it isn't sufficient for us to just provide this, we are legally required to ensure that employees sign for their equipment and we must maintain records for each employee detailing the safety equipment provided. We also have to perform daily checks of all our forklift trucks and weekly checks of the machinery to ensure that it is well maintained and safe for use—all of these checks have to be recorded and any remedial work documented.

Every new employee is taken through a strict induction procedure to ensure that they understand our Health and Safety protocols to ensure that they work safely for both themselves and their fellow work colleagues. These are just three examples of how Health and Safety affects Lonstone operations; the reality is that there are many more checks that we implement.

Reasonableness

Obligations of an employer:

- To maintain plant and equipment and to provide safe systems of working;
- To ensure safe arrangements for handling, use, transport, and storage of hazardous equipment and/or substances;
- To provide all necessary information, training, and supervision in the use of hazardous equipment/substances;
- To ensure that entrances and exits to buildings are safe and maintained;
- To provide adequate facilities and arrangements to ensure welfare at work.

Employers have to provide a safe and healthy place for their employees, and this duty also extends to workers and self-employed people, as the employer is the person who has control of the workspace, and is responsible for the welfare of all people in the building that he is in charge of.

Employers should take steps to ensure people's safety, unless it would not be reasonable to expect them to take such steps.

R v Swan Hunter (1981)

Facts: Swan Hunter ran a shipyard. A fire broke out in a ship leading to the death of eight men. The fire had been caused when an employee of Swan Hunter ignited some leaking oxygen with his torch. The oxygen leak had been caused by an employee of a sub-contractor, Telemeter, who had failed to turn off an oxygen supply the previous evening. Swan Hunter had distributed a book of rules to their own employees for the safe use of oxygen equipment, but this was not distributed to sub-contractor's employees.

Decision: Both Telemeter and Swan Hunter were guilty of a criminal offence. Swan Hunter had a duty to ensure the health and safety of its own employees by the provision of information. If the ignorance of another company's employees placed its own employees at risk, then it was Swan Hunter's duty to inform the employees of the other company of any special risks within its knowledge.

Risk assessments

One of the ways that an employer can find out what steps it should take is by doing risk assessments. This is a duty on employers stated in the Management of Health and Safety at Work Regulations 1999.

A **risk assessment** has been identified as follows:

> A risk assessment should usually involve identifying the hazards present in any working environment or arising out of commercial activities and work activities, and evaluating the extent of the risks involved, taking account of existing precautions and their effectiveness. (The Code of Practice to the Regulations.)

Risk assessments should be regularly reviewed and the results recorded. Once the risk has been assessed, the employer then has to show that he has put in place proper systems to deal with the risk, depending on what the risk is.

Risk assessments can then be taken into account by the employer when drafting a health and safety policy statement, which all employers employing more than five people should have. This sets out issues such as who is responsible for health and safety within the organisation, and what training, etc, is provided.

The employer should also involve employees in the system by appointing some as health and safety representatives to investigate hazards and accidents, to investigate complaints and to carry out regular inspections, and to liaise with health and safety inspectors.

Enforcement of health and safety regulations

The main way that Health and Safety Law is enforced in the criminal courts is by the inspectorates. This can either be the Health and Safety Executive (HSE), or the local authority for the area, depending on the type of workplace. For example, local authorities will inspect offices, hotels, and restaurants, and the HSE will cover manufacturing plants, farms, and construction sites—generally places where specialist expertise is required.

Both the HSE and local authorities have the same powers. The main approach is usually to work with employers to encourage compliance with the law, rather than threaten employers. However, they do have certain powers, and are entitled to turn up without warning and take away samples, and they can require managers and staff to answer questions. They can even go to court to get an injunction to have a place of business closed down.

If the employer has not cooperated, or there are issues that the inspector decides should be addressed, he has the power to issue either:

1. An improvement notice specifying what remedial steps the employer must take and by when.

2. A prohibition notice ordering that an activity is discontinued until remedial steps are taken.

If an employer does not comply with such a notice, it is a serious criminal offence, and the employer can be prosecuted and fined in a criminal court. For more wilful or reckless breaches of health and safety regulations, prosecutions can also be brought for the breach of the regulation itself. In either case, magistrates can fine offenders up to £20,000, while the fine in a Crown Court is unlimited, depending on the severity of the offence. In serious cases responsible managers can even be sentenced to prison.

Business Insight

The HSE reports that in 2013–14 there were 133 workers killed at work and approximately 78,000 reported other injuries to employees.

The HSE issued over 10,000 improvement and prohibition notices.

Civil Law

Civil Law is the opposite of Criminal Law. Here, cases are not brought by prosecuting authorities and punishments given, but rather the law deals with the issue of compensation. The civil side of Health and Safety Law consists of people who are injured or who have become ill because of their working environment or practices, bringing court action so that they can be compensated for injuries that occurred as a result of lax health and safety at work.

Negligence

Key Concept Employers owe all employees a general duty of care in respect of their health and safety at work.

Wilsons and Clyde Coal v English (1937)

Facts: Mr English was working underground near the pit bottom at the end of his shift when the haulage equipment was switched on and the claimant was crushed between the equipment and the wall of the mine. The employer said that the claimant could have got out of the pit by a different route or could have called to the operator of the haulage equipment telling him of his presence.

Decision: The House of Lords held that the employer owed the employee a duty of care, and that this could not be delegated. It was the employer's responsibility. The duty included the provision of:

- a safe place of work (including safe access and exit);
- safe equipment;
- a safe system of work and provision of competent employees.

In Chapter 11 we looked at the law of negligence. This also covers employers and employees, as can be seen from the case of *Wilsons and Clyde Coal v English*, which, in 1937, was the first case to say that employers also owed a duty of care to their employees. Most of the cases that allege negligence are in fact alleging vicarious liability, where the employer is liable for the negligent actions of his other employees (see Chapter 11).

Whether an employer is negligent or not depends on the facts of each particular case, just like the criminal law on health and safety. It depends on how much of the risk of injury or illness was foreseeable, and whether or not the employer's response was reasonable given the cost of reducing that risk.

Most cases tend to arise out of problems with plant and equipment, such as the floor being slippery, or systems of work. This can be either because there is no safe system, or because employees do not in practice operate the systems as they are supposed to.

General Cleaning Contractors v Christmas (1952)

Facts: A window cleaner fell and seriously injured himself while cleaning an office window. He had relied on holding a sash window frame and balancing his foot on a windowsill. The window fell and gave way.

Decision: The employer was liable because it was the employer's duty to give general safety instructions and have a safe system of work. Just because he was an experienced window cleaner did not mean they could just leave him to it, instead of providing a proper system that he should follow.

Pape v Cumbria County Council (1991)

Facts: A cleaner developed a skin disorder from the chemicals she had used for her job. The employer had provided her with rubber gloves, but she had not worn them.

Decision: She was awarded compensation, because the employer had never explained to her the risks associated with not using the gloves when working with commercial cleaning fluids.

Defences

An employer can defend itself on a claim of negligence in a number of ways depending on the case.

One way is by showing that it was not negligent (or that one of the elements of negligence was missing, such as foreseeability, etc). In order to do so, it will have to show that proper risk assessments were undertaken and acted upon, and that the actions of the employer were reasonable.

Another, usually partial, defence is where the employee was at least partly to blame. This is known as contributory negligence, and compensation is apportioned depending on what percentage of fault the judge thinks is attributable to each party, for example, 60 per cent employer, and 40 per cent employee. If the employee is wholly to blame, then the compensation could reduce to zero.

Basic Terminology

For an online flashcard glossary visit the Online Resource Centre

Associative discrimination Direct discrimination against someone because they are associated with a person who has a protected characteristic.

Comparator A person, whether real or hypothetical, that a person claiming direct discrimination has to compare him or herself with, who is similar in all respects relating to work except that the comparator does not have the protected characteristic.

Direct discrimination Treating someone less well than someone else because of a protected characteristic.

Disability A serious mental or physical condition that the person has had for at least a year, or is likely to last at least a year, which has a significant effect on his or her day-to-day activities.

Equality Act 2010 Statute which consolidates all previous discrimination legislation.

Gender reassignment A protected characteristic relating to a person who lives as someone of the opposite gender.

Indirect discrimination Having a policy or practice which is applied equally to everyone, but with which it is more difficult for people of a particular protected characteristic to comply, and which cannot be justified.

Occupational requirement When it is essential that a person be of a particular protected characteristic in order to do the job. The requirement must be crucial to the post, and not merely one of several important factors.

Perceptive discrimination Direct discrimination against someone because they are perceived to have a protected characteristic, although they in fact do not.

Pool of comparison Group of people that a person claiming indirect discrimination should compare him or herself with.

Positive action Where measures are allowed to be taken by employers to alleviate disadvantage experienced by people who have one of the protected characteristics. Such measures, such as training, can be targeted to particular groups.

Prohibited conduct Types of conduct in relation to protected characteristics which are not permitted by the Equality Act 2010. These are listed in this chapter.

Protected characteristics A number of characteristics which are protected from

discrimination by the Equality Act 2010. These are listed in this chapter.

Risk assessment An assessment that an employer has to undertake because of health and safety legislation. It has to identify hazards present in any working environment, and evaluate the risks involved.

Summary

After studying this chapter students should be able to:

Describe the difference between direct and indirect discrimination

- Direct discrimination is deliberate treatment (whether well-motivated or otherwise) towards someone because of a characteristic such as sex or race, and which has a less favourable effect on that person than on someone else who is in a similar situation.
- Indirect discrimination is not deliberately targeted, but applies to a number of people. Some of those people, who are of a particular characteristic, such as sex or race, will find it harder to comply than the others in the pool.
- Direct discrimination cannot be justified.
- Direct discrimination can be the subject of an occupational requirement, which is a justification for a reason that is essential to the job, such as having a black actor play the role of Othello.
- Indirect discrimination can be justified if the employer has a proportionate means of achieving a legitimate aim.

Understand the difference between positive discrimination and positive action

- Positive discrimination is unlawful.
- Positive action is lawful.
- Positive discrimination is when a person treats someone more favourably than another because of a protected characteristic.
- Positive action is when an employer is allowed to take measures to address disadvantage, such as stating that they encourage applications from ethnic minorities and older people, without shortlisting such people, or giving them jobs based solely on their protected characteristic.
- It is lawful to take action that is more favourable to a disabled person.

Explain how the protected characteristics and prohibited conduct interact

- Direct discrimination and victimisation apply to all protected characteristics.
- Discrimination by association and perception apply to all except marriage/civil partnership and pregnancy.
- Harassment and third party harassment apply to all except marriage/civil partnership and pregnancy.
- Indirect discrimination applies to all except pregnancy.
- Almost all characteristics are symmetrical, apart from pregnancy, disability, and marriage/civil partnership.

Explain the difference between criminal and civil health and safety

- The Criminal Law is enforced by local authorities and the HSE.
- Criminal prosecutions result in a fine.

For an online printable version visit the Online Resource Centre

- Civil cases are brought by injured individuals.
- People who bring civil cases are seeking compensation for their injuries.
- For both kinds of cases the employer can defend itself if it did a risk assessment, and took appropriate action to avoid the risks present.

Questions

For outline answers visit the Online Resource Centre

1. What is a risk assessment, why is it important, and how should an employer go about conducting one? Give an example to illustrate your answer.

2. Explain the differences between the different types of prohibited conduct.

3. Jo is a transsexual who has undergone surgery to change her sex from male to female. She applies for a job as a hairdresser, but is rejected because the owner of the salon thinks that she does not really look the part. Does she have any legal remedy? Would your answer be any different if she applied for a job as a changing room assistant?

4. Sarah is a Druid. She wants to have time off to celebrate the summer solstice at Stonehenge, but her employer refuses. At about the same time, he allows some Muslims to take a few days off for Eid. Advise Sarah.

Further Reading

Emir, *Selwyn's Law of Employment*, 18th edn (Oxford University Press, 2014) Chapters 4, 5, and 11.

Sargeant and Lewis, *Employment Law*, 7th edn (Pearson, 2014) Chapters 5 and 6.

Strevens and Welch, *Employment Law*, 3rd edn (Pearson, 2013) Chapter 7.

Taylor and Emir, *Employment Law: an Introduction* (Oxford University Press, 2012) Chapters 4–11 and 18–19.

Wadham, Ruebain, Robinson, and Uppal, *Blackstone's Guide to the Equality Act 2010* (Oxford University Press, 2012).

Online Resource Centre

Test your knowledge by trying this chapter's **Multiple Choice Questions**. Visit:

www.oup.com/uk/orc/law/company/jonesibl3e/01student/mcqs/ch14/

For more information, updates, and multiple choice questions, please visit the Online Resource Centre at:

www.oup.com/uk/orc/law/company/jonesibl3e

PART 5

THE STRUCTURE & MANAGEMENT

Business Organisations

Introduction

UK law permits a range of different types of business organisations, from the simple, one person unincorporated business which can be set up without legal formality, to the public limited company for which a structured legal framework has been devised to govern its internal and external relations. An **unincorporated business** organisation has no separate legal identity and the owners of the business may have no financial protection if the business fails, and their personal assets may be used to pay off business debts. An **incorporated business** organisation has a separate legal identity, its debts are its own, and the personal liabilities of its owners are limited to the amount invested in the business. The choice of legal structure can depend on a variety of different factors, linked to the nature of the business, the persons involved with it, the scale of the operation, and finance and working capital requirements.

Learning Objectives

After studying this chapter you should be able to:

- Identify common types of business organisations and explain the difference between unincorporated and incorporated businesses.
- Outline the rules relating to partnerships.
- Explain the relationship between partners.
- Explain the relationship between partnerships and outsiders.
- Demonstrate an understanding of the main aspects of limited liability partnerships.
- Outline the nature of companies.

Unincorporated and Incorporated Business Organisations

Unincorporated Business Organisation

Business organisations can be either unincorporated or incorporated. An organisation that is unincorporated has no separate legal identity of its own. The risks and liabilities involved in running a business in an unincorporated form belong to the individuals who own or manage it. Those individuals enter into contracts on behalf of the organisation, and they are responsible for its debts and other liabilities. This means that their personal assets are at risk if the assets of the business are not sufficient to cover all the debts and liabilities. Unincorporated organisations can operate relatively informally which gives flexibility but can result in unclear powers and processes for decision-making. An unincorporated business may be owned by one person who runs the business as a sole trader, or by two or more persons who have come together for the common purpose of running a business.

There are different types of unincorporated associations, not all of them run as businesses. An unincorporated association may be formed for non-profit-making purposes such as running a sports club or a trade union. Where the purpose of an unincorporated association is to run a business with a view to making a profit, then it is a general (ordinary) partnership.

Incorporated Business Organisation

An incorporated organisation is a legal entity in its own right. It must be created by a legal process and it continues in existence despite change in membership until the relevant legal procedure takes place to dissolve it. The organisation itself has obligations and liabilities and this means it carries out functions such as entering into contracts, employing staff, and leasing property in its own name. The owners of an incorporated business organisation have limited personal liability. The debts and obligations of the organisation are its own responsibility and not the responsibility of individual members, shareholders, or directors. If a limited company fails to carry out its health and safety obligations or discharges effluent into a river, it is the company itself that is liable and it may be sued or prosecuted. However, with incorporation and limited liability come regulation and disclosure requirements.

There are different types of incorporated organisations, and those most commonly used for running a business are private limited companies and public limited companies, and since 2001 there has been a growing use of limited liability partnerships (see Figure 15.1).

Figure 15.1 Business organisations

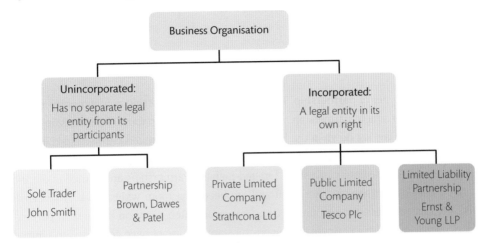

Sole Trader

The simplest business organisation to set up and the most flexible to operate is that of a sole trader. There are no regulations, disclosure, or public accountability requirements, nor are there rules governing the conduct of the business. However, a sole trader must comply with the same general obligations as all businesses, in relation to issues such as employment law and health and safety law. A sole trader is self-employed and, although his business is likely to be small, there is no limit to the size of the business. A sole trader could have a large turnover and numerous employees.

Any person can set up a business trading either under their own name or using a business name. If the business is carried on under a name that is different from the owner then the business name must comply with the Companies Act 2006 (ss 1200–1206). Under this Act, if a sole trader uses a business name that is not his own surname (with or without initials) he must state his name and address on various documents such as business letters, invoices, and orders, and display it on business premises where suppliers and customers have access. In addition, he must supply his name and address if requested by anyone who does business with the firm.

A sole trader can decide how to organise and run his business. He takes the profits and incurs the losses of the business. He is taxed as an individual, and, therefore, pays income tax on any profits made and may be liable for capital gains tax. A sole trader must inform HM Revenue and Customs when the business commenced, keep records showing the business expenses and profits, and make an annual self-assessment tax return.

A sole trader has unlimited liability, which means he is personally responsible for all the debts and liabilities of the business. If the business fails the sole trader will have to meet its debts with his own property and, if he is unable to do this, he may be declared bankrupt. A sole trader can cease trading at any time without any formalities for ending the business, and if he dies the business will automatically end.

Partnerships

There are three types of **partnership**. The first is a general partnership, sometimes referred to as an ordinary or simple partnership, which is the most common form of partnership and is governed by the law set down in the Partnership Act 1890. A limited partnership is formed under the Limited Partnerships Act 1907. It is not a common type of partnership, but it is used by some private equity investors. Limited Liability Partnerships are formed under the Limited Liability Partnerships Act 2000 and are becoming more widespread. Professional persons such as solicitors, accountants, and surveyors often carry on business in partnerships, usually as general partners although a substantial number have converted to Limited Liability Partnerships.

General (Ordinary) Partnership

In a partnership, the partners have come together for the purpose of carrying on a business with a view to making a profit. Each partner is self-employed and takes a share of the business profits and usually participates in the decision-making. A general partnership is an unincorporated association and has no legal existence distinct from the partners themselves. The partners are personally responsible for any debts and liabilities that the business runs up. It is important for people in a general partnership to trust each other because each partner is liable for all the debts of the whole partnership and, if one partner disappears, the other partners will be liable for his share of the partnership debts. A partnership can come into existence either by written or oral agreement or even be implied by the conduct of the parties.

Section 1 of the Partnership Act 1890 (PA 1890) defines a partnership as '... the relationship which subsists between persons carrying on a business in common with a view to profit'.

Therefore, a partnership is a relationship between two or more persons to carry on a business together with the intention of making a profit. The relationship between the partners is contractual. There must be two or more persons but a 'person' includes a 'legal person' and, therefore, companies as well as natural persons can be in partnership. There is no maximum number of partners that may be in a partnership. In December 2002 legal restrictions limiting some partnerships to a maximum of 20 partners were removed. In order for a partnership arrangement to be implied from a joint venture, there must be some sort of business activity. This can be an ongoing venture, or a single transaction where partners act together to complete a deal.

Mann v Darcy (1968)

Facts: An oral agreement was made between parties for the purchase and resale of 350 tons of potatoes.
Decision: The agreement was a single venture partnership.

Key Concept A partnership is an agreement between two or more persons to carry on a business together with the intention of making a profit. A general partnership is an unincorporated business where the partners have unlimited liability for the debts of the business.

Establishing a general partnership

There are no specific legal requirements governing the formation of a general partnership. It is a contractual situation and the general rules of contract apply. Being a contract, the partnership agreement is subject to the same contractual rules as other contracts relating to issues such as mistake, illegality, and misrepresentation. The partners can, within certain limits, agree to whatever terms they wish between themselves and any rights and duties as between partners set down in the PA 1890 can be varied by express or implied agreement.

A partnership can be created by **deed**, in writing, orally, or arise from conduct. Usually there is a written agreement made by deed setting out the terms of the partnership. This document is sometimes referred to as the 'Articles of Partnership' or the 'Partnership Deed'. It is advisable for partners to have a written partnership agreement so that, in the event of a dispute, the partners can seek guidance from the agreement as to how issues should be resolved. Many professional partnerships are governed by a complex, carefully constructed agreement. The partners can include whatever terms they wish in the agreement subject to the general restrictions of contract law. The agreement normally covers the issues such as the names of the partners and amount of capital provided by each partner, and whether interest is payable on capital contributions; the business name and type of business the partnership will be engaged in; how the profits (and losses) of the business are to be divided between the partners; matters governing management and employment; and rules about partnership disputes, new partners, and dissolution of the partnership.

If there is no partnership agreement, written or otherwise, or the agreement does not cover all issues, then the rules set down in PA 1890 apply in default. For example, a Partnership

Agreement may state that profits are to be divided 60 per cent to partner A and 40 per cent to partner B, but if the Agreement is silent about the share of the profits the rules set down in the PA 1890, s 24, will apply and profits will be divided equally.

Viewpoint Joseph Lott, Partner, Field Seymour Parkes

I am a solicitor and became a partner in my firm's Dispute Resolution Team in April 2008. My firm is a general partnership and currently has 17 partners made up of a mix of equity and salaried partners.

It has been very important for me to understand partnership law for two main reasons. Firstly, it was crucial that, when deciding whether to accept the offer of partnership, I weighed up the advantages (including non-financial incentives such as a greater say in the management of the firm) against the potential risks (such as the possibility, however remote, of having to contribute personally to the firm's debts). I am, however, fortunate to work for an extremely well run business where the advantages far outweigh the risks.

Secondly, I use my knowledge of partnership law in my day-to-day role within the litigation team. My team regularly acts for or against both general and limited liability partnerships, so understanding who can be sued, for what, and against whose assets Court judgments can be enforced, is fundamental. By way of example, we often advise on disputes involving partners' duties to each other (such as a breach of the duty of good faith), acrimonious dissolutions (where partners fall out and cannot agree on how partnership assets should be divided up), and insolvency proceedings against firms and/or individual named partners.

Commencement of a general partnership

A partnership begins when the partners begin their business activity. It does not begin when an agreement is made which could be prior to or after the parties embark upon business activities. One factor used by the Inland Revenue to ascertain when a partnership commences is the date of opening a partnership bank account. The business does not necessarily have to be actually trading for the partnership to be established.

Khan v Miah (2000)

Facts: The defendants wished to open an Indian restaurant and, having little money, agreed to go into partnership with the claimant who was going to provide some of the finance for the venture. Premises were found and arranged to be converted into a restaurant, and equipment was purchased. However, before the restaurant opened a dispute arose between the parties and the agreement between the defendants and the claimant was terminated. The question the court had to decide was whether a partnership had existed even though the restaurant had not yet begun to trade.

Decision: A partnership had existed. Many businesses require expenditure before commercial trading commences and, as this had been a joint venture undertaken with a view to profit, it had been a partnership.

The persons embarking upon the joint venture or running the business must have the intention of making a profit even if they actually make a loss. Therefore, a charitable scheme cannot be a partnership, nor is a partnership established if a group of traders agree to share expenses by contributing to a special fund which will be used to pay those expenses. This is because the traders have no intention of making a profit but are only intending to share expenses.

In order for a partnership to exist it is not necessary that all the partners take a percentage of the profits or have contributed to the capital of the partnership, although they are indications of the existence of a partnership. A partner who is entitled to a share of the profits is called an **equity partner**. In deciding if a partnership exists, a court will look at all the circumstances and sometimes, although a person only receives a fixed salary, and is referred to as a **salaried partner**, he may be deemed to be a full partner.

Stekel v Ellice (1973)

Facts: An accountant took on the claimant as a salaried partner and agreed that a partnership agreement would be drawn up and he would become a full partner after seven months. No agreement was drawn up and, when a disagreement between the parties arose, the court had to decide if the claimant was a partner.

Decision: The term 'salaried partner' could not as a matter of law be said necessarily to be or not to be a partner in the true sense. The question of whether a salaried partner is a 'full' partner depended on the substance of the relationship and the facts of the particular case. On the facts of this case the claimant was a full partner.

In the following case, although the defendant took no part in running the business and described himself as a '**sleeping partner**', the court stated that, in the circumstances of the case, he was a full partner and liable for debts of the partnership.

M Young Legal Associates Ltd v Zahid (2006)

Facts: A group of newly qualified solicitors wanted to set up in partnership but, in order to comply with legal requirements, they needed a partner with at least three years' experience. Lees, who had been qualified for over 25 years, agreed to be a partner and was paid a monthly sum. He did not take a share of profits and had not contributed to the setting up of the business. He claimed he was akin to a 'sleeping partner'. When the firm got into financial difficulties, the court had to decide if Lees was a partner and liable to the claimant.

Decision: Although Lees was paid a fixed sum irrespective of the firm's profits and had made no contribution to capital, the firm could not lawfully practise without Lees and therefore he was a full partner and liable to the claimant.

Key Concept *Salaried partner:* Many professional firms, such as accountants and solicitors, often have 'salaried partners' who are listed as partners on the firm's stationery but receive a salary rather than a share of the profits. Whether they are treated by the courts as general (full) partners depends on the circumstances of each situation.

Equity partner: This is a general (full) partner who takes a share of the profits after all expenses are met.

Sleeping partner: This is not a legal term but is sometimes used to describe a partner who invests capital in the firm but takes no part in the running of the business. Such a partner may be treated as a general (full) partner in respect of a firm's liabilities.

Name of a partnership

A partnership may be collectively known as a 'firm' (PA 1890, s 4). Business can be carried on under the firm's name and legal proceedings may be taken by and against the partners in the firm's name, but if the firm is found liable in a court action, judgment is made against the partners. The firm's name may be made up of the surnames of individual partners, with or without forenames or initials, and the corporate names of the corporate partners. If the name is not a combination of the partners' names then the choice of name is subject to restrictions set out in the Companies Act 2006 (CA 2006). Written approval of the Secretary of State for Business, Innovation and Skills is required before a business can use any name that is likely to imply that the business is connected with the Government or a local authority, or uses words such as 'Bank' or 'University'. A partnership can include the word 'company' or 'co', e.g. 'John Smith & Co', but must not use the term 'limited' or 'ltd' as part of its name. If a partnership does not trade under the name of all the partners, the name of each partner and their address for service of documents must be displayed in a prominent place on the business premises and on the firm's business documents (CA 2006, s 1200). Business premises include premises to which suppliers or customers have access. Obviously, if the partnership is very large, this may cause problems on stationery; therefore, the CA 2006 provides that, if there are more than 20 partners, the individual names do not have to be listed on business documents, but a list of partners must be kept at the firm's principal place of business, and there must be a statement in the documents referring to the list and its location. The list must be available for public inspection during office hours.

If the partnership (or any other business organisation) uses a name which is similar to a name already used by another business, the partnership may commit the tort of 'passing-off'. This is where the firm's name is so similar to that of another business that it is likely to confuse the public. The business with the original name can sue the other business for damages and obtain a court order to prevent the name being used. Under the CA 2006 (s 69) if a company registers a name which is the same as that of the partnership or so similar to suggest a connection then the partnership may make a complaint to the Company Names Adjudicator requesting that the company's name is changed (see Chapter 17).

Business Insight Domain names

Many businesses have a presence on the web and will wish to register a domain name (web address). Having decided on a domain name a check needs to be made to ensure the domain name is available for use. Nominet is the Internet registry for UK domain names and a free check can be made on their website to ensure that a name such as lucylovely.co.uk has not already been registered.

Some businesses trade in registering and then selling on domain names. In March 2009 it was reported that toy retailer Toys R Us paid $5.1m (£3.6m) for the Toys.com domain name. In 2010 sex.com was sold for $13m (£8.2m).

Key Concept A partnership can be collectively known as a 'firm'. Business can be carried on under the firm's name which may be the names of the partners or may be a different name. There are some restrictions on the names that can be used.

Relationship between Partners

A partnership is based on trust and good faith. Partners owe each other the duty to act honestly and for the benefit of the partnership as a whole. The partnership relationship is a fiduciary one (based on trust) as well as a contractual one. The partners owe certain duties to each other, in addition to any obligations set out in the partnership agreement or agreed orally between them. The PA 1890, s 5, states that partners are agents of the firm and of their fellow partners; therefore, the duties they owe to each other are similar to those owed by an agent to a principal.

Duties of partners

Partners owe each other a general duty of care in relation to the conduct of partnership affairs. They must act honestly and in good faith. The PA 1890, ss 28–30, set out a number of specific duties.

- *Duty of disclosure (s 28):* Partners must provide true accounts and full information on all things affecting the partnership, to all the other partners or their legal representatives.

- In *Law v Law*, considered next, the duty to disclose had been breached by one of the partners and, had the parties not already agreed to settle, the court would have set the contract aside.

Law v Law (1905)

Facts: Two brothers (William and James Law) were in partnership as woollen manufacturers. The business was carried on in Halifax. William lived in London for 30 years and had acted as the London representative of the firm but latterly had taken no part in the business. The accounts were irregularly prepared, and James was in the habit of paying William monthly sums of his share of the profits. James offered to buy his shares for £10,000. After the sale, William learnt that certain assets had not been disclosed to him.

Decision: The court stated that there was a duty of disclosure, and would have set the contract for sale aside but the brothers had agreed to settle for payment of £3,550 to William.

- *Duty to account (s 29):* Partners must account to the firm for any benefit obtained without consent from any transaction concerning the partnership, its property, its name, or its business connection. This duty is very wide and covers situations where a partner uses partnership property for his own benefit, makes a personal profit out of acting on behalf of the partnership, or uses any business connection gained from the partnership.

- *Duty not to compete (s 30):* Where a partner competes with partnership business without consent of other partners, that partner is liable to account to the partnership for any profits made in the course of the competing business. Profits will only have to be accounted for if the partner had not disclosed that he was competing with the firm.

Don King Productions Inc v Warren (1999)

Facts: King and Warren promoters set up in partnership working together promoting and managing boxers in Europe. Warren entered into some personal contracts with boxers.

Decisions: The partnership was entitled to the profits from Warren's personal contracts.

Rights of partners

The PA 1890, s 24, sets out the rights of partners; however, partners can agree not to be bound by the rights set out in the Act and instead make their own arrangements. If the partners have not made an agreement on all or some of the issues covered by s 24, then this section applies in default. The rights set out in s 24 are as follows:

- *To share equally in the capital and profits of the business (also to contribute equally to losses) (s 24(1)):* Although a partnership agreement may be silent on this matter, a court will look at the conduct of the partners to ascertain if there is evidence of a contrary intention to share capital and profits equally. For example, if the partners have put unequal amounts of capital into a business, a court may presume that the partners by their conduct intended to rebut s 24, and intended their share of capital would be divided according to the percentage of capital originally invested.

- *To be indemnified by the firm for any liabilities incurred or payments made in the course of the firm's business (s 24(2)):* A partner is entitled to recover any expenses incurred by him whilst carrying out partnership business, and he is also entitled to expenses incurred while doing anything that was necessary to preserve the business or property of the firm. If a partner travels to London to look at the possibility of purchasing partnership property, the partner will be able to claim his travel expenses from the partnership. The second part of s 24(2) is similar to that of an agency by necessity (see Chapter 9) and, although a partner does not have to prove he was unable to communicate with his partners before he acted, if he is able to communicate with them and acts without doing so, he may find he has failed in his duty to act in good faith.

- *Entitled to interest of 5 per cent on payments made to the partnership which are beyond the amount of capital which it was agreed that the partner would contribute (s 24(3)):* Partners are not entitled to interest on the capital sums agreed to be contributed to the partnership by a partner (s 24(4)) but extra payments are treated as loans to the partnership. In practice, if capital payments or loans are made to partnerships, the partners usually make their own agreements about rates of interest.

- *To take part in the management of the business (s 24(5)):* All partners may take part in the management of the business. The partnership agreement may limit the extent of one or more of the partners' control of the business but it should not totally exclude a partner from management, as the essence of a partnership is the 'carrying on of a business in common'. However, there is nothing in the PA 1890 to state that a partner must take part in the management of a partnership. A partner may be a 'sleeping partner' and have no management responsibilities if he wishes but, unless he is also a limited partner under the Limited Partnerships Act 1907, he will be responsible for all the partnership debts and liabilities.

- *A partner is not entitled to a salary (s 24(6)):* The basic rule is a partner will take a share of the profits rather than be entitled to a salary. However, in many partnerships it is agreed that one or more of the partners should take a salary, either because they do a greater amount of work for the partnership, or they have less of a share in the profits. Although this section is often altered by a partnership agreement, if it is not altered, one partner will not be entitled to a salary or a greater share of the profits merely because he does the majority of the work for the business.

- *No person can be introduced to a partnership without the consent of all the existing partners (s 24(7)):* A partnership is based on mutual trust and any new partner brought into a firm will have the power to impose financial burdens on the other partners, so it is important that all the partners approve of a new partner. Sometimes a partnership agreement will override this section and allow for persons, often relatives of the existing partners, to be brought in without approval of all existing partners.

- *No changes can be made to the nature of the partnership business unless all partners agree, but ordinary matters connected with the partnership can be decided by a majority of partners (s 24(8)):* This means, for example, that a decision to change the partnership business from a fruit wholesaler to a taxi service would require a unanimous decision by all the partners, but a decision to advertise on radio would only need a majority decision.

- *The firm's books must be kept at the firm's place of business or the principal place of business if there is more than one, and every partner must have access to the books to inspect and copy any of them (s 28(9)):* It is important that partners are aware of financial issues relating to partnership business as they will be personally liable for partnership debts.

Key Concept Partners have duties and rights under the Partnership Act 1890. They owe each other a general duty to act honestly and in good faith. They have a duty of disclosure, a duty to account, and a duty not to compete. Partners may make their own agreement on rights but if there is no agreement then the provisions of the Partnership Act 1890 apply in default.

Partnership property

The assets of a business may be owned collectively by all the partners or, alternatively, it is possible for property to be in the ownership of one partner and be used by the partnership. Any property bought with money belonging to the firm is deemed to have been bought on account of the firm, and is partnership property. It is important to distinguish between partnership property and the personal property of the partners, because partnership property must only be used for the purposes of the business and any increase in value belongs to the partnership. On dissolution of a partnership its assets are used to pay any debts or other liabilities before personal property is utilised. When a partnership is being dissolved, disputes may arise as to whether assets used by the partnership were purchased by one of the partners and lent to the partnership, or were purchased by one of the partners on behalf of the firm and are owned jointly by the partnership. To avoid such disputes, express agreements should be made by the partnership as to which assets are owned jointly by the partnership.

Expulsion from partnership

The majority of partners cannot expel a partner unless power to do so has been conferred by express agreement between the partners (PA 1890, s 25). This is to prevent a partner from being victimised by other partners; however, partners may be justified in expelling a partner if they no longer totally trust him. Often a partnership agreement will state that a partner who breaks partnership rules can be expelled by the majority, but even if the partnership agreement allows expulsion, the other partners must act in good faith and cannot unjustifiably expel a partner.

Blisset v Daniel (1853)

Facts: The partnership agreement allowed expulsion by majority. The majority of partners purported to expel one partner in order to obtain his share of the partnership at a discount.
Decision: The expulsion was not carried out in good faith and, therefore, was not valid.

Kelly v Denman (1996)

Facts: The partnership agreement allowed expulsion by majority. The majority of partners wanted to expel one of the partners for some time and did expel the partner after he was involved in a tax fraud.
Decision: The expulsion was for a legitimate reason and carried out in good faith and, therefore, was valid.

Any changes to the rights of partners can be varied by express or implied agreement of all the partners (PA 1890, s 19).

Partners and Third Parties

The PA 1890 covers the relationship of partners with persons outside the partnership. It deals with contractual situations where a partner enters into a contract with a third party on behalf of the partnership, and tortious situations where a partner commits a tort while carrying out partnership business, such as negligently crashing into another vehicle while driving on partnership business.

The authority of partners to bind the firm

In the course of running a business it is inevitable that a partnership will enter into contractual relationships with third parties; for example, a partnership manufacturing goods may enter into a contract with a third party to purchase raw materials. It is important to understand when an agreement entered into by an individual partner will bind the whole firm. The key to this question depends on the application of agency law. Every partner is an agent of the firm and all the co-partners (PA 1890, s 5). Actions done in the usual course of the firm's business will bind the firm, unless the partner had no authority to act and the third party knows this, or the third party does not know or believe him to be a partner. If the third party genuinely believes a partner has authority to act, it is likely the partnership will be bound by the transaction unless the transaction is clearly outside the ambit of the usual course of business. It is assumed that all partners in a trading partnership business have authority to bind co-partners in matters such as selling and buying goods, receiving payments of debts due to the firm, employing staff, borrowing money, and using the firms' goods as security for a loan.

The partners may by agreement restrict the general powers of one or more of the partners and, if a partner acts outside the restrictions imposed, the action will still be valid if the co-partners gave prior approval to exceed authority or approval after the event, or if the partner acted within the usual scope of the firm's business and the third party was not actually aware of the restriction on the partner's authority (see Figure 15.2).

Mercantile Credit v Garrod (1962)

Facts: Parkin and Garrod were partners in a garage business which mainly dealt with letting garages and repairing cars. The partnership agreement expressly precluded the sale of cars. Parkin sold a car which he had no authority to sell to the claimant; the owner of the car reclaimed the car from the claimant, who then sought to recover the money he had paid for it from Garrod.

Decision: It was within the usual authority of persons in a garage business to sell cars and, as the claimant had no knowledge of the restriction on Parkin, he could recover the cost of the car from either partner.

Liability for contracts

Partners are **jointly and severally liable** for the firm's contracts. This means that they are each liable for the whole contract in addition to being liable together. A claimant will usually sue the partnership using the firm's name and if the claimant wins the action, each of

Figure 15.2 Liability of the partnership

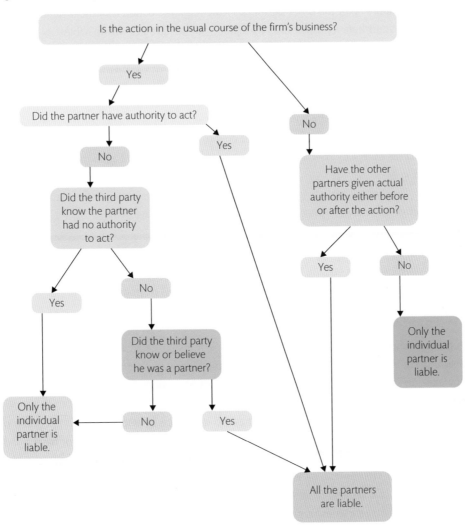

the partners is liable to pay the claim in full. If one partner pays more than his share, he has the right to a contribution from the other partners. If a claimant only sues one partner and obtains judgment against him but is unable to recover the sum owed from him, the Civil Liability (Contribution) Act 1978 allows for a further court action to be taken against the other partners.

Liability for torts

Partners are jointly and severally liable for torts, or for other wrongful acts, committed by a partner in the ordinary course of business, or done with the actual authority of the co-partners

(PA 1890, s 10). If the action is outside the ordinary course of business it must be committed with express approval of the other partners. However, if the action is in the ordinary course of business, even where a partner acts wrongfully, all the partners will be liable.

Dubai Aluminium Co Ltd v Salaam (2003)

Facts: A solicitor committed a tort by setting up fraudulent agreements for his clients which induced the claimant to pay out sums amounting to $50 million. The solicitor did not benefit from the frauds except by payment of his ordinary fees. The claimant sued the partners of the acting solicitor.

Decision: The solicitor had committed a wrongful action but was acting in the course of business; therefore, the other partners were liable under s 10 of the PA 1890.

If the wrongful action is outside the ordinary course of business and has not been authorised by the other partners, only the partner committing the act is responsible.

Liability of outgoing and incoming partners

A partner who retires from a firm is liable for partnership debts and obligations incurred before his retirement (PA 1890, s 17). However, the retiring partner may be discharged from any existing liabilities by an agreement to that effect between himself, members of the firm as a newly constituted partnership, and the creditors.

This agreement, known as a *novation*, may be expressed or implied from the course of dealing between the creditors and the newly constituted firm. Creditors do not have to accept a novation, and if it is not accepted, the retiring partner is responsible for any debts due at the time of his retirement, although the other partners may agree to indemnify him. The retiring partner is also liable for future contracts with people who were customers of the firm unless notice of the retirement is given to those existing customers. Notice must also be given to potential future customers who are aware that the partner is a member of the firm, but for potential customers notice is assumed by placing an advertisement of the retirement in the London Gazette. Notice does not have to be given to future customers who were unaware of the partnership.

A person who is admitted as a partner into an existing firm is not liable to the creditors of the firm for anything done before he became a partner unless the new partner accepts existing liability by agreeing to a novation.

'Holding out' as a partner

Persons 'hold themselves out' to be partners if they lead others to believe they are partners when in fact they are not. Where a person, either expressly or through their conduct, represents themselves or allows themselves to be represented as a partner in a particular firm, then that person is liable as a partner (PA 1890, s 14). In order to be liable as a partner, the third parties must have relied on the representation.

Nationwide Anglia Building Society v Lewis (1997)

Facts: Lewis, a sole practitioner solicitor, employed Williams as his salaried partner. Williams' name was added to the headed paper. Lewis acted negligently and was sued by the claimant building society. The court had to decide if Williams was a partner and, therefore, liable, and even if he was not a partner whether he was liable as 'holding himself out' as a partner.

Decision: The court found on the evidence that Williams had not been a partner in the firm, nor was he liable under PA 1890, s 14, as the claimant had had no dealings with Williams, there was no evidence that they noticed he was a partner, and they could not show they had relied on him being held out as a partner.

Dissolution of Partnership

A partnership may be brought to an end either by agreement, automatically under the PA 1890, or by a court order. As a partnership is a contract, it is possible that the partnership agreement itself expressly states how the partnership can be terminated.

Unless the partnership agreement states otherwise, the PA 1890, ss 32–34 provide for the automatic dissolution of a partnership on the following grounds:

- The expiry of a fixed term: this is where a partnership is for a limited term and expires at the end of the agreed term.

- The expiry of a particular purpose: this is where a partnership is entered into for a single adventure or undertaking and it expires when that adventure or undertaking is completed.

- By giving notice: if a partnership is entered into for an undefined time, it may be dissolved by any partner giving notice to the others of his intention that the partnership be dissolved. Once notice is given it cannot be withdrawn, except with the consent of the other partners. Some partnerships state that the partnership can only be dissolved through mutual consent, in which case one partner will not be able to end the partnership by notice unless the others consent.

- The death or bankruptcy of any partner: the partnership agreement often provides that, on the death of one partner, the surviving partners are to continue the business.

- A partner's share in the partnership becomes subject to a charge: the other partners can dissolve the partnership where there is a charge put on one of the partner's share in the partnership.

- Where the continuation of the partnership is illegal: in the following case, the partnership was dissolved because solicitors can only legally practise if they hold a current practising certificate.

Hudgell, Yeates and Co v Watson (1978)

Facts: One of the partners in a firm of solicitors forgot to renew his practising certificate. It was illegal for him to practise as a solicitor without a certificate.

Decision: The partnership automatically ended as it was illegal.

A court may order the dissolution of a partnership on the application by a partner in the following circumstances (PA 1890, s 35):

- A partner becomes mentally ill or permanently incapacitated for some other reason.

- A partner's conduct prejudicially affects the carrying on of the business. This includes conduct not directly associated with the business, and, therefore, may include conviction of a criminal offence not connected to the business but which might lead to loss of business if customers knew of it.

- A partner persistently breaches the partnership agreement or conducts himself in such a manner that it is not reasonably practicable for the other partners to carry on in business with him.

- The business can only be carried on at a loss.

- It is just and equitable to dissolve the partnership. This ground allows a court to dissolve a partnership where there has been a breakdown of the relationship between partners.

When a partnership is dissolved all the partnership assets are gathered and payments are made in the following order:

1. All debts to outsiders.

2. Loans made to the partnership by the partners.

3. The individual partners will be repaid the capital sum they put into the partnership. If there is not enough in the partnership funds to repay all the capital, unless previously agreed, the partners contribute to the lost capital in the same proportion as they share in the profits.

4. The remaining sums are paid to the partners in the same proportion as they shared in the profits.

Where a partnership is insolvent and does not have enough assets to pay its debts, the losses are first paid out of profits, then capital and finally the partners individually in the proportion in which they were to share profits. However, where a partnership is insolvent and one or more of the partners is personally insolvent and is unable to pay their share of the losses, the solvent partners will be liable to pay the shares of insolvent partners.

Limited Partnerships

The Limited Partnerships Act 1907 provides for the setting up of a limited partnership. This is not a business structure that is often used and must not be confused with Limited Liability Partnerships which have been in existence since 2001 (see later). A limited partnership allows for one or more of the partners to have limited liability, provided at least one of the partners has full liability. There is no upper limit to the number of limited partners provided at least one partner has full liability. The partner or partners who have full liability are liable for all debts and obligations of the firm and are referred to as general partners. Limited partners are not liable for any of the debts and obligations of the firm beyond the sum they have contributed as capital to the partnership. A limited partner contributes money or property with a stated monetary value to the partnership, which usually cannot be withdrawn until the partnership ceases. If some or any of it is withdrawn, the limited partner will be liable up to the amount withdrawn. A limited partner may be a natural person or a company.

Limited partners cannot bind their firm in any transaction, and in order to retain their limited status, they must not participate in the management and running of the business. A limited partner who does take part in the management of the firm will be liable for all the debts and obligations incurred while doing so.

All limited partnerships must be registered at Companies House and, until registered, the limited partnership will be regarded as a general partnership. On registration, various details must be given, including the date when the partnership commenced, its name and place of business, the nature of its business, the names of the general and limited partners, and the sum contributed by each limited partner.

The restrictions on the choice of name are similar to those of general partnerships. In addition, the Registrar will not register a name that is the same or similar to a company, other legal body, or limited partnership already on the register, and from 1 October 2009, all new limited partnerships have to include either 'Limited Partnership' or 'LP' at the end of their names (or Welsh equivalent). In practice there are few limited partnerships in existence, as generally someone wishing to limit their liability or participation of management in a business is more likely to become a shareholder in a limited company.

Limited Liability Partnerships

The Limited Liability Partnerships Act 2000 introduced a new form of business structure, a Limited Liability Partnership (LLP). The Act came into force in April 2001 and additional rules relating to the organisation and running of LLPs have been made by secondary legislation including the Limited Liability Partnerships (Application of Companies Act 2006) Regulations 2009. An LLP is very different from a general partnership or a limited partnership, and in some respects it is more like a limited company. An LLP is a body corporate and is a legal entity, which means similar to a company; it has a legal personality separate from that of its members. The persons involved in LLPs are called members as opposed to partners. The LLP itself is liable up to the extent of its assets but the liability of each of its members is limited. The LLP can do all the things a natural individual or company can do, such as enter into contracts, hold property in its own name, and sue or be sued. Any alteration of membership of an LLP does not affect its existence, and, therefore, if a member leaves, the LLP will continue to exist.

An LLP must register its annual audited accounts with the Companies Registrar, and the accounts are available for public inspection. Although similar to a limited company in many respects, the LLP has the organisational flexibility of a partnership and is taxed as a partnership. The tax position may be an advantage to members of LLPs because they are taxed on their share of the profits, whereas a company must pay corporation tax and its shareholders must pay income tax on dividends they received.

Setting up a Limited Liability Partnership

An LLP may be formed where two or more persons are associated for the purpose of carrying on a lawful business with a view to profit. As with general partnerships, businesses must be run with a view to making a profit. Any general partnership in existence may convert to an LLP, transferring any partnership assets from the partners to the LLP. Alternatively a new business may be formed as an LLP, but a limited company cannot convert to an LLP.

An incorporation document setting up an LLP must be registered with the Registrar of Companies at Companies House. The incorporation document states the name of the LLP and where its registered office is situated (in England, Wales, or Scotland), the address of the registered office, the name, address, and date of birth of each member, and which of its members are to be designated members. The members must all sign, stating they consent to act, and there must be a statement of compliance which is completed by a solicitor or one of the members.

The name of an LLP must end either with the words 'Limited Liability Partnership', or 'LLP' (or Welsh equivalent). The rules relating to the choice of name are similar to the rules for the naming of companies. Certain names such as 'National', 'Trade Union', and 'British' need special approval, and names that are too similar to names of other LLPs or companies on the register will not be registered. The details of the internal relationship between the members of an LLP are not registered at Companies House, and are a private matter dealt with by the partnership itself. Unlike a company, there are no requirements for the LLP to be managed in a particular way, nor is there any limitation on the type of business that an LLP may carry on.

Members of an LLP

The participants of an LLP are called members, and the members may be individuals or companies. There must be at least two members of an LLP. If membership falls to only one member, and the partnership continues to carry on business for more than six months, that one member will no longer have limited liability but will be personally liable for all debts of the business. There is no maximum number of persons who may be members.

There must be at least two designated members, and if at any time the number of designated members falls below two, all members will be treated as designated members. Designated members have the same rights and duties towards the LLP as any other member, but the law places extra responsibilities on them. In particular, they are responsible for ensuring certain documents are properly prepared and registered at Companies House. Their duties are similar to those of company directors and secretaries, and include signing the accounts on behalf of all the members and delivering them to the Registrar of Companies, and notifying the Registrar of any changes in membership or registered address of the LLP.

Membership ceases on death (or dissolution in the case of a corporate member), by agreement with the other members, or by giving reasonable notice to the other members.

Key Concept A Limited Liability Partnership is a body corporate and has a legal entity separate from that of its members. However, it has the organisational flexibility of a partnership and is taxed as a partnership.

Rights and Duties of Members

The mutual rights and duties of members to each other and between members and the LLP itself are governed by the limited liability partnership agreement and the general law. The agreement may be made before an LLP is set up or on its formation. There is no legal requirement for an LLP to have a written partnership agreement although in practice they generally do. If the members have not agreed on various matters, the membership will be subject to the rules set out in the Limited Liability Partnerships Act 2000 (LLPA 2000) and the 2009 Regulations (as amended). These default provisions are similar to those made by the PA 1890 except, unlike general partners in a partnership, the members of an LLP will not have to share the losses of the LLP as the LLP is responsible for its own losses.

The default provisions in the LLPA 2000 and the 2009 Regulations are as follows:

- All members are entitled to share equally in the capital and profits of the LLP.
- The LLP must indemnify every member for payments made or liabilities incurred, in carrying out the ordinary and proper business of the LLP, or for anything done that was necessary to preserve the business or property of the LLP.
- Every member may take part in the management of the LLP.
- No member is entitled to payment for participating in the business or management of the LLP.
- No person can be introduced as a new member or given an interest in an LLP without the consent of all existing members.
- Any differences arising from the running of the business may be decided by majority decision, but no change can be made to the type of business carried on without the consent of all members.
- The books and records of the LLP must be made available for inspection at the registered office or an alternative address. Every member must have access to inspect and copy them.
- Each member shall provide true accounts and full information on all things affecting the LLP to any other member or his legal representative.
- If a member, without the consent of the LLP, carries on any business of the same nature as the LLP, competing with it, he must account for and pay over to the LLP all profits made by him in that business.
- Every member must account to the LLP for any benefit he gets from any transaction concerning the LLP or from any use of the LLP's property or business connection, unless the benefit is received with the consent of the LLP.
- A member cannot be expelled by the majority of other members unless there is an express agreement between all members.

The default provisions will be assumed to be part of the partnership agreement unless the members have agreed different rules.

Every member of an LLP is an agent of the LLP and as an agent is able to enter into contracts on behalf of the LLP (LLPA 2000, s 6). However, the limited liability partnership agreement may limit the authority of members to make particular contracts. If there is a limitation on authority, the LLP will still be bound by a contract made by a member acting outside his authority, unless the third party knew the member had no authority or the third party did not know or believe him to be a member of the LLP. Unlike a general partnership where each of the partners will be bound by a contract entered into by one of the partners, it is the LLP that will be bound. An LLP is liable for the torts committed by its members provided they were committed in the course of the business of the LLP or authorised by the LLP (LLPA 2000, s 4).

Liability and Creditor Protection

Members' liability is limited to the amount of capital introduced into the partnership. There are no restrictions that apply to maintaining the capital in the partnership, and members can agree to withdraw capital sums. Creditors get some protection from the requirement for LLPs to file accounts.

Financial Disclosure

LLPs are required by law to prepare and publish annual accounts. The form and content of the accounts and the audit requirement are the same as for limited companies. The necessity of having to publish accounts and other financial information is a major disadvantage of an LLP over a general partnership. There has been criticism of the need of disclosure as, although a company does have to publish the same financial material, the rules are there to protect shareholders (the owners of the company) against the directors (the managers of the company), whereas in an LLP this is not the case as there are no shareholders and the members are the managers.

Insolvency and Winding Up

An LLP does not dissolve when a member leaves but it may be wound up in the same manner as limited companies. Once an LLP is wound up it ceases to exist. An LLP may be wound up compulsorily by a court order or voluntarily by its members. The provisions relating to winding up and insolvency of companies also apply to LLPs. If an LLP has any remaining assets these are distributed in the same order as a company's assets. The laws relating to wrongful and fraudulent trading also apply to members. (For further information on insolvency and winding up see Chapter 18.)

Business Insight

Ernst & Young (Accountants) were the first partnership to convert to an LLP in June 2001. By November 2014 over 52,500 active LLPs were registered at Companies House. In comparison, in November 2014 there were over 3 million active limited companies registered.

Companies

The company form of organisation is used by many businesses of widely different purposes, functions, and sizes. The flexibility of its structure can meet the needs of the one-man business up to the international corporation. The most important feature of a company is that, once formed, it has its own distinct legal personality separate from its members (shareholders), directors, or employees. The most common type of company is a registered company which has been formed by complying with the procedure set down by the Companies Acts.

A company may be created in three ways:

- *Grant of Royal Charter:* This is a charter granted by the Crown under special powers given to the Crown by Parliament or through the common law. Charters are used to incorporate learned societies and professional bodies such as the Institute of Chartered Accountants in England and Wales. Some universities have been set up under Royal Charter, as was the BBC. This form of incorporation is no longer used for trading companies, but was used to set up such companies in the past. The P&O Ferry Company was incorporated by Royal Charter in 1840 as the Peninsular & Oriental Steam Navigation Company.

- *Act of Parliament:* Statutory companies are created by a special Act of Parliament which also sets out the powers, rights, and liabilities of the company. This was formerly used for public utilities such as gas, electricity, and the railways. However, under privatisation legislation, these former statutory companies were replaced by public limited companies. There are still some organisations set up under statute such as the Health & Safety Executive. The Olympic Delivery Authority was set up by the London Olympic Games and Paralympic Games Act 2006.

- *Registration under the Companies Acts:* A business may be incorporated as a registered company. Since 1844 companies have been permitted to acquire the status of a corporation by complying with the registration procedure through the Registrar of Companies. The current legislation is in the CA 2006 which came into force between 2006 and 2009. Previously, companies were regulated by earlier Companies Acts.

Today, most companies have been and are created by complying with the registration requirements contained in the Companies Act in force at the time of registration.

The Registered Company

A company is created by registration under the CA 2006 or, if formed before 2009, under the procedures set out in the Companies Act 1985 (or previous company legislation). The registration process involves sending certain documents to the Registrar of Companies at

Companies House. The Registrar checks the documents are in order, and issues a certificate of incorporation. Once the certificate is issued the company exists as a separate legal person.

There are different types of registered companies. A company may be a public or a private company. A public company must be limited by shares, and a private company is usually limited although it is possible to have an unlimited private company. A private company may be limited by shares or by guarantee.

Since 2005 a public or a private company may be set up as a community interest company. A company limited by shares, which could be either a public or a private company, is owned by its members (shareholders) but managed by its directors. In a small company, the shareholders are often the directors and manage the company as well as own it. A large company is usually run by a board of directors and its shareholders have little to do with the day-to-day running of the company.

Key Concept A company has a legal personality separate from its members. A registered company limited by shares may be either a public limited company or a private limited company.

Public companies

A public company is a company whose certificate of incorporation states that it is a public company. To obtain this certificate, from the Registrar of Companies, the company needs to comply with the following conditions:

- The company's constitutional document must state that it is a public limited company.

- The name of the company must end with 'public limited company', 'plc', or the Welsh equivalent.

- The company's allotted share capital must not be less than the statutory minimum, which is currently set at £50,000.

- The company must have limited liability.

A company cannot commence trading as a public company until the Registrar of Companies has issued a certificate (CA 2006, s 761). Only public companies are allowed to seek finance from the general public by making a general offer to the public at large to buy their shares. Private companies cannot offer their shares to the public. Public companies make up about one per cent of all registered companies, but are usually much larger than private companies. A public company may also be a listed company, in which case its shares can be traded on the London Stock Exchange. Public companies that are not listed on the Stock Exchange can trade their shares on the Alternative Investment Market. The majority of shareholders of public companies do not take part in the management of the company. Public companies are subject to additional restrictions designed to protect shareholders. For example, there are greater controls over the distribution of payments to shareholders and public companies have to have at least two directors, whereas a private company needs only one director.

It is possible for a private company to re-register as a public company if it meets the necessary criteria. The majority of public companies started life as private limited companies and converted to public limited companies after they had become successfully established in business.

Private companies

These are often, but not always, small-scale enterprises operated and owned by individuals who are actively involved in the day-to-day running of the venture.

Private unlimited companies

Although the majority of companies have limited liability, it is possible to form a private unlimited company. This is quite a rare type of company and, although the company is a separate legal entity and therefore enters into its own transactions, each member of the company is fully liable for the company's debts. The members are, therefore, in a similar position to that of partners in a partnership. The advantage of an unlimited company over a limited company is that it does not have to file its annual accounts or reports at Companies House, and, therefore, its business is not open to public inspection. The advantage it has over a general partnership is that the company is still a separate entity and has perpetual succession (it does not end on the death of a member). However, because members are liable for the debts of the company, an unlimited company is not usually used as a trading company but is more likely to be used for holding land or other investments.

Private limited companies

A private limited company may be limited by shares or limited by guarantee (see Figure 15.3). The majority of limited companies are limited by shares. Where a company is limited by shares, the liability of its shareholders is limited to any amount unpaid on their shares. A private limited company must have at least one director, and at least one shareholder, who could be the same person. In a company limited by guarantee there are no shareholders. The members give a guarantee to contribute towards the assets of the company in the event of its being wound up insolvent. However, the guarantee is usually nominal, frequently just £1. Most companies limited by guarantee contain a non-profit distribution clause, and, therefore, members do not have a right to a share in dividends or any surplus on the winding up of the company, but the company normally has a one member, one vote system so all its members can have an equal voice. As companies limited by guarantee have very limited capital they are not a suitable form of organisation to use for a trading company. They are traditionally associated with charities, trade associations, and not-for-profit ventures.

Figure 15.3 Types of registered companies

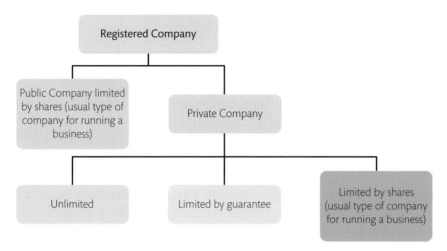

Community Interest Company

A Community Interest Company (CIC) is a relatively new type of company set up under the provisions of the Companies (Audit Investigations and Social Enterprises) Act 2004 which came into force on 1 July 2005. A CIC combines the flexibility of the company structure with special features, ensuring that CICs carry on their activities and use their assets for the benefit of the community. In order to become a CIC, a company has to satisfy a community interest test, confirming that it will pursue purposes beneficial to the community and will not serve an unduly restricted group of beneficiaries. A CIC may be a private company limited by guarantee, or a public or private company limited by shares. There are now almost 10,000 registered CICs and these companies are involved in a range of different social enterprises. If the CIC is set up as a company limited by shares it can provide dividends to investors from profits it makes, but these dividends are subject to a limit. Any capital the company makes is locked into the company and, if the company is dissolved, surplus assets must be transferred to another CIC or a charity (see Figure 15.4). CICs are subject to oversight by the Independent Regulator of Community Interest Companies, who determines whether companies are eligible to be CICs.

Holding and subsidiary companies

Some business enterprises operate through a linked structure of separate companies. Each of these companies exists as a separate corporate entity in its own right. A *holding company*, sometimes called a parent company, is a company that has a dominant interest in its subsidiary companies. The holding company controls the subsidiary companies by holding the majority of the voting rights, and having the right to appoint or remove the majority of the board of directors of the subsidiary companies. Under the CA 2006 there is a duty to disclose this relationship, and the holding company must file additional group accounts.

Figure 15.4 Structure of Community Interest Companies

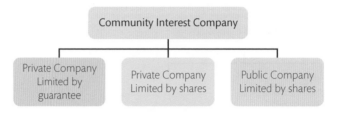

Corporate Entity: Separate Legal Personality

Once a company is formed it has its own **separate legal personality**, distinct from its shareholders, directors, or employees; it is a corporate entity. In the following case the court stated that the company was liable for its own debts.

Salomon v Salomon & Co (1897)

Facts: Salomon carried on business as a leather merchant and boot manufacturer. In 1892, he formed a limited company to take over the business. He was the major shareholder and his wife, daughter, and four sons had one share each. The company paid £39,000 to Salomon for the business by issuing him with 20,000 shares at £1 each, £10,000 in debentures (loans from Salomon) secured by a floating charge on the company's assets, and the balance in cash. The floating charge on the assets made Salomon a secured creditor, which meant that in the event of the company failing he would get paid before an unsecured creditor. The company fell on hard times less than a year later, and a liquidator was appointed. The assets were enough to pay off the debentures but not the unsecured creditors. The unsecured creditors claimed that Salomon and the company were one.

Decision: The House of Lords stated that the company was a separate and distinct legal person. It had been formed without any fraud by Salomon, and the creditors knew they were dealing with a limited company. As Salomon was a separate person from the company, he was entitled to the remaining assets in payment of the secured loan he had made to the company.

Contracts and torts

A company as a separate entity has contractual capacity and it can enter into contracts and sue and be sued in its own name. The company acts through its directors. It is the directors who actually negotiate and sign contracts on behalf of the company, but it is the company itself that has the rights and liabilities that the contract creates. If the company suffers a breach of contract, it is for the company to take the appropriate remedial action. In the following case the director was not personally liable for negligent advice.

Williams v Natural Life Health Foods Ltd (1998)

Facts: C invested their savings into a franchise business on the basis of statements made negligently by a director of the franchisor company. The company became insolvent and C made a claim against the director.

Decision: The veil of incorporation would only be lifted in exceptional circumstances. A company director was not personally liable for negligent advice given by him as director unless he had willingly accepted personal responsibility. In this case there was no evidence to show the director had assumed personal responsibility.

Criminal liability

Companies may be liable in criminal law for committing crimes and subject to financial penalties. Offences vary in seriousness from minor issues such as failing to file documents with Companies House to major offences such as corporate manslaughter under the Corporate Manslaughter and Corporate Homicide Act 2007.

Ownership of property

Business assets are owned by a company in its own name. If a company needs to borrow money, its own property can be used as security for a loan. As business assets are owned by a company, it is the company that is responsible for insuring them.

Macaura v Northern Assurance Co Ltd (1925)

Facts: Macaura was the owner of a timber estate and he formed a company and sold the timber to it for £42,000. The company was financed by the issue of 42,000 fully paid up shares to Macaura and his nominees. Macaura was also an unsecured creditor for £19,000. Macaura took out an insurance policy in his own name. Later most of the timber was destroyed by fire. Macaura claimed on his insurance.

Decision: Macaura could not claim as he did not have an insurable interest in the timber (a person cannot claim for loss of goods owned by another party). The company owned the timber and the insurance policy should have been taken out in the company's name.

Perpetual succession

A company has **perpetual succession**. This means that it continues in existence indefinitely unless it is liquidated by its shareholders or by a court order. If a shareholder dies, his shares are inherited by others. When a company is liquidated all its assets are realised, and distributed to creditors and shareholders according to legal rules of priority. If the assets do not cover all the liabilities, the shareholders will not be asked to make up the shortfall for creditors, but they will have lost the money they invested in the company.

Lifting the veil of incorporation

The principle of a company having its own legal entity, separate from that of its shareholders, means that only the company is responsible for its liabilities and its shareholders are said to be protected by 'a veil of incorporation'. The shareholders are hidden from view and protected from incurring liabilities. However, there are circumstances where the veil of incorporation will be lifted and the business treated as if it were being run by its individual shareholders or directors. Lifting the veil of incorporation can be authorised by a court or by statute. A court will look behind the company façade if the company is being used for a fraudulent purpose to evade legal responsibilities as in the following two cases.

Gilford Motor Co v Horne Ltd (1933)

Facts: Horne had been employed by GMC Ltd and in his contract of employment he agreed that, if he left GMC Ltd's employment, he would not approach the company's customers to try and get them to transfer their custom to any similar business which Horne might run himself. Horne left and formed a limited company in which he was the major shareholder, and sent out circulars to customers of GMC Ltd inviting them to do business with his company. GMC Ltd sought an injunction (court order) from the court restraining Horne from soliciting their customers.

Decision: The court granted an injunction preventing Horne and his company from soliciting GMC Ltd's customers. The corporate structure could not be used by Horne to evade his contractual duties and engage in business under a cloak or sham.

Jones v Lipman (1962)

Facts: Lipman entered into a contract to sell land to Jones; however, before the transaction was completed, he changed his mind about selling the land. To avoid a court order of specific performance (an order to complete the contract), he transferred the land to a company which he had bought for that purpose. He had bought all the shares of the company in his own name and that of a nominee. Lipman contended that, as he no longer owned the land, he could not be ordered to transfer it to Jones.

Decision: The company was a sham set up for the purpose of evading specific performance of the original contract for sale. The court ordered the transfer of the land to Jones.

Where companies are part of a group of companies they are usually treated as separate entities. In *Adams v Cape Industries* (1990) the court stated that the corporate veil of subsidiary companies would only be lifted if the subsidiary acted as an agent of the parent company, if the corporate structure is a sham, or if there is a statutory provision to treat the group as a single economic unit.

→ corporate veil wasn't lifted.

In *Petrodel Resources Ltd v Prest* (2013) the Supreme Court confirmed that courts had the power to pierce the corporate veil but only in very limited circumstances where it was necessary to do so and there is no other effective remedy. The legal personality of a company can only be disregarded by a court where a person is under an existing legal obligation or restriction which he deliberately evades by using a company which is under his control.

→ corporate veil lifted.

There are various statutory instances where the veil of incorporation may be lifted, and liability imposed on directors, shareholders, or others. For example, if a company is wrongfully trading, the Insolvency Act 1986 imposes personal liability on its directors. Under the CA 2006, directors of a public company are liable if a company trades without a Trading Certificate.

Table 15.1 The distinction between registered limited companies and partnerships

Registered Limited Company	General Partnership	Limited Liability Partnership
It is a legal entity separate from its members.	It is not a legal entity separate from its members.	It is a legal entity separate from its members.
Members' liability is limited.	Members' liability is unlimited.	Members' liability is limited.
Directors manage the company affairs.	Partners have a right to manage the partnership's affairs.	Members have a right to manage the partnership's affairs.
Directors are the agents of the company.	Partners are the agents of the partnership.	Members are the agents of the partnership.
Members can transfer their shares to others.	Partners cannot transfer their interests to others.	Members cannot transfer their interests to others.
Company assets belong to the company.	The partners own the assets jointly.	LLP assets belong to the LLP.
Can create a floating charge over assets.	Cannot create a floating charge over assets.	Can create a floating charge over assets.

Table 15.1 (*continued*)

Registered Limited Company	General Partnership	Limited Liability Partnership
Documents must be registered with Registrar of Companies.	Can be created without formalities.	Documents must be registered with Registrar of Companies.
Annual returns and accounts must be registered and are open to inspection by the public.	Affairs are completely private.	Annual returns and accounts must be registered and are open to inspection by the public.
Company pays corporation tax.	Receive a share of the profits and pay income tax on the share received.	Receive a share of the profits and pay income tax on the share received.
Perpetual succession. Change in membership does not alter its existence.	Dissolved when a partner leaves.	Change in membership does not alter its existence.

Basic Terminology

For an online flashcard glossary visit the Online Resource Centre

Deed A written legal agreement which states on the agreement that it is a deed. It must be signed by the persons making it in the presence of a witness.

Equity partner A partner who takes a share of the profits after all expenses are met.

Incorporated business A legal entity in its own right.

Jointly and severally liable Liable both individually and together with others.

Partnership A relationship between two or more persons to carry on a business together with the intention of making a profit.

Perpetual succession Continues in existence indefinitely until liquidated.

Salaried partner Listed as a partner on the firm's stationery but receives a salary rather than a share of the profits.

Separate legal personality In law the body has rights of a natural person.

Sleeping partner Usually used to describe a partner who invests capital in the firm but takes no part in running the business.

Unincorporated business No separate legal identity of its own.

Summary

For an online printable version visit the Online Resource Centre

After studying this chapter you should be able to:

Identify common types of business organisations, and explain the difference between unincorporated and incorporated businesses

- Sole trader: this is the simplest business to set up. There are no disclosure or public accountability requirements or rules governing the conduct of the business, other than those relating to choice of business name and the general law on issues such as employment and health and safety.

- There are three types of partnership: a general partnership, a limited partnership (LP), and a Limited Liability Partnership (LLP).
- A company may be a private or a public limited company. A private company may be limited, or unlimited (this is unusual). If a private company is limited then it may be limited by shares or by guarantee.
- An unincorporated business organisation, such as a general partnership, has no separate legal identity and the owners of the business may have no financial protection if the business fails.
- An incorporated business organisation, such as a limited company or an LLP, has a separate legal identity, its debts are its own, and the personal liabilities of its owners are limited to the amount invested in the business.

Outline the rules relating to partnerships

- A partnership is a relationship between two or more persons carrying on a business together with a view to profit.
- Each partner is self-employed and takes a share of the profits and usually participates in the decision-making.
- A general partnership has no legal existence distinct from the partners themselves, and the partners are personally responsible for any debts and liabilities that the business runs up.
- A partnership can be created by deed, in writing, orally, or arise from conduct.
- A partnership may be brought to an end either by agreement, automatically under the Partnership Act 1890, or by a court order.

Explain the relationship between partners

- A partnership is based on trust and good faith. Partners owe each other a general duty of care in relation to the conduct of partnership affairs.
- Duties are rights as set out in the Partnership Act 1890 but the partners can agree not to be bound by the rights set out in the Act and instead make their own arrangements.

Explain the relationship between partnerships and outsiders

- Every partner is an agent of the firm and all the co-partners.
- Actions done in the usual course of the firm's business will bind the firm unless the partner had no authority to act and the third party knows this, or the third party does not know or believe him to be a partner.
- Partners are jointly and severally liable for the firm's contracts and tortious actions of the partners acting in the course of the business.
- A partner who retires from a firm is liable for partnership debts and obligations incurred before his retirement.

Demonstrate an understanding of the main aspects of Limited Liability Partnerships

- An LLP, introduced by the Limited Liability Partnerships Act 2000, is a body corporate and has a legal personality separate from that of its members.
- An LLP has the organisational flexibility of a partnership and is taxed as a partnership.
- There must be at least two members of an LLP.
- The rights and duties of members to each other and between members and the LLP itself are governed by the limited liability partnership agreement and the law.

Outline the nature of companies

- A company has its own distinct legal personality separate from its members. It can enter into contracts, be liable in tort and criminal law, and own assets and property.
- A company has perpetual succession.

Questions

For outline answers visit the Online Resource Centre

1. Gita and Luis are partners in a catering business called Meals4U. They regularly order fresh fish from Bespoke Foods Ltd. To cut costs, Gita asks Luis not to order any more fish from Bespoke but instead to buy it at the local supermarket. The next day Luis gets a new customer and, wanting to make a good impression, she again orders fish from Bespoke, who know nothing of Gita's request. Two months later, Bespoke's bill has not been paid and Bespoke is threatening to sue Gita and Luis as the partners of Meals4U. Gita blames Luis for the situation.

    a) Advise Gita whether she will be liable to pay the debt from her personal resources if Meals4U has insufficient assets to pay it.

    b) If Meals4U was a limited company rather than a partnership, explain, giving reasons, who would be liable for the debt to Bespoke.

2. For some years Zadie carried on a computer repair business as a sole trader. In 2015 she expanded into computer sales and incorporated the business, assigning the whole of its assets to the company, Comdeal Ltd. Payment was effected by the allotment to Zadie and her husband of £5,000 fully paid shares in Comdeal Ltd. Zadie continued to insure the business assets in her own name as she had done prior to the incorporation of Comdeal Ltd. This year, the premises of Comdeal Ltd were burgled and some £30,000 worth of equipment stolen. Zadie has made a claim on the policy but the insurance company refuses to meet her claim.

    Advise her.

3. Explain the core rights and duties of general partners set out in the Partnership Act 1890.

4. Outline the differences between a registered limited company, a general partnership, and a limited liability partnership.

Further Reading

Bourne, *Bourne on Company Law*, 6th edn (Routledge, 2013).

Dignam and Lowry, *Company Law*, 8th edn (Oxford University Press, 2014).

Dine and Koutsias, *Company Law*, 8th edn (Palgrave, 2014).

Morse, *Partnership Law*, 7th edn (Oxford University Press, 2010).

Wild and Weinstein, *Smith & Keenan's Company Law*, 16th edn (Pearson, 2013).

Government Services and Information: https://www.gov.uk.

Companies House: http://www.companieshouse.gov.uk/.

Department for Business Innovation & Skills: https://www.gov.uk/government/organisations/department-for-business-innovation-skills.

Online Resource Centre

Test your knowledge by trying this chapter's **Multiple Choice Questions**. Visit:

www.oup.com/uk/orc/law/company/jonesibl3e/01student/mcqs/ch15/

For more information, updates, and multiple choice questions, please visit the Online Resource Centre at:

www.oup.com/uk/orc/law/company/jonesibl3e/

Company Law I
Formation and Finance

Introduction

Chapter 15 introduced companies as a business structure. The following three chapters consider the law relating to registered companies limited by shares, which are the usual form of companies used as vehicles for running businesses. Persons who own shares in a company are called the shareholders or members of the company. This chapter considers how companies limited by shares are formed and looks at the contents of companies' constitutions. Company law is currently set out mainly in the Companies Act 2006 (CA 2006) and regulations made under that Act. The CA 2006 is the longest statute ever passed by Parliament and governs both public companies and private companies. In order to run a business, companies need to raise capital sums. The CA 2006 sets out detailed rules about the raising of capital through the issuing of shares, and maintaining the capital at a certain level once it has been raised. The Act also regulates the raising of capital through loans made to a company. A company can give security to creditors by creating a charge on some or all of the company's assets, but these secured loans must be registered with the Registrar of Companies.

Learning Objectives

After studying this chapter you should be able to:

- Explain the role of promoters in setting up a company.
- Explain what is meant by a company 'off the shelf'.
- Identify the steps for registering a company.
- Outline the rules relating to a company's name.
- Describe the constitution of a company.

- Explain the different types of share.
- Show an understanding of how a company is financed through the issue of shares and debentures.

Setting Up a Company

Promoters

When a person or persons decide to set up a new business intending that it should be run as a company, they may try to interest other people in their venture by persuading them to contribute capital sums and/or to take part in the management of the business. Anyone who takes procedural steps to set up a company and who makes business preparations for the company, such as finding the first directors and shareholders, or entering into contracts on behalf of the new company, is known as a **promoter**. The promoter may seek professional advice on the procedure for forming a company from a solicitor, accountant, or other professional person. The person who gives the professional advice does not become a promoter. The duties of promoters vary, but they are always responsible for ensuring that the registration process is complied with. They may also be involved in setting up a business that the company will run before the company is formed.

Duties of promoters

Promoters have a general duty to exercise reasonable care and skill and a fiduciary duty towards the company. A fiduciary duty is one of trust and confidence. This means that if a promoter makes a profit from his position, for example, by selling his own property to the company, he must disclose his profit either to a board of directors of the company independent of himself, or he may make the disclosure to the existing and prospective shareholders. A promoter is often one of the first directors of a company or is connected to the directors and, therefore, is not independent of them, in which case he must make the disclosure to the shareholders. Although a promoter may also be a shareholder of the new company, he will be making the disclosure to all the shareholders.

 Key Concept   Companies are run and managed by directors. The owners of public and private companies limited by shares are the shareholders.

Where a promoter fails to make proper disclosure, the company may rescind a contract for the purchase of property (have the contract set aside) or recover any profit made by the promoter out of the transaction. There is no automatic right to payment of expenses for a promoter but usually the articles of the company set up will authorise repayment of expenses.

A promoter may be disqualified from being a director or promoter by a court under the provisions of the Company Directors Disqualification Act 1986, for up to 15 years if he is convicted of an offence in connection with the promotion, formation, or management of a company.

Key Concept Promoters are the persons who take procedural steps to set up a company and who make business preparations for the company. They are responsible for registering the necessary documents with the Registrar of Companies and have a general duty to exercise reasonable care and skill and a fiduciary duty towards the company.

Pre-incorporation contracts

A contract entered into by promoters purporting to be made by or on behalf of a company before the company comes into existence is not binding on the company but the promoters are personally liable unless the contract states otherwise (CA 2006, s 51). The contract cannot be ratified by the company after incorporation because, in order for a contract to be ratified, the party ratifying it must have been in existence at the time the contract was made.

The promoters may sue or be sued on the contract whether or not the other party knew that the company did not exist. In the following case the promoter, Lane, was liable even though the claimant knew the company did not exist at the time the contract was made.

Phonogram Ltd v Lane (1982)

Facts: A pop group was going to be set up called 'Cheap Mean and Nasty' and it was intended that a company called Fragile Management Ltd would be formed to manage the group. Before the company was formed, negotiations took place between the defendant promoter, Lane, and the claimant, Phonogram Ltd, about finance for an album. Phonogram, knowing the company was not yet formed, sent £6,000 to Lane as a first instalment of finance. Lane accepted the money and signed a letter for and on behalf of Fragile Management Ltd, undertaking to repay the £6,000 if the terms of the contract were not fulfilled within a month. The company was never formed, the contract was not fulfilled, and the claimants sought recovery of their £6,000 from the defendant.

Decision: The defendant was personally liable to repay the £6,000 under the Companies Act 1985, s 36C (now CA 2006, s 51). The fact that the claimant knew the company was not in existence at the time the contract was made did not alter the defendant's personal liability.

In business it is sometimes commercially prudent to enter into contracts quickly to obtain a financial advantage and, therefore, promoters may be tempted to enter into contracts even before a company is formed. It is possible to avoid personal liability, if the third party expressly agrees that the promoter will not be liable on the contract, or by completing a draft contract with the third party before the company is formed and entering into the contract once the company is incorporated. Alternatively, rather than setting up a bespoke company, it is possible to buy a company 'off the shelf' (see later in the chapter) in which case the company will exist before the contract was made, and even though not yet purchased, the company will be able to ratify the contract.

Contracts (Rights of Third Parties) Act 1999

The Contracts (Rights of Third Parties) Act 1999 does not free the promoter from liability for contracts entered into before a company is formed, but its provisions do allow a person (including a non-natural person) to be given rights in a contract even though they are not party to the contract or not in existence when the contract is made. Therefore, a promoter and a third party can agree to give a company that has not yet been incorporated rights in a contract made between them. When the company is incorporated it will be able to sue and be sued on the contract.

Companies 'Off the Shelf'

It is possible to purchase a company **'off the shelf'** rather than setting up a new company. Various businesses offer ready-made private limited companies for sale. These companies have already been registered at Companies House and then left dormant. Annual accounts do not have to be prepared or auditors appointed where a company is dormant. These companies have never traded, although they may have been in existence for some years. When a ready-made company is purchased, the shares are transferred to buyers, and the Registrar of Companies is notified of the new directors and any changes made to the name and constitution of the company. Some businesses benefit from being run by a company that appears to be well-established, as customers feel more confident dealing with older companies rather than new companies.

Registration of a New Company

In order to form a new company limited by shares, an application must be made electronically or by paper to the Registrar of Companies. The documents that must be 'delivered' are a memorandum of association, an application for registration together with the documents required by the application, a statement of compliance, and the appropriate fee (CA 2006, s 9).

The **memorandum of association** is a document that states that the subscribers wish to form a company and have agreed to become members of the company and take at least one share each.

The application for registration must state or include a copy of the following:

- The company's proposed name.

- Whether the company's registered office is to be situated in England and Wales, Wales, Scotland, or Northern Ireland.

- Whether the liability of the company is to be limited, and if so, whether it is to be limited by shares or guarantee.

- Whether the company is to be a public company or a private company.

- If the company is to be limited by shares, the application must contain a **statement of capital and initial shareholdings**. This means it must give details of the total number of shares to be taken on formation by the subscribers, the nominal (face) value of those shares, and particular rights attached to those shares. If the shares are not fully paid up then the extent to which these shares have been paid up. If the company is to be a public limited company, the nominal share capital must be at least £50,000.

- The intended address of the company's registered office. (This is the full postal address as opposed to a statement of the country in which the registered office is situated.)

- A statement of the company's proposed officers (the first directors and first secretary). (A private limited company may decide not to appoint a secretary, in which case only the first directors are named.)

- A copy of any proposed Articles of Association to the extent that these differ from the default model articles. (There are a series of model articles produced by the Government for different types of companies.)

- A statement of compliance which states the legal requirements of registration have been fulfilled. It is a criminal offence to knowingly or recklessly make a false statement of compliance, and, on conviction, a person may be fined or imprisoned for up to 12 months.

On registration of these documents, the Registrar of Companies issues the company's certificate of incorporation (birth certificate), which is conclusive evidence that the company exists and has been registered under the Act (CA 2006, s 15(4)). A company also gets a registration number and a notice is published in the London Gazette.

On receipt of a Certificate of Incorporation, a private company may start its business. A public limited company must obtain an additional certificate from the Registrar which confirms that the company has the minimum allotted share capital (at present £50,000) (CA 2006, s 761).

The company name

Part 5 of the CA 2006 governs the requirements relating to a company's name. A company must not have the same name that is already on the register (CA 2006, s 162). The register includes companies in the UK and overseas companies with a UK branch and other business entities.

Sections 58 and 59 provide that private limited companies (unless exempted) must end their names with 'limited' or 'Ltd', and public limited companies with 'public limited company' or 'plc'. If the registered office is in Wales, then the company can use the Welsh equivalents of 'cwmni cyfyngedig cyhoeddus' or 'ccc' (CA 2006, ss 58 and 59).

Names which, if used, would constitute a criminal offence or are offensive are prohibited (CA 2006, s 53). In the following case the Registrar refused to register 'Prostitute Ltd' as a company name.

R v Registrar of Companies ex p Attorney-General (1991)

Facts: Lindi St Claire asked the Registrar if the name 'Prostitute Ltd' was available for registration as a company. The Registrar refused to register the name and also refused to register 'Hookers Ltd'. The Registrar did agree to register the company in the name of Lindi St Claire (Personal Services) Ltd. Later there was an application by the Attorney-General to strike off the company because it had been set up to carry on the business of prostitution.

Decision: The court ordered the Registrar to strike off the company from the register. Although carrying on the business of a prostitute may not involve a criminal offence, the prime purpose of the company was considered to be contrary to public policy.

Permission from the Secretary of State has to be sought before words that suggest connection with central or local government can be used as part of a company name (CA 2006, s 54). The Secretary of State also has power to make regulations prohibiting the use of sensitive words (CA 2006, s 55). There are regulations prohibiting the use of words such as 'charity', 'university', 'police', 'midwife', 'British', 'English', 'Scottish', and 'Welsh' without permission.

Names with symbols

It is possible to use a symbol as part of a company's name. A company could, therefore, be registered as MotorCity@Brighton Ltd. The use of a symbol may distinguish one company's name from another.

Change of company's name

Shareholders of a company can change a company's name by special resolution at a company meeting or by other means provided for change in its articles (CA 2006, ss 78 and 79). A special resolution is one passed by a majority of not less than 75 per cent. The Registrar must be informed of the change of name.

The Secretary of State can compel a company to change its name if the name is the same as another company that is or should have been on the register, if misleading information or assurances were given at the time of registration, or if the company's name gives so misleading an indication of its activities as to be likely to cause harm to the public.

In addition, any person (not just another company) can object to a company's name, if it is the same as a name in which the objector has goodwill, or if it is so similar to an existing name that it is likely to mislead the public by suggesting a connection between the company and the objector (CA 2006, s 69). An application is made to a Company Names Adjudicator and if the objection is upheld, then the company will have to change its name. The mere use of a symbol or an abbreviation may not be enough to distinguish a name. Therefore, an owner of a business called LoopyLoo may object to a name of a new company registered as Loopy + Loo Ltd.

Passing off

A company or other business may also bring an action in the tort of passing off, where its name has been 'taken' either intentionally or accidentally and the use of its name is likely to cause confusion or take customers away. The claimant business must be able to demonstrate that actual damage has been or is likely to be caused to the goodwill and reputation of the business.

Ewing v Buttercup Margarine Co Ltd (1917)

Facts: The claimant was the owner of a business which sold goods including margarine. He had 150 shops and had been trading since 1904 as Buttercup Dairy Co. He sought an injunction (court order) to prevent a newly-formed company trading as Buttercup Margarine Co Ltd, which intended to sell margarine to the public.

Decision: There would be confusion between the two businesses and, therefore, an injunction was granted to prevent the company using the name Buttercup Margarine Co Ltd.

Internet names

A variation of passing off is using company names on the internet. A person who has a website can obtain exclusive use of a domain name by registering its address with its internet provider. If the internet address registered bears a close resemblance to the name of another business which the public might confuse with the internet site, then an action for passing off may arise.

British Telecommunications plc v One in a Million Ltd (1998)

Facts: The defendants were dealers in internet domain names and registered well-known names without the consent of the businesses. The defendants registered a series of names including bt.org, marksandspencer.com, sainsburys.com, and virgin.org, and then offered to sell the names to the claimants' companies. A court order was applied for by the claimants, which required the defendants to transfer the domain names to the companies and prevented the defendants from registering similar names.

Decision: The court granted the order to the claimants as they were the owners of the goodwill in the name. There had been a threat to pass off by the defendants. The defendants were prevented from using the names and they had to transfer the names to the claimants.

Nominet UK is the internet registry for '.uk' domain names. They register names on a first come, first served basis. If names have been registered primarily to sell them, or if the name is too similar to a well-known company's name or trade mark, disputes can be settled either through Nominet UK's dispute resolution service or by court action.

Business Insight

Nominet is a not-for-profit company limited by guarantee. It took charge of the .uk domain name in 1996 when there were 26,000 .uk sites. There are now over 10 million .uk domain names. Nominet provided a Dispute Resolution Service (DRS) to help resolve .uk domain name disputes.

In 2010 the domain name 'ihateryanair.co.uk' registered by a private person was found by DRS to be an abusive registration and transferred to complainant, Ryanair Ltd. In 2014 names considered to be abusive registration included Natweest-online.co.uk, e-natwest.co.uk, gumtreefreeads.co.uk and inland-revenue.co.uk.

Display of company's name

The company's registered name must be displayed outside the registered office, at all places of business, and on all business letters, notices, cheques, orders, receipts, and invoices (paper and electronic). The law does not require a company to have a common seal but, if it does, that seal must include the company's name. In addition, the company must provide its name and address (if requested) to any person it does business with. If the company is trading under a different name to its registered name, it must display its registered name on all premises, and letters, and other documents.

If a company does not display its name on its premises or documents as required without reasonable excuse, the company and its officers (directors and secretary) are committing a criminal offence and are liable on conviction to a fine.

The company's registered office

The application for registration must state which country the company is registered in: England and Wales, Wales, Scotland, or Northern Ireland. This cannot be changed. The actual address of the registered company is also on the application but this can be changed. To change the address of the registered office, the company must give notice to the Registrar, who publishes changes in the London Gazette. The registered address has to be stated on all business correspondence.

Limited or unlimited

In the application form, the subscribers must state whether the company is limited or unlimited. The majority of companies have limited liability, although it is possible to form a private unlimited company. An unlimited company is a separate legal entity and, therefore, enters into its own transactions, but each member of the company is fully liable for the company's debts. A private limited company may be limited by shares or limited by guarantee. Where a company is limited by shares, the liability of its members (shareholders) is limited to the paid up value of their shares. In a company limited by guarantee, there are no shareholders. The members give a guarantee to contribute the amount specified in the guarantee (usually a nominal amount) in the event of the company going into liquidation. Public companies must be limited by shares.

Statement of capital and initial shareholdings

Where a company is limited by shares, the application must contain a statement of capital and initial shareholdings. This is the amount of money that the company holds or is entitled to hold at the date of registration. It is the total number of shares to be taken on formation by the subscribers. For example, if two subscribers of company X Ltd were intending to take 1,000 shares, each with the face value of £1, the share capital of the company would be £2,000 at its conception.

The statement of capital and initial shareholdings must contain the total number of shares of the company, the aggregate nominal (face) value of the shares, and rights attached to those shares. Sometimes a company may issue different types of shares. Types of shares are called classes of shares. If a new company is issuing different classes of shares, for each class of share the application form must state the particular rights attached to those shares, the total amount, and the aggregate nominal value. If the shares are not fully paid up, then the extent to which the shares have been paid up must be stated.

Later on, after the company has traded, it may require additional capital, and increase its share capital by issuing additional shares. Under former company law, a company had to have an authorised share capital, but new companies set up under the CA 2006 are not required to have an authorised share capital, although they may have one if they wish. An authorised share capital is the maximum number of shares of a stated value that a company is authorised to issue. It acts as a ceiling on the amount of capital that a company can issue, although this limit can be increased by ordinary resolution of the company's shareholders (see Figure 16.1).

Public or private company

Usually a company will begin life as a private limited company and later convert to a public limited company. However, a company may be registered as a public limited company from conception, in which case the application must state that the company is a public company, and the nominal share capital must be at least £50,000 of which at least 25 per cent (£12,500 minimum) must be paid up.

Statement of proposed officers

This statement details the names of the director or directors, and the company secretary if there is one. Public companies must have at least two directors and a company secretary (the company secretary may also be a director). Private companies only have to have one director and do not have to have a secretary. The directors and secretary must provide an address for service which does not have to be their own address but may be a different address, such as the company's registered office or the address of the company's solicitors. Private addresses of directors and secretaries are kept at Companies House on a separate register to which the public do not have access.

A company's articles

The application for registration must include a copy of the company's articles if they are to differ from the model default articles. The Secretary of State prescribes default model articles for companies that have not registered any articles of their own or have not made any provision for a particular matter in their articles.

Figure 16.1 A company with authorised share capital

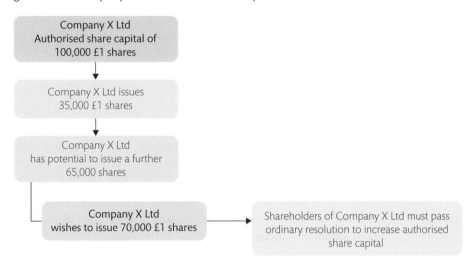

The Constitutional Documents of a Company under the Companies Act 2006

Companies set up under the provisions of the CA 2006 have one major constitutional document, the **Articles of Association**, which are divided into numbered paragraphs and signed by each subscriber. In addition to the articles, the company's constitution includes any special resolutions and unanimous agreements made by the members. These documents form the rules that govern all the workings of the company.

The CA 2006, s 19 gives the Secretary of State the power to prescribe model articles, and regulations have been made setting out model articles for different types of companies. The model articles are often adopted by private limited companies, although the companies may make a few alterations; however, public limited companies usually draft their own articles.

The articles state all the rules necessary for the conduct of the company's business and contain information relating to such matters as:

- Company name.
- Any restrictions on the company's objects.
- Appointment, powers, and proceedings of directors.
- Appointment of a company secretary, if there is to be one.
- Proceedings at meetings of the company.

- Voting rights of members (shareholders).
- Payment of dividends.
- Keeping accounts.
- Issue and transfer of shares.

The Constitutional Documents of Companies Incorporated before October 2009

The provisions relating to constitutions of companies in the Companies Act 2006 came into force in October 2009; companies set up before that date were governed by the provisions of the Companies Act 1985 (or earlier Acts) and were incorporated with two constitutional documents: the **memorandum of association** (concerned with the company's external relations) and the Articles of Association (concerned primarily with the internal workings of the company).

Both these documents could be altered by resolutions of the shareholders. The CA 2006 provides that, where companies have been set up under previous legislation and have an old style memorandum, then its provisions are generally treated as part of its articles (CA 2006, s 28). Therefore, a provision that is in the old style memorandum which, if drafted today would form part of the articles of a new company, is treated by the law as though it were part of the articles. A company with the old style documents may alter its constitution to reflect the changes in the law but it is not required to do so and can carry on with the two documents.

Today, companies set up under the 2006 Act have one constitutional document: the Articles of Association. The memorandum of association is not part of the company's constitution. It is now only used as evidence that the subscribers intend to form a company and become shareholders of it, taking at least one share each on incorporation. The new style memorandum, once registered, cannot be altered.

Section 18 - CA 2006.

Key Concept Companies set up under the 2006 Act have one main constitutional document: the Articles of Association. These are the rules that govern all the workings of the company. They can be altered by resolutions passed by the company's shareholders.

Restrictions on the Objects of a Company

Companies formed under the provisions of the CA 2006 are deemed to have unrestricted objects unless the company's articles specifically restrict its objects. This means that the capacity of the company to enter into legal transactions, such as entering into contracts, borrowing funds, creating charges, or giving gifts, is unrestricted. However, there may be cases where the persons forming the company, or later, the members of the company wish there to be some restrictions on the company's powers. Companies that are charities will have to restrict their objects under charitable legislation, and some companies set up as social enterprises may want to ensure that the company acts within certain boundaries. If the persons forming the company wish to restrict the company's objects, the restriction must be contained in the articles.

Companies formed pre-Companies Act 2006

Companies formed under the pre-2006 legislation did have an objects clause stating what the company could do. Objects clauses tended to be drafted very widely and, therefore, it was unlikely that a company would ever trade outside its objects clause. It was also possible to have a single object of being a 'general commercial company' which empowered the company to 'carry on any trade or business whatsoever' and to do all such things as are incidental or conducive to the carrying on of any trade or business. A company formed under the old legislation may alter its constitution and remove its objects clause if the shareholders agree, but if the company does not alter its constitution, then its objects clause is read as a restriction on what the company can do. If the company enters into a transaction that is beyond its objects clause, that transaction is said to be *ultra vires* (beyond its powers).

Companies acting outside the powers stated in their constitution

The validity of an action taken by a company cannot be questioned on the ground of lack of capacity because of anything in the company's constitution (CA 2006, s 39). This means that if a company has articles that contain restrictions on the objects or purposes of its business, and that company enters into a transaction which is beyond its powers, the transaction will be valid. The capacity of a company itself is different from the question of the powers of directors. A company may have the capacity to enter into an agreement but the powers of a particular director to make that agreement may be limited by the company's articles. However, the powers of the directors to bind the company in any transaction with a person acting in good faith are deemed to be free of any limitations (CA 2006, s 40). Directors have a duty to act in accordance with the company's constitution (CA 2006, s 171) and, therefore, where a director allows a company to act outside the restrictions stated in its articles, although the transaction may be valid as far as a third party and the company are concerned, the directors may become liable to the company.

If a company does have restrictions in its articles and acts outside those limitations on entering into a transaction with a third party, the position will be as follows.

- The company is treated as having capacity to enter into any contract. A third party acting in good faith can sue the company on the transaction and enforce it.

- The third party is presumed to have acted in good faith unless the contrary is proved. He is not regarded as acting in bad faith merely because he knew that an act is beyond the powers of the directors under the company's constitution.

- The company can sue and be sued on any contract it enters into, despite the fact that it is outside its powers.

- Shareholders of a company can apply to the court for an order preventing directors exceeding their powers. This can be used where the shareholders know in advance that the directors intend to enter into such a transaction.

Transactions where the third party is an 'insider'

An 'insider' is either a director of the company or a person connected to a director, for example, his spouse. Where the transaction is with an insider, the company can treat the contract as voidable (CA 2006, s 41). This gives the company the choice whether to have the contract set aside, or to continue with it. If the company wishes to continue with the contract, the insider is bound by it. Irrespective of whether the contract is set aside, the insider and any director who authorised the transaction must account to the company for any gain they have made or indemnify the company for any loss or damage that the company has incurred. If the insider is not a director of the company it may be possible for him to avoid liability if he can prove that, at the time he entered into the transaction, he was not aware that the directors were exceeding their powers.

Binding Power of the Constitution

The provisions of the constitution of a company bind the company and its members to the same extent as if there were covenants on the part of the company and each of the members to observe those provisions (CA 2006, s 33). This means that the articles and any additional resolutions and agreements form a contract between the company and its shareholders, and the shareholders and each other.

- The shareholders are bound to the company.

- The company is bound to the shareholders in respect of their rights as shareholders.

- Shareholders are bound individually to each other shareholder.

The following case demonstrates that the articles are enforceable by the company against its shareholders.

Hickman v Kent or Romney Marsh Sheep Breeders Association (1915)

Facts: The articles provided that, in any dispute between a member (shareholder) and the company, the matter should go to arbitration before court proceedings were commenced. Hickman, a shareholder, sued the company in the High Court in respect of various matters. The company applied to the court to have the court action suspended on the grounds that Hickman should have sought for the dispute to be decided by arbitration.

Decision: The court case was suspended because the shareholder was contractually bound by the articles and had to first take his dispute to arbitration.

The articles are also enforceable between the shareholders and, therefore, one shareholder can take an action against another shareholder. In the following case the directors, who were also shareholders, were bound to obey the articles.

Rayfield v Hands (1960)

Facts: The articles required all directors of the company to be shareholders of the company and to purchase shares at a fair price from any shareholder who wished to sell their shares. The directors refused to buy another shareholder's shares. The shareholder applied to the court for an order requiring the directors to buy his shares.

Decision: The court ordered the purchase of the shares. The contents of the articles were binding on the shareholders and could be enforced by shareholders individually.

The following case illustrates that the company is bound to the shareholders as regards their rights in the articles.

Pender v Lushington (1877)

Facts: C Ltd's articles entitled every shareholder to one vote per 10 shares with a maximum of 100 votes, no matter how many shares were held. Pender transferred a number of shares he had in the company to nominees, who agreed to use their voting rights to support a resolution that Pender wanted to be passed. At a general meeting, when the resolution was being voted on, the chairman refused to accept the votes of the nominees. Pender brought a court action against the company and the chairman to force them to accept the votes of the nominees.

Decision: The nominees were shareholders and had a contractual vote given to them in the articles. The court ordered that the votes were accepted.

Although the articles bind the company and its shareholders to each other in respect of its rights as shareholders, they do not form a contract between the company or its shareholders and 'outsiders'.

Eley v Positive Life Assurance Co (1876)

Facts: The articles contained a clause that stated that the claimant, Mr Eley, a solicitor, should be the solicitor to the company for life. When the company dismissed him, he brought an action for breach of contract for not employing him as their solicitor as stated in the articles.

Decision: The articles did not form a contract between the company and the claimant in his capacity as a solicitor. Although the claimant was a shareholder of the company, this only gave him rights as a shareholder and in his capacity as employee he was an 'outsider'.

The Contracts (Rights of Third Parties) Act 1999 does not apply to articles and, therefore, outsiders cannot gain any rights by using the provisions of the Act as might be the case in an ordinary contract.

Alteration of the Articles

The articles of a company can be amended by special resolution (CA 2006, s 21). Section 283 states that a *special resolution* is one passed by a majority vote of not less than 75 per cent (CA 2006, s 283; see further Chapter 17). Any alteration to a company's articles must comply with company legislation, and the alteration must be made in good faith for the benefit of the company as a whole. Generally, a court will not interfere in the business decisions of a company, and if the majority of shareholders honestly believe they are exercising their powers for the benefit of the company, then the alteration to the articles will be allowed. Where there is evidence that the shareholders were not acting honestly or where no reasonable shareholder could consider the alteration as beneficial to the company, the court may intervene.

The court will not permit an alteration of the articles to be enforced if it is to give the company power to expel shareholders for no particular reason.

Brown v British Abrasive Wheel Co (1919)

Facts: A company needed further capital and the majority of shareholders, who held 98 per cent of shares, were willing to provide the capital if they could buy up the minority shareholders. The minority shareholders refused to sell, and it was proposed that the articles were changed to force the minority shareholders to transfer their shares to the majority at a fair price. The minority shareholders took action in court.

Decision: The alteration was not allowed as it was not for the benefit of the company as a whole that any one or more shareholders should be expelled for no good reason.

If the articles are being altered to expel a shareholder because he is competing with the company, the alteration will be allowed as it is for the benefit of the company as a whole.

Sidebottom v Kershaw Leese (1920)

Facts: Sidebottom was a shareholder of a company with a minority of shares. He carried on a business which competed with the company. The articles were altered to include a clause stating that a shareholder who competed with the company had to transfer his shares at a fair value to persons nominated by the directors.

Decision: The alteration was valid. It was beneficial to the company to have the power to expel a shareholder who was a competitor of the company.

A court may amend the articles of a company where they have been altered and that alteration had an obvious error which did not reflect the true intention of the shareholders.

Folkes Group Plc v Alexander (2002)

Facts: The Folkes family held a substantial proportion of the voting shares in a company. The articles of the company were amended, and as a result of a clerical error the amendment reduced the voting power of the Folkes family so they no longer had control of the company.

Decision: The court amended the articles, as an obvious error had been made that did not reflect the intention of the shareholders.

Making a Company's Constitution Entrenched

A company may have entrenched articles (CA 2006, s 22). The articles may state that specified provisions can only be altered by certain means which are more restrictive than a special resolution. The articles may provide for entrenchment when they are first registered on formation of the company, or can be altered to be entrenched with the unanimous consent of all the shareholders. If a company does have some entrenched provisions in its articles, then the Registrar of Companies must be notified of the entrenchment, and a notice is put on the company register so that people searching the register will be aware that there are some entrenched provisions.

Financing a Company

A company that is set up to run a business will aim to make money from that venture. In order to carry out a business, a company will need to raise a certain amount of capital. This can be obtained by selling **shares** in the company (share capital) or by taking out loans (loan capital). Both shareholders and lenders can be seen as investors in a company, who put capital into it and want to receive some return on their capital while it is invested in the company. Buyers of shares in a company become **shareholders** and are members of the company. They receive a return on their capital investment by way of dividends. There are different categories of share capital, and the CA 2006 sets out detailed rules about the raising and maintenance of share capital. Once capital has been raised through the sale of shares, it is important to ensure that the capital is maintained to act as a reserve in case the company gets into financial difficulties. Where loans are made to a company, the lenders do not become members of the company but they are creditors of the company. Their loans may be unsecured, or secured on company property. The return that creditors receive from the money invested in the company is by interest on the loan (see Table 16.1).

Becoming a Shareholder

A person (who could be another company or a natural person) may become a shareholder by subscribing to the memorandum of association, or by agreeing to become a shareholder. On registration of a company, the subscribers become its first shareholders and their names are entered on the register of members. Every company must keep a register of its members detailing their names, addresses, and the extent of their shareholding (CA 2006, s 113). On agreeing to become a member of a company, a person's name is entered on to the list of members. Membership begins from the date of entry on the register. A person agrees to become a member by purchasing or obtaining shares from the company or by acquiring shares from an existing member. A person who obtains the shares only becomes a member of the company when the company registers his name on the company register.

Obtaining Shares from the Company

When shares are issued, a person who applies to buy the shares is making an offer. The company accepts the offer to buy the shares by sending a letter of allotment. The letter of allotment is the acceptance. A share certificate must be issued within two months of the allotment of shares (CA 2006, s 769). A certificate specifying any shares held by a member is evidence of the member's ownership of those shares (CA 2006, s 768).

Transfer of Shares

Shares can be freely transferred between parties unless the company's articles impose restrictions on transfer. Public companies quoted on the Stock Exchange are not permitted to have restrictions on the transfer of shares. Non-listed public companies and private companies may have restrictions in their articles. For example, a private company may give its directors the right to refuse to register shares that have been transferred to others. Where shares can and have been transferred, the company must be notified of the change of shareholder. Within two months of the notification, the company must issue a new certificate of registration (CA 2006, s 776). Once registration is completed, the new shareholder acquires all the rights attached to the shares (such as a right to vote at meetings, or a right to receive a dividend) and is part-owner of the company.

Rights of Shareholders

A shareholder is a member of the company and has a number of rights which include:

- *A right to transfer his shares subject to any restriction in the articles*
- *A right to receive any dividend declared by the company*

   A **dividend** is a payment from profits paid to the shareholders by the company. A company must have sufficient distributable profits to declare a dividend. It is up to the board of directors to recommend that a dividend is paid, and the amount of the dividend. The shareholders must agree to the dividend at a general meeting. The shareholders can vote to reduce the dividend that has been recommended by the board of directors, but cannot increase the amount or compel the directors to recommend a dividend is paid even if they hold preference shares. A dividend must be paid from distributable profits. If it is paid out of capital, the directors may be liable to repay dividends to the company. If the shareholders knew or had reasonable grounds to believe that a dividend was unlawful, the company will be able to recover the dividend for its shareholders. If a dividend is unlawful because of negligently prepared accounts, the company may be able to claim against the company's auditors.

Business Insight Supermarket price wars: Share prices fall and dividends are cut

In August 2014 shares in a number of supermarkets fell sharply as investors feared an industry-wide price war. It was reported that shares in Tesco had fallen 31 per cent that year reaching an 11-year low after the firm cut its full-year profit forecast to £2.4bn from £2.8bn. The half-year dividend was cut by 75 per cent compared with the previous year.

- *Attend and vote at meetings*
  All shareholders must be given notice of meetings and they are entitled to attend and vote (although shareholders of certain shares may have restricted voting rights). Shareholders may appoint proxies to attend and vote for them. Notices of company's meetings can be sent to members electronically.

- *Receive the company's accounts*
  All shareholders are entitled to a copy of the company's accounts after the end of the company's financial year. The accounts for a public company must be available within six months, and the accounts for a private company must be available within nine months. A company does not have to send out the full accounts, unless requested by the shareholder, but can instead send each shareholder a summary financial statement giving the key financial information from the accounts. A company's articles may permit the accounts and financial statement to be sent electronically to shareholders or to be accessible from the company's website.

Issuing Shares

Shares are first issued when the company is registered, and later on further shares can be issued by the company. The directors of public and private companies with more than one class of shares (shares that have different rights) cannot issue further shares without the express authority of their shareholders (CA 2006, s 549). If a private company has only one type of shares, the directors have authority to issue further shares without shareholder approval provided the articles do not expressly state otherwise (CA 2006, s 550). However, this section only applies to new companies set up after 1 October 2009, and to existing companies where the shareholders have passed a resolution adopting this provision. Where approval for the issue of shares is necessary it is usually given at a general meeting of the shareholders by passing an ordinary resolution. The shareholders can pass a resolution allowing for the issue of a particular allotment of shares, or can give the general power to allot shares to the directors for a period of time up to a maximum of five years. The authority to issue shares can always be varied or revoked by the shareholders.

A public company may advertise its shares for sale to the public. Certain public companies, but not all of them, have the right to sell their shares through the Stock Exchange.

Pre-emption rights

Unless the articles state otherwise, when allotting new shares a company must first offer them for sale to the existing shareholders in the same proportion as their existing holdings. The right to purchase additional shares is called **pre-emption rights**, or **rights issue**. These rights can be excluded by the shareholders passing a special resolution relating to a particular issue of shares, or passing a special resolution disapplying pre-emption rights for a period of time up to a maximum of five years. After five years a further special resolution can be passed. A private company may, if it wishes, permanently exclude pre-emption rights in its articles.

Payment for Shares

The CA 2006 places certain restrictions on shares relating to their price, and the purchase of its own shares by a company. The general rule is that shares must be paid for in money or money's worth, and must not be allotted at less than their nominal value (face value) (CA 2006, s 582). However, a company can issue shares that are partly paid.

The price for shares may be money or money's worth, and private companies can give shares in return for services, but there are stringent rules relating to payments for shares in public companies and non-cash consideration must be independently valued.

Shares can be issued at a premium. A premium is the amount paid to a company in excess of the nominal value of the share. Therefore, if the nominal value of a share is £1 and the shares are issued at £3.20, the premium is £2.20. Any money raised by issuing shares at a premium is regarded as capital of the company and not part of a company's profits. The amount raised must be credited to a share premium account and this account can only be used for certain purposes, such as writing off the expenses on the issue of the shares and issuing bonus shares to shareholders (CA 2006, s 610).

Purchase by a Company of its own Shares

Generally, under the CA 2006 a company cannot acquire its own shares by purchase, subscription, or any other method (CA 2006, s 658). However, the Act does provide the following exceptions.

- Where a court orders the purchase of shares by the company, for example, to protect the interests of the minority shareholders.
- Where redeemable shares have been issued.
- Where shares are forfeited or surrendered by the shareholder failing to pay any sum due on them.
- In accordance with the provisions set out in the CA 2006, Part 18.

A company may buy its own shares provided the articles do not contain a restriction (CA 2006, s 690). The shares purchased must have been fully paid up and the company must pay for them in full on the date of purchase. There are restrictions on how the company finances the purchase of the shares and the purchase must be approved by the shareholders. The rules allowing companies to buy back employees' shares were relaxed in the Companies Act 2006 (Amendment of Part 18) Regulations 2013 to encourage employee share schemes. Some employees had been reluctant to accept shares, particularly in private limited companies, as it could be difficult for them to find a buyer for the shares at a later date. Where a company does purchase its own shares, there must always be some remaining non-redeemable shares. A public limited company must always have an allotted share capital of at least £50,000.

The company generally purchases its own shares out of the profits or proceeds of issue of new shares, although a private company can purchase its own shares from capital under strict conditions to ensure the company does not make itself insolvent.

Share Capital

A share is a form of property which carries rights and obligations. Subject to any restrictions in the articles, a share is transferable. A company may create different types of shares which have different rights as regards payments of dividends, voting at meetings, and return of capital on liquidation of the company or reduction of share capital (see Figure 16.2). The rights attached to a particular type of share are called class rights. A company issues ordinary shares or preference shares. A company may choose to make certain ordinary or preference shares redeemable by the company at a future date (CA 2006, s 684).

> **Key Concept** Dividends are the payments made by a company to its shareholders. They can only be paid out of profits made by the company and must not be paid out of capital sums that the company holds.

Ordinary shares

Ordinary shares are issued without any special rights being attached to them. The majority of a company's share capital usually consists of ordinary shares, and some companies will only issue ordinary shares. Ordinary shares generally have the most voting rights and, therefore, shareholders with ordinary shares have greater control of the company. It is possible to create ordinary shares with either no or limited voting rights, or to create shares with enhanced voting rights. This means that some shares may carry a greater voting power than other shares. For example, a company may issue ordinary shares A with 100 votes per share and ordinary shares B with one vote per share. Both shares will be entitled to an equal payment of dividends but ordinary shares A will have a greater voting power.

The amount of the dividend payable on ordinary shares depends on the profits made by the company, and, therefore, dividends vary according to the company's performance. Dividends on ordinary shares are paid after the dividends on preference shares (see next). The amount of dividend that shareholders of ordinary shares receive will depend upon the distributable profit left after the dividends have been paid to the shareholders of preference shares. When a company is wound up, repayment of capital on ordinary shares is paid after the payment due on preference shares. If a company only issues one class of share it need not be explicitly described as 'ordinary'.

Preference shares

These shares carry rights in preference to other shares. They typically have the right to receive an annual dividend of a fixed amount, before a dividend is paid on ordinary shares. A company pays its dividends out of distributable profits. If there are no profits, it will not be able to pay any dividends to shareholders. The rights of preference shares depend on what is expressly stated in their terms of issue, although a preferential dividend is deemed to be cumulative unless expressly described as non-cumulative. Cumulative means that, if the company is unable to pay the dividend in one year because of financial difficulties, it must pay the outstanding dividend in the following year or at some future date. This has to be paid before any payment is made to ordinary shareholders. Once the preference dividend has been paid in full, preference shareholders usually have no right to share in any surplus profits that the company may have made. The surplus profits are used to pay dividends to the ordinary shareholders. It is possible to issue participating preference shares which are an exception to the general rule, as these shares give the shareholders a right to share in any surplus profits, after a dividend has been paid to the company's ordinary shareholders.

Usually preference shares have a priority right to the return of capital if a company is wound up. This means that, if there is not enough money to repay all the shareholders for their shares, the preference shareholders will be paid before the ordinary shareholders. Preference shares often do not carry any voting rights, except to vote in special circumstances such as a move to vary the rights set out in the shares.

Redeemable shares

Redeemable shares can be either issued as ordinary shares or preference shares, but when they are issued they carry a right by the company to redeem or buy back the shares at some future date. As buying back shares reduces the capital of a company, there are strict rules about the issue of such shares. If the company is a public limited company it must have prior authorisation in its articles to issue redeemable shares (CA 2006, s 684). This enables the public who purchase shares to know whether a company can issue redeemable shares. A private limited company does not need express authorisation to issue redeemable shares in its articles, but the company can restrict or prohibit the issuing of redeemable shares by a provision in its articles.

Redeemable shares can only be issued if the company also has other shares which cannot be redeemed. Therefore, a company limited by shares can never end up with no shareholders leaving only a Board of Directors, who are not shareholders, running the company. Redeemable shares may be issued with a fixed date for redemption, or issued as redeemable between certain dates or at a time to be decided by the Board of Directors. Redeemable shares are useful where a company needs to raise short-term capital to develop its business, and once the business is flourishing it buys back the shares. Investors may be attracted by redeemable shares because they may know when the company will buy them back and often dividends payable on them are reasonably high.

Treasury shares

When a company buys back its own shares it is usually required to cancel out those shares. However, companies that are on the official list of the Stock Exchange or traded on the Alternative Investment Market or equivalent markets in the European Economic Area can decide not to cancel the shares that have been bought back but keep them 'in treasury'. A share held in treasury can be sold at a future date. Shares held in treasury do not require prior authority from the company's shareholders to be sold, which means that the directors can sell these shares quickly if the company needs capital. There are limits to the number of shares that can be held in treasury.

Figure 16.2 Types of shares

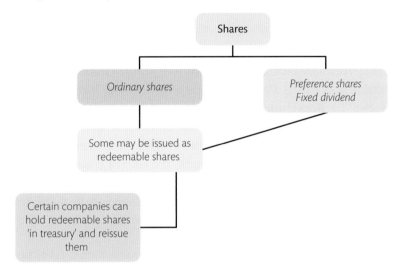

Loan Capital

A trading company has an implied power to borrow money for purposes incidental to its business and charge its assets as security for a loan. However, the articles usually contain the express power to borrow, and may state how far a company's assets may be used as security for the loan. When a loan is made to a company, the document setting out the terms of the loan is called a debenture.

Debentures

A **debenture** is the written document issued by a company setting out the terms of a loan. It normally contains provisions as to payment of interest and terms of repayment of principal. A debenture can be secured on some or all of the company's assets or it may be unsecured. An ordinary mortgage of freehold land by a company is a debenture. The CA 2006 provides certain rules applicable to debentures but it does not provide a comprehensive code, and on a number of points the lender and the company can make their own bargains, subject to the law of contract.

There are three main types of debenture:

- *A single debenture:* This is a loan obtained from a single person or company such as a bank to secure an overdraft.

- *Debentures issued as a series:* This is where different lenders have provided loans which may be for different amounts. Although each transaction is a separate loan, the intention is that the lenders should rank equally between themselves and, therefore, have equal rights to repayment. Each lender, therefore, receives a debenture in an identical form. The debentures are transferable and normally a company must keep a register of debenture holders.

- *The issue of debenture stock:* Only a public company can use this method of raising loans. Debenture stock can be offered through the Stock Exchange in the same way as shares are traded. The stock is usually subscribed to by a large number of lenders. Each lender has a holding of a specific value, and has the right to be repaid his capital at a specific date and, until that date, to receive interest on his loan. Debenture stock can also carry with it other rights such as discount tickets. The issue of debenture stock is treated as a single loan in which each holder has a specified fraction. There must be a trust deed setting out the terms of the loan and providing safeguards for the lenders, such as agreeing to insure the company's assets or restrict the company's total borrowings.

Debenture stock is transferable in multiples of pounds and, therefore, can be transferred in the same way as shares. A holder of debenture stock can sell all or part of his holding. This is an advantage over a single or debenture series, where the loan can only be transferred as a whole. A company is normally required to hold a register of debenture holders.

Business Insight Perks that can be attached to debentures

The All England Lawn Tennis Ground plc issues Centre Court Wimbledon Debentures every five years to raise funds for capital expenditure. Holders of debenture tickets enjoy many privileges, including a centre court seat for every day of the championships (or a no. 1 court seat for the first 10 days of the championships), use of the debenture holders' lounges and exclusive dining facilities, and—for a small, additional fee—the right to enter into a ballot for a car parking space.

Table 16.1 Debentures and shares compared

Debentures	Shares
Provide finance to companies.	Provide finance to companies.
If public companies, may be dealt with on the Stock Exchange.	If public companies, may be dealt with on the Stock Exchange.
Transferable.	Transferable.
A debenture holder is a creditor and their interest is an expense on the company.	A shareholder is a member of the company and can vote at meetings.

Table 16.1 (*continued*)

Debentures	Shares
Company may freely purchase its own debentures.	There are restrictions on a company purchasing its own shares.
Interest is a debt which may be paid out of capital if there are no profits.	Dividends have to be paid out of taxed profits.
Can be issued at a discount.	Cannot be issued at a discount.
If a company is wound up, debenture holders are paid back before shareholders.	If a company is wound up, shareholders are paid back after debenture holders.

Charges

When a company requires a loan, the creditor may require security for the loan (debenture) in the form of a charge on the company's assets. A company which has express or implied power to borrow also has implied power to have a charge put on its assets as security for a loan. A company's assets include its property, machinery, tools, stock, and intangible property such as goodwill, copyrights, and patents. A charge is an impediment upon property granting the holder certain rights over that property. Where a debenture is secured by a charge on assets, the creditor has prior claim over other creditors to payment of his debt out of those assets. In addition to creating a fixed charge over land or on other assets, a company has the unique ability to create floating charges over any assets, fixed or current, present or future.

Fixed charge

A fixed charge is one that relates to specific assets of a company and attaches to those assets as soon as it is created. Assets that are subject to a fixed charge cannot be disposed of without repayment of the charge. If a company defaults on payment of the interest on a loan, the holder of the charge will be entitled to apply to court for the sale of the asset to recover monies owing. It is possible to have more than one fixed charge on any one asset. For example, a company may have a mortgage on its business premises, and then take out a second mortgage on the same premises. If the company is wound up, creditors who hold fixed charges are paid before unsecured creditors. If there are two fixed charges on an asset, usually the first charge created will have priority of payment. If the value of the asset does not cover the amount of all the charges on it, any amount unpaid becomes an unsecured debt. If a fixed charge is created to secure a debt, the charge may be invalid if the company becomes insolvent within six months.

Floating charge

A floating charge does not attach to any particular property but is taken on some or all of a company's assets, both present and future. The types of assets that a floating charge will generally be made on are those that are constantly changing, such as stock or book debts (debts owing to the company). Where a floating charge has been created, a company can carry on business selling and trading the assets subject to the charge, until the charge crystallises. On crystallisation, the charge converts to a fixed charge on the assets secured by the floating charge that the company has at that moment in time. The value of the assets may have fluctuated during the period of time of the floating charge.

A floating charge crystallises and attaches to particular assets when the following events happen:

- The company is wound up.
- The company ceases to trade.
- A receiver is appointed.
- An event occurs which the charge contract stipulated would lead to the floating charge crystallising, and being converted into a fixed charge.

Identification of charges

Whether a floating charge or a fixed charge has been created depends on the freedom given to the company to deal with the charged property in the course of its business. Labels attached to charges by creditors are not conclusive. The general rule is that a charge will be a floating charge if a company remains in control of the assets and can use them and withdraw them from the security. In the following case, although the charge had been described as a fixed charge, the court stated that it was a floating charge because the company was not totally restricted from dealing with the debts or their proceeds.

National Westminster Bank plc v Spectrum Plus Ltd (2005)

Facts: A company created a charge to National Westminster Bank over book debts. The charge was described as a fixed charge. It required the company to pay all the monies it received from book debts into their account with the bank but placed no restriction on the use that could be made of the balance on the account.

Decision: The charge was a floating charge.

Registration of charges

Both fixed charges and floating charges must be registered with the Registrar of Companies within 21 days of being created. If a charge is not registered, it is not enforceable by the debenture holder, who will then be treated as an unsecured creditor.

Basic Terminology

Articles of Association Constitutional document of a company.

Company 'off the shelf' A dormant company that can be purchased from a business.

Debenture A written document issued by a company setting out the terms of a loan.

Dividend Payment made by a company to its shareholders.

Memorandum of Association under the Companies Act 1985 Together with the articles, forms the constitution of the company.

Memorandum of Association under the Companies Act 2006 Document that states that the subscribers wish to form a company and have agreed to become members of it.

Pre-emption rights/rights issue Where new shares are offered to existing shareholders in proportion to their current shareholding.

Promoter A person who takes procedural steps to set up a company.

Share An interest in a company measured by a sum of money.

Shareholders Members of a company limited by shares. They are the owners of the company.

Statement of capital and initial shareholdings The amount of money that the company holds or is entitled to at the date of registration.

For an online flashcard glossary visit the Online Resource Centre

Summary

After studying this chapter you should be able to:

Explain the role of promoters in setting up a company

- Promoters take procedural steps to set up a company and make business preparations for the company.
- They have a general duty to exercise reasonable care and skill and a fiduciary duty towards the company.

Explain what is meant by a company 'off the shelf'

- A company off the shelf is one that has already been registered at Companies House and left dormant.

Identify the steps for registering a company

- To form a new company a memorandum of association, an application for registration, a statement of compliance, and the appropriate fee must be lodged with the Registrar of Companies.
- The application of a company limited by shares must include a statement of capital and initial shareholdings and a copy of the company's articles where they differ from the model default articles.
- A public company must have at least two subscribers and the nominal share capital must be the minimum of £50,000, of which 25 per cent must be paid up.

Outline the rules relating to a company's name

- A company must not have the same name as one that is already on the register.
- Private companies (unless exempted) must end their names with 'limited' or 'Ltd' and public limited companies with 'public limited company' or 'plc'.
- A person may apply to the Company Names Adjudicator objecting to a company's name if it is the same as a name in which he has goodwill or if it is so similar to an existing name that it is likely to mislead the public. The tort of passing off may also be available.

For an online printable version visit the Online Resource Centre

- A company can change a company's name by special resolution or by any other means provided for in its articles.
- The company's registered name must be displayed outside the registered office and at all places of business and on company documents, etc.

Describe the constitution of a company

- Constitutional document is the Articles of Association which state all the rules necessary for the conduct of the company's business.
- The constitution of a company binds the company and its shareholders.
- Articles can usually be amended by special resolution.

Describe the different types of shares

- A share is a form of property which carries rights and obligations. Subject to any restrictions in the articles it is transferable. A company may create different types of shares.
- Ordinary shares are issued without any special rights being attached to them.
- Preference shares have the right to receive an annual dividend of a fixed amount before a dividend is paid on ordinary shares.
- Redeemable shares carry a right by the company to redeem or buy back the shares at some future date.

Show an understanding of how a company is financed through the issue of shares and debentures

- A company can raise capital by selling shares in the company, or by taking out loans.
- The price for shares may be money or money's worth.
- A trading company has an implied power to borrow money for purposes incidental to its business and charge their assets as security for a loan.
- A debenture is the written document issued by a company setting out the terms of a loan. They may be single debentures, debentures issued as a series, or debenture stock.
- A debenture can be secured by a fixed or a floating charge. All charges must be registered at Companies House.

Questions

For outline answers visit the Online Resource Centre

1. Shreena and Gita wish to run a business buying and selling organic vegetables. They have decided to set up a private company limited by shares and are thinking of calling their company 'VegRus'. They will be the subscribers and the first directors of the company. They have already found premises but the owner is insisting that a contract to lease the premises is signed immediately, despite the fact the company will not be registered for about four weeks.

Advise Shreena and Gita what documents will have to be delivered to the Registrar of Companies before a certificate of incorporation of the company is issued, any restrictions on choice of name of the company, and any liabilities they may personally incur if the lease is signed before the company is incorporated.

3. Fabrics Ltd currently supplies soft furnishings to wholesalers, largely on credit terms. Its share capital comprises 100,000 £1 ordinary shares. The company has recently decided to raise more capital as it wants to extend its business via an internet site selling mail order curtains to non-trade customers.

Fabrics Ltd seeks your advice on the following points:

a) In the event that it issues preference shares instead of ordinary shares, what are the differences between the two?

b) If it issues secured debentures, what are the differences between a floating charge and a fixed charge?

4. Explain the options available for financing a company.

5. Discuss the general content and effect of a company's articles.

Further Reading

Bourne, *Bourne on Company Law*, 6th edn (Routledge, 2013).

Dignam and Lowry, *Company Law*, 8th edn (Oxford University Press, 2014).

Dine and Koutsias, *Company Law*, 8th edn (Palgrave, 2014).

Wild and Weinstein, *Smith & Keenan's Company Law*, 16th edn (Pearson, 2013).

Companies House: http://www.companieshouse.gov.uk/.

Department for Business Innovation & Skills: https://www.gov.uk/government/organisations/department-for-business-innovation-skills.

Nominet: http://www.nominet.org.uk/.

Online Resource Centre

Test your knowledge by trying this chapter's **Multiple Choice Questions**. Visit:

http://www.oup.com/uk/orc/law/company/ jonesibl3e/01student/mcqs/ch16/

For more information, updates, and multiple choice questions, please visit the Online Resource Centre at:

http://www.oup.com/uk/orc/law/company/ jonesibl3e/

17 Company Law II
Company Officers and Liabilities

Introduction

A company is a separate legal entity and can enter into agreements and sue and be sued in its own name. However, it is an artificial person and, therefore, it needs natural persons to act on its behalf and manage its affairs. The shareholders of a company own the company, but their main interest is usually with the company's performance, the amount of the dividend declared, and the value of their shares. They are not responsible for the day-to-day running of the company; that is the responsibility of the Board of Directors. Shareholders ultimately have the authority to appoint and dismiss directors and to reduce their powers, but once appointed it is the directors of a company who provide the management of a company. The directors do not have to be shareholders, unless there is a special clause in the company's articles that states directors must be shareholders. Commonly, even where not required by the articles, directors do own some shares in their company. In small private companies the directors may be the major or only shareholders. Even if the directors are the only share-holders and, therefore, own the company, when they act on behalf of the company they carry out their duties as directors and not as owners.

A private company may, and a public company must, appoint a company secretary who has various administrative responsibilities and must ensure compliance with legal require-ments. A company is also required to appoint external auditors for each year who are re-sponsible for ensuring a company's accounts give a fair and accurate view of the company's financial position. The accurate auditing of company accounts is very important. There has been considerable media attention on inaccurate reporting where companies have failed amid financial scandal.

Much of the law relating to directors and other company officers can be found in the Companies Act 2006 (CA 2006). Other important legislation relating to company officers includes the Company Directors Disqualification Act 1986 and the Insolvency Act 1986.

Learning Objectives

After studying this chapter you should be able to:

- Define 'director' and understand the position of the Board of Directors.
- Outline the appointment and removal of directors.
- Describe the powers and duties of directors.
- Explain the appointment and the role of a company secretary and **company auditors**.
- Understand the meaning of corporate governance.

Directors

A director is an officer of a company who acts as an agent of the company, and, therefore, can bind the company by his acts without incurring personal liability. The directors are responsible for the day-to-day management of the company and for developing company strategy and policy.

Key Concept A public limited company (plc) must be registered at Companies House as a public limited company and is subject to additional rules and greater regulation than a private limited company (Ltd). A plc can offer its shares for sale to the public.

All companies must have at least one director and public limited companies (plcs) must have at least two directors (CA 2006, s 154) (see Figure 17.1). In practice, large companies usually have many more than one or two directors. There is no legal maximum number of directors; however, a company's articles may state a maximum number and/or a minimum number (provided it is not less than the legal minimum). There are no legal qualifications necessary to become a director but certain persons may be disqualified from being a director under the Company Directors Disqualification Act 1986, or the company's own articles may exclude certain persons from being directors. A company can be a director of another company (corporate director) but all companies must have at least one director who is a natural person, and, therefore, it is not possible to have a sole corporate director. There is no statutory maximum age limit for a natural person, but there is a minimum age of 16 for both public and private companies.

Figure 17.1 Minimum number of company directors required by law

Companies Act 2006
All companies must have at least one director
who is a natural person aged 16 or above

Companies Act 2006
Public Limited Companies must have an
additional director who may be a natural
person or another company

Articles of a Company
The articles of a company may provide for
additional directors

The Board of Directors

Directors meet and make decisions at **board meetings**. The Board of Directors is the 'mind' of the company and has responsibility for managing its affairs. The Board may delegate some of its powers to individual directors to act on its behalf. Certain decisions, such as approving the annual accounts and recommending a dividend to the shareholders, must be taken by the Board. Directors have a duty to attend board meetings, although these do not necessarily have to be conducted face-to-face. It is possible to hold a board meeting at which all the directors are not in the same room, but are in communication with each other through such means as conference call facilities. Unless the articles state otherwise, any director can call a board meeting, provided reasonable notice is given, or all the directors agree to meet without notice.

Key Concept Board meetings are for directors only and must be distinguished from general meetings which are meetings where all the members (shareholders) of a company have the right to attend.

The quorum (minimum number of persons required) for a board meeting is usually stated in the company's articles, but if it is not fixed, the default model articles fix the minimum number at two. If the number of directors at a board meeting falls below quorum, the Board can only act to fill vacancies, or to call a general meeting of the shareholders. The Board of

Directors usually appoints one of the directors as chairman of the Board. The chairman is responsible for providing an agenda for meetings, ensuring that all meetings proceed in an efficient manner, and that the functions of the Board are competently carried out. Unless the articles state otherwise, each director present at a board meeting has one vote, and resolutions made by the Board are passed by majority. The articles may give the chairman a casting vote. The minutes of meetings must be kept, and the directors and auditors have the right to inspect them.

Categories of Directors

A director includes 'any person occupying the position of director, by whatever name called' (CA 2006, s 250). In Company Law this means whether or not a person is a director is a question of fact rather than terminology. The word 'director' in a job title such as 'Quality Director' does not necessarily mean the person is actually a director of a company. A person is deemed to be a director, even if not appointed as such, if he carries out the functions of a director, such as taking part in decision-making at board meetings. Anyone who acts as a director, although not validly appointed, is called a '*de facto director*' (a director in fact). He becomes a director through conduct and has the liabilities, duties, and powers of a properly appointed director (see Figure 17.2).

Executive and non-executive directors

A company with a relatively large number of directors may have both executive and non-executive directors. The **executive directors** have management responsibilities in the company. They may be appointed to different tasks, such as finance director, managing director, and sales director. Generally, although not a legal requirement, one or more of the directors is appointed as **managing director**. The Board delegates powers to the managing director, giving that director the responsibility for the day-to-day overall management of the company. Executive directors usually work full time for a company and have a contract of employment, making them employees of the company.

Non-executive directors are lay directors who are not employed by the company, and do not receive a salary but may be paid a fee. Their primary function is to attend board meetings, check the executive directors are managing the company properly, and ensure high standards of financial integrity. Although the appointment of non-executive directors is not a legal requirement, it is seen as 'best practice' in corporate governance. The presence of non-executive directors on a Board is a valuable asset for a company, as they can provide an objective and independent view of company policy, and ensure that the Board acts in the interests of the company. However, criticism has been levelled at non-executive directors as being too easily influenced by the executive directors and not fully conversant with the mechanics of the company. Non-executive directors share the same duties and

Figure 17.2 Types of directors

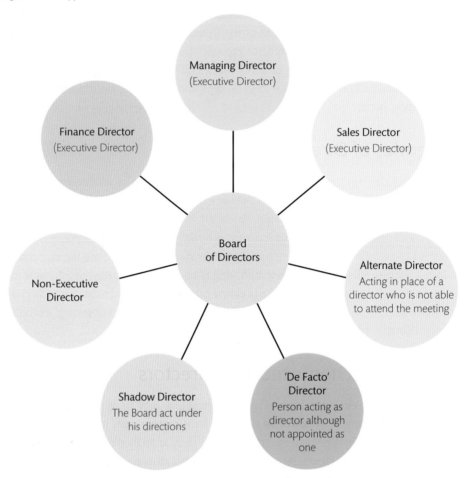

potential liabilities as executive directors; therefore, if the company acts wrongfully or illegally, all directors (both the executive and non-executive directors) may be held liable in law.

Shadow directors

A shadow director is a person (natural or corporate) whose directions or instruction the directors of a company are accustomed to follow (CA 2006, s 251). The shadow director must be 'pulling the strings' of the directors on a regular basis. A shadow director is subject to some of the same liabilities of appointed directors. Persons who give advice to a Board of Directors in their professional capacity, such as solicitors or accountants, are not usually regarded as shadow directors, but any person working too closely with a Board and constantly advising the Board how to act may be regarded in law as a shadow director.

Alternate directors

Where a director is unable to attend a board meeting, he may be allowed to appoint a person to act in his place and vote on his behalf as an alternate director provided the articles allow for such an appointment. Some articles do not allow appointment of alternate directors, but usually articles do allow appointment, provided the alternate director is approved by the Board. In practice, it is often one of the other directors rather than an outsider who is appointed.

Key Concept The directors of a company are responsible for the management of the company and for developing company strategy and policy. A director includes any person occupying the position of director whether validly appointed or not. Public companies must have at least two directors and private companies at least one director.

Appointment, Retirement, and Removal of Directors

When a company is first formed, one of the documents sent to the Registrar of Companies is an application for registration, which states the person or persons who have consented to act as directors. The persons named in the application automatically become the first director or directors of the company. No appointment or confirmation of appointment is necessary. Subsequently, new directors may be appointed, either to replace the existing ones or as additional directors. The procedure for appointing directors is set out in the company's articles (see Figure 17.3). Usually directors are appointed by **ordinary resolution** at a general meeting or by the existing directors. A director's actions are valid even if his appointment is subsequently found to be void or defective.

In public companies, new directors are generally appointed by the Board, and their appointment lasts until the next annual general meeting of the company, when the shareholders are asked to vote to re-appoint the new directors. A directorship in a public company is usually for a set number of years. There is a separate vote for each individual director as opposed to one vote for a team of directors. Generally, the articles also allow the shareholders to propose persons as directors, which they might do if they are dissatisfied with the Board as it stands. In contrast, the articles of small companies may allow for the directors to be appointed permanently.

Retirement and resignation

A director can retire from office at the end of a set period and not seek re-election, or can resign from office at any time. Some articles allow for retirement and re-election of directors

Figure 17.3 Appointment of directors

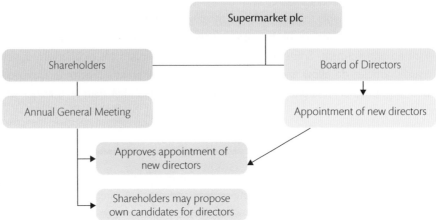

after a set number of years. The articles of public companies and large private companies often require non-executive directors to retire by rotation every three years, but allow them to stand for re-election if they wish to do so.

Removal of directors

In addition to any provision in the articles, the CA 2006, s 168 states that a director can be removed before the expiration of his term of office by an ordinary resolution of the shareholders at a general meeting. This section cannot be excluded by a company. A shareholder who wishes to make a proposal that a director is dismissed must give the company at least 28 days' notice (**'special notice'**) of their proposal prior to the meeting. The director in question has the right to attach his written statement to the proposal for dismissal before it is circulated to shareholders, and has the right to speak at the meeting.

Although s 168 cannot be excluded, its effect may be limited by other means. It is possible for private companies to have **weighted voting rights on shares** which protect directors from being removed by ordinary shareholders. In the following case, the articles gave weighted voting rights to shareholders (who were also the directors) if there was a resolution to remove them as directors.

Bushell v Faith (1970)

Facts: A company had a capital of £300 in £1 shares. There were three shareholders, a brother and two sisters, and each held 100 shares. The three shareholders were also the directors of the company. The articles of the company stated that, in a resolution to remove any director, any shares owned by that director should carry three votes per share. The two sisters voted for a resolution to remove their brother as director. The brother claimed that he had defeated their resolution by 300 votes to 200 votes.

Decision: The Companies Act 1948 (now CA 2006, s 168) allowed companies to have weighted voting rights on shares. The article was valid and the resolution to remove the brother as director was defeated.

Allowing weighted voting rights is not the only technique to prevent the removal of a director. As an alternative, it is possible to divide shares into different classes with each class having the exclusive right to appoint and remove a director (see Figure 17.4). It would also be possible to have a shareholders' agreement that states that each class of shareholder has to be present at a general meeting to constitute a quorum. A shareholder director could absent himself from a meeting where there was to be a vote on a resolution to dismiss him as director.

It would be inappropriate to allow directors of public companies to be a permanent fixture, and a company with weighted voting rights would be refused listing on the London Stock Exchange. Although private companies can usually dispense with general meetings, provided the members all agree (passing only written resolutions), if a director is to be dismissed it must be by a general meeting.

Removal of an executive director may result in a breach of contract of employment if the director has a contract of service with the company. In practice, when a director is going to

Figure 17.4 **Example of dividing shares into classes**

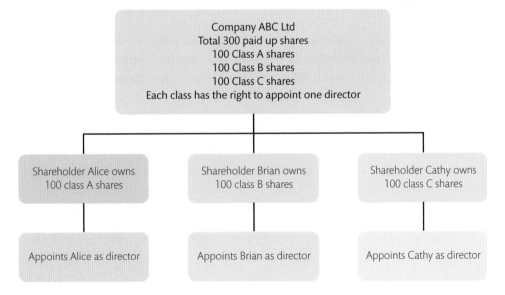

Company ABC Ltd
Total 300 paid up shares
100 Class A shares
100 Class B shares
100 Class C shares
Each class has the right to appoint one director

Shareholder Alice owns
100 class A shares

Shareholder Brian owns
100 class B shares

Shareholder Cathy owns
100 class C shares

Appoints Alice as director

Appoints Brian as director

Appoints Cathy as director

be removed from office he is usually asked to resign rather than go through the formal process of removal, and terms of dismissal are negotiated.

Business Insight Barclay's chief executive resigns

In July 2012 Bob Diamond, Chief Executive of Barclays, resigned after news broke of the bank's attempt to manipulate the interbank lending rates, Libor and Euribor (key benchmark interest rates used around the world to help set the price at which individuals and businesses can borrow). The regulators in the US and UK fined Barclays £290 m ($450 m) for attempting to rig the rates. Other banks have also been fined for rate fixing; the Swiss bank USB £940 m ($1.5 b) and Royal Bank of Scotland £390 m ($612 m).

Vacation of office under the articles

It is usual for the articles of a company to provide that a director's office is automatically vacated if the director becomes bankrupt, suffers from a mental disorder, or has been absent from board meetings for a consecutive period of time (such as six months) without permission, and the Board resolves that he must vacate his office. A directorship ceases on the death of a director and, generally, it also ceases if the company becomes **insolvent** and goes into liquidation. If the articles of a company require its directors to be the registered holders of a certain number of shares, a director's office will be vacated if he fails to obtain or ceases to hold the requisite number of shares.

Disqualification under the Company Directors Disqualification Act 1986

The Company Directors Disqualification Act 1986 (CDDA 1986) was introduced partly to prevent directors of failed companies being able to walk away from the failed company without any personal liability towards the creditors, and start a new company carrying on a similar business.

The CDDA 1986 allows a court to disqualify any person (including persons who have not previously been directors) from being a director, liquidator, administrator, receiver, or manager of a company, or being concerned with the promotion or management of a company. Under the CDDA 1986, in some circumstances a court has the discretionary power to disqualify persons as directors and, in other circumstances, the court must disqualify them.

A court may make a disqualification order for up to 15 years in the following circumstances:

- Where a person has been convicted of a serious offence in connection with the formation, management, or liquidation of a company.
- Where, on the winding up of a company, it appears that a person has been guilty of fraudulent trading (see Chapter 18).

- Where a director is guilty of certain breaches of competition law or participating in wrongful trading (see Chapter 18).

- Where the Secretary of State considers it to be in the public interest that a person is disqualified from acting as a director.

A court may make a disqualification order for up to five years in the following circumstances:

- Where a person has persistently failed to comply with company legislation requirements of filing returns, accounts, or other documents with the Registrar of Companies. (Three failures in five years is conclusive evidence of persistent default.)

A court must make a disqualification order for between two and 15 years in the following circumstances:

- Where a person has been a director of a company which has become insolvent either while he was a director or subsequently, and his conduct as a director makes him unfit to be concerned in the management of a company. Schedule 1 to the CDDA 1986 lists the matters to which the court is to have regard when deciding if a director's conduct makes him unfit to act, and includes breach of director's duties, transactions defrauding creditors, and misapplication of company property.

Generally, the court's approach is to view ordinary commercial misjudgement as insufficient to justify disqualification, and usually will only disqualify a director who has committed a breach such as **insider dealing** or failure to keep proper accounting records; however, a director may be considered unfit to act where he has been totally incompetent.

Business Insight Directors of the Accident Group declared unfit to act as directors for four years

In 2008, two former directors of a company formerly known as the Accident Group, which went into liquidation with a deficiency of £81.2 million, were held by the High Court to be unfit and were disqualified under the Company Directors Disqualification Act 1986. The company had been managed partly by an inner group of directors taking decisions without notice to or consent of the rest of the Board. The company had made payments of £3 million of dividends, when there were insufficient reserves of profit out of which to pay them.

Register of Directors

A company is required to register particulars about directors at Companies House (CA 2006, s 167). The residential addresses of company directors do not have to be made available to the public. This is to protect directors against some of the tactics used by certain campaigners, for example, where the company is connected with the use of animals in research. The company must also keep its own register of directors, and if it is a public company, a register of secretaries. Members of the public are entitled to inspect the registers. Any change in directors should be noted in the company's register of directors and Companies House must be informed within 14 days of the change. A company and its officers are liable to fines, on conviction, for any failure to comply with the registration requirements.

The Powers of Company Directors

The extent of the directors' powers is defined by the articles of a company. The model articles provide that the directors shall manage the company's business and exercise all the powers of the company for any purpose connected with the company's business. This is an extensive power and includes activities such as borrowing money and, in some circumstances, issuing shares. Although the power to manage the company's business is given to the Board of Directors collectively, it is open to the Board to sub-delegate powers to individual directors or others.

Key Concept The Secretary of State prescribes model articles for the most common types of company. They apply where the company either has not provided its own articles, or where its articles do not cover a particular subject. Companies are subject to the model articles that were in force at the time the company was registered unless the company adopts the new model articles, which apply to companies registered from 1 October 2009.

Restrictions on powers of directors

The Companies Act 2006 states that a company has unrestricted objects unless specifically restricted by the articles (for example, community interest companies may restrict their objects to activities beneficial to the community). If the articles do restrict the objects of the company, the directors can only exercise their powers subject to those limitations. However, even if an action is within the power of a company, the articles may limit the powers of the directors to act, for example, by setting out the maximum sum the directors can borrow without express authority from the shareholders at a general meeting. Any alteration of the articles must be by **special resolution**.

Directors are required, by the CA 2006, to exercise their powers for the proper purpose for which they were given and what they honestly believe to be in the best interests of the company.

Directors' Authority to Act

A company as an artificial person can only act through its agents. Under the principle of agency law, agents must act within their actual or apparent authority (see Chapter 9). When the Board of Directors, acting collectively, or one director, acting on his own, enters into a contract on behalf of the company, the contract will be binding on the company, provided the actions are within their authority. Actual authority can be express or implied. A managing director's actual authority is what he is given by the Board but, if the Board does not give him actual authority to make business contracts, he will have implied authority to do so, from his position as managing director. Other executive directors, such as sales directors and finance directors, have no implied authority to make general contracts but have the authority that attaches to those management positions.

Key Concept It is not a legal requirement for a company to appoint a managing director but many companies do so. A managing director is responsible for the day-to-day overall management of a company.

In addition to having actual authority, either express actual authority or implied actual authority, a director may also have apparent (or ostensible) authority. This is where actual authority does not exist but the company holds out a director as having authority to a person who relies on it. The company will be bound by any resulting transaction the director enters into with the third party. For example, if a Board of Directors allows a director to behave as if he were a managing director or give the impression that he is, even though he has not been appointed as one, he will have the apparent authority of a managing director.

Freeman & Lockyer v Buckhurst Park Properties Ltd (1964)

Facts: The Board of Directors comprised four directors. One director made all the contracts as if he were appointed as the managing director, but he had never been appointed as a managing director and, therefore, had no actual authority to bind the company. The other directors knew and acquiesced to this. The company refused to pay out on one of the contracts entered into by the unauthorised director.

Decision: The company was liable on the contract, as they had held out the director as having the necessary authority, and the third party had reasonably relied on this representation. The director had apparent authority to bind the company.

Directors acting without authority: protection for third parties (CA 2006, s 40)

Where directors act without any authority, or surpass the authority they have been given either in the articles or delegated by the Board, the position is governed by CA 2006, s 40. Under this section, the powers given to directors (or persons authorised by the directors) to enter into any transactions between a company and a third party acting in good faith are deemed to be free of any limitations under the company's constitution. This means that, even if the company's articles contain restrictions on the powers of directors, the company will be bound by the transaction, provided a third party is acting in good faith. The third party is presumed to be acting in good faith unless the contrary is proved by the company. A third party is not regarded as 'acting in bad faith' just because he knows that an action is beyond the powers a director has under the company's constitution. Section 40 covers all transactions or dealings between companies and third parties acting in good faith.

However, s 40 does not apply when the 'third party' is a director of the company or a person connected with a director (CA 2006, s 41). Connected persons include the director's spouse or partner, children and step-children, and companies where the director holds 20 per cent or more of the share capital, or can exercise 20 per cent of the voting rights. If the transaction is with a connected person, the transaction may be **voidable** (set aside) by the company, and the connected person is liable to account to the company for any gain he has made and to indemnify the company for any loss that the company has incurred (see Figure 17.5). It may be possible for the connected person to avoid liability if he can show, at the time of making the transaction, that he was unaware that the directors were acting outside or exceeding their powers.

Key Concept A company is bound by a transaction entered into by a director and a third party, acting in good faith, even if the director acted outside or beyond the powers given to him by the company.

General Duties of Directors

Directors are in charge of a company's assets and have extensive management powers, and, therefore, it is important that some safety measures exist to protect the company from directors misusing their powers. These safety measures must be balanced to allow for effective control without stifling innovative and progressive management. The control comes in the form of directors' duties. The CA 2006 codified most of the general duties of directors which were previously to be found in common law rules and equitable principles. Although these duties are now set out in ss 171–177, the CA 2006 makes it clear that the duties should be

Figure 17.5 Flow chart showing when a company is bound by a transaction with third parties

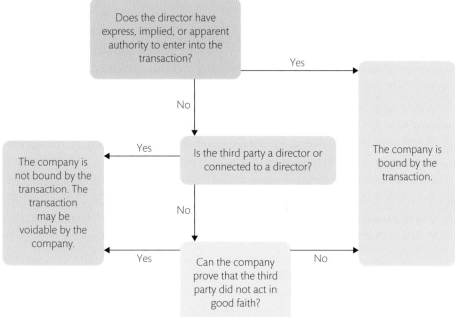

interpreted and applied in the same way as the common law rules or equitable principles that they replaced, and the law should be developed on these principles (CA 2006, s 170(4)). Therefore, some of the cases relating to directors' duties that pre-date the CA 2006 are relevant today.

There are seven codified duties (see Figure 17.6) and, apart from one (the common law duty to exercise reasonable care, skill, and diligence: CA 2006, s 174), all the duties are regarded as fiduciary duties. The word 'fiduciary' is related to trust and confidence. Persons who act on behalf of others are in **fiduciary relationships**, and the law of equity imposes a duty of trust and loyalty on them. This means that the directors, acting both individually and collectively in running a company and dealing with a company's assets, are under an obligation of good faith and loyalty to their company. They must act in a manner that they believe to be in the best interests of the company, and must not put themselves in a position where there would be a conflict of interest.

Section 170(1) makes it clear that these general duties are owed by a director to his company. The duties are owed to the company as a whole, and are not owed to individual shareholders, or other stakeholders such as employees and creditors. It is the company that decides whether or not to take action against a director for breach of duty, and any compensation received as a result of court action is payable to the company.

In carrying out their duties, the directors also have to take into account the interests of employees, suppliers, customers, and others (s 172). General duties apply to executive and non-executive directors.

A duty to act within powers: s 171

Directors must act in accordance with the company's constitution (the articles plus later resolutions and agreements made by the company), and only exercise their powers for the purposes for which they were given.

Where directors act outside their powers or where they have powers to act for one purpose, and they use these powers for a collateral purpose, the transaction may be ratified (approved) by the shareholders in a general meeting. The ratification may be retrospective, i.e. after the powers have been used for an improper purpose.

The CA 2006 allows ratification where a director's conduct amounts to negligence, default, breach of duty, or breach of trust in relation to the company (CA 2006, s 239). The CA 2006 sets down minimum standards for ratification. The director, if he is also a shareholder, or any shareholder connected with him, cannot take part in the vote to ratify the wrongful action.

If the company is insolvent, the transactions must not prejudice the interest of company creditors. Any shareholder can apply to the court to declare that a transaction by the directors is void. If the directors have used their power for an improper purpose, a court may order that a meeting of the shareholders should be held to decide whether or not to validate the transaction.

A duty to promote the success of the company: s 172

A director must act in a way which in good faith (honestly) he considers would most likely promote the success of the company for the benefit of its members (shareholders) as a whole. This means that a director must act in the company's best interests. However, in exercising this duty, a director must also take into account other factors, including the following:

- The likely long-term consequences of any decision.
- The interests of the company's employees.
- The need to develop good business relationships with the company's suppliers, customers, and others who deal with the company.
- The impact of the company's activities on the community and the environment.
- The desirability of maintaining a reputation for high standards of business conduct.
- The need to act fairly between members (shareholders) of the company.

It is up to the directors to decide whether a particular factor is relevant to any decision they make, and how much weight to give it. The directors must always act honestly, in good faith, and with due care, skill, and diligence. The list of factors stated in the CA 2006 is not exhaustive, and directors should also, if appropriate, consider other relevant issues. For example, if the company is a community interest company, it may have additional objectives relating to the local community.

In addition, in some circumstances the law requires the directors to primarily consider the interests of creditors. If a company is insolvent, the directors will be liable for wrongful trading unless they take action to minimise the loss to creditors.

In the following case a director was in breach of both s 172 and s 175.

Odyssey Entertainment Ltd (In Liquidation) v (1) Kamp & others (2012)

Facts: C traded in film distribution rights and D was a director of C. D decided that he would have better prospects working on his own account. He started to undertake work keeping it secret from C's Board of Directors. D told the Board that C's financial prospects were poor and shortly afterwards the Board resolved to wind up C.

Decision: In working behind C's back to develop his own opportunities D was not acting in the way that would promote C's success and therefore had broken his duty of good faith under s 172. He was also in breach of his duty under s 175 to avoid a conflict of interest by undertaking work on his own account.

A duty to exercise independent judgement: s 173

Directors are required to decide questions for themselves, and not merely to act on instructions from others. It is particularly important to ensure directors are exercising their own judgement when their company is a wholly owned subsidiary of another company. However, directors will not be in breach of this duty if they act in a way authorised by the company's constitution, or in accordance with an agreement entered into by the company that restricts the future exercise of discretion by its directors, provided that, when the agreement was made, it was in the best interests of the company. In other words, directors can agree that their company will act in a particular way, provided at the time it appears to be in the best interest of the company. In the following case, the directors of Fulham Football Club Ltd had not breached their duty when they made an agreement with Cabra Estates plc.

Fulham Football Club Ltd & Ors v Cabra Estates plc (1992)

Facts: The directors of Fulham Football Club Ltd made an agreement in writing with Cabra concerning the future development of the ground, involving the payment of substantial sums of money to the club. Later the directors did not want to be bound by the agreement and alleged that they could not fetter their discretion to act in a particular way.

Decision: Directors are under a duty to act in the best interests of their company but that did not mean they could never make a contract which bound themselves to the future exercise of their powers in a particular way. The agreement was binding on the company.

A duty to exercise reasonable skill, care, and diligence: s 174

This duty has an objective and a subjective test. It requires directors to exercise the care, skill, and diligence that would be expected from a reasonably diligent person with the general knowledge, skill, and experience that may reasonably be expected of a person carrying out that director's functions. This is the objective part of the duty in that the test is based on how a reasonable director would have acted. In addition, the section requires a director to exercise the care, skill, and diligence that would be expected from a reasonably diligent person with the director's actual knowledge, skill, and expertise. This is the subjective part of the test because it relates to the attributes of that particular director.

If a director is found to have acted through ignorance, he will be in breach of this duty if a reasonable director in his position would have had the knowledge to act differently. If a director has a particular skill that is of a higher standard than an ordinary director, that director will be expected to perform with that higher level of expertise. Even someone with no business experience is required by the CA 2006 to act with the same level of care expected of a reasonable person fulfilling the position of a director. All the general duties of directors apply to both executive and non-executive directors.

Dorchester Finance Co Ltd v Stebbing (1989)

Facts: A money lending company had one executive director and two non-executive directors who were both accountants. The non-executive directors occasionally visited the company and signed blank cheques for the executive director to use. The executive director made loans that the company could not reclaim. The company brought an action for negligence against all three directors. The two non-executive directors claimed they were not liable.

Decision: All the directors were liable for failing to exercise reasonable skill, care, and diligence. The court did not distinguish between the standards expected of executive and non-executive directors.

In the following case the director who was in breach of his duty under s174 could not claim against the company when he was injured.

Brumder v Motornet Service and Repairs Ltd (2013)

Facts: B, who was the sole director of a company disregarded health and safety issues. This resulted in the company breaching its health and safety duty and B losing a finger. B sued the company.

Decision: B was in breach of his duty under s174. He could not claim against the company.

It is the company that decides whether to sue the directors for their negligence. A company, acting through its shareholders, may ratify a director's failure to exercise his duty of care, skill, and diligence (see earlier CA 2006, s 239).

A duty to avoid conflict of interest: s 175

A director must avoid a situation in which he has, or could have, a direct or indirect interest that conflicts or possibly may conflict, with the interests of the company. This general duty applies particularly (but not only) to the exploitation of property, information, or opportunity regardless of whether the company suffers a loss. It is clear that, where a director acts in competition with his company, he will be in breach of this duty. He is also in breach if he uses an opportunity gained through his position in the company. The following case demonstrates that there can be a conflict of interest where a director takes advantage of information and an opportunity he knows about through his directorship, even though the company itself would not have been able to take up the opportunity.

IDC v Cooley (1972)

Facts: Cooley was an architect and managing director of a building consultancy company. Cooley was in charge of negotiations for a contract with Eastern Gas Board, and when it became clear that the Gas Board were not going to award a contract to the consultancy company, Cooley accepted the work privately, and resigned from the company, falsely claiming ill health. The company sued Cooley for profits made on the contract.

Decision: Cooley was accountable to the company for profits he had made. He had breached his duty as a director by allowing a conflict of interest and taking advantage of an opportunity presented to him.

There is no breach of duty where a director declares his interest to the Board of Directors, and the Board votes to authorise his actions. The vote of the director who declared an interest is not included in the vote at the board meeting. If the company is a private company, the authorisation can only be made if proposed to the Board and nothing in the company's articles invalidates such authorisation. If it is a public company, the articles must expressly include a provision allowing authorisation. Where a Board gives authorisation, additional approval by the shareholders is not necessary, unless the company's articles state otherwise.

A director continues to be subject to this duty even after he has ceased to be a director and is liable if he exploits any property, information, or opportunity which he became aware of whilst a director.

Killen v Horseworld Ltd and others (2012)

Facts: K, a former director of Horseworld Ltd exploited a media broadcasting opportunity which arose whilst she was on the board of Horseworld Ltd to gain a contract for her own company.
Decision: Despite no longer being a director of Horseworld Ltd, K was in breach of her duty to avoid conflicts of interest under section 175. She was ordered to pay any profits her company had made to Horseworld Ltd.

A duty not to accept benefits from third parties: s 176

A director must not accept benefits from a third party given to him because of his position as a director, or for his doing or not doing anything as a director.

Benefits can be financial or non-financial and include bribes and gifts. Large companies generally have strict rules about acceptance of gifts and corporate hospitality from other businesses that may be seeking contracts with the company. A third party is defined as any person, other than the company, its subsidiaries, or persons acting on behalf of the company or its subsidiaries. There is no provision for the Board to authorise acceptance of bribes; however, the articles or the shareholders may authorise acceptance of gifts. It is not a breach of duty if the benefit could not reasonably be expected to give rise to a conflict of interest or a conflict of duties.

A duty to declare an interest in any proposed transaction or arrangement with the company: s 177

A director must disclose any direct or indirect interest he may have in a proposed transaction or arrangement with his company. He must inform all the other directors, at a board meeting or by written or general notice, of the nature and extent of his interest. Indirect interest may arise if, for example, a director's partner or wife is involved in the proposed transaction. Proposed contracts (not yet finalised) with the company are included as transactions. All declarations of interest have to be made before the company enters into the transaction or arrangement, and if the declaration becomes inaccurate or incomplete, the director has a duty to amend it. A director only has to declare an interest if he is aware of the transaction. But he is treated as being aware of a transaction if he ought reasonably to have known of it. A director will not have breached this duty if his interest in a transaction cannot reasonably be regarded as likely to give rise to a conflict of interest, or the other directors are already aware, or ought reasonably to have been aware, of his interest.

Example

S Ltd is negotiating a contract with Naz, the owner of Angora farms, for the supply of goat's cheese. Naz's wife, Julie, is a director of S Ltd. Julie will have a duty under the CA 2006, s 177 to disclose the nature and extent of her indirect interest in Angora farms to the other directors of S Ltd. If she fails to do so, any contract entered into between S Ltd and Naz can be set aside by S Ltd and Julie will be liable to the company for any losses they sustain.

Shareholders of a company do not have to approve or consent to a proposed transaction where a director has disclosed an interest, unless the articles of the company expressly require it (CA 2006, s 180). However, substantial transactions (see later in the chapter) between the company and a director do require the approval of shareholders.

Figure 17.6 General statutory duties of directors

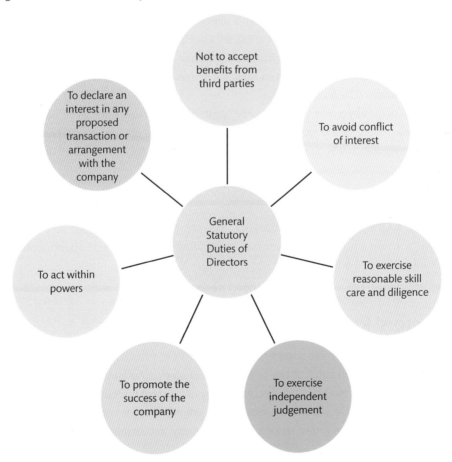

Breach of Duties by Directors

A director who has breached his duties will be required to make up any losses suffered by his company. In addition, any secret profit gained by a director, as a result of his breach of duties, can be claimed by the company. Any contract entered into where the director failed to disclose an interest will be voidable, and can be set aside by the company. If a director has taken any property from the company, this can be reclaimed provided it is still in the director's possession, or has not passed to a third party who acquired the property for value and in good faith. Where the breach is continuing, or if the breach has not yet occurred (but it is clear that a director intends to commit a breach), the company can seek an injunction (order) from a court, preventing the director from breaching his duty or requiring his action to stop.

If more than one of the directors is in breach of their duties, their liability is joint and several. This means that the company can take action against any or all of the directors. A director not in breach is not liable for acts of other directors in breach, but if he becomes aware of serious breaches of duty he must inform the shareholders.

The articles of a company can impose more onerous duties on a director, but they cannot reduce the statutory ones. Provisions, including those in contracts with directors or in the articles, are void if they purport to exempt a director from or indemnify him against liability for breach of duty or negligence (CA 2006, s 232). However, the company is permitted to provide insurance for a director against such liabilities. It is also open to a court to treat a director leniently, and release him from liability if he has acted honestly and reasonably in all the circumstances (CA 2006, s 1157).

A breach of duty by a director may also be negated by the shareholders giving authority, by ordinary resolution, for a director to act in a way which would otherwise be in breach of his duties. The resolution will only be effective if the director has fully disclosed all the relevant details to the shareholders.

Key Concept The Companies Act 2006 sets out seven general statutory duties of directors. The articles of a company can impose more onerous duties on a director but they cannot reduce the statutory ones.

Directors' Remuneration: Salaries and Fees

Where a director is to receive remuneration for his services to a company, the remuneration must be allowed either by the articles or a contract of service. Authorisation is in the articles if the payment is to a non-executive director by way of fees, and in a contract of service if the payment is a salary to an executive director (as an employee of the company). An executive director's service contract must be kept by the company, and shareholders of the company can inspect it and obtain copies. If the shareholders are intending to attempt to remove a director before his term of office expires, it is important for them to know how much it might cost the company if the director sues for breach of contract of service.

Normally the articles state that the amount of fees paid to directors have to be approved by ordinary resolution of the shareholders, but generally the Board of Directors has the authority to deal with contracts of service. However, where a company is listed on the Stock Exchange, there is some control through statutory regulations, and the UK Corporate Governance Code. This Code sets out standards of good practice for the governance of companies, and listed companies must either declare that they comply with its recommendations, or else explain their non-compliance. A listed company must set up a committee of independent non-executive directors to make recommendations about remuneration packages and publish an annual report on directors' pay. The report has to be approved by the Board of Directors and voted on by the shareholders at a general meeting. A copy of the report is sent to the Registrar of Companies.

Business Insight Directors' remuneration

In 2014 a number of companies faced shareholder rebellion over remuneration packages, particularly in relation to large pay awards to senior executives. At the AGMs shareholders of a number of companies rejected the company's remuneration report.

According to the High Pay Centre in 2014 the average annual salary of a top chief executive was almost 180 times greater than the average annual salary. Research from the Incomes Data Services revealed that the median total earnings for a FTSE 100 director was £2.4 m, rising to £3.3 m for chief executives. The highest paid chief executive of any of the FTSE 100 companies was Sir Martin Sorrell, chief executive of media and advertising company WPP whose total remuneration package rose to almost £30 m.

Shareholders have to approve, by ordinary resolution, any contracts of employment given to directors for more than two years that cannot be terminated by notice given by the company (CA 2006, ss 188 and 189). If shareholders' approval is not obtained, the directors' contracts of employment can be terminated by reasonable notice. This provision is useful because directors can no longer give themselves, without shareholders' approval, very long service contracts under which large amounts of compensation are payable if the contract is terminated early.

Loans by the Company to Directors

Loans made by the company to its directors and persons connected to directors (wives, partners, etc) are permitted, provided the shareholders have approved the loan by resolution

(CA 2006, s 197). All transactions involving loans to directors must be disclosed in the company's accounts.

Directors' Contracts

A director must declare an interest in an existing transaction or arrangement with his company (CA 2006, s 182). He must disclose the nature and extent of any direct or indirect interest to all the other directors. If the director has made a relevant declaration, at the point when the transaction was proposed, he does not need to make a second declaration. He does not have to declare an interest which he could not reasonably have known about. Any contract involving an undeclared conflict of interest may be voidable by the company, and any profit gained by the director may be claimed by the company. Failing to make a disclosure under s 182 is a criminal offence.

Substantial and Material Property Transactions

Section 190 of the CA 2006 is designed to prevent directors acting without the approval of shareholders, and buying company assets for less than their market value, or selling assets to their company for more than their value. The section provides that substantial property transactions, involving the sale or acquisition of non-cash assets by the company to or from its director or a connected person, require the approval of the shareholders. A substantial asset is one that exceeds 10 per cent of the company's asset value and is more than £5,000, or its value exceeds £100,000. A connected person includes a director's wife, husband, partner, children, and any company that the director or connected person holds 20 per cent or more of the share value.

If the shareholders have not given their approval, the transaction is voidable by the company, and the director or connected person is liable to the company for profits arising from the contract. Any directors who gave their approval may also be liable. The section applies to transactions that are contracts as well as those that are non-legally binding agreements. However, the company and director can enter into substantial and material property transactions which are conditional on shareholders' approval.

Company Secretary

A company secretary is an officer of a company, an agent of the company, and an employee of the company. A public company must appoint a company secretary, and a private company may appoint one but is not required by law to do so. Prior to the CA 2006, all companies had to appoint company secretaries, and although private companies are no longer obliged to have a secretary, many will choose to appoint one. In some companies, the company secretary is also one of the directors. A company secretary is responsible for much of the company's administrative work, and if one is not appointed, a director, or someone authorised by the directors, will need to be responsible for the tasks previously carried out by a secretary. The directors are usually given the power to appoint and remove a secretary by the company's articles. As an officer of the company, a secretary is potentially liable in criminal and civil law for failure to meet any statutory requirements, such as filing accounts at Companies House. Where a company appoints secretaries then the company must keep a register of them, which must be available for inspection.

For private companies, there are no special qualifications required for company secretaries. In public companies, the directors must be satisfied that their appointee has the knowledge and experience to do the job, and that he satisfies one or more of the qualification requirements set out in the CA 2006, s 273. These state that a secretary must appear to the directors to be capable of discharging his duties as a secretary and must:

- have been a secretary of a public company for at least three years out of the last five prior to his appointment, or

- be a qualified UK lawyer, or

- be a member of one of the named professional bodies (these include Institute of Chartered Accountants in England and Wales, Association of Chartered Certified Accountants, Institute of Chartered Secretaries and Administrators, Chartered Institute of Management Accountants, and Chartered Institute of Public Finance and Accountancy), or

- have experience through being a holder of another office or body.

Key Concept All companies must appoint at least one director who is a human being. Public companies must have at least two directors. Public companies must have a company secretary. Private companies may have one. The company secretary may also be one of the directors.

Duties and Authority of a Company Secretary

There are no specific duties of a company secretary set out in the CA 2006. The duties of a secretary and his role vary according to the size and nature of the company. A secretary generally plays a key role in ensuring procedures of the Board of Directors are observed, and he should be a source of guidance and information for directors on their responsibilities. A secretary's actual duties are assigned to him by the Board, and typically include organising the shareholders' meetings and the directors' meetings, issuing agendas, and drafting the minutes of meetings. A secretary is also responsible for ensuring the statutory registers are kept up to date, and the annual return and other documents are completed and filed at Companies House within the required time limits. The annual return is an update of certain company information required by the CA 2006, ss 855 and 859. It is an offence for the company directors and secretary of a company to fail to submit a return (CA 2006, s 858). In a small company, a secretary may also be responsible for general administration and staff matters.

The company secretary has the authority to act as the company's agent, and should carry out the responsibilities they have been given by the directors. However, if the secretary acts outside their actual authority, but with the apparent authority of a secretary, any contract entered into with a third party acting in good faith is enforceable against the company. In the following case, the court made it clear that the usual role of a secretary covered much more than just administrative tasks, and included entering into certain contracts on behalf of the company.

Panorama Dev v Fidelis Furnishing Fabrics Ltd (1971)

Facts: The company secretary of Fidelis hired cars on the company's behalf, claiming that the cars were being used to transport clients. He used the cars for his own private purposes, and the company refused to pay the hire charges, stating that the secretary had no authority to hire cars.

Decision: The company was liable to pay the car hire charges because contracts for the hire of cars fell within a secretary's apparent authority.

There are some transactions that clearly fall outside the role of a company secretary, such as borrowing money on behalf of the company.

Company Auditors

Companies generally employ an accountant to prepare their accounts unless they are very small companies. The company accountant is appointed by the directors, and is employed by the company. The auditor is a different accountant, who is an independent contractor, appointed to check that the company accounts are accurate and properly prepared, and to report to the shareholders.

Appointment of an Auditor

Companies are required by law to appoint an auditor each financial year to carry out an audit of the accounts. A company may be exempt from an annual audit if it is dormant, a small private company, or a not-for-profit company (whose accounts are subject to a public sector audit). A **dormant company** is one where no significant accounting transactions have occurred. A small private company is one that has an annual turnover of less than £5.6 million and whose total assets do not exceed £2.8 million. However, even where an exemption might apply, an audit is necessary if insisted upon by 10 per cent of the shareholders, or by a shareholder holding at least 10 per cent of the nominal value of the company's shares.

The first auditor is generally appointed by the directors and thereafter appointed by an ordinary resolution of the shareholders. If it is a public company, the shareholders appoint an auditor at the meeting where the annual accounts are produced. If the shareholders fail to appoint an auditor, the Secretary of State has the power to appoint one. As a private company is not obliged to have any meetings, the auditor is generally appointed within 28 days of the circulation of the annual accounts, or if there is a meeting, at the meeting where the accounts are produced. If the private company does not make an appointment, the auditor in office is automatically deemed to be reappointed.

In order to be eligible for appointment, an auditor must be a member of a recognised accountancy body, such as the Institute of Chartered Accountants, and must be independent of the company. The auditor cannot be an officer or employee of the company or in partnership with someone who is an officer or employee of the company.

Rights and Duties of Auditors

An auditor has the duty to audit the company accounts, and to report to the shareholders on whether the accounts give a true and fair view of the financial position of the company and have been properly prepared in accordance with the CA 2006. In order to ensure that the company accounts accurately reflect the financial position of the company, an auditor will need access to a range of information. The auditor has the right of access to the company's books and accounts, and can require explanations and information from officers of the company. It is a criminal offence for anyone to knowingly or recklessly give an auditor misleading, false, or deceptive information. It is also a criminal offence for an auditor to knowingly or recklessly cause a report to be misleading, false, or deceptive, either by including wrong information, or not including relevant information.

An auditor's work is performed under a contract made with the company. The auditor owes the company an implied contractual duty of care in the performance of his work. If he fails to carry out his work with reasonable care and skill, he will be liable to the company for breach of contract. The auditors also owe the company as a whole a duty of care in tort of negligence. This duty is not owed to members of the public or the shareholders as individuals.

Caparo Industries v Dickman (1990)

Facts: The claimants, Caparo, owned shares in Fidelity plc. The accounts of Fidelity plc were audited by Dickman. Caparo, a shareholder, read and relied on the statutory audited accounts when making their decision to purchase additional shares in Fidelity plc and then to mount a successful takeover bid. However, the accounts were inaccurate and showed a profit of £1.3 m instead of a loss of £465,000. Caparo sued Dickman for negligent misstatement.

Decision: Dickman was not liable because auditors owed no duty to the public at large or to individual shareholders who rely on the accounts to buy further shares. The purpose of a statutory audit was to enable shareholders to exercise proper control over a company and not to provide information for share dealings or takeovers.

An auditor may be liable for negligent misstatements if he knew that his report was to be prepared for a specific transaction and he knew his report would be communicated to particular persons (see Chapter 11 on negligent misstatements).

Removal of Auditors

A company may wish to remove an auditor if the auditor is very critical of the company practice; however, the Companies Act 2006 ensures that an auditor cannot just be silenced, and he has the right to bring his criticism to the shareholders' attention. In order to remove an auditor before the expiry of his term of office, the shareholders must pass an ordinary resolution with special notice (28 days) at a meeting. The auditor has a right to make written representations, which the company must send to every shareholder, and the auditor has a right to speak at the meeting where the resolution for his dismissal is being proposed.

An auditor who ceases to hold office, either because he has been removed before the expiry of his term or because he has not been reappointed, must make a statement of the circumstances, or a statement that there are no circumstances, which the auditor wishes to bring to the attention of the shareholders or creditors. This statement is deposited with the company's office, and sent to shareholders and the Registrar of Companies. If it is a public company listed on the Stock Exchange, a copy may also have to be sent to an audit authority.

Corporate Governance

Corporate governance is concerned with how the company is governed and its objectives and strategic direction. As the number of shareholders in a company increases, it becomes impossible for them all to be involved in the strategic management of the company. In larger companies, problems arise mainly from the separation of ownership and control. Powers to make decisions about the company lie with the Board of Directors, who control the company but are accountable to the shareholders for the way in which the company has performed. The directors should ensure the company is managed in the best interests of the shareholders. (The interests of other stakeholders such as employees and creditors may also be taken into account.) However, there is always the risk that the company is not being run for the benefit of the shareholders at all but actually in the interests of the executive directors themselves. It may become difficult for shareholders to restrain management excesses, such as the award of large salaries, and the concealment of incompetence and fraud. One measure of achieving a balance of power is ensuring that there are independent non-executive directors on the Board of Directors. These non-executive directors can oversee financial reporting and risk management and check that the executive directors are not solely acting in their own interests.

The basic rules of good corporate governance apply to all companies and include rules such as the requirement to produce annual audited accounts for shareholders. However, most of the rules on corporate governance relate to large companies that can offer their shares for sale to the general public, and in particular, companies listed on the London Stock Exchange. Some of the rules are compulsory and can be found in Company Law; however, many work through compliance with a voluntary code of practice. The UK **Code on Corporate Governance**, first published in 1992 (and revised since that date) sets out standards of good practice. (The Code is normally updated every two years; the last one was published in September 2014.) It relates to issues such as the composition and accountability of the Board of Directors, remuneration of executive directors, auditing, and relations with shareholders. Public companies are required to report to shareholders on how they have applied the principles of the Code, and either to confirm that they have complied with the Code's provisions, or provide an explanation where they have not complied with the Code.

Business Insight The collapse of the Enron Company demonstrates the importance of ensuring high standards of corporate governance

Enron was established in 1985 with the merger of two companies. It grew rapidly and Enron Online, the company's website for trading commodities, soon became one of the world's largest business sites. In 2000, the company reported annual revenue of approximately $100 billion and its shares were trading at $90. In October, Enron reported a loss and, as the depth of deception became increasingly apparent, investors and creditors withdrew their support. In December 2001, Enron filed for bankruptcy. Shares fell to less than $1, and billions of dollars were lost by shareholders. It emerged that Enron had exaggerated and lied about its profits, and concealed its debts so that the true financial position of the company was not revealed in the company's accounts. A number of top Enron executives have since been convicted of fraud.

Basic Terminology

For an online printable version visit the Online Resource Centre

Board meetings Meetings of Board of Directors of a company.

Code on Corporate Governance A published document which sets out standards of good practice for the governance of companies.

Company auditor An accountant appointed to check that the company accounts are accurate and to report to the shareholders.

Corporate governance The manner in which a company is governed and its aims and planned development.

Dormant company A company in which no significant accounting transactions have occurred.

Executive director Responsible for a company's affairs and performs a specific role in a company as an employee of the company.

Fiduciary relationship Relationship of confidence and trust between two parties.

Insider dealing Where directors or employees of a company or connected persons use confidential price-sensitive information relating to shares for their own gain or the gain of their associates.

Insolvent Unable to meet debts and other liabilities.

Managing director Director who is appointed by the Board of Directors to be responsible for the day-to-day overall management of the company.

Non-executive director Does not work for the company but is involved in its governance.

Ordinary Resolution A decision voted on by more than 50 per cent of members, either present at a general meeting or voting by proxy.

Special Notice 28 days' notice.

Special resolution A decision voted on by more than 75 per cent of members, either present at a general meeting or voting by proxy.

Voidable Transaction that is binding on one party but the other party has the option to have it set aside. Until set aside it has full legal effect.

Weighted voting rights on shares Shares that have more votes per share.

Summary

For an online flashcard glossary visit the Online Resource Centre

After studying this chapter students should be able to:

Define 'director' and understand the position of the Board of Directors

- A director is an officer of a company who acts as an agent of the company. He can bind the company by his acts without incurring personal liability.
- Directors are responsible for the day-to-day management of the company and for developing company strategy and policy.
- All companies must have at least one director and public limited companies must have at least two directors.
- The Board of Directors is the 'mind' of the company and has responsibility for managing its affairs. The Board may delegate some of its powers to individual directors to act on its behalf.

Outline the appointment and removal of directors

- The first director or directors of a company are those named on registration of the company.
- The procedure for appointing new directors is set out in the company's articles. Usually directors are appointed by ordinary resolution at a general meeting or by the existing directors.
- Some articles allow for retirement and re-election of directors after a set number of years.
- A director can be removed before the expiration of his term of office by an ordinary resolution of the shareholders at a general meeting.

- The Company Directors Disqualification Act 1986 allows a court to disqualify any person from being a director.

Describe the powers and duties of directors

- The extent of the directors' powers is defined by the articles of a company.
- The directors must always exercise their powers for the proper purpose for which they were given and what they honestly believe to be in the best interests of the company.
- Directors must act within their actual or apparent authority, but where directors act outside their powers, protection is given to third parties acting in good faith: CA 2006, s 40.
- Directors' duties set out in the CA 2006 are to act within their powers, to promote the success of the company, to exercise independent judgement, to exercise reasonable skill, care, and diligence, to avoid conflict of interest, not to accept benefits from third parties, and to declare an interest in any proposed transaction or arrangement with the company.
- A director who has breached his duties will be required to make up any losses suffered by his company and account for any secret profit gained.
- The articles of a company can impose more onerous duties on a director but they cannot reduce the statutory ones.

Explain the role of a company secretary and company auditors

- A company secretary is an officer and agent of a company and plays a key role in ensuring procedures are observed.
- A public company must appoint a company secretary and a private company may appoint one.
- An auditor is an independent contractor appointed to check that the company accounts are accurate and properly prepared, and to report to the shareholders.
- Companies are required, by law, to appoint an auditor each financial year to carry out an audit of the accounts.

Understand the meaning of corporate governance

- Corporate governance is concerned with how the company is governed and its objectives and strategic direction.
- Some of the rules are found in the CA 2006 and other rules work through compliance with the Code on Corporate Governance which sets out standards of good practice.

Questions

1. Herb Ltd has three directors: Parsley, Sage, and Rosemary. Occasionally Parsley and Rosemary come into the company's premises but all decisions about running the company are left to Sage, who acts as managing director although he has never been appointed as such. In January, Sage enters into a contract with Supermarkets Ltd to supply organic herbs at a fixed price for a year. Shortly afterwards the price of organic herbs increases enormously, and Herb Ltd seeks to have the contract with Supermarkets Ltd set aside on the grounds that Sage had no authority to act on his own. Advise Herb Ltd if they are bound by the contract.

2. Pike, Harri, and Raj are directors of a beauty products company. Pike is responsible for negotiations with suppliers and customers. He agrees a contract between the company and Bleach Ltd for the supply of various chemicals. Bleach Ltd give Pike a commission of £3,000 which he does not declare. Pike enters into negotiations for the supply of hair dye with Julie, who owns a fleet of hairdressers. Unknown to Pike, Julie is Harri's wife. Raj is responsible for research into new products and, during trials to produce a new

For outline answers visit the Online Resource Centre

face cream, he accidentally discovers a formula that promotes rapid hair growth. Raj does not inform the other directors of his discovery but resigns and forms a new company on his own to market the hair growth product. The new company is very successful and makes substantial profits. Discuss.

3. Under the Companies Act 2006, directors owe various duties to a company. Outline the seven general duties of directors which are set out in sections 171–177 of the Companies Act 2006.

4. Explain where a director gets authority to act on behalf of a company and how third parties are protected if a director acts outside his authority.

Further Reading

Bourne, *Bourne on Company Law*, 6th edn (Routledge, 2013).

Dignam and Lowry, *Company Law*, 8th edn (Oxford University Press, 2014).

Dine and Koutsias, *Company Law*, 8th edn (Palgrave, 2014).

Wild and Weinstein, *Smith & Keenan's Company Law*, 16th edn (Pearson, 2013).

Companies House: http://www.companieshouse.gov.uk/.

Department for Business Innovation & Skills: https://www.gov.uk/government/organisations/department-for-business-innovation-skills.

Financial Reporting Council: http://www.frc.org.uk/.

Online Resource Centre

Test your knowledge by trying this chapter's **Multiple Choice Questions**. Visit:

www.oup.com/uk/orc/law/company/jonesibl3e/01student/mcqs/ch17/

For more information, updates, and multiple choice questions, please visit the Online Resource Centre at:

www.oup.com/uk/orc/law/company/jonesibl3e/

Company Law III
Company Meetings,
Shareholder
Protection, and
Liquidation of
Companies

Introduction

A company is owned by its shareholders, who have invested their money in it. Although the shareholders have rights, they have no obligations or duties towards the company. They do not have to police a company's activities to ensure that the company is not using child labour or polluting the environment. The management of the company is in the hands of its directors, and shareholders rely on the directors to safeguard and enhance their investment. Some shareholders take an active interest in a company's affairs, whilst others throw away all the information they receive from the company, and are interested only in the payment of dividends and whether their shares are increasing in value. Shareholders do exercise some control over the directors, and have the right to attend meetings and pass resolutions on company matters. These resolutions are passed by majority decisions. Public companies usually have numerous shareholders, many of whom have relatively small shareholdings. Where a shareholder has only a minority interest in a company, there is a risk of becoming 'oppressed' by majority decisions. The Companies Act 2006 (CA 2006) does provide some protection for minority shareholders, who may, as a last resort even apply to have the company wound up. A company will cease to exist if it is wound up.

Learning Objectives

After studying this chapter you should be able to:

- Outline the different types of company meetings and explain how meetings are convened and managed.
- Distinguish between different types of resolutions and appreciate the rights of shareholders to propose resolutions.
- Show an understanding of protection given by law to minority shareholders.
- Explain the meaning of insider dealing and market abuse.
- Describe the methods under which a company can be wound up.
- Differentiate and explain wrongful and fraudulent trading.

Company Meetings

The purpose of company meetings is to enable shareholders to attend in person, and discuss and vote on matters that affect the company. Although the directors of a company manage the general running of the company, certain key decisions, such as amending the company's constitution, reducing the share capital of the company, and approval of loans to directors, must be made by the shareholders. Decisions made by shareholders are known as **resolutions**. The shareholders of public companies must hold meetings in order to pass resolutions. The shareholders of private companies may pass resolutions in meetings or, alternatively, most decisions can be made by passing written resolutions.

 Key Concept Resolutions (decisions) of shareholders are either passed at the Annual General Meetings or General Meetings. It is possible for private limited companies to pass written resolutions without holding a meeting.

Resolutions made by shareholders passed in meetings are only valid if the meeting is properly convened and conducted, therefore the rules on matters such as notice, quorum and voting must be adhered to. For a company meeting to be valid it is not necessary for all shareholders to be in the same room, provided everyone can see and hear what is going on through audio visual links.

A meeting that all shareholders are invited to attend is called a **General Meeting** and a meeting that only one type of shareholder is entitled to attend is called a **Class Meeting**. A 'General Meeting' may be the company's **Annual General Meeting**. Public companies must hold an Annual General Meeting each year, and in between the Annual General Meetings, they may hold General Meetings. Private companies do not have to hold an Annual General Meeting but may do so if they wish. Almost all of the business of a private company can be conducted through written resolutions, without the need to meet at all. There are some issues, such as the removal of auditors or directors, that do require approval of the shareholders at a General Meeting, and, therefore, in these circumstances it would be necessary to hold a meeting.

The power to call meetings is set out in the company's articles and the CA 2006. Usually the directors call meetings, although in certain circumstances shareholders holding sufficient shares can compel the directors to hold a meeting. A circular is sent to the shareholders explaining the purpose of the meeting, setting out proposed resolutions and giving the directors' views on the proposals (see Figure 18.1).

Key Concept   There are different types of company meetings. General Meetings and Annual General Meetings are meetings where all the members of a company have the right to attend. Class Meetings are meetings where only shareholders holding a particular class of share are entitled to attend. These should be distinguished from **Board Meetings** which are only for directors.

Annual General Meeting

Every public company must hold an Annual General Meeting (AGM) within six months of their financial year end (CA 2006, s 336). All shareholders and directors of the company are invited to attend AGMs. Private companies are not required by law to hold an AGM, but may do so if they wish. Directors and secretaries of public companies that fail to hold an AGM can be prosecuted, and, if convicted, are liable to a fine.

It is at the AGM that the directors report on the initiatives, achievements, and developments of the company. The shareholders have the opportunity to discuss the company's performance and vote on issues. Directors of a public company have to produce the annual accounts and reports of the company every year for approval by shareholders, and this is normally done at the AGM. Other business conducted includes the declaration of dividends, and the appointment or re-appointment of directors and auditors.

> **Business Insight** Shareholder spring
>
> 2012 became known as the 'shareholder spring' when an increasing number of shareholders voted against companies' remuneration reports. Shareholders rarely reject company remuneration reports but they were clearly showing their displeasure at directors' awards in times of recession. The insurance company Aviva, bookies William Hill, Mirror Group newspapers' owner Trinity, mining company Xstrata, and Premier Foods are among those who have faced shareholder anger about pay levels for executives. In some companies the chief executive resigned after the majority of shareholders voted against the remuneration report.

General Meetings

A General Meeting is one to which all shareholders and directors are invited, and it is usually called by a company's directors. The power to call General Meetings at any time is given to the directors by CA 2006, (s 302).

The directors of a public company have a duty to call a General Meeting to discuss the financial position of the company with the shareholders, if there has been a serious loss of capital and the net assets of the company fall below half of the share capital (CA 2006, s 656).

Shareholders may wish for a meeting to be called because they are concerned about the management of the company, and want to put forward certain proposals which the directors may oppose. Shareholders of private and public companies, holding at least 5 per cent of the voting shares in the company, can require directors to convene a General Meeting (CA 2006, s 303). If the directors fail to call a meeting, the shareholders themselves can convene a meeting and recover their expenses of doing so from the company.

Figure 18.1 Power to call company meetings

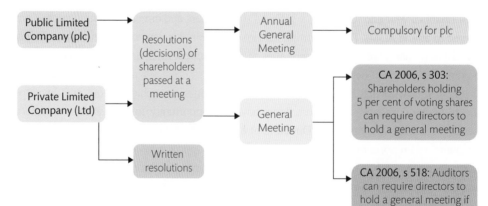

A company's auditors may demand the directors call a meeting if they intend to give notice of their resignation (CA 2006, s 518). In the meeting, the auditors have the right to explain, to the shareholders, the reason for their resignation. Where it is impracticable for a meeting to be called by the directors (for example, they are refusing to speak to each other) the CA 2006, s 306 gives a court the power to call a meeting.

Notice of general meetings and annual general meetings

Notice of meetings must be given to every member and every director. The notice must state the time and place of the meeting, and the general nature of the business to be conducted. It is important that the content of the proposed resolutions is clearly stated in the notice in order that shareholders can decide whether to attend the meeting or to appoint a **proxy** (someone to vote in their place) (See Chart 18.1).

A resolution passed at a meeting will only be valid if the correct notice of the meeting and resolution have been given to shareholders (CA 2006, s 301). The notice must be in writing, but it can be sent out electronically or published on a website. Usually notice of a general meeting must be sent at least 14 days before the date of the meeting, although the articles can provide that longer notice is required. If the meeting is the AGM of a public company then 21 days' notice is required. On occasions **special notice** of at least 28 days is needed for a meeting. Special notice is necessary when there is going to be a proposal at the meeting to remove an auditor or director. Shorter notice is only allowed where shareholders, holding at least 90 per cent of the voting shares of the company, agree to shorter notice. The number of days always refers to clear days, excluding the day of the meeting and the day on which the notice is given (See Table 18.1).

Chart 18.1 Example of a notice for an AGM

Notice of Annual General Meeting

Notice is hereby given that the twenty-first Annual General Meeting of V.G. Plc will be held at The New Conference Centre, East Road, Brighton, BN1 4AM on Tuesday, 20 July 2015 at 11.00 a.m. to transact the business set out in the Resolutions below. Resolutions 1 to 5 (inclusive) will be proposed as Ordinary Resolutions and Resolutions 6 and 7 will be proposed as Special Resolutions. Voting will be by poll.

The Board of Directors believe that the proposals are in the best interests of the Company and its shareholders as a whole, and recommend a vote FOR all Resolutions.

1. To receive the Company's accounts and reports of the directors and the auditor for the year ended 31 March 2015.

2. To re-elect the following directors who are retiring by rotation, Sidney Smart, Jamel Jones, Freda Fox.

3. To declare a final dividend of 7.5p per ordinary share.

4. To approve the Remuneration Report of the Board for the year ended 31 March 2015.

5. To re-appoint Deloitte LLP as auditors to the Company until the conclusion of the next general meeting at which accounts are laid before the Company.

6. A general meeting other than an annual general meeting may be called on not less than 14 clear days' notice.

7. The Articles of Association of the Company be amended by deleting all the provisions of the Company's Memorandum of Association which, by virtue of section 28 of the Companies Act 2006, are to be treated as provisions of the Company's Articles of Association.

By Order of the Board

Martin Rose

Secretary

V.G. Plc, The Steine, Westminster, London SW1

10 May 2015

Where a general meeting has been called, the shareholders who hold at least 5 per cent of the total voting rights, or 100 shareholders who hold on average £100 shares, can require the company to circulate a statement of up to 1,000 words about a proposed resolution, or about any issue due to be considered at the meeting.

Table 18.1 Notice period required for company meetings

Type of meeting	Notice period
General Meeting (and AGM of a private company)	14 Days
Annual General Meeting of a public company	21 Days
Special Notice for certain resolutions (e.g. removal of a director)	28 Days
Shareholders holding at least 90 per cent of voting shares	May agree to shorter period of time for meetings

Procedure at meetings

In order for a meeting to be properly constituted, the correct notice must be given and there must be a quorum (minimum number) of shareholders in attendance. The number of persons necessary for a quorum is usually two, unless the company only has one shareholder (in which case the quorum is one) or the articles provide for a larger number (CA 2006, s 318). The persons attending may be shareholders, their proxies, or corporate representatives (where the shares are owned by another company). A proxy is someone appointed by the shareholder to attend the meeting and vote on his behalf. The proxy may also speak at the meeting. The proxy might be a specially appointed person or, more commonly, the chairman of the Board of Directors. Directors are invited to attend General Meetings but cannot vote unless they also hold shares and are voting in their capacity as shareholders. If the minimum number of persons necessary for the quorum do not attend the meeting, any resolutions passed by the meeting are invalid.

Key Concept The minimum number of shareholders necessary for a company meeting to be quorate is two, unless a higher number is required by the company's articles, or the company only has one shareholder, in which case the quorum is one.

A company's articles usually state that the chairman of the Board of Directors should chair General Meetings. The chairman will supervise the meetings and decide on procedural issues. He must conduct the meetings fairly, taking into account the interests of shareholders and the interests of the company. If the chairman is not available, another director normally acts as chairman, or if necessary the meeting can appoint a chairman.

Decisions are taken by passing resolutions which shareholders vote for or against. Voting may be by a show of hands or by poll.

Voting by a show of hands is where each member or his proxy present at the meeting votes by raising a hand. Each shareholder has one vote irrespective of the number of shares that shareholder may have. This is a quick and simple method of voting and is convenient for non-controversial matters and where there are only a small number of shareholders and proxies present at a meeting. However, it does mean that a shareholder owning one share has the same voting power as a shareholder owning 1,000 shares.

Voting by poll is where each shareholder or his proxy present at the meeting uses as many votes as his shareholding allows him. Usually each shareholder has one vote for each share that he holds, but in some cases the articles of the company may provide that a shareholder is entitled to more than one vote per share.

There is no law about whether a decision should be made by a show of hands or a poll, but because one method is generally one vote per person and the other is generally one vote per share, the two methods can produce different results. Therefore, it is important to know which method of voting is being used. The model articles provide that a decision is to be taken by a show of hands unless there is a demand for a poll (a company does not have to use the model articles). A demand for a poll can be made before or even after a vote by a show of hands. The right to demand a poll cannot be excluded by the company's articles (except for the election of the chairman or adjournment of the meeting) (CA 2006, s 321). However, this section does permit the articles to limit the calling for a poll so that it does not have to be held if it has been demanded by less than five shareholders, or by shareholders holding less than 10 per cent of the voting rights. Companies quoted on the stock exchange must publish the results of each poll taken at General Meetings on its website.

Class Meetings

Where a company has more than one class of shareholders, it may be necessary to call separate meetings for each class because their interests differ. Attendance at a Class Meeting is restricted to shareholders holding that class of share (or their proxy), unless there is unanimous consent that others may attend. The purpose of Class Meetings is usually to vote on a matter that affects that class of shareholder. For example, it may be necessary to hold a meeting of preference shareholders if the company wants to vary the special rights attached to preference shares.

Key Concept Ordinary shares are issued without any special rights being attached to them. Preference shares have the right to receive an annual dividend of a fixed amount before a dividend is paid on ordinary shares. Shareholders holding one type of share may be called to a separate Class Meeting.

Resolutions

The decisions made by shareholders are called resolutions. The shareholders of public companies can only pass resolutions at General Meetings or at the AGM. Resolutions are generally proposed by the directors of a company, but shareholders holding a sufficiently large number of shares may also propose resolutions. Notice of the proposed resolutions must be given to every shareholder in writing. This can either be in hard copy, electronically, or by means of a website. Each resolution proposed is voted on separately. In a meeting, a resolution may be amended provided the amendments are minor and do not take the scope of the resolution beyond the business stated in the notice. The percentage of shareholders needed to agree to pass any resolution depends on the type of resolution to be passed. There are two major types of resolutions: ordinary resolutions and special resolutions. Decisions are made by ordinary resolution unless either the CA 2006 or the articles state that the decision must be made by special resolution (see Figure 18.2).

Figure 18.2 Voting for resolutions

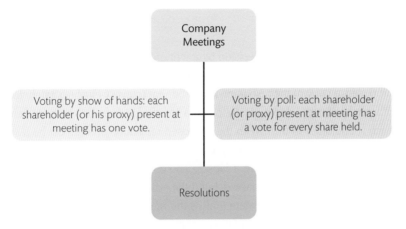

Ordinary Resolutions

An ordinary resolution is one that is passed by simple majority (CA 2006, s 282). This means that it is passed by more than 50 per cent of shareholders who vote in person or by proxy at a general meeting. An ordinary resolution can be passed by a show of hands or by poll. Shareholders must be given at least 14 days' notice of the content of the proposed resolution. Ordinary resolutions are used for the more routine decisions.

Key Concept Voting at General Meetings can be by show of hands, where each shareholder (or their proxy) present at a meeting has one vote. Alternatively voting can be by poll, where the number of votes is determined by the number of shares held.

Special Resolutions

A special resolution means a resolution passed by a majority of not less than 75 per cent of the shareholders (CA 2006, s 283). This type of resolution can also be passed by a show of hands or by poll. Shareholders must be given at least 14 days' notice of the proposed special resolution and the notice must set out the exact text of the proposed special resolution and state that it is a special resolution. A meeting can only make very minor amendments to special resolutions, such as correcting grammatical errors. A copy of every special resolution passed must be filed at Companies House. Special resolutions are required for major changes, such as changing the company's name, altering the company's articles, re-registering the company from a private to a public company, and winding up a company.

Written Resolutions

A private company may pass any decision by a written resolution, apart from a decision to dismiss a director or auditor before the expiry of their term of office. Where a written resolution is proposed, a copy of the resolution has to be sent to every eligible shareholder. It can be sent either in hard copy, electronically, or via a website, or even by one copy being circulated to each shareholder in turn. With the proposed resolution, there must be a statement telling shareholders how to signify their agreement to the resolution, and the date by which the resolution must be passed before it lapses. The company's articles may state the time scale for a written resolution to be passed, but if the articles are silent on this, the resolution lapses 28 days after the circulation date (unless the required number of shareholders have voted for it). Depending on the nature of the resolution (ordinary written resolution or special written resolution), it either requires a simple majority of 50 per cent of the total votes of the shareholders or requires not less than 75 per cent of the total votes. Written resolutions may be proposed by directors, or by shareholders who hold at least 5 per cent of the total voting rights entitled to vote on the resolution (see Table 18.2).

Where a resolution is passed at a meeting, the votes counted are votes of the shareholders (or their proxies) that are present at the meeting, whereas for a written resolution it is votes of all the shareholders holding voting rights that are counted.

Table 18.2 Types of resolutions

Ordinary Resolution	• Used for conducting most types of business • Require simple 50% + majority of votes cast • Plus 14 days' notice • Can be passed as a written resolution or at a meeting: CA 2006, s 282
Special Resolution	• Used for effecting major changes • Requires 75% + majority of votes cast • 14 days' notice • Can be passed as a written resolution or at a meeting: CA 2006, s 283
Written (for private companies) Resolution	• Used for all resolutions, except removing a director/auditor before term of office ends • Passed by either a 50% + or 75% + (depending on business proposed) of total voting rights

Results can differ depending on whether a resolution is proposed at a meeting and voted on by a show of hands, a poll, or proposed as a written resolution. In the following example, a limited company, Costa Lota Ltd, has five shareholders each holding shares with one voting right per share. An ordinary resolution is proposed and Agnes does not vote at all, Bejal is for the resolution, and Carl, Deepa, and Eric are opposed to it. Note the different results depending on which voting method is used (see Table 18.3).

Table 18.3 Results differ depending on voting method

	Voting by show of hands at meeting	Voting by poll at meeting	Written resolution
Agnes 30 shares	Absent	Absent	Does not vote
Bejal 40 shares	For:1	For: 40	For: 40
Carl 10 shares	Against:1	Against:10	Against:10
Deepa 10 shares	Against:1	Against:10	Against:10
Eric 10 shares	Against:1	Against:10	Against:10
Results	3 to 1: **FAIL** (less than 50% of votes cast at meeting)	40 (57%) to 30 (43%): **PASS** (over 50% of votes cast at meeting)	40% For: **FAIL** (must be over 50% of total shares)

Rights of Shareholders to Propose Resolutions

Resolutions are generally proposed by directors of a company who set the agenda for meetings; however, the CA 2006 does provide opportunities for shareholders to propose resolutions in certain circumstances.

Shareholders of both private and public companies can require the directors to convene a General Meeting, and include in their request the text of a resolution which they intend to propose at the meeting (CA 2006, s 303). The content of the resolution must not be ineffective, defamatory, vexatious, or frivolous. The shareholders demanding the meeting must hold at least 5 per cent of the voting shares in the company. The resolution, drafted by the shareholders, is circulated with the notice of the meeting. Shareholders have the right to require a company to circulate a statement of no more than 1,000 words in support of their proposed resolution (or relating to any other business to be dealt with at the meeting) (CA 2006, s 314). The statement must be circulated to every member of the company entitled to get a notice of the meeting; the cost of circulating the statement may have to be borne by the shareholders making the request.

Business Insight Shareholder demands meeting

In October 2014 the *Guardian* newspaper reported that Rangers International Football Club Plc had received a notice under section 303 from Mike Ashley, (who also owns Newcastle United), a director of MASH Holdings Limited. MASH state they hold 4,265,000 ordinary shares amounting to 5 per cent of the voting rights of the company. The notice requires the company to call a general meeting of the shareholders to put forward resolutions for the removal of Graham Wallace and Philip Nash as directors of the company.

Rather than call a meeting to deal with a particular issue, shareholders of public companies can require notice of resolutions to be placed on the agenda of the AGM (CA 2006, s 338).

Business Insight Tesco's chickens: a campaign for improved welfare conditions for chickens in the UK

After launching a national campaign for higher welfare conditions for chickens, Hugh Fearnley-Whittingstall bought a single share in Tesco plc. He gained the support of over 100 shareholders with a minimum of 200,000 shares between them and he was then able to propose a resolution relating to chicken welfare at the 2008 AGM using the provisions of the Companies Act 2006. Voting at the AGM was by poll and the resolution gained approximately 10 per cent of votes; although this was not enough to pass the resolution, it did give publicity to the welfare of chickens.

Shareholders of private companies can require the company to circulate written resolutions provided the content of the resolutions are not ineffective, defamatory, vexatious, or frivolous, together with a statement of not more than 1,000 words about the resolution. The shareholders must hold at least 5 per cent of the voting rights of all shareholders entitled to vote on the resolution, but for written resolutions the 5 per cent rule can be altered by the articles to a smaller percentage, although it cannot be increased to require a larger percentage of shareholders (CA 2006, s 292). Unless the company agrees otherwise, the expenses of circulating the written resolution and any statement must be met by the shareholders making the request. The company can demand a deposit to meet these expenses and, if it is not paid, the company is not obliged to circulate the proposed resolution.

Protection of Minority Shareholders

Although a company is managed and run by its directors, the shareholders own the company and those with the majority of voting rights can control the company by passing resolutions. Shareholders controlling over 50 per cent of the voting rights have control over passing ordinary resolutions and, therefore, could vote to remove directors and appoint others to run the company. Shareholders holding 75 per cent or more of the voting rights have control over additional issues that require special resolutions, such as amending the company's articles or ratifying a director's conduct which is in breach of his duty to the company. Shareholders with 25 per cent of the votes or less will have no control, even to block special resolutions from being passed. Problems may arise if the directors of a company are also the majority shareholders, and the minority shareholders believe that the company has been wronged by its directors and wish the company to take action against them.

Rule in *Foss v Harbottle*

A company is a separate legal person and legal rights belong to the company itself. The rule in *Foss v Harbottle* (1843) states, where a wrong is done to a company, it is the company itself that should take court proceedings to enforce its rights. As the Board of Directors controls and runs a company, it is normally up to the Board to decide to start legal proceedings in the company's name. But if the directors are in breach of duty to the company it is unlikely that the directors will start an action against themselves. There are exceptions to this rule, where a claim can be brought without the authority of the directors.

The common law rules about when a shareholder can take action have been largely overtaken by statute, and today a shareholder would usually take action under the CA 2006 or seek to have the company wound up.

Protection of Minority Shareholders under Statute

The CA 2006 gives protection to minority shareholders by allowing a shareholder to bring a legal action known as a statutory **derivative claim** against a director whose actual or proposed actions or omissions involve negligence, breach of duty, or breach of trust (CA 2006, ss 260–264).

Alternatively, a shareholder may apply to a court for an order that the company's affairs are being or have been carried out in a manner that is unfairly prejudicial to its members generally or to particular members (CA 2006, s 994).

As a last resort, under the provisions of the Insolvency Act 1986, s 122, a shareholder may petition a court to have a company wound up on just and equitable grounds, although a court will generally refuse to wind up a successful company if there is the possibility of an alternative remedy.

Derivative actions: CA 2006, ss 260–264

A shareholder can bring a derivative claim on behalf of the company (CA 2006, s 260). The action is described as derivative because the shareholder's right to sue is not personal to him but derives from a right of the company to sue. In a **derivative action**, the shareholder brings the claim in the name of the company. The claim can be brought against a director, a former director, or a shadow director, even if the director has not personally gained from the breach.

The claim must be for an actual or proposed act or omission involving negligence, default, breach of duty, or breach of trust. The act or omission may have taken place before the claimant became a shareholder. The directors who are in breach do not necessarily have to have control of the majority of shares in the company. If the claim is successful, it is the company as a whole that will benefit and not the individual shareholder who took the derivative action. Any compensation awarded by the court will go to the company, although the shareholder will be able to recover his legal costs of bringing the claim.

A derivative claim requires two stages of permission before the claim is heard. At the first stage, the claimant shareholder must seek the permission of the court to bring the claim. The court will consider the issue on the basis of the evidence filed by the claimant shareholder. The court will dismiss the application if there is not sufficient evidence to justify further investigation. The company is not required to participate at this stage. The reason for this is to ensure the shareholder has adequate grounds for pursuing the claim and to minimise the expense for a company if a claim has no merit.

At the second stage, the court will decide whether the case should continue, after hearing evidence from both sides. Permission must be refused if a notional director acting properly in promoting the success of the company would not continue with the claim, or if the claim arises from an act or omission that the company has authorised to be carried out, or if the act or omission has already taken place and the company has ratified it. Shareholders have the power to ratify directors' conduct, which amounts to negligence, default, breach of duty, or breach of trust, by ordinary resolution (CA 2006, s 239). Even if a director breaches his statutory duties, the shareholders can ratify the action. The directors holding shares and involved in the breach of duty cannot vote on the resolution to ratify their act or omission.

If none of the 'mandatory grounds' requiring the court to refuse permission applies, then in deciding if permission should be given to continue the claim, the court will take into account a number of issues. These include whether the claim would promote the company's success, the views of the other shareholders who have no personal interest in the matter, whether there could have been ratification, and if the shareholder seeking to continue with the claim is acting in good faith.

In the following case a minority shareholder was given permission to continue a derivative claim against directors where a company had made substantial interest-free loans.

Stainer v Lee (2010)

Facts: S had a small shareholding in C Ltd. He sought permission from the court to continue a derivative action against the directors of C Ltd who had allowed C Ltd to make substantial interest-free loans to E Ltd, a company owned by one of those directors.

Decision: The judge allowed the derivative claim to continue stating that the failure to obtain interest over a period of almost nine years on lending to E Ltd, that rose from £4.6 million to £8.1 million, constituted very strong grounds for a claim that the directors were in breach of their fiduciary duties.

Key Concept The Companies Act 2006 gives a shareholder the right to bring a derivative action on behalf of the company against a director, former director, or shadow director, for negligence, default, or breach of duty or trust.

Unfairly prejudicial conduct: CA 2006, s 994

Rather than commence court action by making a derivative claim, a shareholder may bring a petition to a court on grounds of unfair prejudice (CA 2006, s 994). If successful, the shareholder may be awarded compensation on his own behalf, rather than for the company as is the case in a derivative action. Any shareholder has the power to petition the court that the affairs of the company are going to be, are being, or have been, conducted in a manner that has unfairly prejudiced the shareholders generally, or a section of shareholders which includes at least himself. Whether the company's conduct or proposed conduct amounts to unfair prejudice will be up to the court to decide on the circumstances of each case. The conduct must be both unfair and prejudicial to the minority shareholder(s), but it does not have to be illegal, and the directors do not have to have acted negligently or in bad faith.

In order to succeed in a claim, the minority shareholder will have to show that the conduct complained of is unfair and prejudicial. The starting point is to examine the articles of the company and see if the conduct is in contravention of the terms of the articles. Generally, a shareholder will not be able to complain about something that is provided for in the articles, although there may be cases where using the strict legal rights in the articles is contrary to equity (fairness) and the rules of good faith.

Conduct that has been found to be unfairly prejudicial to minority shareholders includes the following:

- Where director shareholders paid themselves excessive fees with the result that the sums available to be paid out as dividends were very limited; therefore, the non-director shareholders were unfairly prejudiced.

- The diversion of company business to another company controlled and owned by the directors.

- A director using company assets for his own personal benefit.

- Directors making an inaccurate statement to shareholders, which led the shareholders to accept a bid by another company which the directors were connected to.

- Directors refinancing the company to the detriment of the company but to the benefit of another company owned by the directors.

Courts do not generally interfere if it is just a case of poor management of a company, unless there is continuous mismanagement which causes serious financial damage to minority interests. Conduct may still be unfair even though it would not be sufficient to wind a company up.

If unfair prejudicial conduct is present, a court has wide discretion in what type of remedy to award (CA 2006, s 996). Remedies include orders to refrain from continuing the act complained of, to regulate the company's future conduct, to amend the company's articles, and to require the company not to make any alterations to its articles without leave of the court. However, the most common remedy is an order for the petitioner's shares to be purchased by the controlling shareholders or the company at a fair value. This ends the shareholder's relationship with the company, which may have broken down beyond repair in any event.

Breakdown of relationship is clearly evident in the following case.

Rodliffe (Simon) v Rodliffe (Guy) and Home & Office Fire Extinguishers Ltd (2012)

Facts: S and G were directors and shareholders of C Ltd. S had asked G for a salary advance from C Ltd, but G had refused on the basis that C Ltd was struggling financially. A fight occurred between G and S at C Ltd's premises; both alleged that the other had attacked them with a hammer. The court found that on the evidence S had instigated the attack.

Decision: The court ordered the compulsory purchase of S's shares. His attack on G with a hammer constituted unfairly prejudicial conduct and made it impossible for them to continue their association as directors and shareholders.

Investigation by Department for Business, Innovation and Skills

The Department for Business, Innovation and Skills (BIS) has the power to investigate companies where serious corporate illegalities are suspected. Powers to investigate are provided for by Part XIV of the Companies Act 1985 (CA 1985). Inspectors may be appointed to investigate on the application of the company itself, or on the application of either 200 or more shareholders or shareholders holding at least 10 per cent of the company's shares (CA 1985, s 431). The Secretary of State has the power to initiate an inspection if it appears to him that the company's affairs have been conducted with the intent to defraud its creditors or for any other unlawful or fraudulent purpose, or there has been fraud or misconduct by the company's officers or the shareholders have not been given all the information relating to the companies affairs that they might reasonably expect (CA 1985, s 432).

The officers and inspectors conducting investigations have considerable powers to demand company documents and other information, and to enter company premises.

As a result of the investigation, the Secretary of State may petition the court that the company is wound up on just and equitable grounds (Insolvency Act 1986, s 124A). In addition, or as an alternative, if there is evidence of unfair prejudice to all or a section of the shareholders, the Secretary of State may petition the court for an order similar to a shareholder's petition under CA 2006, s 994. Information obtained from an investigation may later provide the basis for a subsequent criminal investigation by the police.

Insider Dealing and Market Abuse

A Stock Exchange is a marketplace where company shares and other securities are bought and sold. In order to maintain public confidence in the reliability of the Stock Exchange, it is important that the same information relating to shares and securities is available to all users, and false information likely to affect the value of a company's shares is not spread, thereby creating a false market. Persons who have inside information about a company are prohibited under statute from using it to gain an unfair advantage in transactions involving company shares and other securities.

Insider Dealing

Insider dealing is a criminal offence under section 52 of the Criminal Justice Act 1993 (CJA 1993). The offence can only be committed by individuals and not by other companies. The word 'deal' encompasses both buying and selling company shares and other securities, and a person 'deals' whether he himself deals or whether he enables another person to deal. An individual may be guilty of insider dealing if he uses price-sensitive information, which has not been made public, relating to the present or future value of company securities (such as shares and debentures) for his own profit. Price-sensitive information is information known to an individual but not generally known, and acquired by virtue of the individual's position. The company usually has to be listed on a Stock Exchange. The CJA 1993 covers primary insiders and secondary insiders. A primary insider has information about a company through being a director, employee, or shareholder of a company, or having access to the information because of their office or profession. A secondary insider is someone who has been tipped off directly or indirectly by a primary insider. He must know that the information he uses is from an insider source. It is an offence to disclose inside information to another person, other than in the proper performance of one's job or profession.

There are three general defences available to an individual accused of insider dealing. Firstly, he did not intend to make a profit or avoid a loss; secondly, he had reasonable grounds to believe that information had already been disclosed widely; and finally, he would have done what he did even if he did not have the information. An insider accused of disclosing information to another will have a defence if he can prove that he did not expect the person to whom he disclosed the information to deal, or he did not expect there to be a profit or avoidance of loss.

Insider dealing is a criminal offence and penalties include imprisonment for up to seven years and an unlimited fine. There are criticisms of the CJA 1993 because it does not generally extend to unquoted companies, and it does not provide a civil remedy; therefore, a company or its shareholders do not have the right under the CJA 1993 to recover any losses they may have suffered. As a criminal offence the standard of proof is high (beyond reasonable doubt) and there are relatively few prosecutions each year. The Financial Services and Markets Act 2000 (FSMA 2000) introduced an alternative civil procedure for dealing with market abuse, including insider dealing. Its purpose was to introduce a more effective mechanism to punish unacceptable forms of share dealing and market misconduct.

Market Abuse

Market abuse is improper conduct that relates to investments traded on a financial market. The FSMA 2000, s 118 states that market abuse is behaviour that falls below the standard of behaviour reasonably expected of persons in that market because it involves the misuse of information, or the creation of a false or misleading impression, or the distortion of the market. The conduct may be carried out by one or more persons and must relate to qualifying investments (shares, debentures, etc) traded on certain markets (such as the London Stock Exchange). The prohibited behaviour includes the following:

- The misuse of inside information or information that is not generally available that a regular user would regard as relevant to the transaction in question.

- Creating a false or misleading impression about the supply of, demand for, or the price or value of, investments.

- Behaviour that distorts the market. This includes share dealing which interferes with the normal process of share prices moving up and down in accordance with supply and demand.

The behaviour (which includes action and inaction) must be likely to be regarded by a regular user of that market, who is aware of the behaviour, as below the standard reasonably expected of a person in their position in relation to the market.

The Financial Conduct Authority may take enforcement action under the FSMA 2000. The standard of proof required is the civil standard of 'on the balance of probabilities'. There are a range of penalties that can be imposed including fines, and 'name and shame', which is where a statement is published about the person who has engaged in market abuse. The High Court can issue an injunction, which is a court order to prevent continuing market abuse, and also make an order for restitution.

Winding Up a Company

A company's life is brought to an end when it is wound up. This is also known as liquidation. Once a company has been wound up it ceases to exist. A company may be wound up either by an order of the court, or by a special resolution passed by the shareholders. Where liquidation is ordered by the court it is called **compulsory liquidation**. Where the company's shareholders resolve that the company should be wound up it is called **voluntary liquidation** (see Figure 18.3).

Compulsory Liquidation

Compulsory liquidation is where a liquidator is appointed by the court to wind up the affairs of a company. The liquidator appointed by the court is usually the Official Receiver, who is a government official and an officer of the court. If the Official Receiver ascertains that the company has a number of assets, he may seek to have an insolvency practitioner (usually an accountant or a lawyer) appointed as liquidator. To commence court proceedings for compulsory liquidation, a petition is made to a Court for a company to be wound up. The petition can be presented by a creditor, shareholder, director, or the company itself. The Insolvency Act 1986 (IA 1986) lists a number of grounds on which a company may be wound up. The usual ground is the company is unable to pay its debts.

A company will be regarded in law as being unable to meet its debts if it fails to pay a debt of more than £750 within 21 days of receiving a statutory written demand. Alternatively a company is also considered to be unable to pay its debts if a creditor has a court judgment against the company for any sum, and the court has been unable to recover the debt because the company does not have enough assets to meet the debt or if it can be proved that a company's total assets are less than its total debts.

It is the court that decides whether a company should be put into liquidation, and the court does not have to wind a company up even if it is satisfied that an applicant has good grounds for the petition. The court has the power to call a meeting of all the creditors and persons liable to contribute to the company's assets when the company is wound up (IA 1986, s 195). It may be the case that, although one creditor has petitioned the court to wind up the company, the other creditors believe it is in their best interests to allow the company to continue to trade.

Voluntary Liquidation

Voluntary liquidation is commenced by the shareholders passing a special resolution and takes place without a court order. There are two types of voluntary liquidation: members' (shareholders) voluntary winding up, and creditors' voluntary winding up.

The shareholders, who are the owners of a company, may decide that rather than continue owning the company, they wish the company to be wound up and to share out its assets between them. Members' voluntary winding up can only take place if the company is solvent. All the directors or a majority of directors, if there are more than two, must make a statement saying the company is solvent. The statement, which is called a declaration of solvency, must be made within a five-week period before the shareholders pass a resolution winding up the company. A declaration of solvency is a sworn statement to say the company will be able to pay all its debts in full within the period specified in the statement (the period must not exceed 12 months from the start of the winding up). A list of the company's assets and liabilities drawn up at the latest practicable date before making the declaration must be attached to the declaration. A director who makes a declaration of solvency without reasonable grounds for believing the company is solvent is committing a criminal offence which carries a penalty of a fine and/or imprisonment. It is, therefore, essential for a director to seek professional advice before making such a declaration.

Within five weeks of the declaration of solvency, the shareholders must pass a special resolution at a General Meeting. Once the resolution has been passed, the company must cease trading. A liquidator is appointed by the shareholders.

Where the directors are unable to make a declaration of solvency, there can be a creditors' voluntary liquidation of the company. The shareholders must pass a special resolution which states that it is advisable to wind the company up as it cannot continue in business because of its liabilities. Once the resolution has been passed, the company must cease trading and, within 14 days, the company must call a meeting of all its creditors. The creditors decide who is to be appointed as the liquidator.

> **Key Concept** Liquidation is where a company is brought to an end. The company's assets are sold and the debts of the company are paid. Any surplus money after all the debts are paid is returned to the shareholders.

The liquidator

In a compulsory winding up, the liquidator appointed by the court is usually the Official Receiver. Where there is a voluntary winding up of a company, the liquidator, appointed by the shareholders or the creditors, must be a qualified insolvency practitioner (usually an accountant or a lawyer). Once a liquidator is appointed, the directors' powers to run the company cease. If the company is **insolvent** its employees are automatically dismissed, although they may be re-employed by the liquidator. It is the liquidator's job to collect all the company's assets and distribute them to its creditors. The liquidator will normally write to every known creditor and will advertise in the Gazette (a special paper) and a local newspaper for details of debts to be submitted to him within a certain period. If any money is left over after all the creditors have been paid, the liquidator distributes it among the shareholders of the company.

Figure 18.3 **Company liquidation**

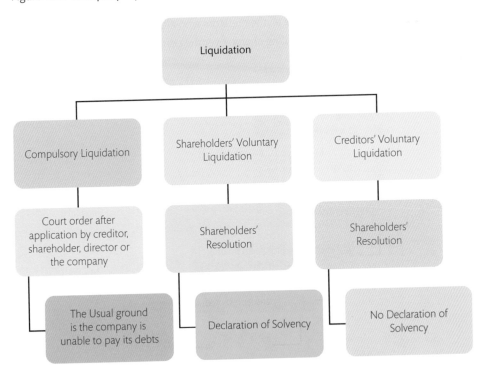

The liquidator sells all the other company property and collects all the money owing to the company. The assets of the company are paid out in a particular order. If there is not enough money to pay all the creditors, those at the end of the list will not receive any money owing to them. The order of payment is the same whether the company is in compulsory or voluntary liquidation (see Figure 18.4).

The assets are distributed in the following order

1. Secured creditors with fixed charges. Where a creditor has a fixed charge over an asset of the company, the asset is sold and the creditor takes the money owed for the charge. Any remaining money goes into the company's general asset pool. If the asset has depreciated and the proceeds do not satisfy the full amount owed, then the creditor becomes an unsecured creditor for the outstanding amount of the debt.

2. The costs of winding up which will include the liquidator's fees.

3. Preferential creditors. These include arrears of salary due to employees (up to a maximum of £800 per employee), holiday pay, and pension contributions.

4. Secured creditors with floating charges. The assets of the floating charge become crystallised and the creditors are paid out of these assets. However, if the floating charge was made after 15 September 2003, a percentage of the assets is set aside for payment of unsecured creditors. The amount set aside for unsecured creditors depends upon the value of the company's assets.

5. Unsecured creditors. These are all the creditors who are not preferential creditors and who do not have a fixed or floating charge over the company's assets.

Figure 18.4 Distribution of company assets by liquidator

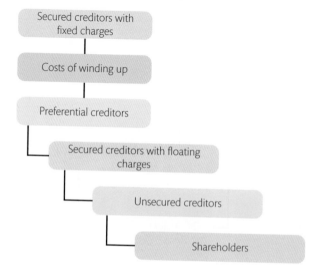

6. Shareholders are paid anything that they are owed. For example, if a dividend has been declared on some shares but not yet paid, then those shareholders will be paid next.

7. Any surplus money will be distributed to the shareholders according to their rights set out in the company's articles.

If there are not enough company assets to pay one class of creditors, then each member of that last class takes an equal percentage of their debt. For example, if there are only enough company assets to pay the secured creditors with fixed charges, and the cost of winding up fully, but not to meet all the debts of the preferential creditors, the preferential creditors will each get an equal percentage of the amount owing to them and the creditors further down the list will get nothing.

Wrongful Trading and Fraudulent Trading

Generally, it is only a company's assets that can be claimed by a liquidator and distributed to creditors; however, where there has been wrongful or fraudulent trading, then the liquidator will be able to apply to court for an order requiring directors and former directors to make a contribution.

Wrongful trading

Wrongful trading is not a criminal offence and it only applies when a company has gone into insolvent liquidation. To prove wrongful trading, the liquidator of a company must show that a company continued to trade when the director(s) knew, or ought to have known, that there was no reasonable prospect that the company could avoid insolvent liquidation, and the director(s) took insufficient steps in the circumstances to minimise the potential loss to the company's creditors. A director will be judged on the standard expected of a reasonably diligent director having the general knowledge, skill, and experience that would reasonably be expected of a person carrying out the same functions as that director. If the director has specialist knowledge, skill, or experience (for example, he is a financial accountant), he will be judged on those higher standards. The level of competence expected of a company director whose company is listed on the Stock Exchange is higher than that of a small company director. If a director (including a shadow director) is found liable for wrongful trading, the court can order that he makes a contribution to the company's assets (IA 1986, s 214). The amount of contribution that a director will be required to make is as the court thinks proper in the circumstances. In addition, the court may make a disqualification order under the Company Directors Disqualification Act 1986, s 10, disqualifying the director from being a company director for up to 15 years.

Fraudulent trading

Fraudulent trading is a civil offence (IA 1986, s 213) and a criminal offence (CA 2006, s 993). In order to be liable for fraudulent trading, a person must have intentionally acted dishonestly according to the standards of ordinary business people.

Only a liquidator can apply for civil action when the company is being liquidated. If any business of a company has been carried on with the intention of defrauding the creditors of the company or for some other fraudulent purpose, the court can make an order requiring any person, who was knowingly a party to the fraud, to make a contribution to the company's assets (IA 1986, s 213). The liquidator makes the application to the court and the amount of the contribution is as the court thinks proper. The court may also make a disqualification order under the Company Directors Disqualification Act 1986, s 10, disqualifying the person from being a director of a company for up to 15 years.

Criminal proceedings can be brought for fraudulent trading whether or not the company is insolvent. A person convicted of fraudulent trading is liable to a fine and/or imprisonment for up to ten years.

Transactions Prior to Insolvency

The liquidator of a company can apply to a court to have a transaction set aside if the company made the transaction at undervalue with any person within two years prior to the insolvency (IA 1986, s 238). This is to prevent a company giving away or selling company assets for less than they are worth in order to defraud creditors. The court can set aside any action by the company which gives preference to a particular creditor, for example, if the company had paid off one unsecured creditor shortly before going into liquidation when there will not be enough assets to pay other creditors.

Figure 18.5 **Actions in event of company in financial failure**

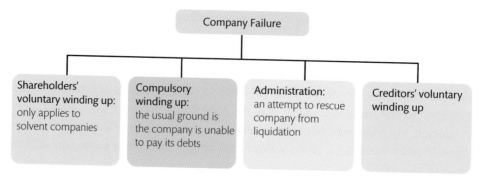

Administration

Administration was first introduced by the IA 1986 as a mechanism for attempting to save a financially unsuccessful company from going into insolvency. An administrator, who is a qualified insolvency practitioner, is appointed to try to rescue a company (see Figure 18.5). An administrator may be appointed by a court order, or on application by a creditor or director of a company. Alternatively, under the provisions of the Enterprise Act 2002, an administrator can be appointed without a court order by the company (resolution of its shareholders), its directors, or creditors with floating charges. A company in administration may continue to trade. The primary purpose of the administrator is to rescue the company as a going concern, and protect the company from its creditors whilst a restructuring plan is introduced. The second purpose is to achieve a better result for creditors than would be achieved by immediate winding up of the company; and the third purpose is to sell company property and distribute the proceeds to one or more secured or preferential creditors.

An administration order generally lasts a year, unless it is extended by a court or with agreement of the creditors. While a company is in administration it is not possible for a winding up order to be made. After appointment, the administrator will require a director or employee of the company to give him a statement setting out the details of the company's creditors and its debts, liabilities, and property. All the creditors must be informed that the company is in administration, and a creditors' meeting will be called where the administrator sets out his proposals for dealing with the company's affairs. All business documents issued by the company must state that the company's affairs are being managed by an administrator and give the name of the administrator. The administrator takes control of the company's property and has the power to do anything necessary for the management of the business.

Business Insight Companies in crisis

In 2010, Portsmouth FC became the first Premier League club to enter administration. At that time the club was estimated to have debts of over £60 m. Administrators were appointed to attempt to rescue the company as a going concern, managing the affairs, business, and property of the company.

In 2011, OpCapita bought Comet Group Ltd for the nominal sum of £2, but the business struggled in the financial climate and later went into liquidation. The unsecured creditors who are owed £232 million are unlikely to receive any money.

In September 2014, despite underlying profit of £105 million made in 2013, Phones 4u went into administration. The company had failed to secure renewal of contracts with mobile phone networks. The chief executive of Phones 4u, stated 'if the mobile network operators decline to supply us, we do not have a business'.

Basic Terminology

For an online flashcard glossary visit the Online Resource Centre

Board Meetings Meetings of Board of Directors of a company.

Class Meeting Meeting of shareholders holding a particular class of share.

Compulsory liquidation Winding up of a company by a court order.

Derivative action Where a shareholder brings a claim on behalf of the company against a director for negligence, default, or breach of duty or trust.

Derivative claim Where a shareholder, in place of the company, pursues a claim against a director of the company.

Fraudulent trading Where the business of a company has been carried on with the intention of defrauding the creditors of the company or for some other fraudulent purpose.

General Meeting and Annual General Meeting Meetings which all the shareholders and directors of a company have the right to attend.

Insider dealing Using price-sensitive information which has not been made public and relates to the present or future value of company securities (such as shares and debentures) for profit.

Insolvent Unable to meet debts and other liabilities.

Market abuse Improper conduct that relates to investments traded on a financial market.

Proxy Someone appointed by the shareholder to attend company meetings and vote on behalf of the shareholder.

Resolutions Decisions of shareholders either passed at the Annual General Meetings or General Meetings. It is possible for private limited companies to pass written resolutions.

Special notice 28 days' notice.

Voluntary liquidation Winding up of a company by its members or creditors.

Voting by a show of hands Each member (or his proxy) present at the meeting votes by raising a hand. Each voter is only counted once irrespective of the number of shares held.

Voting by poll Each shareholder (or his proxy) uses as many votes as his shareholding allows him. Usually each shareholder has one vote for each share held.

Wrongful trading Where a company has been trading and its directors knew or ought to have known that there was no reasonable prospect of the company avoiding insolvent liquidation.

Summary

For an online printable version visit the Online Resource Centre

After studying this chapter students should be able to:

Outline the different types of company meetings and explain how meetings are convened and managed

- A General Meeting is one to which all shareholders and directors are invited and can be called by its directors at any time.
- Every public company must hold an AGM. Private companies are not required by law to hold an AGM but may do so if they wish.
- Class Meetings are where only shareholders holding a particular class of share are entitled to attend.
- The purpose of company meetings is to enable shareholders to attend in person and discuss and vote on matters that affect the company.
- Notice of meetings must be given to every member and every director.
- Decisions are taken by passing resolutions. Voting may be by a show of hands or by poll.
- For a meeting to be correctly constituted, the correct notice must be given and there must be a quorum (minimum number) of shareholders in attendance.

Distinguish between different types of resolutions and appreciate the rights of shareholders to propose resolutions

- An ordinary resolution is passed by a simple majority of shareholders voting in person or by proxy.
- A special resolution is passed by a majority of not less than 75 per cent of the shareholders who vote in person or by proxy.
- A private company may pass any decision by a written resolution.
- Resolutions are generally proposed by directors but there are some opportunities for shareholders to propose resolutions.
- In certain circumstances shareholders can require directors to convene a General Meeting.

Show an understanding of protection given by law to minority shareholders

- A shareholder can bring a derivative claim on behalf of the company.
- A shareholder has the power to petition the court if shareholders, including himself, have been unfairly prejudiced.
- The Department for Business, Innovation and Skills (BIS) has the power to investigate companies where serious corporate illegalities are suspected.

Explain the meaning of insider dealing and market abuse

- Market abuse involves the misuse of information, or the creation of a false or misleading impression, or the distortion of the market.
- Insider dealing is a criminal offence. It is where an individual uses price-sensitive information, which has not been made public, relating to the present or future value of company securities for his own profit.

Describe the methods under which a company can be wound up

- A company may be wound up by a court order (compulsory liquidation) because the company is insolvent or it is just and equitable.
- A company may be wound up by voluntary liquidation of the shareholders, but only if the company is solvent. If the company is insolvent, there may be a creditors' voluntary winding up.
- A liquidator is appointed to collect in all the company's assets and distribute them to its creditors, with any surplus distributed between the shareholders.

Differentiate and explain wrongful and fraudulent trading

- Wrongful trading is where a company has been trading and at the time the directors knew, or ought to have known, that there was no reasonable prospect of the company avoiding insolvent liquidation.
- Fraudulent trading is a criminal offence and applies where the business of a company has been carried on with the intention of defrauding the creditors of the company or for some other fraudulent purpose.

Questions

1. George owns shares in Organic School Dinners plc. He wants to propose a resolution that the company should endeavour to source organic food locally. He has gained the support of a number of other shareholders. Explain to George whether he can require the company to hold a meeting to consider his resolution, or if his resolution could be added to the agenda of the company's Annual General Meeting, or if he could require the company to circulate the resolution as a written resolution.

2. Would your answer be different if the company was a private limited company, Organic School Dinners Ltd?

For outline answers visit the Online Resource Centre

3. Flora Exotic Ltd, a company selling plants, has a large number of debts but continues to trade. Kerry has supplied large quantities of fertiliser to Flora Exotic Ltd but, despite several reminders, their account for £5,000 has not been paid.

    a) Advise Kerry, who wishes to petition the court to have Flora Exotic Ltd wound up.

    b) Consider if the directors of Flora Exotic Ltd may be liable for wrongful trading.

4. Explain the difference between an ordinary and special resolution and how these are made. Can company resolutions be made without the need for a meeting?

5. The Companies Act 2006 gives protection to minority shareholders by allowing minority shareholders to bring 'derivative claims' and also allows minority shareholders to sue for 'unfair prejudicial conduct'. Explain and discuss these actions.

Further Reading

Bourne, *Bourne on Company Law*, 6th edn (Routledge, 2013).

Dine and Koutsias, *Company Law*, 8th edn (Palgrave, 2014).

Wild and Weinstein, *Smith & Keenan's Company Law*, 16th edn (Pearson, 2013).

Department for Business Innovation & Skills: https://www.gov.uk/government/organisations/department-for-business-innovation-skills.

Companies House: http://www.companieshouse.gov.uk/.

Online Resource Centre

Test your knowledge by trying this chapter's **Multiple Choice Questions.** Visit:

http://www.oup.com/uk/orc/law/company/ jonesibl3e/01student/mcqs/ch18/

For more information, updates, and multiple choice questions, please visit the Online Resource Centre at:

http://www.oup.com/uk/orc/law/company/ jonesibl3e/

Intellectual Property Law

Introduction

Intellectual property refers to things that are creations of the mind. It covers a range of different creations and includes inventions, literary and artistic works, symbols, designs, and images. Creators can be given rights to prevent others using their creations and the right to sell them as they become, in essence, their property. It is intangible property and unlike tangible property (such as motor vehicles and furniture) it cannot be touched but it is of vital importance to business. A company that develops a clever process, for example how to change lead into gold, will wish to protect its invention. If it is unprotected and copied by others soon there would be so much gold everywhere that the value of gold would fall and the company would make little money from its invention.

The major intellectual property rights are: copyrights which protect rights in original musical, literary, and artistic works; patents which protect inventions and technical processes; trade marks which protect the use of a particular mark or sign used in business; and design rights which protect the physical and visual appearance of products. It is important to note that there may be more than one form of intellectual property existing in a single product.

The statutes that govern intellectual property law include the Copyright, Designs and Patents Act 1988, the Patents Act 1977, the Trade Marks Act 1994, and the Registered Designs Act 1949. Case law is used to clarify how the Acts apply. The Intellectual Property Act 2014 made some changes in the law, particularly with regard to design and patent law. Some of the provisions of the Act are already in force and it is expected that the whole Act will be in force by late 2015. Most of the changes in the Act seek to make the handling of patents and designs simpler and more cost effective. It also introduces criminal penalties for some design infringements.

The common law also protects business against other persons pretending that their goods or services are those of that business via the tort of 'passing-off'.

Learning Objectives

After studying this chapter you should be able to:

- Define the term 'intellectual property' and understand the difference between copyright, patents, trade marks, and design rights.
- Demonstrate an understanding of the law relating to copyright.
- Show an insight into the law relating to patents.
- Explain what a trade mark is and how it can be protected.
- Show an understanding of design rights.
- Outline the tort of passing-off.
- Demonstrate an awareness of the possibilities of protecting intellectual property rights outside the UK.

Copyright

What is Copyright?

Copyright is the area of intellectual property law that governs the creation and use of goods such as songs, books, films, and computer programs. The law of copyright is governed by the Copyright, Designs and Patents Act 1988 (CDPA 1988) (as amended). Copyright prevents others, for a defined period of time, from reproducing or copying someone else's work without permission. It is an automatic right which means unlike other intellectual property rights it does not have to be registered but is acquired by bringing a work into existence. If an author writes a story and somebody else copies and sells it then they would be in breach of the author's copyright. Copyright is often associated with music artists since when they write a song they will own the copyright for the lyrics and another artist cannot sell music using those lyrics without requesting permission. A product, such as a film may contain different copyrights, for example the story, the dialogue, and the music will all be different copyrights.

In order to ascertain whether copyright has arisen there are a number of questions that must be answered. Firstly, does the work fall within one of the categories protected by the CDPA 1988, is it original, and in permanent form? Secondly, who is the owner of the work and finally, is the work within the time limits for copyright or has copyright expired?

 Key Concept   Copyright is an automatic right (meaning it does not have to be registered) and it is acquired by bringing a work into existence.

Types of Works Protected by Copyright

Although copyright protection is not given to all creative effort, the type of work eligible for protection is very wide (see Figure 19.1). Section 1 of CDPA 1988 states that copyright is a property right that exists in:

(a) Original literary, dramatic, musical or artistic works;

(b) Sound recordings, films, or broadcasts;

(c) The typographical arrangement of published editions.

Original means that the work has not been copied from another source. It relates to the form in which an idea is expressed rather than the idea itself. Copyright does not protect actual inventions or ideas but it may protect an original way of expressing common knowledge. A mathematics examination paper that uses knowledge common to mathematicians can be an original literary work. The work must be created by the author but it is not essential for it to have taken a long time to complete.

Section 3 of CDPA 1988 states that a literary work is any work (other than a dramatic or musical work) that is written, spoken, or sung. This clearly includes works such as books, magazines, and poems. The writing does not have to have any literary merit to be included, for example, business plans, reports, and even instructions on packaging may be literary works. Single words or very short phrases would not be considered to be artistic works. The Act goes on to state that a literary work includes a table or compilation, a computer program, design material for a computer program, and a database. In the following case there was an infringement of copyright when a newspaper published extracts from a personal journal.

HRH Prince of Wales v Associated Newspapers Ltd (2007)

Facts: A newspaper published extracts from a journal written by Prince Charles in which he had recorded details of his visit to Hong Kong. The newspaper had received the journal via an employee of the Prince, who was in breach of her contract of employment.

Decision: The diary was protected by copyright.

The CDPA 1988 does not define dramatic work except to state it includes dance and mime. It must be capable of being performed, so clearly this covers work such as scripts for films and plays as well as choreographic works. A musical work is a work consisting of music. It excludes the words or actions intended to be sung or performed with the music. Where a song is set to music, the lyrics are protected as a literary work and the tune is protected as a musical work.

Artistic works are defined in CDPA 1988, s 4 and cover a wide range of work including paintings, drawings, diagrams, maps, charts, plans, and models made for sculpture. To be regarded as a sculpture an object must have a visual appeal for its own sake. A pile of sand in an art gallery would be a sculpture, but a pile of sand left by a builder in a street would not! In the following case stormtrooper helmets in the Star Wars film were not sculptures within the meaning of CDPA 1988.

Lucasfilm Ltd v Ainsworth (2012)

Facts: Ainsworth (A) had been involved in making the helmets for the 'Stormtroopers' in the first Star Wars film. LucasFilm (L) had provided him with pictures and a clay model on which to base the helmets' manufacture. Some years later A made plastic copies of the helmet which he sold over the internet. L claimed their copyright had been infringed by A's sale of the copies.

Decision: The purpose of the helmet was to be worn as an item of costume in a film. It was a purely functional item and was not a 'sculpture' within CDPA 1988, s 4.

Artistic work also includes works of architecture such as a building or model for a building and works of artistic craftsmanship such as hand knitted jumpers, handcrafted jewellery, and wrought-iron gates.

Sound recordings are a recording of sounds, from which the sounds can be reproduced. A recording of birdsong would gain protection. The definition covers all types of recordings including vinyl, audiotapes, and mp3s. Broadcasts include radio and television broadcasts.

Typographical arrangement of published editions is the layout, font, and lettering of pages of published works. The 'edition' is generally what is between the covers which the publisher offers to the public. A publisher may set out a book in a particular way and that is what is protected as a 'typographical arrangement' rather than the contents of the book.

Acquiring Copyright

To acquire copyright a work must be in permanent form by being recorded in some way, such as writing, filmed, or audio taped. If an author recites a poem, which has not been recorded in any way, it will not attract copyright until it is recorded by the author or some other person. There is no formal process of registration. Copyright is acquired automatically when the criteria set down in CDPA 1988 are met. Sections 154–158 provide that a work will qualify for copyright protection if the author is a British citizen, domiciled or resident in the UK (or if a company, the company is registered in the UK), or the work was first published in the UK. Protection is also given to works created in other countries with which the UK has reciprocal copyright arrangements.

Figure 19.1 Creations in which copyright will exist

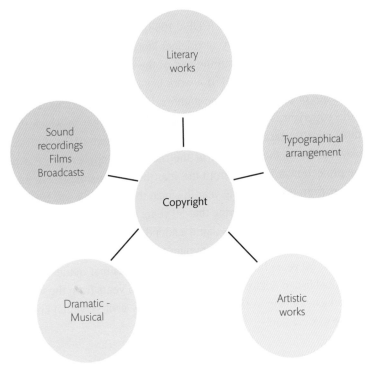

Ownership of Copyright

The creator of the work is usually the owner of the copyright. However, where the work is created by an employee, in the course of his employment, the employer is the owner of the copyright unless the parties have agreed otherwise. What is considered to be 'in the course of his employment' is construed widely. It may include work created by the employee in his own time if it relates to his normal job, even if the employer had not expressly or impliedly requested the employee to create the work. If two or more people have collaborated in producing a work and it is not possible to identify each author's contribution, the work will be considered to have joint ownership even if the authors did not intend to create a joint ownership work and their contributions are not equal.

Key Concept Where work is created by an employee in the course of his employment, the employer is usually the owner of the copyright.

Duration of Copyright

The duration of copyright protection (CDPA 1988, ss 12–15) differs depending on the nature of the work. For the majority of original literary, dramatic, musical, and artistic works the protection is 70 years from the end of the calendar year in which the person who created it dies (see Figure 19.4). If a work has more than one author the 70 years runs from the death of the last of the co-authors. If the work is computer generated the duration of the copyright is 50 years from the end of the year in which the work was made. For films it is 70 years from the year of the latest death of the director, author of the screenplay, author of the dialogue, or the musical composer. If these persons are unknown, the protection is 70 years from the year the film was made. For sound recordings it is 50 years from the end of the year in which the recording was made. However if the sound recording is published during that 50 years then copyright will not expire until 70 years after publication. This means that if a sound recording is made of a pop group in 1966 but not published until 2015 the copyright would last until 2085. The copyright for broadcasts lasts for 50 years from when the broadcast was first made. For typographical arrangements of published editions copyright expires 25 years from the year of first publication. For works belonging to the Crown (created by civil servants) copyright expires 125 years after it was created.

Rights of the Copyright Owner

The copyright owner has the exclusive right to copy, rent, lend, or adapt the work and to perform, play, or show the work in public (CDPA 1988, s 16). The owner also has the right to issue copies of the work, communicate the work to the public, or to authorise others to carry out any of these activities.

Primary and Secondary Infringement of Copyright

Primary infringement of copyright is concerned with the people who are directly involved with copying the material. A person will be liable for primary infringement of copyright if he exercises any of the exclusive rights of the copyright owner without his permission namely:

- Copies the work.
- Issues copies of the work.
- Rents or loans the work to the public.
- Performs, displays, or plays the work in public.
- Communicates the work to the public.
- Makes an adaptation of the work.

The copies must have derived from the copyright work and all or a substantial part of it must have been copied (CDPA 1988, ss 17–21). It makes no difference if the copying is not for commercial purposes and it is irrelevant that the person does not know that the work is protected by copyright or does not intend to infringe copyright. Copying can be done by downloading and storing the material on a computer. A person, who knows nothing about the law on copyright and copies a CD as a gift for a friend is still liable.

It is not only an infringement to exercise the rights of a copyright owner, it is also an infringement to authorise others to do so, although just selling or providing copying equipment does not amount to authorisation.

CBS Songs Ltd v Amstrad Consumer Electronics plc (1988)

Facts: Amstrad sold twin tapedeck recorder machines which could be used to copy taped music to a blank tape. The claimants sought to stop their sale to ensure that their copyrights would not be infringed by its users.

Decision: Facilitating unauthorised copying was not authorisation. The machines could be used for legitimate purposes.

Secondary infringement (CDPA 1988, ss 22–26) is concerned with people in a commercial context who deal with infringing copies or facilitating the copying of materials. It is not the actual copying of the work but the commercial exploitation of the copied work. It includes supplying, importing, or selling infringing copies. In order to be liable for secondary infringement the person must know or have reason to believe the copies are infringing copies and their activities are wrongful.

Key Concept Primary infringement of copyright is concerned with the people who are directly involved with copying the material. Secondary infringement is concerned with people in a commercial context who deal with infringing copies or facilitating the copying of materials.

Permitted Actions/Defences

In order to balance the rights of copyright owners with rights and interests of others the CDPA 1988 lists various acts that are permitted in relation to copyright works. Special exemptions apply to educational establishments, libraries and archives, and parliamentary or court proceedings. Fair dealing can be claimed where the copying is for the purposes of research or private study, criticism or review, quotation, the reporting of current events, parody, or illustration for instruction. Whether the use is fair is a question of degree and depends on issues such as the quantity taken and the use made of the work. Generally the copy must be accompanied by sufficient acknowledgement of the original work. The Act allows making temporary copies of material in some circumstances such as browsing on the internet and backing up a computer. There is also a narrow personal copying exception, which came into force in October 2014. This allows an individual to copy content they own and acquired lawfully to another medium or device for their own private use. It is therefore now legal for an individual to copy a CD he owns to a laptop or MP3 player, but not if he borrowed the CD from a friend.

Licences to use Copyright Material

Property protected by copyright has the potential to be used by a range of different people at the same time. For example music played in shops, pubs and clubs. In some circumstances the copyright owner can license the use of the work directly to the customer and in other cases the copyright owner will use an agency or a collecting society. The licensee pays royalties for using the copyright work.

Business Insight Collecting organisations

The PRS for music is a society of songwriters, composers, and music publishers that license organisations to play, perform, or make available copyright music on behalf of their members and distribute the resulting royalties to them. The PRS for Music currently manage around 13 million musical works. In 2013 it collected over £665 m for its membership from broadcasters, digital services, music sales, public performance, and international use of members' repertoire.
   Extracted from http://www.prsformusic.com/Pages/default.aspx.

Moral Rights

The creator of a work has certain moral rights in his work even he sells or transfers the copyright. Moral rights are not economic rights but if they are infringed a remedy can be sought from a court and damages awarded. The moral rights are firstly, the right to be acknowledged as the author of a literary, dramatic, musical, or artistic work when the work is performed commercially or in public. This is known as the 'paternity right' (CDPA 1988, ss 77–79). The second moral right is the right to object to derogatory treatment of the work (CDPA 1988, ss 80–83). Treatment means altering or adapting the work. Treatment is derogatory if it amounts to a distortion or mutilation of the work or the result is prejudicial to the honour or reputation of the author or director. The third moral right (CDPA 1988, s 84) is not to have a literary, dramatic, musical, or artistic work falsely attributed to a person as author (or if it is a film as a director). The fourth moral right gives a person, who orders the taking of photographs or making of a film for private use, the right not to have the work (or copies of it) shown in public or broadcast.

Remedies for Infringement

Where copyright has been infringed the owner can take civil action, usually applying to a court for an injunction to prevent further breaches and damages. The owner can seek an order claiming any profits made by the infringer and that the infringer hands over any copies in his possession. There are also a number of criminal offences that relate to secondary infringement of copyright (where the defendant knew or had reason to believe that copyright in the articles existed). For example, selling or distributing copied DVDs.

Patents

What is a Patent?

A **patent** is an exclusive right given to an owner of an invention to make use of and exploit their invention for a limited period of time in exchange for a full description of the invention. A patentable invention can be a product or a process that gives a new technical solution to a problem. For example a Dyson vacuum cleaner 'cyclone' mechanism would be a product whereas the way of making Vienetta ice cream would be a process. A patent can be taken out when an inventor makes something which is uniquely different from anything that has been made previously. Unlike copyright it does not arise automatically and will only be granted after a series of formal procedures have been completed (see Figure 19.3). The benefit of taking out a patent is that it gives the inventor the exclusive right to make, use, and sell the patented invention for up to 20 years which could result in considerable profits being made by the inventor. Allowing someone to have a monopoly over a product or process is not usually in the public interest. However, having time-limited patents acts as an incentive to inventors and in return the knowledge of technological advances is made public. Patent law is complex and aims to ensure that only innovative products or processes are given protection. It is governed by the Patents Act 1977 (as amended by various other Acts such as the Patents Act 2004, CDPA 1988, and the Intellectual Property Act 2014).

Key Concept A patent is an exclusive right given to an owner of an invention to make use of and exploit their invention for up to 20 years. It is not an automatic right and will only be granted after a series of formal procedures have been complied with.

What can be Patented?

The Patents Act 1977 (PA 1977), s 1(1) states that a patent can only be granted for an invention if:

- The invention is new.
- It involves an inventive step.
- It is capable of industrial application (see Figure 19.2).

There is no definition given in the Act as to what is an invention, but the Act does give a list of things that will not be considered to be inventions for the purposes of applying for a patent (PA 1977, s 1(2)). These include a discovery, scientific theory, or mathematical method; literary, dramatic, musical, or artistic work (these are covered by copyright); a method of performing a mental act, or playing a game; the presentation of information; a computer program (unless the computer program has a technical character, i.e. the program does more than just operate the computer). The invention must be new to the public. It must not be known to anyone in the UK or elsewhere in the world. It is therefore very important that an inventor does not tell people about his invention or write an article about it because, unless the disclosure was made in confidence, the invention will no longer be regarded as new. It is the invention that must be new but not necessarily the item produced. For example a new way of manufacturing stained glass could be patentable. The invention must involve an inventive step. This is defined in the Act as, 'not obvious to a person skilled in the art'. It might be something simple that solves a long standing problem. Although it cannot be something that would be obvious to a person skilled in the relevant field as clearly the next step to take in the development of a product or a process.

The invention must be capable of industrial application. This means that the invention must be able to be used or made in any kind of industry (including agriculture). It has to have some sort of use. It does not have to be better or cheaper than what came before it, but it cannot be something that is useless for any known purpose.

Inventions that are contrary to public policy or morality are excluded from being patented. Also excluded are inventions which relate to new methods of surgery, therapy, or diagnosis on humans or animals.

Figure 19.2 Essential elements for a patent

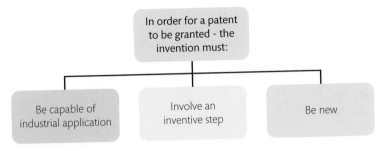

Ownership and Registration of a Patent

It is important to establish who is entitled to a patent because it is a valuable right. The owner of a patent is able to exploit and control its use. They can sell it, license it, or use it as a security for a charge. Granting a licence to another person or company gives them the right to use the invention protected by the patent usually in return for payment, known as royalties. The licence may be an exclusive one allowing only one person to use the patent or a non-exclusive one.

The inventor is usually the person entitled to apply for a patent. Disputes can arise where inventions are made by more than one person or one person adds something to another invention. In the following case the person who suggested the next step was considered to be the inventor.

IDA Ltd v University of Southampton (2006)

Facts: D was the owner of a patent for a cockroach trap using poison carried by electrostatically charged powders that stuck to the insect's legs. In a confidential telephone conversation C suggested to D that magnetic powder may be more efficient. D applied for a new patent using magnetic powder. C claimed that he was the sole inventor.

Decision: When C made the suggestion C did not know whether his idea would work however he had provided the inventive step to an article that was in the public domain. C was entitled to the new patent.

An employer may be entitled to ownership of an invention if the invention was made by an employee in the course of his normal duties or duties specifically assigned to him, and that the circumstances were such that an invention might reasonably be expected. Alternatively, the invention was made in the course of the employee's duties and at the time of making the invention he had a special obligation to further the interests of the employer's undertaking (PA 1977, s 39). Disputes may arise where there is no expectation of the employee making an invention or where the inventor has a top managerial position within the company. If the inventor is a director of a company, she will be under a special obligation to work in the best interests of the company.

In the following case the patent belonged to the employee because he was a salesman and not expected to invent.

Harris' Patent (1985)

Facts: W was employed by R to sell Wey valves and to use his specialist knowledge to deal with customers' problems relating to the valves. W invented a slide valve which was an improvement over a Wey valve. R alleged that the invention belonged to them as W had been their employee when he invented the slide valve.

Decision: W was not employed to invent and did not have a special obligation to further R's interests. W was entitled to the patent.

Where an employer has patented an invention of his employee, the employee may be entitled to be compensated (PA 1977, s 40). If the employer does not voluntarily give compensation to his employee it can be awarded by a court or the Comptroller General. (The Government's Intellectual Property Office is led by the Comptroller General of Patents, Designs and Trade Marks). The invention must be of outstanding value to the employer, taking into account the size of the organisation, the nature of the employer's business, and whether it is just and reasonable to award the employee compensation. The conditions imposed for compensation are restrictive and very few employees' claims are successful, however in the following case the co-inventors were awarded 3 per cent of the company's profits made from their invention.

Kelly v GE Healthcare Ltd (2009)

Facts: K and C were employed as research scientists for G, a pharmaceutical company. They were co-inventors of a radioactive imaging agent which was patented by their employer. It was a highly successful product and K and C claimed compensation from G under PA 1977, s 40.

Decision: In order for employees to be entitled to compensation the patent had to be of outstanding benefit to the employer having regard to the size and nature of the employer's undertaking. In this case the invention was responsible for a large proportion of G's profits and had been particularly beneficial in protecting the business against generic competition. The value of the patent was assessed as £50 million and a just and fair award for K and C was considered to be 3 per cent. K was awarded £1 million and C £500,000 (to reflect the part they each had played).

Key Concept An employer may be entitled to patent an invention if the employee invented it in the normal course of his duties and such an invention might be expected or at the time of making the invention he had a special obligation to further the interests of the employer's business. The employee may be entitled to compensation if the patent is of outstanding benefit to the employer.

Applications to Register a Patent in the UK

Where the inventor is not the person who applies for a patent, the inventor has the right to be named in the application for a patent (PA 1977, s 13). The process of registration of a patent is complex and an applicant may prefer to employ a patent agent to make the application on their behalf. The application is made to the UK Intellectual Property Office (IPO), which is part of the Department for Business, Innovation and Skills and deals with the granting of patents registered trade marks and registered designs. The application may be submitted online or by post. The application must include a description of the invention stating how it works and how it could be made, drawings to illustrate it, the technical features of the claim that are to be protected, and a summary of all the important specifications. The specifications have to be very exact and comprehensible enough for a person skilled in the art to be able to produce the invention. When an application is received initial checks and searches are carried out by the IPO. The IPO will check that the specifications describe something that is new and inventive. Depending on the results of the search the applicant may decide to abandon or to modify his application. Once the application complies with the Act's requirements a substantive examination is carried out. When a patent is granted a notice is published in the Patents Journal. The patent lasts for up to 20 years (see Figure 19.4), but after the first four years it must be renewed annually by payment of a fee. (The fees increase as the patent gets older; in 2014 it was £70 for the 5th year increasing to £600 for the 20th year).

Infringement of Patents

Patent infringement is a complex area of law and can be very costly for businesses. Whether a patent has been infringed will depend upon whether the other product or process is so similar to the patented one that it falls within its scope. In *Dyson Appliances Ltd v Hoover Ltd* (2001) the court decided that Dyson's patent relating to a bagless cyclonic vacuum cleaner had been infringed by Hoover when they produced a similar vacuum cleaner.

The Patents Act 1977 (s 60) states the activities that amount to a breach of a patent include the following:

- Where the invention is a product, infringement is committed by a person making the product, disposing or offering to dispose of it, using, importing, or keeping it.

- Where the invention is a process, infringement occurs where a person uses it or offers it for use knowing, or where he reasonably ought to have known, that he is infringing a patent. Infringement also occurs if a person disposes or offers to dispose of, uses, imports, or keeps any product obtained directly by means of that process.

There are a number of defences to infringement including private, non-commercial use of products or processes, and using products or processes for research and experiments.

An inventor whose patent is infringed may take action in court to seek the following remedies; an injunction, damages, an order to hand over the infringing products and an order to hand over any profits made from exploiting the patent.

Alternatively the inventor or anyone who is in a dispute over the infringement or validity of a patent can make a request to the IPO for an independent opinion. The opinion is based on the papers sent to the IPO by all parties to the dispute. Although the opinion is not binding and the parties can still proceed to court, it does encourage out-of-court settlements.

Viewpoint Tim Aspinall Consultant, DMH Stallard LLP, Solicitors

My work as a lawyer includes giving advice to businesses on intellectual property [IP]. I have produced a guide to Intellectual Property Success which includes the following:

- Value your IP. Work out how much your IP means to your business. How much would it cost to develop if you lost it or had to start from scratch? How much damage would be done if your competitors could access and use your IP without your consent?
- Use a multi-layered approach. Consider securing a number of IP rights at the same time in order to create a package of enforceable rights. Don't just rely on registered rights such as patents, registered designs, and trade marks. Remember copyright and rights in databases, as well as the ability to prevent passing-off.
- Process is important. Don't just think of products you may have designed or made. Look at your processes and the way you do things. Think of protection strategies.
- Protect yourself from unscrupulous customers. Be careful with your customers and keep your trade secrets to yourself. Try to adapt tooling to your way of doing things. Always

assume that your IP is under threat and be aware that customers may even try to patent your IP.

- Do not stand still. Be aware your competitors are still improving. Do everything you can to maximise the IP in your business and protect it.

Trade Marks

What is a Trade Mark?

Trade marks are a type of intellectual property which protect any signs or symbols (like brand names and logos) which distinguish goods and services in the marketplace. A registered trade mark protects a brand owner against a competitor making improper use of its mark. It may also protect a consumer from being deceived into buying the wrong or counterfeit goods or services. Classic trade marks include the rounded tick symbol for Nike sports goods, the apple for Apple products and the 'golden arches' for McDonalds. Trade marks assist customers in recognising products or services belonging to a company and may be of great value to a business. A trade mark can be registered or unregistered but an unregistered trade mark cannot be protected by the Trade Marks Act 1994 (see Figure 19.3). An action in the tort of passing-off may be taken for breach of an unregistered trade mark.

Business Insight The highest ranking global brands

Interbrand, a leading brand consultancy, publishes its annual Best Global Brands ranking each year. In 2014 the top three were Apple valued at $118.9 billion, Google valued at $107.4 billion, and Coca-Cola valued at $81.6 billion (see http://interbrand.com/en/newsroom/15/interbrands-15th-annual-best-global-brands-report.)

The Trade Marks Act 1994 (TMA 1994) governs the law on registered trade marks. Section 1(1) of the Act defines a trade mark as 'any sign capable of being represented graphically which is capable of distinguishing goods or services of one undertaking from those of another'. Most potential trade marks will be signs. A sign is anything that one can see, hear, or even smell. It can consist of either one, or a combination, of logos, words, letters, numbers, colours, images, sounds and jingles, smells, shapes of goods or their packaging. The classic shape of a Coca-Cola bottle can therefore be registered as a trade mark. 'Represented graphically' means that the sign must be able to be clearly described on a

Figure 19.3 Acquisition of Intellectual Property Rights

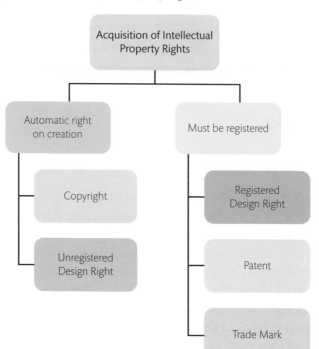

piece of paper in the form of words, images, or numbers. A jingle, for example, can be represented precisely using conventional musical notation or a smell by its chemical formulae. A trade mark needs to be clear and precise so that third parties know exactly what the trade mark consists of in order to avoid infringing it. Although colours may form a trade mark the application must be very clear on the description of things such as the size and coverage of the coloured mark.

Cadbury UK Ltd v Societe des Produits Nestle SA (2013)

Facts: Cadbury's applied to register, 'The colour purple (Pantone 2685C)'. Nestle objected to the registration.

Decision: The Court of Appeal stated that Cadbury's was not entitled to register the colour purple because its description in the application, 'the predominant colour applied to the whole visible surface of the packaging of the goods,' did not satisfy the requirement of a sign, nor the requirement of the graphical representation of a sign.

To be capable of distinguishing goods or services of one business from those of another the sign must be distinctive. If the word is a name it could be distinctive because, it has a particular style of lettering, it is an invented word such as Kodak, or it is an acronym of a real name such as IKEA. It cannot merely describe the type of goods, for example 'lavender soap' would not distinguish one manufacturer's lavender soap from another.

Key Concept Trade marks protect any signs or symbols that distinguish goods and services in the marketplace. They can consist of either one, or a combination, of logos, words, letters, numbers, colours, images, sounds and jingles, smells, shapes of goods or their packaging. A registered trade mark protects a brand owner against a competitor making improper use of its mark.

Excluded Marks

Certain signs are excluded from being registered on absolute grounds (TMA 1994, s 3). In addition to signs not complying with section 1 (discussed earlier), these include the following:

- The mark is devoid of distinctive character. The more striking or fanciful a mark the more likely it will not be considered devoid of distinctive character. The mark should help the reasonable attentive consumer to recognise a company's product so they can either avoid or repeat their purchase in the future.

- The mark consists exclusively of descriptive signs. Descriptive marks include the quality, quantity, intended purpose, value, geographical origin, and other characteristics of the goods or services. Words can be registered when they are descriptive but put in an unusual order. For example, the expression BABY-DRY in relation to nappies could be registered even though it comprises of two words which effectively describe the goods.

- The mark is customary in the language or practices of the trade (unless the use of such marks has already become distinctive of the goods).

Wm Wrigley Jr Co's Trade Mark Application (1999)

Facts: W applied to register a trade mark consisting of a specific shade of light green, for chewing gum.

Decision: The application was rejected; the colour was devoid of distinctive character and may be used by other sweet manufacturers for example to indicate lime or apple favours.

- The mark represents the natural or technical shape of the goods.

Philipps Electronics BV v Remington Consumer Products (1999)

Facts: P registered a trade mark consisting of a picture of a three headed rotary electric shaver. R sold its razors using a similar sign. P took action against R for infringing the trade mark. R alleged that the trade mark was an invalid registration.

Decision: The registration was invalid because it lacked distinctive character and because the mark consisted exclusively of a shape which was necessary to achieve a technical effect.

- The mark is contrary to public policy or morality. Words such as 'SCREW YOU' and 'FOOK' have been rejected for clothing although 'DICK' and 'FANNY' were acceptable.
- The mark is likely to deceive the public, or is contrary to law or obtained in bad faith.

Under section 4 the use of certain emblems, without the consent of the relevant person, cannot be registered. These include words that indicate royal patronage, pictures of the Queen or members of the Royal family, or Royal or national flags.

In order to prevent confusion caused by imitation, the TMA 1994 (s 5) prohibits marks that are identical or similar to other trade marks which are used on similar products or services, and there is a likelihood of confusing the public. Similar marks may not be permitted on dissimilar goods if:

(i) the existing mark has a reputation in the UK, and

(ii) the use of the later similar mark would take unfair advantage of, or be detrimental to, the distinctive character or the reputation of the earlier trade mark.

An application to register VISA for condoms was refused on the basis of Visa International's registration of VISA in relation to credit cards.

Application for Registration

An application to register a trade mark may be made online or by post to the Trade Marks Registry. The application must include representation of the trade mark itself and a statement of the goods or services to which the trade mark is to apply. The Trade Marks Registry classifies goods and services into 45 classes. An applicant has to state which class or classes of goods or services he is applying for. A fee is payable (in 2014 the fee was from £170 online or from £200 by post). The registrar will examine the application and if he has no objections to the application it will be published in the Trade Marks Journal for two months.

During this time anyone can oppose it. Once any objections are resolved the trade mark will be registered and a certificate provided. The Act allows for registration of a **collective trade mark**, which is a mark distinguishing the goods or services of members of an association from other undertakings, for example 'woolmark'.

The Effect and Duration of a Registered Trade Mark

Once a trade mark is registered the owner will be entitled to put the ® symbol next to the brand and will have exclusive rights in that mark. He can therefore use the mark in various ways, including putting the sign on goods or packaging and using the sign on business papers or in advertising. A trade mark is a property right (TMA 1994, s 2) and it can be sold or assigned or licensed for others to use. A limited licence may be granted, for example allowing the mark to be used on a particular type of goods (TMA 1994, s 29). Trade marks are registered initially for a period of 10 years from the date of registration (TMA 1994, s 42). After this time, they can be renewed indefinitely for further periods of 10 years (see Figure 19.4).

Trade Mark Infringement

Actions amounting to an infringement of a registered trade mark are set out in the Act (TMA 1994, s 10). An infringement will only occur if someone uses the trade mark or a similar mark in the course of business. If the goods or services are similar, then the mark must be likely to confuse the public. If the goods or services are dissimilar it will be an infringement where the trade mark has a reputation in the UK or it is detrimental to the character or reputation of the trade mark. 'Using' not only includes fixing a trade mark to the packaging of goods but also offering goods for sale or supplying services under the mark, or importing or exporting goods under the mark. Additionally it is an infringement to use the mark on business papers or in advertising.

In the following case the court considered that confusion could arise between 'Goo Goo' and 'Gaga'.

Ate My Heart Inc v Mind Candy Ltd (2011)

Facts: Lady Gaga's company applied for a court order preventing Mind Candy, a computer game company, from using an animated character (resembling Lady Gaga) on the basis that it infringed its trade mark. The character sang a song in the game that resembled a song released by Lady Gaga. M intended to release the song so that it would be available for purchase.

Decision: The court order was granted. Mind Candy had breached the trade mark. Consumers may think that Lady Gaga and Lady Goo Goo are connected. Lady Goo Goo traded on the reputation of LADY GAGA, a trade mark that enjoyed a huge reputation.

Provided the use of a registered trade mark is in accordance with honest practices in industrial or commercial matters it will not be infringed by a person using his own name or address, or using the trade mark simply as an indication of characteristics of goods or services. For example registration by Pampers of BABY-DRY for nappies will not prevent a competitor from stating in an advertisement 'our nappies will keep your baby dry'. It will also not be infringed if the use of the trade mark is necessary to indicate the intended purpose of a product or service. For example, the registration of BMW will not prevent a trader from advertising 'we repair BMW cars'.

Business Insight Diverting online consumers

The High Court recently ruled, in *Cosmetic Warriors Ltd v Amazon.co.uk Ltd* (2014), that Amazon had breached the copyright of LUSH by attempting to divert customers to similar products through online search results. Amazon had used 'Lush' in its Google sponsored advertisements and in its search facility on the Amazon website. Amazon shoppers searching for Lush products would instead be directed to similar products described as 'lush'.

Remedies for Infringement

Civil actions for infringement of a trade mark may be taken by the owner of the mark. The remedies include damages, an order to account for profits, an injunction to prevent the defendant from continuing to use the mark, an order to erase the offending sign from the goods or to dispose of them.

Figure 19.4 **Duration of Protection**

Copyright	Patents	Trade marks	Design
70 years from death of author	20 years	10 years renewable indefinitely	Registered Design 25 years
50 years for sound recordings			Unregistered Design 15 years

Certain trade mark infringements may also be criminal offences such as counterfeiting, or falsely representing a trade mark as registered.

Designs Rights

What is a Design Right?

A **design right** is a type of intellectual property which protects the visual look of products. It covers the entire outward appearance of a product, including decoration, lines, contours, colours, shape, texture, and materials. Design is concerned with the appearance of articles rather than the articles themselves therefore if the design is put onto other articles there may be an infringement. For example a spoon is an article but if the spoon's handle is in the shape of a human body that shape is protectable under design law. An infringement of the design rights will occur if the shape is used by another business producing spoons or even forks with the same shaped handle. There are two types of design rights in the UK, unregistered and registered.

Unregistered Design Rights

Unregistered design rights are automatic and are treated in a similar way to copyright (see Figure 19.3). The rights are set out in Part 111 of the CDPA 1988 (as amended). An unregistered design right gives the owner the ability to prevent others from copying their design.

Section 213 of the CDPA 1988 states that a design right is a property right which exists in an original design and that design means the shape or configuration (whether internal or external) of the whole or part of an article. Unregistered design rights only cover three dimensional objects and protect both functional and aesthetic aspects of the design. Two dimensional designs or surface decoration, used for example on textiles and ceramics, may be protected by copyright.

The design must be original (i.e. not copied from an existing design), and not commonplace in the industry. Not commonplace means that the design must be a departure from common designs in the field in question at the time of its creation. There is no need for the design to have artistic merit. The design must be in permanent form either in a design document or in an article made to that design (CDPA 1988, s 213).

Duration of Unregistered Design Rights

Design rights automatically protect a design for 15 years from the end of the year in which the design was first recorded (documented) or an article was made to the design, whichever is the earliest (see Figure 19.4). However, if the articles made to the design are available for sale or hire anywhere in the world within five years of creation, the design rights only last for 10 years from the marketing date (CDPA 1988, s 216).

Ownership of Unregistered Design Rights

For all designs, registered and unregistered, created on or after 1 October 2014 the designer is the first owner unless a contract provides otherwise, or the design was produced by an employee as part of their job and under the terms of their contract of employment (CDPA 1988, s 215). (For designs created before 1 October 2014 the person who commissioned a design, as opposed to the designer, is the first owner unless agreed otherwise.)

An unregistered design right is acquired automatically, in the same way as copyright, and gives the owner the exclusive right to make articles in that design or drawings, etc to enable the manufacture of goods made to the design. A design right is personal property and the owner can deal with it in the same way as other property, for example selling it, assigning it, or granting licences to others to use the design (CDPA 1988, s 222).

 Key Concept A design right is a type of intellectual property which protects the visual look of products. It covers the entire outward appearance of a product, including decoration, lines, contours, colours, shape, texture, and materials.

Registered Designs

Some design rights may be registered under the Registered Designs Act 1949 (as amended) (RDA 1949). Greater protection of a design right is gained through registration. The Act defines design as, 'the appearance of the whole or part of a product resulting from the features of, in particular, the lines, contours, colours, shape, texture or materials of the product or its ornamentation' (RDA 1949, s 1(2)). Product covers any industrial or handicraft item other than a computer program. It includes 'packaging, get-up, graphic symbols, typographical type-faces and parts intended to be assembled into a complex product' (RDA 1949, s 1(3)). This means that:

- The design can be of the product itself or part of the product.
- It can be mass produced or a one off item.
- The design need not have aesthetic quality. (It does not have to be artistically beautiful but it must create a different overall impression on the informed user.)
- It covers 3D designs (e.g. the shape of light fittings, toys, and containers) and 2D designs (e.g. patterns for wrapping paper, wallpaper and fabrics).

The design must be new and have individual character (RDA 1949, s 1B). 'New' means that the design, or an almost identical design, has not been made available to the public. To have individual character the overall impression that the design produces on an informed user must be different from other designs.

The RDA 1949 contains similar exclusions for registration of design rights as in the TMA 1994 in respect of trade marks. These include, a design must not be contrary to public policy or morality, make use of protected emblems (e.g. the Olympic rings) or flags of other countries, or conflict with other registered designs.

Key Concept Unregistered design rights are automatic and are treated in a similar way to copyright. Some design rights may be registered under the Registered Designs Act 1949.

An Application for Registration of a Design Right

The owner of a design right can apply for registration. An application is made to the IPO and must include illustrations of the design (drawings, prints and photos, with any necessary labels and explanations), a completed form, and the required fee (in 2014, £60 for a first design and £40 for each additional design). The IPO will examine the application within one month and if there are no objections the design will be registered immediately.

Duration of Registered Design Rights

Once granted a registered design right lasts for five years but it can be renewed every five years (on payment of fees) up to a maximum term of 25 years (see Figure 19.4).

Ownership of Registered Design Rights

The rules relating to ownership of a registered design are the same as those of an unregistered design (see earlier). The design belongs to the designer unless made in the course of employment or agreed otherwise.

The owner of a registered design has the exclusive right to use the design and any design which does not produce on the informed user a different overall impression (RDA 1949, s 7). To use the design includes making, putting on the market, importing, exporting, or using a product in which the design is incorporated or applied. A registered design is personal property and the owner can deal with it in the same way as other personal property such as selling it, giving it away, or licensing its use.

Infringement of Design Rights

A design right is infringed by any person who infringes the rights of the owner for commercial purposes without a licence, or authorises another to do so.

Civil proceedings can be taken by the owner of a design right (registered or unregistered) if the owner's rights are infringed. Remedies available include damages, an injunction, and an order to account for profits.

It is a criminal offence for a person in the course of a business to intentionally copy a registered design so as to make a product exactly to that design or only immaterially different, without permission of the owner. It is also an offence to offer, market, import, use, or stock such products in the course of a business (RDA 1949, s 23ZA). For all offences the accused must know or have reason to believe that the design is a registered design.

The Tort of Passing-off

What is Passing-off?

Passing-off is a tort which is committed where a business markets its goods or services in such a way that they appear to be the goods or services of another business. The offending business does not have to have intended to commit the tort or in fact deceived anyone; it is enough that someone was likely to be deceived.

A passing-off action protects the reputation or goodwill of a business. Goodwill is a very valuable asset to a business. It is the attractive force of business that brings in and keeps its customers. It is linked to the good name, reputation, and connection of a business. For example, a property management business may have few tangible assets as it may rent its premises, lease its cars, and own little equipment. What will be of real value in the sale of the business is its connection with its clients and the probability that old clients will continue to deal with the firm even after it has been sold.

Elements of Passing-off

There is no statute that governs the law of passing-off. The law has developed through case law and to take an action against someone for passing-off certain elements must be present. These elements include:

- The claimant must show he has goodwill or reputation attached to the goods or services.
- A misrepresentation has been made by the defendant (whether intentionally or not) that has led the public to believe that the goods or services offered by the defendant belong to the claimant.

- The claimant has suffered or is likely to suffer damage because of the erroneous belief caused by the defendant's misrepresentation.

The misrepresentation must be made in the course of trade and create some likelihood of confusion. It covers such things as using similar names, descriptions, or packaging.

Reckitt & Colman Products Ltd v Borden Inc (Jif Lemon case) (1990)

Facts: R had been selling lemon juice in a distinctive plastic squeezy container the size, shape, and colour of a lemon since 1956. In 1985, B produced similar lemon-shaped containers for selling lemon juice. R applied for a court order to prevent B from selling it.

Decision: Many shoppers would purchase B's lemon juice when they thought they were purchasing R's. The tort of passing-off had been committed and an injunction was granted.

Key Concept Passing-off is a tort which is committed where a business markets its goods or services in such a way that they appear to be the goods or services of another business.

Extended passing-off protects the collective goodwill that applies to classes of goods, often denoting superior quality. For example the term 'Champagne', may be used by a number of suppliers but only on goods actually originating from the Champagne region, in France. In the following recent case a geographical name had become so distinctive of a product that its use in relation to products from elsewhere amounted to a misrepresentation.

Fage UK Ltd v Chobani UK Ltd (2014)

Facts: F, the main importer of yoghurt made in Greece objected to C marketing its yoghurt in the UK as Greek yoghurt as it was made in the USA. F claimed the use of the phrase 'Greek yoghurt' had sufficient goodwill and reputation to denote a distinctive type of yoghurt made in Greece whereas C claimed that the phrase related merely to the style of the product.

Decision: A substantial number of people in the UK who bought Greek yoghurt thought that it was made in Greece and that was what mattered to them. The phrase 'Greek yoghurt' carried sufficient reputation and goodwill to warrant protection. The tort of passing-off had been committed and an injunction was granted.

An unregistered trade mark can be protected by the tort of passing-off. However, it will usually be advisable for a business to register a trade mark under the Trade Marks Act 1994 because it gives a business additional property rights and greater protection if the trade mark is infringed.

Business Insight Misleading renewal invoices

In 2014, the UK Intellectual Property Office succeeded in their claim for passing-off against two companies trading under the names 'Patent and Trade Mark Organisation' and 'Patent and Trade Mark Office'. The companies had sent letters that looked like official renewal notices to owners of UK trade marks and patents offering to renew their rights at inflated prices. Some owners had paid the higher fees, charged by the two companies, thinking they were dealing with the UK IPO directly.

EU and Worldwide Protection of Intellectual Property Rights

The EU has introduced a number of directives and regulations concerning intellectual property law. The UK is also a member of several international conventions giving protection to intellectual property rights. Usually copyright work is automatically protected outside the UK in the same way as inside the UK.

It is possible to apply for a European patent under the provisions of the European Patent Convention. An application is made either through the IPO in the UK or directly to the European Patent Office. There are over 30 countries that have signed up to the convention including the UK. The application may be for a patent protection in some or all of the states. Under the Patent Cooperation Treaty an application may be made for an international patent either to IPO, the EPO, or directly to the World Intellectual Property Organisation (WIPO), based in Geneva, Switzerland.

Where a business wishes to protect a design or its trade mark in the EU, an application for a Registered Community Design (CD) or a Community Trade Mark (CDM) can be made through the Office for Harmonization in the Internal Market or filed through the IPO. Once granted, a CD can be used to prevent any unauthorised commercial use of the design anywhere in the EU for 25 years. A CTM registration lasts for 10 years but can be renewed indefinitely. It is also possible to register a trade mark or a design internationally by making an application to the WIPO.

An unregistered Community Design gives its owner the right to prevent unauthorised copying of the design throughout the European Union for three years from when the design was first made available to the public.

Basic Terminology

Collective Trade Mark A sign distinguishing the goods or services of members of an association from other undertakings.

Copyright The right of the owner of literary, dramatic, musical or artistic work, to print, publish, perform, film, or record it.

Design Right A right that protects the visual look of products.

Passing-off The deception by one person that his goods or business are that of another.

Patent The exclusive right to use and benefit from a new invention.

Trade Marks Signs or symbols distinguishing the products of one business from that of another business.

For an online flashcard glossary visit the Online Resource Centre

Summary

After studying this chapter you should be able to:

Define the term 'intellectual property' and understand the difference between copyright, patents, trade marks, and design rights

- Intellectual property is something that is a creation of the mind. It covers a range of different creations and includes inventions, literary and artistic works, symbols, designs, and images.
- Copyright protects rights in original musical, literary, and artistic works.
- Patents which protect inventions and technical processes.
- Trade marks which protect the use of a particular mark or sign used in business.
- Design rights protect the physical appearance and visual appearance of products.

Demonstrate an understanding of the law relating to copyright

- Copyright is the area of intellectual property law that governs the creation and use of goods such as songs, books, films, and computer programs.
- The law of copyright is governed by the Copyright, Designs and Patents Act 1988.
- The types of works protected by copyright are original literary, dramatic, musical, or artistic works; sound recordings, films, or broadcasts; the typographical arrangement of published editions.
- To acquire copyright the work must be in permanent form by being recorded in some way.
- The creator of the work is usually the owner of the copyright. An employer is the owner of work created by an employee, in the course of his employment.
- The duration of copyright protection differs depending on the nature of the work. For the majority of original literary, dramatic, musical, and artistic works the protection is the life of the author plus 70 years.
- Primary infringement of copyright is concerned with the people who are directly involved with copying the material. Secondary infringement is concerned with people in a commercial context who deal with infringing copies or facilitating the copying of materials.
- The creator of a work has certain moral rights in his work, even if he sells or transfers the copyright.
- Where copyright has been infringed the owner can take civil action, usually applying to a court for an injunction to prevent further breaches and damages.

For an online printable version visit the Online Resource Centre

Show an insight into the law relating to patents

- A patent is an exclusive right given to an owner of an invention to make use of and exploit their invention for a limited period of time.
- A patent must be registered with the UK IPO.
- A patent can only be granted for an invention if: the invention is new, it involves an inventive step, and it is capable of industrial application.
- A patent lasts for up to 20 years.
- The inventor is usually the person entitled to take out a patent but an employer may be entitled to ownership of an invention made by his employee in certain circumstances.
- Where an employer has patented an invention of his employee, the employee may be entitled to be compensated.

Explain what a trade mark is and how it can be protected

- A trade mark is, 'any sign capable of being represented graphically which is capable of distinguishing goods or services of one undertaking from those of another' (TMA 1994).
- A registered trade mark protects a brand owner against a competitor making improper use of its mark.
- Certain signs are excluded from being registered.
- Once registered, an owner of a trade mark will be entitled to put the ® symbol next to the brand.
- An infringement will occur if someone uses the trade mark or similar mark in the course of business.
- Trade marks are registered initially for a period of 10 years and can be renewed indefinitely.
- Civil and criminal action may be taken where a trade mark is infringed.

Show an understanding of design rights

- A design right is a type of intellectual property which protects the visual look of products.
- There are two types of design rights in the UK, unregistered and registered.
- Unregistered design rights are automatic and are treated in a similar way to copyright. The design must be original and not commonplace in the industry.
- Unregistered design rights automatically protect a design for 15 years from creation or 10 years from first marketing whichever is earliest.
- A design which is new and has individual character may be registered under the Registered Designs Act 1949.
- Once registered a design right lasts for five years but it can be renewed every five years up to a maximum term of 25 years.
- Civil and criminal action may be taken where a design right is infringed.

Outline the tort of passing-off

- Passing-off is a tort which is committed where a business markets its goods or services in such a way so that they appear to be the goods or services of another business.
- The claimant must show he has goodwill in the goods or services, a misrepresentation has been made by the defendant and the claimant has suffered or may suffer damage as a result.

Demonstrate an awareness of the possibilities of protecting intellectual property rights outside the UK

- Through a series of treaties, copyright is generally protected outside the UK.
- An application can be made for a European patent or an international patent.
- To protect a design or trade mark in the EU an application may be made for a Registered Community Design or a Community Trade Mark. An application may be made to the WIPO to protect a trade mark or a design internationally.

Questions

1. Charles, the author of a series of 'the worst wizard' children's books, visits Jane and accidentally leaves behind a copy of the next as-yet unpublished, 'The worst wizard goes camping' novel. Jane takes a copy of the entire book before returning it to Charles, and then gives book-readings, charging an admission fee of £5 per person. Explain how copyright law works and whether there has been a breach of copyright.

2. Pedro believes he has invented a waterproof mobile phone case totally different from anything he has seen or heard of and wishes to patent it. He has not told anyone about it but is thinking of taking his invention to a local trade fair next week. Advise Petro on the steps he will need to take to register a patent and whether he should visit the trade fair with his invention before registration.

3. Natural Beauty Ltd manufactures a range of cosmetic items. The company has expanded over recent years and the managing director believes that they should register the green leaf logo the company puts on its goods as a trade mark. Advise the company on the process and benefits of registering the mark.

4. Outline the type of designs that may be registered under the Registered Designs Act 1949. How long will protection last?

For outline answers visit the Online Resource Centre

Further Reading

Davis, *Intellectual Property Law (Core Text Series)*, 4th edn (Oxford University Press, 2012).

Hart, Clark, and Fazzani, *Intellectual Property Law*, 6th edn (Palgrave, 2013).

Norman, *Intellectual Property Law Directions*, 2nd edn (Oxford University Press, 2014).

Intellectual Property Office: https://www.gov.uk/government/organisations/intellectual-property-office.

Office for Harmonization in the Internal Market: https://oami.europa.eu/ohimportal/en/home.

World Intellectual Property Organization: http://www.wipo.int/portal/en/index.html.

The Institute of Trade Mark Attorneys: http://www.itma.org.uk/.

Online Resource Centre

Test your knowledge by trying this chapter's **Multiple Choice Questions**. Visit:

www.oup.com/uk/orc/law/company/ jonesibl3e/01student/mcqs/ch19/

For more information, updates, and multiple choice questions, please visit the Online Resource Centre at:

www.oup.com/uk/orc/law/company/ jonesibl3e/

PART 6

STUDY SKILLS

& REVISION

Study Skills

Introduction

Law is a fascinating subject but it can be complex. The study of law requires reading, digesting, and understanding a range of material which sometimes can be very demanding. This chapter sets out some guidance on how to study effectively and approach assignments and examinations. With effective and regular study you will find that your knowledge of law and your ability to define, explain, and apply legal principles will develop successfully.

Learning Objectives

After studying this chapter you should understand how to:

- Manage and organise your study time efficiently.
- Take advantage of lectures, tutorials, and seminars.
- Develop technical skills of making good notes.
- Locate case reports and statutes.
- Approach assignment questions.
- Prepare for examinations.

Managing and Organising your Study Time

As a student at university or college, you will be expected to take responsibility for your own learning and develop as an independent learner. Good organisational skills, planning, and consistent study are essential to academic success (see Figure 20.1). At the start of a module it is important to get into a routine of regular study and to keep up momentum throughout the module. However, you need to be realistic about the other demands on your time and ensure that you have allocated a sufficient number of hours for the tasks you need to undertake each week. In addition to contact time in lectures and seminars/tutorials, you will need to plan time for reading, writing notes, research, revision, and preparation and completion of assignments and examinations. You may also wish to set aside some time for small peer group discussions outside formal teaching. When setting yourself a timetable of study, ensure you set achievable goals. Many students find it easier to concentrate in relatively short blocks and then have a break or switch tasks. Note that students often underestimate how long it takes to carry out research for an assignment or prepare effectively for seminars.

Try to get organised from the start of term. Set yourself up with a calendar on your preferred medium (mobile phone, computer, paper), and ensure you write down all the important dates and times including your academic timetable, assignment hand-in dates, examination periods, and term dates. Get into the habit of writing or recording commitments as soon as they arise. You might want to set yourself up with alerts to remind you a week or so before important dates.

Figure 20.1 **Managing your study time**

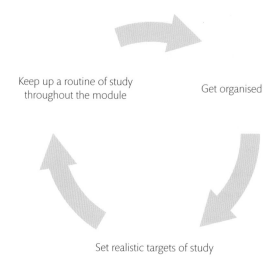

Keep up a routine of study
throughout the module

Get organised

Set realistic targets of study

Lectures and Seminars/Tutorials

Law modules are traditionally delivered through a series of lectures and seminars/tutorials. A lecture is usually a large group session where the lecturer presents material to the students. Before a lecture you may be required to do some pre-reading (or you may wish to do so).

If you are finding the subject difficult, reading relevant chapters in the textbook before a lecture can facilitate your learning and understanding of the topic.

It is important to attend your lectures ensuring you arrive in good time. At the beginning of a lecture, the lecturer may remind the class of where they have got to in the topic area, or give the class an outline of the main points that will be covered (see Figure 20.2). Different lecturers have different styles of presentation and will give students varying amounts of prepared material. Some lecturers give quite detailed lecture outlines and students may only need to make a few additional notes during the lecture. Some lecturers welcome questions and discussions throughout the lecture and others take questions only at the end of the lecture.

A lecture often provides a framework and outlines the main points of a topic area. The lecturer may also deal with specific complex points in detail or highlight new developments in the law. During the lecture, listen to what is being said and make notes. Shortly after the lecture it is essential to re-read your notes and ensure you can decipher your writing and understand the issues. If there are points that you are unclear about, it makes good sense to tackle them early on. At this stage you may want to expand your knowledge and understanding of the topic area by focused reading and adding to your lecture notes. Time spent after the lecture consolidating your learning is invaluable when it comes to writing assignments and examinations.

Figure 20.2 **How to approach lectures**

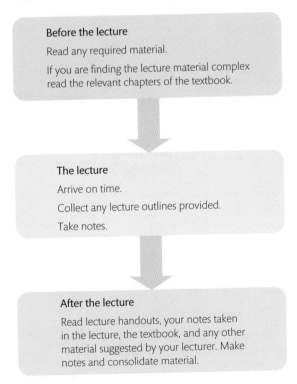

Before the lecture

Read any required material.

If you are finding the lecture material complex read the relevant chapters of the textbook.

The lecture

Arrive on time.

Collect any lecture outlines provided.

Take notes.

After the lecture

Read lecture handouts, your notes taken in the lecture, the textbook, and any other material suggested by your lecturer. Make notes and consolidate material.

Seminars/tutorials are made up of small groups of students who meet regularly with the tutor to discuss questions that have usually been set in advance. Different tutors run seminars/tutorials in different ways but the key to success is attendance, preparation, and participation (see Figure 20.3). Seminars/tutorials are designed to test student understanding of the subject and can be used as a forum to clarify any areas of confusion. Prior to the seminar/tutorial, you will probably be given some relevant reading to complete and be asked to prepare answers to a set of questions. Ensure you write down your answers fully and take your notes to the seminar/tutorial. You will not get much out of a session if you are unprepared and have little knowledge of the subject area. During the session, make sure you contribute even if you are unsure of your answer, and do ask questions even if you think others might view your questions as foolish. If you have found an issue confusing, usually someone else in the group will have a similar problem. There is no need to take notes

Figure 20.3 How to approach seminars/tutorials

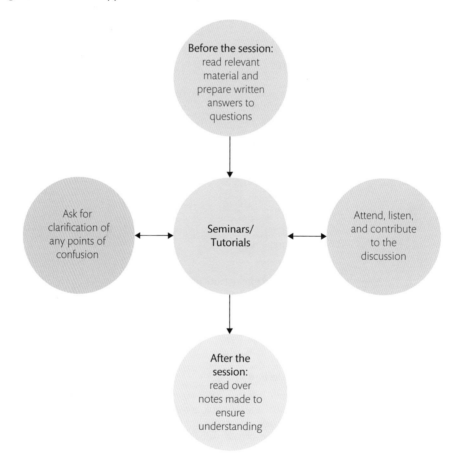

Before the session: read relevant material and prepare written answers to questions

Ask for clarification of any points of confusion

Seminars/ Tutorials

Attend, listen, and contribute to the discussion

After the session: read over notes made to ensure understanding throughout the seminar, but you may want to write down the main issues raised and the outline of any answers that vary from yours. Make sure you read over any notes later and follow up on additional points.

Taking Effective Notes

In addition to taking notes in lectures and seminars, you will need to make notes on your reading. There is no 'right' or 'best' way of note taking. Some students find it helpful to make detailed notes using headings and sub-headings, while other students find taking down key points in a diagrammatic form more useful. It is important to establish a way of taking notes that is organised and easy to use for future reference. Using highlighter pens, numbering points, and underlining issues are all effective ways of bringing order to your notes. In a lecture do not try and write down what is being said verbatim but listen, think about the core messages, and write down the key issues. When you are writing a statement of law it is important to note the appropriate legal authority (a case name or a statute). After reading a textbook or journal article, write notes in your own words, summarising the key points. Do not copy out chunks of text. Being able to put the text into your own words will facilitate your learning. Make sure you keep an accurate note of your source details because you may wish to use and expand on your notes when writing an assignment and you will need to give references for your sources of information and ideas.

It is a good idea to look at all the notes you have made on a particular topic area and consolidate them, soon after you have prepared them. You may find it useful to highlight the core points and write an overview of the topic area.

Locating Case Reports and Statutes

Most of the cases referred to in this textbook have been reported in one or more of the law reports. You will see that in the table of cases (see p. xx) each case has been given a reference (called a citation). This refers to the report that the case can be located in. For example, *Bolton v Mahadeva* has the reference [1972] 1 WLR 1009. WLR refers to Weekly Law Reports. This case is reported in the first volume of the Weekly Law Reports for 1972 at page 1009. If you visited a law library you would be able to locate a copy of the case report by going to the shelves containing the Weekly Law Reports and picking out volume 1 of 1972. Alternatively, you may be able to look up a case by using an electronic database. However, these databases are generally subscription based which means that your college or university would have to pay to subscribe to them.

Case and Tribunal decisions can be located free of charge on the internet at the following sites:

http://www.bailii.org/ (Supreme Court, House of Lords, Court of Appeal, High Court and Tribunals)

https://www.supremecourt.gov.uk/decided-cases/ (Supreme Court)

http://www.publications.parliament.uk/pa/ld/ldjudgmt.htm (House of Lords 1996–2009)

Access to UK legislation free of charge is available on the internet at http://www.legislation.gov.uk/

How to Approach Assignment Questions

Law assignments are usually set as either essays/reports or problem questions/case studies. Essays/reports are discursive questions which focus on your ability to explain, discuss, and evaluate the law. Problem questions/case studies are a set of facts which are often like a mini story. These types of questions focus on your ability to identify legal issues, display your knowledge of relevant legal rules and principles, and apply those rules and principles to factual situations. Both types of question assess a number of common skills such as your ability to present clear, logical, and persuasive arguments. These skills should be your central aims when writing your coursework.

Essays/reports

First steps

It is essential to start by reading the essay question carefully. Ascertain what exactly you are being asked to do. Look to see if a broad or a narrow focused discussion is appropriate and assess what are the limits to the topic. Check to see if you are required to consider one, or more than one, issue. It is unlikely that you will be asked to 'write all you know about' a subject, and, therefore, it is important to focus on the question asked.

In focusing on the question, it is often useful to underline the key words in the question—those that specify the kind of report or essay required. Some examples follow (see Table 20.1).

Sometimes an essay question will include more than one key word, in which case you will need to focus on them all. For example, if you were asked to describe and discuss a legal principle, you would need to describe it by setting out a clear account of the principle, and then to discuss it by exploring it from relevant angles.

Table 20.1 Examples of key words

Compare	Examine similarities and differences.
Contrast	Set in position and show the degree of differences/similarities.
Criticise	Express a reasoned judgement about the merits and demerits.
Define	Set down the meaning. Sometimes it may be necessary to discuss alternative meanings.
Describe	Give a detailed explanation.
Discuss	Examine by argument and content. Give reasons for and against.
Distinguish	Explain the difference between propositions set out.
Evaluate	Assess the importance of something.
Explain	Make plain and clear, give an account of.
Illustrate	Use examples to demonstrate points.
Outline	State the general principles of an issue.
Review	Look at the subject carefully.
Summarise	Give a concise account of the main points.

Gathering material

Once you have determined what the question is about, your answer will need to be researched. Try to use a variety of sources. Re-read your lecture/seminar/tutorial notes and read relevant textbooks and journal articles. If you use the internet ensure you only use reputable websites recommended by your university or college. Keep a notebook, or file of cards with your notes on them. When making notes it is vital that you reference your sources accurately.

Writing your answer

Planning is essential for good writing. It provides a structure, which helps you to write your answer and avoid including irrelevant material. Your plan should consist of a series of brief headings or notes.

An essay/report should always comprise an introduction, main body, and conclusion. In the introduction, comment on the topic and explain your interpretation of the question. You may also wish to outline the order of the discussion you intend to take. In the body of the essay, you should organise your main points in a way which enables your discussion to flow. Arrange your material into paragraphs with each paragraph dealing with one issue. Cite relevant case authority or statute. Aim at clarity and succinctness and ensure you use legal terminology correctly. Check that the main body of your essay answers the question. There should be a continuous thread of argument or discussion throughout your answer. If writing a report, make use of sub-headings to guide the reader through your report. If appropriate, use numbered points. In your conclusion, summarise your main ideas or arguments. Make sure that your conclusion corresponds to the question asked, and that it follows from the discussion in the main body (see Figure 20.4).

Write a first draft and if possible leave it for a short while before checking it carefully. You will find it easier to be objective and critical. Make all the necessary corrections and redraft it. Make sure you keep within any word limit set and remember that poor English, spelling mistakes, and scruffy presentation all detract from your assignment.

Figure 20.4 **Steps to take in writing an assignment**

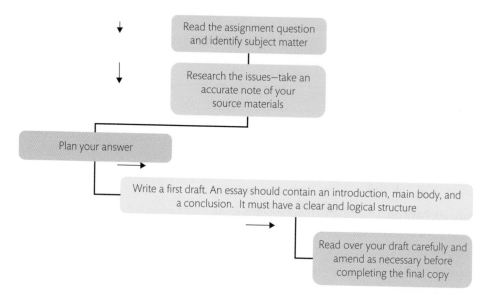

Problem questions/case studies

First steps

Problem questions are essentially factual scenarios that usually contain a number of legal issues, which you are required to identify and discuss. The initial task is to identify the parties involved and the legal issues which the question raises. It is, therefore, essential to read and re-read the scenario very carefully, and note down key issues and relevant points of law. You should accept the facts set down in a scenario and not concern yourself with issues of proof or the improbability of the facts given.

It is important to be aware that crucial facts may be deliberately omitted from a problem question. This may then require you to develop an answer based on a number of grounds. However, do not discuss situations which could not have arisen on the facts (see Figure 20.5).

Gathering material

You need to gather material relating to all the issues raised by the facts. You will need to read round the subject matter to ensure that you have identified all the relevant legal points. Legal principles will need to be supported by authority (statutes or cases). Check that you have covered everything required by the question.

Writing your answer

You need to spend time planning your answer and make sure that it addresses the specific question or questions asked at the end of the scenario. The most appropriate way to structure the answer to a problem question will vary from question to question, depending on the wording and nature of the question, and the subject matter. For example, where a question specifically asks you to advise stated individuals, then you may decide to consider each individual in turn. However, if a question asks you to discuss the scenario then it may be more appropriate to consider potential legal actions as they arise chronologically in the question.

There are mixed views on whether an answer to a problem question should have a general introduction. If you write an introduction it should be short (much shorter than for an essay question). Do not copy out the facts of the question. It uses up the word limit of your coursework and gains you no marks. In the body of your answer, you need to identify and deal with each issue separately. Once you have identified the first legal issue, then set out the relevant principle of law supporting this with a legal authority (case or statute), and apply the law to the facts explaining how the law affects the legal position of the parties. You might find case law with similar facts helpful. Work through the question using this formula for each legal issue identified.

Figure 20.5 Working through problem questions

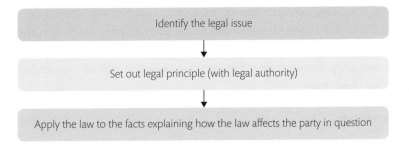

Conclude your answer with a brief summary drawing the issues together. Sometimes it is not possible to reach a conclusion on an issue because you have not been given adequate facts and may have to give alternative possibilities.

Preparing for Examinations

Revision

- *Time planning:* You will need to plan your revision time. Start your revision as soon as possible. If you leave it to the last minute you may find that you do not have enough time to cover the whole module. Prepare a timetable and stick to it. Be realistic with your revision timetable—remember to plan for regular breaks. Once the allotted time for a topic has passed move on to the next topic. Some students think it is better to be selective in their revision and only revise a few topics but this is a risky approach to take. Draft a calendar indicating what areas you will cover on a particular day/timeslot.

- *Revision notes:* Make your own revision notes in a style which suits you. If you have copious notes on topics you will need to reduce them down so that you end up with a manageable quantity of notes. As the examination approaches some students find it helpful to reduce their notes further to short concise points.

- *Practice questions/past examination papers:* Write out draft plans or try writing a timed answer. Look at previous examination papers and attempt to answer the questions using your notes at first and then without your notes.

- *Classes:* Attend any revision classes and prepare thoroughly for them.

The examination

Beforehand

Make sure you are aware of how long the examination is and the format of the paper. You should know how many questions there will be on the paper, whether the paper is divided into sections, how many questions you are expected to answer, and whether the questions carry equal marks. It is a good idea to work out how many minutes you have to answer each question on the paper in advance, so you do not waste time working it out in the examination.

Get sufficient sleep the night before the examination, arrive in good time, and ensure you have adequate pens, etc.

At the examination

Read instructions on the examination paper very carefully and make sure you comply with them. Check the number of questions to be answered. Take 5–10 minutes to read through the whole paper and choose questions that you intend to answer (unless you are required to answer the whole paper). Plan your time carefully. Do not spend more than your allotted time on a question. If you run out of time try to round off your answer and go on

Figure 20.6 Procedure in the examination

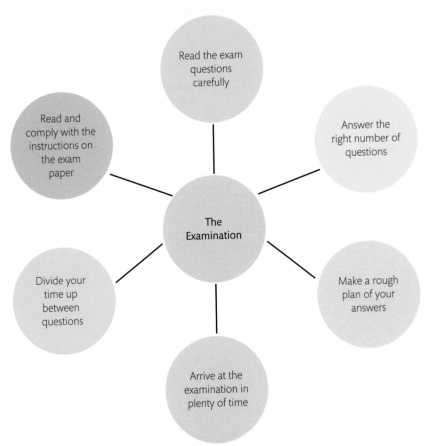

to the next question. Usually more marks are gained from time spent at the beginning of a question as opposed to time spent perfecting a question. You can return to the unfinished question if you have time towards the end of the exam (see Figure 20.6).

For each attempted question you should prepare a short plan before you commence writing. Read the whole question carefully, underline key words, brainstorm, jot down points, and sort into a sensible plan. Remember you must answer the specific question set, rather than write all you know about the subject. Make sure you answer all parts of a question. Do not write out the question as it can waste valuable time. When writing your answer ensure you keep in touch with the question, referring back to it in your answer. Do not forget to start with an introduction and make sure you draw your answer together in a conclusion. Express yourself as clearly and succinctly as you can. Structure and coherence is essential. Try to write legibly. Underline your cases. Give yourself time to read over your work and add in any points that you might have missed.

Online Resource Centre

For further exam advice visit:

**www.oup.com/uk/orc/law/company/
jonesibl3e/01student/examhelp/**

For more information, updates, and multiple choice
questions, please visit the Online Resource Centre at:

**www.oup.com/uk/orc/law/company/
jonesibl3e/**

Index